Crystal Reports® 2008: The Complete Reference

Crystal Reports® 2008: The Complete Reference

George Peck

New York   Chicago   San Francisco
Lisbon   London   Madrid   Mexico City
Milan   New Delhi   San Juan
Seoul   Singapore   Sydney   Toronto

The **McGraw·Hill** Companies

Library of Congress Cataloging-in-Publication Data

Peck, George (George E.)
 Crystal Reports 2008: the complete reference / George Peck.
   p.cm.
 Includes index.
 ISBN 978-0-07-159098-3 (alk. paper)
 1. Seagate Crystal reports. 2. Business report writing—Data
Processing. I. Title
 HF5719.P43433 2008
 651.7'802855785—dc22

                                        2008024972

McGraw-Hill books are available at special quantity discounts to use as premiums and sales promotions, or for use in corporate training programs. To contact a special sales representative, please visit the Contact Us page at www.mhprofessional.com.

Crystal Reports® 2008: The Complete Reference

4 5 6 7 8 9 10 DOC/DOC 1 5 4 3 2 1

ISBN   978-0-07-159098-3
MHID   0-07-159098-6

Sponsoring Editor	**Indexer**
Lisa McClain	Claire Splan
Editorial Supervisor	**Production Supervisor**
Jody McKenzie	George Anderson
Project Editor	**Composition**
Carolyn Welch	EuroDesign - Peter F. Hancik
Acquisitions Coordinator	**Illustration**
Mandy Canales	Lyssa Wald
Technical Editor	**Series Design**
Ian Treleaven	Peter F. Hancik, Lyssa Wald
Copy Editor	**Art Director, Cover**
Bob Campbell	Jeff Weeks
Proofreader	**Cover Design**
Carolyn Welch	Pattie Lee

About the Author

George Peck has been involved in various IT pursuits for close to 30 years. He founded his own consulting and training firm, The Ablaze Group, in 1994 (www.AblazeGroup.com). He has trained, consulted, and developed custom software for large and small organizations throughout the United States, Canada, the United Kingdom, and Puerto Rico.

George works as both a trainer and consultant exclusively with Crystal Reports and the BusinessObjects Enterprise family. This is his seventh title in the *Crystal Reports: The Complete Reference* series, best-sellers published by McGraw-Hill/Osborne. He is also the author of *Crystal Reports Professional Results*, also published by McGraw-Hill/Osborne.

In addition to his software career, George is a broadcaster and voice actor. His voice may be heard on national radio, TV, and web commercials, promotions, and documentaries.

About the Technical Editor

Ian Treleaven is a software engineer working on the Crystal Reports product development team. He has helped create Crystal Reports features as a Senior Developer, Development Lead, and most recently as a Program Manager. Prior to working on Crystal Reports at Seagate Software/Crystal Decisions/Business Objects/SAP, Ian worked for a number of years in the industry at various companies including Microsoft and IBM.

In memory of my Father
My true writing inspiration

Contents at a Glance

Contents

Acknowledgments

With each successive edition of *Crystal Reports: The Complete Reference*, there is a small group of dedicated people who provide immeasurable help in its preparation. Some have helped over and over for each edition, while others are helping me for the first time. Regardless, I so much appreciate your assistance and patience.

First and foremost, some very dedicated people at Business Objects deserve great appreciation. Blair Wheadon and Julie Ingram went above and beyond the call of duty to help make this book a success. And, Ian Treleaven's technical editing is beyond compare. It's good to be "friends" again!

And, as usual, the folks at McGraw-Hill/Osborne are patient and helpful in working towards a successful book. My acquisitions editor, Lisa McClain, deserves the top nod. Your continued support and understanding year after year is so appreciated. Both Lisa and acquisitions coordinator Mandy Canales deserve thanks for putting up with my occasional tantrum. "You may call me again." And, it was terrific to work with Bob Campbell and Carolyn Welch yet again. You both keep me on track and keep the words straight.

Finally, and most importantly, a heartfelt acknowledgement goes to my partner in life and business, Denise. Yet one more time, you've been supportive beyond words. I'm truly grateful.

George Peck, April 2008
author@CrystalBook.com
www.CrystalBook.com

Introduction

In the past, a new version of Crystal Reports could be expected every year to year and a half. With Crystal Reports 2008, Business Objects has elected to wait a while longer before releasing an updated version of its flagship reporting product. And, not only is the software new, so is the organization that created it. With SAP's acquisition of Business Objects in early 2008, Crystal Reports can now be considered in the true "big leagues" of Business Intelligence products. And, the release schedule and vendor organization aren't the only changes. With a brief foray into Roman numeral version number, a new direction has been launched yet again. Crystal Reports 2008 is the first version to make reference to a general release year (even though it was released in late 2007), as opposed to a sequential version number. Regardless, internal version numbering, as well as the Program Files directory structure, indicate that this is a 12.x product release.

While an argument might be made that this is not a "one-dot-oh" upgrade, there are several major changes to Crystal Reports 2008. The look-and-feel change is fairly substantial, with all-new toolbars and various "Office 2007" updates. Some major new features, such as Flash/Xcelsius integration and vastly enhanced cross-tab capabilities, can be found. While all developers may not appreciate the expected deprecation of older Microsoft COM/Visual Studio 6 support, they should appreciate improved web and Windows .NET viewers and integration capabilities. And, with a single-edition, all-encompassing release (there are no longer three editions to keep straight), as well as a substantially reduced "installation footprint," the simplicity of keeping track of editions and installing the product are welcome additions to Crystal Reports 2008.

The 2008 edition of this book largely maintains the layout of previous editions, with a few consolidations. While Part I covers general report design techniques that will apply to virtually everybody who uses the tool, developers will now find a single chapter at the end of this part, devoted solely to Visual Studio .NET integration.

Part II covers various techniques and methods to place your Crystal Reports on the web. While some discussion on simple HTML export helps you get your reports to the web without additional tools, this part concentrates almost entirely on the companion BusinessObjects XI 3.0 product family, which provides an extensive feature set for automating and distributing Crystal Reports. Use chapters in Part II to help you explore this powerful web-based reporting tool.

And, the appendix provides a complete formula language reference. This covers all functions in the formula language (including new functions added to Crystal Reports 2008), along with helpful descriptions and examples that illustrate each function and operator.

As with the previous editions, sample reports and developer applications can be found online. Many of the sample reports illustrated in Part I, as well as sample Visual Studio .NET applications, are available for download. And, an extra online chapter is available to accompany the printed chapters here. All these supplementary materials, as well as any late-breaking changes to the book, can be found on this book's companion web site at **CrystalBook.com**. You may also e-mail the author with suggestions or questions about the book at **Author@CrystalBook.com**.

What's New in Crystal Reports 2008

In addition to the vendor-related and version numbering changes discussed earlier, Crystal Reports 2008 presents significant functional changes. A short description of most of these additions and updates follows, with chapter number references (although some minor new features may be mentioned only here and not covered extensively in the rest of the book). New Crystal Reports 2008-related features in the BusinessObjects Enterprise XI 3.0 family are discussed in Chapters 20, 21, and 22.

- **New Look and Feel**   The first obvious change is the look and feel of Crystal Reports 2008. If you use Microsoft Office 2007, you'll notice a similar organization (including the distinctive color and shading scheme) in Crystal Reports 2008. All toolbar buttons have also been redesigned. Some of these changes are discussed in Chapter 1.

- **Single Edition and Smaller Installation Footprint**   Instead of the three or four editions of previous Crystal Reports versions, all capabilities are combined in a single Crystal Reports 2008 edition that supports all datasources and provides developer enhancements for Visual Studio .NET programmers. And, the installation "footprint" of Crystal Reports 2008 has been reduced to less than 500MB, providing for easier distribution of installation media and faster installation.

- **Interactive Sorting**   Report viewers can now re-sort their reports by way of any visible detail section field. As with other web-based systems, small arrow icons can now be placed on the report to facilitate an interactive sort change. This feature is discussed in Chapter 2.

- **More Flexible Report Layout and Page Orientation Options**   Reports no longer need to be tied to a particular printer. As such, page sizes can be set to any desired width and height, independent of any forms defined on a printer. Furthermore, the Section Expert now allows you to specify mixed page orientations within a single report, whereas some pages appear in portrait orientation, while other appear in landscape orientation. These options are covered in Chapter 6.

- **Product and Viewing Locale Settings**   Crystal Reports 2008 provides much greater control for language and formatting localization. Depending on the language packs you have purchased, the View pull-down menu's Product Locale option allows you to choose from multiple languages to use for the Crystal Reports User Interface (menus, dialog boxes, and so forth). Regardless of the chosen Crystal Reports product locale, the Preferred Viewing Locale option affects various regional-specific settings, such as date formatting in parameter field prompts. Making this choice from the View menu will provide a more appropriate "regional viewing experience" for your report audience, regardless of their local Windows Control Panel regional settings.

- **Saved Data Selection**   This new feature can greatly reduce the number of database refreshes required for interactive report viewing, particularly when used with parameter fields. In previous versions, any time new parameter values were required, a database refresh resulted. Now, saved data selection can change the "viewed data" on the screen based on new parameter values without requiring a database refresh. This feature is discussed in Chapters 3 and 13.

- **Formula/Field Find and Duplicate Enhancements**   The Field Explorer now includes additional options on its pop-up menus to make it easier to find an occurrence of a database field or formula in other formulas. This allows you to assess the impact of changes or deletions by determining where fields/formulas are used throughout the report. Also, you may duplicate an existing formula with a Field Explorer right-click pop-up menu option, allowing you to create a copy of a complex formula. You may then rename and perform minimal edits to the copy for slightly different formula functionality.

- **Optional Parameter Fields and the Parameter Panel**   One of the most powerful enhancements in Crystal Reports 2008, parameter fields can now be defined as optional. This, in combination with the new HasValue formula language function, will permit report viewers to ignore parameter fields they don't wish to provide a value for. The parameter panel also provides the capability to interact with chosen parameter fields right in the Preview tab (or an associated web or Windows viewer in a custom application or BusinessObjects Enterprise). The parameter panel and saved data selection provide for much higher report interactivity with much less database access. Parameter fields and the parameter panel are covered in Chapter 13. The parameter panel is also covered in Chapter 19 (related to custom applications) and Chapter 21 (related to BusinessObjects Enterprise XI 3.0 InfoView).

- **Flash/Xcelsius/Flex Integration**   This powerful new feature allows Flash animation objects to be embedded directly in a Crystal Report. While designed primarily to support integration with Crystal Xcelsius 4.5 and Xcelsius 2008, any Flash .SWF file (whether designed with Xcelsius, Adobe Flash or Flex, or any other Flash development tool), can be added to a report. And, Crystal Reports 2008 even allows values to be passed to the embedded Xcelsius or Flash .SWF file by way of Flash variables, or an enhanced Xcelsius 2008 integration interface. Chapter 11 covers this new feature exclusively.

- **Custom Cross-Tab Rows, Columns, and Summaries** Those familiar with previous Crystal Reports cross-tab capabilities (and limitations) may find new Crystal Reports 2008 cross-tab enhancements to be the most compelling feature in this new release. Now, custom cross-tab rows, columns, and summarized fields can be created with the enhanced formula language. Many reports that couldn't make use of cross-tabs in the past can now make use of a custom cross-tab to provide highly flexible row/column layouts. These new features are covered in Chapter 8.

- **Enhanced Barcode Support** A third-party barcode font, additional formula language functions (provided by a User Function Library), and Convert To Barcode menu options, provide enhanced barcode support in Crystal Reports 2008. This feature is discussed in Chapter 6.

- **New Formula Language Functions** The formula language has been enhanced to provide complete control for customized cross-tab rows, columns, and summarized fields. These new GridValue functions appear when editing or formatting appropriate cross-tab objects. Also, the formula language includes some new functions related to the chosen viewing locale. Some cross-tab functions are covered in Chapter 8, with all new functions covered in the appendix, the Formula Language Reference.

- **Enhanced Support for Web-Based Datasources and CrystalReports.com** Crystal Reports 2008 adds an additional datasource in the Database Expert for Salesforce. com, allowing for direct connection to your Salesforce.com CRM data. XML web services as data sources also receive some updated features (both Salesforce.com and XML web service data sources are covered in Chapter 16). And, you can now open reports and save reports directly to CrystalReports.com, instead of having to manually upload or download already-saved .RPT files.

- **Improved XML Export** Although "standard" XML export capabilities still exist in Crystal Reports 2008, the steps for setting up custom XML exports have changed dramatically. Instead of using the previous built-in dialog box to define the XML export format, Crystal Reports 2008 now provides complete support for XML transforms. This allows virtually unlimited text export capability. New XML exporting capabilities are discussed in Chapter 14.

- **Custom Add-In Developer Hooks** Crystal Reports 2008 provides expanded capabilities for developers to create their own custom add-ins. This capability allows a Visual Studio .NET developer to create a custom Crystal Reports add-in menu and external functionality. Information on creating custom add-ins can be found on the Crystal Reports developer sight, diamond.businessobjects.com.

- **Visual Studio .NET Integration Improvements** As with previous versions, Crystal Reports 2008 will provide additional integration options if installed on a computer already containing a version of Visual Studio .NET. Not only are there additions to the standard Crystal Reports object model, but enhanced support for new Crystal

Reports 2008 features (such as interactive sorting and the parameter panel) are available in a .NET application. These features are discussed in Chapter 19.

- **Hyperlinking Wizard**   If you are using a member of the companion BusinessObjects Enterprise XI 3.0 family, hyperlinking to existing Enterprise-based reports is provided by the new Hyperlinking Wizard. This is covered in Chapter 20.

PART I

Designing Reports

CHAPTER 1

Getting a Feel for Crystal Reports 2008

Information Technology has continued an interesting transition over the past 15 to 20 years. While the direction in the 1980s and 1990s was away from centralized mainframe systems toward decentralized personal computing, IT in the 2000s has moved back toward a centralized environment, with a web browser replacing the dumb terminal of days gone by. Many systems that were converted to PC-based DOS and Windows applications 20 years ago are now being converted, once again, to a centralized web-based environment.

Through the entire transition, however, one central portion of most applications has remained consistent. The SQL database server became the cornerstone of many decentralized applications toward the end of the twentieth century. And, even as applications move back toward a centralized web environment, the database server is still an integral part of most of these emerging systems.

This is where the *database report writer* comes in. No matter what the end-user application interface connects to the core database, a comprehensive reporting tool is one of the most popular approaches available to get data back out of the database. Crystal Reports 2008 continues the tradition of many previous versions of in attaining this goal.

Introducing Crystal Reports 2008

Crystal Reports remains the market leader and de facto standard for business and corporate report writing. In 1984, a Canadian shipping company wanted to produce custom reports from its accounting system. When the vendor said "We can't help you," the company created Quick Reports, the precursor to Crystal Reports. Crystal Reports' first "bundle" was with that vendor's next version of its accounting software. Crystal Reports has continued to grow and expand beyond its humble DOS beginnings. After several transitions through various vendors, Crystal Reports once again finds itself under a new umbrella, based on Business Objects' acquisition by SAP in late 2007. This, without a doubt, places Business Intelligence tools in general, and Crystal Reports in particular, firmly in the big leagues.

NOTE *The "2008" moniker of this release is, yet again, a departure from past version naming conventions. Having long endured standard Arabic numeral version numbering, Crystal Reports took a quick departure toward roman numerals with Version XI. And, while Crystal Reports 2008 once again deviates by using a date as its version basis, you will still find "Version 12" numbering in the Program Files directory where Crystal Reports is installed.*

Crystal Reports is now bundled with hundreds of software packages, both Windows-based PC packages, and web-based centralized systems. Versions of Crystal Reports are also included with various Microsoft packages, including versions of their preeminent development environment, Visual Studio .NET.

Crystal Reports is aimed at several general types of users:

- Casual business users, such as data analysts, executive assistants, and marketing directors, who will design reports around their corporate data to make intelligent business decisions.

- Sophisticated report designers, who will design reports with complex formatting and logic to satisfy recurring enterprise reporting requirements.

- Programmers, who will use Crystal Reports to integrate sophisticated reporting right inside their own Microsoft Windows programs.

- Webmasters, who will use Crystal Reports to provide print-quality reports and graphics over their intranets or the Internet.

Figure 1-1 shows the Crystal Reports 2008 screen when the program is first started. While Crystal Reports 2008 maintains the standard Windows user interface from previous versions, users of older Crystal Reports versions will immediately notice the new "Office 2007" smooth gradient screen layout and color/shading scheme. The Start page will appear, displayed within the first of many tabs used in the Crystal Reports user interface. By default, the Start page includes online content from the Business Objects web site if your computer is connected to the Internet. If you close the Start page by clicking the small *x* on its tab, you may always reopen it by using the Show Start Page option from the Help menu.

When you first start the program, you may want to navigate to some of the online hyperlinks presented on the Start page. However, the only two main functions that you'll usually want to perform are creating a new report and opening an existing report. From within the Start page, you can choose from several new report options, choose from a list of recently opened reports, or click the Open File link to navigate through a standard Open File dialog box for an existing report.

Like most functions in Crystal Reports, these tasks can be accomplished in several ways, in addition to choosing Start page options. Whether the Start page is displayed or not, you may also open an existing report or create a new report with pull-down menu options, keyboard shortcuts, or toolbar buttons, as described later in the chapter.

Crystal Reports Screen Elements

The general look, feel, and layout of Crystal Reports 2008 is similar to previous versions. The Crystal Reports screen consists of several main parts you'll want to familiarize yourself with: the pull-down menus, the toolbars, the report design/preview area, and the status bar.

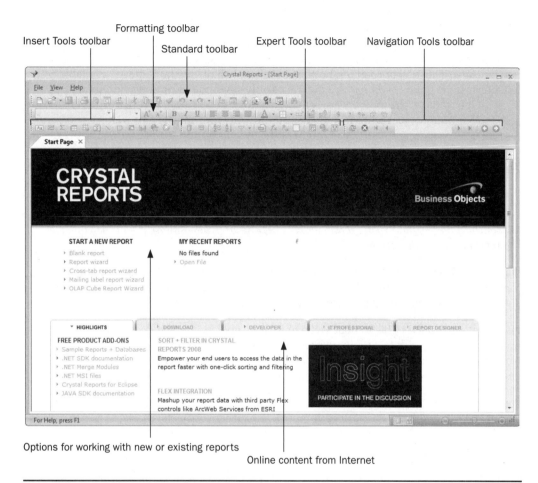

Insert Tools toolbar

Formatting toolbar

Standard toolbar

Expert Tools toolbar

Navigation Tools toolbar

Options for working with new or existing reports

Online content from Internet

FIGURE 1-1 Crystal Reports opening screen

Pull-Down Menus

The pull-down menus are standard Windows-type menus that you can pull down with your mouse. In some cases, you can also use shortcut key combinations (such as CTRL-O to open an existing report) to choose pull-down menu options. You'll notice these shortcut key combinations next to their menu options when you pull down the menus. You can also use the standard Windows convention of holding down the ALT key and typing the underlined letter in the menu, and then choosing a menu option by typing another underlined letter from within the menu. For example, you can open an existing report (File menu, Open option) by typing ALT-F-O.

Toolbars

When you first start Crystal Reports, five toolbars are displayed across the top of the screen by default. Initially, the first two toolbars are displayed by themselves vertically, while the last three toolbars are displayed side by side below the first two. If you've become familiar with toolbar buttons in previous Crystal Reports versions, you'll need to reacquaint yourself with Crystal Reports 2008 toolbars, as many of the button faces have changed.

To selectively turn on or off individual toolbars, choose View | Toolbars from the pull-down menus. The toolbars contain buttons for almost all of Crystal Reports' available functions (some options still require the use of pull-down menu options, but not many). Many of the icons on the toolbars are self-explanatory. In addition, tool tips are available for each toolbar button—just point to a toolbar button with your mouse and wait a few seconds. A small box containing a short description of the toolbar button's function will appear.

TIP *You may "undock" the toolbars from their default positions and place them anywhere you want. Just click the dotted line at the left of the toolbar and drag it to the desired location. If you move it left or right within its current location, it will simply move to a different position. If you move it away from the top of the screen, it will become its own "window." If you place it near the top or bottom of the Crystal Reports screen (or back near its original position), it will snap into place along the edge of the screen.*

The Standard Toolbar This toolbar is the first toolbar just below the pull-down menus. It contains the most often-used Crystal Reports functions, such as opening and saving report files, printing and exporting the report, undoing and redoing actions, and so on.

The Formatting Toolbar This toolbar is the toolbar just below the Standard toolbar. You should be familiar with this toolbar if you've used most any office suite type of tool, such as word processors or spreadsheets. This toolbar enables you to change the format (color, font, size, alignment, and so forth) of one or more objects that you have selected on your report.

The Insert Tools Toolbar The third toolbar (initially, the first toolbar in the third row) contains options to insert new objects onto your reports, such as text objects, charts, maps, and cross-tab objects.

The Expert Tools Toolbar The fourth toolbar (initially, the middle toolbar in the third row) presents buttons that display various Crystal Reports "experts" that guide you through different report functions usually presented with a tabbed dialog box. Such experts include the Database Expert, Group Expert, and Select Expert.

The Navigation Tools Toolbar The fifth toolbar (initially, the last toolbar in the third row) includes buttons that refresh the report's data, stop report formatting that's in progress, and navigate among various report pages.

The External Command Toolbar Crystal Reports 2008 introduces the External Command toolbar. Although not initially displayed, you may turn it on by checking it in the View | Toolbars dialog box. Both this toolbar and the Add-Ins pull-down menu (also not initially displayed) can be populated and controlled with custom programming conducted in various programming environments.

TIP *In addition to using pull-down menus to display the Toolbars dialog box, you may right-click on any portion of a toolbar or the pull-down menu bar. The resulting pop-up menu will allow you to display or hide toolbars.*

Report Design/Preview Area

The large area in the middle of the Crystal Reports screen (you won't see this area until you close the Start page) is the report design/preview area. Here, you actually manipulate fields and objects that make up your report. When you want to have a look at the way the report will eventually appear when printed on paper or exported to another file format, you can preview the actual report in this area, as well.

You'll soon see that you can choose between multiple reports that you may have open simultaneously, as well as different views of the selected report, by clicking a number of tabs that appear at the top of the report design/preview area. When you initially create a new report or open an existing report, you'll see a tab for that report. Below the tab for the currently selected report, you will see one or more other tabs. In particular, you'll always see a Design tab, which shows a design view, or "layout," of your report, simply indicating the location of objects in different report sections. When you preview the report, a Preview tab appears (Figure 1-2) that shows actual data from the database as it will appear in the final report. In addition, as you progress with your report work, you'll see additional tabs for subreports , drill-down views, and report alerts. Simply click the tab you wish to see.

FIGURE 1-2   Multiple report/view tab layout

Status Bar

The status bar appears at the very bottom of the Crystal Reports screen. Although you can hide the status bar by un-checking the Status Bar option on the View menu, you'll probably want to leave it displayed, as it displays very helpful information for you as you design and preview reports. In particular, the status bar will show more detailed descriptions of menu options and toolbar buttons. While the short tool tip that appears when you point to a button is handy, it may not offer a good enough description of what the toolbar button does. Just look in the status bar for more information.

Also, the status bar contains more helpful information on its right side, such as the date and time the report was last "refreshed" from the database, how many database records are being used in your report, the number of database records the report includes, and at what location (X-Y coordinates) on the report page a currently selected object is located.

One new feature in Crystal Reports 2008 comes from Microsoft Office 2007: the Zoom area of the status bar. Once you have opened an existing report, or created a new report, the slider and preset zoom buttons in this area allow you to quickly change the zoom level of your report.

TIP *You may need to resize the overall Crystal Reports window to see all status bar elements. Some items, such as the number of database records included in the report, will not be displayed in the status bar at certain window sizes.*

Starting Out: Opening or Creating a Report

To open an existing report, you may use options from the Start page, choosing a recently used report from the list, or choosing the Open File option. Whether or not you've closed the Start page, you can also use the File menu or Open button in the Standard toolbar. If you want to choose from a list of recently used reports, choose from the recent file list (a list of numbered report filenames) from the File menu, or click the small down arrow on the Open toolbar button in the Standard toolbar.

To choose a report from an Open File dialog box, select File | Open, use the shortcut key combination CTRL-O, or click the Open button in the Standard toolbar. A standard File Open dialog box will appear, showing any files with an .RPT extension in the drive and folder. Navigate to any alternate drives or folders to find the existing Crystal Report .RPT file that you wish to open.

To create a new report, choose options from the Start page, the File menu, or the Standard toolbar. The Start page includes several options for creating new reports, including four report "wizards" and the blank report option. Click the desired choice.

Whether or not the Start page is displayed, you can also start a new report by using pull-down menu options or a toolbar button. If you choose File | New, a submenu will appear presenting the four possible wizards, as well as the blank report option. Pressing the CTRL-N keyboard shortcut or clicking the New Report button in the Standard toolbar will display the Standard Report Creation Wizard.

Using the Report Wizards

The four standard *report wizards* allow you to create "quick and dirty" reports with minimal effort. They're helpful when you want to create a simple report or put together the beginning elements of a more complex report. Using the Start page or File | Menu submenu, choose the wizard that most closely matches the type of report that you want to create.

To create a simple, general-purpose report (for example, an employee phone list or your last year's sales totals), use the Standard Report Wizard (see Figure 1-3). The Standard Report Wizard presents a type of dialog box that's probably familiar to you if you've used other office suites or productivity products. You build your report by choosing options from the different screens in a dialog box. You advance to the next screen by clicking the Next button at the bottom of the dialog box.

To create a report with the Standard Report Wizard, follow these steps:

1. First, choose the database tables (or other data source) you want to use for the report using one of the two categories from the Available Data Sources list. This list allows you to choose any data source Crystal Reports supports, including data connections that you are already connected to previously (from the My Connections folder), and those that are available in the myriad subfolders within the Create New Connection folder. Click the plus sign next to the folder you wish to open to see the available options. For example, if you click the Create New Connection folder, you'll see a list of database types that Crystal Reports can connect to, including PC-style "local" databases, client/server databases (such as Oracle or DB2), BusinessObjects Enterprise Universes, and many other categories (see Chapter 16 for more information on special database types).

FIGURE 1-3 The Standard Report Wizard

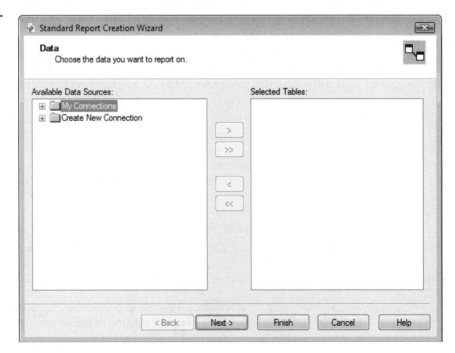

2. As you add tables, you'll see them appear in the Selected Tables list. Once you're finished adding tables, click the Next button. You'll be taken to the Link portion of the wizard (provided that you chose more than one table). This area shows you the tables you've chosen in a visual format, allowing you to *link* the tables together, using common fields. Crystal Reports will *autolink* the tables automatically, showing you lines indicating the fields and tables that are linked. If these links are correct (in the real world they rarely are), you may leave them as is.

3. If you need to delete a link that Crystal Reports added, click the line that connects the tables, and press the DEL key to remove the existing link or click the Delete Link button. If you want to delete all existing links, you may click the Clear Links button. You may then create your own link by dragging from the "from" field and table and dropping on the "to" field and table. A line will appear, indicating your new link. Once you've linked the tables correctly, click the Next button at the bottom of the Wizard.

TIP *Linking tables has quite a few fine points. Look for more information in Chapter 15.*

4. Choose the database fields you actually want to appear on your report. You may choose single fields simply by clicking the field name under the Available Fields list. If you want to choose multiple fields, hold down the CTRL key and click. You'll notice that fields are "multiselected" when you click them. To deselect an already selected field, hold down CTRL and click the field name again. To select a range of fields, click the first field in the range. Then, hold down the SHIFT key and select the last field in the range. Both fields, plus all fields in between, will be selected. Then, click the right-arrow button to move your selected fields to the Fields To Display box. If you, per chance, would like to add all fields from the tables to the report, click the double-right arrow.

5. To search for a particular field (in case the tables you chose contain many fields), click the Find Field button under the Available Fields list. You can enter a full or partial field name to search for. If that field is in any tables in the Available Fields list, the field will be highlighted. If you select a field in the field list and then click the Browse Data button, you'll see a sample of actual data from that database field. This may be helpful in determining whether or not this is the correct field to add to your report.

6. If you'd like to change the order in which the fields appear on the report, you can make those changes in the Fields To Display box by choosing the field you want to move and clicking the up or down arrow above the list. When you're finished, click Next to move on.

TIP *This is all the information the Standard Report Wizard needs to display the report. From this point forward, if you don't want to specify any other report features, such as grouping, totaling, charting, or record selection, you may click the Finish button to display the report.*

7. If you wish to have your report contain report groups, choose one or more fields from the Available Fields list on the Grouping portion of the wizard and click the

right-arrow button. *Grouping* puts all report records together on the report whose chosen grouping fields are the same. Grouping is similar to just sorting records, but groups can have subtotals, counts, averages, or other summaries at the end. Grouping is covered in more detail in Chapter 2.

8. If you choose to group the report, the Next button will then display the Summaries section, where you'll add an entry in the Summarized Fields list for every group you created previously. This is where you choose subtotals, averages, counts, or other summaries that you want to appear at the end of the group. Crystal Reports assumes that you wish to create "sum" summaries for any numeric fields you've placed on your report. You'll notice that these have already been added. You may leave these as-is, change the type of summary by selecting the summary field and choosing from the drop-down list at the bottom of the wizard, or delete the summaries by selecting them and clicking the left arrow. To add new summaries, begin by clicking the group that you wish to create a summary for in the Summarized Fields list. Then, click the field in the Available Fields list that you wish to summarize for that group and click the right-arrow button. The wizard will choose a default summary type (such as Sum or Maximum) and display it below the Summarized Fields list. If you wish to change the type of summary for the field you just added, choose the different summary function from this drop-down list. Note that you'll see more limited summary types for nonnumeric or noncurrency fields.

9. Clicking Next will display the Group Sorting area of the wizard (assuming that you have summary fields on your report). Usually, any groups on your report are presented in alphabetical order (for example, Arizona precedes California, followed by Oregon, Texas, and Wyoming). However, if you want to see the "top or bottom five states in order of sales," select the appropriate radio button to show groups in order of the subtotal or summary amount that you choose in the drop-down list, rather than by the name of the group. Click the Next button.

10. The Chart area lets you show your report data graphically in a bar, line, or pie chart. If you choose one of these options, specify the title for the chart, as well as the fields that the chart should be based on and should use for the size of the bar, wedge, or line. Do this with the Chart Title, On Change Of, and Show Summary options. Chapter 9 explains charting options in more detail.

11. When you click Next, the Record Selection area of the wizard will appear. Use this to limit your report to a desired set of meaningful database records. You likely won't ever want to include every record in the database tables in your report. Many tables contain large numbers of records, and your reports will be much more meaningful if they contain only the relevant set of records. Choose one or more fields to select, and move them to the Filter Fields list by clicking the right-arrow button. When you click a field in the Filter Fields list, an additional drop-down list appears below. You can choose the comparison operator you need in the pull-down list (such as equal to, less than, one of, between, and so on). Then, choose the value you want to compare against in the additional drop-down lists that appear. You may type a comparison value directly in the drop-down list box, or you can click the down arrow in the box to choose from a sample of data that will be read from the database field.

TIP *More detailed information on selecting records is contained in Chapter 3.*

12. Click Next to show the final area of the wizard, the Template area. This area lets you determine the general appearance of your report. If any pre-existing templates have been installed, you'll be presented with a list of them in the Available Templates box. When you select a template, a thumbnail view of the template appears to the right. If you wish to use an existing Crystal Report .RPT file as a template, click the Browse button to locate that .RPT file. Once chosen, the thumbnail view of that report will also appear to the right.

You may now click the Back button if you wish to move backward through the wizard to make any changes. Once you're satisfied with all your choices, click Finish to show the entire report in the Preview tab.

Once you have created the report using the Standard Report Wizard, you can print it on a printer, export it to another file format, save it to the Crystal Reports .RPT file format, or use any other function that Crystal Reports provides. You can click the Design tab to make any manual adjustments to the report that you wish.

Click the Design tab to make manual adjustments to the report
. Save the report
Send the report to a printer

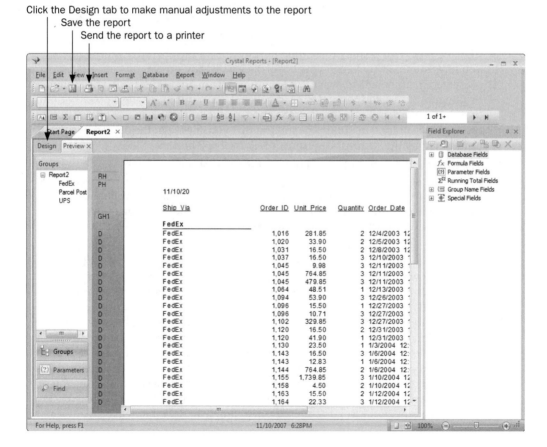

CAUTION *Crystal Reports will not allow you to rerun the Report Wizard to make changes to the report you've already created—you must use the Design tab and make manual adjustments. While the Report Wizard does make "quick and dirty" reporting easier than manually creating reports, you'll probably want to familiarize yourself with general report formatting options in the Design tab so that you can modify reports you create with the wizard.*

Using the Blank Report Option

While the report wizards simplify the report design process by presenting a step-by-step approach, they limit your flexibility to create a report exactly as you'd like it to look. Among other limitations, you are required to accept the fonts, colors, and layout that the wizard chooses. Group total and summary fields are labeled haphazardly, and group fields are repeated over and over again in every report line within the group.

Although it's initially more labor-intensive, using the Blank Report option to create a report gives you absolute control over what you put on your report, where you put it, and how it looks. Even if you use the report wizards, it's important to understand the concepts involved in the Blank Report option, because you'll need to use those concepts to refine many reports that the report wizards create.

To use the Blank Report option, choose Blank Report from the Start a New Report section of the Start page. You may also choose File | New from the pull-down menus and choose the Blank Report option from the submenu. In each case, a new empty report will be created and the Database Expert will appear.

The Database Expert

The *Database Expert,* shown in Figure 1-4, is where you choose the database tables you wish to include in your report. Here, you can select from any database type that Crystal Reports supports, including PC-type "local" databases, such as Microsoft Access, dBASE, Paradox, Btrieve, and others. You can also choose from virtually all popular client/server or SQL databases, such as Microsoft SQL Server, Oracle, Informix, and Sybase. Crystal Reports even supports proprietary data types, such as Web server activity logs, the Windows event log, Microsoft Exchange systems, XML-formatted data, and so forth. These data types are all chosen here.

The Database Expert categorizes types of databases, shown as small folder icons with plus signs next to them. Depending on the type of database you want to report on, click the plus sign next to one of the following database categories:

- **My Connections**   Displays a list of databases you have used previously in other reports. This folder allows you to quickly find a database you've used before, without having to navigate the large number of subfolders within the Create New Connection folder. If you wish to remove a database entry from the My Connections folder, just right-click the desired database connection and choose Delete Connection from the pop-up menu.

- **Create New Connection**   Displays another set of folders that categorize each type of datasource that Crystal Reports will connect to. The folders that appear here are based on what database connection options you chose when you installed Crystal Reports, as well as on database connection software you may have installed on your computer, such as an existing program that contains an Oracle or DB2 client database driver.

Click the Links tab to link multiple tables together

Click to expand data category

Tables already added appear in this list

Right-click item to display shortcut menu

FIGURE 1-4   The Database Expert

NOTE *A more thorough discussion of the different data types that Crystal Reports supports can be found in Chapter 16.*

After you click the plus sign next to the folder you wish to use, you may see a list of available databases within that folder. If you're already logged on to a database in that folder, you'll see the database name and all the available tables underneath the database name. Choose the desired database or subfolder. Depending on the folder or database you choose, additional dialog boxes will appear, asking you to choose a particular database filename, log on to the database, or choose a database server. Eventually, you'll be able to choose one or more *database tables* that you wish to include in your report. You may also see a selection of database object types, such as tables, views, and stored procedures, that you can choose from. Click the plus sign next to the desired object type and choose an object from within the category.

To add a table to the report, select the table and click the right-arrow button. You can also just double-click the table name. When the table has been added to the report, the table name will appear in the rightmost Selected Tables list. If you add a table by mistake, just select it and click the left-arrow button to remove it—it will disappear from the Selected Tables list. If you want to select and add multiple tables, you may multiselect additional tables by holding down the CTRL key while clicking table names. Or, you may SHIFT-click tables to select those two tables, as well as all tables in between. When you've chosen the tables you want to add to the report, click the right-arrow button to add them all at once. And finally, you may simply add all tables in the Available Data Source list to the Selected Tables list by clicking the double-right-arrow key.

TIP *There may be several different ways to connect to the same database. If, for example, you wish to report on a corporate Oracle database, you may connect via ODBC, via OLE DB, or by using a Crystal Reports "native" driver in the More Data Sources category within Create New Connection. If you're unsure of how to connect to your database, check with your database administrator.*

If you choose more than one table for your report, a Links tab will appear in the Database Expert. You must click this tab to link the tables you've added to your report together. If you don't link tables, you'll be presented with the Links tab when you click OK on the Database Explorer dialog box. Use the Links tab to join or link your tables together. There are many fine points to properly linking tables. This is discussed in more detail in Chapter 15.

The Design Tab and Field Explorer

Once you've chosen and linked tables, Crystal Reports will display the Design tab. This is the "template" view that you use to begin designing the look and feel for your report. The first step to beginning report design is choosing fields for the report from the *Field Explorer*, shown in Figure 1-5. If you don't already see the Field Explorer, you can display it by clicking the Field Explorer button in the Standard toolbar, or by choosing View | Field Explorer from the pull-down menus. Begin designing your report simply by dragging fields from the Field Explorer and dropping them on the report where you want them to appear.

The Field Explorer contains categories of fields that are available to place on your report. You'll see a plus sign next to the Database Fields category, indicating that more choices are available in that category. Clicking the plus sign next to it will expand the category, showing all the tables you added from the Database Expert. Plus signs next to the table names, as well as next to the Special Fields category, indicate that fields are available below those levels—click the plus sign to see available fields. The other categories of the Field Explorer will not have any plus signs next to them, unless you've opened an existing report that already contains fields of these types. Once you begin creating new formulas, parameter fields, and so on, you'll see plus signs next to these categories as well. Click the plus signs to see available fields in these other categories.

The simplest way to add a field to the report is to drag and drop the field from the Field Explorer to the report's *design canvas* within the Design tab. When you drag, you'll see an outline of the field object appear on the report as you drag. When you have positioned the field where you want it to appear, simply release the mouse button to drop the field on the report. As an alternative, you may right-click a field and choose Insert To Report from the pop-up menu, or select the desired field and click the Insert To Report button (the first toolbar button) from the Field Explorer toolbar. The field will be attached to the mouse cursor, which you can then position to drop the field.

You're not limited to dragging and dropping one field at a time to the report. If you see several fields you'd like to drag and drop at once, use CTRL-click to select or deselect

Click push pin to shrink Field Explorer to edge of Crystal Reports window
Field Explorer toolbar buttons perform common operations
Drag field from Field Explorer and drop on report

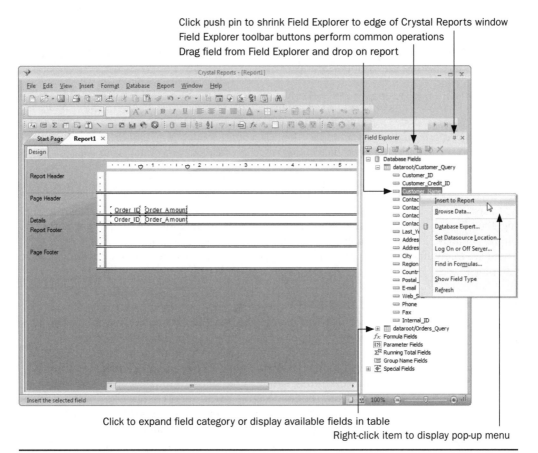

Click to expand field category or display available fields in table

Right-click item to display pop-up menu

FIGURE 1-5   The Design Tab and Field Explorer

multiple fields. If you wish to select a range of fields, click the first field in the range and then hold down the SHIFT key and click the last field in the range. Both fields, as well as all of those in between, will be selected. After you CTRL- or SHIFT-click the desired fields, drag and drop them as a group. After you add a field to the report, you see a small green check mark next to the field in the Field Explorer. This indicates that the field is in use somewhere on the report.

TIP   *Deleting a field you've added to a report is as simple as clicking it, and then pressing DEL. If you wish to delete multiple objects, you may select more than one report object by CTRL-clicking or SHIFT-clicking the desired objects. Then, press DEL to delete all the selected objects.*

You do not have to leave the Field Explorer docked to the side of the Crystal Reports window. If you'd like to expand the size of the Design tab so that you have more room to work without scrolling, "undock" the Field Explorer by pointing to its title bar area at the top. Then, either double-click the title bar or drag the Field Explorer away until you see the outline of a separate, free-floating window. The Design tab will expand to the full width of the Crystal Reports window, and the Field Explorer will now display in its own free-floating window. To redock the Field Explorer, drag it back toward the edge of the Crystal Reports window until the outline of a docked window again appears. You can redock the Field Explorer to the left, bottom, or right of the Design tab. If you double-click the title bar of the free-floating Field Explorer, it will redock to its previous position.

TIP One user interface element appearing in several Crystal Reports dialog boxes (including the Field Explorer) is the push pin. Clicking this icon in the upper right-hand corner of a dialog box will "shrink" the dialog box to the edge of the Crystal Reports screen, freeing up more screen space for report design. Then, if you simply point to the name of the dialog box on the edge of the screen, the dialog box will expand from the edge of the screen. If you wish to return the dialog box to its always-displayed state, just click the push pin again when the dialog box is expanded.

Report Sections

When you first create a new report, Crystal Reports shows five default sections in the Design tab. Table 1-1 outlines where and how many times each section appears in a report, and the types of objects you may want to place in them.

If you drag a database field into the details section, Crystal Reports places a field heading in the page header automatically and aligns it with the database field. If you drag a database field into any other section, no field heading will be inserted, even if you drag the field into the details section later—automatic field headings are only created if you drag a field directly into the details section (and, if you haven't turned off the Insert Detail Field Headings option in File | Options).

Section	Where It Appears	What to Place in the Section
Report header	Once only, at the beginning of the report	Title page, company logo, introductory information that you want to appear once only, at the beginning of the report, charts or cross-tabs that apply to the whole report
Page header	At the top of every page	Field titles, print date/time, report title
Details	Every time a new record is read from the database	Database fields and formulas that you want to appear for every record
Report footer	Once only, at the end of the report	Grand totals, closing disclaimers, charts, or cross-tabs that apply to the whole report
Page footer	At the bottom of every page	Page numbers, report name, explanations for figures in the report

TABLE 1-1 Default Report Sections

Previewing the Report

When you see objects depicted in the Design tab, Crystal Reports is displaying only "placeholders." You'll see the names of fields and objects surrounded by outline symbols, indicating how wide and tall they are. You won't ever see actual data in the Design tab. To see the report containing real data as it might appear when printed on a printer or displayed on a Web page, you need to preview the report.

There are several ways of previewing a report. Choose View | Print Preview or click the Print Preview button on the Standard toolbar to preview the entire report (CTRL-R will also preview the report). To preview a limited number of records, choose View | Preview Sample and specify the number of records you wish to see.

When you preview a report, the Preview tab appears next to the Design tab, as shown in Figure 1-6. You can scroll up and down through the report, use the Zoom control to change the Zoom level of the report, and use the page navigation buttons to move through various pages of the report (Crystal Reports 2008 now displays page navigation buttons both at the

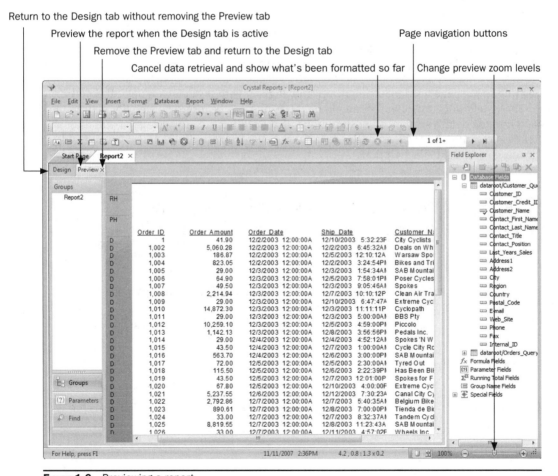

FIGURE 1-6 Previewing a report

top of the report preview screen and in the new Navigation Tools toolbar). You can easily move back and forth between the Design and Preview tabs by clicking them.

Moving and Sizing Objects

Once you've placed objects on your report, you will probably want to move them around the report as your design progresses. Crystal Reports estimates how much horizontal space is required to display string database fields. This may result in string fields on the report that may appear too narrow or too wide. Also, if you change the font size of an object, you'll usually have to adjust the object size accordingly.

The first step in moving or sizing an object is to select the object. Simply click it. A shaded outline and four blocks appear around the object, indicating that it is selected. Now you can move or size it.

Pointing inside the selected object causes your mouse pointer to turn into a four-way pointer. You can then click and drag the object to a new location with the mouse. If you point at one of the little blue blocks—the *sizing handles* at the top, bottom, left, and right of the object—your mouse pointer turns into a two-way size pointer. Clicking and dragging these handles stretches or shrinks the object. Sizing objects requires very precise accuracy with your mouse! Laptop users with trackpads will probably opt for an external mouse after trying this a few times.

Point inside a selected
object to move it

Point at the desired sizing
handle to resize an object

You're not limited to moving or sizing one object at a time. You can select multiple objects before moving or sizing them. CTRL-click or SHIFT-click to select more than one field or field title. You can also surround multiple objects with an elastic box. Before you start to draw the elastic box, make sure you deselect any already-selected objects by clicking an area of the report where there are no objects.

TIP *When the Design tab is displayed, you don't have to use the mouse to move or resize objects. For very fine control of object placement and sizing, use your keyboard's cursor keys. Using the cursor keys by themselves will move selected objects in the direction of the key. If you hold down* SHIFT *and use the cursor keys, objects will be widened, narrowed, made taller, or made shorter in the direction of the keys.*

Using Guidelines to Move Objects

When you insert a database field into the details section, Crystal Reports inserts two other things automatically. The first, the field heading, appears directly above the field in the page header. What might not be so obvious is the *vertical guideline*. You'll notice a little "upside-down tent" (officially known as a *guideline handle*) in the ruler above the report. The guideline is actually a vertical line extending from the guideline handle all the way down the report.

Crystal Reports automatically placed this in the ruler, and it attached the field in the details section and the field heading in the page header to the guideline.

NOTE *By default, only the guideline handles are visible when you first install Crystal Reports. If you'd like to see the dashed guidelines themselves in the Design tab, choose View | Guidelines | Design from the pull-down menus. To see guidelines in the Preview tab, choose View | Guidelines | Preview from the pull-down menus. Note that even if you make the latter choice, you'll see the dashed guidelines in the Preview tab only if you click any object to select it in the preview window.*

You may move objects as a group by dragging the guideline handle left or right inside the ruler. All objects attached to that guideline will move at the same time. If you've placed a database field in the details section and an associated field heading in the page header, and you have inserted several group subtotals in groups and grand totals in the report footer, they will typically all be attached to the same guideline. Just move the guideline left or right to move all the objects together.

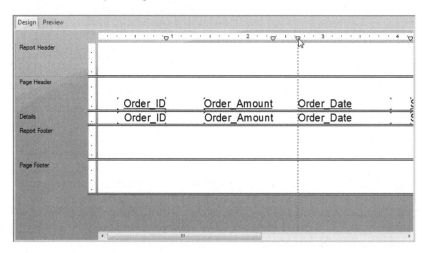

If you created the report with a report wizard, you'll see that Crystal Reports inserted horizontal guidelines on the left side of the Design tab, as well as vertical guidelines described previously. You can also add horizontal guidelines yourself if you use the Blank Report option. Just click in the side ruler to add a horizontal guideline. Then attach objects to them on the top, bottom, or middle. Move the guideline to move whole lines of objects up or down at the same time.

With a little experience, you'll probably quickly develop a love-hate relationship with guidelines. If you have lots of smaller objects positioned closely together on a report, you'll probably give up on the guidelines and just move them by CTRL-clicking or using an elastic box. If you have fewer objects spaced a little farther apart on your report, or lots of aligned objects in several report sections, you'll probably like using the guidelines to rearrange objects. Table 1-2 shows some of the guideline issues that may crop up in your report-design process, along with ways of solving the problems.

What Happened	How Is It Fixed?
You mistakenly dragged a guideline off the ruler when you just wanted to move it left or right. The objects attached to it haven't moved, and the guideline is now gone.	Click the Undo button on the Standard toolbar, or choose Edit | Undo Remove Guideline. This will bring the guideline back. If you notice the missing guideline after you've completed other tasks, and you don't want to Undo, just add a guideline back into the ruler by clicking in the ruler; reattach the objects by dragging them to the new guideline.
You selected and moved an individual object or objects with your mouse, but the guideline didn't move with them. Now, when you move the guideline in the ruler, the objects don't move.	You detach an object from a guideline when you move the object in the Design tab. You cannot reattach guidelines to objects by moving the guideline in the ruler. You have to reattach *objects to guidelines* by moving the objects until they snap to the guidelines. You can tell when an object has been reattached to a guideline by looking at the very small red marks on the edge of the object where it's attached to the guideline.
You've resized or moved objects and they now appear to be attached to two guidelines: one on the left and one on the right. When you move either guideline, the objects stretch rather than move.	Resize the objects away from the guideline you don't want them attached to. By resizing, you detach them from one guideline while leaving them attached to the other.
You notice that when you delete objects from the report, the guidelines stay and clutter up the ruler. When you move other objects around on the report, they're always snapping to the stray guidelines.	Remove any unwanted guidelines simply by dragging them off the ruler.

TABLE 1-2   Guideline Issues

TIP   *You may remove all horizontal or vertical guidelines on the report at once. Right-click anywhere on an empty portion of the report canvas (not on a field or other object) and choose the desired Remove All Horizontal Guidelines or Remove All Vertical Guidelines option from the pop-up menu.*

Formatting Objects

When you place objects on your report, Crystal Reports applies default font faces, sizes, colors, and formatting to the objects. You'll usually want to change some of this formatting to suit your particular report style or standards. There are several ways of formatting objects. As you use Crystal Reports, you may find that one way suits you better than another. Also, all formatting options aren't available with every method, so you may need to use a certain one to perform a specific kind of formatting.

Using the Formatting toolbar is the quickest way to apply standard formatting. The Formatting toolbar is similar to other toolbars you may have used in word processors or spreadsheet programs. To format using the Formatting toolbar, first select the object or objects you want to format, and then change their formatting by clicking Formatting toolbar buttons or choosing items in drop-down lists.

Some formatting options, such as formatting a date field to print in a long date format or designating that only one dollar sign should print at the top of each page, aren't available on the Formatting toolbar. These formatting options, along with all the options available on the Formatting toolbar, can be chosen in the Format Editor, shown in Figure 1-7. To use the Format Editor, first choose the object or objects that you wish to format, and then do one of the following:

- Click the Format button on the Expert Tools toolbar.
- Choose Format Field from the Format menu.
- Right-click the object and choose Format Field from the pop-up menu.

All of these options display the Format Editor. Choose the desired tab on the Format Editor, and make formatting selections by choosing one of the built-in styles, by using a

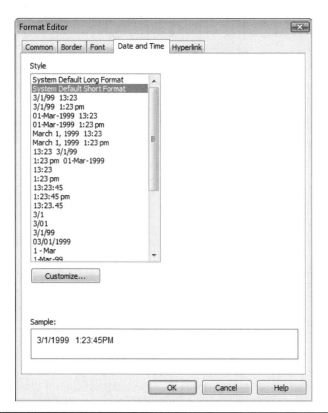

FIGURE 1-7   The Format Editor

custom style, or by choosing other specific formatting options on the desired tab. Click OK on the Format Editor to apply all the formatting you chose and close the Format Editor.

There are two general ways you can choose formats in the Format Editor—with a default style, or by customizing the style. In particular, you'll notice a selection of predefined formats for most non-string data types in the Style list. You can just choose one of these default formats from the list. If, however, the exact format you want isn't in the Style list, click the Customize button at the bottom of the Style list. A Custom Style dialog box will appear where you can make more detailed choices about how to format the field. You'll need to use the Customize button to conditionally format some aspects of the field as well (conditional formatting is discussed in Chapter 6).

TIP *You can add new objects, or move, size, and format existing objects, just as easily in the Preview tab as in the Design tab. Be careful, though, that you move or size objects accurately in the Preview tab. You may inadvertently move an object from the details section to the page header, or make some similar undesirable move, without realizing it. Formatting objects in the Preview tab is great, but it may be better to size or move them in the Design tab.*

Customizing Crystal Reports Behavior

When you first install Crystal Reports, it behaves in a certain way that should serve most report designers well. However, you will probably want to customize the behavior of some Crystal Report options. Other software typically has a Preferences or Options menu item to accomplish this. Crystal Reports has two options that work together to control how the program behaves: Options and Report Options, both chosen from the File menu.

Most often, you will use the Options dialog box, shown in Figure 1-8, to change the default behavior of Crystal Reports. For example, to change the default font face and size from Arial 10 point to something else, you would click the Fonts tab in the Options dialog box, click the button for the type of object you want to change, and choose a different font or size. To change the default format of date fields from the default specified in the Windows Control Panel to mm/dd/yy, you would click the Fields tab in the Options dialog box and then click the Date button.

CAUTION *Many options you choose here don't change items already placed on the current report, or any existing reports—they will affect only new items added to the report. For example, if you change the default font to 8-point Times New Roman, only new objects that you add to the report from that point forward will take on that new formatting.*

There are a number of options that benefit the new user and make report creation a bit easier. You may want to choose File | Options and set each of the following options to your own personal preference.

The Options dialog box is divided into a series of tabs, each categorizing the various options that are available. What follows is a summary of the more often-used options.

FIGURE 1-8 Options dialog box

Layout Tab

- **Design View – Guidelines**   You may wish to turn this option on to display dashed guidelines in the Design tab. The majority of report designing should occur in the Design tab, and guidelines can be useful.

- **Design View – Short Section Names**   Once you're more familiar with the Design tab, you may turn this option on to expand the width of the design canvas. This will change the fully spelled section names at the left of the Design tab to smaller abbreviations.

- **Preview – Section Names**   You'll probably want to leave this option on to help you troubleshoot sectional problems when you're in preview mode. This will show abbreviated section names to the left of the Preview tab.

- **Design View – Show Hidden Sections**   This option will show any sections that you hide or suppress at full height in the Design tab. The hidden or suppressed sections will appear with a repeating diagonal line effect. If you uncheck this option, hidden or suppressed sections will be compacted and will not be visible in the Design tab.

- **Grid Options – Snap To Grid**   Great to turn off when you want to be able to truly use freeform placement of objects. This will allow precise placement without objects snapping to the predetermined grid.

- **Design View – Grid**   If you leave Snap To Grid turned on, this will actually show the grid in the Design tab as a series of dots, so you can see exactly where objects you are moving will snap.

- **Preview – Grid**   You'll probably want to leave this option turned off to improve clarity. You may turn it on if you are moving and resizing objects in the Preview tab and want to see where they will snap.

Reporting Tab

- **Save Data With Report**   Checks the File | Save Data With Report option automatically when you create a new report. This saves data in the Preview tab along with the report design in the report .RPT file. If you don't want this option turned on when you create a new report, uncheck it here in File | Options.

- **Suppress Printing If No Records Selected**   If the particular combination of data and record selection chosen returns no records, this option will suppress printing of every object on the report. If you leave this option turned off and no records are returned, text objects in page/report headers, and other "fixed" objects, will still print.

- **Show All Headers On Drill Down**   Shows all headers above the group being drilled into inside the drill-down tab. See Chapter 7 for information on drill-down reporting.

- **Autosave Reports After x Minutes**   This will automatically save your report files every few minutes, preventing a loss of data if you suffer a power failure or your computer hangs. You may choose how often to automatically save reports. Reports are saved in the drive/folder specified as your Windows "Temp" folder with the file extension .AUTOSAVE.RPT.

- **Save Preview Picture**   This will automatically save a small "thumbnail view" of your report along with the .RPT file when you save the report (you must preview the report before you save it for the Preview Picture to be saved). This is helpful if you plan on posting the report to BusinessObjects Enterprise (discussed in Section II of the book). The preview will also appear in a standard Windows File Open dialog box if you click the Preview button.

Formula Editor Tab

- **Default Formula Language**   This feature allows you to choose the default formula language for Crystal Reports formulas. You may change the language used for formulas within each formula, but this allows you to choose the default. Chapter 4 discusses the different formula language options in more detail.

- **Text Options/Color**   These choices will change the default font and color scheme used in the Formula Editor. You may, for example, wish to increase or decrease the size and style of the font that appears when you create formulas.

Database Tab

- **Sort Tables Alphabetically/Sort Fields Alphabetically**   This will sort tables in the Database Expert and fields in the Field Explorer alphabetically, rather than in the order the database returns them. This may be helpful with large databases when you need to find a particular table or field.

- **Database Server Is Case-Insensitive**   If you check this option, SQL databases that you use (such as Microsoft SQL Server, Oracle, and Informix) will ignore the case of any record selection you may provide. For example, if you supply a record selection or Select Expert comparison value of "USA", the report will still include records if they include "Usa", "usa", or "uSa". This setting also affects case sensitivity in report formulas, such as when using If-Then-Else tests with string fields.

- **Select Distinct Data For Browsing**   You may notice that browsing for sample data in the Select Expert, in the Field Explorer, and in other parts of Crystal Reports takes a significant amount of time. This is probably because the report is set to Select Distinct Data For Browsing. If you turn off this option, only the first 500 records of the report will be read when browsing, instead of reading records until 500 unique values are retrieved. Although this may not supply as many sample values when browsing, it can be significantly faster.

- **Perform Query Asynchronously**   Checking this option will allow you to stop a query sent to a SQL database before it begins returning records to the report. You can do this with the Stop button in the Preview tab (the round red X to the left of the page navigation buttons in the Navigation Tools toolbar). If you leave this option unchecked, you will have to wait until the server completes the query and begins to return records to the report before you may stop report processing.

- **Automatic Smart Linking**   If this option is checked, Crystal Reports will attempt to automatically link tables you add to the Database Expert. This attempt is made by looking for matching field names and data types in adjoining tables. This often results in tables being linked on incorrect fields and not linked on correct fields. You may wish to uncheck this option off, and simply link tables manually on the proper fields.

Fonts/Fields Tabs

These tabs will allow you to choose formatting options for different Crystal Reports data types (such as string, numeric, dates, and so forth) and different types of Crystal Reports objects (such as database fields, summary fields, field titles, and so forth). Click the desired button and choose desired formatting options for the default Format Editor. New objects placed on reports from that point forward will take on the new formatting.

Smart Tag & HTML Preview Tab

This tab presents several options that allow you to preview your report in a web browser to see how it will appear when posted to a custom web application or a Business Objects enterprise web product. In order to make use of this feature, and to properly set options in this tab, you must have a version of a compatible enterprise product (such as BusinessObjects Enterprise or Crystal Reports Server) installed and available on your network. Contact your enterprise software administrator for information about completing items on this tab and viewing the HTML preview of your reports.

A subset of items from the Options dialog box appears on the File | Report Options dialog box.

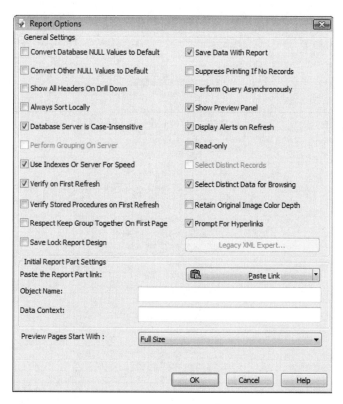

When you create a new report, these options are based on what's set in the File |
Options dialog box. Later, though, these options can be set to be different from the
corresponding File | Options dialog box items. When the report is saved, these options are
saved along with the report. The next time the report is retrieved, they will *supersede* the
corresponding File | Option items.

The Report Explorer

The *Report Explorer* is a tree-like view of all the sections in your report (Report Header,
Details section, Page footer, and so forth) and the report objects within them (database
fields, text objects, and so forth). Navigating through the Report Explorer is another way
to format or delete individual report objects or entire report sections.

To display the Report Explorer, choose View | Report Explorer from the pull-down
menus or click the Report Explorer button in the Standard toolbar. If the Field and Report
Explorers are combined in the single dialog box, you may also click the Report Explorer tab
to display the Report Explorer.

The Report Explorer will appear in the same dialog box space as the Field Explorer, as
shown in Figure 1-9. You may navigate back and forth between the Field and Report
Explorers by clicking the desired tab at the bottom of the dialog box.

Expand nodes or toggle inclusion of
various object types

Click plus or minus signs to
expand or collapse nodes

The *x* in the upper right-hand corner
indicates suppressed section

Magnifying glass icon
indicates hidden section

Right-click report object or
section to display pop-up
menu options

FIGURE 1-9   The Report Explorer

> **NOTE** *By default, the Field Explorer and the Report Explorer are combined into a single tabbed dialog box. You may separate them by dragging the desired tab away from the combined dialog box. If you then wish to redock the explorer, you may discover that the two are no longer combined with their respective tabs. While this may be the way you prefer to display the dialog boxes (especially if you make use of the new push pin feature), you may wish to recombine the two explorer dialogs into a single tabbed dialog. To do this, drag either the Field Explorer or the Report Explorer on top of the other dialog box until a box-with-tab outline appears. When you release the mouse button, the two dialog boxes will recombine. You may actually use this technique to combine other explorers (such as the Workbench or the Dependency Checker) with existing explorers.*

The very top "node" in the Report Explorer represents the report itself—everything else appears within this node. Click the plus sign to expand the report, which will then display a list of report sections (Page Header, Details section, and so forth). If you click the plus sign next to a report section, you'll be presented with either additional sections (if you've created them) or report objects within that section. A different icon will appear for suppressed or hidden sections. And, the type of each report object within a section will also be indicated by a unique icon—a small picture image will appear next to bitmap graphics, the "Aa" characters will appear next to a text object, and so on. Report objects will display either their default names, such as "Graph1", or specific names you've given them in the Common tab of the Format Editor (discussed in more detail in Chapter 6).

If you select a report section, the corresponding shaded section name will be highlighted at the left of the Design or Preview tab. If you click a report object, the object will be selected on the Design or Preview tab of Crystal Reports. Once you've selected the section or object you wish to modify, right-click. A pop-up menu will appear giving you several choices, depending on whether you've selected a report section or an object (this is the same pop-up menu that you'll see if you right-click the report object itself or the shaded section area in the Design or Preview tab). You may choose, among other things, to format a section (which will display the Section Expert), format a report object (which will display the Format Editor), or delete the object or section. If you wish to format multiple report objects at the same time, you may CTRL-click more than one object to select them. Then, options you choose from the pop-up menu will apply to all selected objects (note that you can't multiselect report sections or a combination of sections and objects).

> **TIP** *More information on formatting sections with the Section Expert is presented in Chapter 7. More detailed information on formatting individual objects with the Format Editor can be found in Chapter 6.*

The Workbench

The *Workbench* is an additional "explorer" (similar to the Field Explorer and Report Explorer discussed earlier in the chapter) that allows you to organize sets of reports into "projects."

To display the Workbench, choose View | Workbench from the pull-down menus, or click the Workbench toolbar button in the Standard toolbar. The Workbench dialog appears on the right side of the Crystal Reports screen. As with the other explorers mentioned earlier in the chapter, you may click the small *x* or push pin in the upper right-hand corner of the Workbench to close or shrink the dialog box. You may also combine the Workbench with the Field and/or Report explorers in a tabbed or divided dialog, as described earlier in the chapter.

The Workbench, shown in Figure 1-10, allows you to organize any number of report files into a series of projects. A *project* simply displays as a folder inside the Workbench. You may then add any number of existing reports to a project folder. If you are using Crystal Reports Server or BusinessObjects Enterprise, you may also add Report Packages to the Workbench. By making use of the Workbench, you can organize a series of reports that you wish to treat in some organized fashion, such as a batch of reports that you may be developing for a new Data Warehouse project or a custom software package.

Creating Projects and Adding Existing Reports

You must create at least one project folder before you add reports to the Workbench. If you add reports before you create a project folder, an "Untitled Project" folder will be created for the report automatically. To create a new project, either click the down arrow next to the Add button in the Workbench toolbar and choose Add New Project, or right-click in the Workbench and choose Add | Add New Project from the pop-up menu. An "Untitled Project" folder will be added to the Workbench. The project name will automatically be placed in edit mode so that you can type the desired name for the project folder as soon as you create it. If you wish to rename an existing project folder, select the desired folder and press the F2 key, hold your mouse button down for a short period of time, or right-click and choose Rename from the pop-up menu. The project folder name will be placed in edit mode so that you can type a new name.

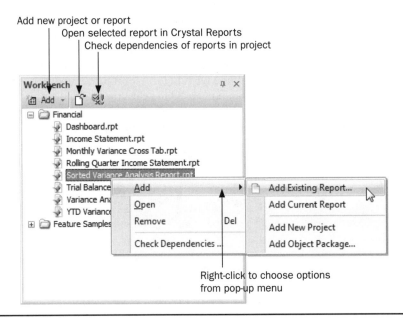

FIGURE 1-10   The Workbench

Once you've created a new project folder, you may add one or more reports to the folder. First, select the project folder you wish to add reports to. Then, click the Add toolbar button in the Workbench toolbar or right-click the desired project folder and choose Add | Add Existing Report from the pop-up menu. An Open dialog box will appear displaying existing .RPT files. Navigate to the desired folder on your local hard disk or network drive and choose the report you wish to add. Once you click Open, the report will be added to the Workbench in the chosen project folder. You may also open a separate Windows Explorer window and select one or more .RPT files. Then, simply drag the files to the desired project folder in the Workbench. The report or reports will be added to the Workbench.

Deleting projects and reports from the Workbench is similarly straightforward. Select either the project folder or report you wish to delete. Then, just press the DEL key or right-click and choose Remove from the pop-up menu. The selected report or project will be deleted from the Workbench. If you delete a project folder, all reports in that folder will be deleted.

NOTE *When you delete reports from the Workbench, you are only deleting their reference in the Workbench dialog box. The actual .RPT file will not be deleted from your hard disk or network drive.*

Once you have organized reports and projects in the Workbench, it's simple to reorganize them by dragging and dropping. You may, for example, wish to move a report from one project folder to another. Just select the desired report and drag with your mouse. You'll see a small underline indicating where the report will be dropped. Drop it underneath the desired folder and the report will be placed in that folder. You may also reorder the lists of project folders by dragging and dropping the folders to different locations.

Opening a report you've added to the Workbench is accomplished by merely double-clicking its name. You may also select the desired report and click the Open toolbar button from the Workbench toolbar, or right-click the desired report and choose Open from the pop-up menu. The report will be opened in Crystal Reports for viewing or editing. If you have renamed, moved, or deleted a report since adding it to the Workbench, the Workbench will be unable to find the report and an error message will appear when you attempt to open the report.

NOTE *You can also publish reports from a project folder in the Workbench to Crystal Reports Server or BusinessObjects Enterprise—either as individual reports, or as a report package. More information on publishing reports can be found in Chapter 21.*

Adding Report Packages

Crystal Reports Server and BusinessObjects Enterprise feature the ability to store a group of related reports as a *report package*. A report package allows multiple reports to be scheduled and viewed as a single unit (more information on report packages can be found in Chapter 21).

The Workbench allows you to connect to your Crystal Reports Server or BusinessObjects Enterprise system and add a report package as a separate entry. Right-click in the Workbench and choose Add | Add Object Package from the pop-up menu (no toolbar button option is available to add report packages). Once you've supplied proper logon credentials to your Crystal Reports Server or BusinessObjects Enterprise system, a list of folders will appear.

Navigate to the desired location and choose the report package you wish to add to the Workbench.

A report package will appear in the Workbench as a separate entry with a unique icon (it won't be placed in a project folder). Click the plus sign next to the report package name to see the group of reports that make it up. As with individual reports you added to the Workbench, you may open a report contained in a report package by double-clicking it, selecting it and clicking the Open toolbar button in the Workbench toolbar, or right-clicking it and choosing Open from the pop-up menu. And, as with reports added to the Workbench from disk drives, any report package reports that are removed or renamed in their source Crystal Reports Server or BusinessObjects Enterprise systems won't open if they're chosen in the Workbench.

The Dependency Checker

The *Dependency Checker* will analyze one or more reports and return a list of potential problems the report may have, including:

- Errors in formulas, SQL Expressions, or Custom Functions
- Hyperlinks set in the Format Editor that are broken
- Invalid database connections that are identified by the Verify Database command
- Repository objects that can't be found in the source repository
- Report part hyperlinks that are broken
- External subreports that can't be found in their original locations

The Dependency Checker can check a single report that is currently open for viewing or editing. It can also be used to check one or more reports as a group from the Workbench (discussed earlier in the chapter). When the Dependency Checker is run, a list of potential problems is presented in a separate dialog box. When you double-click an individual error, the specific part of the report (formula, repository object, and so forth) referenced by the error will be displayed. You may then take steps to resolve the error.

Checking Dependencies in the Current Report

You may check dependencies in the report you currently have open for editing or viewing. You may, for example, have created a large number of formulas and wish to ensure that they all reference proper fields. Or, you may have just opened a report developed by a colleague and wish to look for any obvious problems that the Dependency Checker looks for.

Choose Report | Check Dependencies from the pull-down menus (there is no equivalent toolbar button). A dialog box will appear that indicates the progress of the checking process—the more complex a report, the longer it will take to check dependencies.

The Dependency Checker Dialog Box

Once the dependency checking process is complete, results will be displayed in the Dependency Checker dialog box, shown in Figure 1-11. This dialog box, like other "explorers" discussed in this chapter (Field Explorer, Report Explorer, Workbench, and so forth), can be docked or

Right-click error and choose options from pop-up menu

Double-click error to highlight suspect object

Icon indicates type of error

FIGURE 1-11   The Dependency Checker

undocked to the side or bottom of the Crystal Reports screen, as well as being shrunk and expanded by clicking the push pin icon.

An icon will appear next to each error message, indicating the type of error encountered. These error icons include a green check mark that indicates no errors in the report, a yellow explanation point that indicates a potential problem that generally won't prevent the report from running, and a red *x* that indicates a problem that may prevent the report from running at all.

To display the specific object that resulted in the error message, do one of these things: double-click the error message, select the error message and press ENTER, or else right-click the error and choose Go To from the pop-up menu. The report will display the object referenced by the error (for example, the formula that has an error or the bitmap image that can't be found in the repository). You may then take steps to resolve the problem identified by the Dependency Checker.

Once you've finished viewing Dependency Checker entries, you may close the Dependency Checker dialog box by clicking the small *x* in the upper right-hand corner. However, even closing the Dependency Checker will not clear the entries in it from a previous checking process. You may redisplay the Dependency Checker by choosing View | Dependency Checker from the pull-down menus, or clicking the Dependency Checker toolbar button in the Standard toolbar.

To actually clear errors from the Dependency Checker, select the desired error you no longer wish to display and press the DEL key. You may also right-click the desired error and choose Clear from the pop-up menu. Or, if you'd like to clear all errors in the Dependency Checker, right-click and choose Clear All from the pop-up menu. Once you've cleared errors, running the Dependency Checker process again with the Report | Check Dependencies option will redisplay any leftover errors in the report.

Dependency Checker Options

By default, the Dependency Checker will check all possible types of errors, including those based on the Crystal Reports Server/BusinessObjects Enterprise repository, hyperlinks, and so forth. You may, however, prefer that the Dependency Checker only check for certain types of errors in your report. To make these choices, check or uncheck options in the Dependency Checker Options dialog box. You may display this dialog box by choosing File | Options from the pull-down menus and then clicking the Dependency Checker tab. Or, you may right-click in the Dependency Checker dialog box and choose Options from the pop-up menu.

Checking Dependencies for Workbench Projects

Not only can you check dependencies in the currently open report, but you can check a single report or group of reports that you've organized in the Workbench (the Workbench is covered in more detail earlier in the chapter). You can even check dependencies in one or all reports contained in a report package that you've added to the Workbench from Crystal Reports Server or BusinessObjects Enterprise.

To check a report or reports contained within a Workbench project, select the desired item you want to check in the Workbench. For example, to check a single report, select it in the Workbench. If you want to check all reports in a project, select the project folder. If you want to check a single report in a report package, select the individual report within the package. Or, select the report package name if you wish to check all reports within the package. Once you've made your selection, click the Check Dependencies button in the Workbench toolbar, or right-click and choose Check Dependencies from the pop-up menu.

Crystal Reports will open all selected reports and check dependencies in each one. The Dependency Checker dialog box will appear with all errors found in all reports. You can determine which report an error belongs to by looking at the Location column in the Dependency Checker. To evaluate or correct a particular error, double-click the error, select the error and press ENTER, or right-click the error and choose Go To from the pop-up menu.

Sorting and Grouping

When you first create and preview a report, the report shows details sections in *natural order*. That is, the records appear in whatever order the database sends them to Crystal Reports. This order can vary widely, depending on what database you are using, how you link tables, and the actual order in which records were entered into the database.

You'll probably want to control the order in which information appears on your report. An employee listing, for example, isn't very useful if it isn't in alphabetical order. A sales breakdown is probably more helpful if you see your sales figures in a particular order. You're probably interested in a highest-to-lowest sequence of order quantities if you're about to send gifts to your best customers at the holidays. On the other hand, lowest-to-highest sequence is probably more appropriate if you're about to send your marketing department out to talk to lower-performing customers.

Sorting Your Report

If you simply want to reorder your report's details sections into a particular order, you need to *sort* the report. Sorting is useful for simple reports that need to present information in a certain order. To sort a report, choose Report | Record Sort Expert from the pull-down menus, or click the Record Sort Expert button on the Expert Tools toolbar. This displays the Record Sort Expert dialog box.

The left Available Fields box shows all the report fields that you've placed on the report, followed by a list of all tables and fields you initially added to the report. If you wish to sort on a field you haven't placed on the report, scroll down through the Report Fields list until you find the list of tables and fields you added to your report. Choose one or more fields to control how you want your report sorted. Simply double-click the field you wish to sort on, or select the field and then click the right arrow button, or drag the field from the Available Fields list to the Sort Fields box. You may then choose between the Ascending and Descending radio buttons to choose the sort order.

An *ascending* sort organizes the records alphabetically in A to Z order; if the records start with numbers, they will appear before any letters, sorted 0 through 9. In a *descending* sort, the order is reversed. Records appear in Z to A order, followed by any numbers in 9 to 0 order.

You may sort by as many fields as you like—you're not limited to one. This is handy, for example, if you want to sort your customers by state, and within state by customer name. Simply add the additional sort fields to the Sort Fields box and choose the Ascending or Descending radio button for each field. The first field in the list will be the *primary*, or first, sorting field, the second field will be *secondary* (will be used to sort multiple records that have the same primary field), and so forth. If you wish to change the order of sorting priority, select a field in the Sort Fields list and click the up or down arrow above the list to reorder the sort fields. You may also drag one field above or below another field in the Sort Fields box to change the order of fields. When you click OK, Crystal Reports will sort by the higher (primary) field first, and then the lower fields.

TIP *You can sort just as easily on formula fields (covered in Chapter 4) as you can on database fields. This is often required if you want to customize some aspect of the way records are sorted. Just remember that if you're using a SQL database, such as SQL Server or Oracle, sorting on a formula field makes Crystal Reports sort the records instead of having the database server do the work, which may affect the performance of your report (albeit slightly). This is covered in more detail in Chapter 15.*

New Interactive Sorting

Crystal Reports 2008 introduces a new feature to allow more interactive sorting by the report viewer after the report has been displayed in a Crystal Reports preview tab, when embedded in a custom Windows or Web application, or when viewed in a compatible version of Crystal Reports Server, BusinessObjects Edge, or BusinessObjects Enterprise. *Interactive sorting* mimics the behavior of typical columnar web page displays by placing sort arrow controls in the page header next to a field title. When a report viewer wishes to re-sort the report, he or she merely need click one of the sort arrow controls to change the report sort order without refreshing the report or running a new database query.

Setting up interactive sorting requires two steps:

- Adding fields to the Record Sort Expert dialog box, as discussed earlier in the chapter
- Binding a field title or text object to one of the previously added sort fields

Using techniques described earlier in this section, sort the report by all fields you wish to use for interactive sorting. If you wish to sort the report on additional fields besides those used for interactive sorting, make sure to place fields not used in interactive sorting after those you wish to use for interactive sorting. Otherwise, report viewers may be confused when a primary sort field that they are unable to control takes precedence over the field they are sorting on interactively.

Once desired fields have been added to the Record Sort Expert, you may then *bind* a text object to one of the sort fields to display a sort arrow control next to the text object (text objects are discussed in more detail in Chapter 7). Typically, this text object is the field heading that's already been added to the page header when the corresponding database field was added to the report. However, you may use any existing text object on the report, even if it's not a field heading above the desired field.

To bind a text object to a sort field, right-click the desired text object. Choose Bind Sort Control from the pop-up menu. The Sort Control dialog box will appear. Select the sort field you wish to bind to and click OK. You may also insert a new text object and bind it to a sort field at the same time. Choose Insert | Sort Control from the pull-down menus. The Sort Control dialog box will appear. Select the sort field you wish to bind the new text object to and click OK. The mouse cursor will then change to a cross-hair cursor. Draw the desired text object on the report canvas.

These steps will add a sort arrow control to the right of the text object. Now, preview the report. Click the up arrow on the desired sort arrow control to sort the report in ascending order by the chosen field. Click the down arrow to sort the report in descending order by the chosen field. If you wish to see the resulting changes to the Record Sort Expert, display it by using one of the methods described earlier in the chapter. Notice that fields are moved up and down in the Sort Fields box, and that their sort direction changes from ascending to descending, depending on which field you most recently used in interactive sorting, and whether you clicked the ascending or descending arrow.

To remove an interactive sort arrow control from a text object, simply repeat the steps used to originally bind it; right-click the text object and choose Bind Sort Control from the pop-up menu. Select <Not Interactive> in the Sort Control dialog box and click OK. The interactive sort arrow control will disappear from the text object. You may need to redisplay the Record Sort Expert to ensure that the field that was bound to the just-removed sort control is either removed, or moved below any remaining sort fields that are still bound to text objects. Otherwise, the remaining sort controls may not behave as expected, as they won't be the topmost fields in the Sort Fields box.

TIP Because a sort arrow control appears to the right side of the text object or field heading it is bound to, it may spill over on top of an adjacent field heading if fields are placed close together on your report. Also, it's sometimes difficult to easily determine which text object a sort arrow control is bound to, as there will often be a large amount of white space between the text and the sort arrow control. You may need to return to the Design tab and add more space between fields to reduce this problem. You may also want to consider formatting field headings or text objects bound to sort arrow controls with borders on all four sides to outline the entire text object. This may make it easier for a viewer to determine which field a sort arrow control refers to, even if the border doesn't encompass the sort arrow.

Sort arrow control on text object   Adding a border and horizontally spacing fields may make sort control easier to see

Customer Name	City	Region	Country
UAE Cycle	Abu Dhabi	Abu Dhabi	United A
Benny - The Spokes Person	Huntsville	AL	USA
Psycho-Cycle	Huntsville	AL	USA
The Great Bike Shop	Huntsville	AL	USA
Sports Alsace	Strasbourg	Alsace	France
Mulhouse Vélos	Mulhouse	Alsace	France
Ankara Bicycle Company	Ankara	Ankara	Turkey
Lourdes Sports	Lourdes	Aquitaine	France
Bordeaux Sports	Bordeaux	Aquitaine	France
Bikefest	Little Rock	AR	USA
Mountain View Sport	Auckland	Auckland	New Ze
Auvergne Bicross	Vichy	Auvergne	France
Arsenault et Maurier	Clermont-Ferrand	Auvergne	France
McDonald Klein Sports	Bristol	Avon	Englanc
Bicycle Races	Tempe	AZ	USA
Biking and Hiking	Phoenix	AZ	USA
Bangkok Sports	Bangkok	Bangkok	Thailan
France Sports	Cherbourg	Basse Normandie	France
Vélos Basse Normandie	Caen	Basse Normandie	France
Berlin Biking GmBH.	München	Bayern	Germar
Bikes for Tykes	Vancouver	BC	Canada
Cycles and Sports	Vancouver	BC	Canada

Grouping Records

Sorting records is handy for lists or other simple reports that just need records to appear in a certain order. It's more common, however, to want not only to have your report sorted by certain fields, but also to have subtotals, counts, averages, or other summary information appear when the sort field changes. To accomplish this, you must use Crystal Reports *groups*. In other reporting tools and mainframe development languages, this was often referred to as report *level breaks.*

When you create a report group, you both sort the records on the report and create two additional report sections every time the group field changes. You may place subtotals, averages, counts, and many other types of summary information in these sections. In addition, grouping your report adds an Explorer-like Groups option to the preview panel on the left side of the Preview tab. The group portion of the preview panel gives you a quick overview of the organization of your report and enables you to navigate directly to a particular group that you want to see.

To create a report group, you may either choose Insert | Group from the pull-down menus or click the Insert Group button from the Insert Tools toolbar. The Insert Group dialog box appears. It contains two tabs: Common (shown here) and Options (discussed later).

There are two drop-down lists and a check box/conditional formula button in the Common tab that you use to insert a group. Follow these steps to complete the dialog box:

1. Click the top drop-down list to select the field you want to group on. The list will display fields on your report, as well as other fields in the tables that the report is using. You can group by a field already on the report or by a database field that you didn't put on the report. You can also group by a formula field.

2. Click the second drop-down list to select the order in which your groups will appear on the report. There are four options: *ascending order* shows the groups in A to Z order alphabetically; *descending order* shows the groups in Z to A order; *specified order* lets you create your own groups (described later in this chapter); and *original order* groups records in the order in which they appear in the database. (This last option is an interesting feature, but rarely useful in most reports.)

3. You may also choose to sort groups in ascending or descending order by use of a formula, rather than the choice made in the second drop-down list. This is helpful if, for example, if you wish to prompt your report viewer to choose an ascending or descending group order via a parameter field and create a formula using the parameter field to control group sorting. Should you desire to provide this level of control, check Use A Formula As Group Sort Order and click the conditional formula button. Create a formula that returns the values crAscendingOrder (for ascending order grouping), crDescendingOrder (for descending order grouping), or crOriginalOrder (for original order grouping).

NOTE *Parameter Fields are discussed in more detail in Chapter 13, while conditional formatting formulas are discussed in Chapter 6.*

If you wish to allow Crystal Reports to make "typical" choices for the way groups appear, you may simply click OK now to create the new group. However, if you want to set additional options for the group, click the Options tab.

Make Options tab choices as follows:

1. If you simply want to have the database field itself appear in the groups on the report and the preview panel, leave the Customize Group Name Field check box empty. However, if you'd like to customize the way the groups appear (perhaps you'd like a month fully spelled out along with a four-digit year for a date field), click the Customize Group Name Field check box. You can then make additional choices to determine what appears for the group. "Customizing Group Name Fields" appears later in the chapter.

2. Click the Keep Group Together option if you want Crystal Reports to try to keep your groups from breaking at the end of a page. If you leave this option unchecked, the beginning of a group and just a few detail records in the group may print at the bottom of a page, while the rest of the group's detail records and its subtotals may appear at the top of the next page.

3. The New Page After option (new in Crystal Reports 2008) will insert an automatic page break after the specified number of group footer sections (described later in the chapter) appear on any given page. For example, if you check this option and specify 3 as the number of visible groups, a new page will appear after the third group footer on a single page. If you create larger groups that typically span more than one page, this option will have no effect if three distinct group footers never appear on a single page. If you wish to supply the number of visible groups with a formula value (perhaps set by a parameter field), click the conditional formula button to the right of the visible groups field and create a numeric formula (formulas are covered in Chapter 4).

4. Click the Repeat Group Header on Each Page option if you think you will have large groups that will span more than a single page. This option will print the group header section (described later) at the top of each page where a group continues. This allows you to look at details sections on subsequent pages and know which group they belong to.

NOTE *The File | Report Options screen contains the Respect Keep Group Together On First Page option, which is turned off by default. However if this option is inadvertently checked, choosing Keep Group Together can cause odd behavior if the first group in your report won't fit on a page by itself. In this case, Crystal Reports will detect that it can't fit the group on the first page of the report and will start a new page before it starts printing the group. The result will be a blank first page. If this is not the desired result, return to File | Report Options and uncheck the Respect Keep Group Together On First Page option.*

Figure 2-1 shows the two new sections that are added to the Design tab, the group header and group footer. These sections appear at the beginning and end of every group. Note that Crystal Reports places an object in the group header section automatically. This *group name* object will automatically print the contents of the field on which the group is based in each group header. The group footer section is empty.

Group Header will print at the start of each group
Group Footer will print at the end of each group

FIGURE 2-1 Group added to a report

Tip *You may turn off the Insert Group Name With Group option in File | Options if you don't want Crystal Reports to automatically insert a group name object in the group header when a group is created. If this is turned off, or if you inadvertently delete a group name object, you can insert a group name from the Field Explorer by dragging and dropping a group name object after opening the Group Name Fields category.*

Figure 2-2 shows the Preview tab with the now-active group portion of the preview panel. You can see your groups in an outline form and navigate directly to the beginning of one of the groups by clicking the desired group in the preview panel. You can also turn the display of the preview panel on and off by clicking the Toggle Preview Panel button on the Standard toolbar.

Tip *In addition to the steps previously outlined, you may use the Group Expert (discussed later in the chapter) to create a new group.*

Click a group to navigate directly to it   Click to toggle preview panel display on or off

Resize the preview panel

Click to display the groups portion of the preview panel

Figure 2-2   Groups portion of the preview panel in Preview tab

Manipulating Existing Groups

After you create a group, you may wish to delete it so that only detail records print again without grouping. Or, you may wish to change the field that the group is based on, change the order of the groups from ascending to descending, customize the group name field, or choose one of the formatting options to control the way Crystal Reports deals with page breaks inside groups.

One way to do this is to point your mouse to a group header or footer section in the "shaded section area" of the left side of the Design or Preview tab (the section will be abbreviated "GH" and "GF" in the Preview tab). You must point to the group header or group footer for the group you wish to delete, right-click, and choose Delete Group from the pop-up menu. The group header and group footer sections will be removed from the report, along with any objects in them. You may also use the Group Expert, discussed in the following section, to delete a group.

```
Group Footer #1: dataroot/Customer_Query.Customer_Name - A

Hide (Drill-Down OK)
Suppress (No Drill-Down)

Section Expert...
Change Group...

Show Short Section Names

Insert Line
Delete Last Line
Arrange Lines
Fit Section

Insert Section Below

Delete Group

Select All Section Objects
```

There are also several ways to change existing groups by redisplaying the dialog box that appeared when you created the group. You may change the field that the group is based on, change the order of groups (ascending, descending, specified, original), add a formula to conditionally set the order, customize the group name field, or select the Keep Group Together, New Page After *n* Visible Groups, or Repeat Group Header On Each New Page option.

As when deleting groups, you may point to the group header or group footer section of the group you want to change in the Design or Preview tab. Then right-click and choose Change Group from the pop-up menu. The Change Group Options dialog box will reappear, where you can change group settings on either the Common or Options tab and then click OK when you're finished. You may also use the new Group Expert, discussed in the following section, to change a group.

Group Footer #1: dataroot/Customer_Query.Customer_Name - A

Hide (Drill-Down OK)

Suppress (No Drill-Down)

Se_c_tion Expert...

Change _G_roup...

Show Short Section Names

I_n_sert Line

_D_elete Last Line

A_r_range Lines

_F_it Section

Insert Section Below

D_e_lete Group

Select _A_ll Section Objects

The Group Expert

Another Crystal Reports approach to group manipulation is the *Group Expert,* which is designed to let you perform most of the grouping options described previously in the chapter, such as creating new groups, modifying existing groups, reordering groups, and deleting groups. To display the Group Expert, choose Report | Group Expert from the pull-down menus, or click the Group Expert button in the Expert Tools toolbar. The Group Expert will appear, as shown in Figure 2-3.

Here, you can add a new group to the report by selecting the field from the Available Fields list that you want to use, and clicking the right arrow to add the group. If you have an existing group on the report that you wish to remove, select that group in the Group By list and click the left arrow to remove it. And, if you want to choose options for a group on the report (either a new group you just added or an existing group that was added previously), select the group in the Group By list that you want to modify and click the Options button. The Group Options dialog box will appear. Choose the Common or Options tab and choose or change appropriate options.

If your report contains more than one group (discussed in more detail later in the chapter, under "Multiple Groups"), you may wish to change the order in which the groups appear. For example, you may have initially grouped your report first by Customer, and within Customer by Region. If you want to change the order of the groups to be by Region and then Customer, you would select a group in the Group By list and use the up and down arrows above the Group By list to change the order of the groups.

Adding Summaries

So, what's the difference between just sorting the report and creating a group? Not only is the preview panel useful with grouped reports, but you now have a section available for subtotals, averages, counts, and other summary functions at the end of each group. Although the group footer is empty when first created, you can insert summary functions into it with ease.

Click to add selected field(s) or all fields
in Available Fields list as report groups

Click to reorder selected group
in the Group By list

List of available
fields to create
report groups

List of existing
report groups,
in order of
hierarchy

Click to remove selected group(s) or all
groups in the Group By list from the report

Click to display Group Options dialog
box with Common and Options tabs

FIGURE 2-3   The Group Expert

Inserting summaries in your report requires several steps:

1. Choose Insert | Summary from the pull-down menus, or right-click the field you
   want to summarize in the Details section and choose Insert | Summary from the
   pop-up menu. To insert a summary, you can also click the Summary button on the
   Insert Tools toolbar. The Insert Summary dialog box will appear.

2. If you selected a field on the report before you chose an Insert Summary option, that field will be preselected in the Choose Field To Summarize drop-down list. Otherwise, choose the field you wish to total, average, or otherwise summarize, in this list.

3. Choose the summary function (sum, average, and so on) that you wish to use. Then, either choose to insert a grand total for the entire report (the default), or choose the existing group in which you want to place the summary. If your report contains multiple groups and you wish to add the summary to all group footers, click the Add To All Group Levels check box. If you wish to create a new group on the report for your summary, click the Insert Group button to create a new group.

4. If you want to create a percentage summary field, click the Show As A Percentage Of check box and choose from the drop-down list the field that you want to show the percentage of (percentage summary fields are discussed in detail later in the chapter). You must choose a report group before you can check this box—Percentage Summaries can't be created in the report footer.

5. If the group you've chosen is a hierarchical group (discussed later in the chapter, under "Hierarchical Groups"), you may check the Summarize Across Hierarchy check box to include the summary in all hierarchical groups.

6. Click OK to place the subtotal or summary in the group footer or report footer directly below the detail field that you're summarizing.

7. Since Crystal Reports doesn't label group summaries for you, you should add text objects next to the summaries to indicate what they display. For example, a subtotal won't be confused with an average if you place a text object containing "Subtotal:" next to the subtotal object (text objects are covered in more detail in Chapter 6).

Here are a few pointers to keep in mind when inserting summaries:

- Although Crystal Reports places subtotals and summaries in the group footer or report footer by default, you don't have to leave them there. If you move them to the group header or report header, they'll print the same information, but at the beginning of groups or the report.

- Once a summary or subtotal has been created, you don't have to delete it and insert a new summary if you want to change its function (for example, to change a subtotal to an average). Simply click the subtotal or summary and choose Edit | Edit Summary from the pull-down menus, or right-click the summary and choose Edit Summary from the pop-up menu.

- If you want to insert a summary in one or more group footers and the report footer (to summarize for multiple groups and the entire report), you don't have to use the Insert Summary options over and over for each group and the entire report, or use the Insert For All Groups check box. Just insert the summary into one group and then copy the summary from that group footer to the other groups or the report footer by using Edit menu options, or just CTRL-dragging the summary from a group footer to copy it to another section.

Table 2-1 shows the different summary functions that are available in Crystal Reports and what each does.

Function	Results
Sum	Returns the subtotal of the chosen field; available only for number or currency fields.
Average	Returns the average of the chosen field; available only for number or currency fields.
Sample Variance Sample Standard Deviation Population Variance Population Standard Deviation	For number or currency fields only, these functions return the statistical result for the group or report values. For detailed descriptions on the specific steps performed to arrive at the results, consult a statistics text or Crystal Reports online help.
Maximum	For number or currency fields, returns the highest number in the group. For string fields, returns the last member of the group alphabetically. For date fields, returns the latest date in the group.
Minimum	For number or currency fields, returns the lowest number in the group. For string fields, returns the first member of the group alphabetically. For date fields, returns the earliest date in the group.
Count	Simply counts the records in the details section and returns the number of records in the group. Although you are required to choose a database field before selecting this option, the Count function will return the same number no matter which field you choose (with the exception of fields that contain null values).
Distinct Count	Similar to the Count function, but returns only the distinct number of occurrences of the field. As opposed to Count, the field you choose in the details section before choosing Distinct Count is very significant. For example, if five records contain the strings Los Angeles, Chicago, Vancouver, Chicago, and Miami, the Count function would return 5, whereas Distinct Count would return 4.
Correlation Covariance	For number or currency fields only, these functions return the statistical result for the group or report values. When you choose these functions, an additional drop-down list appears where you may choose an additional report field to complete the function. For detailed descriptions on the specific steps performed to arrive at the results, consult a statistics text or Crystal Reports online help.
Median	For number or currency fields only. Returns the median, or middle, number in the group. If there is one number in the group, it is returned. If there are two numbers, their average is returned.

TABLE 2-1   Summary Functions

Function	Results
Mode	Returns the most frequently occurring value from all the detail records in the group. For numeric fields, Mode returns the most frequently occurring number. For string fields, Mode returns the most frequently occurring string (for example, with detail records containing five occurrences of FedEx, three occurrences of UPS, and eight occurrences of Parcel Post, Mode would return Parcel Post).
Nth Largest	Returns the third, fifth, or tenth (and so forth) largest value in the group, depending on the value you enter for N. For example, Nth largest, with N equaling 1, returns the largest value in the group. When you choose this function, an additional box appears in which you can enter the value for N. For numeric fields, this function returns the Nth-highest numeric value. With string fields, it returns the Nth value alphabetically (for example, if there are three records containing FedEx and two records containing UPS, Nth largest when N equals 2 will be UPS, and Nth largest when N equals 3 will be FedEx).
Nth Smallest	Returns the third, fifth, tenth (and so forth) smallest value in the group. For example, Nth smallest with N equaling 1 returns the smallest value in the group. When you choose this function, an additional box appears in which you can enter the value for N. This function behaves similarly to Nth highest with both numeric and string fields.
Nth Most Frequent	Returns the third, fifth, tenth (and so forth) most frequent occurrence in the group. This is similar to Mode, except that you're not limited to just the *most* frequent occurrence.
Pth Percentile	For number or currency fields only. When you choose this function, an additional box appears in which you can enter a number between 0 and 100 for P. This function returns the number that indicates what the percentile is for P, based on all the numbers in the group.
Weighted average	For number or currency fields only. This will calculate an average of group or report values, but apply the "weight" of another field to adjust the average. When you choose this function, an additional drop-down list appears where you may choose an additional report field to complete the function.

TABLE 2-1 Summary Functions *(continued)*

Caution *If the details field that you summarize contains null values (a special database value where the field actually contains nothing, as opposed to a zero or empty string), the summary function won't "count" that record. For example, a Count or Average won't figure the null record into its calculation. If you wish to avoid this problem with the current report, you can convert database null values to zero or empty string values by choosing File | Report Options and clicking Convert Database NULL Values To Default. If you want this to be the default option for all new reports, you can choose the same option on the Reporting tab from File | Options.*

Percentage Summary Fields

Although the default summary functions satisfy most needs for analytical reporting, sometimes you may prefer to calculate percentages rather than numbers. For example, if your report groups sales by sales rep within each month, you may want to know both the actual dollars and the *percentage* of revenues each sales rep is responsible for in that month. And, you may also want to calculate the percentage of total sales for the entire year that each month is responsible for. Such an example is shown in Figure 2-4. Crystal Reports features the *percentage summary field,* which creates this type of calculation without the need for a formula.

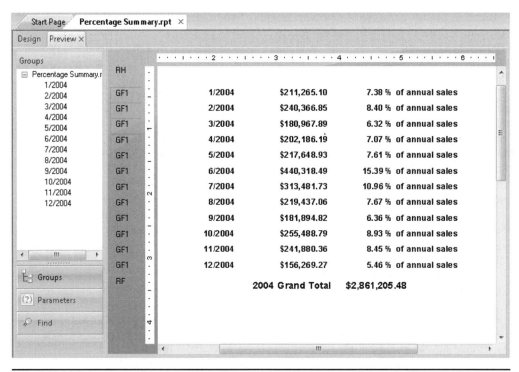

Figure 2-4   Percentages created with Percentage Summary field

To create a percentage summary field, follow the steps previously outlined to insert a summary field. Choose the field you want to use to calculate the percentage (the "numerator") and the group in which you want the percentage placed, as though you were creating a regular summary. Then, click the Show As A Percentage Of check box and use the drop-down list to choose the higher-level group or grand total you want used as the "denominator." If you are placing the percentage in the highest-level (or only) group on the report, you'll only be able to choose a grand total for the denominator. Click OK.

Crystal Reports will place a summary field in the group footer of the group you specified. When you preview the report, however, you'll see a percentage number rather than a count, subtotal, or other number. The percentage summary field will already be formatted to display a percent sign.

Multiple Groups

Crystal Reports does not limit your report to just one level of grouping. In fact, many powerful reporting features can be provided to your report viewer by creative use of multiple groups. The key to many sophisticated reporting requirements lies in creative use of formulas (covered in Chapter 4) in conjunction with multiple levels of grouping.

Multiple groups form a report hierarchy, with increasing levels of detailed information being presented by inner groups. For example, a report might be grouped by country first. Within the country group would be a geographic region group (Northwest, Southwest, and so forth), and then a group by state, a group by county or township, a group by city, and finally detail records showing individual customers or orders within that city. Each group has its own group header and group footer sections, and subtotals and summaries can exist for each group.

The group portion of the preview panel handles multiple levels of grouping very elegantly, following the general style of Windows Explorer. Plus signs (expand buttons) are displayed next to groups that can be expanded to display inner groups; minus signs (collapse buttons) are shown beside expanded groups that can be collapsed. Figure 2-5 shows a report with multiple groups. Notice that you can navigate through the preview panel by clicking the plus and minus signs to open and close group levels. When you find the group you want to see, click the group name in the preview panel to go directly to the beginning of that group in the report, no matter how deep the group is in the hierarchy.

To create additional levels of grouping, simply repeat the process described previously for inserting a group, using either the Group Expert or the Insert Group options. The groups will appear in the order that you create them. You can use the Insert Summary options to add subtotals and summaries to the group footer and group header sections.

You may inadvertently create groups in the wrong order. For example, if you wish to have your report grouped by state and then by city, make sure to create the groups in that order. If you create the city group first, followed by the state group, you'll have one group for each city, with whatever state that city is in as a lower-level group. You'd have, for example, a group for Boulder containing a Colorado group. Below that, you'd have a group for Denver containing another Colorado group.

This isn't as much of a problem as it might seem. You don't have to delete groups and reinsert them in the desired order—moving them around is surprisingly easy. Simply return to the Design tab and point to the gray Group Header or Group Footer area on the left side

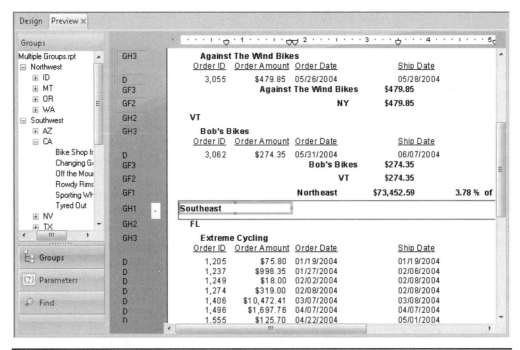

Figure 2-5   Multiple levels of grouping

of the screen. Point to the group that needs to be moved, and hold down the left mouse button—the mouse cursor turns into a hand symbol.

You can now simply drag and drop the group header or group footer on top of the group that you wish to swap it with. When you release the mouse button, the groups swap locations. Don't be confused by the fact that the groups stay numbered in sequential order—the groups have been moved. In the preceding example, simply dropping the state group header (Group Header #2) on the city group header (Group Header #1) will swap the groups. The state group header becomes Group Header #1, and the city group header becomes Group Header #2.

TIP *The Group Expert also allows you to easily swap the order of groups.*

Specified Order Grouping

Sometimes, you may need data grouped on your report in a special order that the database doesn't offer. For example, the database may contain a state field, but not a field indicating what geographic location the record belongs to (Northwest, Southwest, and so on). One option that may be appropriate for more sophisticated customized grouping is basing a group on a sophisticated formula. However, if your customized grouping is not particularly complicated, *specified order grouping* may be more straightforward. This allows you to create customized groups without having to know the Crystal Reports formula language.

Specified order grouping lets you use a dialog box similar to the Select Expert (discussed in Chapter 3) to create your own groups, based on an existing database field. In the geographic location example used previously, you could create a Northwest group consisting of Washington, Oregon, Idaho, and Montana. The Southwest group could include Nevada, California, Texas, and Arizona. The Northeast group could consist of New York, Maine, Vermont, and New Hampshire. Southeast could include Florida, Alabama, Louisiana, and Mississippi. All the other states not in these four groups could either be ignored, placed in their own individual groups, or lumped together in one final group given a name of your choice, such as Midwest.

To specify your own groups, choose Specified Order in the Group dialog box instead of Ascending or Descending order when you create a new group or change an existing group. When you choose Specified Order, a Specified Order tab is added to the Change Group Options dialog box.

NOTE *The Use A Formula As Group Sort option does not allow you to choose Specified Order based on a formula. You may only choose Specified Order grouping with the formula option unchecked.*

Click the New button to create a new named group. This will display the Define Named Group dialog box. Type the name the group should have on the report, such as Northwest. Then, using options in the tabs, indicate which records will be included in the group. For example, you may want the Northwest group to include records in which Customer.Region is one of WA, OR, and ID.

If you need to use several different criteria for the named group, you can click the <New> tab and add additional criteria for the group. When you're finished, click OK on the Define Named Group dialog box. The named group will be created and will appear in the list of named groups in the Group Options dialog box. You can now click the New button again to add additional named groups (for example, Southwest, including AZ, CA, and TX).

TIP *Remember that clicking the <New> tab to create more than one selection tab still only allows you to select by one field—the field your group is created on. The criteria on the tabs will be joined using a logical Or operation—this is different from the Select Expert.*

As you add new named groups, they appear in the Specified Order tab of the Change Group Options dialog box in the order that you created them, *not* in alphabetical order. If you wish to change the order in which the named groups appear on the report, select a named group and use the up or down arrow next to the list of named groups to change its position. The Others group, however, will always be last, no matter what you name it or how you position named groups with the arrow buttons.

After you create at least one named group, the Others tab appears in the Group dialog box. You use this tab to deal with any records that haven't been caught by your specific named groups. You can discard the remaining records, place them in one "catchall" group with the name of your choice, or leave them in their own groups based on the database field. In the geographic example, Northwest, Southwest, Northeast, and Southeast have all been created as named groups. The Others tab is used to lump any regions that weren't otherwise specified into a Midwest group.

TIP *You might have noticed the Named Group drop-down list on the Specified Order tab. This list will browse the database, showing you samples of the actual field you're grouping on. If you choose one of these samples, Crystal Reports will create a named group with the same name as the actual database field. This is handy if you want to create the same groups as you would by using Ascending or Descending order, but place the groups in the specific order you desire.*

After you create your named groups and click OK on the Change Group Options dialog box, the report will reflect your new grouping. Figure 2-6 shows a report grouped by the five geographic areas described previously. If you wish to change any of your specified grouping options, or remove them altogether so that records appear in their own groups, just use the steps mentioned previously to change an existing group. The Change Group Options dialog box will open, and you can edit your specified groups or change grouping to ascending or descending order, which will remove specified grouping.

Drilling Down on Data

One of the most powerful features of Crystal Reports is its online reporting capability. Although you can print reports on a printer and export them to other file formats, such as Word or Excel, the real power of many reports becomes available only when users can view and interact with them *online*. This means that the user directly views the .RPT file that Crystal Reports creates. This affords two benefits:

- A user can rerun the report whenever they want, seeing an updated view of the database at that moment.

- A user can interact with the report by using the preview panel and drill-down capabilities.

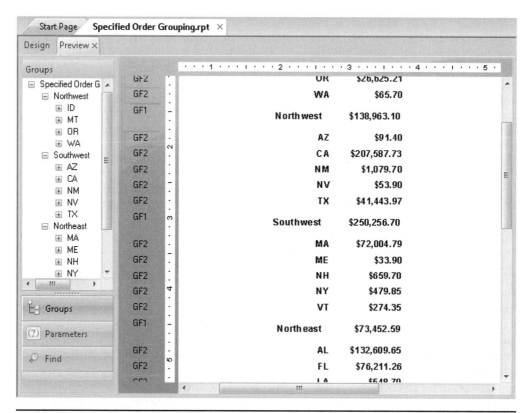

FIGURE 2-6   Report with Specified Order grouping

Various Crystal Reports editions offer online interactive reporting to users in several ways:

- Giving users their own copy of Crystal Reports, letting them open, view, and modify reports at will

- Reporting with a Web browser and a Business Objects enterprise reporting product (covered in Part II)

- Including a Crystal Report in a custom-designed Windows or web application (covered in Chapter 19)

- Providing any one of a number of available third-party tools to users to allow them to run reports online (many of these tools are highlighted on this book's companion web site. Visit CrystalBook.com for information).

All of these interactive methods allow a user to *drill down* on data in the report. This technique, a feature that has been carried over from early PC-based decision-support system software, allows a report viewer to initially look at higher-level data. For example, a report might start at the country level. If the viewer sees a subtotal or summary number (or an element in a pie chart or other chart) for a particular country that interests them, they can double-click that number. This will drill down to the next level in the report, possibly the region or state level, where they can see summary numbers for each of those states or regions. If the report is designed with several levels of drill-down ability, the user could then double-click a region that piqued their interest to display all the cities in that region. The drilling down could progress further, allowing users to drill down on cities and finally ZIP codes, where individual detail items at the ZIP-code level would appear.

Crystal Reports automatically sets up a drill-down hierarchy when you create groups. Every group you create can be drilled into, exposing the lower-level group and finally the details section. So, for the just-described drill-down example to work, you would create multiple groups on the report in the following order: country, region (state), city, and finally ZIP code.

After you create groups, you can drill down on the group name (automatically placed in the group header) or any summary or subtotal that you place in a group header or group footer. When you point at these objects, you'll notice that the mouse pointer changes from an arrow to a magnifying glass (or a finger cursor in a web page), called a *drill-down cursor*. This indicates that you can drill down on the group by double-clicking this object (or single-clicking in a web page). When you double-click, a *drill-down tab* appears next to the main Preview tab, containing the lower-level group or detail data. Every time you drill down, a separate drill-down tab appears.

If you drill down enough times, there won't be enough room to see all the drill-down tabs, along with the main Preview and Design tabs. In this situation, two small arrows appear next to the last drill-down tab. You can click these arrows to move back and forth among the tabs to see tabs that have disappeared off the screen. You can also close any drill-down tab by clicking the small *X* on the selected tab. This closes the current tab and displays the tab to the left. You can close every tab this way (including the Preview tab), except for the Design tab.

TIP *If you wish to print the report to a printer or export it to another file format, only the material appearing in the current tab will print or export. If you're displaying the Preview tab at the time, the summarized report will print or export. If, however, you have a drill-down tab selected when you print or export, only the material in that drill-down tab will be included.*

Figure 2-7 shows a report with several drill-down tabs visible. There isn't enough room to show all the tabs, so small arrows appear to the right of the last drill-down tab. Also notice that the mouse cursor has changed to a magnifying glass because it is over a group name object.

You can drill down on any report that has at least one group on it, even if all the details sections are showing already. Drill-down ability is really helpful with summary reports that start out showing only high-level data. A viewer will only want to see the lower-level groups and the detail when they drill down. Therefore, you'll want to hide the details section, as well as the lower-level group headers and group footers, to create a truly useful drill-down report. You'll see how to hide or suppress sections in Chapter 7.

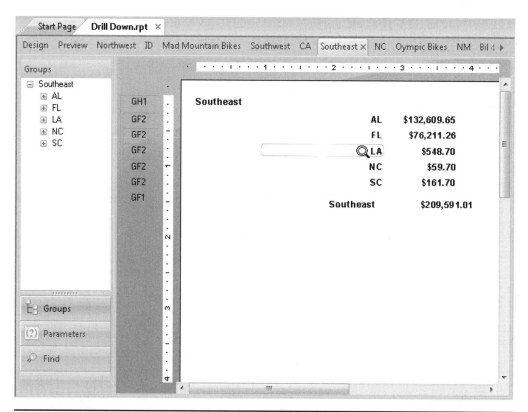

FIGURE 2-7   Drill-down report

TIP *Controlling detailed drill-down behavior, such as deciding if you want to show all higher-level group headers when you drill down, or whether to show a particular group header in some drill-down tabs, but not others, may require use of Crystal Reports formulas or conditional formatting. A DrillDownGroupLevel function is available in Crystal Reports to help with this custom drill-down behavior. Look in the Print State category of the Formula Editor Function Tree to find this function. Formulas are covered in more detail in Chapter 4, and conditional formatting is covered in more detail in Chapters 6 and 7.*

Grouping on Date Fields

When you create report groups based on date fields, you probably don't want a new group to appear every time the date changes from one day to another. You may only want a new group for every week, month, or calendar quarter. You could create a complicated formula that breaks down groups in this manner and groups on the formula, but Crystal Reports provides a much easier way.

When you select a date field to group on, Crystal Reports automatically adds an additional drop-down list to the Insert Group dialog box.

You can choose how often a new group will be created by selecting the appropriate item from the list. Then click OK. The groups will now appear in the preview panel for every month, quarter, year, or whatever period was chosen. The group name in the group header will indicate the beginning date for each group (the first month of the quarter, the first day of the week, and so forth).

Customizing Group Name Fields

The group name field takes on the Crystal Reports default format for the data type of the group field. For example, the default format for date fields is the same as your Windows default date format. Thus, a group name for a calendar quarter group may show up as 1/2005, 4/2005, and so on. What if you prefer the group names to appear as "January, 2005" and "April, 2005"?

You can format a group name field just like any other field or object. Click the group name field and then format it just like any other object (by using the Format menu, by using the Format toolbar button in the Expert Tools toolbar, or by right-clicking and using the pop-up menu). For a group name based on a date field, for example, you can choose how the month and year appear, as well as what character should be used as the separator between them.

However, you'll notice that even when you format the group name field as mentioned here, the preview panel will not reflect the change. It continues to use the default formatting regardless of how you format the group name field. Also, you may find situations in which you want to show information for the group that is different from what is actually supplied by the field you group on. For example, you may be grouping by a fiscal month number in a database. You'll want to show the spelled-out month name despite the fact that the preview panel and group headers will show the number (1 for January, 8 for August, and so on). Or, you may be grouping by employee number rather than employee name, to avoid the possibility of lumping employee data together for employees that share the same name. But, you still want the report to show the employee name instead of the number.

You may create a formula and group on it instead of the database field to accomplish this type of specialized group display. However, you'll often not get exactly the results you want (in the numeric month example mentioned previously, you will need to add the month number in front of the spelled-out month if you want to still show the months in chronological order). However, Crystal Reports provides the *customized group name field,* which gives you much more flexibility in controlling what the preview panel and group header display.

You may customize the group name field when you initially create a group. Or, if you decide later that you'd like to customize the group name field in an existing group, you can change the group by using the Group Expert, or by right-clicking the appropriate group header or group footer gray section name and choosing Change Group from the pop-up menu. Once the Change Group Options dialog box appears, perform the following steps to customize the group name field:

1. Click the Options tab.
2. Click the Customize Group Name Field check box.
3. To choose an alternate database field to display (for example, if you'd like to show an employee name field instead of the employee number field the group is based on), click the Choose From Existing Field radio button and then pick the desired database field in the associated drop-down list.
4. To create a specialized formula to display instead of the field the group is based on, click the Use A Formula As Group Name radio button. Then, click the Conditional Formula button next to the radio button. The group name Formula Editor appears, in which you can create a string formula to display instead of the field the group is based on. For example, to show an employee's last name, a comma, and then the employee's first name, you could create the following formula:

```
{Employee.Last Name} & ", " & {Employee.First Name}
```

Look at Chapter 4 for details on creating formulas.

Grouping on Formula Fields

As your reports become more sophisticated, you'll find more and more often that you won't be able to create the groups you need just from database fields. You may be able to use specified order grouping, but even it is limited by its simple Select Expert–like approach. When your "creative grouping with database fields" runs out of steam, you need to create formula fields and group on them. Creating formula fields is covered in Chapter 4.

Grouping on a formula field is very simple (at least the grouping is, after you create the formula). The formula appears at the end of the list of report fields in the Insert Group or Change Group Options dialog box. Simply choose it as the formula field you wish to group on.

One of the immediate benefits of grouping on a formula is being able to change your report grouping on the fly by use of Crystal Reports parameter fields (covered in Chapter 13). By using a parameter field to change the value that a formula returns, and then grouping on the formula, you can dynamically change report grouping depending on user input.

The @Group By formula field can now be used instead of the database field to dynamically group the report on Country or Region, as chosen by the report viewer.

CAUTION *Although you gain great flexibility when you group on a formula field, you may lose a little performance along the way. When you group on a database field, Crystal Reports can have the database server (SQL Server, Oracle, and so on) sort records in the proper group order before sending them to Crystal Reports. When you group on a formula field, the server won't be able to sort the records in advance, leaving that for Crystal Reports to do once the records begin to arrive from the server. You may or may not notice any performance degradation, depending on the size of the report and the speed of your computer. If you really want to maximize performance and still have a customized group, you may be able to substitute a SQL expression for a formula as the source for your group. SQL expressions are covered in Chapter 15.*

Top N Reporting

Figure 2-8 shows a typical order summary report by customer name. This is a great drill-down report example—the details section is hidden, and only the summary information for each customer is showing (hiding sections is covered in Chapter 7). This is a good report for

FIGURE 2-8   Order summary by customer

the sales manager who is asked, "How did Barry's Bikes do last year?" All the viewer has to do is click Barry's Bikes in the preview panel to go directly to its summaries.

However, what if the sales manager has ten boxes of Godiva chocolates that she wants to send to her ten best customers? Or, consider the new sales associate who's been assigned the task of visiting the 15 worst-performing customers to try to bolster sales. The report shown in Figure 2-8 is not very useful if you want to find the top 10 or bottom 15 customers. The sales manager and sales associate would be much happier with a Top *N* report.

A Top *N* report lets you sort your groups by a subtotal or summary function (subtotal of order amount, for example), instead of by the name of the group. That way, your groups will appear, for example, in order of highest to lowest sales or lowest to highest sales. In addition, Top *N* reporting enables you to see only the top or bottom *N* groups, where you specify the *N*.

Crystal Reports uses the Group Sort Expert to reorder your groups by a subtotal or summary. Choose this option from the pull-down menus by selecting Report | Group Sort Expert. You can also click the Group Sort Expert button in the Expert Tools toolbar.

The Group Sort Expert presents a tab for every group you've created on your report (provided that group has at least one summary created for it). Click the tab for the group that you want to reorder. When you first open the Group Sort Expert, the default setting for the first drop-down list is No Sort. This simply indicates that this group initially will not be a Top *N* group and that groups will appear in the order you chose when you created the groups. If none of the groups on your report have subtotal or summary fields in them, the Group Sort Expert won't be available, as it uses summary fields to sort the groups.

There are several choices available in the For This Group Sort drop-down list. Choose the desired option from the following choices:

All	Displays all groups on report, but uses one or more summary fields to determine the order of the groups. You have a choice of whether to show groups in ascending order (lowest to highest) or descending order (highest to lowest).
Top N	Displays only the top N (top 5, top 10) groups based on a summary field in order of highest to lowest.
Bottom N	Displays only the bottom N (bottom 5, bottom 10) based on a summary field in order of lowest to highest.
Top Percentage	Displays the top N percent (top 10 percent, top 25 percent) of groups based on a summary field.
Bottom Percentage	Displays the bottom N percent (bottom 10 percent, bottom 25 percent) of groups based on a summary field.

When you click the down arrow of the second drop-down list, you see all the summaries you've created for that group (only summaries you created with Insert Summary will be there—you won't see any formulas or other fields). Choose the one that you want the Top *N* report to be based on. For example, if you want to see the top 10 customers according to last year's sales, choose Sum of Customer.Last Year's Sales. If you leave the first drop-down list set to All, all groups will remain on the report, but they will be sorted in ascending or descending order, based on the radio buttons at the bottom of the dialog box. If you want the groups sorted by more than one summary (for example, first by sum of order amount and then by count of order ID), select additional summaries from the drop-down list and choose an ascending or descending sort for each.

TIP *Using the All option to sort groups in a different order can be a very innovative way to solve unique reporting problems. If you need to create a group based on one field but then have the groups appear in a different order, insert a summary field in the group footer based on the field you want to sort the groups by. Then, using the All option, choose the summary field you created.*

If you are only interested in the Top *N*, Bottom *N*, Top Percentage, or Bottom Percentage groups, change the first drop-down list from All to the desired choice. The second drop-down list enables you to select one summary or subtotal to use to sort the groups. Choose the summary you want to use. Once you've done that, type the value of *N* or the percentage in the appropriate text box. You also have a check box and text box that let you choose whether to include other groups not in the Top or Bottom *N* or percentage in the report. If you do include them, they will be lumped together in one other group with the name you type. If you want to not increment the *N* or percentage when group summaries are tied (this may change a top 10 to a top 12 if two of the groups are tied), check the Include Ties check box.

TIP *You may also provide the value for N or the percentage by way of a formula. This is helpful if you, for example, want to supply the value for N from a parameter field (Parameter Fields are covered in Chapter 13). Click the Conditional Formula button next to the N text box and supply a formula or numeric parameter field name.*

Using the Godiva and worst-performing-customer example earlier:

- The sales manager's Godiva chocolate report would be Top *N* of Sum of Orders. Order Amount, where *N* is 10 and other groups are not included.
- The sales associate's follow-up visit report would be a Bottom *N* of Sum of Orders. Order Amount, where *N* is 15 and other groups are not included.

The following Top *N* report shows who will be getting chocolates this year:

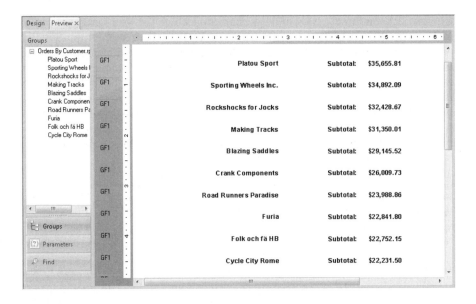

If you wish to change the report from Top *N* to Bottom *N*, change the value of *N*, or remove the Top/Bottom *N* sorting altogether and show all of your groups sorted in the order you originally chose, simply redisplay the Group Sort Expert and change the values. Remember that a group will be sorted in its original ascending or descending order if you set the first drop-down list to No Sort.

CAUTION   *If you create a Top N report and don't include others, any grand totals you place in the report footer will still include all records on the report. If you want to include accurate grand totals in a Top N report, either include others or use a running total instead of grand totals (as explained in Chapter 4).*

Hierarchical Groups

Crystal Reports also features *hierarchical groups,* which can be helpful in certain reporting situations where two fields relate to each other hierarchically. A specific example would be an organizational relationship between employees and supervisors, where the database would contain a single record containing both an employee ID and a supervisor ID. Without hierarchical grouping, creating an organizational chart utilizing this data would be difficult. While you could group by supervisor ID to see all the employees that reported to that supervisor, you still wouldn't see any hierarchical levels, where that supervisor would appear underneath *their* supervisor, and so forth.

With Crystal Reports, you may simply choose hierarchical grouping options to indicate the relationship between the two fields in the same set of data, and to specify how much indentation you wish to show between the hierarchies. As an example, you may create a simple report using the Employee table from the XTREME sample database (available for download from CrystalBook.com). If you create a group based on Employee ID, you'll simply see one group for each employee in the table. To show the reporting relationship among the employees, choose Report | Hierarchical Grouping Options. This displays the Hierarchical Group Options dialog box.

Choose the group (if there is more than one) for which you want to show the hierarchy. Then, click the Sort Data Hierarchically check box and choose the field that relates to the group field in the Parent ID Field drop-down list. Then, type the distance by which you wish to indent the lower-level hierarchies. Click OK.

The report will now create additional occurrences of groups to show the hierarchies created by the relationship of the two chosen fields. Here's an example of hierarchical reporting using the XTREME sample database:

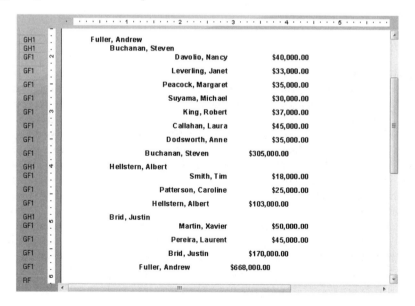

Crystal Reports includes the ability to add subtotals or summaries in hierarchical groups. Once you've created your group hierarchy with the features discussed previously, just use the same Insert Subtotal, Insert Summary, and Insert Grand Total features covered earlier in the chapter to summarize data in hierarchical groups. The Summarize Across Hierarchy check box will appear.

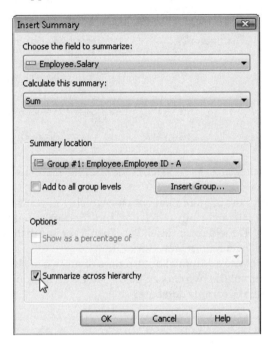

Hierarchical Formula Functions

Crystal Reports provides formula language functions that are helpful with hierarchical grouping. These functions help you determine where in the hierarchy a group appears (both the level of grouping in a multigroup report, as well as how many levels deep a value is within a single hierarchy). The *GroupingLevel* and *HierarchyLevel* functions can be used to determine where, within the hierarchy, a particular group resides (one level deep, two levels deep, and so forth). And, *CountHierarchicalChildren* can be used to determine how many "child" groups exist for a given hierarchy, allowing suppression of group headers and footers if no child groups exist.

In addition, the horizontal position of a field may be supplied via a conditional formula. By choosing the Size And Position option from the Format menu or pop-up menu after selecting the desired field, you can specify the horizontal (or X) position via a conditional formula, rather than just a typed-in number. By using the aforementioned hierarchy formula functions in a conditional formula, you may change the horizontal position of certain fields according to their hierarchy. This gives you more granular formatting control than that provided by the Group Indent setting in the Hierarchical Grouping Options dialog box (which controls indentation of the entire group, not just a single object).

TIP *A detailed explanation of the GroupingLevel, HierarchyLevel, and CountHierarchicalChildren functions can be found in the appendix.*

Analyzing with Advanced Selection Criteria

C reating a simple report is as quick as choosing tables, dragging and dropping fields on the report, and clicking the Preview button. However, if you perform only those few steps, you may have a much larger report show up than you bargained for! One important step missing is *record selection*. If you don't enter some record selection criteria, every record that exists in the tables you choose will appear on the report.

In the case of a small PC-type database with, say, 1,000 records, this won't be terribly time- or resource-intensive. However, if you're connected to a large SQL database with potentially millions of records, the consequences of not including record selection will probably be felt on your network and will certainly be felt on your desktop PC. Since Crystal Reports needs to store the data that makes up a report somewhere, you may run out of memory or temporary disk space in such a situation. Regardless of these concerns, your report will be terribly slow, and probably not very useful, if you have that many records on the report.

Virtually all reports will need record selection criteria. You may want to limit the report to only U.S.A. customers, only orders placed in 2004, or only invoices that are more than 30 days past due. Record selection criteria can be used to limit your report to any of these sets of records. In any event, it's very wise to apply your record selection criteria early on in your report design process—probably *before* you preview or print the report.

Three Different Ways to Select Data

While previous versions of Crystal Reports offered two different selection options (in particular, record selection and group selection), the difference was not always readily apparent. In Crystal Reports 2008, not only has a third type of selection been added, but the three different choices are much more obvious in the various methods of choosing selection criteria discussed throughout this chapter.

- **Record selection** This type of selection limits records initially sent to your report from the database. This is the first type of selection that Crystal Reports performs before it does any further processing or formatting on the report. In the case of reports based on most SQL databases, *record selection* is actually performed on the database server by means of a SQL WHERE clause before any data is even sent to Crystal Reports (more detail on SQL database interaction can be found in Chapter 15). For example, if you set an initial record selection criterion that limits the report to customers in the U.S.A., only customers in the U.S.A. will be sent to the report from the database server. No other countries will be available anywhere in the report at any time after the database is initially queried. Because many corporate databases can be so large, and because the true usefulness of a reporting tool is limiting a report to a useful set of data, virtually every report you design will probably contain at least simple, if not more complex, record selection.

- **Group selection** After the report has read initial data from the database (and has been filtered by record selection), after the report has been sorted and grouped, and after group subtotals and summaries have been calculated, you may perform *group selection*. Because group selection is performed after groups, subtotals, and summaries have been created, you may base group selection on a subtotal or summary value. For example, you may initially set record selection to limit the report to U.S.A. customers only, group the report by State, and subtotal order amounts for each state group. At this point, you may have up to 50 groups on the report (one for each state) with total sales for each state appearing in the group footer (grouping and summarizing are discussed in Chapter 2). You may now use group selection to limit the report to only state groups that have total sales in excess of, for example, $1 million. By using a subtotal or summary value as a group selection field, a limited number of state groups will appear on the report, even if all 50 states were sent to the report from the database.

CAUTION *Group selection occurs after the group tree, subtotals, and grand totals have been calculated. This can lead to apparent inaccuracies on your report if you create group selection that eliminates certain groups from the Preview tab. Even though these groups won't appear on the report, they will still be visible in the group tree. This is inherent behavior of Crystal Reports and cannot be changed.*

- **Saved data selection** Crystal Reports 2008 adds *saved data selection* as a new option. This choice allows you to perform various selection options on data stored locally in your PC's memory after the initial record selection discussed earlier has been performed. By supplying different saved data selection values, you may conduct further analysis on the set of data initially sent from the database without querying the database again (an often slow and time-consuming process). For example, you may have set an initial record selection criterion to limit the report to customers in the U.S.A. As this initial record selection is typically performed by the database server, customers in the U.S.A. will be read by Crystal Reports and stored locally in your PC's memory as *saved data*. You may then perform additional saved data selection on, for example, State. By repeatedly supplying various state values to saved data selection, you may analyze sales performance for one or more states within the U.S.A. without needing to run another query against the database. The saved data selection capability allows for quick "subanalysis" on the larger set of saved data without the need for repetitive, time-consuming re-querying of the database.

NOTE *The remainder of this chapter discusses general selection techniques and approaches that can apply equally to record, group, and saved data selection. The type of selection you choose will depend on how you want to analyze data in your report.*

The Select Expert

Crystal Reports provides the *Select Expert* to help you create useful selection criteria. You can use the Select Expert for simple, straightforward selection, and as a starting point for more sophisticated selection. The Select Expert can be run from the Record Selection section of any of the report wizards, or after you have chosen and linked tables using the Blank Report option. In either case, you'll want to make sure to use it to provide initial record selection for your report before you preview the report.

The only type of selection available in a report wizard is record selection (group selection and saved data selection may be used after the wizard has completed and has initially run the report against the database). To use the Select Expert while using one of the report wizards, choose at least one table in the Data section and, if necessary, link the tables in the Link section (table linking is covered in more detail in Chapter 15). Then progress through the other sections until you reach the Record Selection section, which looks like this:

If you are using the Blank Report option to create a report, you must initially add and link tables. Once the Design tab appears, you can either immediately run the Select Expert or add fields to the report before running the Select Expert. Again, you'll want to run the

Select Expert to supply initial record selection before you preview the report for the first
time.

Run the Select Expert by clicking the Select Expert button in the Expert Tools toolbar.
The default form of selection chosen by the button is record selection. If you click the small
down arrow to the right of the Select Expert button, you may also choose Record from the
resulting pop-up menu. You can also choose Report | Select Expert | Record from the drop-
down menus. If you have already added fields to the report and want to use one of them
from the Design tab or Preview tab for record selection, select the field on the report before
you start the Select Expert. You can also right-click your selected field and choose Select
Expert Record from the pop-up menu. In each case, the Select Expert will start with a tab
already created for the chosen field.

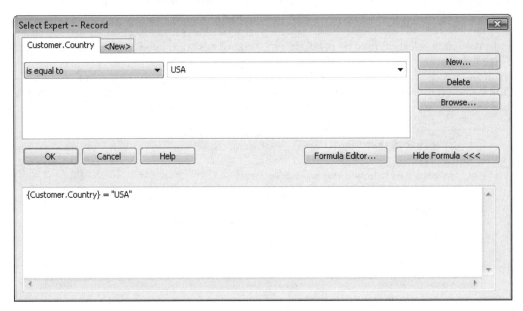

CAUTION *Pre-selected report fields may result in unintentional selection fields. If you
inadvertently select a report field that you don't want to use for selection, and then start the
Select Expert, you'll see a tab for the selected field. Just click the Delete button on the right side of
the expert to delete the current tab. Then click the <New> tab or the New button to choose the
correct field to select.*

If this is the first time you've run the Select Expert, and you haven't chosen an existing
report field, you'll see a Choose Field dialog box listing all report and database fields. You'll
also see this dialog box if you are already displaying the Select Expert and click the <New>
tab or the New button to add additional criteria.

Click the report or database field that you want your record selection to be based on. Whether you click a field in the Report Fields or Database section of the Choose Field dialog box is irrelevant. If a field exists in both sections of the dialog box, the resulting selection will be exactly the same. If you want to see sample data from the database for that field, click Browse. Once you're satisfied with the field you want to use for record selection, select it and click OK. The Select Expert will appear with a tab for that field.

Once you've chosen a field to base selection on, a drop-down list will appear displaying the default Is Any Value criteria. You will use this list to choose the comparison operation you want to use for your selection. The drop-down list will reveal all the comparisons you can use to select records; it may vary somewhat based on the type of field you've chosen for selection. Table 3-1 explains the different operators that may appear in the drop-down list. In addition to those listed in the table, the Select Expert will also provide "Is Not" versions of most of the comparisons. As you might imagine, choosing the "Not" version of the comparison will include records where the condition is *not* true, instead of where the condition is true.

Once you've chosen a comparison operator in the drop-down list, the Select Expert will change based on the choice you've made. If you've chosen an operator that only compares to one item (such as Equal To, Less Than, or Greater Than), one additional drop-down list will appear. If you've chosen an operator that can compare to multiple items (such as One Of, Like, or Starts With), a drop-down list will appear, along with a multiple-item box. You can add and remove items from the multiple-item box by clicking the Add and Delete buttons that appear next to the box.

Operator	Description
Is Any Value	This is the same as having no selection criteria at all. Is Any Value means it doesn't matter what's in the field—all records will be included in the report.
Is Equal To	The field must be exactly equal to what you specify.
Is One Of	You can specify more than one item to compare to by adding multiple comparison items to a list. If the field is exactly equal to any of them, the record will be included.
Is Less Than	The field must be less than the item you're comparing to. If you are comparing numbers, the field must be smaller numerically. If you are comparing dates, the field must be an earlier date. If you're comparing strings, the field must be lower in the alphabet. If you choose the Less Than Or Equal To option, the field can be equal to or less than what you're comparing to.
Is Greater Than	The field must be greater than the item you're comparing to. If you are comparing numbers, the field must be larger numerically. If you're comparing dates, the field must be a later date. If you're comparing strings, the field must be higher in the alphabet. If you choose the Greater Than Or Equal To option, the field can be equal to or greater than what you're comparing to.
Is Between	Allows you to select two items to create a comparison range. The field must be between the two items, or equal to one of them. Is Between uses the same type of comparison as is used with less and greater comparisons: numbers compare numerically, dates compare chronologically, and strings compare alphabetically.
Starts With	Allows you to specify "leading" characters to compare to. If the first characters in the field equal the specified characters, the record will be returned. If you want to perform several Starts With comparisons, you can add multiple criteria to a list. This operator will only appear when you are using a string field.
Is Like	You can look for partial text matches using wildcard characters to search for records that contain particular characters or groups of characters. When you specify your comparisons, you can use a question mark to indicate that one character in the field at that position can contain anything. You can use an asterisk to indicate that the rest of the field from that point on can contain anything. If you want to perform several Like comparisons, you can add multiple criteria to a list. This operator will appear only when you are using a string field.
Is In the Period	Allows you to compare a date field to a group of built-in date ranges, such as the last week, last month, last quarter, current year, etc. These built-in ranges are all based on the system clock of your computer when you run the report. This operator will appear only when you are using a date or date-time field.
Is True	Includes records where the field equates to true. This operator will appear only when you are using a Boolean field.
Is False	Includes records where the field equates to false. This operator will appear only when you are using a Boolean field.
Formula	Allows you to enter any Boolean formula using the Crystal Reports formula language. The resulting formula box is identical to the formula box that appears at the bottom of the Select Expert dialog box.

TABLE 3-1   Select Expert Comparison Operators

The new drop-down list allows you to choose the item you want to compare the field to in either of two ways: you can type it directly or choose it from the drop-down list. You can simply type the literal item you want to compare to directly in the drop-down list.

If you click the arrow on the drop-down list, the Select Expert will browse the database and list sample items from that database field. You may choose one of the items in the drop-down list for comparison.

If the comparison operator you've chosen allows multiple entries, you can add an item you've typed to the multiple-item box by clicking Add. If you choose a browsed database item from the drop-down list, it will be added to the multiple-item box automatically. In either case, you can remove an item from the multiple-item box by selecting it and then clicking Remove.

Note that you can choose *Is Not* versions of the comparison operators as well. This will, in essence, *reverse* the selection criteria you've chosen. If, for example, you chose a country field, selected the Is Not Equal To operator, and specified "USA" as the item to compare to, your report will now include records for every country *except* the U.S.A.

The Select Expert does not limit you to comparing just one field. Once you have added one field, you can click the <New> tab or the New button. This will redisplay the Choose Field dialog box, from which you can pick another field to compare to. Once you pick this field, a new tab will display in the Select Expert, enabling you to create another comparison. You may create as many tabs and comparisons as you need.

TIP *Crystal Reports applies a logical AND to all the tabs in the Select Expert—all the criteria have to be true for a record to be selected. If you would rather have a logical OR applied to some or all of the tabs (so that if any one of them is true, but not all of them, a record is returned), you must manually edit the selection formula created by the Select Expert. This is discussed later in this chapter, in "Manipulating the Record Selection Formula Directly."*

Refreshing the Report Versus Using Saved Data

When you create an initial record selection and preview a report on the screen for the first time, Crystal Reports has to actually read the database and perform record selection, and only thereafter can it format and display the report. To enhance future performance while you work with the report, Crystal Reports creates a set of *saved data*, as discussed earlier in the chapter. This saved data consists of the records that were retrieved from the database, which are then kept either in memory or in temporary files on your hard drive. If you perform simple formatting changes, move fields around, or make other minor modifications that won't require the database to be re-queried, Crystal Reports will use the saved data every time you preview the modified report, thus improving performance. If you add new fields to the report, Crystal Reports knows it has to re-query the database, and it does so without prompting. You may notice a bit of a wait (or maybe a long wait, depending on your database) while it runs the new query.

But when you change record selection criteria, Crystal Reports doesn't know whether or not it needs to re-query the database. You will be given the option to Refresh or Use Saved Data. The choice you make is dependent upon whether you widened or narrowed the selection criteria. If you *narrowed* your selection criteria so that the new selection criteria can be completely satisfied with the existing saved data, you can choose to use the saved data. Since the database doesn't have to be re-queried, the changes will appear very quickly in the Preview tab.

If, however, you *widened* the selection criteria so that the saved data won't contain all the records you're specifying, you need to refresh the report so that the database can be re-queried. Choosing to use saved data in this situation will result in your report showing too few (if any) records, even though they actually exist in the database. However, the new query will take time to perform. If you make the wrong choice and end up with too few, or no, records, you can refresh the report manually by clicking the Refresh button in the Navigation Tools toolbar, pressing the F5 key, or choosing Report | Refresh Report Data from the drop-down menus.

NOTE *With the addition of saved data selection in Crystal Reports 2008, the Refresh/Used Saved Data choice may seem confusing. If you choose saved data when prompted, you are, in essence, turning your record selection into a saved data selection. However, the saved data selection won't appear in the Select Expert for you to change later. Therefore, if you plan on changing criteria with saved data several times for quick analysis, you should use Select Expert options for saved data selection instead of record selection. Only change record selection if you plan on refreshing the report and re-querying the database.*

When you save a report, you have the option to store the saved data in the .RPT file. If you include the saved data, the report will immediately display the Preview tab showing the saved data the next time you open the .RPT file—no database re-query will be required. However, this will also make the .RPT file larger (sometimes significantly so), since it has to keep the saved data along with the report design specifications.

To choose whether or not to save data, check or uncheck File | Save Data With Report from the drop-down menus, and then resave the report after making your choice. You can also make the choice with the appropriate check box on File | Report Options. If you wish to set default behavior for this option for all new reports in the future, turn on or off the Save Data With Report option on the Reporting tab of File | Options.

TIP *Even if you open a report with saved data, the saved data will be discarded and only the Design tab will appear if the Discard Saved Data On Open option is checked on the Reporting tab of File | Options.*

Selection with Date Fields

Many reporting requirements can be satisfied by creatively using date fields in selection. Crystal Reports provides a good choice of built-in date ranges you can use to compare to, or you can use other operators to compare date fields. When you choose a date or date/time field in the Choose Field dialog box, the Select Expert makes the In the Period comparison operator available. If you choose this operator, another drop-down list containing Crystal Reports' built-in date ranges appears.

By using these built-in ranges, you can create a report that will return, say, only orders in the previous month by comparing to the LastFullMonth. What's particularly appealing about using built-in date range functions is the "self-maintenance" of the report. When you use the LastFullMonth range, for example, the report will always use the system clock in your computer to include orders from the previous month, no matter when the report is run. You don't have to manually change the date range every month.

There may be times, however, when you have to manually enter a date range for record selection. If, for example, you want to see all orders for 2005, you need to specify those dates manually. There is no built-in X Years Ago date range. In this case, you choose the date field you want to select on (for example, Order Date) and use a Between comparison operator to indicate orders between January 1, 2005, and December 31, 2005. You can enter a beginning date of 1/1/2005 and an ending date of 12/31/2005.

TIP *Crystal Reports allows a fair amount of flexibility in date formatting with the Select Expert, generally allowing you to type in free-form dates as you wish. However, you'll still receive error messages if you type in dates that Crystal Reports isn't sure about.*

Even if you choose a date/time field for record selection, you may supply just a date (without a time) as the comparison value. While Crystal Reports will allow this, understand that a time of midnight will be assumed with the date you specified. With a Between comparison in particular, this can cause confusing results. Since both dates will be compared to as of midnight, all records on or after midnight for the *first* specified date will be included. However, only records that include times of exactly midnight for the *second* date will be included—any times of even one second after midnight for the second date won't be included. Therefore, make sure you include a time value alongside a date value if you want to select records based on some time other than midnight.

Manipulating the Selection Formula Directly

When you create selection criteria with the Select Expert, it actually creates a formula using the Crystal Reports formula language. Crystal Reports 2008 shows the formula in the lower part of the Select Expert as you build selection with various tabs and selection choices. For most simple selection criteria, you won't have to worry about manipulating this formula directly. Also, by using the Select Expert directly and not manipulating the actual formula that it creates, you will often maximize performance (in particular, when using the Select Expert to create record selection with SQL databases).

However, there are times when the Select Expert itself won't provide enough flexibility for the record selection you need to accomplish. Consider the following scenario—you have two fields on their own tabs included in the Select Expert: Region Is Equal to CO, and Order Amount Is Greater than 2500.

Since the Select Expert performs a logical AND between the tabs (you can confirm this by noting the AND operator used in the resulting selection formula), what do you do if you want to see all orders from Colorado, regardless of the order amount, as well as orders from any other state over $2,500?

In this case, the Select Expert tabs don't provide sufficient flexibility to create this type of special selection. Thus, you must modify the selection formula, manually changing the AND to OR. You can modify the formula in one of three ways:

- By directly editing the formula in the lower part of the Select Expert itself

- By using the drop-down menus to choose Report | Selection Formulas, and then choosing which selection formula you wish to modify from the submenu

- By displaying the Formula Workshop (discussed in more detail in Chapter 5) and choosing the desired selection formula in the Selection Formulas category

TIP *If you know you'll need extra features that the Select Expert doesn't provide, you can skip it entirely and create your selection formula right in the Formula Editor or Formula Workshop using methods just described.*

In the scenario previously mentioned, the formula created by the Select Expert may simply be edited, changing the And initially created by the Select Expert to Or, and then clicking OK.

If you initially display the Select Expert, but decide you want to use the full-featured Formula Editor instead, just click the Formula Editor button in the Select Expert dialog box. The formula will be transferred to the Formula Editor, where you can modify it using all the features of the full Formula Editor.

Since you will ultimately be using the Crystal Reports formula language for your selection, most of the features of the language are available for use in your selection formula. In this situation, it may be preferable to edit the selection formula in the Formula Editor so that you can see and use all the built-in functionality. The formula that the Select Expert created will appear when you use the drop-down menus to choose Report | Selection Formulas, and then choose the particular selection formula you wish to modify from the submenu.

You can modify this formula to your heart's content, provided that the ultimate finished formula is a Boolean formula—it will ultimately just return true or false (refer to Chapter 5 for more information on Boolean formulas). The formula will be evaluated for each record or group being selected. If the formula evaluates to true, the record will be included in the report; otherwise, the record will be ignored.

Case Sensitivity with Selection

A question you will probably ask yourself fairly quickly when using record, group, or saved data selection is, "Is it case sensitive?" In other words, if you ask to see records where the country is "USA," will a record be returned if the database field contains mixed-case characters, such as "Usa"?

Case sensitivity is generally ignored when using SQL databases and PC databases via ODBC, as well as certain databases using a direct database driver. Although this case insensitivity is the default behavior "out of the box," be sure to check the Database Server Is Case-Insensitive option in the File | Report Options dialog box to affect the current report, or check the same option on the Database tab of File | Options to set the default for all new reports you create in the future.

Even if this option is checked, some databases and ODBC drivers may not support case insensitivity with Crystal Reports. It's best to run a test with your own database to make sure you're retrieving all desired records with your record selection.

NOTE *If you modify the formula the Select Expert created, or you create your own formula, running the Select Expert again is fine. However, if the Select Expert is unable to fully interpret the formula you created, you'll see slightly different behavior for one or more tabs. You may see a tab with a field set to Is Formula and part of the selection formula showing in the third list box. You may also see a message indicating that the formula uses a "composite expression" and prompting you to edit the formula directly.*

Performance Considerations with Record Selection

In many cases, record selection is the most time-consuming portion of the report process, particularly with larger databases. If you're using a PC-style database located on a local or network hard drive, Crystal Reports performs the record selection itself, reading every record in the database and keeping only those that match. If you are using a server-based database (such as SQL Server or Oracle), Crystal Reports will attempt to create a WHERE clause in the query that's sent to the database server, which will cause the database server to perform the query and send only the desired records to Crystal Reports.

In either situation, you'll probably see overall improved performance if you use *indexed fields* for your record selection (with PC-style databases, this is often very critical). Indexed fields are fields that are specially designated when the database is designed. The field's index stores all the values in the field in a presorted state that makes it much faster to select records based on the field. To determine if a field is indexed, you may wish to consult the database designer.

You can also see which fields are indexed by using the Links tab of the Database Expert. Click the Database Expert button on the Expert Tools toolbar, or choose Database | Database Expert from the pull-down menus. Then, click the Links tab (you must have added at least two tables to your report to see it).

Fields with a "tent" character are indexed

You'll notice a small "tent" character appearing next to every indexed field (the different colors you may see are generally insignificant to record selection, as long as you select on a field with the symbol). Make note of the indexed fields and attempt to use them in record selection. If the field you need to select on is not indexed, and record selection appears very sluggish, you may wish to consult the database designer about adding an index for that field.

NOTE *Depending on the database driver you are using, you still may not see the tent index designators in some instances.*

Finally, double-check the setting of the Use Indexes Or Server For Speed option. To check the option for the current report, look in the File | Report Options dialog box. If you wish to check the option for all new reports in the future, look for the option on the Database tab of File | Options. If this is turned off, Crystal Reports won't use field indexes at all.

SQL databases (or PC-style databases accessed via ODBC) present a different set of performance considerations when compared to performance with PC-style databases. As a general reporting rule, you want to always have the database server perform the record selection (via the aforementioned WHERE clause), if at all possible. This can typically be accomplished by using only the Select Expert to create record selection criteria—using the formula portion of the Select Expert or the Formula Editor makes it entirely too easy to introduce functions that Crystal Reports can't move to the database server. This may seriously degrade database server record selection performance. As with PC-style databases, make sure the Use Indexes Or Server For Speed option is turned on in File | Report Options. More information on the relationship between record selection and report performance with SQL databases can be found in Chapter 15.

NOTE *Steps discussed in this section are only pertinent to record selection. Group selection and saved data selection are always performed on the local PC by Crystal Reports after record selection has occurred and the report has been formatted. As such, the techniques discussed will have no effect on group selection or saved data selection performance.*

CHAPTER 4

Using Formulas

When you first start using Crystal Reports, you'll be able to write some simple reports using data that comes entirely from the database. You simply drag fields from the Field Explorer onto the report, and away you go. However, it won't be long until you find that you want some information to appear on your report that isn't contained in the database. Or, you may find that you want to display a field differently on the report than it appears in the database. For these, and many similar situations, use Crystal Reports *formulas*.

A formula can be thought of as a math calculation or a small piece of computer programming code. If you're not used to them at first, creating formulas can appear to be very complicated. Depending on your background, you may like the fact that some formulas are very much like programming, or this may be one characteristic of formulas that you would prefer not to deal with. Formulas can be as simple or as complex as you want to make them—you can start with simple math computations and, as you get more comfortable, graduate to full Basic-like formulas using Case statements, variables, and other advanced programming techniques. You can even share your formula expertise with your coworkers using Crystal Reports custom functions (covered in Chapter 5) and the Repository (covered in Chapter 18). Formulas bring the ultimate power and flexibility to Crystal Reports.

You can create formulas with either the Design or the Preview tab displayed, although creating them in the Design tab is probably better because you will have a more accurate idea of where the formulas will really end up when you place them on your report. You may create a new formula or modify an existing formula in two places in Crystal Reports—either the Field Explorer's Formula Fields category, or from the Formula Workshop.

The Formula Workshop

The *Formula Workshop* is a dialog box that presents a unified approach to examining, creating, and modifying different types of formulas in your reports. The Formula Workshop not only allows you to display and modify standard report formulas, but also allows creation of report custom functions (covered in Chapter 5) and provides the capability to store custom functions in the central repository (covered in Chapter 18). The Formula Workshop provides access to record, group, and saved data selection formulas, and custom formatting formulas.

 To display the Formula Workshop, either choose Report | Formula Workshop from the mail pull-down menus, or click the Formula Workshop toolbar button from the Expert Tools toolbar. The Formula Workshop will appear, as shown in Figure 4-1.

Formula Editor toolbar will become
enabled when actually editing a formula

Formula Workshop toolbar provides
quick access to various functions

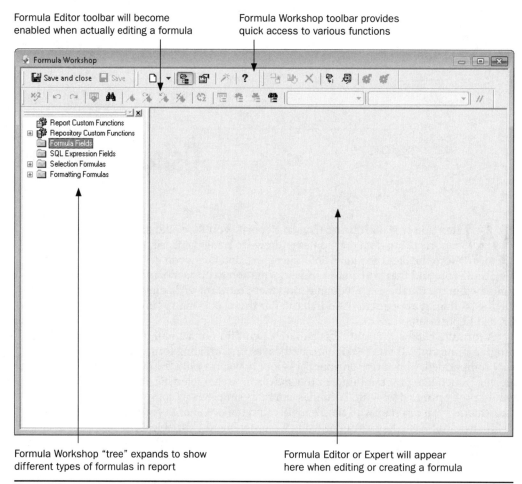

Formula Workshop "tree" expands to show
different types of formulas in report

Formula Editor or Expert will appear
here when editing or creating a formula

FIGURE 4-1 The Formula Workshop

The Formula Workshop consists of a folder "tree" view on the left, two toolbars on the
top, and a large area below the toolbars and to the right of the tree view where the Formula
Expert or Formula Editor (both discussed later in the chapter) will appear when actually
working with a formula.

The tree view contains a list of formula categories available in the Formula Workshop.

- **Report Custom Functions**   "Sharable" functions that can be used by any formula
  in your report (covered in Chapter 5).

- **Repository Custom Functions**   "Sharable" functions that have been saved in the
  repository to be used by every copy of Crystal Reports connected to the repository
  (the repository is covered in Chapter 18).

- **Formula Fields**   Formulas that you create for use in just this report (covered in the
  rest of this chapter).

- **SQL Expression Fields** Server-based formulas, using the Structured Query Language (covered in Chapter 15).

- **Selection Formulas** Formulas used to control record, group, and saved data selection. These are the same formulas created using the Select Expert, or the Report | Selection Formulas pull-down menu options (covered in Chapter 3).

- **Formatting Formulas** Formulas that set appearance of report objects and sections conditionally. These are the same formulas created using the conditional buttons in the Format Editor and Section Expert (covered in Chapters 6 and 7).

If there are available formulas or functions in the desired category, a plus sign will appear next to that category—just click the plus sign to open up that category and show the available formulas or functions in it. The lack of a plus sign next to a category indicates that no formulas or functions in that category have yet been created.

As Table 4-1 shows, the Formula Workshop toolbar at the top of the dialog box provides quick ways to perform more common Formula Workshop options.

Icon	Description
or **CTRL-S**	Saves the current formula or function and closes the Formula Workshop. If Crystal Reports detects any errors in the formula or function, you'll be prompted whether or not you wish to save with the error. You may also close the Formula Workshop by clicking the X in the window's upper right-hand corner.
or **ALT-S**	Saves the current formula or function but leaves the Formula Workshop open. If Crystal Reports detects any errors in the formula or function, you'll be prompted whether or not you wish to save with the error.
or **CTRL-N**	Creates a new formula. If you click the button directly, you'll create a new formula or function based on the category selected in the tree view. If you click the small down arrow next to the button, you'll be given a choice of type of formula to create. You may also create a new formula by right-clicking the desired tree view category and choosing New from the pop-up menu.
	Toggles display of the Formula Workshop tree view on and off.
	Toggles between viewing the actual code of a selected custom function or the custom function's properties, such as arguments, author, and so forth (this button has no effect when editing a formula). See Chapter 5 for more information on this button.
or **ALT-X**	Toggles between displaying the formula in the Formula Expert (discussed later in the chapter and in Chapter 5) or in the Formula Editor. If you are displaying a formula that consists of something other than use of a single custom function, you'll be warned that clicking this button will erase the current formula. Also, this button won't work while you're creating a custom function.

TABLE 4-1 Formula Workshop Toolbar Buttons

Icon	Description
? or **F1**	Displays context-sensitive Formula Workshop, Formula Expert, or Formula Editor online help (depending on which portion of the Formula Workshop is currently displayed, which function or operator is highlighted, or where the cursor appears).
	Copies the formula currently selected in the tree view, adding a sequential number to the new formula name. This allows you to copy a complex formula to a new formula without having to reenter all formula text again, or without having to copy the entire formula text to the clipboard and then paste it into a newly created formula. You may then select the new formula in the tree view to rename it and modify its copied contents as needed.
	Renames the formula currently selected in the tree view. Clicking this button will place the formula name in the tree view in Edit mode. You may also rename a formula by right-clicking the formula in the tree view and choosing Rename from the pop-up menu, or by just holding your mouse button down for a few seconds after selecting the formula name in the tree.
X	Deletes the formula from the Formula Workshop and the report. You may be notified that the formula is being used in the report or that repository function deletions can't be undone and asked to confirm the deletion. You may also delete by right-clicking the formula in the tree view and choosing Delete from the pop-up menu.
	Expands the folder you currently have selected in the tree view (the same as clicking the plus sign to the left of the folder itself). For example, if you have the Formula Fields folder selected, clicking this button will open that category and show all the report formulas within the category. If the folder is already expanded, clicking the button again will do nothing.
	Toggles between showing all Formatting Formula category report objects in the report or only those objects that already contain formatting formulas. For example, if you click this button while viewing the expanded Formatting Formulas category, a limited set of report objects will appear (or none, if there are no existing formatting formulas in the report). This button affects only the Formatting Formulas category in the tree view.
	Adds the selected report custom function to the repository (see Chapter 18 for more information on adding your own custom functions to the repository).
	Copies the selected repository custom function to the current report. The custom function will then appear in the Custom Functions portion of the Formula Editor functions tree. See Chapter 17 for more information on adding repository custom functions to your report.

TABLE 4-1   Formula Workshop Toolbar Buttons *(continued)*

Not all of the toolbar buttons will be enabled all of the time. Certain buttons and their functions are enabled only when an appropriate formula is selected in the tree view. For example, you can't rename custom functions in the repository or click Delete when the record selection formula is highlighted.

TIP *The Formula Workshop toolbar actually consists of several separate toolbars, each of which can be "undocked" from the top of the Formula Workshop window. Just click on the small gray vertical bar to the left of the different parts of the toolbar and drag to a new location.*

You're not limited to using the Formula Workshop to create, rename, and delete formulas. You can also use the Field Explorer. By choosing the Formula Fields category of the Field Explorer, you can access Field Explorer toolbar buttons, right-click pop-up menus, and keyboard shortcuts as well. Accordingly, there are numerous ways to create a new report formula by using the Field Explorer's Formula Fields category or the Formula Workshop. Once you've chosen to create a new formula, you'll be asked to supply a formula name. Remember that you're *not* creating a file on disk when you add a formula, so you don't need to worry about file-naming conventions—the formula is simply stored inside the .RPT file of your report. Your formula names can contain upper- and lowercase letters, spaces, and anything else that makes them descriptive. Use an easy-to-understand formula name—not only does it help you to recognize what the formula is when you look at the list of formulas you've created, but it also is used for the field title when you place a formula in the details section.

The Formula Expert

When you initially create a new formula, the Formula Editor will appear (the Formula Editor is discussed in detail later in the chapter). However, if you click the "magic wand" toolbar button in the Formula Workshop toolbar before you type any formula text, the Formula Expert will appear instead. Also, if you edit an existing formula that's based on a single custom function, the Formula Expert will also appear.

The Formula Expert is shown in Figure 4-2. This expert is designed to help you create a formula without having to use the Crystal Reports formula language. While this sounds tempting to those who may, at least initially, be slightly put off by the Crystal formula language, the Formula Expert immediately introduces one substantial caveat: only formulas using a single custom function can be created in the expert. If you want to create a formula using regular Crystal Reports formula language functions or math operators, the Formula Expert won't provide appropriate capabilities. And even if you are using a custom function, the Formula Expert won't allow you to enclose it inside another custom function or use the custom function with any other Crystal Reports formula language syntax. In any situation where you can't use the Formula Expert, you'll need to use the Formula Editor to create your desired formula.

The first step in using the Formula Expert is to determine the custom function you want to base your formula on. Choose this function in the Custom Function list. In the initial version of Crystal Reports 2008, you must choose a function from the Report Custom Functions category (these are custom functions that are already part of your report)—attempting to choose the Repository Custom Functions category will result in a message

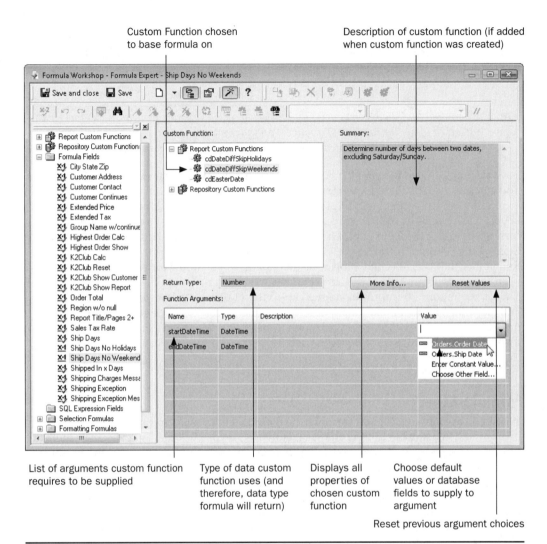

Custom Function chosen
to base formula on

Description of custom function (if added
when custom function was created)

List of arguments custom function
requires to be supplied

Type of data custom
function uses (and
therefore, data type
formula will return)

Displays all
properties of
chosen custom
function

Choose default
values or database
fields to supply to
argument

Reset previous argument choices

FIGURE 4-2   The Formula Expert

box indicating incompatibility. If you use an updated version of Crystal Reports 2008 that
allows connection to an associated member of the BusinessObjects Enterprise family, you
will be able to make a choice from the Repository Custom Functions category (these are
custom functions that reside in your BusinessObjects Enterprise repository). Click the plus
sign next to the desired category and navigate through the tree until you find the desired
custom function you wish to use. Once you select that custom function, a description of the
function will appear in the Summary area (if the description was added when the custom
function was created). The data type that the function will return (string, number, and so
forth) will appear in the Return Type area. And, any necessary parameters or *arguments* that

the function requires to be supplied will be added to the Function Arguments area at the bottom of the Formula Expert.

Then, simply choose the database fields, other formula fields, or typed-in values that you want to supply as arguments to the custom function. You may do this by typing in a number, string, date, or other value directly in the Value area for the desired argument. Or if you click the down arrow to display a drop-down list, you'll see a list of fields you've previously added to the report that match the data type of the argument (for example, if the argument requires a date-time value, only date-time fields that you've previously added to the report will appear in the drop-down list). You may also choose drop-down list options to Enter Constant Value, which will display a separate dialog box where you may choose or type a value (which is just the same as typing the value in directly without clicking the down arrow). You may also select Choose Other Field from the drop-down list, which will display a separate dialog box listing all fields in all database tables that match the data type of the argument.

If you've supplied several values to arguments in the Function Arguments list and wish to discard them all, click the Reset Values button above the Function Arguments list. All previously supplied arguments will be discarded, and you'll need to choose arguments again. If you want more general information on the custom function you've chosen to base your formula on, click More Info to see a dialog box showing all the function's properties.

Once you've supplied all the necessary arguments, click the Save And Close button in the Formula Workshop toolbar. If the formula you're creating in the Expert is based on a function from the repository, you'll be reminded that creating this formula will add the chosen repository custom function (and any other repository functions that it may be based on) to the report. This will be required to use this formula, so click Yes to acknowledge this message.

The formula will be created and added to the Field Explorer, where it may be dragged to your report just like any other field. If you later wish to edit this formula, either right-click the formula in the report's Design or Preview tab and choose Edit Formula from the pop-up menu, choose Field Explorer options to edit the existing formula, or display the Formula Workshop and choose and edit the formula from within the Formula Fields tree. The Formula Workshop containing the Formula Expert will reappear with the formula already in it. If you wish to see the formula displayed in the Formula Editor instead of the Formula Expert, click the "magic wand" button in the Formula Workshop toolbar—the formula will be displayed in the Formula Editor instead.

NOTE *Creating your own custom functions that you may base Formula Expert formulas on is covered in more detail in Chapter 5.*

The Formula Editor

When you first create a new formula or edit an existing formula that is based on something other than a single custom function, the Formula Editor will appear inside the Formula Workshop, as shown in Figure 4-3. It may look a little foreboding at first, but don't worry— it will soon become second nature to you as you create and edit more formulas.

Formula Editor toolbar provides access to
the most common Formula Editor functions

Choose the formula language
syntax to use for this formula

Field Tree box contains a hierarchical
tree of database fields, other formula
fields, group subtotals, etc.

Function Tree box contains a
hierarchical view of available
Crystal Reports functions
and custom functions

Operator Tree box contains a
hierarchical view of built-in Crystal
Reports math, string, comparison
operators, etc.

FIGURE 4-3   The Formula Editor inside the Formula Workshop

TIP *If you wish to customize the font face, size, colors, and other appearance options that the
Formula Editor uses, select File | Options on the pull-down menus and make your choices on
the Formula Editor tab.*

Before you actually create a formula, familiarize yourself with the layout of the Formula
Editor. Notice that the Field Tree, Function Tree, and Operator Tree boxes can be closed,
resized, moved, and undocked (detached from the main window and put in their own
windows). You have a great deal of flexibility in customizing the way the Formula Editor
looks. You may also undock the Formula Editor toolbar (the second toolbar at the top of the
Formula Workshop) and move it to another location on the screen.

PART I

Tip *If you mistakenly undock and then close the toolbar, you can get it back by closing and re-opening the Formula Workshop. The toolbar will then reappear.*

When you're working with the Formula Editor, you'll want to familiarize yourself with the Formula Editor toolbar (titled the *Expression Editor toolbar* if you undock it), because you'll need to use it on a regular basis. There are buttons to check for proper formula syntax; undo and redo editing changes; hide and show the field, function, and operator trees; and so forth. If you're unfamiliar with a toolbar button's function, point to it with your mouse and wait a second or two—a tooltip for that button will appear. Table 4-2 shows the functions of the Formula Editor's toolbar buttons.

Button/Key Combo	Name	Function
x·2 or **ALT-C**	Check	Checks the syntax of the formula and reports any errors.
or **CTRL-Z**	Undo	Undoes the latest editing or typing.
or **CTRL-Y**	Redo	Redoes the latest editing or typing.
or **ALT-B**	Browse Data	Displays sample data from the database for the selected database field. This button will work only when you've highlighted a database field, not a custom function.
or **CTRL-F**	Find/Replace	Allows searching and replacing for specific characters in the current formula, or in multiple formulas. If you choose the option to search in multiple formulas, a Find Results box will appear below the Formula text box.
or **CTRL-F2**	Toggle Bookmark	Places a bookmark at the current line of formula text. If a bookmark is already there, removes it.
or **CTRL-ALT-F2**	Next Bookmark	Moves the cursor to the next bookmark in the current formula.
or **SHIFT-F2**	Previous Bookmark	Moves the cursor to the previous bookmark in the current formula.
or **CTRL-SHIFT-F2**	Clear All Bookmarks	Removes all bookmarks from the current formula.
or **ALT-O**	Sort Trees	Sorts the contents of the three Tree boxes alphabetically, instead of in the default logical order.

TABLE 4-2   Formula Editor Toolbar Buttons

Button/Key Combo	Name	Function
[icon] or **ALT-F**	Field Tree	Displays/hides the Field Tree box.
[icon] or **ALT-U**	Function Tree	Displays/hides the Function Tree box.
[icon] or **ALT-P**	Operator Tree	Displays/hides the Operator Tree box.
[icon]	Display Find Results	Displays/hides results of a Find in Formulas operation below the formula text portion of the Formula Workshop. Find in Formulas is discussed later in the chapter.
Crystal Syntax ▾	Syntax	Chooses syntax (Crystal or Basic) to use for this formula only.
Exceptions For Nulls ▾	Null Treatment	Chooses to treat null values encountered in a formula as nulls, or to convert nulls to the default value for the data type of the null field.
// or **ALT-M**	Comment/ Uncomment	Adds comment characters (two slashes for Crystal Syntax, an apostrophe for Basic Syntax) to all formula lines that are highlighted. If the lines already are commented, this button removes the comment characters. Lines that are preceded with comment characters are ignored by the formula.

TABLE 4-2 Formula Editor Toolbar Buttons *(continued)*

TIP   There are other shortcut keys you can use while in the Formula Editor, many of them being standard shortcuts that are common across most Windows applications. Search Crystal Reports online Help for "Key controls for Formula Editor" for specifics.

There are two general approaches to building a formula: type in the parts of the formula directly or double-click or drag and drop in the tree boxes. Once you become more familiar with the Crystal Reports formula language, you will probably create at least some parts of your formula by typing the formula text right into the Formula text box at the bottom of the Formula Editor. For example, simply typing an asterisk when you want to multiply numbers often is easier than clicking around in the Operator Tree box to find the multiplication operator.

Other parts of your formula, however, are best created automatically by double-clicking or dragging and dropping elements in one of the three tree boxes. For example, to include a database field as part of your formula, just find the field you want to include in the Field Tree box and double-click it. The field will be placed at the cursor position in the Formula text box, using proper formula language syntax. You may also drag it from the Field Tree box to the desired location in the formula.

Using the trees is easy. Simply find the general area of the tree that you are interested in and click the plus sign next to the category that you want to use. All the functions or operators within that category will appear. Double-click the one you want to use and it will be placed at the cursor position in the Formula text box. You may also drag the function or operator to the desired location within the Formula text box. If you choose a function that requires *arguments* (or parameters), such as an UpperCase function that needs to know what you want to convert to uppercase, the function name and parentheses will be placed in the formula with the cursor positioned at the location of the first argument. You can either type it in or move to another tree (the field tree, for example) and double-click or drag and drop the field you want to add as the argument. After a while, you'll be able to find the functions or operators you're looking for quickly and create fairly large formulas simply by double-clicking or dragging and dropping.

Notice the syntax that Crystal Reports uses when it places objects in the Formula text box (the small formula illustrated in Figure 4-3 is a good example). If you decide to type material into the formula yourself, you'll need to adhere to proper formula language syntax. Table 4-3 identifies special characters and other syntactical requirements of the formula language.

Crystal Syntax	Basic Syntax	Uses
. (period)	. (period)	Used to separate the table name from the field name when using a database field. You must always include the table name, a period, and the field name—the field name by itself is not sufficient.
{} ("curly" or French braces)	{} ("curly" or French braces)	Used to surround database fields, other formula names, and parameter fields. The formula won't understand fields if they're not surrounded by curly braces.
// (two slashes)	' (apostrophe) or Rem	Denotes a comment. These can be used at the beginning of a line in a formula, in which case the Formula Editor ignores the whole line. You can also place two slashes or an apostrophe anywhere in a formula line, in which case the rest of the line will be ignored. You may use the Formula Editor Comment/ Uncomment toolbar button to add these characters to multiple selected lines at one time.

TABLE 4-3   Formula Editor Special Characters

Crystal Syntax	Basic Syntax	Uses

" " or ' ' (quotation marks or apostrophes)	" " (quotation marks)	Used to surround string or text *literals* (fixed-string characters) in formulas. With Crystal syntax, you can use either option, as long as they're used in matched pairs. For example:
		`If {Customer.Country} = "USA" Then`
		`"United States" Else 'International'`
		If you are using Basic syntax, you must use quotation marks only—an apostrophe will be interpreted as a comment.

() (parentheses)	() (parentheses)	Used to force certain parts of formulas to be evaluated first, as in the following:
		`({Orders.Amount} +`
		`{Orders.Amount}) * {@Tax Rate}`
		Also used to denote arguments of built-in functions, as in this example:
		`UpperCase({Customer.Customer Name})`

@ ? # %	@ ? # %	Crystal Reports automatically precedes certain fields with these characters. The @ sign precedes formulas, ? precedes parameter fields, # precedes running total fields, and % precedes SQL expression fields. When including these types of fields in a formula, make sure you surround the field with curly braces.
# (pound sign)	# (pound sign)	If you don't include curly braces around a pound sign, Crystal Reports will expect a value appearing between two pound signs that can be converted to a date/time value, as in this example:#2/10/2000 1:15 pm#

, (comma)	, (comma)	Used to separate multiple arguments in functions. For example:
		`ToText({Orders.Amount},0," ")`
		Don't add a comma as a thousands separator when using a numeric constant in a formula. For example:
		`{Orders.Amount} + 2,500`
		will cause a syntax error.

; (semicolon)	: (colon)	If your formula contains multiple statements, you must separate them with a semicolon in Crystal syntax (putting statements on separate lines without a semicolon will still cause a syntax error). With Basic syntax, you must either put each statement on a separate line or separate multiple statements on the same line with a colon. Note that in Basic syntax, some statements (such as those making up For loops) must be placed on separate lines—separating these statements with a colon will still cause a syntax error.

TABLE 4-3   Formula Editor Special Characters *(continued)*

Crystal Syntax	Basic Syntax	Uses

ENTER key	_ (space followed by underscore)	In Crystal syntax, you may press ENTER to start a new line in your formula anywhere between a field or function and an operator (don't put new lines or spaces in the middle of field or function names). Long formulas are more readable on multiple lines. For example:
		`If {Order.Amount} > 5000 Then`
		`   "Qualifies for bonus"`
		`Else`
		`   "Not eligible for bonus"`
		In Basic syntax, you may press ENTER only at the end of a complete statement. If you want a line break in the middle of a statement, you must use a line continuation sequence (a space, followed by the underscore). For example:
		`If {Order.Amount} > 5000 Then`
		`    Formula = _`
		`    "Qualifies for bonus"`
		`Else Formula = _`
		`    "Not eligible for bonus"`
		`End If`

:= (colon followed by equal sign)	= (equal sign)	Used for variable assignment, such as:
		`NumberVar Quota := 1`
		In Crystal syntax, don't confuse this with the equal sign alone, which is used for comparison:
		`If {Customer.Region} = "BC"`
		`Then`
		`"Canadian Customer"`
		In Basic syntax, the equal sign is used for both comparison and assignment, as in
		`If {Customer.Region} _`
		`   = "BC" Then`
		`Formula = "Canadian Customer"`
		`End If`

TABLE 4-3   Formula Editor Special Characters *(continued)*

Formula Syntax Choices in Crystal Reports

The syntax you use for individual formulas can be chosen with the syntax drop-down list, located at the right end of the Formula Editor toolbar. When you choose the desired syntax, you'll notice that the function and operator trees will change, showing all the built-in functions and operators for the chosen syntax. When you check the formula with the Check button, the formula must conform to the syntax chosen in the drop-down list. If, for example, you create a formula that is correct for Crystal syntax and then choose Basic syntax in the drop-down list, you'll probably get an error message if you check the formula. Crystal Reports will not automatically convert from one syntax to the other when you change the syntax drop-down value in an already existing formula.

The choice of syntax is largely one of personal preference. If you are a Basic programmer who often encounters syntax errors with Crystal syntax because you instinctively use Basic, you'll probably be pleased with Basic syntax. If you've used previous versions of Crystal Reports and aren't a Basic programmer, you'll most likely want to continue to use Crystal syntax because you're familiar with it. You don't have to do this at the expense of flexibility, either—virtually all of the Basic-like constructs in Basic syntax are also available in Crystal syntax. You can always choose which syntax to use in each formula that you create (the notable exceptions being record, group, and saved data selection formulas—these can use only Crystal syntax, and you aren't given a choice). You may choose the default syntax for all new formulas by choosing File | Options and clicking the Formula Editor tab.

The remainder of this chapter focuses largely on Crystal syntax, showing most examples in the Crystal Reports "original" formula language. This choice has been made for two reasons:

- If you are using previous versions of Crystal Reports, most of this chapter will still apply to you.

- The Basic language is well documented in many other texts. Since this book is specific to Crystal Reports, language syntax that is specific to Crystal Reports is best documented here.

Any examples or issues that are specific to Basic syntax will be so noted.

Crystal Reports Formula Autocomplete

If you develop computer programs in certain programming languages, or develop web pages with certain tools, you may be familiar with autocompletion, which will often anticipate what you are typing and complete portions of your code for you. Crystal Reports features a limited form of this technology as part of the Formula Editor.

In addition to double-clicking functions in the group tree, you may begin typing portions of your formula directly in the formula text area of the Formula Editor. If you'd like to choose from a list of possible formula functions you can use, press CTRL-SPACE. A list will appear with possible functions you can use.

The list of functions you see in the drop-down list will be based on what you've typed so far before pressing CTRL-SPACE—if you've typed enough letters to narrow down the list of available functions to a small group, only the few that fit will appear. If you type CTRL-SPACE with no characters typed beforehand, the whole list of Crystal Reports functions will appear in the drop-down list. And, if you have typed enough characters to narrow the available functions to just one, the drop-down list won't be displayed at all—the complete function name will just be typed in for you.

To choose a function from the drop-down list, use the DOWN ARROW key to choose the desired function and press SPACE or ENTER, or click on the desired function with your mouse. You may also just continue to type, narrowing down the list of available functions as you go. When you get to a single unique choice, the completed function name will be typed for you.

Instead of choosing a field from the Field Tree box, you may type the field name directly into the Formula Text box. When you type a left curly brace, Crystal Reports will display a list of possible fields. As you continue to type, the list will continually update, showing only the narrowed-down list of available fields. You may use the UP ARROW or DOWN ARROW keys, in combination with ENTER, to choose an available field in the list. If you choose a table in the list and press ENTER, a new list of fields within that table will appear, whereby you can continue to type additional characters to narrow down the field list, or use cursor keys to pick the desired field.

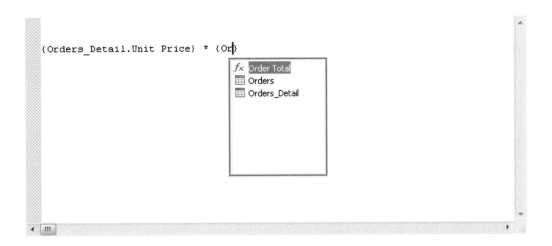

Finding Text in Multiple Formulas

There may be situations where you've used a certain database field, formula function, variable name, or the like, in multiple formulas throughout your report. If you wish to change this reference throughout all these formulas, you don't have to manually edit each and every formula in your report, looking for occurrences of the desired text or field. You may use the Find in Formulas option to search all formulas in the report for the specific occurrence.

You may start this search in several areas of Crystal Reports. First, if there is a particular database field, formula, SQL Expression, or the like, that you wish to search all formulas for, simply expand the desired category of the Field Explorer and select the field you wish to search for (you must first close the Formula Editor/Workshop before you use the Field Explorer). Right-click and choose Find In Formulas from the pop-up menu. The Formula Workshop will appear with the Find Results box appearing below the Formula text box and the first formula containing the search text displayed in the Formula Editor.

If you are already editing a formula, you may use the search option (the "binoculars" button in the Formula Editor toolbar). Type in the full or partial text you wish to search for (for example, if you are looking for a specific database field, you needn't type in the surrounding French braces). Then click the All Formulas or All SQL Expressions radio button, depending on which type of formula you wish your search to encompass. The Find Results box will appear below the Formula text box.

The Find Results box displays each occurrence of the specified text in a formula. If the text appears in the same formula more than once, that formula will appear multiple times in the Find Results box. You may now double-click any line in the Find Results box to display that formula in the Formula Editor (you may also use the arrow keys to select the desired formula and press ENTER, or you may right-click the desired line in the Find Results box and choose Go To from the pop-up menu). The search text will be highlighted in the formula.

You may also right-click any entry in the Find Results list and choose options from the pop-up menu to clear this particular occurrence from the list, clear all occurrences, undock the Find Results box from the Formula Workshop, or hide the list (it may be redisplayed by clicking the appropriate toolbar button in the Formula Editor toolbar or by performing a new search).

Data Types

As you begin to work with formulas, it's very important to understand the concept of *data types*. Every database field has a certain data type, and every formula you create will result in a single data type. These concepts are important, because if the formula you create doesn't deal with data types properly, you'll get errors when you try to save the formula, or the formula won't give you the result you're looking for. You can't, for example, add the contents of a number field to the contents of a string field with a plus sign—both fields have to be numbers. You can't convert a date field to uppercase characters, because only a string field can be converted to uppercase.

By default, Crystal Reports doesn't display objects in the Design tab by their data types. It shows their names instead. You may prefer to see the data-type representation instead of the field name. To do this, choose File | Options from the pull-down menus and turn off the

Show Field Names check box in the Field Options section of the Layout tab. Notice the difference between showing field names and showing data types:

Order ID	Order Amount	Order Date	Courier Website
-5,555,555	($55,555.56)	3/1/1999 1:23:45PM	xxxxxxxxxxxxxxxxxxxxxxxx

You may want to turn off Show Field Names when you first start working with formulas. Seeing the data types can help you determine the types of operators and functions that will work with the database fields you're including in your formulas. Also, whenever you *browse* database fields in the Formula Editor, the data type shows up in the Browse dialog box. In the preceding illustration, the fields have the following data types:

- **Order ID**   A *number* data type, which can contain only numbers (along with a period to indicate a decimal point, and a hyphen or minus sign if it's a negative number). You can add, subtract, multiply, divide, and perform other math operations on number data types.

- **Order Amount**   A *currency* data type (available only from certain databases). This is similar to a number data type, but it avoids rounding errors that sometimes occur when performing math operations on number data types.

- **Order Date**   A combined *date/time* data type (again, supported only by certain databases). This can contain a date, a time, or a combination of both. Other databases have date-only data types, and some have time-only data types.

- **Courier Website**   A *memo* data type. The memo data type, like another type called *string*, allows any combination of characters to be placed in the field. However, because letters and punctuation marks can reside in the field, you normally can't perform mathematical calculations with the field.

You may encounter other data types in your databases that aren't shown in this example:

- **Boolean**   Represents data that can have only a true or false value.

- **BLOB**   Designed to contain photos, graphics, or large amounts of plain ASCII text. Sometimes these appear as "Picture" data types.

CAUTION   *BLOB (Binary Large Object) fields can be placed on the report only for display. They cannot be used or manipulated inside formulas. While they may show up in the Formula Editor Field Tree box, you'll receive an error message if you attempt to use them inside a formula.*

You may also show data types alongside field names in the Field Explorer. Just select the Database Fields category, a table name, or an individual database field and then right-click. Choose the Show Field Type option from the resulting pop-up menu (the option will then show a check mark next to it). The data type will then appear next to each field name in any database table.

Creating a New Formula

Creating a simple math calculation is easy. Using the Orders Detail table of the sample XTREME sample database available for download at the book's companion web site, CrystalBook.com, you can calculate the extended price of each order-line item with the following formula.

To create this formula, follow these steps:

1. Create a new report using the XTREME Microsoft Access sample database available for download from CrystalBook.com. Choose the Orders Detail table from this database.

2. Select the Formula Fields category and then click the New button in the Field Explorer toolbar. Or, you may launch the Formula Workshop and create the new formula from there.

3. When asked to name the formula, type **Extended Price**, and click OK.

4. When the Formula Editor appears, double-click the Orders Detail.Unit Price report field in the Field Tree box (you may need to click the plus sign next to the database name to be able to see the Orders Detail table) to add it to the Formula text box. If the field you want to add has already been placed on the report, you will actually find it in the field tree under both the Report Fields section and the database name—there is absolutely no difference if you choose the field from either area.

5. Click the plus sign next to Arithmetic in the Operator Tree box to see all the arithmetic operators that are available. Double-click the multiply operator. (You can save yourself some mouse clicks by typing an asterisk directly in the Formula text box, if you'd like. Although you don't have to put a space before or after the asterisk, the formula is easier to read if you do.)

6. Double-click the Orders Detail.Quantity field in the Field Tree box to place it after the asterisk.

7. If you wish to add a comment explaining the use of the formula (for your own information, or perhaps for others who may be working with your report later), you may precede the comment lines with two slashes, or just type the comment lines, highlight them with your mouse, and click the Comment button in the Formula Editor toolbar.

TIP   You may drag and drop fields, functions, and operators from their respective boxes to the Formula text box, as well as double-clicking.

After you finish the formula, you have several ways to save it and close the Formula Editor and the Formula Workshop. When you first start to use formulas, you'll probably want to check for correct syntax of the formula before you save it. This will ensure that Crystal Reports can at least understand the different parts of the formula and how they are supposed to be calculated or manipulated. Check the formula's syntax by clicking the Check button in the Formula Editor toolbar, or press ALT-C. If Crystal Reports can understand all parts of the formula, a dialog box will appear indicating that no errors were found. (If you've ever written computer programs or used spreadsheet formulas before, though, you know that correct syntax doesn't guarantee that the formula will return the right answer!)

If there is a syntax error in the formula, Crystal Reports will display an error message and highlight the portion of the formula where it stopped understanding it. As you can see here, sometimes these messages may be very descriptive:

or they can be very cryptic:

even though both of these examples result from simply forgetting curly braces. You'll learn over time what most error messages indicate and how to resolve them.

CAUTION *Even though you may not get any syntax errors when you first check the formula after you create it, you may still get an error when the report runs, depending on the actual data in the database. This may happen, for example, if you create a formula that divides two fields, but the "divided by" field returns a zero during a certain record. You'll then get a Divide by Zero syntax error in the middle of the report process. If there's a chance that this type of error may occur given particular data, you'll probably want to add some type of "If {field} > 0 Then. . ." logic to ensure these types of run-time syntax errors won't occur.*

After you determine that there are no syntax errors, it's time to save the formula. You may either save the formula and remain in the Formula Workshop or save the formula and close the Formula Workshop by using the appropriate buttons in the Formula Workshop toolbar. If you try to create a new formula or edit another formula without first saving the current formula, you'll be asked if you want to save the current formula before you proceed to the next formula.

If you choose to skip the syntax check and immediately save the formula, Crystal Reports will check the syntax anyway. If there is an error, you'll be given the opportunity to save the formula with the error. This makes little sense, because Crystal Reports will stop as soon as you try to run the report and display the error message in the Formula Editor. If you try to save and get a syntax error, correct the error and try to save the formula again. If there are no errors, you'll no longer get a syntax error message and the formula will be saved.

Once the formula has been saved and the Formula Workshop has closed, you will see the formula name under the Formula Fields category of the Field Explorer. You can simply drag and drop the formula on the report, just like a database field. In the case of the Extended Price formula, notice that the formula has taken on the currency data type. This occurred because a currency field was multiplied by a number field, resulting in a currency formula.

Run-Time Debugging Features

As mentioned previously in the chapter, it's possible that an error may occur when the report actually runs, but not be detected when you initially create a formula. It's frustrating to create a formula, click Check, and receive a "No Errors Found" message, only to have the formula return with an error when the report runs. This situation is known as a *run-time error*. Run-time errors are often caused by formulas not anticipating the type of data that may be encountered as the report progresses. For example, the formula may perform division on a database field that could possibly return zero for certain records. Or, the formula might extract certain specific characters from a string, only to encounter an error at run time when a record contains a null value for a string, or not enough characters to satisfy the formula's requirements.

Run-time errors can be easily debugged using the *call stack*. If you encounter a run-time error, you'll first see the error message indicating what the error is (such as "Divide By Zero"), followed by the Formula Workshop showing the offending formula. However, the left-hand tree of the workshop will now show the formulas and functions that led up to the error.

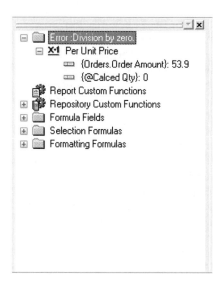

By viewing different entries in the call stack, you can see what the values of variables, fields, and other parts of the formula currently contain. This can be helpful in determining the cause of the error more quickly so that you can supply additional logic to avoid the error in the future.

Editing, Renaming, or Deleting an Existing Formula

After you create a formula, you may wish to change its calculation or add to its function. There are many ways for you to *edit* the existing formula in either the Field Explorer or Formula Workshop. To edit by using the Field Explorer, perform any of these steps:

- Select the formula you wish to change and click the Edit button in the Field Explorer toolbar.
- Right-click the formula and choose Edit from the pop-up menu.

Or, you may display the Formula Workshop by clicking the Formula Workshop toolbar button or choosing Report | Formula Workshop from the pull-down menus. You may then expand the Formula Fields category and click the formula you want to edit.

Any of these options will redisplay the Formula Workshop and Formula Editor with the formula in it.

An even quicker method of editing is available after you've placed the formula on your report. In either the Design or Preview tab, click the formula. Notice in the status bar that the formula name is preceded by the @ sign. Crystal Reports automatically adds this symbol to the beginning of all formulas you create. Now that you've selected the formula, simply right-click and choose Edit Formula from the pop-up menu. The formula will reappear in the Formula Editor, ready for you to modify.

If you wish to *rename* a formula, you may do so either from the Formula Fields category of the Field Explorer or the Formula Workshop. If you are using the Field Explorer, begin by selecting the formula you want to rename. Then, you may either click the Rename button in the Field Explorer toolbar or press the F2 key. You may also right-click the formula and choose Rename from the pop-up menu or even just click on the formula and then hold the mouse button down for a second or two. The name will become "editable"—type the new name and either click outside the formula name or press ENTER. If you've used this formula inside other formulas or elsewhere on your report, Crystal Reports will change the name there, too. To rename a formula in the Formula Workshop, use identical steps to select and rename the formula in the workshop tree.

If you select a formula on the report and press the DEL key, you remove that particular occurrence of the formula from the report. However, the formula remains in the Field Explorer and takes up memory and storage space when you save the report. If you're sure you no longer need the formula, delete it entirely. This must be done from the Formula Fields category of the Field Explorer or the Formula Workshop. Select the formula you want to delete and press the DEL key. You can also choose the Delete button from the appropriate toolbar, or right-click the formula name and choose Delete from the pop-up menu. The formula will be removed from the dialog box.

CAUTION *If you remove a formula that is in use somewhere else on the report, such as in another formula or in a hidden section, you'll be given a warning, as deleting a formula that other formulas depend upon may stop the report from working properly. In some cases, Crystal Reports won't even allow you to delete a formula if it is being referenced in some other formula in the report. While a message will indicate that you cannot undo a formula deletion, you may perform a single undo that returns the formula to the Field Explorer. However, anything prior to this in the "undo stack" will no be longer available.*

Copying Formulas

As your reports become more complex, so will your report formulas. The most complex of report formulas may consist of many lines of formula logic, declaration and assignments of variables, and so forth. After you spend a great deal of time creating and testing a formula, you may wish to make use of it as the basis for another report formula. While you can edit the first formula, highlight the entire formula in the Formula text box, copy it to the clipboard, create a new formula, and paste the previously copied text into the Formula text box, Crystal Reports gives you quicker ways to copy a formula—either within the same report, or from one report to another.

If you wish to copy a formula within the same report, simply right-click the formula you wish to copy in the Formula Fields category of the Field Explorer. Choose Duplicate from the pop-up menu. A new copy of the formula will be created in the Field Explorer with the same name as the original formula, appended by a sequential number. You may now edit the copied formula as you would any other formula, rename it to have a more meaningful name, or drag and drop it to the report.

Other situations may require that you copy a formula from one report to another. Again, you may choose to edit the original formula, copy the formula's text to the clipboard, switch to the other report, create a new formula, and paste in the copied text. However, there's a simpler way. Make sure that the formula you wish to copy is placed somewhere on the report canvas of the first report. Select it and choose Copy from the File menu, toolbar, or right-click options. Then, select the tab of the already-open report you wish to copy the formula to, or open the report with the File menu or toolbar options. With either the Design or Preview tab of the second report visible, choose the File menu, toolbar, or right-click options to paste the copied formula. You may also simply drag the formula from one report to another, if you have tiled or cascaded multiple report windows in Crystal Reports.

CAUTION   *If any parts of the formula you copied to the new report don't apply to that report (for example, database tables referenced in the formula aren't included on the second report), your formula may not operate properly. Make any necessary changes to the copied formula to ensure it will work properly on the new report.*

Number Formulas

Probably the most common type of formula is a number formula, such as the Extended Price formula discussed earlier. Number formulas can be as simple as multiplying a database field by 1.1 to increase its amount by 10 percent, or as complex as calculations that include sophisticated statistical math. There is no special procedure required to declare a formula as a "number formula"—the formula simply takes on that data type because of the fields and operators that you use in the formula. The Extended Price sample formula (shown here), multiplying a currency field by a number field, will return a resulting currency data type:

```
{Orders Detail.Unit Price} * {Orders Detail.Quantity}
```

Many number formulas will use a mathematical *operator,* such as a plus sign, a hyphen or minus sign, an asterisk for multiplication, or a slash for division. You may also need to use built-in *functions* that Crystal Reports supplies or custom functions that you create yourself or that others create for you. You'll find all these functions listed in the Function Tree box (if you are using BusinessObjects Enterprise, you may need to add a custom function to your report from the repository first—see Chapter 18 for more information). When you double-click a function, the function name is placed in the Formula text box with the cursor located in between the opening and closing parentheses. You can then either type in the function's arguments, or double-click other fields or formulas in the Field Tree box to add them as arguments to the function.

For example, if you have a group on the report and want to include a group subtotal in a formula, you would use the Sum function. You'll find that three Sum functions actually are available, with one, two, or three arguments. Here are some examples:

```
Sum({Orders.Order Amount})
```

returns a total of all order amounts for the entire report.

```
Sum({Orders.Order Amount},{Customer.Region})
```

returns a total of just the order amounts in the region group where the formula is evaluated. If the formula was evaluated in the Colorado group, the formula returns the order amount subtotal for Colorado only.

```
Sum({Orders.Order Amount},{Orders.Order Date}, "weekly")
```

returns the order amount subtotal for the current order date group, calculating the subtotal based on a week of orders. Note that this third argument corresponds to the time periods that are available when creating a group based on a date field. (Refresh your memory about date-field grouping by looking at Chapter 2.)

So, you could calculate each order amount's percentage of the region subtotal by using the percentage operator and the Sum function as follows:

```
{Orders.Order Amount} % Sum({Orders.Order Amount},{Customer.Region})
```

There are built-in functions to calculate all the summary-type information discussed in Chapter 2, such as average, subtotal, *P*th percentile, and on and on. By opening the Arithmetic category of functions in the Function Tree box, you'll also find functions to calculate remainders, determine absolute value, and round numbers.

TIP *If you need to calculate a group subtotal as a percentage of a grand total or higher-level group total, there's no need to create a formula. Instead, use percentage summary fields as described in Chapter 2. However, you'll still need to create a formula, as described previously, if you want to determine what percentage of a group subtotal a particular detail field is responsible for.*

The Basic Syntax Formula Variable

When you use Crystal syntax, the formula simply returns the results of the last statement in the formula. If the formula consists of only one statement, such as the multiplication in one of the previous examples, the formula returns the results of the multiplication. If the formula contains several statements separated by semicolons, the last statement determines what's returned to the report.

But if you are using Basic syntax, you must keep in mind one slight difference from any Basic-like programming languages you've used. In a Basic computer language, you typically assign and manipulate variables throughout your code. When you wish to display the value of a variable, you may use a Debug.Print (or similar) statement or set the value of a text box or other form element to the value of the variable. Because Crystal Reports has no Print statement, you need an alternative method of displaying a value on the report. This is accomplished with the *Formula variable*.

The word "Formula" is a reserved word in Basic syntax—you can't use it for any other purpose, such as using it as your own variable name with a Dim statement. By assigning a value to the Formula variable, you determine what the formula returns to the report. You can use the Formula variable over and over within a formula, just like any other variable (as an accumulator, for example). The last occurrence in the formula where a value is assigned to the Formula variable determines what the formula returns to the report. Consider the following Basic syntax formula:

```
' Calculates extended price
Formula = {Orders Detail.Unit Price} * {Orders Detail.Quantity}
If {Customer.Region} = "CO" Then
    ' add 4.25% sales tax to Colorado orders
    Formula = Formula * 1.0425
End If
```

Here, the Formula variable is used like a regular variable (it doesn't even have to be declared with a Dim statement first). It's first used just to calculate the extended price. Then, it's included in an If statement to add sales tax for Colorado orders. If the If statement is true, the existing value of the Formula variable is multiplied by 1.0425 to add 4.25 percent. If the If test fails, the last statement that assigns a value to the Formula variable (the extended price calculation) will be what's returned to the report.

Order of Precedence

You'll sometimes find situations where you're unsure of the order in which Crystal Reports evaluates a formula's operators. For example, if you wish to add sales tax to an extended price, you might use the following formula, which is supposed to add 8 percent sales tax to the extended price of an order (already calculated in the @Extended Price formula):

```
{@Extended Price} + {@Extended Price} * .08
```

The question of how Crystal Reports calculates this is crucial. Does it perform the addition operation first and then the multiplication operation, or does it perform the multiplication operation first and then the addition operation? The results will vary dramatically, depending on the calculation order. Consider an Extended Price of $100 with addition performed first:

```
100 + 100 = 200
200 * .08 = 16.00
```

or with multiplication performed first:

```
100 * .08 = 8.00
100 + 8.00 = 108.00
```

While your customer might be very pleasantly surprised by the first calculation showing up on their invoice, the second calculation is certainly the correct one. But looking at the formula, you'll notice that the multiplication operator is the second operator. Will it be evaluated second?

The answer is no, because of the *order of precedence.* Although it may sound like a computer concept, order of precedence is actually a concept that you should recall from your ninth-grade math class. In this formula, multiplication and division are evaluated first from left to right across the formula; then, addition and subtraction are evaluated from left to right across the formula.

The order of precedence for both Crystal syntax and Basic syntax is as follows:

- Exponentiation (^)
- Negation (−)
- Multiplication, division, left to right (*, /)
- For Crystal syntax only, percent (%) is evaluated at the same time as multiplication and division
- Integer division (\)

- Modulus (Mod)
- Addition and subtraction, left to right (+, –)

Given this syntax, the formula to add tax to the Extended Price shown earlier will work just fine. But what if, for some reason, you want the addition performed first, not the multiplication? Again, thinking back to ninth-grade math, you surround the part of the formula you want evaluated first with *parentheses*. The following formula will perform the addition before the multiplication:

```
({@Extended Price} + {@Extended Price}) * .08
```

NOTE *If you use one formula inside another formula, as in this example, Crystal Reports calculates the embedded formula first (using the order of precedence) and then calculates the outer formula.*

String Formulas

Many times, the database will contain string or text data that is insufficient for your reporting needs. For example, you may want to sort a report by ZIP code, but the database contains ZIP codes only as part of a combined City_State_Zip field. Or, you may want to write a report to print checks, spelling out the dollar amount in words, using a number or currency field in the database. All of these are applications for a formula that either manipulates or creates string data.

Strings can be *concatenated*, or "tacked together," using the plus sign or the & sign (ampersand). Although the plus operator is the same one used to add numbers, the results will be very different depending on the data type. For example, the formula

```
25 + 7 + 100
```

returns a numeric result of 132. Because all the elements of the formula are numbers, the plus sign will add the numbers together and return a numeric answer.

Contrast that with this formula:

```
"25" + "7" + "100"
```

or

```
"25" & "7" & "100"
```

which returns a string result of 257100. When you enclose the numbers in quotation marks, Crystal Reports interprets the values in the formula as strings, not numbers. When you use a plus sign or ampersand with strings, the result is the concatenation of the individual string elements.

This is very useful for many situations you'll encounter when reporting against databases. The following illustration shows the beginning of a form letter that simply uses database fields on the report.

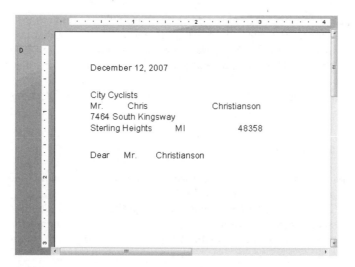

Notice the spacing problems for the contact name, city-state-ZIP line, and salutation. While you may be able to improve the appearance of this report slightly by resizing and moving the individual database fields, you'll never achieve a perfect result. By placing the database fields on the report in fixed locations, the report will never be able to accommodate varying widths of first names, last names, cities, and so on.

The next illustration shows the same report using formulas to concatenate the database fields together.

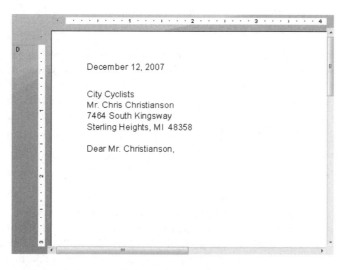

The results are obvious: No matter how wide or narrow names or cities are, they are placed right next to the other items (with a space in between).

While you can conceivably combine these database fields in text objects to accomplish the same result (refer to Chapter 6 for information about combining data in text objects), formulas give you a lot more flexibility as to how your report looks. For example, you can display only the first initial of a contact name on the report using a formula. You can't do that with a text object.

Concatenating string fields is as simple as using the ampersand (&) operator, as in the following:

```
{Customer.Contact Title} & " " & {Customer.Contact First Name} &
" " & {Customer.Contact Last Name}
```

Notice that a space is hard-coded into the formula using a *string literal,* which is simply a fixed string surrounded by quotation marks. You'll use string literals often in concatenation formulas and If-Then-Else formulas (discussed later in this chapter). So, the literal space in this formula will separate the title from the first name, and the first name from the last name.

You could create a salutation line using database fields and several string literals, as follows:

```
"Dear " & {Customer.Contact Title} & " " &
{Customer.Contact Last Name} & ","
```

Notice that the word "Dear" and a space precede the title, a space separates the title from the last name, and a comma follows the last name.

NOTE *The ampersand concatenation operator is available in both Crystal and Basic syntaxes. An concatenation operator held over from earlier Crystal Reports versions, the plus sign (+), is also available in Crystal syntax.*

There are many situations in which you may want to use only certain parts of strings in a formula, not the whole string. For example, you may want to use only a first initial as part of the contact name on a form letter. By following a string field with a number or range of numbers enclosed in square brackets (Crystal syntax) or parentheses (Basic syntax), you can extract certain characters from the string field. This function is known as the *subscript* function. For example, look at this formula in Crystal syntax:

```
{Customer.Contact Title} & " " & {Customer.Contact First Name}[1] &
". " & {Customer.Contact Last Name}
```

Notice that only the first character from the first name will be included in the formula, and a period has been added to the space literal between the first and last names.

Many older database systems contain date information in string fields because earlier versions of mainframe systems or older database systems did not include a date data type. To allow dates to sort correctly, the year needs to precede the month and day in these fields as well. Thus, it is very common to find January 10, 1999, coded into a string database field as 19990110.

If you want to display the date in an mm/dd/yyyy format to make the date more readable, you could use string subscript operators to pick out the individual parts of the date, add some string literals, and rearrange the date's appearance. Assuming that the hire

date in a "legacy" database is an eight-character string field in the form yyyymmdd, this
formula will redisplay it as mm/dd/yyyy:

```
{EMP.HIRE_DATE}[5 to 6] & "/" & {EMP.HIRE_DATE}[7 to 8] &
"/" & {EMP.HIRE_DATE}[1 to 4]
```

Notice that the subscript operator can also return a *range* of characters, not just one.

In addition to the subscript operator, there are many built-in string functions that you
can use in your formulas. There are functions to return characters from the left of a string,
the middle of a string, and the right of a string. Using these, the preceding date formula
could be rewritten in Crystal syntax as follows:

```
Mid({EMP.HIRE_DATE},5,2) & "/" & Right({EMP.HIRE_DATE},2) &
"/" & Left({EMP.HIRE_DATE,4})
```

In this case, the Mid function takes three arguments: the field or string to use, the
position in the string from which to start reading, and the number of characters to return
(there's also a two-argument version of Mid). The Right and Left functions take two
arguments: the field or string to use and the number of characters to return.

TIP *You can find complete explanations of all built-in Crystal Reports formula functions, including
samples of usage, in the appendix.*

Dealing with Null Database Values

Crystal Reports may return odd results with formulas that encounter a database field
containing a *null value* (a special database value equating to empty, as opposed to zero
for a number field, or an empty string for a string/text field). Several factors determine
whether or not the database will contain null values. In many cases, this is determined
by the way the database is initially designed. If you prefer to avoid null values appearing
on the report, Crystal Reports allows you to convert them en masse to a "default" format
(typically a zero for number fields, and an empty string for string fields). To do this for
all new reports in the future, check Convert Database NULL Values To Default on the
Reporting tab of the File | Options pull-down menu. You'll also find the Convert Other
NULL Values To Default option to deal with other non-database values (such as other
formulas) that may return null values. To set these options for just the current report,
check the same options after choosing File | Report Options from the pull-down menus.

String formulas are particularly susceptible to problems resulting from null values.
If any field in the string formula that you're using returns a null, the entire formula will
return null (this type of formula is sometimes referred to as a formula that returns an
exception).

There are several ways of dealing with nulls and the resulting oddities in formulas.
One way is to use an If-Then-Else formula, along with the IsNull built-in function
(described later in the chapter), to deal with potential null situations. Or, you may check
the Convert Database NULL Values To Default options described earlier in this box.

Crystal Reports provides yet one additional way of dealing with nulls in formulas (string or otherwise). A drop-down option choice appears in the Formula Editor toolbar presenting two choices for dealing with nulls: Exceptions For Nulls and Default Value For Nulls. The first point to keep in mind is that *neither* of these options will be relevant if your formula doesn't encounter any nulls. Thusly, if you've chosen to Convert Database NULL Values To Default as described previously, no formulas in your report will ever encounter a Null and neither of these options will have any effect.

If, however, you may encounter null values in a formula, this new option allows you to make a choice, on a formula-by-formula basis, on how to deal with them. If you choose Exceptions For Nulls, nulls will be treated as an *exception* if they are encountered in a formula. For example, a string concatenation formula that encounters a null anywhere within it will return a null (or *exception*) to the report—no data will actually appear. By choosing Default Value For Nulls, you in essence choose the Convert Database NULL Values To Default for *this one formula only*. In this case, a string concatenation formula that would otherwise return a null "exception" value will, instead, return the results of the string concatenation with an empty string appearing for the field that would have otherwise evaluated to a null.

If you wish to set a default choice for this setting for all new formulas you create in the future, you may make this choice by choosing File | Options from the pull-down menus. Then, make your desired default choice on the Formula Editor tab.

The ToText Function

A crucial built-in function that you will probably use very often in string formulas is ToText, which is used to convert other data types to a string data type so that you can use them in concatenation or comparison formulas. You can use ToText to convert numbers, dates, times—virtually any other data type—to strings. You need this functionality to avoid the type of problem shown here:

This problem occurs because you can't concatenate a number field onto a string literal (or any other combination of mismatched data types). To convert a number or currency field to a string, such that you can concatenate it to another string, use ToText. The following will solve this problem:

```
"Thanks for purchasing " + ToText({Customer.Last Year's Sales}) +
" in merchandise last year."
```

That formula will return

```
Thanks for purchasing $32,421.27 in merchandise last year.
```

If you look in the Function Tree box under Strings, you'll see several permutations of ToText, with anywhere from one to five arguments. You may also notice the CStr function containing the same set of arguments. CStr and ToText are equivalent—you may use either function.

TIP *If you use the ampersand operator (&) to concatenate strings, you reduce your need to use ToText, as this operator performs an automatic conversion if you are mixing data types in your formula. However, if you want to control formatting of the converted values in your formula, you'll still need to use ToText to provide customized formatting.*

While the best place to look for all the ToText details is Crystal Reports online Help or the appendix, here are a few additional ToText examples:

- Determine the number of decimal places.
    ```
    "Thanks for purchasing " & ToText({Customer.Last Year's Sales},0) &
    " in merchandise last year."
    ```
    will return
    ```
    Thanks for purchasing $32,421 in merchandise last year.
    ```
    A second number argument to ToText determines how many decimal places Crystal Reports uses when it converts the number or currency field to a text string.

- Determine the thousands separator.
    ```
    "Thanks for purchasing " & ToText({Customer.Last Year's Sales},0,"")
    &
    " in merchandise last year."
    ```
    will return
    ```
    Thanks for purchasing $32421 in merchandise last year.
    ```
    A third string argument to ToText determines what thousands separator Crystal Reports uses when it converts a number or currency field to a text string. In this example, the two quotation marks side by side indicate an empty string, so ToText doesn't use a thousands separator.

- Format date fields.
    ```
    "Your order was placed on " &
    ToText({Orders.Order Date},"dddd, MMMM d, yyyy.")
    ```

will return

```
Your order was placed on Monday, January 12, 2004.
```

This version of ToText uses a *format string* as the second argument. The format string (sometimes referred to as a *mask*) uses special characters—pound signs; zeros; decimal points; the letters *d, m, y*; and so forth—as placeholders to indicate how data should be formatted when converted to a string. In this example, the *dddd* characters specify the day of the week to be spelled out fully. *MMMM* specifies a fully spelled month, *d* specifies the day of the month without a leading zero, and *yyyy* specifies a four-digit year. Any characters included in the format string that can't be translated into placeholders (such as the commas and periods) are simply added to the string as literals.

TIP *It's important to remember that the case of the placeholder characters is significant. When formatting time fields, for example, lowercase h characters indicate hours with a 12-hour clock, whereas uppercase H characters indicate hours with a 24-hour military clock. Apart from that, if you use placeholder characters of the wrong case, Crystal Reports will just include the characters in the resulting string as literals.*

Another built-in function, ToWords, comes in handy when writing checks with Crystal Reports. Consider the following formula:

```
ToWords({PAYROLL.NET_CHECK_AMT})
```

When placed on the report, this formula returns the following for an employee record with net pay of $1,231.15:

```
one thousand two hundred thirty-one and 15/100
```

Picking Apart Strings

In more complex reports, you may wish to pick out only certain parts of strings (the first initial of a name was mentioned previously as an example). Crystal Reports contains many interesting formula functions to handle even more complex "substring" requirements.

For example, you may wish to make use of the ToWords function discussed previously, but not to print checks. If you are printing legal contracts, real estate documents, or bank notes, for example, you may need to print both the numeric and text forms of the same number, as in

```
This contact expires in thirty (30) days.
```

For the sake of this example, assume that the data indicating the number of "expire days" is contained in a numeric database field. Accordingly, you may try creating a formula to print the previous example. The formula might initially look like this:

```
"This contract expires in " & ToWords({Contracts.Expires}) & " (" &
ToText({Contracts.Expires},0) & ") days."
```

In this example, the ToWords function is used to convert the numeric field to "spelled out" text, and ToText is used to convert the number to a numeric string, with no decimal places.

However, the result of this formula will be

```
This contract expires in thirty and xx / 100 (30) days.
```

Because ToWords is designed for printing checks, it returns not only the "whole number" part of the numeric field, but the hundredths part as well. For the contract example shown previously, this won't work. How, then, can you create a formula to return just the whole number portion?

If you look closely at ToWords, you'll notice that the whole number portion is always separated from the hundredths portion with the word "and." If you can search through the result of ToWords for the "and" characters, and return just the portion *before* these characters, you will have a successful formula.

Look at this example:

```
"This contract expires in " &
Left(ToWords({Contracts.Expires}),
     InStr(ToWords({Contracts.Expires}), " and "))
& "(" & ToText({Contracts.Expires},0) & ") days."
```

There are several functions and techniques used in this formula that require further explanation:

- **The Left function**   The Left function returns a certain number of characters from the left side of another string (and as you might imagine, there is also an available Right function to return characters from the right side of a string). In this formula, the desire is to return the left portion of the words returned by ToWords up until the characters "and" are encountered. So, if ToWords returns "thirty and xx / 100", you wish to extract the first six characters from the left (up until the "and" is encountered). But, how do you determine where the characters "and" are?

- **The InStr function**   There are several different versions of InStr in the formula language. The version shown in the previous example takes two arguments: the string you want to search, and the "substring" you want to search for within the first string. By supplying the ToWords function as the first argument, and the characters "and" as the second argument, you are asking InStr to find the *numeric position* in "thirty and xx / 100" where the word "and" is. Here the word "and" begins at position 8, which is the numeric result from the InStr function.

So, by using the InStr function within the Left function, you can extract the proper number of characters to get just the whole number portion of the spelled-out number. The only adjustment you must consider is that InStr returns a value of 8, but you want only the first 6 characters (or 7, if you don't mind having a trailing space). This is why you see the "– 1" subtraction of the value returned by InStr. This will return the leftmost 7 characters, including the trailing space, resulting in the characters "thirty " appearing as the spelled-out text.

There are many other built-in string functions that can perform similar functions. Look in the functions tree under Strings, or in the appendix, for information on other versions of ToText, InStr, Mid, and many others.

Date/Time Formulas

There are many reporting situations in which you need to manipulate date, time, or date/time data types. Most PC and SQL databases support some or all of these data types. Although date and time fields don't appear on the report as pure numbers (they often include other characters and words, depending on how they're formatted), they are actually stored by the database and Crystal Reports as numbers. Therefore, it's possible to do mathematical calculations on date fields. There are also built-in date and time functions that return just parts of date and time fields and that convert other data types to date or time fields.

Number of Days Between Dates

When Crystal Reports performs math on date-only fields, the result of the calculation is in whole days. Crystal Reports returns fractional days if fields in the formula are date/time fields. For example, if you subtract a date-only field containing the value May 1, 2007, from a date-only field containing the value May 5, 2007, the result will be the whole number 4. If the fields are date/time fields and the May 1 field contains a time of 12 noon and the May 5 field contains a time of midnight, the result will be the fractional number 3.5.

So, determining how long it took to ship an order is as simple as creating the following formula:

```
{Orders.Ship Date} - {Orders.Order Date}
```

Even though both the database fields in this formula are dates (or date/time if these fields are coming from the sample XTREME database referred to elsewhere in this book), the result of the formula will be a number—the number of days between the two dates. This formula will return the number of calendar days between the two dates—it uses all days in the calendar. When you perform this type of date arithmetic, you may find fractional days returned, if the date/time fields contain actual time values. This can cause differences between two dates to be "3.5" or "5.75." This can sometimes be difficult if you really want to know just the number of days between two dates, not including time. In these cases, you can use the *Date* built-in function to convert the Date/Time data types to just dates. It may be preferable, for instance, to use the following formula to determine the number of days between two dates:

```
Date({Orders.Ship Date}) - Date({Orders.Order Date})
```

Or, you may also consider using the Round or Truncate function to adjust the numeric result. *Round* (not a Date-related formula function, but helpful in this example) will round a number to a specified number of decimal places—rounding up or down, depending on the fractional value. *Truncate* will simply "throw away" the fractional portion of the result, not rounding in the process. Accordingly, this would also work to avoid fractional dates resulting from time values in the date/time fields:

```
Truncate({Orders.Ship Date} - {Orders.Order Date}, 0)
```

If you wish to exclude weekends from this calculation, it gets a little trickier. Crystal Reports provides the Visual Basic–like function DateDiff in both syntaxes to do more flexible date math. An example of using DateDiff to exclude weekends from this type of calculation can be found in Crystal Reports online Help. Search for "DateDiff function."

You can calculate a date in the future. If, for example, you want to create an accounts receivable report that shows the actual due date of an invoice, the date itself could be calculated by using the invoice date (a date field) and terms (a number field), as follows:

```
{AR.INV_DATE} + {AR.TERMS}
```

Although you don't explicitly define this formula as a date formula, it returns a date data type showing the date on which the invoice is due, provided the terms field contains the number of days required for payment (30, 45, and so forth).

Another function in both Crystal Reports formula syntaxes can be a lifesaver with future and past date calculations. The DateAdd function operates much like its Visual Basic counterpart. For example, to determine a date exactly one month prior to today's date, you would use this formula:

```
DateAdd("m", -1, CurrentDate)
```

The "m" argument indicates an interval of a month. The second argument indicates the number of "time intervals" to add (in this case, a negative one, thereby subtracting a month). The third argument is the date or date/time value to add to (Crystal Reports' *CurrentDate* function returns the date from your PC's system clock). What's particularly powerful about DateAdd is the automatic adjustment for various numbers of days in months and years. For example, if you evaluated this formula on March 31, 2004, it would return February 29, 2004 (there is no February 31, but 2004 was a leap year, therefore resulting in February 29).

Number of Hours and Minutes Between Times

You can also perform mathematical functions directly on time fields. When you calculate two time fields together, the result is in seconds. For example, the following formula will return the elapsed time, in seconds, between a starting time formula and ending time formula (assuming that both formulas are designed to return a time data type):

```
{@Course End Time} - {@Course Start Time}
```

Since most industry-standard database systems don't support time-only field data types, you'll often find that database fields containing the time are actually date/time data types. If you'd rather not return days between the dates, but seconds between the times, you'll need to use the built-in *Time* function to return just the time portion of a field. For example,

```
Time({COURSE.EndDateTime}) - Time({COURSE.StartDateTime})
```

You may not want the time returned as seconds, but perhaps as hours and minutes, minutes and seconds, or any combination separated with colons. To accomplish this, you have a bit more work to do, but not as much as you might think. Examine the following:

```
Time(0,0,0) + ({@Course End Time} - {@Course Start Time})
```

You'll notice that parentheses force the time calculation to be performed first, resulting in the number of seconds between the two times. The Time built-in function (used in a different format in this example) is also being used to return a time data type using three arguments: hour, minute, and second. The particular time being returned by the Time function is midnight. By adding the seconds between the two times to midnight, you essentially have the number of hours, minutes, and seconds that have elapsed since midnight.

When you place this on your report, you'll see hours, minutes, and seconds, followed by AM or PM (AM if the time difference is less than 12 hours, PM if more, assuming that you're using Crystal Reports' default *hh:mm:ss AM/PM* date format). Now it's simply a matter of using the Format Editor to suppress the AM/PM indicator by choosing 24-hour time display. You can also suppress any combination of hours, minutes, and seconds to show the elapsed time the way you wish.

TIP *The DateDiff function is not limited to just calculating differences between dates. You can also do time calculations similar to the previous example with DateDiff.*

Month, Day, Year, Hour, Minute, and Seconds Functions

There are many built-in functions to help you use date and time fields. You can use the Month, Day, and Year functions with a date or date/time field as an argument to return just the month, day, or year of the date as a number. Conversely, with the Hour, Minute, and Seconds functions, you can supply a time or date/time field as a single argument and have just the hour, minute, or second of the field returned as a number.

DateValue Function

Two very important functions are DateValue and CDate, both of which are functionally equivalent. While there are several variations on DateValue, probably the most intriguing is the variation that accepts one string argument. This string can contain several variations of date-like strings, such as 10/1/99, March 17, 2005, 21 Feb 2008, and so on. Crystal Reports will evaluate the string to determine where the month, day, and year portions reside, returning a "real" date value as the result.

NOTE *If you supply a two-digit year to DateValue, Crystal Reports applies a "sliding scale" approach to determining the century. If the two-digit year is between 0 and 29, Crystal Reports assumes the century is 2000. Otherwise, the two-digit year will be converted to the 1900s.*

This greatly simplifies date conversion in Crystal Reports. For example, if your legacy database contains dates in string fields formatted as "mm/dd/yyyy," simply use the following:

```
DateValue({EMP.HIRE_DATE})
```

There may be times when DateValue can't properly evaluate a date string, due to misspellings or other nonconforming string contents in a database field. This is a prime candidate for a run-time formula error. When you check the formula in the Formula Editor with the Check button, you'll get the popular No Errors Found message. However, when the report runs and the formula encounters the nonconforming string value, you'll see the following:

To avoid these run-time errors, use an If-Then-Else statement (described later in the chapter) in conjunction with another function, IsDate, to perform the conversion to a Date value only if the string can be interpreted by Crystal Reports as a date.

TIP   *A number of related Time and DateTime conversion and detection functions are also available in Crystal Reports. Look in the functions tree, the online help, or the appendix for DateTimeValue, TimeValue, IsDateTime, and IsTime.*

If-Then-Else Formulas

One of the complaints that's sometimes heard in the competitive community of database report writers is, "Crystal Reports is too complex—it's made for programmers." While this complaint may or may not ring true, there is no doubt that elements of common programming languages can be found in the Crystal Reports formula languages. The first of these programming-oriented features is If-Then-Else logic. The If-Then-Else combination is the cornerstone of much computer programming code, so once you learn If-Then-Else concepts, you'll be on your way to performing really sophisticated report customization.

If-Then-Else formulas perform a test on a database field, another formula, or some combination of them. Your test can be as simple or as complex as you need it to be— perhaps just checking to see if a sales figure exceeds the $1,000 bonus threshold. Or, you may want to check the number of days a product took to ship, in conjunction with the carrier who shipped the product and the sales level of the customer, to determine if a shipment met your company's shipping goals. If the test passes (returns *true*), the formula will return a certain result. If the test fails (returns *false*), a different result will be returned.

If-Then-Else formulas are created with the following syntax:

```
If <test> Then <result if true> Else <result if false>
```

The test portion of an If-Then-Else formula must use comparison operators found in the Operator Tree box (or a Boolean formula, discussed later in the chapter). You'll find a Comparisons section of the box that, when opened, shows operators that test for equal, less than, greater than, and other combinations of conditions. These can be used in conjunction with And, Or, and Not Boolean operators to combine multiple conditional tests together. Here's a simple If-Then-Else formula that will return a string based on an order amount:

```
If {Orders.Order Amount} > 5000 Then "Bonus Order"
Else "Regular Order"
```

The Order Amount database field is tested to see if its value is greater than 5,000. If the test is true, the formula returns the "Bonus Order" string. Otherwise, the formula returns the "Regular Order" string.

Boolean operators can also be used to combine multiple comparisons together. You can use And, Or, and Not Boolean operators. The preceding formula has been slightly enhanced in the following formula, using a Boolean operator to combine two comparisons:

```
If {Orders.Order Amount} > 5000 And Month({Orders.Order Date}) = 12 Then
    "Holiday Bonus Order"
Else
    "Regular Order"
```

Here, the order amount has to exceed 5,000 *and* the order must have been placed in December for the formula to return Holiday Bonus Order. Orders over 5,000 in other months will still be regular orders. If you change the And to an Or in the preceding formula, then *all* orders in December will be bonus orders, regardless of amount. Orders over 5,000 will also be considered bonus orders the rest of the year.

Data Types in If-Then-Else Formulas

While creating If-Then-Else formulas, you must pay special attention to the data types that you're using in the formula. In the If test of the formula, make sure you use similar data types in each individual comparison operation. For example, if you want to test whether Customer.Country is USA, the test will be

```
If {Customer.Country} = "USA"
```

Since Customer.Country is a string field, you need to compare it with a string literal, enclosed in quotation marks or apostrophes (just quotation marks in Basic syntax). If the field you are testing is numeric, you need to use a number constant, as in the Orders.Order Amount sample shown previously. If you mismatch data types, such as these:

```
If {Orders.Order Amount} > "5000"
```

you'll receive an error.

If you use multiple comparisons separated by Boolean operators, each comparison can have a different data type. For example, if you want to combine the two tests mentioned previously, your formula would start out as follows:

```
If {Customer.Country} = "USA" And {Orders.Order Amount} > 5000
```

In this case, the different data types in the If part of the formula are fine, as long as each "side" of each comparison is of the same data type.

For example, you may have an existing formula on your report, @Ship Days, that calculates the number of days it took to ship an order. But since @Ship Days is a numeric formula, it will display a zero on your report if the order was placed and shipped on the same day. Therefore, you would write the following If-Then-Else formula to show the words "Same Day" on the report if @Ship Days is zero, or to show just the contents of the @Ship Days formula if it is not zero:

```
If {@Ship Days} = 0 Then
    "Same Day"
Else
    {@Ship Days}
```

But if you use the Check button in the Formula Editor to check the syntax of this formula, you'll receive an error:

The problem is that Crystal Reports doesn't know what data type to assign to the formula. If the test returns true, the formula will return a string for the words "Same Day". However, if the test returns false, the formula will return @Ship Days, which is a number. Crystal Reports must assign a data type to a formula when it's first created—it can't wait until the report is running. Therefore, even though the If part of a formula can contain various data type tests, the Then and Else parts must contain the same data types.

Remember the function that converts other data types to strings? The following will solve this problem:

```
If {@Ship Days} = 0 Then
    "Same Day"
Else
    ToText({@Ship Days},0)
```

This result is better, because it doesn't show zero as the number of ship days. But we want to take it a step further to make the report more readable. Look at the enhanced version of this formula:

```
If {@Ship Days} = 0 Then
    "Shipped Same Day"
Else
    "Shipped in " + ToText({@Ship Days},0) + " days"
```

This looks better on the report, particularly if the report isn't a straight columnar report. You might want to put this in a group header for an order, before the individual line items for the order show up in the details section. But there's just one more problem. What will this formula return if it took only one day to ship the order?

```
Shipped in 1 days
```

While this probably won't mean your dismissal from the report development team, why not go one easy step further to make the report look even better? Try the following:

```
If {@Ship Days} = 0 Then
   "Shipped Same Day"
Else
   If {@Ship Days} = 1 Then
      "Shipped in 1 day"
   Else
      "Shipped in " + ToText({@Ship Days},0) + " days"
```

This is an example of a *compound* or *nested* If-Then-Else statement. Notice that you're not limited to one If, Then, or Else clause in a formula. You can make another If statement the result of the first Then, or the result of the first Else, and on and on. There is no specific limit to how many levels you can nest these, but obviously the formula becomes hard to follow after only one or two levels. Also, don't forget that the Else clause isn't required, so when you nest these, you won't have to always have a matching Else clause for every If.

Multiple Actions with One If-Then-Else Statement

You'll notice in all the preceding examples that only one action occurred as the result of the Then and Else parts of the statement. While this is okay for many types of formulas, sometimes you may want several things to happen, particularly when you need to set the contents of several variables as the results of a single Then or Else clause (variables are discussed later in this chapter). In this situation, you can simply repeat the If-Then-Else test several times, with a different result for each Then and Else clause. Just be sure to separate each If-Then-Else statement from the next with a semicolon. For example, to set the contents of several variables in one formula, you might use the following:

```
NumberVar GroupBonus;
NumberVar GroupFollowUpCount;
NumberVar ReportBonus;
NumberVar ReportFollowUpcount;
StringVar GoodCustomer;

If {Orders.Order Amount} > 5000 Then
   GroupBonus := GroupBonus + 1
Else
   GroupFollowUpCount := GroupFollowUpCount + 1 ;

If {Orders.Order Amount} > 5000 Then
   ReportBonus := ReportBonus + 1
Else
   ReportFollowUpCount := ReportFollowUpCount + 1 ;

If {Orders.Order Amount} > 5000 Then
   GoodCustomer := {Customer.Customer Name}
```

All of these If statements will be evaluated and the resulting variables will be set. The formula will display the result of the last action in the If statement on the report. In this example, if the Order Amount is over $5,000, all the bonus variables will be incremented by one and the GoodCustomer variable will be assigned the customer name. But because the GoodCustomer variable assignment is the last action that executes, the customer name is what the formula actually displays on the report. If the Order Amount is less than $5,000, then the two FollowUpCount variables will be incremented by one. But because the last statement still tries to set the GoodCustomer variable and fails (and there's no Else clause), the GoodCustomer variable won't be assigned a value and the formula will return an empty string.

If you look at the previous example, you see quite a bit of duplicate typing (the If test is repeated three times). This duplication can be eliminated by creating just one If-Then-Else statement, but supplying several actions to the Then and Else clauses, separating the action statements with a semicolon and surrounding them all with parentheses. Here's the same formula created using this shortened approach:

```
NumberVar GroupBonus;
NumberVar GroupFollowUpCount;
NumberVar ReportBonus;
NumberVar ReportFollowUpcount;
StringVar GoodCustomer;

If {Orders.Order Amount} > 5000 Then
    (GroupBonus := GroupBonus + 1 ;
    ReportBonus := ReportBonus +1 ;
    GoodCustomer := {Customer.Customer Name})
Else
    (GroupFollowUpCount := GroupFollowUpCount + 1 ;
    ReportFollowUpCount := ReportFollowUpCount + 1;
    GoodCustomer := "")
```

CAUTION *In the preceding example, you'll need to make sure to include the statement to assign the GoodCustomer variable an empty string in the Else clause. Otherwise, you'll receive the "A String Is Required Here" error. This is because the Then and Else clauses must still return the same data type. Without the GoodCustomer assignment in the Else clause, the Then clause will return a string value (a string variable is being assigned) and the Else clause will return a numeric value (a numeric variable is being assigned).*

Enhanced Crystal Reports If-Then-Else Options

If the If-Then-Else logic described so far isn't enough to propel you toward (or perhaps away from) a programming career, Crystal Reports includes a bevy of other If-Then-Else possibilities to help you reconsider!

First, the If-Then-Else statements in Basic syntax differ from those Crystal syntax versions described previously. Basic syntax follows the more typical If-Then-Else-EndIf approach familiar to Basic language programmers. In particular, this makes performing multiple actions as the result of a single If-Then-Else statement more straightforward by introducing the End If clause:

```
If <test> Then
   <statement>
   <statement>
   <more statements...>
Else
   <statement>
   <statement>
   <more statements...>
End If
```

Also, you can use the Basic syntax ElseIf clause (don't forget it's one word—no space) to allow nesting of multiple If conditions in one statement:

```
If <first test> Then
   <statements...>
ElseIf <second test> Then
      <second test statements...>
Else
   <statements if first test fails...>
End If
```

Yet another permutation of If-Then-Else logic exists in both Crystal and Basic syntaxes. If you've used Microsoft Office products, such as Microsoft Excel, you may be familiar with the IIF *Immediate If* function. This shortened version of protracted If-Then-Else logic is actually a single function, similar to ToText or UpperCase (it appears in the function tree under Programming Shortcuts) that accepts three arguments. The function syntax is as follows:

```
IIF(<boolean expression>, <result if true>, <result if false>)
```

This function can simplify If-Then-Else logic for small, simple formulas, or when you want to perform a "mini" If-Then-Else statement as part of a larger formula. For example, consider the following string formula using traditional If-Then-Else logic:

```
If {Customer.Country} = "USA" Then
   {Customer.Customer Name} & " requires domestic shipping charges"
Else
   {Customer.Customer Name} & " requires international shipping charges"
```

By using the Immediate If function, this can be simplified to the following:

```
{Customer.Customer Name} & " requires " &
IIF({Customer.Country} = "USA", "domestic", "international") &
" shipping charges"
```

Helpful Built-in Functions for If-Then-Else Formulas

If you look in the Function Tree box of the Formula Editor, you'll notice a Print State category. Opening this category shows a variety of built-in functions that you can use in If-Then-Else (and other) formulas to enhance your reporting flexibility. For example, the special fields found in the Field Explorer, such as Page Number, Total Page Count, Print Date and Time, Record Number, and Group Number, are available. There are other special functions that you can use to test for a null database value in the current, next, or last record; to check whether the current database record is the first or last; to check whether the formula appears in a repeated group header. By using these special built-in functions, you can create formulas that make your reports more intuitive and easier to read.

Here are some examples.

IsNull Function

```
If IsNull({Customer.Region}) Then
    ""
Else
    ", " + {Customer.Region}
```

The IsNull function is critical if you want to actually test for null values in database fields that you include in your formulas. By using the If-Then-Else test with the IsNull function, you can check whether the region field contains a null value. If so, the formula will return an empty string (denoted by the two sets of quotation marks). Otherwise, the formula will return a comma, a space, and then the region name. This formula can then be concatenated with city and ZIP database fields in another formula to form a city-state-ZIP line. If the region in the database is null, the other formula won't become null.

TIP *A more complete discussion of null values and how to deal with them can be found earlier in this chapter, under "Dealing with Null Database Values."*

Next Function

```
If {Customer.Customer Name} = Next({Customer.Customer Name}) Then
    {Customer.Customer Name} + " continues on next page..."
```

The Next function reads a field in the next record of the database. This formula compares the field in the next record to the same field in the current record. If the values are the same, you know that the same customer will appear in the first record on the next page, and you can note this with a text message. This formula would typically be placed in the page footer.

TIP *Notice that there is no Else clause in this formula. Crystal Reports doesn't require an Else clause in an If-Then-Else formula in Crystal syntax. If you leave the Else off and the test returns false, the formula will produce an empty string.*

InRepeatedGroupHeader Function

```
If InRepeatedGroupHeader Then
    GroupName ({Customer.Customer Name}) + "   - continued -"
Else
    GroupName ({Customer.Customer Name})
```

If you place this formula in the group header of a group with the Repeat Group Header On Each New Page option turned on (this can be set when you create or change a group—see Chapter 2), "- continued -" appears only when the group header is repeated. This also uses the GroupName function to return the group name field for a particular group. An InRepeatedGroupHeader test also comes in handy if you are resetting variables in formulas you are placing in the group header (assuming that you'll always be encountering a new group when the group header prints). Because you don't want to reset your variables in a *repeated* group header, you can condition your variable assignment statement on the value of InRepeatedGroupHeader. You might use something similar to the following:

```
If Not InRepeatedGroupHeader Then GroupBonus := 0
```

Other Crystal Reports Logic Constructs

Many advanced users (particularly those with programming backgrounds) will often find some of the procedural capabilities of high-level computer languages useful when designing reports. If you fall into this category (perhaps you are a Basic programmer), not only will the typical procedural constructs in Basic syntax open up enhanced flexibility for you, but similar logic constructs in Crystal syntax will also make your reporting life easier. Even if you're not a programmer, you'll probably soon find that these features come in handy in the more advanced reporting situations you'll encounter.

The term *logic construct* refers to the features of the Crystal Reports formula language that enable you to go beyond basic If-Then-Else logic. For example, it can be tedious to write long repetitive If-Then-Else formulas to perform tasks such as testing for more than a small number of conditions, picking apart strings, or cycling through multiple-value parameter fields or other arrays. Crystal Reports logic functions such as Select Case, For loops, and Do loops make these tasks much easier. These functions enable Crystal Reports formulas to move closer and closer to a full procedural language, such as Visual Basic.

Select Case Statement

Select Case is very similar to its Visual Basic counterpart. It provides a much simpler and cleaner approach to testing for multiple conditions and returning appropriate results—those complex If-Then-Else statements can now be replaced with more readable and easy-to-maintain logic.

Look at the following compound If-Then-Else statement:

```
If {@Ship Days} = 0 Then
    "Shipped Same Day"
Else
    If {@Ship Days} = 1 Then
        "Shipped in 1 day"
    Else
        "Shipped in " & ToText({@Ship Days},0) & " days"
```

This is a relatively simple formula that checks whether the @Ship Days formula returns a 0 or a 1, returning a different string value in each case. If neither of these conditions is true, a catchall Else clause displays another string value. While this particular example isn't particularly complicated, it could quickly become much more difficult to interpret and maintain if testing for more than two conditions.

Select Case is much better suited to this type of logic. Consider the following:

```
Select {@Ship Days}
    Case 0:
        "Shipped Same Day"
    Case 1:
        "Shipped in 1 day"
    Default:
        "Shipped in " & ToText({@Ship Days},0) & " days"
```

You may choose Select Case from the Control Structures category of the Formula Editor Operator Tree or simply by typing the correct syntax. Begin with the word "Select" followed by a database field, formula, or other expression. Then, supply multiple Case clauses, each testing the value of the Select expression (make sure the value you supply to each Case clause is the same data type as the Select expression). If you want to have the formula return the same result for several different values of the Select expression, you may separate the values after the Case clause with commas. You may also supply one value, the To operator, and a second value to supply a range of values. After the Case clause, supply a colon (don't use a semicolon—this isn't the end of the statement) and then supply the expression you want the formula to return if the Select value equals the Case clause. Remember that all expressions that result from a Case clause must be the same data type—you can't have one Case clause return a string and another Case clause return a number. After the Case clauses have been defined, you may supply an optional Default clause, followed by a colon, and the expression you want the formula to return if none of the Case clauses match the Select value.

For Loop

Basic programmers have always enjoyed the capability to loop through fragments of program code over and over to perform repetitive logic. This also becomes helpful in certain reporting situations (if, for example, you need to cycle through a multiple-value parameter field or iterate through a number array).

Crystal Reports includes the ubiquitous For loop in both syntaxes (except there's no Next clause in the Crystal syntax version). The For loop uses a counter variable to keep track of how many times a specified piece of logic has been cycled through. The For clause sets both the beginning and ending values of the counter variable. The optional Step clause tells the For statement how to increment the counter variable (the default is 1 if the Step clause is left out). The For statement is closed off by the word Do, followed by one or more statements enclosed in parentheses (use a semicolon to separate more than one statement within the parentheses). The statements inside the parentheses will be executed once for every increment of the counter variable.

The following formula displays all the entries a user has chosen in the multiple-value Region parameter field:

```
NumberVar Counter;
StringVar Message := "Regions Chosen: ";

// cycle through all members of the multivalue
```

```
// ?Region parameter field
For Counter := 1 to Count({?Region}) Step 1 Do
(
    // build the Message variable, along with comma/space
    Message := Message & {?Region}[Counter] + ", "
);

// strip off last comma/space added by the loop
Left(Message, Length(Message) - 2)
```

First, this formula declares two variables: Counter to increment the For loop, and Message to accumulate the parameter field values (look at the next section of the chapter for information on using variables). The For loop then cycles Counter from 1 to the number of elements in the parameter field (returned by the Count function). For each loop, Counter is used to retrieve the next element of the parameter field and accumulate it, along with a comma and a space, in Message. The final statement of the formula, which is not associated with the loop, strips off the last comma and space that were added inside the last occurrence of the loop.

NOTE *Although Crystal Reports allows string formulas and variables to return up to 64K of characters, good formula logic dictates adding a test in this formula that uses the Exit For statement to exit the For loop if the Message variable may ever approach approximately 64,000 characters in length. If the loop tries to accumulate more than 64K characters in the variable, a run-time error will occur.*

Using the Join and Split Functions to Avoid Loops

While the previous code is a great For loop example, there's actually another built-in formula function that negates the need for the variable declarations, the looping logic, and the removal of the trailing comma/space when creating a single string containing multivalue parameter field entries. Look at the following code:

```
"Regions chosen: " + Join({?Region}, ", ")
```

This formula uses the *Join* function, similar to its Visual Basic counterpart, which takes all the *elements* of the array supplied in the first argument (a multivalue parameter field actually is an array), concatenates them together, and optionally separates each with the string supplied in the second argument. Join performs the same thing as all the looping logic and variable manipulation demonstrated earlier, with one simple function.

Conversely, you may wish to take a string value or variable that contains multiple strings separated by a common delimiter (such as a slash) and create an array of string values. You could create a loop that cycles through the string one character at a time, looking for the delimiter (the slash), and performing complex logic to extract the substring and add it to an array. But the *Split* function, like its equivalent in Visual

Basic, will perform all this logic for you automatically. Look at the following code fragment (this is not a complete formula):

```
StringVar array Regions;
Regions :=
Split("Northwest/Southwest/Northeast/Southeast/Midwest", "/")
```

The second line of code will populate the Regions array variable with five elements by looking through the string and separating the five substrings that are separated by slashes.

But, don't forget your looping capabilities just yet—the Join and Split function work only with string values. If you have a multivalue parameter field that is designated as a number, date, or other non-string type, you'll still need to use loops to extract the individual elements. And if you want to build a non-string array, you may need to use loops as well, as Split works only with strings.

While Do Loop

A looping construct similar to the For loop described previously can be used to repeat statements while a certain condition is met. Whereas the For loop uses a counter variable to determine how many times the loop executes, the While Do loop evaluates a condition before each occurrence of the loop and stops if the condition is no longer true. This construct is similar to Do and While loops used in Visual Basic and other procedural languages.

The following listing is a formula that sets a variable to a phone number database field and then uses a While Do loop to look for hyphens in the variable. As long as a hyphen exists in the variable, the Do loop will execute a statement to "pick out" the hyphen, leaving behind only the pure numbers from the phone number. When there are no more hyphens in the variable, the While condition will fail and the statement after the closing parenthesis of the While Do loop (the variable name, which will display the number without the hyphens) will execute.

```
StringVar NewPhone := {Customer.Phone};

While Instr(NewPhone,"-") > 0 Do
(
    NewPhone := Left(NewPhone, Instr(NewPhone,"-") - 1) &
    Right(NewPhone, Length(NewPhone) - Instr(NewPhone, "-"));
);

NewPhone
```

Although this is a good example of how a While Do loop can cycle while a condition is true, it's a fairly complex process for the relatively simple "search and replace" function that it performs. For a more streamlined formula, you can use the Crystal Reports Replace function, as in the following example:

```
Replace({Customer.Phone}, "-", "")
```

In this case, the Replace function makes use of three arguments: the first being the string field or value that you want to modify, the second being the character or characters you want to search for, and the third being the character or characters you want to replace the search characters with.

NOTE *The previous logic construct examples are presented in Crystal syntax. Basic syntax logic constructs are very similar, if not identical, to their Visual Basic counterparts. Just remember that you must use at least one instance of the Formula intrinsic variable in Basic syntax to return a result to the report.*

Boolean Formulas

The one remaining type of formula that you may need to create is the *Boolean formula*, which can return just two values, true and false. You can think of a Boolean formula as just the "test" part of an If-Then-Else formula. When the formula is evaluated, it ultimately returns only one of the two states.

Here's a simple Boolean formula:

```
{@Ship Days} > 3
```

In this formula, the existing @Ship Days formula (a number formula) is tested to be greater than 3 (indicating a shipping exception). It simply *is* or *is not* greater than 3. If it is greater than 3, the formula returns a true value—if it's not, the formula returns a false value.

When you then place this formula on your report, it will appear with a Boolean data type. If you have Show Field Names turned off in File | Options (discussed earlier in the chapter), then you'll see the formula show up with the word "True" in the Design tab. If you format the field, you'll notice a Boolean tab in the Format Editor that lets you choose how you want the true/false values to appear on the report.

Although you may occasionally find Boolean formulas helpful when they're actually placed on the report, you'll probably use them much more often as a cornerstone for other formulas. For example, the Boolean formula shown previously indicates that Xtreme Mountain Bikes considers orders that took longer than three days to ship as exceptions. But, Xtreme really wants to break down the shipping exception rule according to Last Year's Sales. If the customer purchased more than $50,000 in merchandise last year, the three-day shipping exception will apply. However, if a customer purchased less, a six-day shipping exception applies.

This requires a *compound* Boolean formula, such as

```
({@Ship Days} > 3 And {Customer.Last Year's Sales} > 50000)
Or {@Ship Days} > 6
```

which uses a combination of And and Or operators, along with the comparison operators, to create a more complex Boolean formula. What's important to remember, though, is that the ultimate result will still be either true or false. You can make a Boolean formula as complex as you want, using combinations of comparison operators along with And, Or, and Not operators, but in the end, only true or false will result.

TIP *Notice the parentheses around the first part of this compound Boolean formula. They ensure that both @Ship Days is less than 3 and Last Year's Sales is greater than $50,000 before "Or'ing" the @Ship Days greater than 6 test. Although this may make the formula more understandable, it is optional. Crystal Reports considers all Boolean operators (And, Or, and Not) equally in the order of precedence (discussed previously in this chapter). That is, it evaluates them equally as it travels through the formula from left to right.*

There are several benefits to creating Boolean formulas in this fashion:

- After you create a complex Boolean formula, you can include it in other formulas as the test part of an If-Then-Else formula, as in the following:

```
If {@Shipping Exception} Then
    "*** Shipping Exception ***"
Else
    "Shipped Within Goal"
```

This makes the second formula much easier to read and understand.

- By using the Boolean formula throughout the report, you eliminate the need to retype the complex Boolean test repeatedly, thus reducing the chance of errors. Even more important, you have only one formula to change if the report requirements change down the road. For example, if you use the @Shipping Exception formula as the cornerstone for 50 other formulas in your report, and you later decide to reduce the Last Year's Sales qualification from $50,000 to $35,000, you have only *one* formula to change on your report, not 50. All the rest will follow the change.

- You can use the Boolean formula in record, group, and saved data selection (covered in Chapter 3) and conditional formatting (covered in Chapter 6) to limit the report to certain records or to have certain objects on the report appear with different formatting.

TIP *Every Crystal Reports built-in formula function and operator is illustrated in the appendix. Also, you can find extended online help for these when displaying the Formula Editor. Just select the function or operator you want more information on in the appropriate Function or Operator Tree and press F1.*

Variables in Formulas and Evaluation Times

As a general rule, formulas maintain the results of their calculation only for the duration of one database record. If you put a formula in the details section, it will evaluate every time a new record is processed and put its result in the details section. If you put a formula in a group footer, it will be evaluated when each group footer prints. In every case, the formula will not "remember" anything from the previous record or previous group footer. Once the next record or footer comes along, the formula evaluates completely "from scratch."

Sometimes, though, you may need a formula to remember material from record to record or from group to group. You may want to accumulate some value as the report progresses so that you can print a total in a group footer or report footer. For example, you may want to check the value of a subtotal in a group footer. If it exceeds a certain threshold, you may want to increment a counter so that you can show how many groups exceeded the threshold at the end of the report.

To accomplish this, you need to somehow store information from record to record or from group to group. This can be accomplished by using *variables*. A variable is simply a "placeholder" that Crystal Reports sets aside in the computer's memory. As the report progresses from record to record or from group to group, your formula can refer back to the variable or change its contents. You can then use the variable in other formulas or display its accumulated contents in a group or report footer.

Declaring a Variable

The first step in any formula that uses a variable is to *declare* the variable. This sets aside a specific amount of memory for the variable, based on its data type. You'll find variable declarations listed in the Operator Tree box of the Formula Editor under Variable Declarations.

Notice that a different variable declaration statement exists for each Crystal Reports data type. You must consider in advance what kind of data your variable is going to hold, and declare the correct type of variable accordingly. If, for example, you want to keep track of a customer name from record to record, and the customer name field in the database is a string data type, you need to declare a string variable to hold the information.

***

NOTE *Crystal syntax and Basic syntax use different statements to maintain variables. Just like in Microsoft Visual Basic, Crystal's Basic syntax requires use of the Dim statement to declare a variable before use. And as when working in Visual Basic, you can either assign a data type to a variable when you Dim it, or simply assign a value to it after you have used Dim without a data type (and the variable will automatically take on the data type of the value you assign it). Because of this similarity to Visual Basic, Basic syntax variables won't be discussed here, because they are well documented in Visual Basic texts. The rest of the discussion on variables applies to Crystal syntax.*

***

You must also give each variable a name. You can give it any descriptive name you wish, provided it doesn't start with a number, contain spaces, or conflict with another Crystal Reports formula language *reserved word*. You can't, for example, use variable names such as Date, ToText, or UpperCase—these are reserved by the formula language for its own built-in functions (you'll know if your variable names are reserved words by looking at their color in the Formula Editor—Crystal Reports turns all reserved words blue).

To declare a variable, type the appropriate variable declaration keyword followed by the variable name, such as this example:

```
NumberVar BonusAmount;
```

This declares a number variable called BonusAmount that can later be assigned a numeric value. The semicolon at the end of the statement separates this statement from the next one in the formula (presumably a statement to assign or test the contents of the variable).

If you wish to use more than one variable in the formula, you may declare them together, again separated by semicolons. For example,

```
NumberVar BonusAmount;
StringVar BonusCustName;
DateVar DateBonusReached;
```

***

TIP *You may be used to assigning variables in programming languages. Remember that Crystal Reports probably treats variables differently. You must declare a variable in each formula where you want to refer to the variable. However, even if you declare a variable and assign it a value in one formula, and then declare it again in a formula that appears later in the report, it will retain the value from the first formula. Unlike in many other languages, declaring a variable more than once in Crystal Reports does not reset its value to zero or empty (with the exception of local variables, as described in the following section). These considerations apply to both syntaxes, Crystal and Basic. Even if you're used to using the Dim statement only once in Visual Basic, you must use it with Basic syntax in every formula where you want to refer to a variable. If the variable has been declared with a Dim statement in another formula, declaring it again will not reset its value.*

Variable Scope

The whole idea and benefit of variables is that they retain their values as the report progresses from record to record or from group to group. So, for variables to be of real benefit, they need to keep their values throughout the report process. And because you may have several formulas that you want to refer to the same variable, you need to be able to refer to a variable in one formula that was already declared and assigned a value in another.

Exactly how long and where a variable keeps its value is determined by the variable's *scope*. If a variable has a narrow scope, it will retain its value only in the formula where it is initially declared—any other formula that refers to a variable with the same name will be referring to a brand new variable. If a variable has a wide scope, its value will be retained for use not only in other formulas, but also in subreports within the main report. (Subreports are covered in Chapter 12.) The following are three additional words you can place in front of your variable declarations (or use in place of the Dim statement in Basic syntax) to determine the variable's scope.

Local	The variable remains in scope only for the formula in which it is defined. If you declare a variable with the same name in another formula, it won't use the value from the first formula.
Global	The variable remains in scope for the duration of the entire main report. You can declare a global variable in one formula, and another formula will be able to use the contents placed in the variable by the first formula. Global variable values, however, are not retained in subreports.
Shared	The variable not only remains in scope for the duration of the entire main report but can also be referred to in formulas in subreports. You can use shared variables to pass data around the main report, back and forth between the main report and subreports, and from subreport to subreport.

Add these keywords in front of variable declarations to determine their scope, as follows:

```
Local NumberVar BonusAmount; //will only be visible in this formula
Global StringVar BonusCustName; //available to the whole main report
Shared DateVar DateBonusReached; //available to main and subreports
```

> **TIP** *If you leave off the variable scope keyword in Crystal syntax, the default scope for a variable will be global—it will be available to other formulas in the main report, but not to subreports. If you use the Dim statement in Basic syntax, the default scope for the variable will be local—it will be available for use only in the rest of the formula where it's declared. If you don't want to use the default scope, make sure you always add the proper scope keyword. And, make sure you add the keyword to the declaration in every formula that will be using the variable.*

Assigning a Value to a Variable

After you declare a variable, it won't do you much good if you don't assign a value to it. You may want to use it as an accumulator (to "add one" to it each time some condition is met for the database record). You may want to assign a string value to it, concatenating additional string values onto the variable as records progress. You then might display the value of the accumulated variable in the group footer, and assign the variable an empty string in the group header to start the whole process over again for the next group.

TIP If you declare a variable but don't assign a value to it, it takes on a default value based on its data type. Numeric and Currency variables default to 0, string variables default to an empty string, Boolean variables default to false, and Date variables default to a "0/0/00" date. Date/ Time and Time variables default to a null value. Standard practice, however, dictates that you assign a value to a variable to ensure that it, in fact, contains a useful value for the remainder of the report.

Crystal syntax provides two instances in which you can assign a variable a value: at the same time the variable is declared, or on a separate line later in the formula. In either event, you must use the assignment operator, consisting of a colon followed by an equal sign, to assign a value to a variable. This is important—it's easy to get confused and just use the equal sign by itself. The equal sign works only for comparison—you must place a colon in front of the equal sign to make assignment work properly unless you are using Basic syntax, in which case the equal sign by itself is used for both assignment and comparison. Here's a Crystal syntax example of assigning a variable a value on a separate line:

```
NumberVar CustomerCount;
CustomerCount := CustomerCount + 1
```

Here, the CustomerCount variable is declared on the first line (terminated with a semicolon) and assigned a value on the second line. In this particular formula, the CustomerCount variable will keep its value from record to record (remember that Crystal syntax variables take on Global scope by default), so it will be incremented by one every time the formula executes.

If you want to reset the value of the CustomerCount variable in a group header, you need to reset it to 0. Here's a Crystal syntax example of how to declare and assign a variable at the same time:

```
NumberVar CustomerCount := 0
```

Here, the variable is declared, followed by the assignment operator and the value to assign the variable. In this example, placing this formula in the group header will reset the CustomerCount variable at the beginning of each group.

TIP Keep in mind that a semicolon doesn't have to appear at the end of the last line of a formula, because it is used to separate one statement from another. If your formula only declares and assigns a variable, you don't need the semicolon at the end of the declaration/assignment statement.

You don't have to assign a value to a variable every time the formula executes, nor do you need to assign the same value every time. Creative use of logic constructs, such as If-Then-Else or Select Case, along with variable assignment, provides report flexibility that rivals that of many programming languages. Look at the following formula, which declares and conditionally assigns several variables:

```
CurrencyVar BonusAmount;
StringVar HighestCustName;
DateTimeVar DateBonusReached;

If {Orders.Order Amount} > BonusAmount Then
    (HighestCustName := {Customer.Customer Name};
     DateBonusReached := {Orders.Order Date};
     BonusAmount := {Orders.Order Amount})
```

Look at this formula closely. Assuming it's placed in the details section, it keeps track of the highest order amount as the records progress. When an order exceeds the previous high amount, the customer who placed the order and the date the order was placed are added to variables. Then, the new high order amount is assigned to the bonus amount. The following are some important points to note about the formula:

- There are multiple variable assignments separated by semicolons inside the parentheses. They will all execute, but only the last statement will determine how the formula appears on the report. In this example, the last statement uses a currency data type, so the formula will appear on the report as currency.

- If you are keeping track of the bonus amounts, dates, and customer names for a certain group, such as a region or country, make sure to reset the variables in the group header. If you fail to reset the variables, and the next group doesn't have an order as high as the top value in the previous group, the previous group's values will appear for the following group as well.

- If you want to keep track of quotas or similar values for both group and report levels (for example, you want to see the bonus customer for each region and for the entire report), you'll need to assign and maintain two sets of variables: one for the group level that is reset in the group header, and one for the report level that's not reset.

Displaying a Variable's Contents

In the preceding example, you saw how to accumulate values in variables in the details section, and how to reset them by assigning them a value of 0 in the group header (or in another area of the report). You also need to have a way to show exactly what's contained in a variable on the report, or to use the variable's value in a formula some other way.

To show the contents of a variable, you simply need to declare it. If the formula contains no other statements, declaring the variable will also return it as the formula value. For example, you might place the following formula in the group footer to show the customer who reached the bonus in the region group:

```
StringVar HighestCustName
```

You neither need to place any other statements in the formula to show the value of the variable nor even need the semicolon at the end of the declaration line—it's the last line in the formula.

You may have situations in which you want to show the contents of a variable but are using other statements to assign the variable in the formula. In that case, just declaring the variable won't display it, because the declaration statement won't be the last line in the formula. In this situation, just add the name of the variable as the last line of the formula. This will then display the contents of the variable when the formula executes. Here's an example:

```
CurrencyVar BonusAmount;
StringVar HighestCustName;
DateTimeVar DateBonusReached;

If {Orders.Order Amount} > BonusAmount Then
    (HighestCustName := {Customer.Customer Name};
     DateBonusReached := {Orders.Order Date};
     BonusAmount := {Orders.Order Amount});

HighestCustName
```

This formula performs the test and variable assignments as before, but the last line of the formula simply shows the HighestCustName variable, a string variable. So, this formula shows up with small x's in the Design tab (if Show Field Names is turned off in File | Options), and the contents of the HighestCustName variable will be shown whenever the formula executes.

You can go even one step further by testing and assigning variables and then using them later in other calculations or concatenations. Here's another permutation of this formula:

```
CurrencyVar BonusAmount;
StringVar HighestCustName;
DateTimeVar DateBonusReached;

If {Orders.Order Amount} > BonusAmount Then
    (HighestCustName := {Customer.Customer Name};
     DateBonusReached := {Orders.Order Date};
     BonusAmount := {Orders.Order Amount});

"As of this order, the amount to beat is " & BonusAmount &
" set by " & HighestCustName & " on " &
ToText(DateBonusReached,"M/d/yy")
```

This formula not only declares variables, it also conditionally assigns them and then concatenates and displays them, automatically converting them to text with use of the ampersand concatenation operator.

Evaluation Times and Report Passes

As you may have gathered by this time, formulas that contain variables are often affected by where they are placed physically on the report. If you want to check values and assign variables during record-by-record processing, you must put the formula in the details section. If you want to show the accumulated totals for each group, you place a formula in the group footer to show the total variables. To reset the variables for the next group, you need to place the formula that resets them in the group header.

However, just placing the formulas in these sections doesn't necessarily guarantee that they will actually evaluate in that section or during the logical "formatting" process of the report (during which a group header prints, then the detail sections for that group print, then the group footer prints, and so on). Consider the following example. Figure 4-4 contains a report that calculates a "running total" using a variable. The variable accumulates the order amounts in each detail section as the report progresses.

As you can see, the report is a simple detail report—there are no groups. The running total is accumulating the orders as the report progresses. The formula contains the following variable assignment:

```
CurrencyVar MonthlyTotal := MonthlyTotal + {Orders.Order Amount}
```

In Figure 4-5, the report is grouped by Order Date, using "for each month" grouping. In this situation, the desire is to reset the running total for each month, as the viewer evaluates each month on its own. Accordingly, the running total variable "MonthlyTotal" must be reset in each group header with the following formula:

```
CurrencyVar MonthlyTotal := 0
```

Order ID	Customer Name	Order Date	Order Amount	Running Total
1	City Cyclists	12/02/2003	$41.90	$41.90
1002	Deals on Wheels	12/02/2003	$5,060.28	$5,102.18
1003	Warsaw Sports, Inc.	12/02/2003	$186.87	$5,289.05
1004	Bikes and Trikes	12/02/2003	$823.05	$6,112.10
1005	SAB Mountain	12/03/2003	$29.00	$6,141.10
1006	Poser Cycles	12/03/2003	$64.90	$6,206.00
1007	Spokes	12/03/2003	$49.50	$6,255.50
1008	Clean Air Transportation Co.	12/03/2003	$2,214.94	$8,470.44
1009	Extreme Cycling	12/03/2003	$29.00	$8,499.44
1010	Cyclopath	12/03/2003	$14,872.30	$23,371.74
1011	BBS Pty	12/03/2003	$29.00	$23,400.74
1012	Piccolo	12/03/2003	$10,259.10	$33,659.84
1013	Pedals Inc.	12/03/2003	$1,142.13	$34,801.97
1014	Spokes 'N Wheels Ltd.	12/04/2003	$29.00	$34,830.97
1015	Cycle City Rome	12/04/2003	$43.50	$34,874.47
1016	SAB Mountain	12/04/2003	$563.70	$35,438.17
1017	Tyred Out	12/05/2003	$72.00	$35,510.17
1018	Has Been Bikes (consignment)	12/05/2003	$115.50	$35,625.67
1019	Spokes for Folks	12/05/2003	$43.50	$35,669.17
1020	Extreme Cycling	12/05/2003	$67.80	$35,736.97
1021	Canal City Cycle	12/06/2003	$5,237.55	$40,974.52
1022	Belgium Bike Co.	12/07/2003	$2,792.86	$43,767.38
1023	Tienda de Bicicletas El Pardo	12/07/2003	$890.61	$44,657.99
1024	Tandem Cycle	12/07/2003	$33.00	$44,690.99
1025	SAB Mountain	12/07/2003	$8,819.55	$53,510.54
1026	Wheels Inc.	12/07/2003	$33.00	$53,543.54
1027	The Great Bike Shop	12/07/2003	$2,972.85	$56,516.39
1028	Bikes and Trikes	12/08/2003	$296.87	$56,813.26
1029	Poser Cycles	12/08/2003	$49.50	$56,862.76
1030	Bikes, Bikes, and More Bikes	12/08/2003	$890.55	$57,753.31
1031	Spokes for Folks	12/08/2003	$33.00	$57,786.31

FIGURE 4-4 Running total using a variable

However, even when this formula is placed in the group header of the report, the desired result is not achieved.

Notice that not only did the running total not get reset to zero from the group header, but that it's showing a *lower* value than it was in the previous group. Why does adding a group result in the oddities with the running total? This happens because the formula is accumulating the running total at a different time from when it's actually displaying it on the report, and because the formula to reset the running total is evaluating at yet another time during report processing.

The formula to accumulate the running total is calculating while records are being read from the database, not when records have been grouped and are actually being printed or formatted. Also, the formula that resets the running total is actually being processed only once, at the very beginning of report processing, not when each group header prints. These formulas are said to be calculating in different *report passes* than the pass that actually formats the report. So, the running total has already been calculated for every record before Crystal Reports sorts the records to be placed in groups. Besides, the running total is actually being reset to zero only once before anything else happens on the report.

D	3183	New Trails	12/12/2003	$959.70	$4,075,786.74
D	3184	Beach Trails and Wheels	12/12/2003	$33.00	$4,075,819.74
D	3185	Forested Hills	12/12/2003	$659.70	$4,076,479.44
D	3186	Bill's Bikes	12/12/2003	$101.70	$4,076,581.14
D	3187	Lisbon Cyclists	12/12/2003	$14.50	$4,076,595.64
D	3188	Evora Family Sports	12/12/2003	$19.90	$4,076,615.54
D	3189	Souzel Bike Rentals	12/12/2003	$31.00	$4,076,646.54
D	3190	Tom's Place for Bikes	12/12/2003	$53.90	$4,076,700.44
D	3191	Coastal Line Bikes	12/12/2003	$101.70	$4,076,802.14
D	3192	Hikers and Bikers	12/12/2003	$959.70	$4,077,761.84
D	3193	Mountain View Sport	12/12/2003	$23.80	$4,077,785.64
GF1					
GH1	1/2004				$0.00
D	1121	Rough Terrain	01/01/2004	$851.77	$164,388.60
D	1122	Hooked on Helmets	01/01/2004	$1,025.40	$165,414.00
D	1123	Clean Air Transportation Co.	01/02/2004	$5,219.55	$170,633.55
D	1124	Off the Mountain Biking	01/02/2004	$59.70	$170,693.25
D	1125	Road Runners Paradise	01/02/2004	$75.42	$170,768.67
D	1126	Platou Sport	01/02/2004	$3,842.55	$174,611.22
D	1127	BBS Pty	01/02/2004	$520.35	$175,131.57
D	1128	Tandem Cycle	01/02/2004	$65.70	$175,197.27
D	1129	The Bike Cellar	01/02/2004	$2,997.25	$178,194.52
D	1130	Rowdy Rims Company	01/03/2004	$23.50	$178,218.02
D	1131	Magazzini	01/03/2004	$357.41	$178,575.43
D	1132	Fulcrum Cycles	01/04/2004	$38.98	$178,614.41
D	1133	Spokes for Folks	01/04/2004	$43.50	$178,657.91
D	1134	Paris Mountain Sports	01/05/2004	$43.80	$178,701.71
D	1135	Blazing Saddles	01/05/2004	$2,584.85	$181,286.56
D	1136	C-Gate Cycle Shoppe	01/05/2004	$3,209.53	$184,496.09
D	1137	Furia	01/05/2004	$6,040.95	$190,537.04
D	1138	Crazy Wheels	01/05/2004	$79.62	$190,616.66

FIGURE 4-5   Formula in group header to reset running total doesn't work

Crystal Reports generally breaks down its report processing into the following three passes, during which certain types of formulas automatically evaluate.

Before Reading Records	Occurs before any records are read from the database. If formulas don't include any references to database fields or summary functions, they calculate in this pass. These formulas are sometimes referred to as flat or constant formulas.
While Reading Records	Occurs as records are being read from the database, but before any record selection, sorting, or grouping is performed. Formulas that include references to database fields, but don't contain any subtotal or summary functions, are calculated in this pass. These formulas are often called first-pass or recurring formulas.
While Printing Records	Occurs after records have been read and are being formatted for display or printing. Sorting and grouping occurs during this pass. Formulas that include sum, average, or other summary functions are included in this pass. These formulas are often called second-pass or print-time formulas.

In most cases, you can trust Crystal Reports to accurately determine in which pass it needs to evaluate a formula. The glaring exception, however, is when a formula uses variables. If a formula simply declares a variable, or declares the variable and assigns it a literal or constant value, Crystal Reports evaluates that formula in the Before Reading Records pass, because it makes no reference to database fields or summary functions. If you assign a variable a database value, Crystal Reports evaluates that formula in the While Reading Records pass (the formula will become a first-pass formula). If you have some type of summary or subtotal function in the formula, or if you make use of one of the functions from the Print State function category, such as PageNumber, Crystal Reports automatically evaluates the formula in the While Printing Records pass (the formula then becomes a second-pass formula).

This default behavior can cause very strange results, as the previous running total example illustrates. The formula to accumulate the running total makes reference to the Order Amount database field and therefore evaluates in the first pass (WhileReadingRecords). This accumulated the running total just fine before the report was grouped. However, when the report was grouped by the Order Date, records appeared on the report in a different order than they were read from the database, resulting in the running totals no longer appearing in a logical order. And to complicate matters even further, the formula that reset the running total variable made no references to database fields at all, so it became a flat formula (BeforeReadingRecords) and processed only once at the very beginning of report processing, instead of at the beginning of every group.

When you use variables in a formula, you may need to force the formula to evaluate in a different pass than it would by default. You do this by changing the formula's *evaluation time*. To do this, add an evaluation-time statement as the first statement in the formula. Look in the Formula Editor Function Tree box and you'll notice an Evaluation Time section. Open that section to see several evaluation-time statements that should now be mostly self-explanatory.

To force the formula that accumulates the running total to the second pass, where it will calculate the running total correctly after the records have been grouped, add the WhilePrintingRecords evaluation-time statement to the formula, as follows:

```
WhilePrintingRecords;
CurrencyVar MonthlyTotal := MonthlyTotal + {Orders.Order Amount}
```

CAUTION *Don't get confused if you can't insert a subtotal, summary, or grand total on a second-pass formula. When you click this type of formula in the details section, no subtotal, summary, or grand total options will be available on the pull-down or pop-up menus, because subtotals, summaries, and grand totals are calculated in the WhilePrintingRecords pass. If the formula is already evaluating in that pass, you can't create a summary or grand total on it.*

Now, to ensure that the formula that resets the running total actually happens when the groups are being formatted, instead of one time only at the beginning of the report, force it to the WhilePrintingRecords pass as well.

```
WhilePrintingRecords;
CurrencyVar MonthlyTotal := 0
```

The one evaluation-time function that may not be self-explanatory is EvaluateAfter, which takes one argument: the name of another formula. This forces one formula to evaluate after another formula when they evaluate in the same pass and are in the same section of the report. Because Crystal Reports automatically evaluates formulas that contain other formulas in the proper order, you'll use this function very rarely. However, it may be necessary to use it with formulas that contain variables.

When Crystal Reports evaluates two formulas that contain the same variable in the same section of the report, the order in which it will evaluate them is not predictable. One example is if you place two formulas in a group footer. The first formula shows the values of the variables (assuming that those values have been set in other formulas in the details section):

```
WhilePrintingRecords;

CurrencyVar BonusAmount;
StringVar HighestCustName;
DateTimeVar DateBonusReached;
"The highest order of " + ToText(BonusAmount) +
" was placed by " + HighestCustName + " on " +
ToText(DateBonusReached,"M/d/yy")
```

The second resets the variables to zero or an empty string to prepare for the next group:

```
WhilePrintingRecords;

CurrencyVar BonusAmount := 0;
StringVar HighestCustName := "";
DateTimeVar DateBonusReached := DateTime(0,0,0);
```

Because there's a chance that the formula that resets the variables will evaluate before the formula that shows them, you have two choices. The first (and probably most logical) is simply to move the formula that resets the variables to the group header. That way, the variables will be reset when a new group begins, after they have been displayed in the previous group footer. But, if there is some logical reason why both formulas must exist in the group footer, you can use EvaluateAfter in the formula that resets the variables, as follows:

```
EvaluateAfter ({@Bonus Show});

CurrencyVar BonusAmount := 0;
StringVar HighestCustName := "";
DateTimeVar DateBonusReached := DateTime(0,0,0);
```

By placing EvaluateAfter as the first statement in the formula, you force the reset formula to evaluate after the display formula. Because you are forcing this formula to evaluate after a formula that's in the second pass, there's no need to include WhilePrintingRecords in this formula (although the formula will work fine if you do).

TIP *As you begin to add formulas that calculate and reset variables, you may find quite a few instances of things appearing in details and group header sections that show zeros or other unnecessary information. You can't delete the formulas from these sections, because then they won't evaluate properly. To hide them, just suppress their display by using the Suppress button on the Formatting toolbar or the Suppress check box on the Common tab of the Format Editor. You'll then see them on the Design tab, but not on the Preview tab or any other report output.*

When Not to Use Variables

It's fairly common to learn how to use certain "spiffy" features of a tool, and then to use them to excess! Variables have that potential. Although they are fast and, if used judiciously, don't consume significant extra memory or resources, they can sometimes be "overkill." If you find a use for variables, first look closely at your report to see whether an easier, quicker way exists to accomplish the same task.

Figure 4-6 is an example of a report that counts orders that exceed a $1,000 bonus level. The number of orders needs to be shown both at the group level and at the end of the report.

Using variables to accomplish this requires the creation of several formulas. Two variables are also required: one to accumulate the bonus order count for each group, and one to count for the whole report. Following are the formulas.

@Bonus Calc is placed in the details section and suppressed:

```
WhilePrintingRecords;
NumberVar CountCustomer;
NumberVar CountReport;
If {Orders.Order Amount} > 1000 Then
    (CountCustomer := CountCustomer + 1;
     CountReport := CountReport + 1)
```

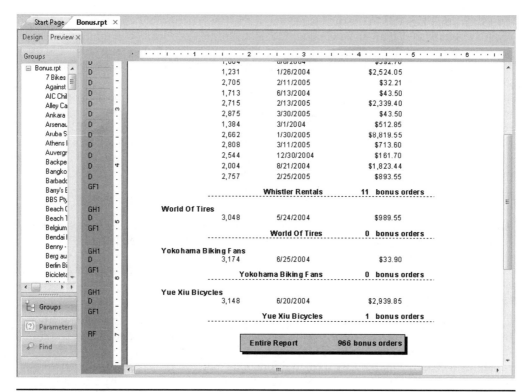

FIGURE 4-6 Over $1,000 Bonus report

@Show Group Bonus is placed in the group footer:

```
WhilePrintingRecords;
NumberVar CountCustomer;
"This customer had " + ToText(CountCustomer,0) + " bonus orders."
```

@Reset Group Bonus is placed in the group header and suppressed:

```
WhilePrintingRecords;
NumberVar CountCustomer := 0;
```

@Show Report Bonus is placed in the report footer:

```
WhilePrintingRecords;
NumberVar CountReport;
"This report had " + ToText(CountReport,0) + " bonus orders."
```

While this will work, there is a much simpler way to accomplish the same task with just one formula using no variables. Create a single formula, place it in the details section, and suppress it. It will simply consist of the following:

```
If {Orders.Order Amount} > 1000 Then 1
```

When you place this in the details section, it will return a number constant of 1 when an order exceeds $1,000. If an order is under $1,000, the number formula will return 0 (because the formula is numeric and there is no Else clause, it will return 0 if the If test fails). You then simply need to insert a group subtotal and a report grand total on the formula to calculate group and report totals.

The result: the same totals with much less effort. This simple technique of assigning a formula a value of 1 if a test is passed can become the cornerstone for a lot of statistics-type reports you may have to write.

You may also be able to save time by using running total fields instead of formulas with variables. The running total report earlier in the chapter that illustrates evaluation times is a perfect example. In this type of report, there's no need to create formulas to calculate the running total. Running total fields are covered later in this chapter.

TIP *Many of the types of formulas illustrated in this chapter are included in samples report on this book's accompanying Web site. Look at CrystalBook.com for FORMULAS.RPT and BONUS. RPT to see how these, and similar formulas, are implemented.*

User Function Libraries

Crystal Reports has been designed as an *extensible* reporting tool. With respect to formulas, that means that you can develop your own functions to add to the Function Tree box if Crystal Reports doesn't provide one that you need. In Crystal Reports 9 and later, this capability has been enhanced with custom functions that you can create directly in your report, or add to the repository to be shared with other Crystal Reports users (custom functions are covered in Chapter 6).

However, versions of Crystal Reports prior to 9 didn't feature custom functions. Also, in some cases, Custom Functions still may not provide sufficient capabilities for your particular business needs. For these situations, you'll still need to create your own functions that appear in the Formula Editor. Look at an example of the built-in functions that appear under the Additional Functions category.

The functions in this category aren't really "built-in." These functions are being supplied to Crystal Reports by *user function libraries (UFLs)*. The UFL is supplied to Crystal Reports by an external dynamic link library developed in another programming language. You can write your own custom functions using a Windows programming language, such as C++, Visual Basic, Delphi, or Java, and have them appear in this section of the Function Tree box. For example, you could write a function that calculates the number of business days between two dates you supply, excluding any weekends and company holidays that are contained in an external database.

Or, you might write a UFL that reads a value from an external piece of proprietary measurement equipment and supplies a value to your report.

The filename that supplies the UFL appears as a category in the Additional Functions list—you may click the plus sign next to the filename to see the available functions supplied by that file. As with other functions, double-click the function name and supply the necessary arguments inside your formula.

The choice of which type of UFLs you wish to appear in your report is made in the Formula Editor tab of File | Options. As Windows-oriented UFLs (Windows-based UFL development typically occurs with Visual Basic, Visual Studio .NET, Delphi, and so forth) can't reside in Crystal Reports at the same time as Java-developed UFLs, you must choose which UFLs you wish to be visible to Crystal Reports. You may choose to include COM/C (Windows-oriented) UFLs, Java UFLs, or no UFLs. Once you make the choice and restart Crystal Reports, only UFLs of the chosen type installed on your computer will appear in the Additional Functions category of the Function Tree box.

TIP *Although the need for external UFLs is probably greatly reduced by Crystal Reports custom function and repository capabilities, you may still need to use them to connect to external databases, external equipment, or any other capability that is not provided by the Crystal Reports formula language (which is what Crystal Reports custom functions use). Information on creating User Functions Libraries with Visual Basic can be found on this book's Web site. Look at CrystalBook.com.*

Running Total Fields

In certain situations, the use of formulas with variables (discussed earlier in the chapter) is inevitable. However, many of the examples shown previously can actually be accomplished without even creating a formula. If you need to accumulate, display, and reset running totals, you will probably prefer the *running total field*. A running total field can be inserted just like a database field. It gives you great flexibility to accumulate or increment values as the report progresses, without the need for formulas or variables.

Figure 4-7 shows a Top *N* report (discussed in Chapter 2) that shows regional subtotals for the top five regions in the U.S. This particular Top *N* report does not include Others. As mentioned in Chapter 2, this causes the report grand totals not to agree with the sum of all the group totals. The grand totals are based on all report records, not just those that fall into the top five groups. Using running total fields is the perfect answer to this problem.

All new running total fields are created from the Field Explorer. First, select the Running Total Fields category in the Field Explorer. Click the New button in the Field Explorer toolbar or right-click the Running Total Fields category and choose New from the pop-up menu. You may also select an existing field in the Details section, right-click, and choose Insert | Running Total from the pop-up menu. The Create Running Total Field dialog box appears, as shown in Figure 4-8.

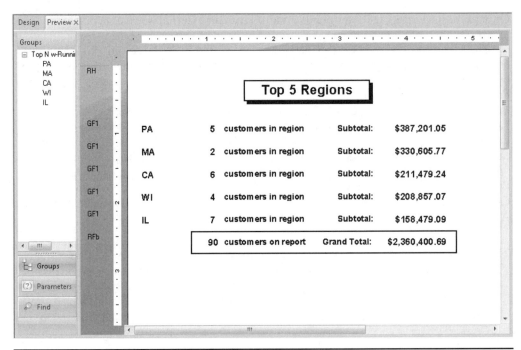

FIGURE 4-7   Grand total problem with Top *N* report and no Others group

Start by giving the running total field a name (if you don't like the default name given by Crystal Reports). It can contain mixed-case characters and spaces and won't conflict with formula or database field names. Crystal Reports will precede the running total field name with a pound sign (#).

If you select a detail field and use the right-click method to insert the running total field, the field you choose will already appear in the Field To Summarize drop-down list, and a default summary function will appear in the Type Of Summary drop-down list. If you're creating a new running total field from the Field Explorer, choose the report, database, or formula field that you want to use to calculate the running total by selecting the field in the Available Tables and Fields list and clicking the right arrow next to the Field To Summarize box. Choose the type of calculation you want to use from the Type Of Summary pull-down list. If you just want to increment the running total by one for certain records, use the Count or DistinctCount summaries, depending on how "unique" the field you are summarizing is, along with any field from the report that won't contain null values (nulls don't increment counts). Other functions available in running totals are the same as those available for summaries. Look back at Chapter 2 for a detailed description of available summaries.

Choose when you want the running total to increment, by making choices in the Evaluate section. Then, choose when you want the running total to reset, by making choices in the Reset section. If you select a field in the Available Tables And Fields list and then click

When the running total will be incremented

Fields available to use
in running total

Field and type of summary used to calculate running total

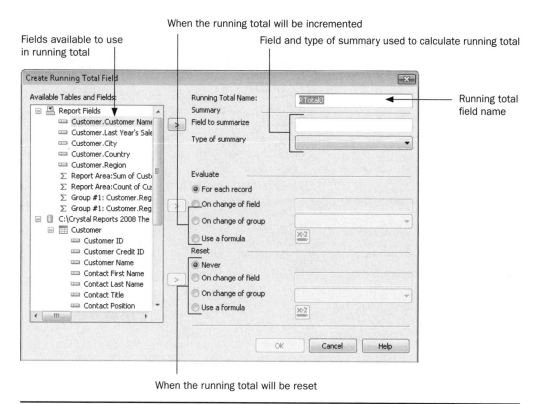

Running total
field name

When the running total will be reset

FIGURE 4-8   Create Running Total Field dialog box

the arrow next to the On Change Of Field radio button, the running total will increment or reset every time a new value appears in that field. If you click the On Change Of Group radio button, you can then choose an existing report group in the pull-down list. The running total will increment or reset every time the chosen group changes. If you click the Use A Formula radio button, you can then click the Formula button next to it. The Formula Editor will appear, in which you can enter a Boolean formula that will trigger when the running total field is incremented or reset.

Click OK when you've completed the Create Running Total Field dialog box. The running total will now appear in the Field Explorer and can be dragged and dropped on the report just like a database field. If you'd like to edit, rename, or delete the running total field, you have these choices in the Field Explorer. You can also right-click a running total field in either the Design or Preview tab and choose Edit Running Total from the pop-up menu.

To solve the problem with the Top *N* report without "Others," simply create two running total fields: one to calculate the number of customers:

and one to calculate the sale grand total:

Place these running totals in the report footer instead of grand totaling the fields from the details section. Because running totals evaluate only during the While Printing Records pass, the extra records in the Others group won't be included in the report footer. Figure 4-9 shows the correct totals now displayed on the Top *N* report.

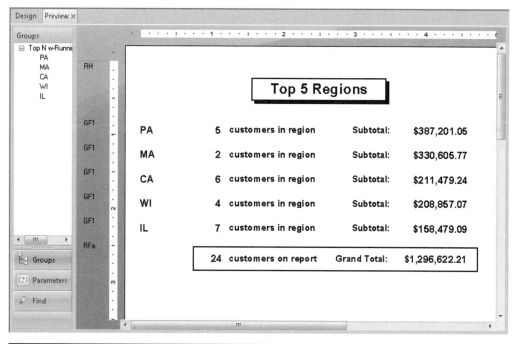

FIGURE 4-9   Correct Top *N* report using running totals

CAUTION   *Because running total fields are calculated in the While Printing Records pass of the report, you cannot create running total fields based on second-pass formulas.*

Creating Custom Functions

One of the most often-heard questions from Crystal Reports users is "How can I share a formula I write with other reports or with other Crystal Reports users?" Often, too, a report designer will find a set of formula logic that is particular to their type of business or type of reports that must be used over and over again in many other formulas. The question then becomes, "Is there any way of reducing the need to type these same parts of the formula over and over again?"

In many cases, the solutions to these requirements typically aren't very elegant. Some users might open two reports side by side, reduce the size of the windows inside the Crystal Report designer, and drag a formula from one report to another. Others might open a report, edit a formula, copy the contents to the clipboard, and paste the contents to a new formula. Or a user might copy the contents of a formula in a report, close the first report, open a second report, create a new formula, and paste the formula text from the first report into the Formula Editor. Still others may keep their own "library" of formulas in a text file or word processing document, cutting and pasting between various formulas in various reports and this document on a regular basis.

However, Crystal Reports makes this much easier by providing the ability to create your own "reusable functions," called *custom functions.* Not only can custom functions be used over and over again in different formulas in the same report, but they can be added to the BusinessObjects Enterprise product family repository for use in other reports and for use by other Crystal Reports users.

Custom Functions Defined

A custom function is very similar to a regular function you will already find in the function tree of the Crystal Reports Formula Editor (learn more about formulas and the function tree in Chapter 4). For example, the built-in ToText function in the Crystal Reports formula language will convert from any non-text data type (such as numbers) to a text data type. The built-in Left function will return a certain number of characters from the left side of a string value. And the built-in Round function will round a numeric value to a specified number of decimal places.

But what if you have a special need in your company to use a function that's not included as part of the built-in Crystal Reports functions? You may, for example, need to calculate the number of business days between two dates, excluding weekends and company holidays. Or you may want to calculate a discount for customers in a large number of formulas. However, you want to base this discount on several factors, including the size of the order amount, the number of orders the customer placed last year, and the length of time they have been a customer. While you can most probably make use of Crystal Reports' extensive formula language to create these special formulas, making use of the logic over and over again in more than one formula, or sharing the logic with other report designers, is where a custom function becomes really useful.

Available custom functions (either that you built after creating the report, or added from the repository) will appear in the Formula Editor just like built-in functions. However, custom functions appear in their own Custom Functions area of the function tree, as shown in Figure 5-1.

A custom function can accept arguments (or parameters), just like a regular function (arguments are discussed in more detail later in the chapter). And as with regular functions, you can use the custom function over and over in as many formulas as you desire. If the core logic of your custom function changes (perhaps business holidays or a discount percentage tier change with the new year), changing the custom function in its one location

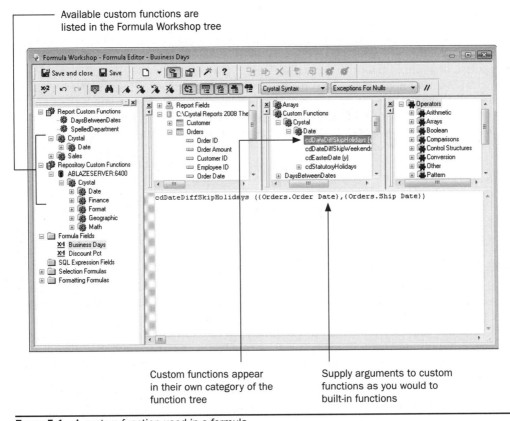

Available custom functions are listed in the Formula Workshop tree

Custom functions appear in their own category of the function tree

Supply arguments to custom functions as you would to built-in functions

FIGURE 5-1 A custom function used in a formula

will be reflected in all formulas that make use of that function—you won't have to edit each and every formula to change the formula logic.

NOTE   *Custom Functions are most helpful when stored in the BusinessObjects Enterprise repository. As of this writing, a matching production version of Enterprise was not yet available for Crystal Reports 2008. As such, descriptions and screens included in this chapter may change when a final version of Enterprise becomes available. Visit the book's companion web site, CrystalBook.com, for significant updates to material based on the shipping version of BusinessObjects Enterprise.*

Creating Your Own Custom Functions

If you install a matching version of the BusinessObjects Enterprise family (Enterprise, Edge, Crystal Reports Server), its repository ships with a "starter set" of custom functions. However, you'll probably soon discover a use for your own. Creating a custom function is very similar to creating a Crystal Reports formula—most of the typical built-in functions and operators otherwise available in regular formulas are available for your use in a custom function (Chapter 4 covers formula creation in more detail).

There are two ways to create a new custom function: base it on an existing formula, or create it from scratch.

Extracting Custom Functions from Existing Formulas

If you have an existing formula in a report that contains the "core" set of logic that you wish to use for your custom function, you may base your custom function on it by *extracting* the custom function from the formula. Do this by performing these steps:

1. Launch the Formula Workshop by clicking the Formula Workshop button in the Expert Tools toolbar, or choosing Report | Formula Workshop from the pull-down menus.

2. In the Formula Workshop tree, right-click the Report Custom Functions category and choose New from the pop-up menu. You may also just click the Report Custom Functions category to select it and click the New button in the Formula Workshop toolbar, or click the down arrow next to the New toolbar button and choose Custom Function from the drop-down list.

3. Type in a name for your custom function. Choose a name within the naming limitations discussed later in this chapter.

4. Click the Use Extractor button to base your custom function on an existing report formula. The Extract Custom Function From Formula dialog box will appear, as shown in Figure 5-2.

5. Make any desired changes to arguments that are substituted for database fields in the original formula. You may also add descriptive text to the function definition that will appear when you use the function in the Formula Expert (discussed in Chapter 4).

6. If you wish to change the original formula to use the function, check the Modify Formula To Use New Custom Function check box.

Choose an existing report formula for your function

Change the previously given function name here

Type in a description of the function (optional)

Give arguments substituted for formula database fields names and descriptions (optional)

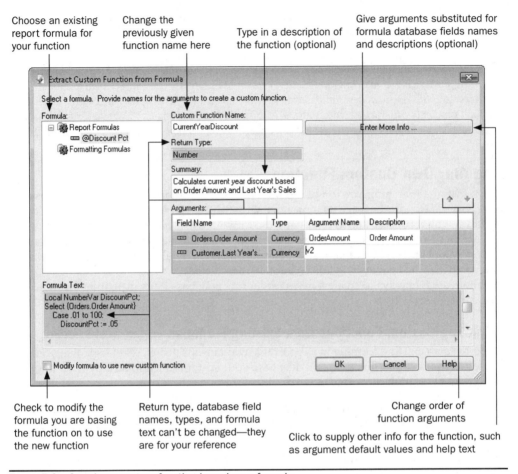

Check to modify the formula you are basing the function on to use the new function

Return type, database field names, types, and formula text can't be changed—they are for your reference

Change order of function arguments

Click to supply other info for the function, such as argument default values and help text

FIGURE 5-2   Creating a custom function based on a formula

7. Click the Enter More Info button to supply optional items, such as default argument values and other descriptive text.

8. Click OK to save the new custom function.

Custom Function Arguments

One of the first adjustments you'll need to make when creating custom functions, as opposed to formulas, is handling function arguments. An *argument* is a parameter that you create within your function to accept a value from the formula that calls it. It then uses this value (possibly along with other arguments that are also supplied) to perform some calculation or logic and return a result to the calling formula.

If you think of Crystal Reports built-in functions, most require that you supply arguments when you use them in formulas. For example, if you use the ToText function to convert a

---

Custom Function Naming Limitations

You are more restricted in choosing names for your custom functions than you are for formulas. Because custom functions appear in the Formula Editor's function tree alongside all the built-in functions, there are several limitations:

- Custom function names must begin with a letter—you can't start a function name with a number. Also, you can include only letters, numbers, and the underscore character in your custom function name—other special characters (such as the % or # signs) cannot be included.

- Custom function names cannot contain spaces—you can use only underscores to separate a multiword custom function name. However, you can use mixed upper- and lowercase letters to help delineate multiword custom function names.

- You cannot use a name that is already used by a Crystal Reports built-in function. For example, you'll receive an error message if you try to create a custom function named ToText or Left.

- Some organizations prefer standardized prefixes for custom-design functions or values. For example, Business Objects–supplied custom function names may include a two-character "cd" prefix (left over from previous Crystal Decisions references). Although adding your own prefix is certainly not required, it may be a handy way of identifying a certain group of custom functions. Prefixing custom function names may also help avoid naming conflicts with other custom functions contained in the repository, as well as conflicts with built-in function names.

---

number, date, or other non-string data type to a string, you must supply at least one argument: the non-string value to be converted. And the Left function, which returns a certain number of characters from the left side of a larger string, requires you to supply two arguments: the string to retrieve a subset of characters from, and the number of characters to retrieve. In cases of built-in functions, arguments you supply must conform to specific data types. The single-argument ToText example requires a string argument to be supplied. The Left function requires a string argument and a number argument.

When you create your own custom functions (by either extracting logic from an existing formula or creating the function from scratch), you must consider if your function will need to accept arguments from the calling formula, how many arguments your function requires, what data types the arguments will be, and if you want to supply one or more default values for each argument.

When extracting a custom function from a formula, such as the function illustrated in Figure 5-2, the number and data types of arguments in your function are automatically determined by the number of unique database fields included in the original formula. In the example shown in the figure, the original formula the custom function is based upon contains two database fields: {Orders.Order Amount} and {Customer.Last Year's Sales}. When the custom function is extracted from this formula, the database fields are removed from the function and replaced with two arguments, both of which require currency data types (the data types of the original database fields) to be supplied.

The arguments that the extract process identifies are listed in the Arguments list of the Extract Custom Function From Formula dialog box. You'll see the original database fields that are being replaced with arguments, the data type of the argument (both of these columns are for your information and can't be changed), the name of the argument in the custom function, and the description of the argument. By default, the extract process will number arguments successively from the number 1, preceding the argument number with the letter *v*.

If you simply wish to allow the default v-numbered arguments to remain, you may ignore this section of the Extract Custom Function From Formula dialog box. However, in that case, the function illustrated in Figure 5-2 would appear like this in the function tree of the Formula Editor:

```
CurrentYearDiscount(v1, v2)
```

It's more likely that you will want arguments in your custom function to have more meaningful names, perhaps replacing v1 with OrderAmount, and v2 with PreviousSaleAmount. To accomplish this, rename the v1 and v2 argument names in the dialog box. You may optionally add descriptions to each argument that will appear in the Formula Expert (described in Chapter 4).

The More Info Button

When you extract a custom function from a formula, you'll notice the Enter More Info button on the Extract Custom Function From Formula dialog box. If you click this button, the Custom Function Properties dialog box appears.

The shaded areas of this dialog box are just for reference—they can't be changed here. The Summary and Argument descriptions are interchangeable with those in the Extract Custom Function From Formula dialog box—changing the descriptions of the function and arguments in either place will change it in the other. However, the Category, Author, Display In Experts check box, argument default values, and help text can be changed only on this dialog box.

Category One of the benefits of the Function Tree in the Formula Editor is the way functions are categorized and subcategorized. Instead of having every function listed together in one category, functions belong to a particular category appropriate for their use (for example, the String category contains functions appropriate only for string fields and values). You may set up categories and hierarchies for your own custom functions. Do this by specifying the category in the Category text box. If you wish to build a hierarchy for the categories, separate the category names with slashes. For example, placing a function in the Sales/ Orders category will show a Sales entry in the Formula Workshop tree with a plus sign. When you click the plus sign, the Orders subcategory will appear with the CurrentYearDiscount custom function in it.

Author This is, in essence, a comment field that you can either leave blank or fill with text of your choice (probably the name of the person who developed the custom function). This value will appear only when you edit the custom function or use it in the Formula Expert. This text won't be available in the Formula Editor.

Display In Experts This check box determines whether or not the custom function will appear in the list of available functions when using the Formula Expert (covered in Chapter 4). If you uncheck this box, then you'll see the custom function in the function tree of the Formula Editor, but not in the list of available custom functions when using the Formula Expert.

Argument Default Values For certain arguments, such as those that may accept department codes, months of the year, or other common values (the order amount/previous period sales examples here probably don't fall into this category), you may wish to supply a list of one or more default values that a user can choose from when they use the custom function in the Formula Expert. To supply these, click the Default Values box for the argument that you want to set the defaults for. This will display the Default Values dialog box.

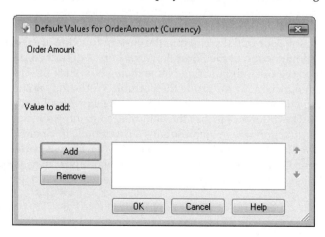

Here, you may type in a default value that you want a user to be able to choose; then click Add. This will add the value to a list in the lower part of the dialog box. If you want to add additional values, type them in and click Add. If you wish to remove a value that's already been added, choose it in the lower list and click Remove. And if you wish to change the order of the default values you've already added, choose the value in the list that you wish to move and click the up or down arrow to the right of the list.

When you click OK, the default value list will be added to the custom function and will appear in the argument list on the original Custom Function Properties dialog box.

Help Text   Clicking the Help Text button will simply display yet another dialog box where you can type in free-form text describing the custom function, providing more detail on its arguments or return value, or other helpful information. This help text will be visible only when editing this function later, or using it in the Formula Expert. This text won't be available in the Formula Editor.

CAUTION   *There are certain requirements an existing report formula must meet to be used as the basis for a custom function. For example (and this list is not all-inclusive), the formula cannot contain any evaluation time functions (such as WhilePrintingRecords), any summary functions used with database fields (such as Sum({Orders.Order Amount})), or any variables scoped other than Local. If you attempt to extract a custom function from such a formula, you'll either receive an error message indicating that the formula can't be used, and explaining why, or have to deal with a function that may not perform the way you expected it to. You may either copy the formula to the clipboard and paste it into the Custom Function Editor when creating the function from scratch (making modifications to the copied formula to allow it to work as a function), or edit the report formula (perhaps explicitly setting variable scope to Local), and then extract the function from the updated formula.*

Creating Custom Functions from Scratch

There may be times when an existing report formula isn't available as the basis for your custom function. Also, you may have a need for a custom function that is more sophisticated than an existing formula, or the existing formula might contain elements that prohibit it from being used as the basis for a custom function (it may use global variables, evaluation time functions, or other limiting features). In these cases, you will want to create a custom function "from scratch" using the Custom Function editor.

In this case, the steps for initially creating the custom function are the same. Create and name the new custom function in the Formula Workshop as described previously in the chapter. However, in the Custom Function Name dialog box, click the Use Editor button to display the Custom Function Editor inside the Formula Workshop, as shown in Figure 5-3.

The Custom Function Editor is almost identical to the Formula Editor discussed in detail in Chapter 4. The difference is that the field tree, containing a list of database fields, is not visible. And the function tree, which contains a list of built-in Crystal Reports functions, contains a slightly reduced set of built-in functions. This variance is because custom functions are designed to be independent of any particular report they are placed in; you can't include database fields in a custom function—there would be no way of ensuring

FIGURE 5-3 The Custom Function Editor

these fields would be available when the function is called from another report. You are also prevented from including the limited set of built-in functions (such as Evaluation Time, Print State, and others) because of the "stateless" nature of a custom function. Even though the function tree contains a reduced set of options, it will still display a Custom Function category where you can choose another existing custom function to use in the current custom function.

TIP *If you find you need to use a function that is missing from the Function Tree, you may create an argument to accept it, and use the argument in the custom function formula where the unavailable function would normally be used. Then, when you call the custom function from a formula, you may pass the function name to the custom function as an argument.*

You may now just create the custom function logic by double-clicking built-in functions in the function tree and operators in the operator tree. You may, of course, type in these items yourself, as well as associated formula code. And as with the Formula Editor, you can check the syntax of your custom function before saving by clicking the Check button in the toolbar or typing ALT-C.

Syntax Choices and Requirements

When you create a custom function, you have the choice of both Crystal Reports formula languages (or syntaxes) just as you do when creating a report formula. Choose the desired syntax from the drop-down list toward the right of the Custom Function Editor toolbar. The function tree and the operator tree will adjust to the chosen syntax. You'll also see a commensurate difference in the formula text that is automatically added by Crystal Reports.

The basic premise of creating a custom function directly in the Custom Function Editor is to design formula logic to accept any necessary values passed into the function arguments from the calling formula; perform evaluations, calculations, If-Then-Else tests, and so forth within the custom function; and return a value back to the calling formula. If you have created functions in a programming language, such as Visual Basic, then this should be a fairly straightforward process. If you haven't programmed in a programming language in the past, then getting the "hang" of custom function creation may take some time. But, if you're familiar with Crystal Reports formulas in general, you should be able to apply your existing knowledge to custom function creation pretty quickly.

Here is an example of a Basic Syntax custom function that returns the spelled-out name of a company department based on an abbreviated name passed in as an argument:

```
Function SpelledDepartment (Abbreviation As String) As String
    Select Case Abbreviation
        Case "HR"
            SpelledDepartment = "Human Resources"
        Case "IT"
            SpelledDepartment = "Information Technology"
        Case "EXEC"
            SpelledDepartment = "Executive"
        Case "ENG"
            SpelledDepartment = "Engineering"
        Case Else
            SpelledDepartment = Abbreviation
    End Select
End Function
```

The basic (no pun intended) layout of a Basic syntax function is formula code within a Function–End Function block. The Function statement declares the name of the function (the same name you used when you created the function), a list of any arguments and data types the function should accept (a string argument named Abbreviation in this case), and the type of data the function will return to the calling formula (the data type "As" portion is optional—if you don't include it, the data type the function returns will be determined by the data type you assign to the function name later inside the function).

The last statement within the Function–End Function block that assigns a value to the function name will determine what the function returns to the calling formula. In this case, the function uses a Select Case construct (from the Control Structures category of the operator tree) to test for various values of the passed Abbreviation argument, setting the function name to a string literal based on the value of the argument.

Here is the same function in Crystal syntax (this is illustrated in Figure 5-3):

```
Function (StringVar Abbreviation)
Select Abbreviation
    Case "HR" :
        "Human Resources"
    Case "IT" :
        "Information Technology"
    Case "EXEC" :
        "Executive"
    Case "ENG" :
        "Engineering"
    Default:
        Abbreviation
```

In this case, there is no Function–End Function block—all the formula text included in the function is implicitly considered to be within this "block." The argument being passed to the function is included in parentheses immediately after the Function keyword, preceded by the data type that the argument is assigned (data type keywords are the same as those for declaring variables—see the Variable Declarations section of the operator tree for proper spelling). Similar to the Basic syntax example, the last statement inside the function to evaluate will determine what the function returns to the calling formula. In this example, the Case statement that matches the passed argument will return a string value to the calling formula.

Complex Data Types and Optional Arguments

In the preceding examples, the custom function accepted a single "simple" string value as an argument and returned a single simple string value as a result. However, you may have more complex custom functions that need to deal with more than one argument, or *complex data types,* such as array and range values. While the Formula Extractor (discussed earlier in the chapter) can create custom functions with multiple arguments, it can't create functions that accept or return complex data types. To accept range values or arrays as arguments, or pass similar data types back to the calling formula, you must use the Custom Function editor.

You also may create a special kind of argument in the Custom Function editor called an *optional argument.* By placing the Optional keyword in front of an argument name, you specify that the formula calling the function does not have to supply this argument. If the formula does supply the argument, it will override the default value for the argument that you must supply if you declare an argument as optional.

For example, if you create the following as the *first* line of a Basic syntax function:

```
Function DaysBetweenDates _
(BDate As Date, Optional EDate As Date = CurrentDate)
```

you will be able to call the function in a formula using one *or two* arguments, as the second argument is optional. If you call the function using two arguments, both will be supplied to the function. If you call the function using only one argument, that argument will be supplied as the BDate argument and the current date from the computer's system clock (CurrentDate is a built-in function) will be supplied as the second argument. Adding optional arguments will create multiple occurrences of the function in the function tree to indicate the ability to call the function with multiple arguments. For example, the single custom function created with the Function statement illustrated previously will appear in the function tree twice.

Optional arguments are declared in Crystal syntax with the Optional keyword as well, but with the standard Crystal syntax data type spellings and colon-equal operator used to assign the default value.

```
Function (DateVar BDate, Optional DateVar EDate := CurrentDate)
```

TIP   Finer points on Crystal and Basic syntax when used in custom functions, such as how to declare complex data types in arguments and syntax differences between custom functions and report formulas, can be found in Crystal Reports online help. Search for Custom Functions | Basic Syntax, or Custom Functions | Crystal Syntax.

Modifying Existing Custom Functions

Once you've created a custom function, you may wish to change it later. One of the benefits of custom functions over copying and pasting the same formula logic over and over again in multiple formulas is that all formulas based on a custom function will automatically reflect the change made in the one custom function. As such, a great deal of effort can be eliminated by sharing custom functions in the repository and making a single change to the repository. The change will automatically be reflected in all formulas in all reports that make use of that function. Storing custom functions in the repository is covered later in this chapter and in Chapter 18.

If you've added the custom function just to one report, you may change a custom function in the same way you would change a formula: select it in the Formula Workshop and make changes directly to the formula text in the Custom Function Editor. When you save changes, any formulas using the function will immediately reflect the change.

NOTE   Even though you were able to initially extract a custom function from a formula using a dialog box, you will need to make changes to the custom function in the Custom Function Editor. Once you've saved any custom function, even by extracting it from a formula, editing must be done in the Custom Function Editor.

If you've added custom functions to your report from the repository, you'll notice that the Custom Function Editor formula text area is disabled for editing when you select the custom function in the Formula Workshop tree. This is because you have not disconnected the custom function from the repository. In order to change the contents of a repository-based function, you must *disconnect* the function—this is similar to "checking out" the function from the repository.

To disconnect a custom function from the repository, right-click the function you wish to edit in the Formula Workshop tree (this must be a function in the Report Custom Functions category—you can't disconnect or edit a custom function that hasn't first been added to the report). Choose Disconnect From Repository from the pop-up menu. You'll notice two changes: first, the custom function can now be edited in the Custom Function Editor, and second, the small icon appearing next to the custom function name in the Formula Workshop tree will no longer display the small "linked" icon.

Repository custom function has been disconnected ———————

Repository custom function is still connected ———————

 You may not only edit the formula text of an existing custom function, but the summary, author, category, and other nonformula items that you specified when first creating the function. With the function you wish to edit displayed in the Custom Function Editor, click the Toggle Properties Display button in the Formula Workshop toolbar, or right-click the function name in the Formula Workshop tree and choose Toggle Property Display from the pop-up menu. The Custom Function Editor will be replaced with a dialog box summarizing all the other properties that can be set for the function. Make any necessary changes on this screen and click the same toolbar button or use the same pop-up menu choice to toggle back to the Custom Function Editor.

Once you've made changes to the custom function and saved the changes, you may wish to add your new custom function to the repository for sharing with other reports or users. If the custom function is a modified version of an existing repository function, you will probably want to "reconnect" the custom function back to the repository with changes. The following section describes how to add a custom function to the repository.

Sharing Custom Functions with Other Users

One of the main benefits of Crystal Reports custom functions is the ability to share them not only among reports you may design, but among reports that other Crystal Reports users design as well. This is accomplished by saving the custom function or functions you wish to share in the repository. And if you've disconnected a custom function from the repository to change it, you'll most probably want to save the updated function back to the repository again. The steps to add a new custom function to the repository for the first time, or to update a custom function that you disconnected, are largely the same. There are actually three different ways to accomplish the same thing:

- Right-click the report custom function you wish to add to the repository in the Formula Workshop tree. Select Add To Repository from the pop-up menu. If you have not already logged on to your BusinessObjects Enterprise system to access the repository, you'll be prompted to do so. If the function already exists (you disconnected it earlier), you'll be prompted to confirm that you want to overwrite the existing repository function.

- Select the custom function you wish to add to the repository in the Formula Workshop tree. Click the Add To Repository button in the Formula Workshop toolbar. If necessary, you'll be prompted to log on to BusinessObjects Enterprise. If the function already exists (you disconnected it earlier), you'll be prompted to confirm that you want to overwrite the existing repository function.

- Simply drag the custom function you wish to add to the repository from the Report Custom Functions category of the Formula Workshop tree to the Repository Custom Functions category. This will automatically add the function to the selected repository. You'll be prompted to log on to BusinessObjects Enterprise, if necessary. If the function already exists (you disconnected it earlier), you'll be prompted to confirm that you want to overwrite the existing repository function.

CAUTION *You may not be able to add a custom function to the repository—either a new custom function you created yourself, or a custom function you disconnected from the repository to edit. Depending on the BusinessObjects Enterprise system you are connected to, and the rights you have been granted, you may not be able to add or update custom functions. If you get an error message when attempting to add a custom function to the repository, contact your system administrator to verify that you have the right to modify the repository.*

Using Custom Functions in Your Formulas

Once you've created a custom function, either for use in just the current report, or to be shared from the repository, using the function in a formula is easy. You may create a formula that makes use of the function with the Formula Expert (covered in detail in Chapter 4). Or if you create a formula with the Formula Editor, custom functions you've created in the current report will appear in the Custom Functions category of the function tree.

Custom functions in the repository, however, won't automatically appear in the function
tree unless you add them to the report first. To add a repository custom function to the
report, expand the Repository Custom Functions category of the Formula Workshop until
you find the custom function that you wish to use (you may be prompted to log on to
BusinessObjects Enterprise first). Select the function you wish to add and click the Add To
Report toolbar button in the Formula Workshop toolbar. You can also right-click the function
name in the Formula Workshop tree and choose Add To Report from the pop-up menu. And
finally, you may simply drag the custom function you wish to add to the report from the
Repository Custom Functions category to the Report Custom Functions category of the
Formula Workshop tree.

Making Your Reports Visually Appealing

Crystal Reports, as a Windows-based report writer, has many features that can help you create eye-catching, visually effective reports. You can often use Crystal Reports to create reports right from the database, whereas you formerly had to use a word processor or page publishing program to create such reports. The next time you're tempted to export database records to a text file and merge them in a word processing or page publishing document, use some of the techniques covered in this chapter and save yourself the extra work.

You may consider using charts and graphs (discussed in Chapter 9), geographic maps (discussed in Chapter 10), or integrated Flash or Crystal Xcelsius files (discussed in Chapter 11) as visual elements to make your reports more appealing and interactive. But even using just the textual elements of Crystal Reports can be very creative. Not only can you use a variety of fonts and typefaces in your reports, you also can set object foreground and background colors, choose unique borders on all four sides of objects, add drop shadows, and use other graphical features. You can then copy that formatting en masse from one object to others. You can include bitmap pictures on your report, either reading them directly from the database (if the database you're using supports and includes them) or adding graphics files right into a report section. You can draw lines and boxes around the report to highlight important portions. You can use Report Alerts to trigger a message when a certain condition is met, as well as highlight portions of the report that met that condition. You can choose a predefined set of object and report formatting and apply it to other reports in one step by use of templates.

Setting Page Size, Orientation, and Margins

Many aspects of your report appearance are dependent upon the page size and layout defined for your report. The default page size, page orientation, and margins that a report takes on when first created are determined by your Windows default printer (or are 8 ½ by 11 inches in portrait orientation if no default printer is chosen). However, you may want to change this default behavior, especially if you won't necessarily be printing reports on your default printer. Reports exported to another file format, such as PDF or Excel, or reports posted to the Web with a custom web application or the BusinessObjects Enterprise family, may benefit from a different set of page size, orientation, and margin settings.

Make these settings by choosing File | Page Setup from the drop-down menus. The Page Setup dialog box will appear, as illustrated in Figure 6-1. If you wish to choose a different printer than the Windows default, choose it from the Printer drop-down list. You may also check the No Printer check box if you wish the report to not make use of built-in printer characteristics, such as paper or form sizes or types. You may then choose the paper or form size you wish the report to use from the drop-down list in the Page Options section of the

FIGURE 6-1 Page Setup dialog box

dialog box. Paper/form sizes defined on the selected printer will appear in this list, unless you choose the No Printer option, in which case a standard set of generic paper sizes will appear.

Crystal Reports 2008 adds several new features to this dialog box to provide more flexibility to accommodate non-standard paper or form sizes, or to more easily design a report for the Web that doesn't necessarily need to conform to a printed paper size. You may choose to display and set width, height, and margin values in inches, pixels, or centimeters, dependent upon the type of report you are designing, the type of printer you are using, and so forth. All existing measurements on this dialog box will immediately change to reflect the radio button you choose. And, while the default orientation of all report pages may be chosen with the Portrait or Landscape radio button, Crystal Reports 2008 allows page orientation to be changed within the report, allowing some pages to appear in Portrait mode, while others appear in Landscape mode. This in-report selection is made with the Section Expert (covered in Chapter 7).

Another new Crystal Reports 2008 option is *Dissociate Formatting Page Size and Printer Paper Size.* This allows you to still maintain the report's connection to a Windows printer, but manually specify the actual horizontal and vertical sizes of the report design and preview area as values different than those of a defined printer form. For example, this is immediately helpful for web reports that may provide better visibility if not tied to a standard 8 ½- by 11-inch page layout. If you have large amounts of detail data that you wish a web viewer to merely scroll down through, rather than having to click page navigation buttons, you may check the Dissociate check box and manually type in a very large vertical page size (in inches, pixels, or centimeters, depending upon the selected Unit radio buttons). The report will then only insert an automatic page break when this physical size has been exceeded.

The initial page margins that appear in the bottom portion of this dialog box are dependent upon the printer choice. You may leave these values as-is for the maximum amount of available design area on your report, or type in a new value for any of the four margins if you wish to increase the amount of white space on any side. A new Crystal Reports 2008 option is the *Adjust Automatically* check box. Checking this will allow Crystal Reports to change your specified page margins when you change page size or orientation. In this case, Crystal Reports will attempt to maintain the same general look and spacing of your report by increasing or reducing margin sizes as it sees fit. You are best advised to look carefully at your report if you select this option and change page sizes. You may find that the look of your report changes dramatically and that you need to manually adjust margin sizes.

Crystal Reports 2008 also allows you to set margin values with a conditional formula (conditional formatting formulas are discussed later in this chapter), changing page margins on the fly as the report progresses. New formula language functions, such as CurrentPageOrientation (detailed in Online Help and the Appendix), can be used with other functions from the Formula Editor's PrintState category (such as PageNumber), database field or group values, and other formula functions, to determine more precise margin changes you wish to make as the report formats. By setting a conditional formula numeric value (in "twips," which are 1,440[th] of an inch), you may customize margin sizes as the report prints. For example, the following Crystal Syntax conditional formula will change the left margin to one-half inch for Robert King's group, but only if the page is appearing in Portrait orientation. For all other conditions, the left margin will be one inch.

```
If GroupName ({@Sales Rep}) = "King, Robert" And
CurrentPageOrientation = crPortrait Then
    720
Else
    1440
```

NOTE *Contrary to behavior of some other standard Windows application, Crystal Reports margin settings do not include your printer's "unprintable area." If, for example, you specify a margin value of 0 for all four margins, no text will be truncated when you actually print the report to your printer, as the actual print margins will still take the printer characteristics into account. However, when you preview the report, the Preview tab will show no white space at all on any side.*

General Formatting

Crystal Reports gives you considerable flexibility in customizing the appearance of objects that you place on your report, such as database fields, text objects (discussed at length later in this chapter), and formulas (covered in Chapter 4). By using various formatting options for these objects, you can change many aspects of their appearance, such as font face, size, color, alignment, and more. The most basic type of formatting is known as *absolute formatting,* in which you simply select the object and make formatting changes with the Formatting toolbar or the Format Editor. In either case, the change applies to all occurrences of the object on the report—if you format a field in the details section absolutely, that field will appear the same every time it prints.

The Formatting Toolbar

The quickest way to format one or more objects on the report is to select the object or objects you want to format and then choose options from the Formatting toolbar. To select a single object, just click it with the mouse. You may select multiple objects to format at once using several methods. By CTRL-clicking or SHIFT-clicking on more than one object, you may select a specific set of objects (you'll notice that all objects you've selected will have a shaded outline around them). You may also select multiple objects with an "elastic box" by first deselecting any already-selected objects (click on a blank area of the report canvas) and then holding down the left mouse button while dragging the box around desired objects. You may also right-click on a shaded section area at the left of the report design canvas (for example the Details shaded area in the Design tab or the D shaded area in the Preview tab) and choose Select All Section Objects from the pop-up menu.

Once you have selected objects that you wish to format, click buttons in the Formatting toolbar to format the selected objects. Table 6-1 outlines each Formatting toolbar button.

The Format Editor

Although Crystal Reports offers a large number of formatting choices on the Formatting toolbar, there are still quite a few formatting options that you can't perform with toolbar buttons. For these formatting requirements, you must use the Format Editor. The *Format*

Editor is not an "editor" per se, but a tabbed dialog box that displays a varying set of tabs, depending upon the data type of the object you're formatting.

Button	Function
Arial ▾ Font Face	Choose a different font face (such as Arial, Times Roman, etc.) from the drop-down list.
10 ▾ Font Size	Choose the font size, in points, from the drop-down list, or enter a value directly in the box.
A⁺ Increase Font Size	Increase the font size (each click of this button increases the font size by one point).
A⁺ Decrease Font Size	Decrease the font size (each click of this button decreases the font size by one point).
B Bold (or CTRL-B)	Format object using bold emphasis.
I Italic (or CTRL-I)	Format the object using italic letters.
U Underline (or CTRL-U)	Add an underline to the object.
≡ Align Left	Align text to the left of the object's defined width.
≡ Align Center	Align text to the center of the object's defined width.
≡ Align Right	Align text to the right of the object's defined width.
≡ Justify	Align on both the left and right sides of the object's defined width. This provides "fully justified" text, similar to that often found in newspaper columns.
A Font Color	Change font color. If you click the button itself, it will set the font color to that displayed on the small line in the button. If you click the down arrow, a dialog box will appear giving you a choice of colors. Once you choose a color, that becomes the default color for the button—you will see the small line in the button change to that color.

TABLE 6-1 Formatting Toolbar Options

Button	Function
Outside Borders	Add border lines on sides of object. If you click the face of the button, all four sides of the object will initially be given a border. If you click the face of the button again, the borders will be turned off. If you click the down arrow, a subset of buttons will appear, which allow you to choose combinations of left, right, top, or bottom borders, all, or none.
Suppress	Toggle display of the object on and off. This is equivalent to clicking the Suppress check box on the Common tab of the Format Editor.
Lock Format	Toggle ability to change other formatting properties on the object. If formatting is locked, all other formatting options, including width and height, will be disabled. This is equivalent to clicking the Read Only check box on the Common tab of the Format Editor.
Lock Size/Position	Toggle ability to change the width or height, or to move the object. This is equivalent to clicking the Lock Position and Size check box on the Common tab of the Format Editor.
Currency	Toggle display of a currency symbol (the symbol chosen as the default currency symbols in the Windows Control Panel) with the object. This button will be enabled only if all objects you've selected are currency or numeric fields.
Thousands Separator	Toggle display of a thousands separator (the symbol chosen as the default thousands separator in Windows Control Panel) within the object. This button will be enabled only if all objects you've selected are currency or numeric fields.
Percent Sign	Toggle display of a percent sign on the right side of the object. This option actually adds a currency symbol, but it changes the symbol to the percent sign and the position to the right side of the object. This button will be enabled only if all objects you've selected are currency or numeric fields.
Increase Decimals	Increase the number of decimal places displayed. For example, if the object is displayed as $121.22 and this button is clicked, the number might display as $121.223. This button will be enabled only if all objects you've selected are currency or numeric fields.
Decrease Decimals	Decrease the number of decimal places displayed. For example, if the object is displayed as $121.22 and this button is clicked, the number will display as $121.2. This button will be enabled only if all objects you've selected are currency or numeric fields, and if at least one decimal place is already showing.

TABLE 6-1   Formatting Toolbar Options *(continued)*

To display the Format Editor, select objects as described earlier in this chapter and then choose one of the following options:

- Choose Format | Format Text, Format | Format Field, or Format | Format Objects from the pull-down menus (the choice of Text, Field, or Objects is determined by the number and data type of objects selected before you choose the option).

- Right-click the selected object and choose Format Text, Format Field, or Format Objects from the pop-up menu.

- Click the Format toolbar button in the Expert Tools toolbar.

The tab that displays in the Format Editor will vary, depending on the data type of the object you're formatting. For example, if you selected one or more date/time fields before displaying the Format Editor, the Date/Time tab will initially display. Number fields will result in the Number tab displaying, and string fields or text objects will cause the Paragraph Formatting tab to initially display. If you select multiple objects of varying data types, the Common tab will display by default, and you'll be able to change only formatting options that apply to all objects you've selected: data type–specific options will be unavailable until you cancel the Format Editor, select one or more objects with the same data type, and reformat them.

In some of the Format Editor tabs (such as the Number tab or Date/Time tab), you'll be able to choose from predefined formatting "styles" that appear in a list. These styles provide more commonly used formatting styles that you may select with one mouse click. If, however, you'd like to use some combination of formatting that these styles don't provide, a Custom Style button at the bottom of the Format Editor will display additional dialog boxes where you can format individual pieces of the field, such as the leading day-of-week for a date field, or the currency symbol for a number or currency field.

Most Format Editor options are fairly self-explanatory in terms of the data type being formatted. For those options that aren't self-explanatory, Crystal Reports online help will provide additional information. Also, additional discussion of various Format Editor options can be found throughout this book in sections and chapters relating to the different types of fields being formatted.

The Highlighting Expert

While the absolute formatting options on the Format Editor will solve many reporting needs, you'll soon find that you may wish object formatting to change according to the data being displayed. This is called *conditional formatting,* which lets you change the appearance of objects depending on their contents or the contents of other fields, objects, or formulas. Although the possibilities of conditional formatting are limited only by your imagination and creativity, some immediate uses of conditional formatting that may come to mind are

- Showing sales figures in red if they fall below a predefined level
- Using a different font to highlight long-time customers
- Adding a border around an invoice number if it's past due
- Showing a report title that's different on the first page than on the rest of the pages
- Graphically indicating with file-folder icons whether a case file has been opened or closed

Probably the simplest conditional formatting tool with Crystal Reports is the *Highlighting Expert,* which lets you vary the appearance of a field when a certain condition is met. If a sales figure falls below a preset goal for the department, you can have it stand out with a white font color on a red background. Or, you can change the border on a Days Overdue formula that exceeds, say, 60 days.

To use the Highlighting Expert with a field, select the field you want to change. Start the Highlighting Expert by clicking the Highlighting button on the Expert Tools toolbar, choosing Format | Highlighting Expert from the pull-down menus, or right-clicking the object and choosing Highlighting Expert from the pop-up menu. Figure 6-2 shows the Highlighting Expert.

The idea of the Highlighting Expert is to allow conditional formatting of a field without intricate knowledge of the Crystal Reports formula language. By using the drop-down lists in the dialog box, you choose a series of conditions (by clicking the New button multiple times), and choose specific formatting for each condition. Begin by clicking New to add a new condition. Then, choose the field you want to use in a comparison test from the first drop-down list in the Value Of section of the dialog box (you may choose any field on the report for this test, not just the field you are highlighting). Then, choose a comparison operator in the second drop-down list. You'll find most of the standard comparison operators you've used in formulas or in the Select Expert, such as Less Than, Greater Than, Equal To,

FIGURE 6-2 The Highlighting Expert

Not Equal To, and so forth. After making this choice, enter a constant value to compare to in the third drop-down list (you can also click the drop-down arrow and choose a value from the sample data in the list). Finally, choose any combination of font and background styles, colors, and border styles you want the field to display if the comparison is true.

For example, to format the sales figure to show up as white text on a red background if it falls below the preset sales figure of $1,000, choose "this field" in the first drop-down list, choose a comparison of Less Than, type **1000**, and then choose a Font Color of White and a Background of Red. You will see a sample in the Sample box in the lower right of the Highlighting Expert, as well as to the left of the now-created condition in the Item List box on the left. When you click OK, the field will show white text on a red background for any sales figures less than $1,000.

You may want to set up multiple conditions if you want more than one formatting option displayed. To expand on the previous example, suppose you want to show bonus sales (over $5,000) in blue, in addition to the existing red background for those that fall below $1,000. Just click the New button below the Item List box. You can enter a new condition and another set of formatting options. Both will apply to the field.

You may have two conditions that conflict with each other. For example, you could have a condition that formats field contents over $1,000 in red, and another that applies blue formatting for contents over $5,000. Since both conditions would satisfy the over-1000 condition, will everything over $1,000 (including anything over $5,000) be in red? It depends on the *priority* you assign the conditions. If the over-1000 condition is higher in the Item List box, everything over $1,000 will be in red. However, if the over-5000 condition is set higher, then it has priority—everything over $5,000 will be in blue. Then, the second item in the list (the over-1000 item) will be tested, placing anything over $1,000 in red. To change priority, click the condition you want to move and then click the up or down Priority arrow.

Conditional Formatting Formulas

The Highlighting Expert is a simple and quick way to format fields, because you don't have to know the formula language to use it. However, the trade-off is in flexibility. As your reports become more sophisticated, sometimes the Highlighting Expert won't provide all the flexibility you need. For example, you may need to apply formatting other than just color and borders. Or, you may need to perform a more complex test than can be done with the comparisons that are in the expert. For these situations, you need to use *conditional formatting formulas*. Conditional formatting formulas use the Formula Editor to create one or more conditions to determine how the object appears.

Absolute Versus Conditional Formatting

Before you learn how to set formatting conditionally, it's important to have a fundamental grasp of absolute formatting, which simply refers to applying normal formatting to objects with the Format Editor. This type of formatting, described earlier in the chapter, makes use of the Formatting toolbar or the Format Editor to apply the same formatting to all occurrences of the field. If you right-click an object and choose Format Field from the pop-up menu, the Format Editor will appear. You can then click the Font tab to change the font face, style, size, or color. If you change the color of the font to Red, *all* occurrences of the object on the report will be red. If you click the Border tab and select the Drop Shadow check box, *all* occurrences of the object will have a drop shadow. This is the process of absolute formatting.

The first rule to follow when it comes to conditional formatting is remembering that you must use the Format Editor. While you can perform absolute formatting with either the Formatting toolbar or the Format Editor, you can set up conditional formatting only with the Format Editor—the Formatting toolbar won't work.

As you approach conditional formatting, it's important to distinguish between two types of Format Editor formatting properties: *multiple-choice* properties and *on-off* properties. On the Font tab, Font and Color are good examples of multiple-choice properties. You can click a drop-down list and choose from any one of several fonts or colors. An example of an on-off property is Drop Shadow on the Border tab, which just has a check box: it can only be turned on or off. Whether a formatting property is multiple choice or on-off determines the type of formula you'll use to set it conditionally. Multiple-choice properties are conditionally formatted with If-Then-Else or Select Case formulas, while on-off properties are conditionally formatted with Boolean formulas.

TIP   *You need to be familiar with the Crystal Reports formula language to use conditional formatting effectively. To refresh your memory, look for information on If-Then-Else and Boolean formulas, as well as Select Case in Chapter 4.*

To set formatting conditionally, click the Conditional Formula button that appears on the Format Editor next to the property that you want to format.

This will display the *Format Formula Editor* inside the Formula Workshop (essentially the same Formula Editor discussed in Chapter 4, but with a new title), shown in Figure 6-3. Notice that you can set conditional formatting with either Crystal or Basic syntax by making your choice from the Syntax drop-down list. If you are formatting a multiple-choice property, all the available options for the property appear at the top of the Function Tree box. If, for example, you are conditionally formatting the Color property, you'll see all the available colors listed. If you're formatting a border, you'll see the different available line styles. And, available options also appear as comments (lines preceded by two slashes in Crystal syntax or an apostrophe in Basic syntax) in many formatting formulas to help you choose proper values.

Use an If-Then-Else or Select Case formula to determine the formatting of the object. Your formula can be as simple or as complex as you need. For example, you may have a formula to set font color that is as simple as the following:

```
If {Customer.Last Year's Sales} > 5000 Then crBlue Else crBlack
```

or a formula to set a bottom border as complex as this:

```
If {Orders.Order Amount} > 5000 And {Orders.Ship Via} = "Fedex" Then
    crDoubleLine
Else
    If {Orders.Order Amount} > 1000 And {@Ship Days} < 3 Then
        crSingleLine
    Else
        crNoLine
```

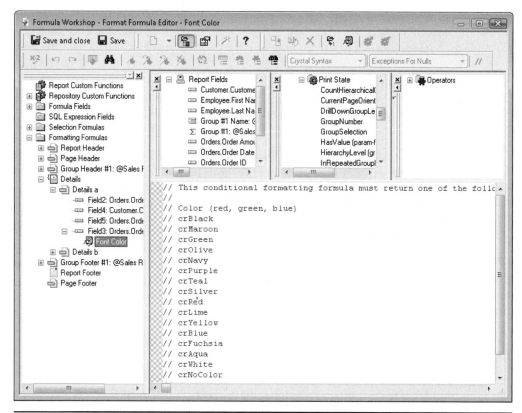

FIGURE 6-3   The Format Formula Editor

TIP   *In most cases, you may type formatting values, such as color or line type, into the formula directly. You may also double-click values shown in the Function Tree box of the Formula Editor. If you double-click, the prefix "cr" will appear in front of the formatting value in the formula. With few exceptions, either the value name by itself or the value name preceded by "cr" is acceptable.*

You can use any type of simple or compound If-Then-Else formula, or a Select Case formula, as long as the results of every Then, Else, or Case are one of the available formatting properties in the Function Tree box.

When you have finished with the formula, you can use the Check button to check for correct syntax of the formula, or save the formula and close the Format Formula Editor with the Save And Close button. The Format Editor will remain on the screen. Notice that the Conditional Formula button changes from blue to red, and the pencil character inside the button points at an angle. This indicates that a conditional formula is set for this property.

To change the existing formula, click the Conditional Formula button again and change the formula that appears in the Format Formula Editor. To delete conditional formatting and return to absolute formatting (or no formatting at all), just highlight and delete the whole conditional formula. Then, click Save And Close. You'll notice that the Conditional Formula button has returned to a blue color with the pencil pointed in its original direction.

NOTE *While most conditional formulas must use a built-in formatting function for the Then, Else, or Case clauses of your formula, the Size property is a little different from other properties. In this case, the result of your conditional formula must be a number, which will indicate the font size to be used.*

If you're formatting an on-off property, the general procedure for conditional formatting is the same. But when you click the Conditional Formula button next to the property, you won't see any additional functions in the Function Tree box of the Format Formula Editor, because you generally won't use an If-Then-Else or Select Case formula to format this property. Because the property can have only one of two states, on or off, you must format it with a Boolean formula that can return only one of two results: true or false.

To add a drop shadow to Customer Name fields of customers who have last year's sales greater than $100,000, start by right-clicking the Customer Name field. Choose Format Field from the pop-up menu, choose the Border tab, and click the Conditional Formula button next to the Drop Shadow property. When the Format Formula Editor appears, type in the following Boolean formula:

```
{Customer.Last Year's Sales} > 100000
```

The Boolean formula will evaluate to only one of two states: true or false. If the formula returns true, the formatting property will be turned on and the field will have a drop shadow around it. If the formula returns false, the property will be turned off and the field won't have a drop shadow.

TIP *If you find If-Then-Else or Select-Case logic simpler to remember, you can use it with a Boolean conditional formula. Just make sure the result of every Then or Else, or every Case clause, is the word True or False. Conditions that return True will turn on the formatting property, while False conditions won't.*

You may be curious about how conditional formatting and absolute formatting interrelate. Consider the following scenario. You choose an absolute color of Red on the Font tab of the Format Editor and click OK. Of course, every occurrence of the field will be red. You then return to the Format Editor and, without changing the absolute formatting, click the Conditional Formula button next to the Color property and add the following formula:

```
If {Customer.Last Year's Sales} > 50000 Then Blue
```

Note the missing Else clause. Remember that Crystal Reports does *not* require an Else clause in an If-Then-Else formula. In a regular formula, if the If test fails and there's no Else clause, the formula returns an empty string, zero, or other default value based on the data type of the formula. But what color will the font take on here if there's no Else clause and absolute formatting is set to red?

Contrary to what might seem logical, when the If test fails in this case, the font will show up in black type, despite the absolute formatting of red. This is by design—if conditional formatting is applied, absolute formatting is ignored. If the conditional formula fails (and there's no condition to "catch" the failure, like an Else clause), the Windows Control Panel default color or format for that type of object will be used. Be careful with this if you don't use Else clauses, especially if you're formatting background colors. A font color of black isn't necessarily problematic, but a background color of black will often cause your report to look like someone plastered electrical tape all over it!

The exception to this rule, and a way to combine absolute and conditional formatting, is to use the DefaultAttribute function, located in the Formatting Functions category of the Function Tree box in the Format Formula Editor. If you use this function with the Then, Else, or Case clause, the formula will use the setting from the absolute formatting property. Hence,

```
If {Customer.Last Year's Sales} > 50000 Then
    Blue
Else
    DefaultAttribute
```

will show sales figures over $50,000 in blue and others in red (provided that the absolute color chosen in the Format Editor is red). If you change the absolute color, then figures over $50,000 will still show up in blue, but the rest will take on whatever color you specified as absolute.

TIP   *If you apply conditional formatting to a field that's also being formatted with the Highlighting Expert, the Highlighting Expert formatting options will take precedence.*

Creative Use of the Suppress Property

If you search through the Format Editor, you'll notice that virtually all formatting properties can be set conditionally. One of the most flexible is the Suppress property on the Common tab. You may consider that absolutely setting the Suppress property is of limited usefulness. (Why even bother putting the object on the report if you're just going to suppress it?) There are some good reasons for suppressing the object; for example, a formula that sets a variable to zero in a group header has to be physically placed in the header to work properly, but you don't want zeros showing up at the top of every group.

There are many more situations in which *conditionally suppressing* an object can be useful. Here are some examples, and the corresponding Boolean formulas you will apply to the Suppress property:

- **Placing the word "continued" in a repeated group header**   In Chapter 2, the repeated group header was introduced. If you select this option in the Group Options dialog box, a group header section will repeat at the top of a page if a group continues from the previous page. Indicating that this group continues from the previous page adds readability to your report. Place a text object that contains the word "continued," or something similar, in the group header close to the Group Name field. You must now suppress it if it is *not* in a repeated group header. Conditionally suppress the text object with the following Boolean formula:

  ```
  Not InRepeatedGroupHeader
  ```

TIP *When you conditionally suppress an object, you use a Boolean formula; when your formula returns true, the object will be suppressed. So, you may have to think "backward" when conditionally suppressing.*

- **Showing a bonus message only for certain records** You may want a report to indicate that a certain record (for example, a certain order or a certain salesperson) has exceeded a predefined goal amount. Simply create a text object that displays something like "Congratulations! You've exceeded the sales goal." Again, you have to think about when you *don't* want the text object to appear, not when you do. Assuming a $10,000 sales goal, conditionally suppress the text object with the following Boolean formula:

```
{AccountRep.Sales} <= 10000
```

- **Showing a different heading on page 2 and later** You may want to have a larger report title, perhaps including the company logo and a large font, on page 1 of the report. However, every other page needs to contain a smaller title without the logo, and perhaps include the word "continued." If you put the large title in the report header, you'll only see it at the beginning of the report. Putting the smaller title in the page header, on the other hand, will result in it showing up on every page, including page 1. Create the text object that contains the smaller title and place it in the page header along with any column headings or other objects you want to appear on every page, but conditionally suppress the text object containing the title with the following Boolean formula (PageNumber is a built-in function from the Print State category of the Formula Editor Function Tree box that returns the current page number):

```
PageNumber = 1
```

TIP *You can also create string formulas that provide roughly the same functionality as these examples and place them in appropriate report sections. However, to minimize potential "formula clutter," it sometimes may be preferable to just create text objects and conditionally suppress them.*

Special Fonts, Graphics, Line Drawing, and Barcodes

As mentioned at the beginning of the chapter, Crystal Reports is a true Windows report writer. This means that it can use most of the fonts and graphical capabilities of Windows.

Using Special Fonts

Don't hesitate to use symbol fonts that are installed on your computer. In particular, the Symbol and Wingdings symbol fonts are included as part of Windows and should be available to most "target" systems that will be running your report.

CAUTION *Don't forget that any fonts you use when designing your reports must also be present on the machine that runs your reports if you expect the report to look identical on both machines. Using Times Roman, Arial, Symbol, and Wingdings fonts, at a minimum, is pretty safe, because they are installed by default on all Windows systems.*

Both Symbol and Wingdings fonts contain typographical symbols instead of letters and numbers. Although you type letters and numbers into a text object or formula formatted with a text font initially, you'll see them replaced with the symbol characters once you change the font from a text font to one of the symbol fonts. You'll need either a font table (typically available from Windows Control Panel) or a little extra time to experiment and figure out what symbols display when you type certain letters, numbers, or special characters.

Figure 6-4 shows a report using the Wingdings font. In this example, the following formula is being displayed on the report next to the order amount, formatted using the Wingdings font:

```
If {Orders.Order Amount} < 1000 Then
    "L"
Else
    If {Orders.Order Amount} In 1000 To 2500 Then
        "K"
    Else
        "J"
```

FIGURE 6-4   Report using symbols as well as text

Using Bitmap Graphics

If you are planning to create reports that approach the quality of output from page publishing programs, you'll soon have a need to use *bitmap graphics* in your reports. Bitmap graphics are common graphics files most often associated with the Web (such as .JPG files) or Windows paint program files (such as .BMP and .PCX, and .WMF files). You may have a company logo that you want included on the title page of the report. Or, you may want to add a smaller graphical element, such as an icon, to another section of the report.

To insert a bitmap graphic, first make sure you are displaying the Design tab. Although it's possible to add a graphic while viewing the Preview tab, this is risky, because you won't always be sure which report section the graphic will end up in. Click the Insert Picture button on the Insert Tools toolbar, or choose Insert | Picture from the pull-down menus. A familiar File Open dialog box will appear, asking you to choose a bitmap format file. Navigate to the necessary drive and folder, and the dialog box will show any files at that location that can be added to the report. Choose the correct file and click OK.

An outline will appear alongside your mouse cursor. Drag the outline to the section of the report where you want the graphic to be placed, and click the left mouse button to drop it there. If the graphic happens to cover more than one report section, it will be dropped in the section where the upper-left corner of the outline is when the mouse is clicked. Once you drop the graphic, you'll see it appear in the Design tab.

You have complete control over how the graphic is sized and cropped. You can simply drag the graphic to a new location on the report, or resize it using the sizing handles on the sides and corners. You can also position the graphic (or any other object on the report, for that matter) with the Object Size and Position dialog box. Select the object that you want to position, right-click, and choose Size and Position from the pop-up menu. You can also choose Format | Size and Position from the pull-down menus.

To format the graphic more precisely, you can use the Format Editor. Make sure the graphic is still selected. Then, click the Format button in the Expert Tools toolbar, right-click the graphic, and choose Format Graphic from the pop-up menu; or choose Format | Format Graphic from the pull-down menus. The Picture tab allows you to specify exact cropping and scaling values.

TIP *Only common bitmap graphic formats are supported in Crystal Reports. It will not recognize specialized formats, such as Adobe Photoshop, or vector formats (other than Windows Metafile), such as those from CorelDRAW or Adobe Illustrator. If you wish to use these graphics in a report, you need to convert them to common bitmap formats before adding them to your report. And if you wish to include graphics from web pages, you must use .JPG format—Crystal Reports won't recognize .GIF files.*

Although using symbol fonts, such as Wingdings, is very powerful, you are limited to what is included in the font itself. Also, the symbols are generally simple two-dimensional images and can be displayed only in a single color. Wouldn't it be nice if you could use smaller bitmap files, such as icon-like graphics that look more three-dimensional and include several colors, on your report?

Because you can suppress bitmap files conditionally, just like other objects, you have real power and flexibility in creating visually appealing and interesting reports using bitmap graphics. Figure 6-5 shows a report with unique icons indicating the status of an order. Orders that have been shipped (or are "closed") have a closed file folder next to them. Open orders (not shipped) have an open file folder next to them.

This report uses a technique that could be called *mutually exclusive suppression*. There are two different bitmap files on the report: an open-file bitmap and a closed-file bitmap. They are placed right on top of each other in the details section. They are conditionally suppressed in such a way that only one will ever be displayed at a time. In this case, they are suppressed using the Shipped field (a Boolean field that returns true or false) from the XTRME Sample Database Orders table (this sample database is available for download from CrystalBook. com, this book's companion web site).

FIGURE 6-5 Using bitmap files formatted conditionally

The open-file bitmap is conditionally suppressed using this formula:

```
{Orders.Shipped}
```

while the closed-file bitmap is conditionally suppressed using this formula:

```
Not {Orders.Shipped}
```

Because of this, only one bitmap will ever be visible at a time.

The success of this technique depends on Crystal Reports allowing multiple objects to be placed right on top of each other. You have the ability to do this with any text or graphic object whenever and wherever you choose. Just make sure you implement some technique similar to this to prevent them from splattering all over each other. You can also use the Move to Back, Move Backward, Move Forward, and Move To Front options from the Format pull-down menu or from the pop-up menu that appears when you right-click an object. These options determine which objects have "priority" when they are placed on top of each other.

Dynamic Graphic Locations

While you choose a specific image file when you first use the Insert Image option, Crystal Reports provides additional flexibility to change the actual source file of the bitmap image dynamically as the report runs. This *dynamic graphic location* capability allows you to use a conditional formula to specify an external graphic image filename and location "on the fly." This provides an additional way to have images change dynamically as the report is processed, besides use of image fields contained in a database table (sometimes known as Binary Large Object, or "BLOB," fields).

To set the location of a graphic file dynamically, click the Graphic Location conditional formula button on the Picture tab of the Format Editor. The Formula Workshop/Formula Editor will appear. Create a formula using any available formula field, function, or operator that returns a string value equating to the location and filename of an image file. For example, the following formula uses a database field to derive the filename of an external .JPG file containing a unique image for each DVD in a DVD collection database record:

```
"C:\Program Files\InterVocative Software\DVD Profiler\Images\"
& {Collection.ID} & "f.jpg"
```

This formula concatenates a drive and pathname to a number taken from the database to the letter *f*, followed by the ".jpg" extension. The result is a unique JPEG filename for each record in the database.

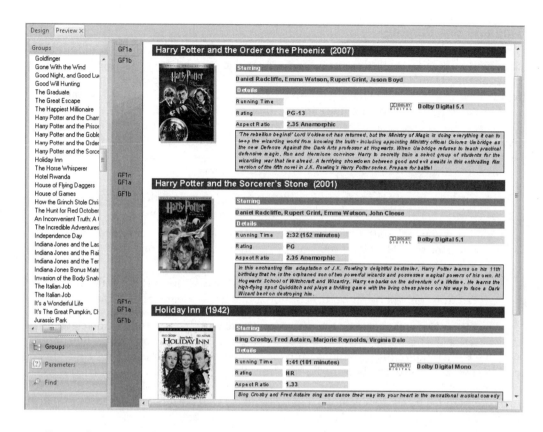

Remember to consider how a "target" computer that runs your report will find images you specify in dynamic graphic location formulas. For example, if the images are stored on a network drive mapped to drive H on your computer, they may not be found when another computer on the network runs the report if the same drive H mapping isn't defined. To reduce this probability, you may choose to use Universal Naming Convention (UNC) path- and filenames, such as:

```
"\\x23\c\Program Files\InterVocative Software\DVD Profiler\Images\"
& {Collection.ID} & "f.jpg"
```

Or, if an image is stored on a web server or Internet web site, you may use a web URL to specify the graphic name:

```
"http://www.ablazegroup.com/DVDData/Images/"
& {Collection.ID} & "f.jpg"
```

Line and Box Drawing

You can use the Border tab on the Format Editor to control line appearance on all four sides of individual objects. While this lets the individual objects stand out by having lines or boxes appear around them, you may want more flexibility to have groups of objects highlighted with boxes or to have lines stretch partially or completely across sections.

Crystal Reports lets you use line and box drawing tools to create these boxes and lines. To create a line or box, ensure that you have the Design tab chosen. Inserting lines or boxes in the Preview tab may give you undesirable results if you don't put them in the right section.

To add a line or box to your report, perform these steps:

1. Click the Insert Line or Insert Box button in the Insert Tools toolbar. You can also choose Insert | Line or Insert | Box from the pull-down menus.

2. When you make either of these choices, your mouse cursor changes to a pencil. Point the pencil to where you want to begin the line or box, and hold down the left mouse button.

3. Drag the line or box to its ending position and release the button. Notice that you can draw only perfectly vertical or horizontal lines—diagonal lines can't be drawn.

The line or box will appear on the report, complete with sizing handles. You can now drag or resize the line or box just like any other object. You may also format the line or box with the Format Editor (using options from the Format pull-down menu, or by right-clicking the line or box and choosing Format from the pop-up menu). You can choose the color, size, and style of the line or box, along with other options (Crystal Reports allows you to create rounded boxes, for example). Figure 6-6 shows a report that uses a horizontal line to delineate group footers, and places a filled, rounded box around report totals.

TIP *You can draw lines and boxes that traverse multiple report sections. This is handy if you want to have a single box enclose a column starting in the page header and ending in the page footer, including all the sections in between. However, this can sometimes result in odd behavior if, for example, you start a line in the page header but end it in the details section or a group footer. If your lines or boxes traverse sections, make sure you preview the report to check that you get the desired results.*

Printing Barcodes

While previous versions of Crystal Reports allowed barcode printing by use of third-party TrueType barcode fonts and utilities, Crystal Reports 2008 now bundles several Code39 barcode fonts from Azalea Software and adds additional capabilities to simplify barcode printing. You may make use of these bundled fonts, or acquire additional TrueType fonts (perhaps for UPC or Code128 barcodes) and use these within your report as well.

Begin by placing the database field or formula you wish to display as a barcode on your report (generally, you should use string or numeric fields for barcode printing—use a formula to convert other data types to numbers or strings and format the formula for barcode printing). Then, right-click the desired field and choose Change To Barcode from the pop-up menu. The Select Barcode Type dialog box appears, showing two bundled Azalea Software

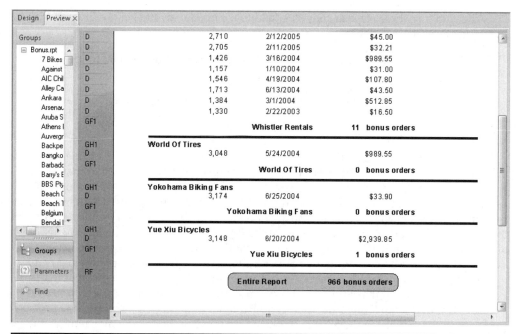

FIGURE 6-6   Line and box drawing

Code39 barcode fonts (one for simple letters and numbers and one for the full ASCII character set, including special symbols). Choose the desired font and click OK to convert the selected field to a barcode.

When you use these steps to convert a field to a barcode, several actions are performed by Crystal Reports automatically:

- The font face is changed to the associated bundled Code39 barcode font.
- The font size is changed to 24 points and the field size is changed.
- The Display Text property on the Format Editor is set to use a bundled User Function Library (UFL) function to convert the actual text of the field to the proper characters to make up a Code39 barcode.

You may wish to make additional adjustments to the converted barcode to make it more appropriate for your particular application. For example, your barcode reader may reliably read a smaller font, or you may wish to use a larger font for specialized applications. In that case, you may select the barcode field and change the font size using the Formatting toolbar or Format Editor. Or, you may wish to adjust or replace the formula that actually sets the text to be converted to a barcode. For example, if the formula you initially added to the report already used a UFL function or other custom formula logic to create the proper barcode text, you may format the barcode with the Format Editor and remove the Display Text formula.

You may also wish to later remove the barcode formatting and return the field to use a normal text font. If you make this determination shortly after converting the field to a barcode, you may simply undo the Change to Barcode step. However, if you have performed other actions in the interim that you don't wish to undo, you may remove the Display Text formula and change the font face and size back to the original values to remove the barcode formatting.

CAUTION   *If you wish to use a different barcode than the bundled Code39 barcode, simply formatting the barcode field to use a different TrueType barcode font won't be sufficient. As various barcode coding techniques are different than Code39, you'll need to modify the Display Text formatting formula, or write your own custom formula, to properly code for the particular barcode font you will use. While the only barcode font included in Crystal Reports 2008 is Code39, the bundled Azalea User Function Library includes functions to code to other barcode formats, such as Code128 and UPC. Additional acquired fonts can be used with these coding functions.*

Text and Paragraph Formatting

Crystal Reports includes various text formatting features that enhance reporting capabilities. Some are designed for use with foreign-language versions of the report writer (such as Japanese), while others simply provide enhanced functionality for more reporting situations.

A subtle feature that may not be immediately noticeable is *fractional point sizes* for fonts. If you use the Point Size drop-down list either in the Formatting toolbar or from the Font tab of the Format Editor, you'll see that only whole-number point-size values are available. However, if you click inside the drop-down list, you can then type values directly into the drop-down list, rather than choosing predefined numbers. If you want to use a 10.5 point size instead of a whole number, simply type **10.5** and press ENTER. You may type in sizes in ½-point increments (10.5 will work, but 10.25 will round to 10.5).

CAUTION   *In the initial release of Crystal Reports 2008, fractional point sizes do not appear in the Format Editor Font tab, even if you have properly typed them in. Only whole number point sizes will appear. However, the Formatting toolbar will display the fractional point size and the object will be properly formatted in the fractional size.*

You'll also notice a *Text Rotation* option on the Format Editor Common tab. This allows you to rotate objects based on TrueType or built-in printer fonts to 90 degrees (sideways from bottom to top) or 270 degrees (sideways from top to bottom). Just choose the desired rotation from the drop-down list. You'll probably need to adjust the height and width of the now-rotated text to properly show all the material in the object.

TIP   *You can make innovative use of text rotation by using multiple report sections and the Underlay section formatting option, described in Chapter 8. For example, by placing a rotated text object in Page Header b (which is formatted with the Underlay option), you can have vertical text flow down alongside the rest of your report on every page. This technique can be helpful for replicating special forms, for example.*

Format Editor Paragraph Formatting Tab

If you format a string or memo database field or a text object, Crystal Reports presents an additional *Paragraph* tab on the Formula Editor, as shown in Figure 6-7. Use these options to determine how multiple lines of text or data will be formatted:

- **Indentation—First Line**   Indicates the amount of space the first line in each paragraph will be indented. The first line of the text or any line after a carriage return is considered the first line of a paragraph.

- **Indentation—Left**   Indicates the amount of space that the entire field will be indented from the left side of the object.

- **Indentation—Right**   Indicates the amount of space that the entire field will be indented from the right side of the object.

- **Spacing—Line Spacing**   Adds vertical blank space between each line in the paragraph. Choose the Multiple option to choose a multiple of the normal spacing (for example, two times normal spacing). Choose the Exact option to choose a specific point size for line spacing (for example, 5 points).

Figure 6-7   Paragraph Formatting tab on Format Editor

- **Spacing—Of *x* Times Normal**   Specifies the associated number for the Multiple or Exact Line Spacing option.
- **Reading Order**   Specifies whether the text in the object that's being formatted will be read from left to right, or right to left. This option generally applies to non-English versions of Crystal Reports, and while it doesn't reverse the display of characters that make up a field, it does rearrange placement of punctuation marks that appear at the end of fields.

Using HTML and RTF Text Interpretation

Figure 6-7 also shows the *Text Interpretation* drop-down list on the Paragraph Formatting tab (you'll see this option only with string or memo database fields—not with text objects).

Available options in this drop-down list are None (the default), HTML Text (Hypertext Markup Language), and RTF Text (Rich Text Format). HTML text is often associated with the Web—web pages are encoded in HTML. RTF is a standard text format that is interchangeable between most popular word processors and page publishing programs.

If you leave the default Text Interpretation option of None chosen, Crystal Reports simply displays the value from the database as it actually appears in the database. If the field contains special formatting codes, they'll just appear on the report directly. If your database string or memo fields contain text with special HTML or RTF formatting codes to describe fonts, colors, and special formatting, choose the appropriate HTML or RTF Text Interpretation option.

Crystal Reports will convert these formatting codes into actual typeface, point size, color, and formatting options. Notice how a Text Interpretation setting of None (as opposed to a setting of HTML) displays a database field that's encoded using the Hypertext Markup Language.

TIP *Not all HTML tags and attributes are supported. For a list of specific HTML tags that Crystal Reports interprets, search online help for "Paragraph tab."*

The Format Painter

The *Format Painter,* which provides capabilities like those of similarly named features in standard office suites, allows you to copy a large number of formatting properties from one previously formatted object to one or more additional objects with simple mouse clicks.

First, decide which object will contain the formatting that you want to copy (this object is known as the *source object*). If necessary, double-check the source object's formatting by displaying the Format Editor after selecting the object. Once you're sure of its formatting, select the source object (you can only select a single object—the Format Painter won't work if you select more than one source object). Then, click the Format Painter button in the Standard toolbar, choose Format | Format Painter from the pull-down menus, or right-click and choose Format Painter from the pop-up menu.

The mouse cursor will change to the Format Painter paintbrush. Now, move the mouse cursor to the report object (known as the *target object*) you want to copy the source formatting to. If you move the mouse cursor over an object that the Format Painter won't work with, a "no-drop" cursor (a circle with a line through it) will appear. For example, you won't be able to copy formatting from a database field to a bitmap image. Objects that can accept Format Painter formatting will show the paintbrush cursor. Click on the target object to apply the copied formatting.

TIP *If you wish to paint formatting from the source object to multiple target objects, double-click the Format Painter toolbar button. You may continue to paste onto multiple objects until you press ESC. Or, if you single-clicked the toolbar button, you may hold down the ALT key while clicking target objects. The paintbrush icon will continue to appear as you click subsequent objects until you release ALT.*

Data types play a significant role in Format Painter behavior. If you've set a combination of formatting properties for the source object that both are and are not dependent upon data type (for example, font color is not dependent upon data type, but number of decimal places is), some of the properties will not "stick" to the target object. Continuing with the previous example, using a numeric field that contains a red font color and three decimal places will only result in the red font color sticking on a non-numeric field—the three decimal place formatting will stick only when the target object is a numeric or currency field.

Conditional formatting is also a consideration when using the Format Painter. First and foremost, any conditional formatting applied with the Highlighting Expert (discussed earlier in the chapter) *will not* be copied to target objects by the Format Painter. However, conditional formatting applied with formulas set with Format Editor conditional formatting buttons will be copied. Again, only those conditional formulas that are applicable to the target data type will be copied—a conditional formula setting the number of decimal places won't be copied to a non-numeric field, while a conditional formula setting font size will.

While data types play a role in determining what will be copied to target objects, the *type* of report object (database field, text object, bitmap image, cross-tab, and so forth) determines whether or not the Format Painter will even work. If you attempt to copy formatting with the Format Painter, you may find the no-drop cursor (circle with line) appearing more often than you might expect. This is often because you are attempting to copy formatting to a dissimilar type of report object.

For example, if you click a database field prior to clicking the Format Painter toolbar button, you'll encounter a no-drop cursor if you hover the mouse over a text object, bitmap field, or other dissimilar report object. Sometimes, this behavior will be completely understandable (you can't change the font color of a bitmap). In other cases, you may wish to paste some common formatting properties (font color, size, or face) onto the text object target from the source database field. Because the objects are dissimilar, the Format Painter won't work. This is a limitation of Crystal Reports.

Report Alerts

In addition to some of the conditional reporting features discussed elsewhere in this chapter, Crystal Reports allows you to highlight records that meet a requirement using Report Alerts. *Report Alerts* enable you to set up a condition that Crystal Reports checks for every time you refresh the report (by clicking the Refresh button in the Navigation Tools toolbar or next to page navigation buttons), by selecting Report | Refresh Report Data from the pull-down menus, or by pressing the F5 key). Report Alerts can also be used to highlight desired conditions or send an e-mail when reports are scheduled with the BusinessObjects Enterprise family of web-based reporting systems (covered in Part II of this book).

While you've always been able to conditionally format report sections and objects in terms of a condition, you might not have always known which customers, sales reps, months, and so forth had "triggered" this condition without going through the report page by page looking for the conditionally formatted sections. Now when a report with Report Alerts defined runs, a separate dialog box will pop up if any of the conditions on the report have been met. You can then click a button on the dialog box to display a separate tab (similar to a drill-down tab) that shows only report records that meet the alert condition.

To work with Report Alerts, choose Report | Alerts | Create Or Modify Alerts from the pull-down menus. The Create Alerts dialog box will appear, as shown in Figure 6-8. If any existing alerts have already been created in the report, they'll appear inside this dialog box. If you wish to modify any existing alert, select it in the dialog box and click Edit. To delete an existing alert, select it and click Delete. If there are no alerts in the report yet, the dialog box will be empty.

To create a new alert, click New. The Create Alert dialog box will appear, as shown in Figure 6-9. At minimum, you must specify the name of the Report Alert in the Name text box, and the condition that will trigger the alert by clicking the Condition button. You may optionally type a message that will appear when the alert is triggered in the Message text box, or customize the message with a string formula you create by clicking the conditional formula button. Clicking Condition will display the Formula Editor, where you enter a Boolean formula that determines when the alert will be triggered (see Chapter 4 for information on Boolean formulas). If you wish to temporarily disable the alert without deleting it entirely, deselect the Enabled check box.

For example, you may wish to create a simple report showing orders that were placed. If the order amount exceeds a certain level ($5,000, for example), you wish to trigger a report alert. Create the report as you usually would and then create a new Report Alert. Give the alert a name of your choosing (perhaps "Order Exceeds 5,000"), type any message you want to appear when the alert is triggered, and then click Condition. Enter a Boolean formula to indicate what records should trigger the alert, such as

```
{Orders.Order Amount} > 5000
```

FIGURE 6-8 The Create Alerts dialog box

Click to create string formula to
display when alert is triggered
(optional)

Give the alert a name ⟶

Type message that will
display when alert is
triggered (optional)

Click to create Boolean
formula indicating when
alert should be triggered

Temporarily
disable alert
without deleting it

Figure 6-9   The Create Alert dialog box

Once you've saved the alert, simply refresh the report. If any order amounts in the report exceed $5,000, you'll receive an alert dialog box indicating that the alert has been triggered.

To see a separate tab showing all report records with orders that exceed $5,000, just click View Records. A separate tab (similar to a drill-down tab, discussed in Chapters 2 and 7) will appear showing just the relevant records.

You don't have to just base Report Alerts on database fields, as in the previous example. You can also base report alerts on summaries or subtotals in group footers (although you can't base Report Alerts on WhilePrintingRecords or "second pass" formulas). For example, you may prefer to create a parameter field (discussed in Chapter 13) to prompt the user for a customer total threshold. You can then create a Report Alert that will be triggered if an order subtotal in a customer name group footer exceeds the value supplied by the parameter field. In this situation, the Boolean formula used to trigger the alert will look something like this:

```
Sum ({Orders.Order Amount}, {Customer.Customer Name}) >
{?Report Alert Threshold}
```

Basing Report Formulas or Conditional Formatting on Report Alerts

While it's helpful to see a dialog box showing that a Report Alert has been triggered, and see a separate tab of report items that triggered the alert, you may appreciate the additional power afforded to your formulas by Report Alerts as well. Three functions exist in the formula language in Crystal Reports to support alerts: *IsAlertEnabled, IsAlertTriggered,* and *AlertMessage.* Each of these new functions takes one argument, the name of a previously created report alert:

- **IsAlertEnabled**   Returns a true or false value, depending on the state of the Enabled check box in the Create Alert dialog box (shown in Figure 6-9, earlier in the chapter). If the alert is enabled, then this function will return true. Otherwise, it will return false.

- **IsAlertTriggered**   Returns a true or false value, depending on whether the record the formula is evaluating for triggers the alert or not. For example, if you create a formula containing the IsAlertTriggered("Order Exceeds 5,000") function, the function will return true for records with order amounts greater than $5,000, and false for records with order amounts equal to or less than $5,000.

- **AlertMessage**   Returns the message specified for the Report Alert. This is either the "hard-coded" message that was typed into the Message text box when the alert was created, or the results of the message string formula that was created with the alert.

For the previously discussed customer subtotal example, you may wish to create a formula that displays a message in group footers that trigger the alert. The formula might look similar to this:

```
If IsAlertTriggered ("Beat 2004 Goal") Then
    GroupName ({Customer.Customer Name}) & " beat the 2004 goal"
```

You may also wish to highlight the entire group footer with a different background color if the group triggered a Report Alert. You can use these new formula functions in conditional formatting formulas, as well as report formulas. For example, you could conditionally set the background color of the Customer Name Group Footer to aqua by using the Section Expert. The conditional formula would be similar to this:

```
If IsAlertTriggered ("Beat 2004 Goal") Then
    crAqua
Else
    crNoColor
```

NOTE *For complete information on formatting sections and the Section Expert, refer to Chapter 7.*

Crystal Reports Templates

You may have created a report that contains a large amount of custom formatting that you'd like to apply to other reports all at once. You may user Report Templates for this purpose. *Report Templates* are just existing .RPT files that are used to format other reports. One of the first places you may notice use of report templates is on the last screen of report wizards that you can use when first creating a new report.

To apply a template in a report wizard, simply select one of the predefined templates in the Available Templates list. When you choose one of the templates in the list, a thumbnail view of the template is shown in the Preview section of the report wizard. You may also choose another .RPT file to use as a template by clicking Browse. This will launch a standard open file dialog box, where you can navigate to the existing .RPT file you wish to use as a template.

Once you've chosen the report, it will be added to the template list, where you may select it to control the formatting of the new report. If the report you added has a value in the File | Summary Info Title field, it will appear as the name of the template. And if the Save Preview Picture check box is checked in the File | Summary Info dialog box of the report you just added, the preview of the report will appear in the Preview area of the report wizard.

NOTE *Any .RPT files you add to the template list won't remain in the list the next time you use the report wizards. You'll need to navigate to the report with the Browse button again if you want to use it as a template.*

The Template Expert

If you want to apply a template to a report you've already created (either with a report wizard or without), you can use the Template Expert to apply a template or undo the previous application of a template. To display the Template Expert, either click the Template Expert toolbar button in the Expert Tools toolbar, or choose Report | Template Expert from the pull-down menus. The Template Expert will appear, as shown in Figure 6-10.

The Template Expert looks very similar to the Template section of the report wizards, with a few additional features. As with the report wizards, you can pick a template from the list to add to your current report. When you select a template in the list, a preview of the template will appear in the Preview area of the Template Expert. And you may also click Browse to add an existing .RPT file to the template list to use to reformat the current report.

However, the Template Expert includes a few more features that don't apply to the report wizards. In particular, if you've already applied a template and aren't satisfied with its results (and this is a real possibility—templates can dramatically change the formatting of your report), you can undo the template application by clicking the Undo The Current Template radio button in the Template Expert. This is the only way to undo a template application—the Undo feature on the Edit menu or the Undo toolbar button won't undo a template application. If you've already undone a template and wish to redo it, you may either choose it in the template list again or click the Re-Apply The Last Template radio

FIGURE 6-10 The Template Expert

button. It's important to remember that the Undo and Redo features will be available only during the current Crystal Reports session. If you apply a template, save the report, and then exit Crystal Reports, you'll be stuck with the template's formatting when you next reopen the report.

TIP *The predefined templates in the Template Expert are supplied by existing .RPT files. By default, Crystal Reports looks in \Program Files\Business Objects\Crystal Reports 12.0\Templates\ <language> for template reports. If you wish to change the location that Crystal Reports uses to populate the Template Expert, you must change the Registry key HKEY_LOCAL_MACHINE/ Software/Business Objects/Suite 12.0/Crystal Reports/Templates/TemplatePath. Ensure you are familiar with manipulating Registry settings before attempting this change.*

Once you've chosen a template to apply to your current report, the report's formatting will change, often drastically. How Crystal Reports applies all the individual object and section reporting of the source template to your current report is not necessarily predictable—you'll want to experiment with several templates to see how they affect formatting. However, as a general rule, Crystal Reports will compare report objects and report sections between the template and the current report, applying many of the formatting properties of both report sections and individual objects in the template to the current report. If, for example, the template report contains two details sections (Details a and Details b) and the current report contains only a single details section, the current report will have an additional details section added when the template is applied. If you have a chart in the template but not in your current report, a chart will be added when the template is applied. And if your template contains ten details section fields formatted with different colors, you can generally expect the template's formatting to be applied to the first ten objects in the details section of your current report.

If you plan on using a template, you probably won't want to do a great deal of formatting to your original report before you apply the template—your pretemplate formatting will be discarded. If you are generally pleased with a report's formatting, you would be well advised to save the report before applying templates. While the Undo capability exists in the Template Expert, you'll want to play it safe in case you may not want to permanently accept a template's formatting changes.

TIP *You are not limited to applying one template to a report, but may apply as many as you'd like by following the previous steps more than once. Depending on which templates you apply, these multiple template applications will "blend" together to form a report that combines the formatting options from all templates applied. In other cases, one template will completely replace another.*

Creating Your Own Templates

As was mentioned previously, templates are merely other Crystal Report .RPT files whose formatting is copied to the current report. While the few sample templates that are already provided by Business Objects are acceptable for exploring the capabilities of adding templates, you'll probably want to develop a set of templates that conform to your company's "look and feel," perhaps including a company logo, preferred font face and size, and various object and section formatting standards that you wish to commonly apply to reports.

You may want to begin by just picking some already-created "standard" reports that approximate the look and feel you desire. You can then experiment with using them as templates. You may wish to save them in a temporary folder and modify the original reports to make better use of them as templates. Once you've modified the existing "template" reports to meet your needs, you may add an appropriate name to the Title field in the File | Summary Info dialog box, as well as checking the Save Preview Picture check box in the same dialog box. Then, preview the report (this is required to generate the preview picture) and save the report into the template directory. That report will now appear as a template in the Template Expert and Report Wizard Template section.

You may also wish to create a new report from scratch to act as a template. Crystal Reports includes a special type of field known as the template field to help in this endeavor. A *template field* is a special kind of field you can add to a report to act as a placeholder for a report object when applying the template to the main report. A template field doesn't initially display any data—it just contains formatting information that is carried over when the template is applied to the main report. To insert a template field, choose Insert | Template Field Object from the pull-down menus. An object outline will be placed on your mouse cursor. Drag the object to its desired location on the report and click to drop it. The template field will be added to the report.

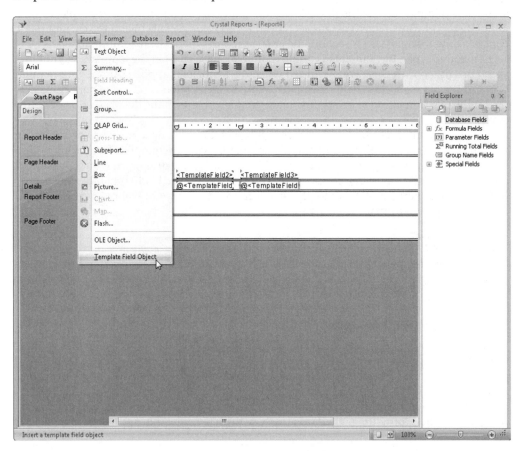

You now select the template field and format it with any of the methods discussed earlier in this chapter. However, you'll notice one unique difference between template fields and regular database fields when you format them with the Format Editor: tabs for every possible data type will appear in the Format Editor when formatting a template field. This additional template field flexibility lets you set up formatting for various target report fields that you may use with this template report. For example, if you're not sure whether the first field in the details section of the target report will be a string, number, or date, you can use the Paragraph tab, the Number tab, and the Date and Time tab to set formatting for the template field. When the template field is used to apply formatting in the target report, the formatting you've chosen in the appropriate tab will filter to the target fields.

When using template fields in a template report, it may be difficult to see what the actual target report formatting may look like. This is because template fields, by default, aren't connected to any database fields. As such, they won't show any data if you try to view your template report in the Preview tab. However, you can set template fields to display a value in the Preview tab by using the Formula Workshop. Notice that when you add a template field to the report, a corresponding formula is added to the Field Explorer. If you edit the template field formulas (editing formulas is discussed in detail in Chapter 4), you can change the formula to return something other than ten spaces, which are initially returned by the formula by way of the Space(10) function. You may replace the Space(10) function with a database field from the Field tree, or another function from the Function tree that will return data. When you display the template report in the Preview tab, you'll now be able to more accurately determine how the resultant formatting will be applied in the target report.

Once you've used template fields to create the template report, supply a name for the template in the Title field of File | Summary Info. You may also wish to check Save Preview Picture, preview the template report (which is required to save the preview picture), and then save the template report to the folder where other template reports are located. You will then see the new template appear the next time you need to apply a template with the Template Expert or in the report wizards.

Adding Custom Text

There are many times during the report design process that you need to just drop some *literal text* into your report. This could be a report title that you place in the report header, a label next to a subtotal in the group footer, or a whole paragraph that you place in the report footer (perhaps explaining the methodology of the report). You can accomplish this with *text objects.*

To insert a text object, choose Insert | Text Object or click the Text Object button on the Insert Tools toolbar. Crystal Reports 2008 will display a cross-hair cursor. Move this cursor to where you want the text object to appear. Then hold down your mouse button to drag the text object to its desired width and height. The text object will be dropped at that location, and you'll be immediately placed in *edit mode.* You'll always know when you're in edit mode because you'll see a flashing cursor inside the text object and a small ruler at the top of the Design or Preview tab, as shown here:

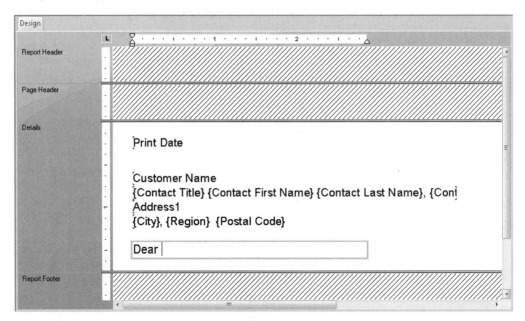

Now, just start typing. The material you type will appear inside the text object. When you're finished, just click outside the text object to save your changes.

The small ruler that appears while editing a text object gives you additional capabilities for text layout, much as rulers in text editing and word processing programs do. There are four items that can be customized within a text object ruler:

- **Left Margin**   Drag the small up-arrow-with-block icon in the lower left of the ruler to change the left margin within the text object. All text you type will start from this position, regardless of the width of the actual text object on the report.

- **Right Margin**   Drag the small up-arrow icon in the lower right of the ruler to change the right margin within the text object. All text you type will end or word-wrap at this position, regardless of the width of the actual text object on the report.

- **Left Indent Position**   Drag the small down-arrow icon in the upper left of the ruler to change the indent position within the text object. The first line of text in the text object, as well as any text appearing after you press enter, will start at this position. You may drag this arrow to the left of the left margin arrow to create out-dented paragraphs, if you choose.

- **Tab Stops**   Click anywhere on the ruler to add a tab stop. A small "L" icon will appear by default, indicating a left-alignment tab stop. Pressing TAB while adding or editing text will position text at the corresponding tab stop. You may choose from three other types of tab stops: center-alignment, right-alignment, and decimal-alignment. Make your choice by clicking the small "L" icon to the left of the text object ruler. Each click will cycle through the available types of tab stops. When the desired type is displayed, click in the text object ruler to add that type of tab stop. You may move any of the existing tab stops to a new location by dragging the associated icon. Remove a tab stop by dragging its icon off the text object ruler.

There are several ways to edit the contents of an existing text object. To use the "long way," select the text object and then choose Edit | Edit Text from the pull-down menus, or right-click the text object and choose Edit Text from the pop-up menu. The "short way" is simply to double-click a text object, which places you in edit mode. Once in edit mode, use the cursor keys, BACKSPACE key, and DEL key to move around and edit the text. You may also use the CTRL key, in combination with cursor keys, to move forward and backward an entire word. And, to highlight portions of the text object (perhaps to delete a group of text), use the SHIFT key in combination with cursor keys.

CAUTION *It's commonplace to attempt to exit edit mode by pressing the ENTER key. Not only will this not end editing, it will start a new line in the text object. This can often cause the contents of the text object to partially or completely disappear. If you want to put line breaks in your text object, go ahead and press ENTER, but make sure you resize the text object when you're finished so that you can see all of your text. You may also format a multiline text object with the Can Grow formatting option.*

The Field Heading Text Object

A special kind of text object is the *field heading text object*. This is created in the page header automatically by Crystal Reports when you place a field from the Field Explorer into the details section. If you then select the text object in the page header, you'll notice that the Crystal Reports status bar indicates that you've selected a field heading. While this object can be edited and formatted just like a regular text object, it will now move along with its matching details field—if you move the field in the details section left or right, the field heading will follow. Even if you move the details field vertically to a new section (to the page or report header or footer, for example) and then move the field left or right, the field heading will still move left or right with it. And, if you delete the original database field, the field heading will be deleted along with it.

The only time you may detach the field heading from its associated details field is if you move the details field out of one section into another *and* move it horizontally at the same time. In this case the two objects will be separated—the field heading won't follow the original details field anymore. However, to hook the two objects together again, simply move the details field left or right in its new section until it lines up with the field heading. The two will become "reattached."

TIP   *If you inadvertently delete a field heading while leaving the original database or formula field on the report, or you drag a field from the Field Explorer to a section other than Details, you'll end up with a field with no matching Field Heading. You may create a field heading by selecting the field and choosing Insert | Field Heading from the drop-down menus, or by right-clicking on the field and choosing Insert | Field Heading from the pop-up menu.*

Combining Database Fields

Simply typing literal text into text objects is a waste of their capabilities! Text objects are powerful elements that can help you create very attractive reports. Consider Figure 6-11, the beginning of a form letter that uses the Customers table from XTREME.MDB (available for download from the book's companion website, CrystalBook.com). Note the spacing problems with the contact name, city, state, and ZIP code. These lines are composed of separate fields from the Customers table. No matter how much you try or how creative you get sizing and moving these fields, they will not line up properly for every customer. They appear in the same horizontal location in every details section, no matter how wide or narrow the fields are sized.

This type of problem is a dead giveaway that this is a computer-generated letter. Although most consumers are savvy enough to assume that a computer had something to do with the form letters they receive, you don't want to make it obvious. Crystal Reports gives you a better way with text objects.

In addition to containing literal text, text objects allow you to *embed* database fields inside text objects with literal text. When the text object appears, it automatically sizes the contents of these embedded fields so that there is no extra space. Figure 6-12 shows the same form letter as Figure 6-11, but text objects are used to combine the database fields with literal text and spaces.

To combine fields inside a text object, follow these steps:

1. Insert a text object, as described previously. If you need to include any literal text, you may type it either now or after you've inserted the database fields. It doesn't matter whether you leave the text object in edit mode or end editing.

2. From the Field Explorer, choose the field or fields you want to combine in the text object. Drag them from the Field Explorer into the text object. Note that your mouse cursor will change when you move over the text object, and a blinking cursor will appear in the text object at the same time:

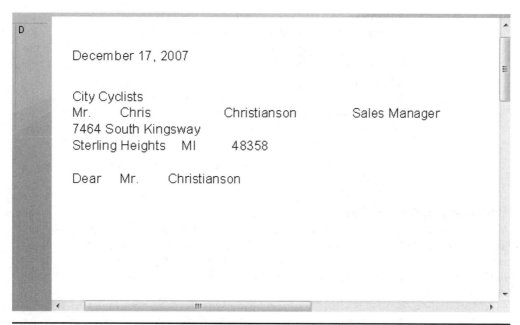

Figure 6-11   Spacing problems using database fields

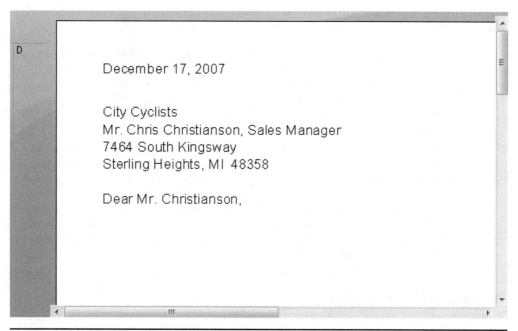

Figure 6-12   Spacing problems solved with text objects

3. Before dropping the database field or fields in the text object, look very carefully at the location of the blinking text object cursor. Wherever the cursor is located is where the field or fields will go when you release the mouse button. Release the button when the cursor is in the proper position.

4. If you were already editing the text object when you dragged the field into it, it will stay in edit mode. You may now type more literal text or add another field, if you need to. If the text object wasn't in edit mode, the field will be dropped inside without going into edit mode. If you wish to add more text, double-click the text object to place it in edit mode.

5. When you're finished combining fields and literal text, end editing by clicking outside the text object.

Combining Special Fields

You're not limited to combining database fields inside text objects. You can use *special fields* as well. Special fields are system-generated fields, such as the print date, print time, page number, and total page count. You may place them directly on the report, just like database fields. And, like database fields, they'll give you spacing problems if you try to place them near literal text.

To combine special fields with literal text inside text objects, perform the same steps as for database fields. Just drag the fields from the Special Fields category of the Field Explorer, instead of from the Database Field category. In fact, you can embed any type of field from the Field Explorer in a text object just by dragging and dropping from the desired category.

Figure 6-13 shows the benefits of combining special fields with literal text in text objects.

The following pointers will help you as you combine fields and literal text inside text objects:

- If you place a database or special field in the wrong location inside the text object (suppose you place the Last Name field in between the letters *a* and *r* in the word "Dear"), you can simply use your cursor keys and the BACKSPACE or DEL key to make the correction. In this case, it is easier to just delete the text following the special field, and reenter it before the special field. You may also use CTRL-C to cut text and CTRL-V to paste text inside the text object.

- If you inadvertently drop a subtotal, a summary, a database field, or some other item inside a text object by mistake (it's pretty easy to do, even if you're careful), you have two choices. If you catch the problem immediately, you can choose Edit | Undo, or click the Undo button on the Standard toolbar. The field will move back where it was. However, if you notice that you accidentally dropped a field inside the text object after it's too late to reasonably undo it, edit the text object, click the field that was mistakenly added to highlight it, and press the DEL key. The field will be removed from inside the text object. You will then need to recreate it and place it in its correct position on the report.

The Can Grow Formatting Option

When you combine database fields or special fields inside text objects, you may often find that the text object is no longer wide enough to show its entire contents. Crystal Reports features the Can Grow formatting option that allows a text object to grow vertically, if

Special fields combined with literal text inside text objects
  Special fields and text as separate objects

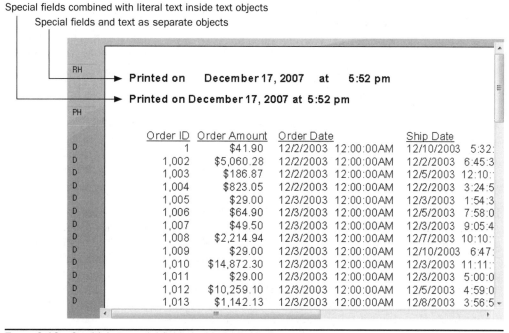

FIGURE 6-13   Combining special fields inside text objects

necessary, to show its entire contents. You may choose this option, as well as change the Maximum Number Of Lines option that the text object can grow from the Format Editor.

To display the Format Editor, use one of these options:

- Select the text object and then select Format | Format Text from the pull-down menus.

- Right-click the text object and choose Format Text from the pop-up menu.

- Click the Format button on the Expert Tools toolbar.

The Can Grow option is found on the Common tab of the Format Editor.

With Can Grow turned on, the text object will automatically grow taller to show all the text inside it. You can specify the maximum number of lines that the text object will grow, or leave the number set to zero for unlimited size. When Can Grow is turned on, the text object will display only as wide as it appears on the report. However, it will word-wrap at spaces in the text, creating additional vertical space up to the maximum number of lines.

This automatic behavior lets you size a text object so that it's only one line high. If the contents of the text object can be displayed in one line, the text object will remain one line tall. If it needs more lines, it will expand only by the amount of vertical space necessary to show the material inside the text object (limited by the maximum number of lines).

TIP *Can Grow is helpful for other types of objects as well, not just text objects. You can set the Can Grow formatting option for string fields and memo fields. This is particularly helpful for "description" or "narrative" types of fields that could contain as little as a few characters and as much as several paragraphs of text. Can Grow isn't available for any type of object other than a text object, string field, or memo field.*

The Suppress Embedded Field Blank Lines Formatting Option

Another handy formatting option for text objects is *Suppress Embedded Field Blank Lines*. This option will eliminate blank lines from a text object created by embedded fields that don't return a value. For example, if you were to embed a Company Name field in a text object, press ENTER, embed the Address 1 field, press ENTER, embed the Address 2 field, press ENTER, and then embed City, State, and ZIP fields side by side with appropriate spaces and commas, a blank line would appear in the text object for any records where the Address 2 field was empty. By checking Suppress Embedded Field Blank Lines on the Common tab of the Format Editor, the blank line resulting from the empty Address 2 field will be eliminated.

By combining this option with Can Grow, you can create text objects that will not only grow taller as needed, but eliminate blank lines based on the database or formula field embedded in the text object. These "variable-height" text objects, while flexible, may cause difficulty when placed directly above other fields or objects in the same report section. As you can't be sure how many lines tall the text object will be when the report is formatted, the possibility will exist that the text object will grow right over the top of an object just below it. To avoid this scenario, you may create an additional report section of the same type just below the section containing the text object and place other fields or objects in the additional section. This way, the section containing the variable-height text object will expand vertically, as necessary, to accommodate the text object, while the other objects in the subsequent section will appear directly below the text object, regardless of how tall it grows. Multiple sections are discussed in Chapter 7.

Formatting Individual Parts of Text Objects

You can format a text object as you would any other object, using the Formatting toolbar or Format Editor. When you select a text object and change the formatting, as by setting a color or font size, the entire text object takes on that format. This may be the behavior you want.

However, at other times you may want certain characters or words in a text object to take on different formatting than the rest of the text object. This is actually quite simple. Start editing the text object by double-clicking it. You are then free to select individual characters or words by dragging over them with your mouse or by holding down the SHIFT key while using the cursor keys. You can then use the Formatting toolbar or Format Editor to change the formatting for just those selected characters.

Even more prevalent is a situation in which you need to format individual database fields or special fields that are embedded *inside* a text object. For example, when you insert the Print Date special field inside a text object, it takes on the default formatting from File | Options (perhaps an mm/dd/yyyy format). If you select the text object and display the Format Editor, there is no Date tab in which to choose an alternate date format—this is a text object you're formatting! Similarly, if you've placed a number field inside a text object, you may want to change the formatting to show no decimal places or to add a currency symbol.

One way to accomplish this is to initially place fields from the Field Explorer on the main report design canvas and format them directly. Then, if they are dragged into a text object from the design canvas, they will retain their formatting within the text object. You may also format the object after it's been embedded in the text object. To change the formatting of a database or special field inside a text object, edit the text object and then click the field you wish to format. You'll know you've selected the field when it becomes highlighted inside the text object. You can then use the Format Editor (either from the Format menu or by right-clicking—the number-formatting buttons on the Formatting toolbar won't work here) to change the formatting of the object.

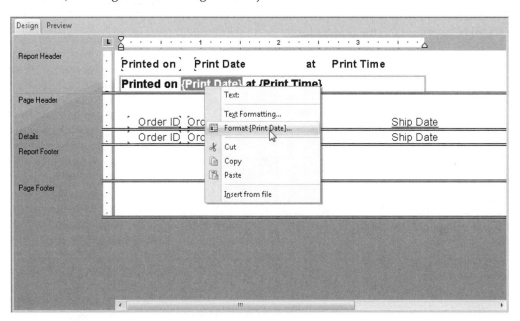

Importing Text from a File

If you have large amounts of text that you want to use in Crystal Reports text objects, you may either type it into a text object directly or copy and paste from the Windows Clipboard. However, data for text objects can also be imported directly from plain text, Rich Text Format (RTF), or Hypertext Markup Language (HTML) files.

To import text into a text object, add a text object as described previously in the chapter (using the Insert menu or toolbar button). If the text object isn't already in edit mode, double-click it to place it in edit mode. Then, right-click and choose Insert From File from the pop-up menu.

A File Open dialog box will appear. Navigate to the drive and folder where the text, RTF, or HTML file is that you wish to import into the text object. Choose the desired file and click OK. The file will be imported into the text object, alongside any existing text that may already be in the text object. If the text file contains plain text, it will simply be displayed in the text object in the default font style for text objects (set on the Fonts tab of File | Options). If the imported text is in HTML or RTF format, Crystal Reports automatically interprets most (but not all) of the embedded font and formatting specifications and includes them in the text object. If you wish to reformat portions of the text object, simply use techniques described previously in the chapter for formatting individual parts of text objects.

Using Sections and Areas

In previous chapters you learned how to change the appearance of individual objects on the report, such as by changing the color of a field or adding a drop shadow to a text object. However, you also have the ability to format *entire sections* of your report. Just a few of the section formatting options available to you are to

- Add a gray background to every other details section
- Format a group header so that every group starts anew on its own page
- Create multiple columns in your details section for labels
- Add a light-colored watermark graphic in its own page header section that appears behind the rest of your report
- Mix both portrait and landscape page orientations in one report (new in Crystal Reports 2008)

Formatting Sections with the Section Expert

There are several ways to change the appearance of an entire report section. You'll often just want to change the *size* of a section. Consider this "single-spaced" report:

Notice the details sections appearing very close to each other. Maybe you'll just want to "double-space" the report. However, there is no double-space, space-and-a-half, or similar function available in Crystal Reports. Instead, you choose how tall you want a section to be by using one of several techniques.

The simplest technique is simply to drag the bottom border of a section down to make the section taller. Point to the line at the bottom of the section you want to resize—the mouse cursor will turn into two lines with up and down arrows. This section-sizing cursor indicates that you can drag the section border down to make a section taller, or drag the border up to make the section shorter.

When you simply make the details section taller, the white space that's exposed becomes the "double-space" when you re-preview the report, as shown here:

Although this is the most straightforward way to resize a section, you have other options available. By right-clicking in the shaded section name on the left side of the Design tab, you display the section pop-up menu. For example, right-clicking the Details section brings up this menu.

This pop-up menu contains four additional features for resizing sections, as listed here:

Insert Line	Adds an additional horizontal guideline to the section ruler on the left side of the section. If the section isn't tall enough to show the additional guideline, the section grows taller.
Delete Last Line	Removes the bottom guideline in the section and shrinks the size of the section proportionally. If you choose this option and a report object is attached to the guideline that you would remove, you'll receive an error message.
Arrange Lines	Rearranges any horizontal guidelines in an even fashion. If there aren't enough horizontal guidelines to fill the section, additional guidelines will be added.
Fit Section	Automatically shrinks the size of the section to the bottommost object in the section. If there are any horizontal guidelines below the bottom object, they are removed before the section is resized.

Although you may sometimes use the Insert Line, Delete Last Line, or Arrange Lines option from the section pop-up menu, you'll most likely find Fit Section the only useful option. It's particularly useful if the section is very tall (perhaps you've deleted a large map, chart, or picture from the sec tion and all the white space it took up is still there), and you want to shrink it without having to scroll down to find the bottom section border.

The Section Expert

Whereas the Format Editor is used to format individual objects, you use the *Section Expert,* shown in Figure 7-1, to format entire sections of your report. The Section Expert has a large number of options for formatting individual report sections. Using these options provides a high level of flexibility for your reports.

The Section Expert can be displayed in several ways. You can click the Section Expert button on the Standard toolbar, choose Report | Section Expert from the pull-down menus, or right-click in the gray area of the section you wish to format and choose Section Expert from the pop-up menu. If you choose the toolbar button or menu option, the first section will be highlighted in the Section Expert. If you right-click in the gray area of a section and use the pop-up menu, that particular section will be highlighted.

By selecting different sections of the report in the Section Expert, you can view and set formatting properties for the section. Some options may be dimmed and unavailable, and some new properties may appear, depending on the report section that you are modifying. For example, as the Print at Bottom of Page property makes little sense for a page header, it will be dimmed when the Page Header is selected. And, the Format With Multiple Columns option will only appear when the Details section is selected. Table 7-1 explains the different section formatting properties available in the Section Expert's Common tab.

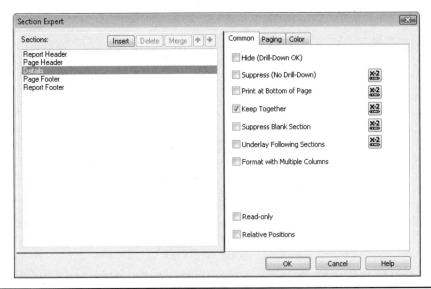

<figure>**FIGURE 7-1**   The Section Expert</figure>

CAUTION   *Don't confuse the Keep Together section property and the Keep Group Together group property on the Options tab of the Change Group dialog box. Keep Together in the Section Expert just prevents the particular section from splitting over two pages; whereas Keep Group Together will attempt to keep the group header, all details sections, and the group footer for the same group from printing across multiple pages.*

Property	Function
Hide (Drill-Down OK)	Hides a section and all objects in it. However, if the section is within a higher-level group and that group is drilled into, this section *will* appear in the drill-down tab.
Suppress (No Drill-Down)	Suppresses a section and all objects in it. If the section is within a higher-level group and that group is drilled into, this section *will not* appear in the drill-down tab, even though a drill-down tab will appear.
Print at Bottom of Page	Prints the section at the bottom of the page. This is typically used for invoices, statements, or other, similar reports that require a group footer with a total to print at the bottom of the page, regardless of how many details sections print above it.
Keep Together	Prevents Crystal Reports from putting a page break in the middle of this section. For example, this would avoid having the first few lines of a multiple-line details section appear on the bottom of one page and the last few lines appear on the next page.

TABLE 7-1   Section Expert Common Tab Formatting Properties

Property	Function
Suppress Blank Section	Suppresses the entire section if all the objects inside it are blank. This is useful in situations where you want to avoid white gaps appearing in your report if all the objects in a section have been conditionally suppressed or suppressed "if duplicated."
Underlay Following Sections	Prints the section, and then all following sections print right on top of the section. This is useful for printing maps, charts, or pictures alongside data or underneath the following sections.
Format with Multiple Columns	Creates multiple newspaper- or phonebook-style columns. The Layout tab will appear when this property is checked. This is only available when the details section is chosen.
Clamp Page Footer **(New in Crystal Reports 2008)**	Places the page footer immediately below the last report section that contains data, rather than adding vertical white space to make a full page before displaying the page footer. This is typically helpful for online reports that don't necessarily benefit from an 11-inch page height, even if there isn't sufficient data to fill a full 11-inch page. When printing to a standard printer or exporting to a page-oriented format, such as Adobe Acrobat, you'll probably find it best not to use this option. This is only available if the Page Footer is selected.
Reserve Minimum Page Footer	Reserves only enough vertical space to show the largest page footer section (if you have added multiple page footers, such as Page Footer a, Pager Footer b, and so on, and have conditionally suppressed them). If you have multiple conditionally suppressed page footers and don't check this option, Crystal Reports will leave enough vertical space for all the combined page footers, even if they are not all displayed. This option is only visible if the main Page Footer area is selected (not Page Header a, b, and so forth).
Read Only	Prevents formatting, moving, or sizing of all objects in the report section. This is, in essence, the same as selecting all objects in the section and using the Lock Format and Lock Size And Position options from the Formatting Toolbar or Format Editor.
Relative Positions	When selected, this will automatically move any objects that are placed to the right of a cross-tab or OLAP grid in the section, according to the size of the cross-tab or OLAP grid. For example, if you place report fields or text objects to the right of a cross-tab, the cross-tab may very well print right over the top of the other object, as it grows horizontally to match the data it shows. By checking this option, you assure that any objects to the right of the cross-tab or OLAP grid will automatically move right to avoid being overprinted.

TABLE 7-1   Section Expert Common Tab Formatting Properties *(continued)*

In Crystal Reports 2008, options for controlling page breaks and orientation are contained on the Paging tab. Note that the properties will vary slightly, some new properties may appear, and some won't be available, depending on which section you select. For example, the New Page Before property doesn't make much sense for a page header section, so it will be grayed out when a page header is selected. Table 7-2 explains the different section formatting properties available in the Section Expert's Paging tab.

TIP *In addition to the ability to change page orientation section by section, Crystal Reports 2008 introduces the CurrentPageOrientation formula language function. This allows you, in a conditional formatting formula, to determine the current page orientation as the report is formatting and change some aspect of report behavior (page margins, for example), based on whether the current page is displaying in portrait or landscape orientation. More information on CurrentPageOrientation can be found in the appendix.*

Property	Function
New Page Before	Starts a new page before printing this section. This is useful in a group header if you want each group to start on its own page, or in a form letter if the entire letter is in the Details section and each letter should print on its own page.
Reset Page Number After	Resets the page number back to 1 after printing this section. This is useful in a group footer if you want each group to have its own set of page numbers, regardless of the total number of pages on the report. This also resets the Total Page Count field.
New Page After – End of Section	Starts a new page after printing this section. This is useful in a group footer if you want the next group to start on its own page. If the Details section is selected, the End Of Section check box performs the same function as New Page After for non-Details sections.
New Page After – Visible Records **(New in Crystal Reports 2008)**	This option, which only appears if the Details section is selected, will advance to the next page after the specified number of "visible" records have displayed. Visible records are those that actually appear on the report—if a conditional suppression formula has been supplied that might not print certain details sections, only details sections that actually print will count toward the visible record count. This option may be helpful if you wish to limit the number of records that print on any one page.
Orientation **(New in Crystal Reports 2008)**	Allows selection of an alternate page orientation for the selected section. The default will use the same page orientation specified in the File | Printer Setup dialog box. Choosing Portrait or Landscape will override the default setting and change the page orientation for the selected report section. Note that even if you don't specify a New Page Before or New Page After choice, changing page orientation will start the selected report section on a new page, as it's impossible to mix different page orientations on the same page. This option is not available for a Page Header or Page Footer section.

TABLE 7-2 Section Expert Paging Tab Formatting Properties

You'll also notice Conditional Formula buttons for many properties on the Common and Paging tabs. These properties can be set conditionally with a Boolean formula, if necessary (an exception is the Visible Records property on the Paging tab, which must be supplied a numeric value). There are many uses for both absolute and conditional properties. Here are some common examples.

Starting a Group on Its Own Page

Checking New Page Before in a group header or New Page After in a group footer (but not both) will cause each group to start on a new page. There is one problem with setting this property absolutely—you can end up with "stranded" pages. If you set New Page Before on a group header, you'll often encounter a stranded first page, because the report header will print and Crystal Reports will skip to the next page before printing the first group header. Conversely, if you set New Page After on a group footer, you'll often encounter a stranded last page, because the last group footer will be followed by a page break before the report footer prints.

To avoid these pitfalls, you have two choices:

- Suppress the report header and/or report footer if you have no data in them to show.
- Set the New Page Before or New Page After property conditionally.

If you have material in the report header or report footer that you want to print on the same page as the first group header or last group footer, you must do some conditional formatting. To avoid a stranded first page, you can use a conditional formula to set the New Page Before property only on the second and subsequent groups—the first group will stay on the first page with the report header. Since the first group header will print at the same time the first record is printing, you can use the following Boolean conditional formula for New Page Before:

```
Not OnFirstRecord
```

To avoid a stranded last page, you want a new page after every group footer *except the last one*. Since the last group footer will only occur on the last record of the report, you can use this conditional formula for New Page After:

```
Not OnLastRecord
```

Printing an Invoice Total at the Bottom of the Page

You may be creating invoices grouped by invoice number, or statements grouped by customer number. You want the invoice or statement total, located in the group footer, to print at the bottom of the page, regardless of how many detail records print. Crystal Reports' normal behavior is to print the group footer immediately following the last detail record. If there are only a few invoice items or statement lines, the total will print high up the page, right after the last detail line. If you want the total to print at the bottom of the page in this situation, check the Print at Bottom of Page property for the group footer.

Starting Page Numbers Over for Each New Group

You might have a large report grouped by department that you want to "burst" apart and distribute to each individual department. Initially, you'll want to make sure to use the New

Page Before property with the group header or the New Page After property with the group footer so that you won't ever have the end of one department appearing on the same page as the beginning of the next.

However, you also don't want to confuse those who may look at page numbers on later groups in the report. Even though a page may be the first one for the IT department, it will probably have a much larger page number than 1. Simply check the Reset Page Number After property for the department group footer. Page numbers will then start over at 1 for each department.

Reducing the Vertical Size of the Page, Regardless of Printer Paper Size Settings

Reports displayed in a web page (perhaps via a custom Visual Studio .NET or Java web application, or with the BusinessObjects Enterprise product family) may not lend themselves to a full 8½-inch page height (or whatever other height may be chosen in the File | Printer Setup dialog box). Prior to Crystal Reports 2008, a report page viewed on the web always displayed with a fixed height based on the printer page size setting, regardless of how much data actually appeared on the page. If less than a full page of data was included on a page, white space appeared between the last line of data and the bottom of the page.

The new Clamp Page Footer option, available in the Common tab when the Page Footer is selected, allows the bottom of the page (represented by the Page Footer) to appear immediately after the last report section showing data. No white space is added to the report to create a full page height. This allows online reports to only take up only the vertical space actually required to show report data.

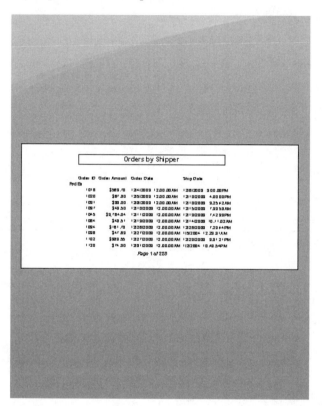

NOTE *Choosing this option for a report that will actually be printed on a printer, or exported to a page-oriented file format such as PDF, may result in unacceptable display, as contents of the page footer (such as page numbers) will appear immediately below report data, and not at the bottom of the physical page.*

Changing Color for Entire Sections

The Color tab in the Section Expert, shown in Figure 7-2, lets you change the background color for an entire section, separate from any color formatting that individual objects in the section may have.

If you check the Background Color property, you can then choose from various colors from the color palette below it. You may also select More and choose from a wide array of additional colors from the standard Windows color dialog box. This will set the background color for the entire section. This lets you highlight entire sections with different colors, if

FIGURE 7-2 Setting the background color for a section

you choose—for example, a report with the group footer section showing a different background color:

Creating a "Banded" Report

Notice the Conditional Formula button on the Color tab. This lets you set the background color conditionally, which can be helpful if you want to base a background color on some particular condition.

Mainframe reports often were printed on "green bar" or "blue bar" paper with alternating shades of color and white. This was designed to make columns of numbers easy to follow across the page. Now that many PC-based reports are printed by laser printers on plain paper, you must create your own "banded" reports if your reports would benefit from this kind of look.

Simply giving the details section a silver background color isn't visually appealing, as shown here:

However, setting every other details section to silver provides a good way to help report readers follow columns of material across the page. You can set the background color conditionally to accomplish this. Use the following conditional formula:

```
If RecordNumber Mod 2 = 0 Then
    crSilver
Else
    crNoColor
```

This uses several built-in Crystal Reports functions. The Mod function (which performs Modulus arithmetic) divides one number by another but returns the *remainder* of the division operation, not the result of the division. The RecordNumber built-in function simply counts records consecutively, starting at 1. Therefore, *every other* record number, when divided by 2, will return 0 as the remainder. This will alternate the details section background color for every record.

You can make modifications to this formula to shade more than just every other line. If you want *every two* lines shaded, you could change the formula slightly:

```
If RecordNumber Mod 4 In [1,2] Then
    Color(187,219,242)
Else
    crNoColor
```

This divides the record number by 4 and checks for remainders of 1 or 2. This will be true for every two records. The resulting color will be a light pastel cyan, based on the Red-Green-Blue (RGB) color combination supplied with the Crystal Reports Color function. The result is shown here:

TIP *Determining the three color numbers to supply to the Color function is easy. Just choose absolute color formatting somewhere in the Section Expert and click More to display the Windows color palette. Use this dialog box to find the desired custom color you wish to set for the report section. Then, note the Red, Green, and Blue numbers that appear in the dialog box. Cancel the Windows color palette dialog box, return to the conditional color formula, and supply those three numbers to the Color function.*

You probably get the general idea of how this works. You can now modify the formula in any number of ways to change the way background shading works. You may consider that when setting the background color of a section, as well as background colors for individual objects, using NoColor instead of White may be preferable to indicate a normal color. By using White, you will have solid white colors that can sometimes look unpleasant in combination with other solid colors. If you use NoColor, you often achieve a certain amount of transparency that will look better when mixing colors on the report or when using watermarks (discussed later in the chapter).

Creating Summary and Drill-Down Reports

A *details report* shows every individual detail record in the database. This may often be preferable for certain listings or smaller transaction-type reports. Often, however, a viewer will only want to see subtotals, counts, averages, or other summary information for certain groups on the report. The details information used to arrive at those summaries isn't as important. This calls for a *summary report*.

In its simplest form, a summary report is a report with one or more groups with the details section hidden or suppressed. Consider Figure 7-3, a details report of orders, grouped by customer.

FIGURE 7-3   Orders detail report

This shows every order for the customer, with order count and order amount subtotals appearing in the group footer. While this may be useful for a report viewer concerned about individual orders, the sales manager or account representative may often just be interested in the summary information for each customer—just the *bottom line*. All the order details just get in the way of their analysis.

In this case, simply hiding or suppressing the details section will create a much more meaningful report for these viewers. You can hide or suppress the details section from the Section Expert. As a shortcut, there are Hide and Suppress options available right in the section pop-up menu, as well. Just right-click the shaded details section name at the left of the Design or Preview tab and choose Hide (Drill-Down OK) or Suppress (No Drill-Down) from the pop-up menu.

The details section will simply disappear from the Preview tab, while the group header and footer still show up. Figure 7-4 shows the resulting summary report, which is much more succinct and meaningful to a viewer looking at the big picture.

If you later want to change your report back to a details report, you need to have the details section reappear. Just display the Section Expert by using the toolbar button or pull-down menu option. Select the details section and turn off the Hide or Suppress property. You can also display the Design tab and right-click the shaded area to the left of the screen

FIGURE 7-4 Orders summary report

where the details section is hidden or suppressed. To redisplay the details section, choose the opposite of the Suppress or Hide option you initially set.

TIP *You can choose how a hidden or suppressed section appears in the Design tab. Choose File | Options from the pull-down menus and look for the Show Hidden Sections option in the Design View section of the Layout tab. If this is checked (the default), hidden or suppressed sections will still appear in the Design tab, but they will have gray shading. If you turn this option off, they will only show the bottom border of the hidden or suppressed section in the Design tab.*

Choosing whether to hide or suppress a section determines whether or not you want a report viewer to drill down into the section. Also, note that the Suppress property can be conditionally set in the Section Expert, while the Hide property cannot.

Drill-Down Reports

One of the most powerful features of an online reporting tool like Crystal Reports is interactive reporting. You may be creating a report to distribute to a large audience via a Web page in the BusinessObjects Enterprise software family (covered in Part II of this book), or as part of a custom web or Windows application (covered in Chapter 19). A truly useful report will initially present viewers with higher-level summary or total information. If the viewer sees a number or other characteristic of the report that interests them, you want them to be able to drill down into just that particular area.

NOTE *Drill-down is an interactive feature only applicable to viewers looking at a Crystal Report in its "native" format. Drill-down isn't available in any reports exported to another format, such as Word or Excel. And obviously, drill-down isn't a feature that applies to reports printed on paper!*

In its simplest form, a drill-down report can be created by hiding the details section (hence, the Drill-Down OK notation alongside the Hide property) in a report that has one or more groups. When you point at the group name field, or a subtotal or summary object in a group header or footer, you'll notice your mouse cursor change to a magnifying glass, or *drill-down cursor.* When you double-click, a separate drill-down tab will appear, showing the group header, footer, and details sections for that group. You can then navigate to the main Preview tab to see the summary report, or back to individual drill-down tabs to see the details information. You can double-click in the Preview tab as many times as you want in order to create additional drill-down tabs.

More complicated drill-down reports can be created by using multiple levels of grouping, along with creative use of section hiding. Figure 7-5 shows a drill-down report containing a details section and three groups: country, region, and city. Initially the report just shows countries and their totals. If you drill down on a country, you'll find region subtotals for that country. Drilling down on a region will show city totals. And finally, drilling down on a city total will show individual orders placed from that city.

TIP *Make note of the Show All Headers On Drill Down option. When you turn this option on (it's off by default), your report will display all higher levels of page and group headers when you drill into a group, instead of showing just the previous level of group headers. Choose this option for the current report only by selecting File | Report Options. To choose the option for all new reports in the future, set the option on the Reporting tab after choosing File | Options. While this may provide better visibility for certain reports, it often displays too much data in many drill-down reporting situations. In these cases, leave the option turned off and use techniques described later in this chapter under "Creative Use of Column Headings and Group Headers in Drill-Down Reports" for precise drill-down header control.*

Click the Design, Preview, or
any drill-down tab to display it

Click the *x* on a tab to close that tab

Click to print or export the contents of the current tab

Moves among the tabs, if there
are too many to display at once

The Groups portion of the preview panel shows the drill-down hierarchy

Double-click to drill down when you see the magnifying glass

FIGURE 7-5 A more complex drill-down report

If you're interacting with a report, it's important to remember what will print or export if you click the Print or Export button on the Standard toolbar, or choose File | Print or File | Export from the pull-down menus. Only what's shown in the current drill-down tab (or Preview tab) will print or export. If you want to just print one drill-down tab, choose the drill-down tab and then click Print. If you want to print all the summary information in the main Preview tab, make sure it's selected before you print or export. If you want to print or export both summary and details information *in the same report,* you must either display the details section and print from the Preview tab, or create a separate report more appropriate for printing.

Using Tool Tip text (under the common section of the Format Editor) can help a viewer determine what will happen when they double-click an object. By either typing text into the Tool Tip text box directly, or by creating a string formula with the Tool Tip text Conditional Formula button in the Format Editor, you can give a viewer more information about what the object contains. For example, this tooltip will appear when you enter the following Tool Tip text conditional formula. This formula is added to the Tool Tip Text property of the summary field in the Country group footer:

20🔍	Subtotal:	$28,813.
Double-click to see regional totals within Austria		
1	Subtotal:	$659.

```
"Double-click to see regional totals within " &
   GroupName ({Customer.Country})
```

Creative Use of Column Headings and Group Headers in Drill-Down Reports

If you leave Crystal Reports' default column headings in the page header and simply hide or suppress lower-level group headers in your drill-down reports, you may get undesirable results when the viewer sees the initial Preview tab.

The first problem will be the appearance of column headings in the Preview tab above the first group header, but with no matching detail records. But when you eventually drill down to the details level, the page header won't appear, so the viewer won't see the column headings.

There are two ways of resolving this problem, depending on how many levels of grouping exist on the report. If you only have one level of grouping, perform the following steps:

1. Move the column headings from the page header to the group header, either above or below the group name field (or remove the group name field altogether), depending on how you want the drill-down tab to appear.

2. Copy the group name field from the group header into the group footer.

3. Hide the group header along with the details section.

This way, the summary report will just show one line per group until you drill down. Then, the group header (containing the column headings) will appear inside the drill-down tab, along with the details sections.

However, if you have more than one level of grouping, the previous technique won't work properly—you'll see the column headings appear over and over again at the last group level. In this case, use this approach:

1. Create a second details section (Details b) and move the column headings into it.

2. Swap Details b and Details a so that the column headings are on top of the details section that contains database fields.

3. Select the text objects that comprise the column headings. You may multiselect them with CTRL-click or an elastic box. Using the Format Editor, choose the Suppress If Duplicated formatting option.

4. Using the Section Expert, choose the Suppress Blank Section formatting option for Details a.

This technique, while a little more time-consuming, provides perfect results. When the lowest level of grouping appears, there will be no column headings (because they've been moved to the details section). But when you drill down to the details level, the column headings only show up once at the top of the drill-down tab, because of the Suppress If Duplicated/Suppress Blank Section formatting combinations.

If you simply choose the Hide (Drill-Down OK) formatting option on group header sections, your report may suffer from extra sets of group headers that appear when you drill down. For example, if you drill down into a country group to see all the regions within the country, the region group header will print before every group footer. To solve this problem, you may try to suppress the region group header so that it will never show up. However, when you then drill into a region group to see cities within the region, the region group header won't print at the top of the list of cities.

In theory, you'd like the region group header to show up when you've drilled into the region group to see cities, but *not* show up when you're looking at the region group at its summary level. But, what conditional formula can you use to suppress the region group header so that it only shows up when there isn't a country group header there as well?

Crystal Reports features the *DrillDownGroupLevel* function in the Crystal Reports formula language. This function allows you to test for a certain drill-down level and conditionally suppress a group header (or perform any other functions or calculations, for that matter), depending on the level of the drill-down. Making use of this function to conditionally suppress group headers will allow you the ultimate control over your report behavior when the viewer drills down.

Using the previous Country/Region/City drill-down scenario as an example, you suppress the region group header (Group Header 2) conditionally, so that it won't appear when you drill down to the country level, but will appear when you drill down to the region level. This is simply a matter of using this formula to conditionally suppress Group Header 2:

```
DrillDownGroupLevel = 1
```

This will suppress the group header when a Country drill-down occurs (level 1), but will not suppress it when a Region drill-down occurs (level 2). You may also use the DrillDownGroupLevel function to determine if the main Preview tab is being displayed. If the DrillDownGroupLevel function returns a zero, no drill-down is occurring at all.

Examples of the drill-down techniques discussed here can be found in a sample report on this book's companion Web site. Look for the Drill Down.RPT sample report at CrystalBook.com.

Multiple-Column Reports for Labels and Listings

Crystal Reports is designed to replace much of the repetitive printing that you may have used a word processor for in the past. Immediate uses include form letters and mailing labels. You can also use the multicolumn feature of Crystal Reports to create newspaper-style columns in your reports. If you have just a few fields that you'd like to print in columnar form, the Section Expert provides the necessary section formatting.

To create mailing labels in Crystal Reports, use the Mailing Label Report Wizard from the Start page or File | New menu when first creating a new report. This wizard takes you step-by-step through the process of choosing the table and fields that make up your mailing label, and choosing from a predefined list of continuous-feed and laser printer labels. Figure 7-6 shows the section of this wizard where you may select predefined labels or make fine adjustments to label specifications.

On the Layout tab, you determine the specifics of the columns you want to create. Although you might expect to see a "number of columns" setting, this is actually determined by page margins (set with File | Page Setup), the width of the details section, and the horizontal gap between details. For example, if you have quarter-inch margins with standard letter-size paper in portrait orientation, you'll have 8 full inches of printable space. If you choose a details-size width of 2.5 inches and a horizontal gap of a quarter inch, you'll have three evenly spaced columns with a quarter inch on all sides.

Since there is no similar expert for creating newspaper-style reports, you have to create such reports using the Blank Report option and the Section Expert. Recall from Table 7-1 one of the Section Expert's formatting properties, Format with Multiple Columns. This property is only available for the details section—it won't even appear in the Section Expert if you have any other section selected. Once you check this property, the Layout tab appears in the Section Expert, as shown in Figure 7-7.

FIGURE 7-6   Mail Label Report Creation Wizard

Specify width of the column (height is unused here—details section height is determined in the Design tab)

Specify horizontal gap (gutter) between columns and vertical gap between details sections

Choose the order in which to print details sections

Choose whether to print group headers and footers in the same columnar format as the details sections

FIGURE 7-7   Section Expert for multicolumn report

When you choose to format the details section with multiple columns, the Design tab changes slightly. You'll notice that the width of the details section's bottom border shrinks to equal the width you set in the Layout tab. The other sections of the report retain the full width of the page.

The exception to this rule occurs when you check the Format Groups With Multiple Column check box on the Layout tab. In this case, all group headers and footers take on the same width as the details section. This can make a marked difference in the appearance of your report, depending on the size of your groups. As a general rule, not formatting groups with multiple columns will cause smaller groups to print only in one column on the left side of the page. Usually, the only small groups that print across multiple columns are ones that start at the bottom of the page. Figure 7-8 shows the difference. You'll typically experience more predictable behavior by formatting groups with multiple columns.

Using Multiple Sections

To be precise, the five default sections that first appear in a new report, and any additional group headers and footers that are added later, are referred to as *areas.* This is in contrast to

the term "section," which really refers to "subareas." Because Crystal Reports lets you create multiple occurrences of the same area, such as multiple details or multiple group headers, each of the individual occurrences is called a *section.* Creating multiple sections can be accomplished from the Section Expert or by using the pop-up menu that appears when you right-click in the gray area on the left side of the screen.

To insert an additional details section, for example, right-click in the details shaded area on the left side of the Design tab and choose Insert Section Below from the pop-up menu. Or, from the Section Expert, select the area that you wish to duplicate and click Insert. You'll see the details area split into two sections: Details a and Details b. Once you've created multiple sections in an area, the pop-up menu (shown here) and Section Expert (shown in Figure 7-9) take on a great deal of additional capability.

TIP *You can also rearrange the order in which sections appear right in the Design tab. Simply point to the gray section name on the left of the screen, hold down the mouse button, and drag the section you wish to move—the mouse cursor will change to a "hand." Drop the section in its new location in the same area. Although the section contents will swap, the consecutive lettering will not change—the first section will still be lettered a; the second, b; and so on.*

You can insert as many sections in an area as you wish—there can be Details a, b, c, d, and on and on (when Crystal Reports runs out of letters, it starts doubling them up, as in "Details ab"). Any area can consist of multiple sections. Nothing prevents you from having three report headers, five details sections, two group footer #1s, or any other combination.

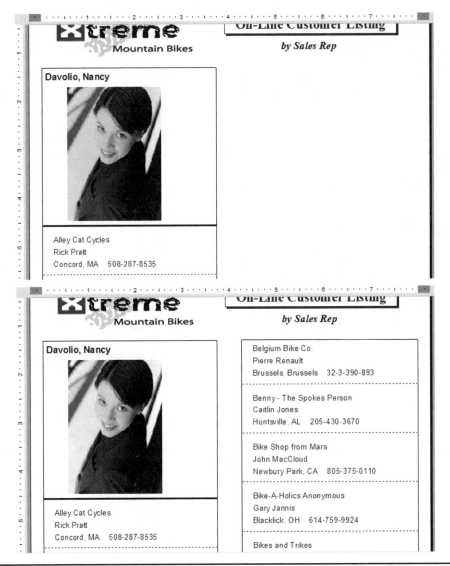

FIGURE 7-8 Report groups formatted without and with multiple columns

Once you've created the multiple sections, you can add objects to any of the sections. You can even add the same object to some, or all, of them. When the report prints, the sections will simply print one right after the other, with the objects showing up one below the other. Probably the biggest question you have right now is, "What's the benefit of multiple sections anyway? Everything just prints as though it were in one bigger section!"

Deletes the current section, and all objects in it

Merges the current section with the section below it. All objects in the section below will be placed in the current section.

Creates a new section directly below the currently selected one

Rearranges the order in which sections appear

FIGURE 7-9   Manipulating multiple sections in the Section Expert

Figure 7-10 is a great example of the benefit of multiple sections. This shows portions of a form letter based on the Customer table from the sample XTRE ME Mountain Bike database available from the book's companion web site, CrystalBook.com. Notice that the letter consists of four different details sections. Details a contains the logo, print date, customer name, and address 1; Details b contains address 2; Details c contains the city-state-ZIP and salutation; and Details d contains the body of the form letter. When you preview the report, it just shows the details sections one on top of the other, as though everything were in one big details section.

But what will happen to a customer with no address 2 data? You would see an empty line where the Address 2 database field would appear. This behavior, again, is identical to what you'd expect if you had put all the objects in one tall details section.

Here's the benefit: you may *conditionally suppress* individual sections—in this case, Details b—so that they appear or disappear according to your specifications. To eliminate the blank line that appears when there's nothing in address 2, format Details b with Suppress Blank Section. If the objects contained in it all contain empty values, the section will not appear at all. You can also use the Conditional Formula button next to the Suppress property to suppress according to any condition you need.

FIGURE 7-10   Multiple details sections

These techniques, and others that make good use of multiple sections and conditional formatting for form letters, are illustrated in the sample Form Letter.rpt report. Find it on this book's companion web site at CrystalBook.com.

TIP   *The more you work with areas and sections, the more you may notice the large amount of space the area and section names take up on the left side of the Design tab. If you wish to have more space for actual report objects, you can change the way Crystal Reports shows section names. Choose File | Options and check Short Section Names in the Design View section of the Layout tab. You can also right-click in a shaded section name in the Design tab and choose Show Short Section Names from the pop-up menu. "Report Header" will now be abbreviated "RH," "Page Header a" will become "PHa," and so on. You'll now have more room to work with actual report objects.*

Conditionally Suppressing Sections

There may be times when conditionally suppressing a single section is beneficial (for example, you may wish to conditionally suppress a single group header, depending on DrillDownGroupLevel). But, conditional suppression really comes in handy with multiple section reports. Using the Conditional Formula button next to the Suppress property lets you supply a Boolean formula to determine when the section appears or doesn't appear. Consider the following examples.

Printing a Bonus Message for Certain Records

You are designing a list of orders by salesperson. You want a bonus message and a "lots o' money" graphic to appear below the order if it exceeds $2,500. However, if the order doesn't exceed the bonus level, you *don't* want the large blank space to appear where the graphic and message are located. If you just use the Format Editor to conditionally suppress the graphic and text object containing the message, they won't appear, but the empty space still will.

Simply create a Details b section and place the graphic and text object in it. Then, suppress Details b when the bonus isn't met, using the following conditional formula for the Suppress property:

```
{Orders.Order Amount} < 2500
```

Figure 7-11 shows the result.

Printing a Different Page Header on Page 2 and Later

You may wish to print a title page or other large page header on page 1 of the report, perhaps containing a logo and large formatted title. However, on subsequent pages of the report, you want a less flashy header with smaller type and no graphic. You want column headings and the print date and time to show up on all pages of the report, including the first.

This presents a special reporting problem. The flashy page header can simply be put in the report header section. It will then appear only on the first page. However, if you put the smaller report title in the page header along with the column headings and other information, it will appear on page 1 along with the report header. You can use the Format Editor to suppress the object containing the smaller header, but then extra white space will appear on page 1.

FIGURE 7-11 Multiple details sections with conditional suppression

The solution is to create a second page header section. Put the smaller report title in Page Header a and put the column headings and print date/time in Page Header b. Then, conditionally suppress Page Header b so that it won't show up on page 1. Here's the conditional formula, which uses the PageNumber built-in function:

```
PageNumber = 1
```

Printing Odd and Even Page Headers or Footers

You may be printing your report on a "duplex" laser printer that can print on both sides of the paper. Or, you may want to photocopy your report from one to two sides and place it in a three-ring binder or other bound format. Crystal Reports lets you create separate odd and even page headers and footers to add a real page-published look to your report.

Simply create separate Page Headers a and b (and, perhaps, Page Footers a and b). Place the appropriate material in each section and position it properly for odd/even appearance. Now, conditionally suppress the sections. The sections containing the material for odd page numbers will be suppressed for even page numbers with the following conditional formula:

```
PageNumber Mod 2 = 0
```

Also, the sections containing the material for even page numbers will be suppressed for odd page numbers with the following conditional formula:

```
PageNumber Mod 2 = 1
```

These formulas use the PageNumber built-in function illustrated previously. In addition, they use the Mod function, which will indicate whether a page number is even or odd (even page numbers divided by 2 return a remainder of 0, and odd page numbers return a remainder of 1, as explained earlier in the chapter).

Underlaying Sections

The Section Expert includes the Underlay Following Sections property. As described earlier, in Table 7-1, this property prints the underlaid section in its usual position but prints the following sections right over the top. Initially, this may seem of limited usefulness. How readable will a report be if sections are printing right over the top of earlier sections?

Look at Figure 7-12 to get an idea. This report includes a large, light "Draft" graphic that has been placed in the page header. When Underlay Following Sections is checked for the page header in the Section Expert, all the other sections will print right over the top of the page header, creating the watermark effect.

If you want to include column headings in the page header, along with the watermark, you experience a problem. The watermark will be underlaid as you desire, but so will the column headings! The solution, as you might expect, is to add a Page Header b. Place the watermark graphic in one page header section and format it to Underlay Following Sections.

FIGURE 7-12   Using Underlay Following Section to print a watermark

Place the column headings in the other page header section and don't underlay it. Which page header you place the objects in will d etermine whether or not the column headings are underlaid. If you put the watermark in Page Header a (which is formatted to Underlay Following Sections) and the column headings in Page Header b (not underlaid), the watermark will underlay the column headings. If you choose the other way around, the column headings won't be underlaid.

NOTE *When you underlay a section, all sections will print over the top of it, until Crystal Reports comes to its "companion" section, which will not underlay it. For example, if you underlay a page header, all sections will print on top until Crystal Reports gets to the matching page footer. If you underlay Group Header b, all other sections will print on top until the report hits Group Footer b, which will not be underlaid.*

You can also use the Underlay Following Sections feature to place maps or charts beside the data they refer to, rather than on top or bottom of the related data. Figure 7-13 shows a report containing a chart. Notice that the chart appears alongside the data that the chart refers to, rather than above. The chart is contained in a second report header (Report Header b), but the chart object has been moved to the right of the section, and the report header section is formatted to Underlay Following Sections.

Placing the chart in Report Header b permits the report title and logo to remain in Report Header a (which isn't underlaid), so that the report title and logo aren't also underlaid along with the chart.

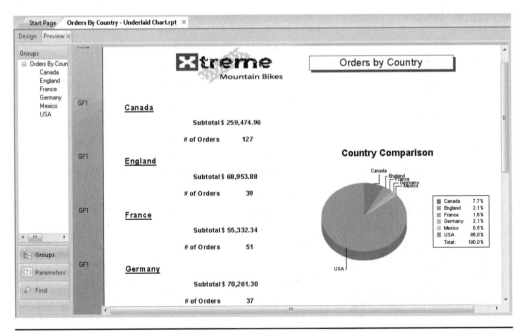

FIGURE 7-13   Chart in an underlaid section

TIP *Underlay Following Sections can also be handy when dealing with subreports (covered in Chapter 12) that may take up extra vertical space, even if you choose to suppress all subreport objects. Since you can't suppress the entire section a subreport appears in to eliminate the vertical space it occupies (suppressing a section containing a subreport will not allow the subreport to process), underlaying the section containing the subreport will eliminate any vertical space it may occupy while still allowing it to process.*

Analyzing with Cross-Tabs

Database report writers and spreadsheet programs are typically considered to be two completely separate products. The database report writer sorts and selects data very well, while the spreadsheet is great for analyzing, totaling, and trending in a compact row-and-column format. Crystal Reports provides a tool that, to a limited extent, brings the two features together: the cross-tab object. A *cross-tab* is a row-and-column object that looks similar to a spreadsheet. It summarizes data by using at least three fields in the database: a row field, a column field, and a summarized field. For each intersection of the row and column fields, the summarized field is aggregated (summed, counted, or subjected to some other type of calculation) in a "cell."

Consider two common summary reports. The first summary report shows total sales in dollars for each state in the United States. The second report shows total units sold by product type. If a marketing analyst wanted to combine these two reports to more closely analyze both sales in dollars by state and units sold by product type, you would be limited in what you could offer with the standard grouped summary report.

You can create a report, similar to that shown in Figure 8-1 (initially grouped by state, and within state grouped by product type), that provides the information the analyst desires. But if the analyst wanted to compare total mountain bikes sold in the country with total kids' bikes sold in the country, this report would make the process very difficult. Product type is the inner group, so there are no overall totals by it. Also, comparing Alabama totals with Illinois totals would be difficult, because they would be several pages apart on the report.

This scenario is a perfect example of where a cross-tab object would be useful. A cross-tab is a compact, row-and-column report that can compare subtotals and summaries by two or more different database fields. Whenever someone requests data to be shown by one thing and by another, it's a cross-tab candidate. Just listen for the "by this and by that" request. Figure 8-2 will probably be much more useful to the analyst.

Creating a Cross-Tab Object

When you look at a cross-tab, it's tempting to think of it as an entire report unto itself, much as an Excel spreadsheet is entirely independent. In fact, a cross-tab is just an object that resides in an existing report section. Even when you choose the Cross-Tab Report and Wizard choices from the Start page or the File | New menu item, Crystal Reports just

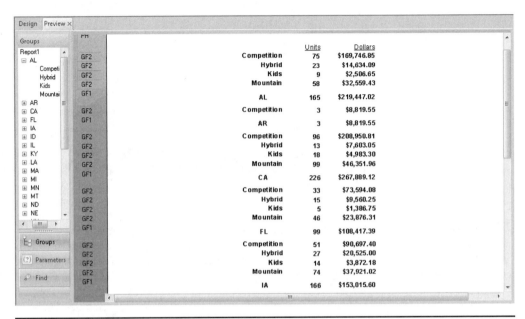

FIGURE 8-1 Standard summary report with two groups

	Total	Competition	Hybrid	Kids	Mountain
Total	2,585.00 $2,804,815.67	917 $1,962,965.54	397 $272,789.66	210 $57,894.96	1,061 $511,165.51
AL	165.00 $219,447.02	75.00 $169,746.85	23.00 $14,634.09	9.00 $2,506.65	58.00 $32,559.43
AR	3.00 $8,819.55	3.00 $8,819.55	0.00 $0.00	0.00 $0.00	0.00 $0.00
CA	226.00 $267,889.12	96.00 $208,950.81	13.00 $7,603.05	18.00 $4,983.30	99.00 $46,351.96
FL	99.00 $108,417.39	33.00 $73,594.08	15.00 $9,560.25	5.00 $1,386.75	46.00 $23,876.31
IA	166.00 $153,015.60	51.00 $90,697.40	27.00 $20,525.00	14.00 $3,872.18	74.00 $37,921.02
ID	156.00 $166,838.79	54.00 $117,076.14	34.00 $21,824.45	18.00 $4,962.62	50.00 $22,975.58
IL	365.00 $379,353.54	119.00 $263,124.29	38.00 $25,855.88	28.00 $7,689.28	180.00 $82,684.09
KY	1.00 $313.36	0.00 $0.00	0.00 $0.00	0.00 $0.00	1.00 $313.36
LA	2.00 $548.70	0.00 $0.00	0.00 $0.00	2.00 $548.70	0.00 $0.00
MA	105.00	38.00	18.00	5.00	44.00

FIGURE 8-2 Cross-tab showing units/dollars by region and by product type

creates a new report, placing a cross-tab object in the report header. You can create more than one cross-tab per report, if you wish. In fact, you can even copy an existing cross-tab and put it in several different sections of the same report. It's just an object, like a text object, chart, or database field.

A cross-tab can exist by itself on a report (as evidenced by the Cross-Tab Report Wizard, which creates a report containing nothing but a cross-tab), or it can be placed on a report that already contains fields in the details section, as well as one or more groups. The report can be completely functional in every respect before the cross-tab is added—the cross-tab is simply dropped in.

The first step in creating a cross-tab is to ensure that the tables you've chosen and linked for your report contain enough data to populate the cross-tab. If, for example, you want to look at order totals for the years 2004, 2005, 2006, and 2007 by state, make sure you choose tables that include the order amount, the year or date the order was placed, and the state of the customer who placed the order. While this may seem rather obvious, you may not have enough data to adequately populate your cross-tab if you don't think ahead carefully.

You may or may not want to use actual report fields as cross-tab fields. If the fields are already on the report, you can add them to the cross-tab object. Or if you've added completely different fields to the report, you can still base the cross-tab on other fields that exist in the tables you chose when creating the report, even if those fields haven't been placed anywhere else on the report.

You can use the Cross-Tab Report Wizard option from the Start page, the Cross Tab Report option from the File | New menu, or add a cross-tab to an existing report you've already created. To begin with the Cross-Tab Report Creation Wizard, simply choose it from the Start page, or choose File | New | Cross-Tab Report. In addition to the familiar Data, Link, Chart, and Record Selection dialogs seen in other report wizards, the Cross-Tab Wizard displays a Cross-Tab row/column dialog and a Grid Style dialog similar to those discussed in more detail later in the chapter.

If you've already created another report using another wizard or the Blank Report option, you may insert a cross-tab object whenever you want. To create a cross-tab object, it's best to select the Design tab first. Although you can place a cross-tab on the report in the Preview tab, you may not be able to accurately tell where it's being placed. In the Design tab, there's no question. Click the Insert Cross-Tab button on the Insert Tools toolbar, or choose Insert | Cross-Tab from the pull-down menus. An object outline will be attached to your cursor. Drop the outline where you'd like the cross-tab to appear. You can drop the cross-tab object in the report header or footer, or in a group header or footer. Cross-tabs can't be placed in the details section or in a page header or footer—you'll get a "no-drop" cursor (a circle with a line through it) if you try to position the cross-tab in these sections.

Once you've dropped the empty cross-tab object in the desired reports section, you may drag fields directly from the Field Explorer onto the Cross-Tab object to determine your row, column, and summarized field selections.

Begin by choosing the field you wish to appear as the cross-tab row or column field. Drag it from the Field Explorer to the right of the Total column (to make it the column field) or below the Total row (to make it the row field). The mouse cursor will appear as a piece of paper with a plus sign, and a small arrow will appear beside the column total or below the row total. Release the mouse button to drop the field in the cross-tab. You may add additional row or column fields (when using multiple rows or columns, a cross-tab will create a hierarchy between the two fields) by dragging them from the Field Explorer. Drop a field above an existing column or to the left of an existing row to place that field at the top of the hierarchy. Or, drop a field below an existing column or to the right of an existing row to place it at the bottom of the hierarchy (hierarchical relationships based on multiple row and column fields are discussed later in the chapter).

Once you've chosen row and columns fields, drag the field you wish to summarize (sum, average, and so forth) on top of the Insert Summarized Field cell. The cell will turn a different shade when you have the field properly positioned. Release the mouse button to drop the field in the summary cell. As with rows and columns, you may include more than one summary field in a cross-tab (for example, you may choose to summarize both quantity and extended price for the cross-tab). Just drag the additional field on top of the existing summary in a summary cell. The additional summary will be added to the cross-tab.

You're not limited to dragging and dropping fields from the Field Explorer onto the cross-tab object. You can also drag a field or formula from another location on the Design tab onto the cross-tab object, which will add it to the cross-tab and remove it from its original location. If you wish to add an existing Design tab report field or formula to the cross-tab while also leaving it in its original position, hold down the CTRL key while dragging the object to the cross-tab.

NOTE *A default behavior of using the drag-and-drop cross-tab creation method is that a total row and column will appear before any data rows or columns, rather than after them. If this is not the desired appearance for your cross-tab, select the desired row or column name object in the cross-tab, right-click, and uncheck Totals On Top from the Row Grand Totals pop-up menu choice, or Totals On Left from the Column Grand Totals pop-up menu choice. You can also display the Cross-Tab Expert (discussed later in the chapter) and turn off the Row Totals On Left and Column Totals On Top options on the Customize Style tab.*

In addition to the ability to drag and drop fields directly on the cross-tab object, and to control cross-tab behavior from right-click pop-up menus, complete cross-tab control is available with the *Cross-Tab Expert*. First, you must select the entire cross-tab object (you can't display the Cross-Tab Expert if you've selected an individual cross-tab field or summary). Do this by clicking either the small white space in the upper-left corner of the cross-tab (above the first row and to the left of the first column) or one of the grid lines between cells. You'll know you've selected the entire cross-tab if the status bar displays "Cross-Tab" (you can select the cross-tab in either the Design tab or the Preview tab). Then, choose Format | Cross-Tab Expert from the pull-down menus, or right-click the cross-tab and choose Cross-Tab Expert from the pop-up menu. The Cross-Tab Expert dialog box will appear, as shown in Figure 8-3.

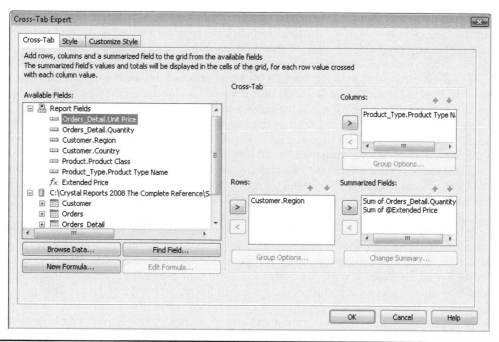

FIGURE 8-3   The Cross-Tab Expert dialog box

The Cross-Tab Expert dialog box has three tabs: Cross-Tab, Style, and Customize Style. The Cross-Tab tab is used to define the database fields or formulas that make up the rows and columns of the cross-tab. The Style tab lets you choose a predefined formatting style for the grid on the cross-tab. And, the Customize Style tab displays a large number of custom formatting options to precisely control the appearance of the cross-tab.

You'll notice fields you've already dragged and dropped onto the cross-tab appearing in the Rows, Columns, and Summarized Fields boxes on the Cross-Tab tab. If you wish to change a row, column, or summarized field item, you may select existing items and remove them with the small left arrows, or choose additional fields in the Available Fields box to add. Just drag your chosen field from the Available Fields box and drop it on the Rows or Columns box. You can also select the field in the Available Fields box and click the right-arrow button beside the Rows or Columns box. If you don't want to scroll the Available Fields box to find your field, you can click Find Field and type all or part of the field name in the resulting dialog box. The first field name containing that string will be highlighted in the Available Fields box.

You may also remove fields from or add fields to the Summarized Fields box. These will typically be number or currency fields, such as Quantity Sold or Order Amount, but they don't have to be. If you choose a number field, the default summary type will be a sum (subtotal) of the field for each cell. If you choose a field with another data type, the default summary type is a count of the number of occurrences of the field for each row/

column combination. Drag the field to be summarized from the Available Fields box to the Summarized Field box, or select the field and click the right arrow next to the Summarized Fields list. If you need a different summary type, use the Change Summary button, as discussed in more detail later in this chapter.

If you'd like to use an existing formula for a row, column, or summarized field, just select the formula in the Available Fields box. If you'd like to create a new formula or edit an existing formula before using it in the cross-tab, click the New Formula button or Edit Formula button, either of which launches the Formula Editor, where you can create or edit the formula. The formula will then appear in the Available Fields box; you can then drag it to the Rows, Columns, or Summarized Field box.

If you're not concerned initially about doing any customized formatting for your cross-tab object, you can click OK to close the Cross-Tab Expert (formatting options on the other two tabs of the Cross-Tab Expert dialog box are discussed later in the chapter). When you click OK on the Cross-Tab Expert dialog box, you are returned to the report.

When you preview the report, Crystal Reports will cycle through report data to properly summarize the totals for all row and column combinations—you may note some extra time required to do this. The cross-tab will then appear in the section where you placed it.

The section in which you place a cross-tab is critical in determining the data that the cross-tab will encompass. If you place a cross-tab in the report header or footer, only one occurrence of the cross-tab will appear on the report (remember, the report header and footer appear only once, at the beginning and end of the report, respectively). This cross-tab will encompass all the data on the report. If you place a cross-tab in a group header or footer, you get as many cross-tabs on your report as there are groups, each encompassing only data for that group.

Figure 8-4 shows a cross-tab created using the XTREME sample database available for download from the book's companion web site, CrystalBook.com. This cross-tab includes product names as the rows, and cities as the columns. Notice that all cities in all states show up in the cross-tab.

Contrast this with Figure 8-5, which is the exact same cross-tab object that's just been moved to a state group footer. Now there will be a cross-tab on the report for every state group, but each cross-tab will contain data only for that particular group. If you choose to, you can copy the cross-tab object between a group header or footer to the report header or footer and actually see cross-tabs for individual groups, as well as an all-encompassing cross-tab for the whole report.

Editing an Existing Cross-Tab

After you create a cross-tab and drop it on your report, making changes to it is easy. If you wish to add an additional row, column, or summarized field, you may drag and drop desired fields or formulas from the Field Explorer just as you could when you initially created the cross-tab (you'll want to make sure the Design tab is active before you do this). Or, you may make more detailed changes using the Cross-Tab Expert.

As mentioned earlier, you must first select the entire cross-tab object, not just one of its individual pieces, before you can start the Cross-Tab Expert. Once you've selected the desired cross-tab, choose Format | Cross-Tab Expert from the pull-down menus, or right-

FIGURE 8-4   Cross-tab in report header

click and choose Cross-Tab Expert from the pop-up menu. This simply displays the Cross-Tab Expert dialog box, where you may also change row, column, or summarized fields on the Cross-Tab tab, or format cross-tab styles with the Style tab or the Customize Style tab.

FIGURE 8-5   Cross-tab in group footer

You can also *pivot* the cross-tab, which simply means swapping the rows and columns around so that what used to be the row will now be the column, and vice versa. Choose Format | Pivot Cross-Tab from the pull-down menus, or right-click the selected cross-tab object and choose Pivot Cross-Tab from the pop-up menu.

Creative Use of Grouping and Formulas

As discussed previously, Crystal Reports chooses a default calculation for the summarized field when it creates the cross-tab. If you choose a number or currency field for a summarized field, Crystal Reports will use the Sum function to place a subtotal in each cell. This typically is what you want for this type of field (for example, the total sales figure for Green Bikes in the U.S.A.). If you use any other type of field (string, date, Boolean, and so forth), Crystal Reports will default to the Count function to count the occurrences of the particular summarized field for each row/column combination.

You are, however, completely free to change the function that Crystal Reports assigns to the summarized field. If you want to see the average sales figure in each cell instead of the total figure, it's easy to change. In either the Design or Preview tab, click the object in the cell (the intersection of the row and column). The status bar will indicate that you've selected Sum or Count of <summarized field>. Change the summary operation to any other available summary by choosing Edit | Edit Summary from the pull-down menus or by right-clicking and choosing Edit Summary from the pop-up menu. This brings up the Edit Summary dialog box.

You can change the field that's summarized, if desired, or just the summary operation itself. If you've used a nonnumeric field for the cross-tab summarized field, you can change the summary operation from Count to Minimum, Maximum, Distinct Count, or any other summary function that is available for nonnumeric fields. You can also choose to express the summary as a percentage of another total or summary. These options are similar to how you can change the summary operation with existing group summaries and subtotals, as discussed in Chapter 2. In fact, the cross-tab, in essence, groups database records for every row/column combination, creating the summary or subtotal field for each cross-tab "group." Chapter 2 has more information on available summary functions and what they calculate.

TIP   *Although cross-tabs are typically used for numeric analysis, you may sometimes find them of value when using string fields. For example, by using Minimum or Maximum summary functions with string fields, you can display textual information within a cross-tab cell. This may be helpful for certain types of string-oriented cross-tabs, such as schedules.*

Changing Cross-Tab Grouping

Because Crystal Reports uses a procedure to create cross-tabs that's similar to its procedure for creating groups, you have some of the same flexibility to change the way the cross-tab is organized. You can change a cross-tab "group" when first creating the cross-tab or when editing an existing cross-tab. This can be done with a pop-up menu from the cross-tab object, or through the Cross-Tab Expert.

If you want to change group options when displaying the cross-tab in the Design or Preview tab, select the desired row or column name object (at the top of a column or left of a row) and right-click. Choose Row Options | Group Options or Column Options | Group Options from the pop-up menu. If you're using the Cross-Tab Expert, select the row or column field you want to change in the Cross-Tab tab, and then click Group Options. The Cross-Tab Group Options dialog box appears.

The Common tab allows you to change the field the cross-tab is grouped on, as well as the order in which the groups are displayed. For a non-date field, there are three order choices, along with the choice to determine order by using a formula:

- **Ascending Order**   Shows the cross-tab row or column in A to Z order.
- **Descending Order**   Shows the cross-tab row or column in Z to A order.

- **Specified Order**   Lets you create custom rows or columns, based on the contents of the database field you chose for the row or column. This works identically to Specified Order Grouping, discussed in Chapter 2.
- **Use A Formula As Group Sort Order**   Displays the Formula Editor, where you can create a formula that chooses between ascending and descending order.

NOTE   *Even though the OriginalOrder option is available in the Formula Editor, you'll receive an error if your formula returns this option. Original Order is not a valid choice for cross-tab grouping.*

On the Options tab, the Customize Group Name Field check box, radio buttons, and formula button work the same as the identical options in the Change Group dialog box discussed in Chapter 2. You may customize the appearance of the text that displays in the row or column of the cross-tab with these options.

If the row or column field is a date field, time field, or date/time field, the Cross-Tab Group Options dialog box offers additional options that give you even greater flexibility, similar to creating report groups with similar fields.

The pull-down list under "The row/column will be printed:" gives you a choice of how often you want a new row or column to appear in the cross-tab. Choices include every day, every week, every two weeks, every hour, every minute, and so on. Again, these are identical to the date/time grouping choices discussed in Chapter 2.

The pull-down list under "The value printed for the row/column will be:" gives you two choices: the first date in the period and the last date in the period. If you choose the first-date option with, say, a quarterly date period for 2004, the cross-tab will show 1/2004, 4/2004, 7/2004, and 10/2004. If you choose the last-date option, the cross-tab will show the exact same data in the cells, but the dates will be 3/2004, 6/2004, 9/2004, and 12/2004.

NOTE *Remember that cross-tab row and column settings have no relation to any existing report groups. Changes you make in the Cross-Tab Expert will have no bearing on existing report grouping, and vice versa.*

Using Formulas in Cross-Tabs

Even with the powerful grouping options and the ability to change the summary function used to calculate cell values, you may not always be able to display material in a cross-tab exactly the way you want using just fields available in the database. You are completely free to use formulas in your cross-tabs as a row, column, or summarized field. You can create the formulas in advance with the Formula Editor and drag them to the cross-tab. Or, if you are using the Cross-Tab Expert, you can use an existing formula in the Available Fields box, or click the New Formula button right in the Cross-Tab Expert dialog box to display the Formula Editor. After you create the formula, it will appear in the Available Fields box under the Report Fields category. Simply drag it to the Rows, Columns, or Summarized Field box.

TIP *You may also use running totals as summarized fields in a cross-tab. Just drag and drop the running total from the Field Explorer to the summary area of a cross-tab in the Design or Preview tab. You'll also find running totals in the Available Fields box in the Cross-Tab Expert— just drag the running total to the Summarized Fields box. Note, however, that you can't use a running total as a row or column field in a cross-tab.*

Multiple Rows, Columns, and Summarized Fields

If you drag and drop a field onto an existing row, column, or summary cell in a cross-tab, you'll notice that the arrow icon or plus-sign icon still appears, indicating that you can add more than one field to a row, column, or summarized field. And, if you are using the Cross-Tab Expert, the Rows, Columns, and Summarized Field boxes obviously are more than one field tall. Yes, that means that you can add more than one database field or formula to any of these cross-tab sections. It's important to understand, though, how this will affect cross-tab behavior and appearance.

Probably the simplest place to start is with multiple summarized fields. If you add more than one summarized field, the cross-tab will simply calculate the additional summary or subtotal in each cell. You could, for example, use Product Name as the row, Region as the column, and both Quantity and Price as summarized fields. The cross-tab would simply include two numbers in each cell—the total quantity and total price for that particular product and region.

You can even add the same field as a summarized field more than once and choose a different summary function for each occurrence, using the change summary option (by right-clicking the summarized field in the cross-tab and choosing Edit Summary from the pop-up menu, or using the Change Summary button in the Cross-Tab Expert). You could, for example, add both the Quantity and Price fields as summarized fields again, and then choose a different summary operation for these summaries, such as Average. Alternatively, you might add them as Sum functions again, but this time choose the Percentage Of summary function for the second occurrence of the summed fields.

In the Edit Summary dialog box, when you select the Show As A Percentage Of option, you are given a choice between the Row total and the Column total as the target comparison number. In this example, the sums will be shown as a percentage of the column totals, so the resulting cross-tab shows four numbers in every cell: total quantity, percentage of total quantity for the quarter, total price, and percentage of total price for the quarter. It's interesting to note that the Row totals also display their percentage of the column totals, so the report is very effective as an analysis of each product type by quarter and for the whole year:

	1/2004	4/2004	7/2004	10/2004	Total
Competition	156	171	159	136	622
	37.96%	38.34%	34.57%	31.55%	35.58%
	$335,269.00	$368,869.72	$338,316.55	$284,565.82	$1,327,021.09
	72.75%	74.19%	68.80%	65.26%	70.37%
Hybrid	54	37	83	81	255
	13.14%	8.30%	18.04%	18.79%	14.59%
	$37,515.27	$23,902.97	$57,585.41	$56,495.59	$175,499.24
	8.14%	4.81%	11.71%	12.96%	9.31%
Kids	35	28	39	40	142
	8.52%	6.28%	8.48%	9.28%	8.12%
	$9,717.48	$7,693.14	$10,821.47	$11,074.23	$39,306.32
	2.11%	1.55%	2.20%	2.54%	2.08%
Mountain	166	210	179	174	729
	40.39%	47.09%	38.91%	40.37%	41.70%
	$78,354.83	$96,699.68	$85,004.71	$83,914.27	$343,973.49
	17.00%	19.45%	17.29%	19.24%	18.24%
Total	411	446	460	431	1,748
	100.00%	100.00%	100.00%	100.00%	100.00%
	$460,856.58	$497,165.51	$491,728.14	$436,049.91	$1,885,800.14
	100.00%	100.00%	100.00%	100.00%	100.00%

Adding multiple row or column fields causes a little different behavior that is important to understand. Whereas multiple summarized fields simply calculate and print in the same cell, multiple row or column fields don't just print over and over, side by side. When you add multiple row or column fields, you create a grouping hierarchy between the fields. Consider a cross-tab in which you add the Product Type field as the first row field, and the Product

Name field as the second row field. Crystal Reports will create a group hierarchy by Product Type, and within that, by Product Name. The resulting cross-tab would look like this:

		1/2004	4/2004	7/2004	10/2004	Total
Competition	Descent	$240,479.79	$262,234.66	$209,023.38	$180,800.80	$892,538.63
	Endorphin	$33,024.51	$34,779.22	$21,596.40	$25,645.75	$115,045.88
	Mozzie	$61,764.70	$71,855.84	$107,696.77	$78,119.27	$319,436.58
	Total	$335,269.00	$368,869.72	$338,316.55	$284,565.82	$1,327,021.09
Hybrid	Romeo	$24,720.81	$11,486.42	$37,206.06	$37,330.89	$110,744.18
	Wheeler	$12,794.46	$12,416.55	$20,379.35	$19,164.70	$64,755.06
	Total	$37,515.27	$23,902.97	$57,585.41	$56,495.59	$175,499.24
Kids	Micro Nicros	$3,840.90	$5,720.19	$5,212.65	$5,761.35	$20,535.09
	Mini Nicros	$5,876.58	$1,972.95	$5,608.82	$5,312.88	$18,771.23
	Total	$9,717.48	$7,693.14	$10,821.47	$11,074.23	$39,306.32
Mountain	Nicros	$22,264.90	$31,995.55	$23,914.15	$24,573.85	$102,748.45
	Rapel	$30,926.36	$32,197.98	$32,293.94	$25,839.98	$121,258.26
	SlickRock	$25,163.57	$32,506.15	$28,796.62	$33,500.44	$119,966.78
	Total	$78,354.83	$96,699.68	$85,004.71	$83,914.27	$343,973.49
Total		$460,856.58	$497,165.51	$491,728.14	$436,049.91	$1,885,800.14

Notice that rows are created for both the "inner" and "outer" groups—each product name has its own row within its product type, and each product type has its own subtotal row. And, at the end of the cross-tab is a grand total row for everything.

You can set up this multiple-field group hierarchy for either rows or columns with as many fields as you want (although it may not make much sense if you go beyond two or three levels).

So, a cross-tab that consists of two related row fields, two related column fields, and two summarized field might look like this in the Cross-Tab Expert:

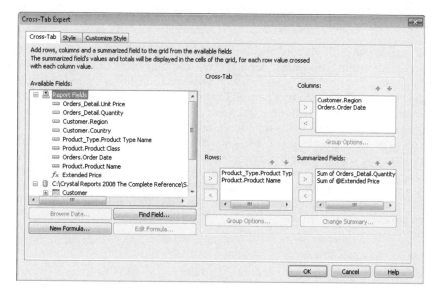

Here's a portion of the resulting cross-tab:

NOTE *What section of the report you place the cross-tab in is particularly important when you are using multiple row or column fields. If you create a cross-tab that's based on Country, and then Region, you'll see different behavior, depending on where you put the cross-tab. If you put it in the report header or footer, you'll have rows or columns for each country, and all the regions within those countries. However, if you have already grouped your report by country, and you place the cross-tab in a country group header or group footer, you'll then have one cross-tab for every country. However, that cross-tab will have only one country row or column in it, followed by any regions within that country. If you find cross-tabs at group levels with only one high-level row or column, there's not a great deal of benefit to using multiple row or column fields in that cross-tab.*

If you plan to use multiple row or column fields, choosing fields that have a logical, hierarchical relationship with each other is crucial. You may think of this relationship as being *one-to-many.* The Product Type/Product Name relationship is a good example—every one product type has many product names. Country/Region is another good example—every one country has many regions.

Using two row or column fields that don't have this relationship will cause an odd-looking cross-tab. For example, if you add Customer Name and Address fields to the same row or column, you'll simply see the customer name row or column, immediately followed by a single address row or column. The summaries in each will be exactly the same, because there's no logical one-to-many relationship between the fields. (The exception would be if a single customer had more than one office location—then this would be a valid multiple-field cross-tab example.)

NOTE *You may yearn for a cross-tab that allows multiple row or column fields that don't act as groups. You might, for example, want to see Actual $, Budget $, Variance $, and Variance % all as separate column fields that just calculate and print side by side. New Crystal Reports 2008 Calculated Members and Embedded Summaries offer this capability. This is discussed later in the chapter, under "New Derived Rows, Columns, and Cells."*

Reordering Fields in the Rows, Columns, or Summarized Field Boxes

The multiple fields you add as rows or columns not only have to have a logical relationship, they also need to appear in the right order. Using the previous Country/Region example, Country must be the first field row or column, followed by Region. If they're added the other way around, then each region will appear first, followed by a single row or column containing numbers from the country the region is in.

If you happen to add fields in the wrong order, you may reorder them either directly in the cross-tab object on the report, or by using the Cross-Tab Expert. If you wish to reorder them directly on the report, simply drag and drop one row or column name on top of the other (you may do this either in the Design or Preview tabs). A small "double-swap-arrow" cursor will appear, indicating that the fields will swap locations. Or, if you use the Cross-Tab Expert, you can reorder them by one of two methods: either click one of the fields and then click the up or down arrow for that box to move it up or down, or click and drag a field in any of the boxes and drop it in a different location in the box.

New Derived Rows, Columns, and Cells

While cross-tab objects have always been a powerful Crystal Reports feature, they've also had certain limitations. In some cases, reports that appeared to initially lend themselves to cross-tabs eventually had to be designed with alternative report-design approaches to emulate cross-tab behavior. For example, a basic cross-tab limitations in past versions was that cross-tab rows and columns could only follow database records that were the source of report data. If there wasn't a particular database record or group of records in the report, there was no way to derive a row or column in the cross-tab. Another core cross-tab requirement was that it summarize database or formula values internally as it processed. You were unable to create your own summarization formulas to calculate, for example, the difference between two other existing summarized fields in the cross-tab.

Crystal Reports 2008 has eliminated these restrictions. One of the most powerful new features, if not *the* most powerful, in Crystal Reports 2008 is the ability to derive your own rows, columns, and cells within a cross-tab object. This capability, using the new *Calculated Members* feature, allows you to insert your own rows and columns at any desired point in a cross-tab object, calculating the values in the resulting cells based on other row and column values anywhere in the cross-tab, or based on any other database field or formula available in the report. You may also create additional calculated cell values in existing rows or columns using *Embedded Summaries*. These additional calculated cells can also display any type of value you can calculate with a Crystal Reports formula, not requiring use of a cross-tab summary function to display a value.

A Calculated Member will create an additional row or column in a cross-tab. However, the Calculated Member isn't visible within the Cross-Tab Expert. Embedded Summaries create an additional summary value (or *cell*) within the existing cross-tab row/column structure. Even though Embedded Summaries are not created in the Cross-Tab Expert, they do appear within the Cross-Tab Expert Summarized Fields box.

Calculated Members create rows/columns
that don't appear in Cross-Tab Expert

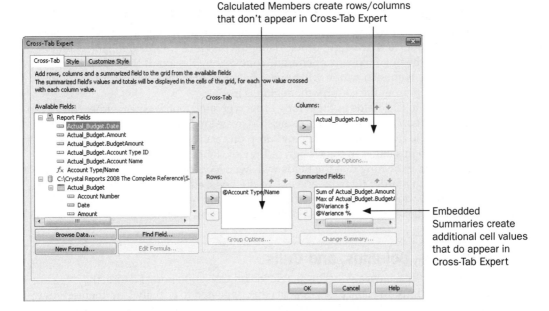

Embedded Summaries create additional cell values that do appear in Cross-Tab Expert

Creating Calculated Members

Prior to creating your own derived rows or columns with Calculated Members, you'll probably want to build the basic structure of your cross-tab using existing available database fields and formulas. Don't forget that, even before you add Calculated Members, you have the flexibility to create fairly sophisticated cross-tabs by using formulas as row, column, or summarized fields. But, as your cross-tab requirements grow, you'll eventually encounter a situation where no combination of database fields or formulas can adequately meet a requirement that lends itself to a cross-tab.

Consider the report illustrated in Figure 8-6. This is a typical financial report represented in a cross-tab that consists of an account description specified as the row, a date specified as a column (grouped by month), and two summarized fields from the database appearing in cells for each row/column combination: the sum of a transaction amount (labeled Actual) and the maximum of a budget amount (labeled Budget).

NOTE *Formatting and customization techniques, such as editing of the summarized field labels, suppression of row and column totals, and organizing accounts together in income/expense categories by use of a concatenation formula and customized group name field, are described later in this chapter and elsewhere in the book. Also, the Cross-Tab With Calculated Members.rpt sample report can be downloaded from this book's companion web site, CrystalBook.com.*

2004 Actual vs. Budget	January		February			March	
	Actual	Budget	Actual	Budget		Actual	
Bike Sales - Competition	$297,290.05	$149,396.01	$199,405.43	$363,525.31		$94,572.06	$
Bike Sales - Hybrid	$53,482.84	$7,191.46	$18,304.47	$11,965.54		$15,799.35	$
Bike Sales - Kids	$11,492.69	$491.77	$5,008.53	$282.00		$5,020.80	
Bike Sales - Mountain	$91,266.96	$29,197.58	$14,223.81	$1,256.16		$62,599.69	$
Sales Gloves	$2,602.17	$858.04	$590.50	$881.65		$442.21	
Sales Helmets	$10,585.64	$8,069.89	$1,733.77	$2,266.26		$1,634.82	
Sales Locks	$1,275.31	$522.95	$155.99	$57.01		$366.83	
Sales Returns	$4,825.37	$14,835.10	$1,664.70	$3,249.45		$5,351.02	
Sales Saddles	$1,649.98	$1,251.59	$944.35	$450.76		$532.13	
Accounting & Legal	$7,014.74	$1,000.00	$0.00	$0.00		$0.00	
Advertising & Promotions	$946.62	$10.46	$0.00	$0.00		$0.00	
Amortization Expense (Building)	$25,560.24	$2,045.94	$2,045.94	$2,045.94		$2,045.94	
Amortization Expense (Machinery)	$26,668.88	$2,134.68	$2,134.68	$2,134.68		$2,134.68	
Bank Charges	$259.11	$29.50	$24.26	$2.28		$29.16	
Bikes (Competition) Cost	$135,502.94	$35,911.66	$91,037.79	$128,541.67		$42,927.30	$
Bikes (Hybrid) Cost	$24,284.41	$3,745.90	$8,422.25	$4,974.55		$7,278.26	
Bikes (Kids) Cost	$5,259.47	$259.82	$2,272.86	$1,778.43		$2,259.36	
Bikes (Mountain) Cost	$41,587.63	$13,504.04	$6,464.81	$9,968.92		$28,213.04	$
Couring & Dartorn	$1,000.07	$202.41	$172.02	$04.54		$125.22	

FIGURE 8-6   Typical financial report in cross-tab

The initial organization of this cross-tab presents several limitations:

- There is no subtotal row at the end of Income or Expense accounts.

- A Net Sales subtotal will need to subtract the Sales Returns account from the remaining Sales accounts.

- There is no Net Revenue row that subtracts expenses from sales/income.

- There's no ability for cross-tabs in earlier versions of Crystal Reports to include extra blank rows and label rows without cell values to help delineate the Income and Expense areas of the cross-tab.

- Additional cells need to be provided to determine the difference between the Actual and Budget summaries represented as a number (variance in dollars) and as a percentage (variance in percentage).

While it might be possible to create additional formulas and add additional rows or columns based on the formulas to bypass some of these limitations, not all of them can be adequately eliminated without using derived rows (for the various subtotals) and derived cells (to calculate the variance figures). In particular, the extra row requirements can be solved by inserting additional derived rows by use of Calculated Members. Figure 8-7 illustrates the results.

Label Rows and Blank Rows make the cross-tab more readable, while showing no cell data

	January		February			March
	Actual	Budget	Actual	Budget		Actual
Income						
Bike Sales - Competition	$297,290.05	$149,396.01	$199,405.43	$363,525.31		$94,572.06
Bike Sales - Hybrid	$53,482.84	$7,191.46	$18,304.47	$11,965.54		$15,799.35
Bike Sales - Kids	$11,492.69	$491.77	$5,008.53	$282.00		$5,020.80
Bike Sales - Mountain	$91,266.96	$29,197.58	$14,223.81	$1,256.16		$62,599.69
Sales Gloves	$2,602.17	$858.04	$590.50	$881.65		$442.21
Sales Helmets	$10,585.64	$8,069.89	$1,733.77	$2,266.26		$1,634.82
Sales Locks	$1,275.31	$522.95	$155.99	$57.01		$366.83
Sales Returns	$4,825.37	$14,835.10	$1,664.70	$3,249.45		$5,351.02
Sales Saddles	$1,649.98	$1,251.59	$944.35	$450.76		$532.13
Net Sales	**$464,820.27**	**$182,144.18**	**$238,702.15**	**$377,435.26**		**$175,616.87**
Expenses						
Accounting & Legal	$7,014.74	$1,000.00	$0.00	$0.00		$0.00
Advertising & Promotions	$946.62	$10.46	$0.00	$0.00		$0.00
Amortization Expense (Building)	$25,560.24	$2,045.94	$2,045.94	$2,045.94		$2,045.94
Amortization Expense (Machinery)	$26,668.88	$2,134.68	$2,134.68	$2,134.68		$2,134.68
Bank Charges	$259.11	$29.50	$24.26	$2.28		$29.16
Bikes (Competition) Cost	$135,502.94	$35,911.66	$91,037.79	$128,541.67		$42,927.30
Bikes (Hybrid) Cost	$24,284.41	$3,745.90	$8,422.25	$4,974.55		$7,278.26
Bikes (Kids) Cost	$5,259.47	$259.82	$2,272.86	$1,778.43		$2,259.36
Bikes (Mountain) Cost	$41,587.63	$13,504.04	$6,464.81	$9,968.92		$28,213.04
Courier & Postage	$1,898.07	$392.41	$173.62	$94.54		$125.33
Gloves Cost	$1,180.13	$241.05	$269.78	$355.85		$201.83
Helmets Cost	$4,813.88	$3,609.19	$789.44	$497.81		$739.98
Insurance	$15,596.05	$2,028.15	$1,225.87	$199.58		$1,467.56
Interest Expense	$24,612.36	$2,051.03	$2,051.03	$2,051.03		$2,051.03
Internet	$1,444.08	$159.77	$120.34	$13.09		$120.34
Locks Cost	$582.45	$590.66	$70.40	$81.95		$168.57
Miscellaneous	$749.16	$20.95	$62.43	$1.21		$62.43
Office Supplies	$2,926.31	$92.32	$436.78	$96.17		$0.00
Repair & Maintenance	$321.66	$0.00	$0.00	$0.00		$552.71
Saddles Cost	$746.78	$216.47	$427.73	$573.67		$244.58
Telephone	$4,201.93	$267.83	$432.71	$20.47		$374.62
Utilities	$4,627.44	$290.40	$385.62	$52.61		$385.62
Wages & Salaries	$667,999.98	$44,114.18	$51,384.61	$36,684.20		$51,384.61
Total Expenses	**$998,784.31**	**$112,716.42**	**$170,232.93**	**$190,168.64**		**$142,766.94**
Net Revenue	**($533,964.04)**	**$69,427.76**	**$68,469.22**	**$187,266.61**		**$32,849.93**

2004 Actual vs. Budget

Net Sales, Total Expenses, and Net Revenue rows perform custom calculations based on existing cross-tab data

FIGURE 8-7 Derived rows using Calculated Members

There are three ways of creating a Calculated Member: using one of four built-in calculation methods, inserting a blank row or column, or using the Calculated Members Expert dialog box.

Using a Built-in Calculation

The simplest way to add a Calculated Member is to use one of the four built-in calculation methods: Sum (addition), Difference (subtraction), Product (multiplication), and Quotient (division). This process merely allows you to select an existing row or column as the first portion of the Calculated Member, and then choose a second row or column as the second portion, selecting one of the four calculation methods to use in creating the new derived row or column.

Begin by right-clicking the row or column header of the row or column you want to use as the first portion of your calculation. For example, if you wish to create a derived row that displays Sales Saddles minus Sales Returns, right-click the Sales Saddles row heading at the left of the cross-tab (note that you must be displaying the cross-tab in the Preview tab, as no actual data rows will appear in the Design tab). Select Calculated Member | Select "Sales Saddles" As First Value from the pop-up menu (note that the actual value displayed in the pop-up menu will change, depending on the value you selected).

Then, right-click the second row or column header you want to use for the calculation (if you initially chose a row header, you must choose another row header, not a column header). For example, to complete the aforementioned Sales Saddles minus Sales Returns calculation, right-click the Sales Returns row header. From the pop-up menu, choose Calculated Member | Difference Of "Sales Returns" And "Sales Saddles" (again, the available values on the pop-up menu will change, based on the header values you have selected). A new row or column will appear below the last row you selected, or to the right of the last column you selected, containing a single new derived row or column. The row or column will be labeled according to the type of calculation you selected. For example, the Saddles minus Returns row will be labeled Difference.

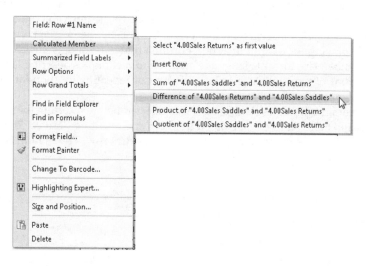

Depending on the requirements of your cross-tab, this single derived row or column may prove sufficient. However, there are several possible modifications you may need to make if the row or column appears in the wrong location, if you want to change the default text that appears as the column or row header, if the row or column needs to be repeated at a regular interval throughout the cross-tab, or if the new cells require a more involved calculation that one of the four built-in options doesn't provide. Changing this default behavior will require you to modify any of four possible properties of the Calculated Member; the Insertion Formula, the Header Formula, the Calculation Formula, or the Row or Column Value Formula.

- **The Insertion Formula**   This formula determines *where* and *how many times* in the cross-tab the derived row or column appears.

- **The Header Formula**   This formula determines what text appears in the row or column header at the left of the row or top of the column.

- **The Calculation Formula**   This formula determines *what value appears in the cells* within the derived row or column.

- **The Row/Column Value Formula**   This formula allows you to specify a unique name for the Calculated Member that can be used to refer to the derived row or column in other Calculated Member formulas.

In the case of the Sales Saddles minus Sales Return example, all four of these formulas require modification: the Insertion Formula needs to be modified to change the location of the derived row; the Header Formula needs to be modified to change the row header text; the Calculation Formula needs to be modified to encompass all of the sales rows, not just the Saddles row, to determine Net Sales; and the Row Value Formula needs to be modified so that the Calculated Member may be referred to later in another Calculated Member formula used to display Net Revenue.

The Insertion Formula   If the derived row or column resulting from the Calculated Member appears in the wrong location or needs to repeat multiple times throughout the cross-tab, you'll need to modify the Insertion Formula. Do this by right-clicking the row header at the left of the derived row or the column header at the top of the derived column. Choose Calculated Member | Edit Insertion Formula from the pop-up menu. The Formula Workshop will appear displaying the default Insertion Formula that was initially created with the Calculated Member. Use formula language syntax and techniques described in Chapter 4, and other portions of the book, to specify a different or repeating location for the Calculated Member.

For example, since the Sales Returns row was selected before inserting the Difference of Sales Returns and Sales Saddles Calculated Member, the resulting derived row appeared below the Sales Returns row and above the Sales Saddles row. The default Insertion Formula appears as

```
GetRowGroupIndexOf(CurrentRowIndex) = 1 and
GridRowColumnValue("@Account Type/Name") = "4.00Sales Returns"
```

By changing the specific row referenced by the GridRowColumnValue function, the row will move to the end of the Sales rows and above the Expense rows.

```
GetRowGroupIndexOf(CurrentRowIndex) = 1 and
GridRowColumnValue("@Account Type/Name") = "4.00Sales Saddles"
```

An alternative method might be to actually reference the number of rows in the cross-tab and place the derived row at a specific row location. Also, since this particular cross-tab consists of only one row "group," the GetRowGroupIndex function is not required:

```
CurrentRowIndex = 9
```

These examples result in a single Calculated Member row at a specific location. While this is the default behavior of a row or column created with a Calculated Member, you may encounter situations where you wish a derived row or column to appear at a repeating interval through the cross-tab. For example, if your cross-tab contains a database field that returns one of two string values, "Actual" or "Budget", and an associated dollar value, you may base the cross-tab column on this database field. If you set up a grouping relationship in the cross-tab by placing the Actual/Budget field within a date field, grouped by month, you will have repeating Actual/Budget columns appear within each month.

Creating a Calculated Member by subtracting Actual from Budget will result in only one derived Difference column at the particular position where you create the initial Calculated Member. It won't automatically repeat for each additional month in the cross-tab. The default Insertion Formula, referencing a specific month group, will look something like this:

```
GetColumnGroupIndexOf(CurrentColumnIndex) = 2 and
GridRowColumnValue("Command.Date") = CDateTime(2005,01,01,00,00,00)
and GridRowColumnValue("Command.Amount_type") = "Budget"
```

In order to have the variance column appear for each month, you'll need to modify the Insertion Formula for the Calculated Member. The modified formula may look like the following, just removing the GridRowColumnValue reference to a particular month column. The resulting derived column will appear after every column in the cross-tab in the second column "group" named Budget.

```
GetColumnGroupIndexOf(CurrentColumnIndex) = 2 and
GridRowColumnValue("Command.Amount_type") = "Budget"
```

NOTE *Even if you modify an insertion formula to create a repeating row or column, the default Calculation Formula that determines the cell value will remain an "absolute" formula, displaying the same value each time it repeats. In order to have the repeating row or column calculate cell values "relatively," you'll need to modify the Calculation Formula, as described later in this chapter.*

The Header Formula   When you use one of the four built-in calculation features to create a derived row or column via a Calculated Member, the row or column heading takes on the name of the type of calculation. So, for the Sales Saddles minus Sales Returns Calculated Member example used earlier, the derived row will be labeled "Difference." While this may be acceptable in some situations, you'll probably want to change the row or column label to be more descriptive. This is done my modifying the Header Formula. Do this by right-clicking the row header at the left of the derived row or the column header at the top of the derived column. Choose Calculated Member | Edit Header Formula from the pop-up menu. The Formula Workshop will appear displaying the default Header Formula that was initially created with the Calculated Member.

Depending on your reporting requirement, you may want to provide a more sophisticated formula based on database fields or formula functions. The formula must return a string value. Or, you may just want to change the default string literal provided. For example, since the Sales Saddles minus Sales Returns Calculated Member will eventually display Net Sales, the "Difference" string literal that's created by default can just be modified to

```
"Net Sales"
```

NOTE   *If you modify the referenced name of the Calculated Member by setting a value for the Row or Column Value Formula (discussed later in this chapter), the row or column header will display the value specified in the Value Formula. If you still wish to set a different row or column header value, any value you supply to the Header Formula will override what may be displayed by the Row or Column Value Formula.*

The Calculation Formula   It probably goes without saying that the purpose of a Calculated Member is to create some sort of custom calculation. As such, the standard summarized fields used in the remainder of the cross-tab aren't sufficient for use with Calculated Members. And, while the four built-in calculations described earlier may solve basic Calculated Member requirements, you'll probably want to modify the values in a Calculated Member's cells to solve more sophisticated custom cross-tab requirements. This is where the Calculation Formula comes in.

A Calculation Formula is created to match each existing summarized field already in the cross-tab. So, for the Budget/Actual example used throughout this section, two Calculation Formulas were created when the Sales Saddles minus Sales Returns Calculated Member was created. Both formulas appear in the derived row where the standard cross-tab summaries appear in database-based rows. Modify the desired Calculation Formula by right-clicking the desired formula in the derived row or column. Choose Calculated Member | Edit Calculation Formula from the pop-up menu. The Formula Workshop will appear displaying the default Calculation Formula that was initially created with the Calculated Member.

Since the example Sales Saddles minus Sales Returns Calculated Member was created using the Difference built-in calculation, the default Calculation Formula subtracts two cells in the same column as the Calculation Formula with the following formula:

```
GridValueAt(GetRowPathIndexOf("4.00Sales Saddles"), CurrentColumnIndex,
CurrentSummaryIndex) -
GridValueAt(GetRowPathIndexOf("4.00Sales Returns"), CurrentColumnIndex,
CurrentSummaryIndex)
```

Because this Net Sales Calculated Member really needs to sum all sales row cells, not just Saddles, and then subtract the Sales Return cell, the formula needs to be modified.

There are several approaches that might be taken. One will reference all sales rows by specific name, as in

```
GridValueAt(GetRowPathIndexOf("4.00Bike Sales - Competition"), CurrentColumnIndex,
CurrentSummaryIndex) +
GridValueAt(GetRowPathIndexOf("4.00Bike Sales - Hybrid"), CurrentColumnIndex,
CurrentSummaryIndex) +
GridValueAt(GetRowPathIndexOf("4.00Bike Sales - Kids"), CurrentColumnIndex,
CurrentSummaryIndex) +
GridValueAt(GetRowPathIndexOf("4.00Bike Sales - Mountain"), CurrentColumnIndex,
CurrentSummaryIndex) +
GridValueAt(GetRowPathIndexOf("4.00Sales Gloves"), CurrentColumnIndex,
CurrentSummaryIndex) +
GridValueAt(GetRowPathIndexOf("4.00Sales Helmets"), CurrentColumnIndex,
CurrentSummaryIndex) +
GridValueAt(GetRowPathIndexOf("4.00Sales Locks"), CurrentColumnIndex,
CurrentSummaryIndex) +
GridValueAt(GetRowPathIndexOf("4.00Sales Saddles"), CurrentColumnIndex,
CurrentSummaryIndex) -
GridValueAt(GetRowPathIndexOf("4.00Sales Returns"), CurrentColumnIndex,
CurrentSummaryIndex)
```

The other method will reference cells by row number, not row label. This formula is simpler to write, but assumes that the number and location of sales rows will not change—any additional data that may cause the cross-tab to have more or fewer sales rows directly above the Calculated Member will cause this formula to return inaccurate results:

```
GridValueAt (CurrentRowIndex-9,CurrentColumnIndex,CurrentSummaryIndex) +
GridValueAt (CurrentRowIndex-8,CurrentColumnIndex,CurrentSummaryIndex) +
GridValueAt (CurrentRowIndex-7,CurrentColumnIndex,CurrentSummaryIndex) +
GridValueAt (CurrentRowIndex-6,CurrentColumnIndex,CurrentSummaryIndex) +
GridValueAt (CurrentRowIndex-5,CurrentColumnIndex,CurrentSummaryIndex) +
GridValueAt (CurrentRowIndex-4,CurrentColumnIndex,CurrentSummaryIndex) +
GridValueAt (CurrentRowIndex-3,CurrentColumnIndex,CurrentSummaryIndex) -
GridValueAt (CurrentRowIndex-2,CurrentColumnIndex,CurrentSummaryIndex) +
GridValueAt (CurrentRowIndex-1,CurrentColumnIndex,CurrentSummaryIndex)
```

As discussed earlier, you may be required to modify the Insertion Formula for a Calculated Member to repeat the resulting derived row or column at regular intervals through a cross-tab. If this is required, you'll probably need to modify the associated Calculation Formulas as well. For example, if you create a single derived column using the Difference Calculated Member option, the Calculation Formula will make specific reference to fixed column locations, such as

```
GridValueAt(CurrentRowIndex, GetColumnPathIndexOf(CDateTime (2005,01,01,00,00,00),
"Actual"), CurrentSummaryIndex) -
GridValueAt(CurrentRowIndex, GetColumnPathIndexOf(CDateTime (2005,01,01,00,00,00),
"Budget"), CurrentSummaryIndex)
```

In this example, the specific Actual and Budget columns for January 1, 2005, are referenced. Even if you modify the Calculated Member's Insertion Formula to repeat the derived column for every month group, the resulting cells will show the variance for January 1, 2005, as the formula specifically references these cells. In order for a cell to calculate relative to its current position, you need to modify the Calculation Formula to reference cells one and two columns to the left of the calculating cell, as in

```
GridValueAt(CurrentRowIndex, CurrentColumnIndex-2, CurrentSummaryIndex) -
GridValueAt(CurrentRowIndex, CurrentColumnIndex-1, CurrentSummaryIndex)
```

TIP *If you modify the cross-tab to add a new summarized field after you've created a Calculated Member, a matching Calculation Formula won't be readily visible in the Calculated Member derived row or column. In order to create this new Calculation Formula, you must use the Calculated Members Expert to set the matching Calculation Formula for the new summary. This is described later in the chapter, under "The Calculated Members Expert."*

The Row/Column Value Formula   In preceding examples of various Calculation Formulas and Insertion Formulas, you may have noticed specific references to other rows or columns with such functions as GridRowColumnValue and GetPathIndexOf. Many Calculated Member–related functions in the formula language make use of specific row or column references, based on the values in the associated database or formula row or column name. But, since Calculated Members that you create aren't based on database fields or formulas, there's no immediate way to refer to your own Calculated Members in other Calculated Member formulas you create later. Providing a specific name for a derived row or column is the function of the Row Value Formula and the Column Value Formula.

Set the value for a Row or Column Value Formula by right-clicking the row header at the left of the derived row or the column header at the top of the derived column. Choose Calculated Member | Edit Row Value Formula Or Calculated Member | Edit Column Value Formula from the pop-up menu. The Formula Workshop will appear displaying an empty formula. You may use built-in database fields and functions to create a value formula, ensuring that the formula result is a string. Or, you may supply a fixed row or column name by supplying a string literal, surrounded by quotation marks.

For example, if you've created a single derived row Calculated Member that determines Net Sales, you may wish to give it a Row Value Formula consisting of

```
"Net Sales"
```

And, if you've created another derived row Calculated Member that determines Total Expenses, you may wish to give it a Row Value Formula consisting of

```
"Total Expenses"
```

Then, when you create yet one more Calculated Member row to calculate Net Revenue, you may reference cells in the two previously named Calculated Members, utilizing the Row Value Formulas you supplied:

```
GridValueAt (GetRowPathIndexOf("Net Sales"),CurrentColumnIndex,CurrentSummaryIndex)
-
GridValueAt (GetRowPathIndexOf("Total
Expenses"),CurrentColumnIndex,CurrentSummaryIndex)
```

New Crystal Reports Grid Value Functions

A quick glance through the various sample formulas used earlier in this chapter will give you a feel for the large number of new formula functions available for use with Calculated Members and Embedded Summaries. In order to provide the flexibility for controlling where and how often derived rows and columns appear in a cross-tab, as well as providing the ability to refer to other parts of the cross-tab in Calculation Formulas, a large number of new functions are now presented in the Grid Value section of the Formula Editor Function Tree.

While an exhaustive discussion of every Grid Value function is best left for Crystal Reports online help, or the appendix (the Formula Language Reference), here are examples of some of the functions you'll often use, and that are used in the sample *Cross-Tab With Calculated Members.rpt* report available for download from the book's companion web site, CrystalBook.com.

- **GridRowColumnValue**   Allows navigation to a specific row or column in the cross-tab, based on the value of the row header or column header. For example,

```
GridRowColumnValue("@Account Type/Name") = "4.00Sales Saddles"
```

will search the cross-tab for a row or column based on the @Account Type/Name formula, and find the specific row or column based on the "4.00Sales Saddles" value. GridRowColumnValue is typically used in Insertion Formulas to determine where to add a derived row or column.

- **GridValueAt**   Returns the value contained in the specified cell, based on the row, column, and number of summarized fields for each row/column combination. For example,

```
GridValueAt (3, 0, 1)
```

will return the cell value in the fourth row, the first column, and the second summarized field at the row/column combination. Another example is

```
GridValueAt (CurrentRowIndex-2,CurrentColumnIndex,CurrentSummary
Index)
```

which will return the cell value two rows above the current row, but in the same column as this cell. If there are multiple summarized fields in the row/column combination, the summarized field in the same position as this cell is used. Note that arguments provided to GridValueAt are zero-based—that is, the first row/column/summarized field is numbered 0, instead of 1.

- **GetRowPathIndexOf, GetColumnPathIndexOf**   Returns a number indicating the row or column with a label matching that of the supplied argument. For example,

```
GetRowPathIndexOf("4.00Sales Locks")
```

will return the number 7 if the eighth row in the cross-tab is 4.00Sales Locks.

```
GetColumnPathIndexOf(CDateTime (2005,01,01,00,00,00), "Actual")
```

will return the number of the column labeled Actual, within a higher-level column for January 1, 2005. Supplying multiple arguments allows searching within a cross-tab that consists of multiple nested rows or columns.

GetRowPathIndex and GetColumnPathIndex are zero-based—the first row or column in the cross-tab is numbered 0, not 1.

- **CurrentRowIndex, CurrentColumnIndex, CurrentSummaryIndex**   Indicates the number of the current row, the number of the current column, or the number of the current summarized field (if more than one summarized field has been added to a row/column combination). For example, a cell located 11 rows from the top of the cross-tab, in the February column of a 12-month set of columns, and in the position of the third summarized field (in a set of four summarized fields for the row/column combination), will return a CurrentRowIndex of 10, a CurrentColumnIndex of 1, and a CurrentSummaryIndex of 2. Note that indexes are zero-based—the first row or column in the cross-tab is numbered 0, not 1. Also, note that neither header/title rows at the top of columns nor label columns at the left of rows will increment index counts.

Inserting a Blank Row or Column

While simpler cross-tab applications may benefit adequately from the four types of default calculations that can used when inserting Calculated Members, you'll probably find more flexibility by inserting your own individual blank derived rows or columns. The four formulas discussed earlier in the chapter (Insertion, Calculation, Header, and Row/Column

Value) can be modified as described previously in the chapter for your blank row or column, allowing complete control over the placement, header text, and cell values of a Calculated Member.

You may, for example, want to simply insert a blank row or column to make the cross-tab more visually appealing (perhaps to add more visual separation between Income and Expense rows in a cross-tab). Simply select the header for the existing row or column you want the blank to appear below or to the right of and right-click. From the pop-up menu, choose Calculated Member | Insert Row/Insert Column. A new row or column will appear in the cross-tab.

If you want the new column or row to simply display white space, you may leave the Header Formula and Row Value Formula/Column Value Formula as-is. The row or column header will be blank. However, you must deal with the zero values that appear in the new row or column cells by default. To eliminate the zero values, either perform custom formatting on the cell values using Suppress or Display Text properties of the Format Editor (discussed later in the chapter, under "Customizing Cross-Tab Appearance"), or remove the 0 value that is placed in the Calculation Formula by default. To eliminate the default 0 value, right-click each summarized field cell of the new derived row or column. Select Calculated Member | Edit Calculation Formula from the pop-up menu. Delete the 0 the appears in the Formula Editor. This will then display an empty cell once you save the Calculation Formula.

TIP *If you later wish to add some sort of calculation back into the Calculation Formula, you must access it via the Calculated Members Expert, as described later in the chapter. Once you eliminate the Calculation Formula, you are no longer able to right-click the cell and choose the Calculation Formula option from a pop-up menu.*

In addition to creating blank "spacer" rows or columns, you may modify various formulas belonging to your just-inserted blank row or column (as described earlier in the chapter) to customize its appearance and behavior. You may, for example, modify the Insertion

Formula to have the row or column repeat at some interval in the cross-tab. Modifying the Header Formula will change the value that appears in the column or row header. You may write your own Calculation Formula to populate the new row or columns cells with any calculation that can be created with the Crystal Reports formula language, well beyond the Sum, Difference, Product, or Quotient calculations available by default. And, by specifying a value for the Row or Column Value formula, you may reference the new derived row or column elsewhere in other formulas.

For example, you may wish to simply create a new "label" row or column that doesn't show any values in cells but displays a header value. Looking back at the sample cross-tab displayed in Figure 8-7, you'll notice two label rows; one at the top of the Income area of the cross-tab, and another at the top of the Expenses area of the cross-tab. In both these cases, the Header formula is set to the corresponding "Income" or "Expenses" string literal and the cells are conditionally suppressed in the Format Editor.

And, for more complex Calculated Members that the four default calculation types don't accommodate, you may start with a blank row or column and modify the various formulas to your needs. Again, looking at the sample cross-tab displayed in Figure 8-7, you'll notice a Calculated Member to subtotal Net Sales (described earlier in the chapter), another to calculate Total Expenses (very similar to the Net Sales row), and a third to show Net Revenue. The Net Revenue row consists of a blank row Calculated Member that is inserted at the end of the cross-tab (after another blank "spacer" row that contains no data). The Header Formula contains the string literal "Net Revenue," and the Actual and Budget Calculation Formulas contain a reference to the Net Sales and Total Expenses Calculated Members (referenced by way of values entered for the Net Sales and Total Expenses Row Value Formulas):

```
GridValueAt (GetRowPathIndexOf("Net Sales"), CurrentColumnIndex,
CurrentSummaryIndex) -
GridValueAt (GetRowPathIndexOf("Total Expenses"), CurrentColumnIndex,
CurrentSummaryIndex)
```

The Calculated Members Expert

As you work with various pop-up menu options to create and modify Calculated Members, you may notice that there's no option to remove a Calculated Member you no longer want. And, if you eliminate a Calculation Formula in a blank row or column, you may notice that you can no longer select the cell to add the Calculated Formula back in. Both these capabilities require use of the *Calculated Members Expert*, a dialog box that offers another way to create, remove, and modify Calculated Members. And, the Calculated Members Expert can also be used to add new Calculated Members or modify any of the formulas used to affect Calculated Member behavior.

To display the Calculated Members Expert, you must select the entire cross-tab object (you may be viewing either the Design or Preview tab) by clicking a grid line intersecting a row and column, or by clicking in the white space at the upper-left corner of the cross-tab. Then, right-click and choose Advanced Calculations | Calculated Member from the pop-up menu. The Calculated Members Expert will appear, as illustrated in Figure 8-8.

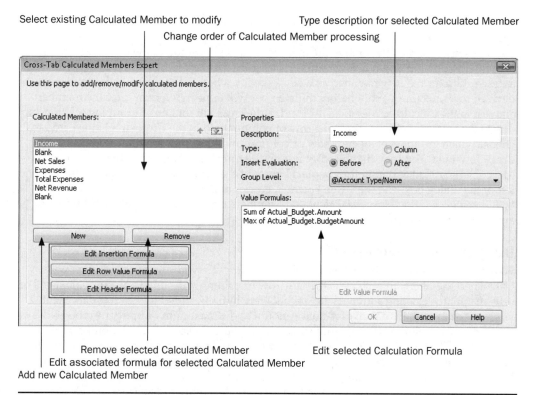

FIGURE 8-8   The Calculated Members Expert

The Calculated Members Expert can be used to modify existing Calculated Members, to remove Calculated Members you no longer wish to include in the cross-tab, as well as to add new Calculated Members. The first thing you may choose to use the Calculated Members Expert for is to provide helpful descriptive text for any existing Calculated Members you've already created. Otherwise, the series of "Please enter a description" default descriptions will make it difficult to determine which Calculated Member each entry in the dialog box refers to. If you're not sure which calculated member you are editing, select it in the Calculated Members list and click one of the associated formula buttons to help determine its properties. Then, type a description for the member in the Description text box.

To remove a derived row or column you no longer wish to use, select the desired entry in the Calculated Members list. Then, click Remove. To modify some aspect of a member, select the desired Calculated Member in the list and click the corresponding Edit Insertion Formula, Edit Row/Column Value Formula, or Edit Header formula buttons. To edit the Calculation Formula for an associated Calculated Member, select the desired Calculation Formula in the Value Formulas list in the lower right of the dialog and click the Edit Value Formula button below the list.

And, you can create a new derived row or column with the Calculated Members Expert. Click New button to add a new Calculated Member to the bottom of the Calculated Members list. You may then move the member to a new position in the Calculated Members list with the up- and down-arrow buttons. Using the Properties area of the dialog, provide a description for the new member, as well as specify whether the new member will create a derived row or column and whether the member will appear before or after the member above it in the Calculated Members list. And, if the cross-tab contains a grouping relationship due to the existence of more than one row or column field in the Cross-Tab Expert, you may choose which group level the new row or column should appear in with the Group Level drop-down list. You may then modify any of the four Calculated Member formulas (described in detail earlier in the chapter) by use of the three Formula buttons at the lower left of the dialog box, and the Value Formula entries at the lower right of the dialog box. When you click OK to close the Calculated Members Expert, the new row or column will appear on the cross-tab.

Using Embedded Summaries

So far, this section of the book has discussed creating derived rows and columns with Calculated Members. In each case, the new row or column will contain an equivalent cell or cells that match existing summary fields that were initially added to the cross-tab. So, if your cross-tab contains a sum of Actual Amount and a maximum of Budget Amount, the derived row or column will contain two cells that you can use the Calculation Formula to customize. However, because cross-tabs prior to Crystal Reports 2008 allowed you to add only cells based on summarizations of existing database or formula fields, you were often limited in your ability to create your own custom cells, such as variances. Crystal Reports 2008 now allows complex cross-tabs to benefit from the ability to add custom cells to either existing database/formula-based rows and columns, or your Calculated Member derived rows and columns. These *Embedded Summaries* don't add additional rows or columns—they simply add additional cells to existing rows and columns that can contain custom calculations that aren't limited to summarizations.

Looking back at the finished cross-tab illustrated in Figure 8-7, you'll notice two variance cells; one showing variance in dollars between the Actual and Budget figures, and another showing variance in percentage. These common values are often required in standard financial reporting and have largely been unavailable in previous Crystal Reports cross-tabs because they rely on calculations based on *existing* summaries in the cross-tab, rather than on summaries of a database or formula field. Crystal Reports 2008 offers the ability to create these kinds of calculations with Embedded Summaries.

To create an Embedded Summary, select the summary cell that you wish to add an Embedded Summary after (you may be viewing the cross-tab in either the Design or Preview tab). Right-click and select Embedded Summary | Insert Embedded Summary from the pop-up menu. A new cell will appear in the cross-tab with a default "Edit this formula" string literal displaying in the cell, and with @Embedded Summary used as the cell title text object. Two additional steps may then be taken to customize the Embedded Summary: changing the title by modifying the text object, and customizing the cell's contents with the Calculation Formula.

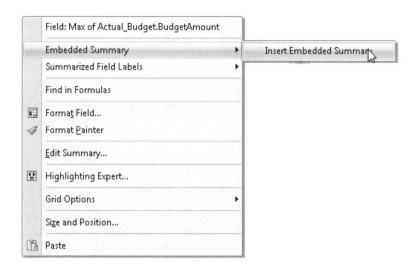

Just as with a regular cross-tab summarized field, an Embedded Summary's title is simply a text object that may be changed by double-clicking it, or right-clicking and choosing Edit options from the Format or pop-up menus. So, you are free to customize the title for your embedded summary by simply changing the default text.

To customize the calculation performed by the Embedded Summary, right-click on the newly created "Edit this formula" cell. Choose Embedded Summary | Edit Calculation Formula from the pop-up menu. The Formula Editor will appear with the "Edit this formula" string literal appearing. Use techniques discussed earlier for customizing Calculated Member cells to calculate the value returned by the Embedded Summary. The same Grid Value functions discussed earlier; such as GridValueAt and column, row, and summary index functions; can be used to create a custom calculation. In particular, remember that Embedded Summaries will appear in each row or column of the cross-tab, as opposed to Calculated Member derived cells, which will initially only appear once. This typically requires you to consider "relative" Embedded Summary Calculation Formulas that don't refer to fixed-location cells but refer to cells a certain number of positions to the left or right of the current cell location.

So, to calculate a Variance in Dollars amount with an Embedded Summary, the following Calculation Formula may be specified. Note that the formula makes relative reference to other summaries in the same row and column, but appearing two positions to the left of the current cell, and one position to the left from the current cell:

```
GridValueAt (CurrentRowIndex,CurrentColumnIndex,CurrentSummaryIndex-2) -
GridValueAt (CurrentRowIndex,CurrentColumnIndex,CurrentSummaryIndex-1)
```

And, to calculate the Variance as a percentage, another Embedded Summary can be created to the right of the Variance $ summary. After the text objects is modified to properly display the Variance % title, the Calculation Formula may be customized to create a "relative" formula to calculate the percentage, such as

```
If GridValueAt (CurrentRowIndex,CurrentColumnIndex,CurrentSummaryIndex-2)
<> 0 Then
    GridValueAt (CurrentRowIndex,CurrentColumnIndex,CurrentSummaryIndex-1) %
    GridValueAt (CurrentRowIndex,CurrentColumnIndex,CurrentSummaryIndex-2)
Else
    0
```

The Embedded Summaries Dialog Box

As with Calculated Members, there is an additional way beyond right-click pop-up menus to reorder, create, and remove Embedded Summaries, as well as modify their Calculation Formula. The *Embedded Summaries dialog box* can be used to manipulate existing Embedded Summaries, or create new ones. First, select the entire cross-tab object (you may be viewing either the Design or Preview tab) by clicking a grid line intersecting a row and column, or by clicking in the white space at the upper-left corner of the cross-tab. Then, right-click and choose Advanced Calculations | Embedded Summary from the pop-up menu. The Embedded Summaries Dialog Box will appear, as illustrated in Figure 8-9.

Reorder selected Embedded Summary

Remove Selected Embedded Summary
Edit selected summary's Calculation Formula
Add new Embedded Summary
Embedded Summaries are preceded with an @ sign

FIGURE 8-9   The Embedded Summaries dialog box

A list of existing cross-tab summarized fields, as well as existing Embedded Summaries, will appear in the dialog box (Embedded Summaries will be preceded by an @ sign). You may reorder the combination of cross-tab summaries and Embedded Summaries by selecting the desired summary and moving it with the up- and down-arrow buttons. Removing an Embedded Summary you no longer want is as simple as selecting it and clicking Remove. You may modify the Calculation Formula for an Embedded Summary with the Edit Embedded Summary button. And, creating a new Embedded Summary is as simple as clicking New.

TIP *You can also change the order of Embedded Summaries, or remove them from the cross-tab, with the Cross-Tab Expert, as Embedded Summaries appear in the Cross-Tab Expert (unlike Calculated Members). Select the entire cross-tab object and display the Cross-Tab Expert via the Format menu or right-click pop-up menu. To reorder the Embedded Summary, select it in the Summarized Fields box and drag and drop it to a new location or use the up- and down-arrow buttons. To remove an Embedded Summary, select it in the Summarized Fields box and click the left-arrow button.*

Customizing Cross-Tab Appearance

So far, this chapter has concentrated on the steps required to create cross-tabs, grouping options, some of the finer points of multiple row, column, and summarized fields, and new Calculated Member and Embedded Summary features of Crystal Reports 2008. In all of these examples, the resulting cross-tab object looks fairly plain. In keeping with the ability of Crystal Reports to create publication-quality reports, you have numerous options available to help you improve the appearance of your cross-tab reports.

The most basic type of formatting options for cross-tabs lies in the individual cross-tab objects themselves. A cross-tab actually consists of a series of individual objects. The best way to see this is to look at a cross-tab in the Design tab.

	Column #1 Name	Total
Row #1 Name	of @Extended Price	Extended Price
Total	of @Extended Price	Extended Price

Notice the row and column name fields, which are similar to group name fields in a regular report—they display the database fields that make up the row and column headings. The Total text objects indicate the subtotal and total rows and columns. These are standard text objects—simply double-click them to change their contents, if you wish. And, in the actual cells, notice the subtotal or summary functions that calculate the cross-tab totals.

Each of these individual objects can be resized or formatted to change the appearance of the cross-tab. For example, if a column in the cross-tab isn't wide enough to show its contents, the contents will just be cut off, or truncated. Examine the following cross-tab:

	1/2004	4/2004	7/2004	10/2004	Total
Compet	#########	#########	#########	#########	#########
Hybrid	$37,515.27	$23,902.97	$57,585.41	$56,495.59	#########
Kids	$9,717.48	$7,693.14	$10,821.47	$11,074.23	$39,306.32
Mountai	$78,354.83	$96,699.68	$85,004.71	$83,914.27	#########
Total	#########	#########	#########	#########	#########

Notice that the row labels are being truncated. Also, note that many of the cells contain pound signs, indicating that the cells aren't wide enough to show all the data in them. (Remember that if Allow Field Clipping is turned on in the Format Editor, you won't see pound signs when numbers are truncated.)

Although you may be tempted to point to a line between columns in the cross-tab object to get a sizing cursor, or look on one of the tabs of the Cross-Tab Expert dialog box for some sort of column width setting, you simply need to select the individual object that makes up the column and resize it. This can be done in either the Design or Preview tab. Simply select the object, noting that all other similar cells are selected as well. Then, point to the desired sizing handle (one of the small blue blocks on all sides of a selected object) until the mouse cursor changes to the two-way sizing cursor. Then, simply resize the object to its desired width.

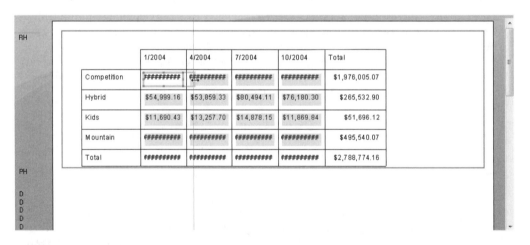

Tip *If the summarized values in your cross-tab are just too large to fit into a tidy grid, there is also a custom formatting formula you can use to abbreviate thousands or millions with the standard "K" or "M" notation. See "The Display String Formatting Property" later in this chapter.*

You can format the individual pieces of the cross-tab just like any other text object or number field, using either the Formatting toolbar or the Format Editor. You can change the object's color, font face and size, horizontal alignment, or any other standard formatting option. If you choose one of the summary or subtotal objects in the middle, you can choose one of the default formatting styles, or choose a custom style to specify the number of decimal places, whether to include a thousands separator or currency symbol, or any other formatting option available to numeric or currency fields. If you base a row or column on a date or time field, you can choose how the field is displayed—month/year, month/day/year, hour:minute, hour:minute:second, or any other variation provided by the Format Editor.

TIP   *You can select multiple objects in a cross-tab by using* CTRL-*click or* SHIFT-*click. You can then format them all at the same time with the Formatting toolbar or the Format Editor. Note, however, that the elastic box selection method doesn't select multiple objects within in a cross-tab. You'll need to* CTRL-*click or* SHIFT-*click to do this.*

The Style Tab

When you select a cross-tab object and choose Format | Cross-Tab Expert or right-click and choose Cross-Tab Expert from the pop-up menu, the Cross-Tab Expert dialog box will appear. Two tabs in this dialog box control formatting: Style and Customize Style. The Style tab lets you choose from several predefined formatting styles for the cross-tab object.

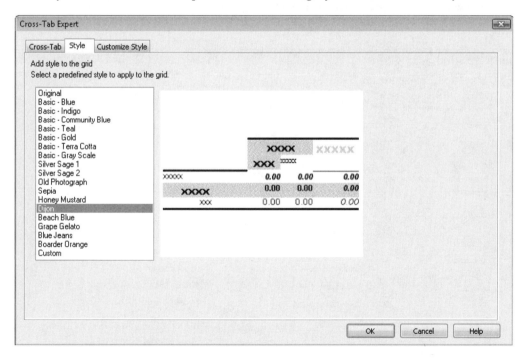

The Original option simply displays the cross-tab object with no special formatting—this is the original formatting option when a cross-tab is first created. You may choose from any of the predefined styles in the list. When you click a style, a sample of the style appears in the right side of the Style tab. Then, just click OK. The cross-tab will be formatted according to the built-in style that you chose.

CAUTION *Crystal Reports behaves somewhat oddly when using the Style tab on the Cross-Tab Expert dialog box. Even if you haven't chosen any customized settings, you'll always receive a warning that you'll lose customized settings when you choose one of the built-in styles. And if you return to the Style tab later after choosing one of the built-in styles, the Custom setting will be highlighted, not the built-in style you chose before. Just remember that if you don't like a style setting, you may simply press CTRL-Z or use Edit | Undo to revert to your previous formatting.*

The Customize Style Tab

For very specific formatting of a cross-tab object, you need to use the Customize Style tab on the Cross-Tab Expert dialog box. This tab contains advanced cross-tab options that more precisely control cross-tab behavior. The Customize Style tab is shown in Figure 8-10.

If you've already chosen one of the built-in styles on the Style tab, you'll see the settings for that built-in style when you choose the Customize Style tab. For example, you'll see background colors for each row or column item that the built-in style selected. If the built-in style shows totals before rows and columns instead of after, you'll see those options chosen. If you haven't chosen one of the built-in styles, or you want to change some of the settings that the built-in style selected, you may choose the various options in the Custom Style tab. The various options are explained in Table 8-1.

FIGURE 8-10 The Customize Style tab of the Cross-Tab Expert dialog box

Option	Description
Customize Grid's Style	
Rows list	Select the row that you want to format. If you've added multiple row fields, you'll see each row field listed. You can also choose separate formatting options for the row grand total.
Columns list	Select the column that you want to format. If you've added multiple column fields, you'll see each column field listed. You can also choose separate formatting options for the column grand total.
Summarized fields	When you have multiple fields summarized, you can choose whether to display them in a vertical stack (this is the default) or horizontally side by side. The Show Labels option prints the summarized field name(s) in the column header area (you can't customize the labels here, but can edit them in the Design or Preview tabs just like text objects). Figure 8-11 shows the horizontal summaries with labels.
Group Options	
Suppress Subtotal	If you select this option, the subtotal row or column (depending on what's selected in the Rows or Columns list) won't appear. In this case, the cross-tab still shows the hierarchical grouping relationship among the multiple row or column fields, but the subtotals for the selected field won't appear. This option is available only for higher-level fields when you've chosen multiple row or column fields—the option is disabled if you select the lowest-level (or if you added only one) row or column field.
Suppress Label	If you choose the Suppress Subtotal option, this option becomes enabled. Checking this option will completely eliminate the field you chose from the row or column. The grouping hierarchy will remain, but the higher-level group won't appear at all in the cross-tab. If you have also checked Indent Row Labels (described later in this table), this option will be checked and you can't change it.
Alias for Formulas	Used to refer to an entire row or column when performing conditional formatting on the cross-tab. See "Conditionally Formatting Cross-Tabs" later in the chapter.
Background Color	Sets the background color for the entire row or column that's chosen in the Rows or Columns list. This color is independent of any individual cell colors you may choose by selecting an object in the cross-tab and using the Format Editor.
Grid Options	
Indent Row Labels	Checking this option will indent the label for the chosen row from the left of the cross-tab. You may specify how much to indent the row in the text box after the Indent Row Labels check box. This is typically used to highlight a hierarchical grouping relationship when you've added multiple row fields to the cross-tab.

TABLE 8-1   Customize Style Tab Options

Option	Description
Indent Column Labels	Checking this option will indent the label for the chosen column from the top of the cross-tab. You may specify how much to indent the column in the text box after the Indent Column Labels check box.
Repeat Row Labels	If Keep Columns Together is checked, this option will repeat the row labels when a cross-tab exceeding the width of the page is printed on two or more pages.
Keep Columns Together	Prevents columns from being cut in half when a cross-tab exceeding the width of the page is printed.
Column Totals on Top	Displays column totals on top of the actual columns containing the data being totaled, rather than at the bottom of the columns (this is the default when dragging fields directly from the Field Explorer to a new cross-tab object).
Row Totals On Left	Displays row totals to the left of the actual rows containing the data being totaled, rather than on the right of the rows (this is the default when dragging fields directly from the Field Explorer to a new cross-tab object).
Show Cell Margins	Pads cells with white space on all sides. Turning this option off will place cells right next to each other.
Suppress Empty Rows	Rows with no data will not appear in the cross-tab.
Suppress Empty Columns	Columns with no data will not appear in the cross-tab.
Suppress Row Grand Totals	Prevents row grand totals from appearing in the cross-tab.
Suppress Column Grand Totals	Prevents column grand totals from appearing in the cross-tab.
Format Grid Lines button	Displays the Format Grid Lines dialog box (described later in the chapter) to customize where and how grid lines appear in the cross-tab.

TABLE 8-1   Customize Style Tab Options *(continued)*

Several of the options on the Customize Style tab, particularly the Repeat Row Labels and Keep Columns Together options, dictate how a cross-tab appears when printed on paper. This is significant, because Crystal Reports displays cross-tabs differently in the Preview tab than it will print them on a printer. Even if the cross-tab width exceeds the width of the page, the Preview tab will show the entire cross-tab across the screen. You can continue to scroll farther right to see the rest of the cross-tab.

When Crystal Reports prints the cross-tab on paper, however, it must add page breaks if the cross-tab exceeds the width of the printed page. You can control how Crystal Reports formats the cross-tab across multiple pages with the options in the Customize Style tab. When you display the cross-tab in the Preview tab, you can see where Crystal Reports will insert page breaks when the cross-tab is printed on paper. In Figure 8-11, notice that the page break occurs between columns (it's not running right through the numbers of a column) and that the row labels are repeating after the page break. This is the result of turning on both Keep Columns Together and Repeat Row Labels.

TIP *In Crystal Reports, some of the options available on the Custom Style tab are also available by right-clicking directly on a column or row name field in the cross-tab and choosing options from the Summarized Field Labels, Column/Row Options, Grid Options, or Column/Row Grand Totals pop-up menus.*

Formatting Grid Lines

Crystal Reports provides the ability to customize grid line appearance, including which grid lines appear and how they look. To customize the grid lines, select the entire cross-tab (you can't just select an individual cross-tab cell), right-click, and choose Grid Options | Format Grid Lines from the pop-up menu. If you are using the Cross-Tab Expert, click the Format Grid Lines button in the Grid Options area of the Customize Style tab. The Format Grid Lines dialog box will appear, as shown in Figure 8-12.

Summarized field names appear when "Show Labels" activated

Repeat Row Labels will show row names for each "virtual" page

	1/2004		4/2004
	:ended Price	Quantity	@Extended Price
	$444,161.41	293	$625,777.60
	$54,999.16	76	$53,859.33
	$11,690.43	48	$13,257.70
	$108,284.64	312	$148,707.69
	$619,135.64	729	$841,602.32

	7/2004	
	Quantity	@Extended Price
Competition	238	$478,281.91
Hybrid	119	$80,494.11
Kids	54	$14,878.15
Mountain	259	$122,151.72
Total	670	$695,805.89

Summaries print side by side with horizontal option

Dashed line indicates where page break will appear when printed on paper, with row labels repeated after break

FIGURE 8-11   Cross-tab with Repeat Row Labels, Show Labels, and Horizontal summaries activated on Customize Style tab

Choose particular grid line to format

Turn on or off all grid lines

Choose formatting options for chosen grid line

FIGURE 8-12   The Format Grid Lines dialog box

You may simply choose to not show any grid lines at all by unchecking the Show Grid Lines option. Or to control individual grid lines, you may either select the grid line you want to customize in the grid line list or actually click a particular line in the grid lines diagram at the top of the dialog box. Then, choose individual options for the grid line in the Line Options portion of the Format Grid Lines dialog box.

Labels or Legends with Cross-Tabs

If you add multiple summarized fields to a cross-tab, it may not be clear to your viewer what the numbers mean—they may be totals, averages, or counts. The Show Labels option, demonstrated earlier in Figure 8-11, is effective with one or two summaries. With more than one or two summaries, they may become unwieldy and hard to fit in the column or row headers.

One way of reducing the size of labels is to change their content. Initially, they display the field name of the summarized field, including any special characters (such as the @ sign that precedes formula or Embedded Summary names). These labels are actually special text objects added to the cross-tab that you can manually change. As with other text objects, you may edit cross-tab row and column labels by simply double-clicking on them, by clicking them and choosing Edit | Edit Text from the pull-down menus, or by right-clicking and choosing Edit Text from the pop-up menu.

Conditionally Formatting Cross-Tabs

You may wish to conditionally format cross-tab cells, depending on their contents. Conditional formatting (discussed in more detail in Chapter 6) is the process of changing the appearance of a cross-tab cell according to its contents. You may wish to highlight certain cells that exceed a certain sales goal or shipping level; you can change the color, shading, or border of just those cells.

Select the summary or subtotal object that you want to conditionally format. Then, choose Format | Highlighting Expert from the pull-down menus, or right-click the cell and choose Highlighting Expert from the pop-up menu. You can choose Highlighting Expert conditions and formats to highlight certain cells.

You can also use conditional formulas. After selecting a summary or subtotal object in the cross-tab, display the Format Editor by choosing options from the Format pull-down menu or by right-clicking and choosing options from the pop-up menu. You can click a Conditional Formula button anywhere on the Format Editor to set that formatting property conditionally.

You may also wish to conditionally format the labels for derived rows or columns created with Calculated Members. For example, if you wish to set bold or underline formatting for label values on certain rows only, you might add a conditional formatting formula similar to this to the proper property in the Format Editor:

```
If GridRowColumnValue ("@Account Type/Name") In ["Income","Expenses","Net
Sales","Total Expenses","Net Revenue"] Then
    crBold
Else
    crRegular
```

What Is CurrentFieldValue?

When you choose to use conditional formulas instead of the Highlighting Expert, you must be careful about the tests you use to conditionally format cross-tab summaries. Since the summaries are calculations based on database fields, but are not actually the database fields themselves, you can't just test a database field to conditionally format the cross-tab. And contrary to what you see if you've placed subtotals or summaries in a group footer, you won't see the summaries or subtotals that make up the cells in the field list of the Formula Editor.

You must test the built-in CurrentFieldValue function when conditionally formatting cross-tabs. CurrentFieldValue, as its name suggests, returns whatever the cell or "field" being tested contains. You can, therefore, use a conditional formula similar to the following to apply a silver background color to cross-tab subtotals that exceed $30,000:

```
If CurrentFieldValue > 30000 Then crSilver Else crNoColor
```

Figure 8-13 shows a cross-tab with this formatting.

What Are GridRowColumnValue and the Alias for Formulas?

Using the CurrentFieldValue function described in the preceding section, you can set conditional formatting in the cross-tab only based on the value of the current cell. However, you may also want to set conditional formatting based on the row or column that the cell is

	1/2004	4/2004	7/2004	10/2004
Descent	$313,682.06	$448,915.16	$284,283.56	$271,789.16
Endorphin	$42,877.87	$66,903.88	$49,851.72	$44,992.55
Micro Nicros	$3,840.90	$7,338.85	$6,831.31	$6,556.96
Mini Nicros	$7,849.53	$5,918.85	$8,046.84	$5,312.88
Mozzie	$87,601.48	$109,958.56	$144,146.63	$111,002.44
Nicros	$29,505.11	$44,744.27	$36,959.74	$36,580.42
Rapel	$39,083.81	$45,681.81	$42,130.89	$34,957.13
Romeo	$30,921.83	$37,663.83	$47,860.15	$53,020.68
SlickRock	$39,695.72	$58,281.61	$43,061.09	$44,858.47
Wheeler	$24,077.33	$16,195.50	$32,633.96	$23,159.62
Total	$619,135.64	$841,602.32	$695,805.89	$632,230.31

Figure 8-13 Cross-tab conditional formatting with CurrentFieldValue

in, not just the value in the cell. Crystal Reports provides this capability using two functions: GridRowColumnValue and Alias for Formulas.

When you conditionally format a cell, notice the GridRowColumnValue function in the Formatting Functions category of the Functions box in the Format Formula Editor. By using this function with an If-Then-Else formula (when setting a multiple-choice formatting property) or a Boolean formula (when setting an on/off formatting property), you can determine which row or column the cell is in and format accordingly. Consider the following Boolean formula that conditionally sets the Drop Shadow property on the Format Editor Border tab:

```
GridRowColumnValue("Product.Product Name") = "Nicros"
```

The result is shown in Figure 8-14. Notice that only cells in the Nicros row have drop shadows applied to them. By supplying an alias name as the parameter for the GridRowColumnValue function, you can determine which row or column the formula will refer to. In this scenario, Product.Product Name is supplied as the alias name. So the GridRowColumnValue for the Product Name row is tested. If the value of the row is Nicros, the drop shadow is applied.

By default, each row or column's alias is the field or formula name of the row or column (without the curly braces). If you want to change the alias name to something more meaningful (perhaps just the field name instead of the entire table/field name combination),

	1/2004	4/2004	7/2004	10/2004
Descent	$313,682.06	$448,915.16	$284,283.56	$271,789.16
Endorphin	$42,877.87	$66,903.88	$49,851.72	$44,992.55
Micro Nicros	$3,840.90	$7,338.85	$6,831.31	$6,556.96
Mini Nicros	$7,849.53	$5,918.85	$8,046.84	$5,312.88
Mozzie	$87,601.48	$109,958.56	$144,146.63	$111,002.44
Nicros	$29,505.11	$44,744.27	$36,959.74	$36,580.42
Rapel	$39,083.81	$45,681.81	$42,130.89	$34,957.13
Romeo	$30,921.83	$37,663.83	$47,860.15	$53,020.68
SlickRock	$39,695.72	$58,281.61	$43,061.09	$44,858.47
Wheeler	$24,077.33	$16,195.50	$32,633.96	$23,159.62
Total	$619,135.64	$841,602.32	$695,805.89	$632,230.31

FIGURE 8-14   Cross-tab conditional formatting with GridRowColumnValue

you may change it on the Customize Style tab of the Cross-Tab Expert dialog box (refer back to Figure 8-10).

Select a row or column field in the Rows or Columns list. Then, type a new value in the Alias For Formulas text box. You may then use the new text you typed as the parameter for the GridRowColumnValue function to refer to the row or column. If you're unsure of the row or column name aliases that are available, you may expand the Row or Column names subcategory of the Formatting Functions function tree category to see them.

> **TIP** *If you're formatting a Calculated Member, the value you specified for the Row or Column Value formula is used to refer to the row or column in conditional formatting formulas.*

The Display String Formatting Property

Another handy formatting function for custom cross-tab formatting is the Display String property on the Format Editor. By using this conditional string formula, you may actually format the cross-tab to show a different value in cells than the actual value displayed in the cell. Do this by selecting the cell that you want to customize. Then, use the Format pull-down menu, or right-click and choose Format Field from the pop-up menu. The Format Editor will appear. Select the Common tab and click the Display String conditional formula button. You may then create a Crystal Reports string formula to replace the actual contents of the cell with the results of the formula.

For example, if you wish to replace the actual formula contents with a shorter number followed by an "M" (indicating millions) or "K" (indicating thousands), you might use a Display String formula similar to this:

```
If CurrentFieldValue / 1000000 > 1 Then
    CurrentFieldValue / 1000000 & "M"
Else If CurrentFieldValue / 1000 > 1 Then
    CurrentFieldValue / 1000 & "K"
Else
    ToText(CurrentFieldValue)
```

CAUTION *As much as you might like to, you cannot drill down on a cross-tab object. If you include a cross-tab in a summary report, you can drill down on the summary report groups, but not on the cross-tab.*

Cross-Tab Virtual Page Formatting Options

Crystal Reports deals with cross-tabs that span multiple pages in an inconsistent manner between the Preview tab and what actually is printed or exported from the finished report. If a cross-tab contains so many columns that it exceeds the chosen Crystal Reports page width, it simply expands the Preview tab horizontally and shows the cross-tab across a single page. However, when you print or export the report, the cross-tab will actually be broken into multiple pages that print one after the other.

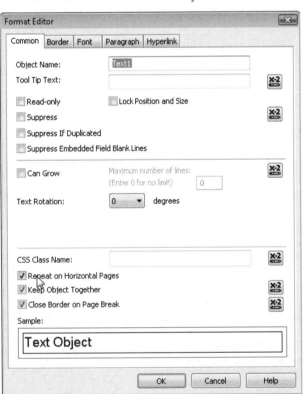

Several options are available to make these "virtual pages" appear more palatable when printed or exported. A formatting option in the Format Editor, as well as a horizontal page number special field, are available to enhance cross-tab appearance.

The Repeat On Horizontal Pages formatting option appears on the Format Editor Common tab. You may select this formatting property for virtually all Crystal Reports object types—database fields, bitmap graphics, text objects, and so forth. Any object that you apply this formatting option to will repeat on each subsequent page that a cross-tab object appears on, whether in the Preview tab or on a printed or exported report.

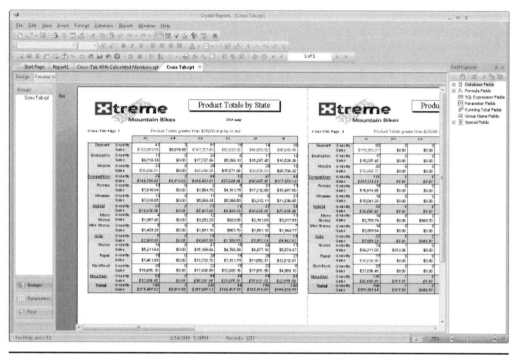

FIGURE 8-15   Multipage cross-tab

The other feature that's helpful with multipage cross-tabs is the Horizontal Page Number special field. Available along with other special fields in the Field Explorer, Horizontal Page Number will increment as cross-tabs span multiple pages, whereas the standard Page Number special field won't. Simply drag and drop the Horizontal Page Number special field onto the report as you would any other field. The page numbers will increment as cross-tabs span pages.

Figure 8-15 illustrates these features. Notice that the XTREME logo and a text object indicating custom formatting in the cross-tab appear on multiple horizontal pages displayed in the Preview tab. Also, notice that the Horizontal Page Number special field automatically increments when the cross-tab spans multiple pages.

Creating Charts

Depending on your reporting audience requirements, you may find that graphical representation of data either supplements, or perhaps even replaces, traditional textual presentation—sometimes "a picture is worth a thousand words." Crystal Reports' rich charting capability complements its complete formatting capabilities for textual information. Not only can you create attractive, meaningful text-based reports, you can present the information graphically as well. Using Crystal Reports charting and graphing capabilities, you can see your database data presented in colorful bar charts, in pie charts, in three-dimensional area charts, and in many other ways. These charts can be seen in the Preview tab right inside Crystal Reports, on Web reports, included in reports exported to other external file formats, or printed on a black-and-white or color printer.

There are some very fundamental questions you should initially ask before you add a chart to a report. Either you or your reporting audience should answer these questions satisfactorily before you proceed:

- Will my viewers really benefit from a graphical representation of the data?
- What kind of chart best matches the information to be shown?

While it's tempting to load up reports with lots of pretty, colorful charts, they aren't always an appropriate way to get across the "message" of the report. But for the many instances when a chart will add value to a report, you have a great number of charting options available to you.

Types and Layouts of Charts

Once you've decided to use a chart, you have two general choices to make about how you'll create your chart: what type of chart to use, and how the chart will be laid out. The *chart type* refers to what the chart will look like—whether it will show the data in bars, lines, a pie, or some other graphical representation. The *chart layout* refers to the data that will be used to make up the chart, whether it comes from the details section, group summaries, or a cross-tab or OLAP grid (OLAP reporting is discussed in Chapter 17).

Chart Type

The first consideration is which type of chart best represents the data to be charted. Although some types may be prettier than others, you again need to consider what type of chart will add real meaning to the data, allowing the viewer to get the most benefit from the report. Table 9-1 discusses the main types of charts available in the Crystal Reports Chart Expert and where they are best used. When you begin to use the Chart Expert, you'll notice that many of these main chart types actually have several variations.

Chart Type	Usage
Bar	Shows a series of bars side by side on the page, which is effective for showing how items compare to each other in terms of volume, size, dollars, etc., and may also be effective in plotting growth over time.
Line	Shows trends over time, particularly for multiple groups of data.
Area	Similar to a line chart, except that the area below the line is filled in with a color. Like the line chart, it is helpful for showing trends over time, but for just one or a few groups of data.
Pie	A circle with colored slices for each item, which is good for showing which item is the biggest "piece of the pie." The pie chart represents percentages for each item and is effective for small to moderate numbers of items.
Doughnut	Similar to a pie chart, showing who has the biggest bite of the donut. The only difference from a pie chart is that the doughnut has a hole in the middle, where the grand total for the chart is displayed.
3-D riser	A three-dimensional version of the bar chart. You can choose what shape you want for the bars—a cone, a pyramid, etc. Because this chart is three-dimensional, it can show multiple groups of data side by side.
3-D surface	A three-dimensional version of the area chart; it shows multiple groups of data in a three-dimensional view.
XY scatter	Plots data as points on two axes, allowing you to see if a correlation exists between the individual items.
Radar	Looks a little like a radar screen, with concentric circles expanding from the center. Each group of data is drawn as a line from the center to the outside of the chart, with the subtotal of that group displayed on the line in its relative location.
Bubble	Very similar to an XY scatter chart, plotting individual points within two axes, but provides more quantitative information by varying the size of the plotted points as well.

TABLE 9-1 Crystal Reports Chart Types

Chart Type	Usage
Stock	Similar to a bar chart in that it displays side-by-side bars. However, not all the bars start at the bottom of the chart. Both the tops and bottoms of the bars are based on data supplied. This chart is helpful for viewing minimum and maximum financial data, such as stock prices.
Numeric Axis	An alternative way of creating bar, line, or area charts (discussed previously in this table), a Numeric Axis chart allows you to use a numeric value or date/time field as the X-axis value for the charts.
Gauge	A gauge chart shows values much as a gauge on an auto dashboard shows the amount of fuel left or the speed of the automobile—a needle points to the value represented by the chart. One gauge appears for each group or single "on change of" value. If there are multiple "on change of" values, multiple needles appear in each gauge.
Gantt	This is the quintessential "project schedule" chart, showing one bar for each "task," plotting the start and end dates. This chart type can only be used with an Advanced Chart (no Group charting is available), and two date or date/time fields must be used with the chart.
Funnel	This chart type, which is very similar to a stacked bar chart where multiple elements make up a single bar, shows multiple elements in a funnel shape. A funnel chart is sometimes used to illustrate sales processes or potential, such as where each sales rep or time element sits "in the funnel."
Histogram	This standard statistical chart breaks down the data being charted into buckets or "bins," displaying a count of occurrences that fall into each bin as a bar in the chart. The number of bin bars typically is seven or eight, regardless of how many different occurrences or ranges are being charted. Values being charted are then dropped into the appropriate bin, based on where they fall in the ranges represented by the bins.

TABLE 9-1   Crystal Reports Chart Types *(continued)*

Chart Layout

In addition to the type of chart, you have a choice as to what data the chart will represent. *Cross-Tab charts* and *OLAP charts* are fairly easy to understand—they graph data in existing cross-tab objects or OLAP grids on your report. A *Group chart* graphs data contained in subtotal or summary fields in existing group headers or footers. An *Advanced chart* graphs data based on individual database records. The choice you make will be based on your individual report design and the way you want to graphically display the data.

It's particularly important to understand the difference between a Group chart and an Advanced chart, and to know where they can be placed on a report. Consider the following illustration:

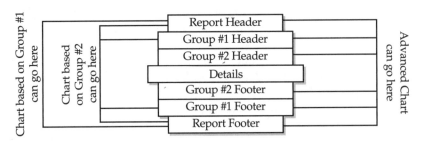

In essence, a chart must always be placed *at least one level higher* than the data it's graphing. An Advanced chart must be placed in a group header or footer or the report header or footer. A Group chart must be placed in a group header or footer of a higher-level group (if there is one), or the report header or footer. Because of the one-level-higher requirement, you can *never* place an Advanced chart or Group chart in the details section—cross-tab and OLAP charts can't go there either.

Cross-Tab and OLAP charts don't fit the one-level-higher scenario. Because they depict data in a specific cross-tab or OLAP grid, they make sense only if they're in the same section as the cross-tab or OLAP grid they're based on. If you base a chart on a cross-tab or OLAP grid, it must be placed in the same section. If you later move the cross-tab or OLAP grid to another report section, the chart will automatically move along with it. If you try to move a cross-tab or OLAP grid chart to a mismatching section, you'll be unable to drop the chart.

Where you place a chart determines the data that it depicts. If you create an Advanced chart and place it in a group header, it will depict just the database records for that group—a different chart will appear for each group. If you place the same Advanced chart in the report header or footer, it will depict data for the entire report. You'll see the same behavior for a Group chart. If you place it in a higher-level group, it will graph data only for subgroups within the group where it is located. If you place the Group chart in a report header or footer, it will include data for all groups on the report.

Creating Charts

You can create a limited set of chart types within the Standard, Cross-Tab, or OLAP Report Wizard from the Start Page or wizards available on the File | New pull-down menu. If you're using one of the report wizards, you will eventually arrive at a Chart section that contains a reduced set of charting options. To take advantage of all charting capabilities, you'll need to edit the existing chart or insert a new chart after using the wizards. You may also insert a new chart when creating a report with the Blank Report option.

If you've already created a report with a wizard and simply want to add a chart to it, or if your report is designed with the Blank Report option, you may add a new chart in one of two ways. While you can insert a chart when the Preview tab is displayed, you'll probably find better results if you first display the Design tab. Then, either click the Insert Chart button on the Insert Tools toolbar or choose Insert | Chart from the pull-down menus.

An outline of the chart will be placed on your mouse pointer to be dropped into a particular report section. As discussed earlier in the chapter, charts cannot be placed in all report sections—if you drag a chart over a prohibited section, a "no-drop" cursor (a circle with a line through it) will appear. Once you click the mouse to drop the chart onto the report, two different behaviors can result: either a bar chart will be placed on the report with most options automatically chosen, or the Chart Expert will appear for you to choose specific charting choices. The different behavior is determined by where you drop the chart and how your existing report is designed.

For example, if you insert a chart into the report header or footer when there are no groups on the report (or groups with no associated summary fields), the Chart Expert will appear with the Advanced Chart button selected. However, if you perform the same insertion with a report containing a group with a summary field, a bar chart based on that group will immediately appear in the report header or footer. If your report contains a Cross-Tab or OLAP Grid object and you select it before inserting a chart, Crystal Reports will create an additional section above that containing the Cross-Tab or OLAP Grid and place a bar chart based on the Cross-Tab or OLAP Grid in the new section. You will find other instances of direct placement of bar charts versus display of the Chart Expert too. Ultimately, if you're not happy with the default behavior, just make other choices in the Chart Expert (if necessary, you'll need to select the default chart and select Format | Chart Expert from the pull-down menus or right-click the chart and choose Chart Expert from the pop-up menu).

The *Chart Expert* is a tabbed dialog box that gives you tremendous flexibility for designing your charts. You specify chart options by progressing through the Chart Expert's six tabs: Type, Data, Axes, Options, Color Highlight, and Text (some of which may not appear, depending on the chart type chosen).

The Type Tab

When the Chart Expert first appears, the Type tab will be displayed, as shown in Figure 9-1.

First, choose the general type of chart (such as pie, bar, or area) that you want to use from the list. When you make a general choice, you typically see a more specific set of choices shown as thumbnails on the right. To use the specific type of chart, click the thumbnail that best represents what you want to use. You'll see a description of the layout and uses of the chart in the scroll box below.

Certain chart types give you a choice of horizontal or vertical direction. If you choose vertical with a bar chart, for example, the bars will grow out of the bottom of the chart. If you choose horizontal, they will spread from the left of the chart toward the right. By default, all chart types display in a flat non-dimensional form. However, most chart types will provide a Use Depth Effect check box to allow the chart to be displayed with a three-dimensional appearance. Checking this box will display the thumbnails with a 3-D appearance so that you can get a better idea of how your chart will ultimately appear.

The Data Tab

The Data tab is where you choose the layout for the chart—whether it will be an Advanced, Group, Cross-Tab, or OLAP chart. You also use the Data tab to select the actual summary, database, or formula fields you want Crystal Reports to use when creating your chart, and to specify when you want the chart to "change" graphically (when you want a new bar or pie slice to be created, when you want a new point plotted on the line, and so on).

Begin by choosing the chart layout you want to use. The following four buttons on the left side of the Data tab may or may not be enabled, depending on other elements in your report:

- **Group** Available only if at least one group with at least one summary field has been created on your report.

- **Advanced** Always available, although it is the default button only if nothing else is available.

- **Cross-Tab** Available only if one or more cross-tab objects already are on the report in the same section as the chart (or "companion" section, such as a corresponding header or footer section). If you have more than one cross-tab but haven't selected the cross-tab you want to chart first, this button will be disabled.

- **OLAP** Available only if one or more OLAP grids already are on the report in the same section as the chart (or in a "companion" section, such as a corresponding header or footer section). If you have more than one OLAP grid but haven't selected the grid you want to chart first, this button will be disabled.

Portions of the Data tab will change as you click different chart layout buttons.

Group

A Group chart will graph data from fields in an existing report group. You have to have at least one group defined, with at least one subtotal or summary field, before you can use this button. You also must have placed the chart in the report header or footer or in a higher-level group header or footer (above another group) for this button to be enabled. Figure 9-2 shows the Data tab when the Group button is clicked.

The On Change Of drop-down list lets you choose when you want the graph to start a new element. If, for example, you choose Customer.Customer Name, a new bar will show up in a bar chart for every customer. Or for another example, if you choose Employee.Last Name, a new slice in a pie chart will appear for every employee.

The On Change Of drop-down list's contents change in correlation with where you placed the chart on the report, how many groups are on the report, and which groups contains summary fields. In essence, the On Change Of drop-down list shows you one or two levels lower than where you placed your chart. For example, if you placed the chart in a report header or footer, the On Change Of drop-down list will show the highest-level group on the report. If there is more than one group, it will also show an additional option of showing the highest-level group and the next-highest-level group (assuming both groups contain at least one summary field). If you placed the report in a group header or footer, On Change Of will show the next two lower-level groups, and so on.

Choose the summary field in the group you
want to base the chart on

Choose the group you want to use to create the chart

FIGURE 9-2 Data tab for Group button

Here's an example of what shows up in the On Change Of drop-down list when the chart is placed in the report header and there are country and customer name groups on the report, both containing at least one summary field:

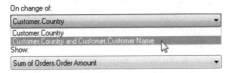

If you choose a single group, your chart will just summarize the values in that group, as shown here:

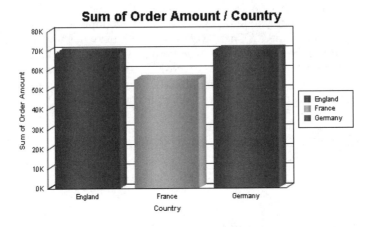

If you choose the two-group option, Crystal Reports actually creates multiple sections of the chart—the first section based on the first group, each containing individual chart elements based on the second group, like this:

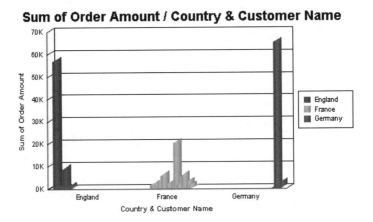

The Show drop-down list lets you choose what makes up the chart element. If, for example, you create a bar chart with On Change Of set to Customer.Country, and Show set to Sum of Orders.Order Amount, you'll see a new bar for every country. The bar's height or width (depending on whether you chose a horizontal or vertical bar chart) will be based on the subtotal of Order Amount for the group.

The Show drop-down list is populated according to what subtotal and summary fields you place in the group header or footer of the group chosen in On Change Of. For a group chart to work, you must have at least one summary or subtotal for the group—if you don't, the Group layout button won't even be available.

Advanced

An Advanced chart graphs data from individual database records in your report. Although you can create an Advanced chart even if you have groups defined, it won't be affected by the groups at all. Figure 9-3 shows the Data tab after you click Advanced.

Choose whether to have a new chart element appear for every record, or just when one or more fields change

List of fields chosen from Available Fields list (available only when On Change Of is chosen from the drop-down list above it)

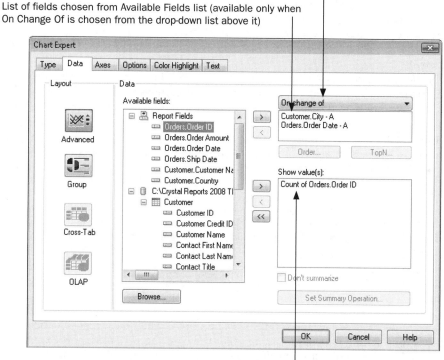

Field(s) and summary function each chart element will represent

FIGURE 9-3   Data tab for the Advanced button

This rather busy dialog box lets you choose data from the report or database to create a chart (fields don't have to be placed on the report to be used to create the chart). Because so many different choices are available, a little more forethought is required when using this dialog box.

The Available Fields list shows report, formula, running total, and database fields in the report. You can select any of these fields that you need for creating your chart. If you're unsure what kind of data is in a database field, select it and click Browse to see a sample of database data. Once you're ready to use a field as either an On Change Of or Show Value(s) field, select the field and click the right arrow next to the box where you want the field placed. It will be copied to the box on the right.

The drop-down list in the upper right gives you three choices: On Change Of, For Each Record, and For All Records. The choice you make here determines how often a new chart element (bar, pie slice, and so on) will appear in the chart.

If you choose For Each Record, a new element appears in the chart for every record in the report. This may be useful for very small tables that have only a few records in them. However, if your database has more than a few records, making this choice will probably render a chart that's too crowded to be of any real value. If you choose For All Records, you essentially create a *grand total* chart, showing just one element that displays a total of all records on the report. If you choose this option, the box below the drop-down list remains empty—you won't be able to add any fields to it from the Available Fields list. If you choose For Each record, you may add one field from the Available Fields list that will label each chart element.

By choosing On Change Of in the drop-down list and choosing one or more fields from the Available Fields list, you can create a chart that summarizes values for the chosen field or fields. This option basically creates an invisible group within the chart, creating a new chart element every time the chosen field changes. For example, if your report contains no groups but you choose On Change Of Customer.Country, your chart will have a new element appear for each unique country that appears in the database. Whatever field you add to the Show Value(s) list will be summarized or subtotaled by country, and the result will be used as the value for the chart.

TIP *You can choose one or two fields to add to the On Change Of list. This works like the Group chart option, described previously, in which you can choose to show the highest-level group and the next-highest-level group. If you choose one field, the chart will contain only one section with all the elements located in it. If you choose two fields, the chart will be broken into side-by-side sections, with the first-chosen field making up the first section. Then, individual elements for the second field will appear within each of the sections based on the first field.*

Although there isn't an actual group on the report, Crystal Reports is creating an "invisible" group within the chart. You have control over the way the Chart Expert uses these groups. The TopN and Order buttons control this. If you click TopN, you'll see the Group Sort Expert dialog box, where you can choose to include only the top N, bottom N, Top N Percentage, or Bottom N percentage groups in your chart, and choose which number to use for N.

If you click Order, you'll see the Chart Sort Order dialog box with a drop-down list containing Ascending, Descending, Specified Order, and Original Order options. You may choose to show the chart elements in A to Z order, Z to A order, or using specified grouping (and, if you recall from Chapter 3, although Original Order is an option, it's probably of little use). If the chosen field is a date, time, or date/time field, you can choose how often you want a new chart element to appear (monthly, weekly, every minute, hourly, and so on). Refer to Chapter 3 for information on Top N, Specified Order grouping, and grouping on date/time fields.

Once you've chosen a field in the On Change Of box to determine when a new chart element will appear, you can add a field or fields to the Show Value(s) list to indicate which values Crystal Reports will use to size the chart element. If you add multiple fields to this list, the chart will contain multiple bars, lines, and so forth—one for each field you add to the list.

If you add a number or currency field to this list (and you haven't chosen For Each Record in the top drop-down list), Crystal Reports automatically uses the Sum function to subtotal the field for each invisible group. If you choose another type of field, Crystal Reports automatically uses the Count function. If you wish to change the summary function (for example, to graph the average sales amount instead of the total), you can select the field you want to change in the Show Value(s) list and click Set Summary Operation. A dialog box will appear with a drop-down list containing the available summary functions for that type of field. Choose the summary function you want used to size the chart element. The Percentage Summary Field option for group summaries, discussed in Chapter 2, is also available here. By checking the Show As A Percentage Of check box, you can choose a higher-level group total or grand total, and chart elements will display the percentage of the higher totals that each of the invisible group totals represents.

NOTE *If you choose On Change Of for an Advanced Chart and add a formula field to the Show Value(s) list, the Don't Summarize check box will be enabled when you select the formula. Clicking this check box for the formula (probably a formula that already does some sort of summarization) allows you to display the formula's value directly in the chart without it being summarized again.*

If you choose For Each Record in the top drop-down list, Crystal Reports will display a new chart element for every record on the report—no invisible group will be created. In this case, any fields you add to the Show Value(s) list won't be summarized—whatever value the fields return for each record will be charted.

Cross-Tab

While there are several ways of creating a chart based on a cross-tab object, the most consistent first step is to select the cross-tab you want to chart on *before* you insert a chart (Chapter 8 discusses cross-tab objects). When you choose the previously described Insert Chart options after selecting a cross-tab, Crystal Reports will add an additional report section above that of the selected cross-tab and place the chart in the new section. To change the way the chart displays the various cross-tabs rows and columns, click the Data tab. Figure 9-4 shows the Data tab after you click Cross-Tab.

The On Change Of drop-down list includes the two outer fields you chose for the cross-tab row and column; if you used multiple row and column fields, only the first row or field can be used. Crystal Reports will create one chart element (bar, pie slice, and so on) for each occurrence of this field in the cross-tab.

The Subdivided By drop-down list changes, depending on the choice you make in the On Change Of drop-down list. It will display options for no subdivision, the row or column that corresponds to the choice you made in On Change Of, or the lower-level group field for the choice made in On Change Of (if the cross-tab contains nested rows or columns). If you choose None, the chart will create only one series of chart elements, based on the field in the On Change Of drop-down list. If, however, you want to create two series of elements for side-by-side comparison, or if you're using a 3-D riser or 3-D area chart and want to see multiple elements three-dimensionally, choose the other row/column field in the Subdivided By drop-down list.

The Show drop-down list shows the summary field or fields you placed in your cross-tab. Choose the field that you want to use in your chart. This field determines the size of the chart elements (height of a bar, size of a pie slice, and so forth).

FIGURE 9-4   Data tab for the Cross-Tab button

The following illustration shows the resulting 3-D riser chart for the Data tab shown in Figure 9-4:

CAUTION *If you edit a cross-tab chart in the Chart Expert, change the chart type to be Group or Advanced, and then click OK to close the Chart Expert, you won't be able to later re-edit the chart and change the chart type back to Cross-Tab. You may use undo options to undo the chart change, or you may re-insert another chart after first selecting the desired cross-tab object.*

OLAP

Charting on OLAP grids (Chapter 17 discusses OLAP reporting) is similar, but not identical, to charting on cross-tabs. The first step is to add an OLAP grid to the desired area of your report. The most straightforward method to chart on the grid is to select it before choosing any of the previously described Insert Chart options. This will create a new report section above the grid and place the chart in the new section. If you have multiple OLAP grids on your report, you *must* select the specific grid you wish to chart on before inserting a chart. If you only have one OLAP grid on a report, the OLAP button will be enabled in the Data tab even if you don't select the OLAP grid first. Figure 9-5 shows the Data tab after you click OLAP.

Creating a chart based on an OLAP grid is very similar to creating a chart based on a cross-tab. There are just a couple of differences between the two. There is no summary field to choose (OLAP grids display only one value, so there is no choice to make). Also, the dimension hierarchy of your OLAP grid may be a little different than the multiple row/column fields you added to a cross-tab object.

Choose a dimension on which to base the chart from the On Change Of drop-down list. A new chart element will be created for every occurrence of this dimension. If you leave the Subdivided By drop-down list set to None, the chart creates only one series of chart elements,

Click to chart off all dimensions in the OLAP
grid. The other controls will be dimmed.

Choose dimension to determine chart element

Optionally choose another dimension for multipart chart

Click to limit the chart to certain values in additional dimensions not
included in the On Change Of and Subdivided By drop-down lists

FIGURE 9-5 Data tab for the OLAP button

based on the dimension in the On Change Of drop-down list. If, however, you want to create
two series of elements for side-by-side comparison, or if you're using a 3-D riser or 3-D area
chart and want to see multiple elements three-dimensionally, choose another dimension in
the Subdivided By drop-down list. You can choose a next "deeper" level dimension here if
you've created multiple levels of dimensions in your OLAP grid.

Depending on how many nested dimensions your OLAP grid contains, and how the fields
that make up the dimension relate to each other (their *hierarchy*), you may need to filter the
chart to just certain field values in a dimension. To do this, click the Other Dimensions button
in the lower right of the Data tab. This displays the Format Other Dimensions dialog box,
where you can choose the particular subdimension of the OLAP grid that you want the chart
filtered by.

Click one of the available Other Dimensions and click Select A Member Value. The Member Selector dialog box appears, with the dimension hierarchy displayed in an Explorer-like fashion.

Navigate through the dimension hierarchy and choose a level that you want to limit the chart to. For example, if you navigate down from All Products and choose Bikes, your OLAP chart will just contain totals for the Bikes in the OLAP grid.

The Axes Tab

The Axes tab will appear if you have chosen a chart type that makes use of X and Y axes (for example, a bar or line chart—pie or doughnut chart choices will eliminate the Axes tab). The Axes tab gives you complete control over how Crystal Reports displays the X, Y, and Z (if you're using a 3-D chart) axes of the chart. Figure 9-6 shows the Axes tab.

By making choices in the Axes tab, you can control how Crystal Reports displays axes on your charts. The *axes* are the areas of the chart that describe or depict the data values in the chart. If, for example, you have a bar chart in which each bar represents sales volume for

Displays major or minor gridlines
for different axes on the chart

Controls automatic or manual setting
of number of divisions on the chart

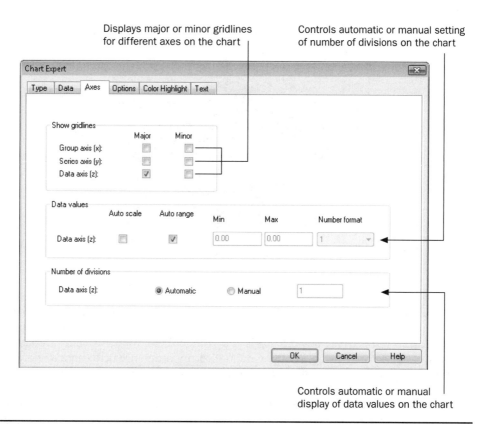

FIGURE 9-6   The Axes tab

a country, the bottom of the chart where each country is listed is called the *group axis* (also sometimes called the *X axis*). The left side of the chart where the numbers representing the volume appear is called the *data axis* (sometimes called the *Y axis*), as shown here:

If you are using a 3-D chart, the data axis is the Z axis, and a new axis called the *series axis* is the Y axis, like this:

Click the Major or Minor check box to add gridlines to the chosen axes. *Major gridlines* fall directly in line with the axis labels that Crystal Reports assigns to the axis. *Minor gridlines* appear in between the axis labels and work only for numeric labels. Depending on the type of chart you're using, you may not notice any difference between major and minor gridlines. Also, some charts will always have a group axis gridline, regardless of what you choose on the Axes tab.

If you leave the Auto Range check box for the Data Values option on, Crystal Reports automatically formats the chart according to the number of elements it includes. If you wish to customize this, you can turn off the Auto Range option and add starting and ending values for the axes, as well as choose the number format (decimals, currency symbols, and so on) to use for the labels. If you choose a certain number format, such as a currency symbol, and then recheck Auto Range, the axes will be automatically renumbered, but the number format you chose will stay in place. The Auto Scale option affects the beginning numeric value that the data axis starts with. If you choose Auto Scale, Crystal Reports uses the values of the chart elements to choose an appropriate starting number for the data axis.

If you leave the Number of Divisions set to Automatic, Crystal Reports will create a predefined number of labels and gridlines for the data axes. Clicking the Manual radio button and specifying a number in the text box will create your specified number of divisions, along with labels and gridlines, for the data axes.

The Options Tab

The Options tab allows you to customize general options for your chart, such as whether to display it in color or black and white, whether to show a legend and where to place it, and other options. The Options tab will change based on the type of chart you've chosen. Figure 9-7 shows the Options tab for a bar chart.

Show nothing, field, or value of
element on chart elements

Report items underneath
chart will show through

Choose size and shape of markers for
line charts and legend for other charts

Show chart in color or black and white

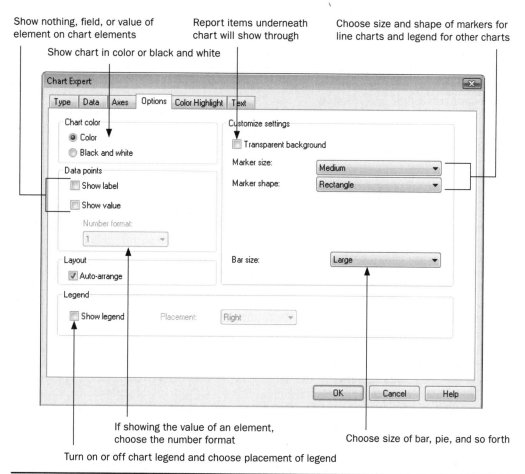

Figure 9-7   The Options tab

If showing the value of an element,
choose the number format

Choose size of bar, pie, and so forth

Turn on or off chart legend and choose placement of legend

Tip   *If you are printing your reports on a black-and-white printer, it may be preferable to leave the chart in color and let the printer assign gray tones to the chart elements. These may actually look better than the ones Crystal Reports assigns. Experiment to determine what works best with your particular printer.*

The Data Points section lets you choose whether you want labels, numbers, or both to appear on your chart elements. If, for example, you choose Show Label with a pie chart, each of the slices of the pie will be labeled with the item that the slice refers to. If you choose Show Value with a bar chart and choose a number format of $1, you'll see the actual dollar amounts (with no decimal places) appear above each bar.

The Marker Size and Marker Shape drop-down lists let you choose how markers look on a line chart. *Markers* are the points on the line chart that are connected by the lines.

The Show Legend check box determines whether or not a legend appears on your chart. The *legend* is the color-coded key that indicates what the elements of your chart refer to. You can also choose where to place the legend with options in the Placement drop-down list. You might want legends for a pie chart with no labels, for example. However, if you are using a bar chart with labels already appearing along the bottom of the chart, a legend is redundant and should be turned off.

Other choices will appear on the Options tab, depending on the type of chart you choose in the Type tab. For example, Pie or Doughnut charts will have choices for detaching or "exploding" the largest or smallest slice. And, 3-D charts will have a choice of several viewing angles.

The Color Highlight Tab

The Color Highlight tab allows conditional formatting of chart element colors. While you can pick individual chart elements, such as an individual pie wedge, or an individual bar, and change the color (as discussed later in the chapter, under "Changing Colors and Shades of Chart Elements"), your change will always affect the same wedge or bar in each chart, regardless of what the value of that element is. In other words, if you change the pie wedge for Colorado, which happens to be the second wedge in the chart, to a light blue color, the second wedge in the chart will be light blue no matter what data populates the chart. If the data changes so that Colorado becomes the fourth wedge, the second wedge will still be formatted as light blue.

The Color Highlight tab works with charts in much the same way that the Highlighting Expert works with text (the Highlighting Expert is discussed in detail in Chapter 6). You may choose one or more conditions that determine the color of a chart element. The Color Highlight tab is shown in Figure 9-8.

By choosing either the "On Change Of" field that the chart is based on or the summary field used to determine the weight of the chart element, you can conditionally set the color of the chart element.

For example, Figure 9-8 shows a condition set up to change the color of the chart element (in this case, the bar of a bar chart) to Red if the value shown by the bar exceeds $35,000. To set this condition, click the New button, which will add a new condition to the Item list. Then, choose the field you want to base the condition on and the comparison operator (such as equal to, greater than, and so forth) from the first two drop-down lists of the Value Of section. Type the value you want to compare to in the text box in the same section. Then, choose the color you wish the chart element to display if the condition is true from the color list on the lower right. Any chart elements that meet the condition will be given the chosen color.

You may add as many conditions as you wish by clicking New multiple times. If you have multiple conditions that may conflict, such as a condition that looks for a value between 100 and 1,000, and another condition that looks for a value greater than 500, you list. Conditions toward the top of the item list take priority.

The Text Tab

The Text tab, shown in Figure 9-9, allows you to assign text to different parts of your chart, and change the appearance of these text items. You can add a chart title, subtitle, and footnote. Also, you can place titles on the group, data, and series (or data2) axes of your chart.

Reorder priority of conditions if
there are more than one

Choose field and condition to
determine element color

Click to add or remove a condition

Choose color for elements that
meet the chosen condition

FIGURE 9-8 The Color Highlight tab

By default, the Auto-Text check boxes are all selected and the text boxes next to them are dimmed. You'll notice that Crystal Reports has added titles into certain items automatically, depending on the data that the chart is based on. If you don't wish to use Crystal Reports' default titles on the chart, uncheck the Auto-Text check box for the desired title and then type the material you want to appear on the chart in the associated text boxes on the Text tab. If you leave a text box blank, that title won't appear on the chart.

To change the appearance of the different items, select the item you want to change in the list on the lower right of the Text tab. Then, click Font to choose the font face, size, and appearance for that item. A sample of the font you choose appears in the shaded box above the Font button.

Figure 9-10 shows a chart with all the labels set. You can see where each of the labels appears on a typical chart.

Placing and Sizing Charts

Once you complete all the information on the Chart Expert and click OK, Crystal Reports redisplays the chart with any changes you chose in the Chart Expert. The chart remains selected after you close the Chart Expert—you'll notice the shaded outline and sizing

Check to automatically generate
text based on data in the chart

If you turn off Auto-Text, type in titles
for various parts of the chart

Choose fonts for different parts of the chart text

Figure 9-9 The Text tab

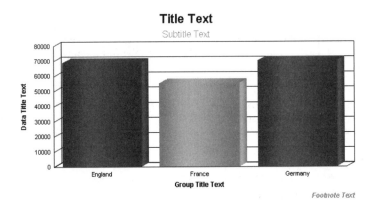

Figure 9-10 Labels from the Text tab

handles around the chart. You can now drag it to another location in the same section, or move it to another section on the report. You can also resize the chart by using the sizing handles, or move and resize the chart by choosing Format | Size And Position from the pull-down menus, or by right-clicking the chart and choosing Size And Position from the pop-up menu.

CAUTION *Make sure you have the entire chart selected before you attempt to move or resize it. If you see sizing handles around any individual chart elements, such as the title, or an individual bar or pie wedge, you'll move or resize the individual element instead of the entire chart.*

Remember that where you place a chart determines the data that it displays. If you place an Advanced or Group chart in the report header or footer, it will display data for the whole report. If you place the chart in a group header or footer, the chart will appear for every group, showing data for only that particular group. Cross-Tab and OLAP charts display the data from the particular objects they're based on. If you place a cross-tab object and matching chart in a group header or footer, the cross-tab and chart will display data only for the group they're in. Since OLAP grids don't change with their location on the report, a matching OLAP chart won't change if you move it.

Cross-Tab and OLAP charts are always in the same section (or a "companion" section, such as a matching footer or header) as their corresponding cross-tab object or OLAP grid object. You may have an OLAP grid in the report footer and its matching chart in the report header, but if you try to move the chart into a group header or footer, it won't work. And if you then move the OLAP grid from the report footer to a group footer, the chart will automatically move to the matching group header.

TIP *If you create a chart based on, say, a Region field, but years appear in the Design tab, don't be surprised. The charts that appear in the Design tab are "dummy" charts that don't depict actual data in the database. When you preview the report, however, you will see live data depicted in the chart.*

Placing Charts Alongside Text

If you initially place a chart in a report or group header, the chart will print before the rest of the report or the group, because the section containing the chart prints first. Sometimes, you may want a chart to appear *alongside* the data it's referring to. Typically, this might be an Advanced chart that you've placed in a group header. Instead of having the chart print by itself, followed by the details that belong to the group, you may want the chart to print alongside the details sections.

By using the Underlay option in the Section Expert, you can format the group header section to underlay the following details sections, thereby printing the chart alongside the other items. For this to work effectively, you need to size and move the details section objects so that they won't be overprinted by the chart. Then, move and size the chart so that it will appear to the side of the details section objects. Using the Section Expert, choose the Underlay Following Sections option for the section containing the chart. If there is a group name, column headings, or other information in the group header that you *don't* want to be underlaid, you need to create a second group header section for the chart that you underlay. Format it to use the Underlay feature and format the first group header containing the textual information with Underlay turned off. See Chapter 8 for more information on multiple sections and the Underlay feature.

Figure 9-11 shows a chart placed in the Report Header with Underlay Following Sections turned on.

Modifying Existing Charts

Once you've created a chart, you may wish to change it. You may not agree with the default choices Crystal Reports makes when it inserts certain charts for you. Perhaps you prefer to see a pie chart instead of a bar chart. Or, you may want to change the titles that appear on the chart. You may even want to change the chart from an Advanced chart to a Group chart, or vice versa.

First, select the chart you want to change in either the Design or Preview tab (make sure you select the entire chart, not just an embedded chart element). Then, choose Format | Chart Expert from the pull-down menus, or right-click the selected chart and choose Chart Expert from the pop-up menu. The Chart Expert will reappear, and you can make any desired changes before clicking OK.

If you place a single chart on the report that may appear multiple times (for example, you place a chart in a group header that prints for multiple report groups), you'll find that a submenu will appear when you attempt to redisplay the Chart Expert. The submenu's choices, Applied To Group Template and Applied To This Instance, determine whether the Chart Expert will apply to *all* charts in all groups (the Group Template choice) or to the individual chart in the group you selected (the This Instance choice).

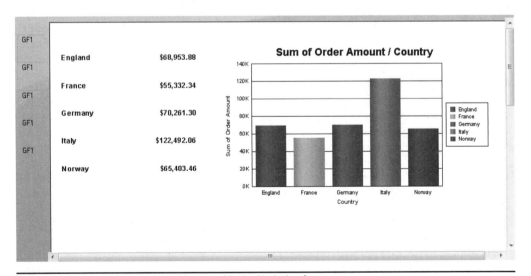

FIGURE 9-11 Chart placed alongside text with the Underlay feature

Tɪᴘ   The Crystal Reports Format Painter works with charts, as well as textual elements. However, note that only the few formatting items that appear on the chart Format Editor, such as a border, drop shadow, and so forth, will be copied from one chart to others. No chart-specific items, such as chart type, legend, or titles, will be copied by the Format Painter.

Zooming In and Out on Charts

You may zoom in and out on a limited number of chart types. If you have created a Bar or Line chart, you'll notice additional options, such as Select Mode and Zoom In, available on the pop-up menu when you right-click. You may also select a chart and use the Zoom options from the Chart pull-down menu.

If you choose the Zoom In option, your mouse cursor will change to a magnifying glass with a plus sign. While you may be tempted to just click somewhere inside the chart expecting to zoom in, you must actually hold down your mouse button and draw an elastic box with the mouse. When you release the mouse button, the chart will zoom in to the area you surrounded. You may continue to highlight additional areas to zoom in further on the chart.

To zoom back out, right-click the chart and choose Zoom Out from the pop-up menu, or choose the associated option from the Chart pull-down menu. The mouse cursor will change to a magnifying glass with a minus sign. Just click anywhere on the chart to zoom back out.

When you're finished zooming in or out on a chart, choose Select Mode from the chart pop-up or pull-down menus. Your mouse cursor will return to its default "four-arrow" state so that you can select the chart to move or resize it on the report.

Drilling Down on Charts

If you create a Group chart, you'll notice the mouse cursor change to a magnifying glass when you point to a chart element. This drill-down cursor indicates that you can double-click a chart element that you're interested in to drill down on the chart. When you drill down on a chart element, another tab appears next to the Preview tab for the particular group you drilled down on. Drill-down allows your report viewer to interact with charts, much as they interact with group footer and group header subtotal and summary fields.

By creative use of Group charts and hiding of details and group header/footer sections, you can create a very visually appealing interactive report for use in online reporting environments. You could, for example, create a large Group pie chart and place it in the report header, along with grand totals and text objects. You might add a text object that directs the viewer to double-click a pie slice for more information. You may also set Tool Tip text for the chart, prompting the viewer to double-click the slice they're interested in. Select the chart and right-click, choosing Format Chart from the pop-up menu. Then, type text into the Tool Tip Text box directly, or use the Conditional Formula button to add Tool Tip text via a string formula.

To add even more interactivity, you could add lower-level Group or Advanced charts in the report's group headers or footers, hiding them with the Section Expert. When the user drills down on the higher-level chart in the report header, a drill-down tab showing a more detailed chart will open. You can create drill-down levels until the user eventually reaches details sections to see low-level transaction data.

Get more information about creating multiple groups, drill-down, and hidden sections in Chapter 2 and Chapter 7.

TIP Drill-down is available and useful only when viewing a report in its native format. Viewers can drill down on reports displayed right on the Preview tab of Crystal Reports, by using a report integrated with a custom Windows or Web application developed in Java or Visual Studio. NET, or by publishing the report to a member of the BusinessObjects Enterprise family (discussed in Part II of this book). Drill-down doesn't work with reports exported to other file formats, such as Word and Excel. Obviously, drill-down won't be effective with printed reports.

Finer Points of Chart Formatting

So far, the discussion on chart formatting has been limited to what can be accomplished in the Chart Expert. However, Crystal Reports provides more granular formatting options by way of in-place chart formatting. *In-place* formatting allows you to select individual parts of the chart, such as chart or axis titles, individual chart elements, or the chart legend, and perform additional formatting functions.

CAUTION While in-place chart formatting reduces the number of steps required to format individual chart elements, it also makes it easier to inadvertently move or resize an individual chart element when you mean to move or resize the entire chart. Pay close attention to what has been highlighted (the entire chart, or an individual chart element) before you move or resize with your mouse.

One of the first chart formatting options that you should become familiar with is the *Auto Arrange Chart* option. Once you've selected a chart, you may choose this option either from the Chart pull-down menu or by right-clicking on the chart and choosing it from the pop-up menu. This option will use default placement, sizing, and formatting for chart elements. If you haven't done any individual element formatting since you've created the chart, this option very well may not do anything at all. However, if you've changed positions of certain items (such as the chart title, legend, or axes titles), you may see them snap back to other positions that you didn't intend. Don't worry too much about this behavior—if you don't like the changes that Auto Arrange makes to the chart, you may undo its effects with Edit | Undo from the pull-down menus, the Undo toolbar button in the Standard toolbar, or by pressing CTRL-Z.

Customizing Charts with Chart Options

While you can control a good deal of chart formatting from within the Chart Expert, there will probably be many times when you wish to have more detailed control over chart appearance. Crystal Reports allows you either to select individual elements of the chart (such as the title, individual bars or pie wedges, the legend, and so forth) and apply formatting to them, or to make more specific changes that affect the overall chart appearance.

To perform generalized formatting on the entire chart, choose Chart | Chart Options from the pull-down menus or right-click the chart and choose Chart Options from the pop-up menu. A tabbed dialog box will appear, showing various detailed options for changing overall chart appearance.

In most cases, you'll notice a thumbnail miniature picture of the chart in the dialog box. As you make changes to the dialog box, you'll see the changes immediately reflected in the thumbnail. When you click OK, the chart will reflect the changes.

TIP *If you make formatting choices while viewing a group chart in the Preview tab, changes will apply only to the particular instance of the chart you selected. If, for example, you choose a chart in the Canada group header and customize it with Chart Options, the other charts in the USA and Mexico group headers won't be affected. If you want to have these changes propagate to all other chart instances, right-click the chart and choose Apply Changes To All Charts from the pop-up menu, or choose Chart | Apply Changes To All Charts from the pull-down menus. If you want to undo the custom settings so that the selected chart matches the remainder of the charts in other groups, choose Discard Custom Changes from the same menu.*

In addition to general chart formatting options available on the Chart Options dialog box, various individual customization options are available for individual portions of a chart, including individual elements (such as line/pie/bar elements), the chart "frame," and individual text portions of the chart (such as titles, axes labels, and footnote text).

Changing Colors and Shades of Chart Elements

When you create a chart in the Chart Expert, your only choices for affecting chart colors are the Color and Black And White radio buttons on the Options tab, and the Color Highlight tab for conditional color selection. By choosing the Color radio button in the Options tab, you have no control over what individual colors or shades the chart elements will have. And, while you can set conditions for coloring chart elements in the Color Highlight tab, this is an unduly complicated task if your desire is to simply change the default colors. The ability to completely customize element colors and shades is a feature available with Chart Options.

Begin by selecting the element you wish to color. This can be an individual bar, pie slice, or line. Note that it may look as though you've selected only part of an element—for example, just one side or just the top of the bar. Whenever you change the color, however, it will apply to the entire element.

Then, choose the appropriate format option from the Chart pull-down menu, or right-click the element and choose the Format option from the pop-up menu. For example, if you select an individual bar in a bar chart and choose Format Series Riser, the following dialog box appears:

Click Border tab to choose various
options for element border

Choose new color from color palette

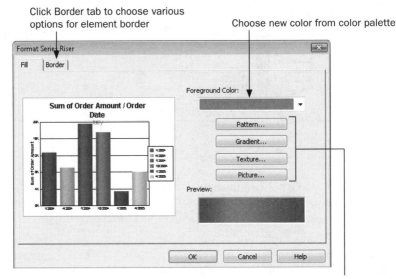

Click one of these buttons to fill with
a pattern, gradient, texture, or picture

You may change not only the color of the chosen chart element, but also the pattern displayed in the element. By default, all charts created with the Chart Expert contain solid colors. However, you may want to replace the solid color with a graduated color, a pattern, or maybe even a picture. You may change the solid color to use for the element by choosing a predefined color from the palette. If you want to use a color that's not in the standard palette, click the More button at the bottom of the palette. A Custom Color dialog box appears, in which you can choose a custom color.

TIP *You may notice that the first release of Crystal Reports 2008 initially displays certain chart types (bar charts, in particular) with a graduated color combination (this automatic behavior may not appear in subsequent releases). While you may prefer this new appearance, you may occasionally want to display chart elements with the "flat" color approach of earlier versions of Crystal Reports. Rather than formatting individual chart elements, you may select the entire chart, right-click, and choose Apply Flat Colors from the pop-up menu. Chart element colors will revert to non-graduated colors. If you wish to re-display the graduated color scheme, you may simply undo the formatting change, or right-click on the chart again and choose Apply Shaded Colors from the pop-up.*

To apply a pattern, gradient, or texture, or to fill the chart element with a picture, choose one of the corresponding buttons on the right side of the dialog box. For example, clicking the gradient button displays a dialog box showing preset color gradients. If you click Advanced Options, the gradient dialog box displays an extra section that lets you design your own gradients.

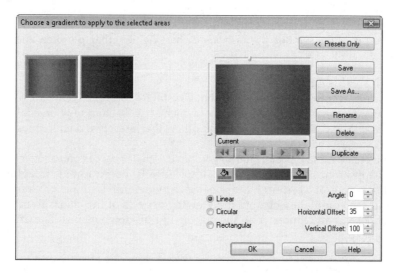

Either choose one of the preset gradients or use the dialog box options to customize your own gradient. When you click OK, the solid color previously appearing in the preview portion of the dialog box will be replaced by the selected gradient.

Click OK on the Formatting dialog box to apply your selected color, pattern, gradient, or picture to the chart element.

TIP   Often, gradients and patterns, or even certain solid background colors, can add visual appeal if applied to the whole background of the chart. To do this, select the entire chart, making sure no individual chart elements are selected. Then, right-click or use the Chart menu options to format the chart background. Color and gradient/pattern options you choose will then apply to the chart background.

Customizing and Moving Chart Titles, Labels, and the Legend

When you add a title, labels, and legend to your chart with the Options and Text tabs of the Chart Expert, Crystal Reports places them in specific locations, using specific colors and alignment. If you choose to display a legend on your chart, you have only a few predefined locations on the Options tab where you can place it. Also, if you choose the Auto Arrange Chart option discussed earlier, chart elements will be repositioned to default locations.

However, chart titles and labels are all objects that you can select by pointing and clicking within the chart in either the Design or Preview tab. Once you've selected an object (as denoted by the "sizing handle" blocks on all sides), you can reposition the text simply by pointing inside the text frame and dragging it to a new location. To resize the object, position the cursor on one of the sizing handles and narrow or stretch the object. Then, use the appropriate Chart menu or pop-up menu format option to display the Formatting dialog box. You may choose alternate colors, fonts, alignment, and other text-related options on the Font and Text tabs of the Formatting dialog box.

If you want to move the legend to a specific place on the chart, just drag it (you can't resize it) to its new location. You can actually select and format three different parts of the legend: the frame, the textual items, and the symbols. Select each piece and use the Chart pull-down menu or pop-up menu formatting option to change them. Note that if you change certain properties of the symbol, the associated chart element (bar, pie slice, and so forth) changes along with it.

Changing 3-D Viewing Angles

Some of the more impressive chart types that Crystal Reports can create are 3-D charts. There are several types of 3-D charts, some of which actually chart only one data item, such as the 3-D bar, pie, and doughnut charts, and others that chart two data items, such as 3-D riser and 3-D surface charts.

Once you create these types of charts, you have a great deal of control over the three-dimensional appearance of the chart. For example, if you choose a single doughnut chart, Crystal Reports gives it a certain 3-D appearance by default. Using choices from Chart Options, you can completely change the viewing aspects of the chart. To make these selections, choose Chart Options from the pop-up or pull-down menus. The Chart Options dialog box will appear.

The Appearance tab contains various sliders and spin boxes that allow you to change all visual aspects of the 3-D doughnut chart.

Dual-data-item 3-D charts, such as the 3-D riser and 3-D surface charts, have even more "whiz-bang" 3-D capabilities. Not only can you choose from a variety of viewing angles right on the Chart Expert's Options tab when you create the chart, but you also can perform almost unlimited 3-D customizations using pull-down or pop-up menu formatting options.

Select the 3-D riser chart you want to adjust. Then, choose 3D Viewing Angle from either the pull-down or pop-up menus. The Choose A Viewing Angle dialog box appears. If you click Advanced Options, the dialog box displays an extra section that lets you completely customize the viewing angle, rather than just choosing presets, as shown in Figure 9-12.

This dialog box offers numerous options for changing the 3-D appearance of the chart. You can simply choose either a custom angle (chosen in the Chart Expert Options tab) or a standard angle by clicking one of the two boxes on the left side of the dialog box, or choose from the Current and Default saved angle definitions by clicking the drop-down list or forward/backward buttons below the main thumbnail. You can also manually change all kinds of 3-D viewing aspects of the chart by making manual adjustments on the Rotate, Pan, Walls, and Move tabs. You'll see the main thumbnail in the middle of the dialog box change as you choose alternative viewing options.

You may be confused by the prompt to name and save a viewing angle that you've customized when you click OK. If you make manual changes to the viewing angle with options on the tab, rather than choosing one of the built-in presets or named angles, you'll be prompted to save the settings before you apply them. While you can replace an existing named angle, or create a new one, before you actually apply the viewing angle to the chart, you don't have to. Just click the Cancel button on the Enter 3D Viewing Angle Preset name dialog box. The changes will still be applied to the chart.

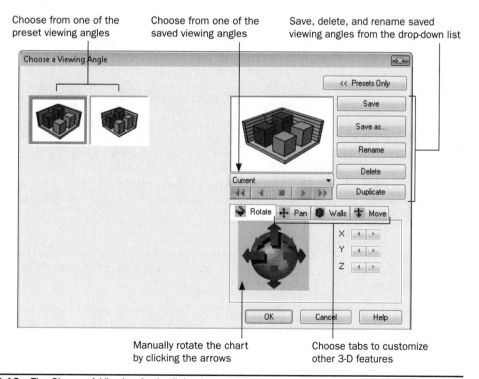

FIGURE 9-12   The Choose A Viewing Angle dialog box

Choosing Additional Chart Types

Although the Chart Expert contains many different types and variations of charts (bubble, scatter, and so forth), the Format Chart option contains even more (provided you selected the Custom Charting option when you installed Crystal Reports). To look at the available additional chart types, select the chart that you want to potentially apply a new chart type to. Then, choose Load Template from either the pull-down or pop-up menu. The Choose A Chart Type dialog box will appear.

This dialog box presents a list of chart categories on the left. When you click each category, a large assortment of chart thumbnails from within that category appears on the right. Scroll down through the different thumbnails until you find a custom chart type that appeals to you. Select it and click OK. The new chart type will be applied to the selected chart. If you want to customize the look of the chart further, use any of the techniques discussed earlier in the chapter.

NOTE *You must have chosen the Custom Charting option when you installed Crystal Reports for these additional chart types to be available. If they're not available, rerun Crystal Reports setup and choose the Custom Charting option.*

Saving and Reusing Chart Templates

If you have a particular set of formatting settings you'd like to use on more than one chart, you can save the settings in a chart *template.* You can then apply the template to another chart that you create or edit.

To save a template, make any desired changes to your chart, such as changing label positions, element colors, perhaps the legend position, and any other settings you want to make. Then, either choose Save As Template from the pull-down or pop-up menu. A Save As dialog box will appear where you can give your chart a name (the template will be saved with a .3tf file extension).

To apply the saved template to a new chart, use the steps described in the preceding section, "Choosing Additional Chart Types." Notice that the last category on the Choose A Chart type dialog box is *User Defined.* When you choose that category, the collection of thumbnails consists of all the templates you've saved. Choose the thumbnail that you wish to apply to your current chart. When you click OK, the template settings will be applied to the existing chart.

PART I

Creating Geographic Maps

Much of the rest of this book discusses techniques for designing textual reports. However, chart and Flash/Xcelsius integration chapters deviate from this direction, as does this chapter. Your reports can include not only textual information (for example, states, cities, and sales totals), but also a colorful map that, for example, plots sales totals by state. Using maps, you can display information in a way that helps to analyze geographical data more easily. In addition to regular groups and details section fields, Crystal Reports allows you to create maps based on online analytical processing (OLAP) grids and groups using specified order grouping.

NOTE *Crystal Reports's installation program does not install geographic map capabilities by default. You must choose a custom installation method and specifically choose the mapping component.*

Different Map Types

Crystal Reports provides five different types of maps. The type you should choose depends on the data that you'll be depicting in the map and the way you wish to show it. Table 10-1 discusses the different types of maps and their uses.

CAUTION *Crystal Reports contains a limited number of maps. If you use a field that contains geographic values that Crystal Reports can't resolve to an existing map, the map may not show any meaningful data, or it may show up as a blank area on your report. Crystal Reports mapping modules are provided by a third party, MapInfo. You may also get more information from MapInfo at mapinfo.com.*

- **Group map** Requires you to use existing groups with their subtotals and summaries for the map. A report grouped by country, for example, can be used to show the concentration of customers by country if you include a summary function that counts customers for each group.

- **Advanced map** Allows you to create a map based on data in the report's underlying database records. You may have a detail report containing a sales figure for each customer. If you include the state each customer is in, you can create an advanced map based on the state and the amount of sales for that state. The map will show

how sales compare by state. In effect, the map will group and subtotal your records by state, even if no state group exists on the report. You also would use an advanced map when you need to map multiple values per geographic region (as in the pie chart and bar chart explained in Table 10-1).

- **Cross-Tab map or OLAP map**   Plots data from a cross-tab object (covered in Chapter 8) or an OLAP grid (covered in Chapter 17). The cross-tab object must have at least one row or column field that's based on a geographic item, such as a country or state. OLAP grids must have a certain type and organization of dimensions (see "OLAP Maps," later in the chapter, for details). Because cross-tabs and OLAP grids can contain multiple summary fields, you can use them to create pie chart or bar chart maps.

Map Type	Description	Uses and Comments
Ranged	Assigns different colors to ranges of numbers. For example, a state that contains over $500,000 in sales would be bright red, a state that contains between $250,000 and $500,000 in sales would be orange, and a state that contains less than $250,000 in sales would be a deep magenta.	Useful for comparing different regions or countries to each other by shade or color. There are four ways to choose how the ranges are colored: **Equal count** Evenly divides the number of map ranges so that an equal number (or as close as possible to an equal number) of mapped values appear in each range. This avoids map views containing almost all one color, which may occur if the data you are mapping is heavily concentrated on the low or high end of the overall range of values. **Equal ranges** Divides the map ranges by the summary numbers being shown on the map. This option assigns equal ranges of summary values, regardless of how many groups or regions make up each range. **Natural break** Also uses the summary numbers to determine map ranges, but bases range breakdowns on the average amounts of the ranges. **Standard deviation** Divides the map ranges such that the middle interval breaks at the average of the summary values. The ranges above and below the middle break at one "standard deviation" above or below the middle.
Dot density	Displays a dot on the map for every occurrence of the item being mapped. A higher concentration of dots appears in areas of the map that have the most occurrences.	Used to show a concentration of activity (for example, quantities or subtotals) in certain states or countries.

TABLE 10-1   Crystal Reports Map Types

Map Type	Description	Uses and Comments
Graduated	A symbol (a circle, by default) represents data, and the size of the symbol is based on the concentration or level of the amount: small amounts are represented by small circles, large amounts by large ones.	Shows just one symbol per country, state, etc., but shows a different size depending on the number the map is based on. The default symbol is a circle, but you can choose from other characters, as well as apply special effects (for example, a drop shadow, halo, etc.) to the symbol.
Pie chart	Displays a pie chart over the related geographic area.	Only useful when comparing multiple related data points for the same geographic area. A pie chart is better for comparing items against each other, where all items total 100 percent. For example, if you are graphing sales by account rep, grouped by state, you would see a pie chart on each state showing how much of the "state pie" each rep has.
Bar chart	Displays a bar chart over the related geographic area.	Only useful when comparing multiple related data points for the same geographic area. A bar chart is better for comparing items over time, or other comparisons that aren't "piece of the pie" oriented. For example, if you are graphing sales for the past five years, grouped by state, you would see a bar chart on each state comparing the sales for the past five years.

TABLE 10-1   Crystal Reports Map Types *(continued)*

Adding a Map

To insert a map on your report, choose Insert | Map from the pull-down menus, or click the Insert Map button on the Insert Tools toolbar. The Map Expert appears, containing three main tabs: Data, Type, and Text.

The Data Tab

The Data tab is where you choose the type of map you want to create, as well as the fields and summaries from the report that you want to base your map on.

Group Maps

To create a group map, click the Group button on the Data tab.

The Place Map drop-down list lets you choose how often you want the map to appear on the report. The options in this list will vary according to how many groups you have on your report. If you only have one group on your report, the only option available in the drop-down list is Once Per Report. If you have more than one group, you also have For Each *Group Field* options for every group, *except* for the bottom-level group, because you must always place a map at least one level higher in your report than the group your map is based on.

For example, if you only have a state group on your report, the only option for a group map is Once Per Report, because you must have the map at a level higher than the group. However, if you have a country group, and a region group within the country group, the drop-down list allows you to choose Once Per Report or For Each Customer.Country. If you choose this lower country level, you'll have a map appearing in every country group, showing the geographic breakdown *by region* for that country.

You can then choose whether to have Crystal Reports initially place the map in the group or report header or footer, by clicking the desired radio button. After the map has been created initially, you can drag the map object from the header to the footer, or vice versa.

Use the On Change Of drop-down list to choose the geographic group that you want the map to be based on. Continuing with the preceding example, if you choose once per report, then the options are on change of Customer.Country or on change of Customer.Country and Customer.Region. However, if you choose to place the map per country, then the only option in the On Change Of list is Customer.Region.

From the Show drop-down list, choose the summary or subtotal field you want the map to depict.

TIP *Because Group Maps must be based on a summary or subtotal field in a group, any groups that don't have at least one subtotal or summary field won't show up in the Map Expert. If you only have one group on your report and it doesn't contain a subtotal or summary field, the Group button in the Map Expert will be dimmed.*

Advanced Maps

To create an advanced map, click the Advanced button on the Data tab.

The Place Map drop-down list lets you choose how often you want the map to appear on the report. The options in this list will vary according to how many groups (if any) you have on your report. If there are no groups, the only option available in the drop-down list is Once Per Report. If you have one or more groups, you also have For Each *Group Field* options for every group.

You can then choose whether to have Crystal Reports initially place the map in the group or report header or footer, by clicking the desired radio button. You are also free to drag the map object from the header to the footer, or vice versa, after the map has been created.

The Available Fields list contains all the report, database, and formula fields available for the map. Choose the geographic field that you want your map to use, and then click the right arrow next to the Geographic Field box to choose the field. The same field will also automatically be placed in the On Change Of box. If you wish to just summarize values for the geographic field (for a range or dot density map, for example), simply leave the same field in the two boxes. If, however, you wish to show a pie or bar chart on the map for another field (for example, to show a pie chart in each country comparing states), then choose the field you want to "compare" in the Available Fields list and click the right arrow next to the On Change Of text box. Finally, click one or more fields (using CTRL-click or SHIFT-click) in the Available Fields list that you want summarized in the map. Use the right arrow next to the Map Values box to add them. If you wish to remove a Map Value field or fields, click it in the Map Values box and click the left arrow. If you wish to remove all the Map Value fields, click the double left arrow.

Even though this is an advanced map (based on individual data records), Crystal Reports still summarizes values by default, as though report groups exist for the fields you've placed in the Geographic Field and On Change Of boxes. You can choose the summary function (Sum, Average, Count, and so on) you want the map to use when summarizing the detail fields you've added to the Map Values box. Select a field in the box, click Set Summary Operation, and choose the function (Sum, Average, Count, and so on) that you wish to use.

Crystal Reports mapping can be picky about the geographic field you base your map on. For example, if the field contains USA, the map will recognize it. If it just contains US, the map won't recognize it. The same holds true for state names. Two-letter abbreviations and completely spelled state names are recognized, whereas inconsistently abbreviated state names or standard two-letter state names followed by periods may not be recognized. Sometimes you'll need to experiment, and in some cases you may want to create a formula (discussed in Chapter 4) that changes the way the geographic data is presented, and then base the map on the formula field. Also, Crystal Reports provides the ability to resolve data mismatches that exist between the geographic names that maps recognize and the actual data in the database (see "Resolving Data Mismatches" later in the chapter).

TIP *If you add a nonnumeric field to the Map Values box, it is automatically summarized with a count function. The only other choice in the Change Summary Operation list is DistinctCount.*

Cross-Tab Maps

To create a cross-tab map, you must initially create a cross-tab object on the report that contains at least one geographically oriented field. Select the cross-tab object you want to base the map on. Then, use either the Insert menu or Insert Map toolbar button to display the Map Expert. The Cross-Tab button on the Data tab will be automatically selected (this button will be grayed out unless you have selected a cross-tab object in your report first).

The Place Map drop-down list will be dimmed, because you must place the map on the same level as the cross-tab (in the same group, once per report, and so forth). You can choose whether to have Crystal Reports initially place the map in the group or report header or footer, by clicking the desired radio button. You can also drag the map object from the header to the footer, or vice versa, after the map has been created.

In the Geographic Field drop-down list, choose the row or column of the cross-tab that contains the geographic field the map will be based on. If you want the cross-tab to be mapped as a pie or bar chart map, choose the other row or column in the Subdivided By drop-down list. In the Map On drop-down list, choose the summary field from the cross-tab that you want depicted. If you have multiple summary fields, you'll have multiple options here.

OLAP Maps

To create an OLAP grid map, you must initially create an OLAP grid object on the report that contains at least one geographically oriented field (OLAP reporting is covered in Chapter 17). If your report contains more than one OLAP grid, you must select the grid object you want to base the map on first. If you only have one OLAP grid object on your report, you don't have to select it first. Use either the Insert menu or Insert Map toolbar button to display the Map Expert. If you have already selected an OLAP grid, the OLAP button on the Data tab will be automatically selected. Otherwise, click the OLAP button on the Data tab to map the one OLAP grid on the report.

The Place Map drop-down list will be dimmed, because you must place the map on the same level as the OLAP grid (in the same group, once per report, and so forth). You can choose whether to have Crystal Reports initially place the map in the group or report header or footer, by clicking the desired radio button. You can also drag the map object from the header to the footer, or vice versa, after the map has been created.

In the On Change Of drop-down list, choose the dimension of the OLAP grid that contains the geographic field the map will be based on (this may be a "lower-level" dimension; go back and look at the results of your OLAP grid if you're unsure where the geographic data is). If you want the OLAP grid to be mapped as a pie or bar chart map, choose another dimension in the Subdivided By drop-down list. Checking the Map Off Entire Grid check box will disable the On Change Of and Subdivided By drop-down lists and will create a map based on all row and column dimensions in the OLAP grid.

NOTE *The initial version of Crystal Reports 2008 exhibits a bug when creating a map in a report that contains just one OLAP grid in a group header or footer. If you don't select the OLAP grid before inserting the map, the map may appear in the report header or footer instead of the matching group header or footer where it belongs. However, if you then move the OLAP grid to a report header or footer, and then move it back to its original group header or footer location, the map will then follow it to a matching group header or footer.*

The Type Tab

After you've chosen the data elements for your map, click the Type tab to choose the type of map you want to display. Click one of the following buttons to select a map type:

- **Ranged**   Presents options for a ranged map, including how many intervals the map will contain, how the intervals are broken down, the beginning and ending color for the intervals, and whether the map should show empty intervals.

- **Dot Density**   Enables you to choose large or small dots for the map.

- **Graduated**   Presents the symbol used for the graduated map. A circle symbol is chosen by default, but you can click Customize to change the symbol and color and add special effects to the symbol, such as a halo or drop shadow.

- **Pie Chart**   Presents options for a pie chart map. You can choose small, medium, or large pies. If you click the Proportional Sizing check box, the pies will be sized according to the quantities contained in the data being mapped: larger quantities create larger pies, and smaller quantities create smaller pies.

- **Bar Chart**   Enables you to choose the size of the bars: large, medium, or small.

NOTE *You are restricted to either the first three or the second two buttons, depending on how many data elements you've chosen for your map. If you chose only one data element to map, you can use only the Ranged, Dot Density, or Graduated option. If your map contains multiple elements from a detail report, or you chose a Subdivided By item with a cross-tab object or OLAP grid, you can use only the Pie Chart or Bar Chart option.*

The Text Tab

The Text tab lets you customize textual elements, such as the title and legend, which appear with the map. Type in the Map Title box the title you wish the map to display. Crystal Reports automatically creates a legend for the map. You can choose whether to display a full legend, a compact legend, or no legend at all by clicking the appropriate radio button. If you choose to include a legend, you can display the map-generated legend or specify your own by using the radio buttons and text boxes in the Legend Title section.

After you choose all the necessary options, click OK. Crystal Reports creates the map and places it in the report or group header or footer that you specified. To modify an existing map, simply click the map to select it in either the Design or Preview tab. Then, choose Format | Map Expert from the pull-down menus or right-click the map and choose Map Expert from the pop-up menu.

Drilling Down on Maps

Crystal Reports lets you drill down on Group maps, just like on group names and summaries (discussed in Chapter 2) and on charts and graphs (covered in Chapter 9). When you view a map in the Preview tab, simply point your mouse to the geographic region you wish to look at in more detail. The mouse cursor turns into a magnifying glass (or a finger cursor in a web page). Double-click (single-click in a web page) the desired area of the map to open up a drill-down tab next to the Preview tab. This drill-down tab will contain just the information for the report group represented by that map segment. If you attempt to drill down on a geographic element that doesn't include any data (perhaps you drill down on a city that's plotted on a map, but there's no group for that city), you'll receive a message indicating the lack of detail data for that city.

To close a drill-down tab, click the small *x* that appears on the right of the drill-down tab. The current tab closes and the next tab to the left is displayed.

TIP *Because an Advanced map is already mapping the lowest level of information on your report, you cannot drill down on this type of map. Nor can you drill down into Cross-Tab or OLAP maps.*

Changing the Map View

While viewing a particular map, you may wish to change your "view" of the map, such as zooming in or out on the map, or panning left, right, up, or down on the map. You may do this by selecting the map you want to change the view of and choosing options from the Map pull-down menu. Or, simply right-click on the map in the Preview tab and choose options from the pop-up menu.

- **To zoom in on a map**   Choose the Zoom In option. This will change the mouse cursor to a magnifying glass with a plus sign. Draw an elastic box around the portion of the map you want to zoom in on. The map will resize to show your chosen area.

- **To zoom out from the map**   Choose the Zoom Out option. This will change the mouse cursor to a magnifying glass with a minus sign. Every time you click on the map, it will zoom out a predetermined level.

- **To pan left, right, up, or down**   Choose the Pan option. This will change the mouse cursor to an arrow/pan cursor. Hold down the mouse button on the map and move your mouse left, right, up, or down. The map will reposition accordingly.

- **To recenter the map to its original position**   Choose the Center Map option.

The Map Navigator

Another way to change your view of a map in Crystal Reports is the Map Navigator. When you click on a map to select it in the Preview tab, a smaller "thumbnail" of the map appears in its own window in the lower right of the map. You may drag the Map Navigator by its title bar to move it around inside the map, as well as resize the window by dragging a border of the window.

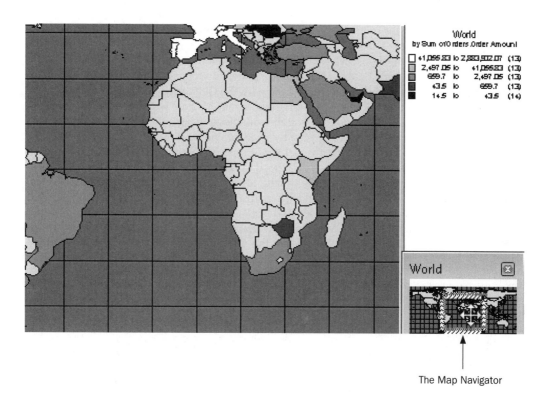

The Map Navigator

A shaded outline in the Map Navigator shows the portion of the map that you see in the rest of the map view. If you zoom in or out on the map (using the pop-up menu options), the outline shrinks or expands, outlining the zoomed-in portion of the map. You can also use the outline in the Map Navigator to zoom in, zoom out, and pan the view to a particular area of the map. If you point inside the outline, your mouse cursor changes to a four-arrow move cursor; simply drag the outline around to pan to a different area of the map. If you point to a corner of the outline, the mouse cursor changes into a diagonal two-arrow cursor. Drag the corner to expand or contract the outline. This zooms in or out on the map.

You may hide the Map Navigator by clicking the *X* on its upper right-hand corner. However, if you then deselect and reselect the map, the Map Navigator will return. If you want to turn the Map Navigator display off on a more permanent basis for all instances of maps, you may uncheck the Map Navigator option in the Map pull-down menu or pop-up menu that appears when you right-click on a map.

Resolving Data Mismatches

One of the peculiarities of geographic maps is potential mismatches of geographic data in the database to what the map understands. If your database contains, for example, spelled-out state names instead of two-letter abbreviations, the map will not be able to resolve the names to actual states. Crystal Reports allows you to resolve data mismatches that may cause database data to be improperly mapped, or not mapped at all.

If you suspect that the map may not be interpreting database data correctly, first select the map that you wish to work with in the Preview tab (you can't resolve data mismatches in the Design tab). Then, choose Map | Resolve Mismatch from the pull-down menus or right-click on the map and choosing Resolve Mismatch from the pop-up menu. This will display the Resolve Map Mismatch dialog box, with the Change Map tab shown first.

The map definition used to display the particular map you are working with will appear as both the "current map" and selected in the Available maps list. If you wish to display a different map definition, scroll through the list of available maps and choose another map. If, however, the mismatch involves a misspelling or misinterpretation of a particular country, state, city, or other geographical field, you'll need to resolve the mismatch on the Resolve Mismatch tab, shown in Figure 10-1 (it may take some time for this tab to appear, as Crystal Reports must build several lists on the fly when you choose this tab).

You'll notice that any database values that have already been matched to map values by Crystal Reports will appear in the Match Results list. However, if there are database values that could not be matched, they will appear in the Assign This Field Name list in the upper

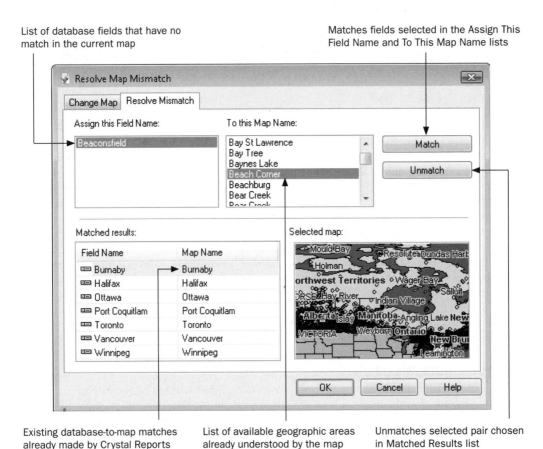

List of database fields that have no match in the current map

Matches fields selected in the Assign This Field Name and To This Map Name lists

Existing database-to-map matches already made by Crystal Reports

List of available geographic areas already understood by the map

Unmatches selected pair chosen in Matched Results list

FIGURE 10-1   The Resolve Mismatch tab

left-hand corner. And, you'll find a list of all the available geographic values that the map understands in the To This Map Name list in the upper right-hand corner.

To match an unmatched database value to a map value, select the value you want to match in the Assign This Field name list. Then, scroll up and down in the To This Map Name list until you find the substitute data, which you can then select (typing letters on the keyboard will often select items in the list more quickly than using the scroll bar). Click the Match button, which adds the match to the Matched Results list. Each match you create is added to the bottom list, along with all assignments that Crystal Reports made previously. If you decide that you don't want to use an assignment (that either you made or was made automatically), select it in the Matched Results list and click Unmatch.

When you're finished assigning values, click OK to show the map with the updated mapping assignments.

Map Layers

A map is displayed in the Preview tab using *layers*. If you are looking at a USA map, for example, the map may be composed of layers consisting of USA, US Highways, and US Major Cities. You can think of a map layer as a transparency containing just that layer's information that lies on top of the lower layers, which lie on top of the map. By using layers, the map can be displayed showing different levels of detail, usually determined by how far in the map is zoomed. If you are fully zoomed out on the map, you'll only see the states. As you zoom in, you eventually see highways appear across the states. And, as you zoom in even further, you see dots and the names of cities within the states.

Although maps include layers in a default order with default settings, you can choose which layers to display, hide, include, or not include. You can also change the order in which the layers "lie" on the map, and change the zoom level at which layers become visible. To work with map layers, select the map you wish to work with in the Preview tab (you can't work with layers in the Design tab). Then, choose Map | Layers from the pull-down menus, or right-click on the map and choose Layers from the pop-up menu. The Layer Control dialog box is displayed.

You see all the layers included in the map by default. You can change the order in which the layers appear by selecting an individual layer and then clicking the Up or Down button to change the order of the layers. If you want to hide a layer so that it doesn't show in the map, select the layer and clear the Visible check box. If you decide that you no longer want the layer at all, select it and click Remove.

If you later decide you want to redisplay a layer you removed earlier, or you want to add a new layer not already on the map, click Add. A File Open dialog box appears. Additional layers are located in \Program Files\Business Objects\MapInfo Mapx\Maps. Point to that folder and look for the appropriate .TAB file. After you choose it, it appears in the Layer Control dialog box.

To change the zoom level at which a layer appears, select the layer and click Display. The Display Properties dialog box for that layer opens.

If you uncheck Display Within Zoom Range, the layer appears in the map at all times, regardless of the Zoom level. If you leave it checked, you can set the minimum and maximum Zoom levels at which the layer will become visible. After you make your choices, you can zoom in or out on the map to see the layer changes.

Figure 10-2 shows the same map at the same Zoom level with different settings for the US Highways layer.

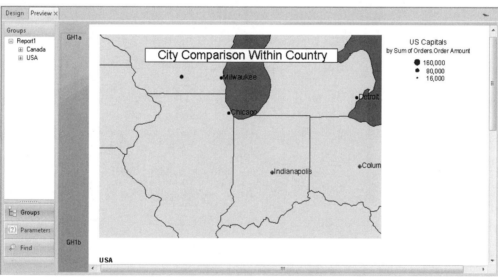

FIGURE 10-2   Maps with different US Highways layer zoom settings

Integration with Crystal Xcelsius and Flash

The Web continues to be the medium of choice for new interactive development efforts. As the demand for richer web content continues to grow, so does the choice of tools to provide it. While some web sites are still based on simple HTML pages, most are taking advantage of more versatile design platforms, such as Java and Adobe's now-ubiquitous Flash platform. The emergence of Flash as a web standard is complemented even further by the growing acceptance of Business Object's companion product to Crystal Reports, Crystal Xcelsius. The final output from an Xcelsius interactive visualization is also Flash-based, making it an ideal tool for web-based interactive analytical dashboards.

Crystal Reports 2008 introduces the ability to include Flash-based content right in a report. Any standard .SWF (Shockwave Flash File) can be added to a report via either a URL or filename reference, or else embedded directly within the report. While this new capability has primarily been added to allow tight integration with Crystal Xcelsius, any standard Flash .SWF file can be added to a report, including those that display video, graphics, audio, web service data connectivity, and so forth.

NOTE *Crystal Reports 2008 can only display already-designed .SWF files created with Crystal Xcelsius, Adobe Flash, Adobe Flex, or other Flash creation tools. With the exception of passing data into an appropriately designed .SWF file (described later in the chapter), you cannot modify the contents or behavior of the .SWF file in Crystal Reports. Any changes to the .SWF file must be performed within the original design tool.*

Adding a Flash .SWF File to a Report

You may add a Flash file to a report while either the Design or Preview tab is visible. However, to ensure you place the Flash object in the proper location, it's probably best to view the Design tab prior to inserting the file. To add an .SWF file to a report, choose Insert | Flash from the pull-down menus. You may also right-click on an empty area of the report and choose Insert Flash Object from the pop-up menu. Or, click the Insert Flash Object toolbar button in the Insert Tools toolbar. The Insert Flash Object dialog box will appear.

Specify the name of the Flash .SWF file you wish to add to the report. You may specify either a Windows-compatible filename (including a UNC filename) or a URL that references an intranet- or Internet-based .SWF file. If you wish to navigate to the desired file on your local hard drive or a network drive, you may click Browse to display a file open dialog box to navigate to the desired file. Click the Embed radio button to include a copy of the .SWF file in your report. Even if the original file is later changed, moved, or deleted, the contents of the original file will stay in your report. If you click the Link radio button, Crystal Reports will look for the existence of the .SWF file every time the report is opened, automatically displaying any changes that may have been made to the .SWF since the report was last opened (and, an error message will appear if the .SWF can no longer be found at the original location).

Click OK. An outline indicating the size of the .SWF image will appear attached to your mouse cursor. Position the outline in the report section where you want the .SWF file to appear and click to drop the .SWF object on the report. The Flash object placeholder in the Design tab will show the first frame of the image. To view the complete Flash object's animation, preview the report.

If the Flash object's animation is set to begin automatically, it will begin to play as soon as the report is previewed. If, however, the Flash object is set to immediately require a mouse click, or some other user interaction, then you must double-click the Flash object in the preview tab to enable interaction. Then, you may interact with the Flash object's user interface just as though it were embedded in a web page.

NOTE *You must have a current version of the freely available Flash player installed on your computer to view Flash objects in a report.*

Flash Formatting Options

Once you've placed a Flash object on your report, you may manipulate it much the same way as you manipulate other report objects (particularly, bitmap image files). Once you've selected the object, you may move and resize it the same as you do other objects, with its sizing handles. You may use Object Size and Position options from pull-down or pop-up menus to set a specific location and size for the object. And, applicable formatting toolbar buttons, such as Border, Suppress, and Lock Format, will also work with a Flash object.

You may also format the Flash object with the Format Editor. Ensure the desired Flash object is selected in either the Design or Preview tab. Then, choose Format | Format Flash from the pull-down menus, click the Format button in the Expert Tools toolbar, or right-click the Flash object and choose Format Flash from the pop-up menu. The Format Editor will appear, displaying Common, Flash, and Border tabs. Formatting options unique to a Flash object will appear on the Flash tab.

You may type specific scaling and width/height entries into the appropriate text boxes. If you wish to return the Flash object to its original size, click Reset. If you initially created an embedded Flash object (you selected the Embed radio button when the .SWF file was added), then you may replace the object's original contents with a different .SWF file by typing a new URL or filename into the SWF Location text box (you may also display a file open dialog to navigate to a new file by clicking the ellipsis button). If the initial Flash object was added as a linked object, you may point to a different object by replacing the filename or URL that refers to the linked .SWF file by typing a new URL or filename into the text box (you may also display a file open dialog to navigate to a new file by clicking the ellipsis button).

The last option in the Format Editor Flash tab is the Image For Printing And Exporting option. Because it's not possible to include a Flash object when the report is printed or exported to most file formats, you may specify an alternative fixed image that will appear in place of the Flash object when exporting or printing your report. Do this by clicking Change. A file open dialog box will appear, allowing you to navigate to a .WMF, .BMP, .TIF, .JPG, or .PNG image file. Once you choose the desire file, a thumbnail view of the image file will appear to the left of the Change button. When you print or export the report, this image will appear in place of the Flash object.

NOTE *An embedded Flash file or Xcelsius visualization will be viewable in a report exported to PDF format. While the initial release of Crystal Reports 2008 limits this to Xcelsius visualizations that don't tie to report data, additional Xcelsius/PDF export capabilities may be provided in subsequent Crystal Reports 2008 updates. Check the Business Objects website for the most current release.*

Integrating Crystal Reports 2008 with Xcelsius

While there are many potential uses for adding Flash objects to Crystal Reports, it's safe to assume one of the primary reasons Business Objects added this capability was to facilitate integration with Xcelsius, Crystal Report's companion dashboard/analysis product. As the final output from an Xcelsius visualization is a Flash .SWF file, Crystal Reports 2008 introduces the ability to integrate an Xcelsius interactive .SWF file right into a Crystal Report. Steps to add and format an Xcelsius .SWF file are the same as those for a non-Xcelsius Flash object and are described in the first portion of this chapter.

One of the immediate limitations you may encounter when basing an Xcelsius visualization on its Excel spreadsheet data model is the lack of ability to use real-time data from your corporate database or data warehouse. One way to accomplish this goal with Xcelsius is to use "Query as a Web Service" connectivity, which allows XML-formatted data to be passed into an Xcelsius .SWF file at view time. However, this connection method requires special preparation and data handling, separate from any standard connectivity methods you may already have set up for database access. Another way to pass data is to add an Xcelsius .SWF file to your Crystal report, tying specific values in the Flash object to data in the report. This allows your Xcelsius visualization to be based on live, current data from a corporate database, without the requirement to implement Query as a Web Service in the Xcelsius visualization itself.

There are several approaches to this scenario, depending on which version of Xcelsius you are using. Crystal Xcelsius 4.5 makes use of Flash Variables to pass values from your report into the Flash object. The latest version, Xcelsius 2008, not only allows Flash variable integration, but additional integration with entire blocks of data via the Crystal Report Data Consumer, including the ability to tie an entire Crystal Reports cross-tab directly to the Xcelsius Flash object.

CAUTION *Only certain editions of Crystal Xcelsius allow data-passing from Crystal Reports 2008. Crystal Xcelsius 4.5 Workgroup Edition and Xcelsius 2008 Engage, Engage Server, and Enterprise Editions are the only editions that provide the ability to receive data passed from a report as described in the remainder of the chapter. If you don't have one of these Xcelsius editions, you can still add an Xcelsius .SWF file to your report, but you will be unable to pass data to it.*

Using Flash Variables with Crystal Xcelsius 4.5

A standard method of passing data into a Flash .SWF file (developed with typical Flash development tools, including Crystal Xcelsius) is by way of *Flash variables*. Flash variables are typically used to pass values into a Flash object from within a web page using Embed tags, on a web URL, and so forth. Crystal Reports 2008 supports the ability to pass values to Flash variables as well.

Consider the following Flash object, created with Crystal Xcelsius 4.5, added to the report header of a Crystal report:

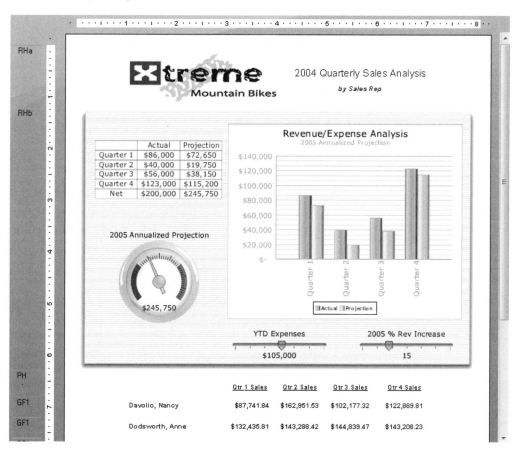

While the complete interactivity provided by the Xcelsius visualization (two slider controls, text grid, gauge control, and column chart objects) is available when previewing the report, the underlying data that the objects are based on consists of a set of fixed values contained in the underlying Microsoft Excel data model that the Xcelsius visualization is based on. You may also notice that, below the Xcelsius object, the remainder of the report consists of quarterly totals displayed for each sales rep by way of report grouping. The ultimate desire for this report is to have the Xcelsius interactive dashboard appear in each group footer, incorporating that particular sales rep's quarterly totals as its underlying data.

Preparing the Xcelsius Visualization

The first step to integrate this particular Xcelsius visualization with Crystal Reports is to modify the visualization to receive values for the four quarterly actual numbers via a Flash variable. Then, the updated Xcelsius .SWF file can be added to the report, and the Flash variable can be tied to the group subtotals included in the sale rep group footer.

In Crystal Xcelsius 4.5 Workgroup Edition, Flash variables are defined in the Export Settings dialog box. Display this by choosing File | Export Settings from the Xcelsius pull-down menus. The Export Settings dialog box will appear.

Select the Use Flash Variables radio button, and choose either the XML Format or CSV Format radio button underneath it. The CSV (comma-separated value) format requires you to send data from Crystal Reports as one or more values, separated by commas. XML (Extensible Markup Language) is a web standard that requires you to send "blocks" of tagged data from Crystal Reports.

TIP *While you may initially find CSV formatting to be more straightforward, there could be certain circumstances where using the XML format is preferable. Crystal Reports 2008 introduces three new formula language functions that will help you in this effort. Look at online help, or this book's appendix, for information on ToXMLColumn, ToXMLRow, and ToXMLData.*

Once you've chosen to use Flash variables, you must define one or more variable names, and specify the individual cell or range of cells in your underlying Excel data model that each variable refers to. Do this by clicking the Define Variables button next to the Use Flash Variables radio button. The Replace Data Selection dialog box will appear, where you may add or remove variables, name each variable, and tie a variable to a cell or range of cells in the underlying Excel data model. This is illustrated in Figure 11-1.

Variables may refer to a single underlying cell or to a range of cells. You will pass either a single value, or a delimited set of values, to the variable from your report, depending on

Add or remove variables

Provide a meaningful name for the variable

Select the cell or range of cells that the variable will refer to

Click to display the underlying Excel data model

FIGURE 11-1   Defining Flash variables in Xcelsius 4.5

whether the variable refers to one cell, or a range of cells. You will want to ensure that the cells you assign Flash variables to contain only static values, as assigning a variable to a cell containing a formula will almost certainly result in undesirable behavior when you pass a value to it from your report.

In the example illustrated in Figure 11-1, two Flash variables have been created. Q1-4Actual refers to a range of four cells containing actual sales for the four 2004 quarters. And, RepName refers to a single cell that is used as the contents cell for the subheading on the column chart. Make note of your Flash variable names before you return to Crystal Reports to tie the Flash variables to report values, as you must use the exact same variable names in the report (Xcelsius .SWF files don't expose their variable names to Crystal Reports automatically).

Once you've defined Flash variables that will receive data from Crystal Reports, you must export the Xcelsius visualization as a Flash .SWF file. Use the File | Export | Macromedia Flash (SWF) option to create the .SWF file that you will then add to Crystal Reports 2008.

Passing Data to the .SWF File with Flash Variables

Once Flash variables have been defined and the resulting .SWF file has been created, you're ready to tie it to the appropriate data values in your Crystal report. First, embed or link the .SWF file to your report, as described earlier in this chapter. You'll want to pay particular attention to the report section you place the Flash object in. If, for example, you are going to pass grand total values to the Flash object for display only once at the beginning or end of the report, you'll want to place the Flash object in the Report Header or Footer. If, however, you wish to display an Xcelsius dashboard that is passed subtotal data for each group (in the case of the current example, for each sales rep), then add the Xcelsius Flash object to the Group Header or Footer, so that an occurrence of the Flash object will appear for each group.

If you simply preview the report before performing any data connection between it and the Flash object, the Xcelsius visualization will show the same data over and over for each occurrence, as no data is yet being passed from the report to the .SWF file. You accomplish data integration by using the Flash Data Binding Expert. First, in the Design or Preview tab, select the Flash object you wish to pass data to (make sure you don't double-click it if you're displaying the Preview tab, as that will activate the object). Then, either choose Format | Flash Data Expert from the pull-down menus, or right-click the selected Flash object and choose Flash Data Expert from the pop-up menu. The Flash Data Binding Expert will appear, as illustrated in Figure 11-2.

To add a reference to a Flash variable created in the Flash object, click the Plus button, or just double-click in a blank variable name cell. Type the exact same variable name that you assigned to the variable in Xcelsius. Then, choose an existing database or formula field to pass to the variable from the drop-down list under the Value column. You may also click the conditional formula button to display the Formula Editor and specify a formula that returns a string value (creating string formulas is discussed in depth in Chapter 4).

The type and contents of the field or formula you pass to a Flash variable are significant, considering that the Flash variable you defined in Xcelsius will be expecting a list of comma-

Add or remove Flash
variable references

Choose existing database field
or formula to pass to variable

Supply exact same variable name
defined in Xcelsius visualization

Supply a formula to pass
to variable

Preview will show effects of
values passed to variables

FIGURE 11-2 Flash Data Binding Expert

separated values (assuming you chose the CSV format option in the Xcelcius Export Options
dialog box). If the referenced Flash variable is tied to a single cell, you must pass a single
value (containing no commas, or surrounded by quotation marks if it contains a comma).
If the referenced Flash variable is tied to a range of cells, you must pass a matching set of
multiple values, each separated by a comma (and, each value can't contain a comma, unless
the values are surrounded by quotation marks). If the range of cells referenced by the Flash
variable is a contiguous set of cells in a single Excel row or single Excel column, the values
you pass will be placed in the cells consecutively from left to right or top to bottom. If the
range of cells referenced by the Flash variable consists of multiple rows and columns, the
values you pass will be placed in the cells consecutively from left to right in the first row,
then left to right in the second row, and so forth.

Considering the "four quarterly sales values for each sales rep" example illustrated earlier,
there are two Flash variables that must be passed values from the report: the four quarterly
sales numbers passed to Q1-4Actual, and the name of the sale rep passed to Rep Name.

A Crystal Reports formula can be created to concatenate the four quarterly sales numbers for the sales rep group, separating each number with a comma. This formula might be similar to

```
ToText(ToNumber(Sum ({@Qtr 1 Sales}, {@Sales Rep})),0,"") & "," &
ToText(ToNumber(Sum ({@Qtr 2 Sales}, {@Sales Rep})),0,"") & "," &
ToText(ToNumber(Sum ({@Qtr 3 Sales}, {@Sales Rep})),0,"") & "," &
ToText(ToNumber(Sum ({@Qtr 4 Sales}, {@Sales Rep})),0,"")
```

This formula uses several techniques to ensure that the values passed to the Flash variable are appropriate for placement in the underlying Excel data model:

- The currency summary values are converted to numbers (using the ToNumber function) to eliminate a dollar sign from appearing in the resulting string value.

- The second argument to the ToText function rounds the numeric value to a whole number, to be consistent with values in the Xcelsius visualization's underlying Excel data model.

- The thousands separator is eliminated by supplying an empty string to the third argument of the ToText function. This eliminates a comma from appearing within a numbers of 1,000 or greater (as commas are used to separate values when using CSV format).

- Commas are added between the four quarterly values to indicate to the Flash variable where each new value begins (this is a requirement of using the CSV, or comma-separated value, format).

Because this particular report contains separate first name and last name fields for the sales rep, and because there is a desire to add the word "for" at the beginning of the sales rep name when it appears as the subtitle in the column chart, a custom formula is specified to pass a value to the RepName Flash variable. This formula might be similar to

```
"for " & {Employee.First Name} & " " & {Employee.Last Name}
```

While this formula is using straightforward string concatenation, it must not include a comma anywhere in the resulting string, as the Flash variable would consider this the end of the value being passed (based on the CSV format specified in the Xcelsius Export Options dialog box).

Once Flash variables have been defined, click OK to close the Flash Data Binding Expert dialog box. Preview the report. You should see a different appearance for each occurrence of the Xcelsius Flash object, based on the data being passed from the report (if you see undesirable results, redisplay the Flash Data Binding Expert and make any necessary changes to properly pass data to the .SWF file). In the quarterly sales by rep example, the four quarterly numbers for each salesperson are passed to the Xcelsius Flash object, creating a custom dashboard for each sales rep.

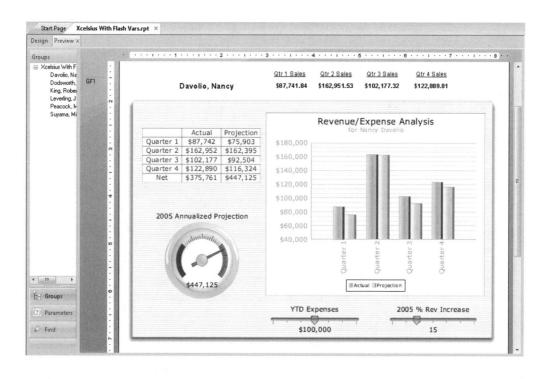

TIP   *You're not limited to tying just Xcelsius .SWF files to your report with Flash variables. Any Flash object that can accept Flash variable values, such as custom objects designed with Adobe Flash or Adobe Flex, can be tied to your report in the same manner.*

Integration with Xcelsius 2008

Xcelsius 2008 Engage, Engage Server, and Enterprise Editions add even more flexibility for receiving data passed from Crystal Reports 2008. If you design a visualization with Xcelsius 2008, you have the choice of defining Flash variables, and using the Crystal Report Data Consumer. You may use either method, or a combination of the two.

To use Flash variables in Xcelsius 2008, display the Xcelsius 2008 Data Manager (look at the earlier portion of this chapter entitled "Using Flash Variables with Crystal Xcelsius 4.5" for complete information on Flash variables). This may be done by choosing Data | Data Manager from the pull-down menus, or by clicking the Data Manager toolbar button from the Standard toolbar. The Data Manager dialog box will appear with existing data connections (if any) already appearing.

Add a connection to set up Flash variables by clicking the Add drop-down list button at the top of the Data Manager. Choose Flash Variables from the list. A Flash Variables connection item will be added to the Data Manager, as illustrated in Figure 11-3. Much as with setting up Flash variables with Xcelsius 4.5 (discussed earlier in the chapter), you may choose the format for the incoming Flash variables (CSV or XML), and add, name, and remove

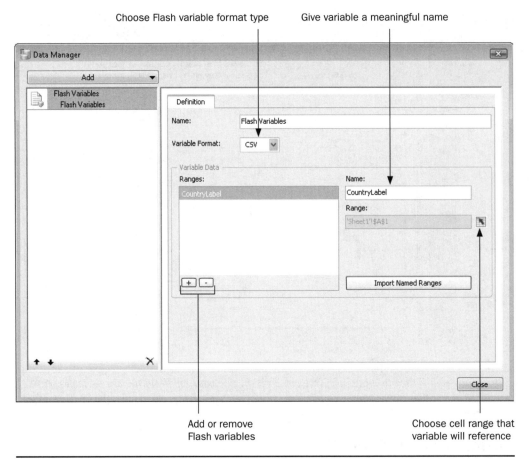

FIGURE 11-3   Adding Flash variables in the Data Manager

variables. For each defined variable, you may choose the cell range in the underlying Excel data model, or choose an existing cell Named Range.

Once you have defined necessary Flash variables, export the Xcelsius visualization to an .SWF file (using the File | Export menu option). Then, you may add the resulting .SWF file to your Crystal report, and pass values via the Flash Vars tab on the Flash Data Binding Expert, as described earlier in the chapter, under "Passing Data to the .SWF File with Flash Variables."

The Xcelsius 2008 Crystal Report Data Consumer

Xcelsius 2008 adds an additional method for receiving data from a Crystal Report. The *Crystal Report Data Consumer* allows a series of underlying cells in the Excel data model to be exposed to Crystal Reports as the Row Headers, Column Headers, and Data range. Then, in Crystal Reports 2008, you can pass a series of values to each of these different cell ranges, or choose an existing cross-tab object in your report to pass these values all at once.

Consider the following Xcelsius 2008 visualization. Particularly important is the underlying Excel data used to create the chart and the text grid. This consists of three rows: England, Germany, and France. In order to provide the three yearly comparisons, the country rows are subdivided into three columns, one each for 2005, 2006, and 2007. And, Excel formulas calculate the totals in the text grid and the projection comparison in the pie chart. The desire is to set up a Crystal Report Data Consumer to pass the matrix of country/year data, including the country row headers and year column headers, into the underlying Excel data model from a Crystal report.

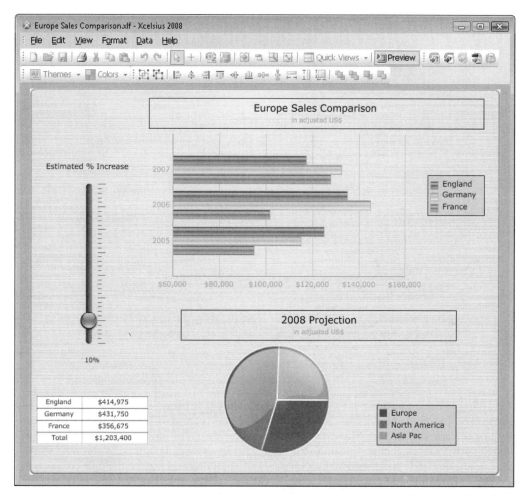

The Crystal Report Data Consumer connection is viewed in the Xcelsius Data Manager. Display the Data Manager with the appropriate pull-down menu command or toolbar button. Then, add the Crystal Report Data Consumer by clicking the Add drop-down list button at the top of the Data Manager. Choose Crystal Report Data Consumer from the list. A new connection item will be added to the Data Manager, as illustrated in Figure 11-4 (you can only add one Crystal Report Data Consumer to the Data Manager).

Select range to act as row headers/labels

Select range to act as column headers/labels

Select range to act as data values

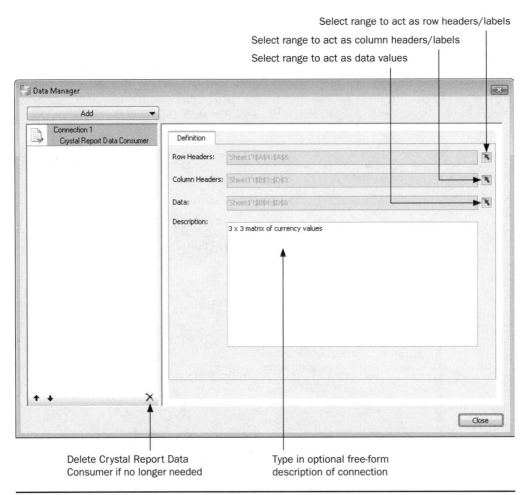

Delete Crystal Report Data
Consumer if no longer needed

Type in optional free-form
description of connection

FIGURE 11-4 The Crystal Report Data Consumer

Using selection buttons in the Crystal Report Data Consumer dialog box, choose the portion of the underlying Excel data model that contains the row headers/labels that you will pass from your report. Make a similar choice for the cells that contain column labels. And, use the Data selection button to highlight the range of cells in the Excel model that contain the actual data values. Finally, you may optionally type in text for the data connection, perhaps providing a description of the type and size of data cells that the data connection refers to.

Figure 11-4 indicates cells A4 through A6 being selected as Row Headers (in the underlying data model, these cells contain three row labels: England, Germany, and France). Cells B3 through D3 have been specified as Column Header cells, containing the values 2005, 2006, and 2007 in the underlying Excel sheet. And, cells B4 through D6 have been chosen as the Data range, containing nine values (a three-by-three cell matrix), containing sales data for each country/year combination.

Once you've completed the Crystal Report Data Consumer screen, click Close to close the Data Manager. Then, export the Xcelsius visualization as a Flash .SWF file. Use the File | Export | Flash (SWF) option to create the .SWF file that you will then add to Crystal Reports 2008.

Using the Crystal Reports 2008 Xcelsius Data Tab

Once the resulting .SWF file has been created, you are ready to tie it to the appropriate data values in your Crystal report. First, embed or link the .SWF file to your report, as described previously in this chapter. Using a Crystal Report Data Consumer adds a limitation to where you can place your .SWF file—you'll only be able to place it in a report header or footer, or a group header or footer. Attempting to place it in another report section will result in a no-drop cursor (a circle with a line through it), indicating that you can't drop the Flash object in that section.

If you simply preview the report before performing any data connection between it and the Flash object, the Xcelsius visualization will appear showing no data, as it is expecting data to be received from Crystal Reports. You accomplish data integration by using the Xcelsius Data tab of the Flash Data Binding Expert. First, in the Design or Preview tab, select the Flash object you wish to pass data to (make sure you don't double-click it if you're displaying the Preview tab, as that will activate the object). Then, either choose Format | Flash Data Expert from the pull-down menus, or right-click the selected Flash object and choose Flash Data Expert from the pop-up menu. The Flash Data Binding Expert will appear. The Xcelsius Data tab will appear, provided you have added an Xcelsius 2008 Flash object containing a Crystal Report Data Consumer. The Xcelsius Data tab is illustrated in Figure 11-5.

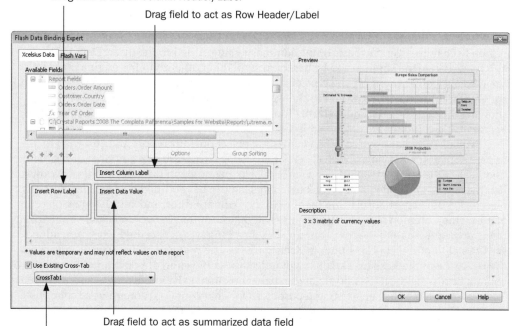

FIGURE 11-5 The Xcelsius Data tab of the Flash Data Binding Expert

There are three ways to connect Crystal Reports 2008 data to an Xcelsius object with the Xcelsius Data tab: by dragging individual database or formula fields from the Available Fields list to the Insert Data Value section in the middle of the dialog box; by dragging fields to supply row and column labels and data values to their respective sections in the middle of the dialog box; or by checking Use Existing Cross-Tab and selecting an existing report cross-tab in the associated drop-down list to supply row, column, and data values.

If you have added an Xcelsius object that has a small number of single-value cells that you wish to pass individual values to, you may drag one or more fields from the Available Field list right to the Insert Data Value section in the middle of the dialog. For each value you drag, you may manually change the column label for the value by overtyping it in the Insert Column Label section.

Most often, however, you will probably want to supply values from your report to fill in a series or range of cells in the Xcelsius object. You may drag the field that contains values to act as row headers/labels to the Insert Row Label box. Data will be read from the field, with the box showing the unique row values that will be passed. Then, choose another field to act as column headers/labels and drag it to the Insert Column Label box. Again, the box will display unique column values from the database field. Finally, choose the field that will act as the "summary" for each row/column intersection and drag it to the Insert Data Value box. Crystal Reports will calculate a summary for each row/column combination and display it in the Insert Data Value box.

NOTE *Values appearing in the Insert Data Value box are not necessarily representative of actual report data, and will often change to different non-representative values as you make additional modifications in the Xcelsius Data tab.*

Much as with the Cross-Tab Expert (discussed in Chapter 8), you can click the Options button to change several aspects of the summary value added to the Insert Data Values box. You may change the summary to be based on something other than the original field you dragged, as well as changing the type of summary (sum, average, count, and so forth). And, the Options button will allow you to choose Top N options for the row field, such as only showing the Top 10 rows, and so forth (Top N reporting is discussed in Chapter 2, and Top N cross-tab techniques are discussed in Chapter 8).

If you already have a predesigned cross-tab object on your report that you wish to use to pass data to the Xcelsius object, check Use Existing Cross-Tab at the bottom of the dialog. Then, select the cross-tab object you want to use to pass data in the associated drop-down list (the names of the available cross-tabs in this list can be modified by selecting cross-tab objects on your report, formatting them with the Format Editor, and supplying an object name on the Common tab). Crystal Reports will match up the row, column, and summarized fields in the cross-tab to the row, column, and data ranges you specified when you added the Crystal Report Data Consumer in Xcelsius 2008. The preview of the Xcelsius object on the right side of the Xcelsius Data tab will reflect the connection. If you manually add more column or row fields in the middle of the dialog box than exist in the ranges specified in the Xcelsius object, or select an existing report cross-tab that contains more rows or columns than the Xcelsius object, the Xcelsius object will read the first set of matching rows/columns and ignore the extras.

Once specifications have been made on the Xcelsius Data tab, click OK to close the Flash Data Binding Expert dialog box. Preview the report. You should see report data reflected in the Xcelsius Flash object (if you see undesirable results, redisplay the Flash Data Binding Expert and make any necessary changes to properly pass data to the .SWF file). In the previously illustrated Europe Sales Comparison, the three country rows, the three year columns, and the data values that drive the Xcelsius object are all being passed via a cross-tab on the report.

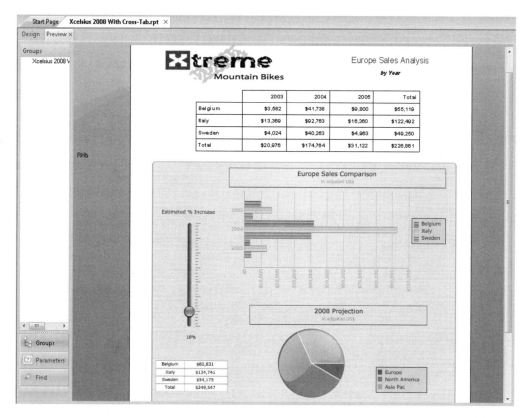

NOTE *Sample report files that integrate Xcelsius objects with both Flash variables and the Crystal Report Data Consumer, along with the commensurate .SWF files, can be downloaded from this book's companion web site, CrystalBook.com.*

CHAPTER 12

Using Subreports

A s you become more sophisticated in your report designing abilities, you will find at times that it's difficult, if not impossible, to create certain kinds of reports. For example, you might want to create one of the following:

- A single-page Company Condition dashboard that contains an accounts receivable bar chart in the upper left, an accounts payable summary in the upper right, a payroll expense gauge chart in the lower left, and a Top 10 sales summary in the lower right. At the bottom of the report, you'd like some grand totals for each of the summary reports.

- A listing of orders by customer for the month that also has a summary of the top five products sold during the month, regardless of customer.

- A sales report grouped by state, with a list of all credit granted in the same state in the group footer.

- A report that combines tables in such a way that duplicate records from certain tables repeat when matching to other tables (often referred to as a "many-to-many" relationship). You wish to properly subtotal records from the affected tables.

- A report that contains a report title, logo, and company information from a separate Company Information table in the database that doesn't contain any field that can be linked to other fields in other tables.

In each of these cases, you can't create the report using traditional Crystal Reports methods. The first three instances are prohibitive because a report, by nature, can use only a single result set, or a single group of fields returned all at once, from the database. The fourth instance exhibits a common problem that occurs when multiple tables contain more than one matching record. And the fifth instance (a fairly common situation), exhibits the problem encountered when there are no common fields that can be linked between the two tables.

Crystal Reports provides an innovative way to deal with these types of reporting challenges. *Subreports* allow you to solve these problems by, in essence, placing one report inside another report. A subreport is simply another report that appears inside the original *main report* as an object. Even though both reports have separate layouts and separate Design tabs, they appear together in the same place. The main report is created initially, after which one or more subreports are added to the main report.

Each subreport is designed separately, based on its own database tables and fields. You can preview each subreport in its own Preview tab, format individual objects in each subreport, and create unique selection criteria for the subreport. However, when you return to the main report's Preview tab or print the main report, the subreports will be processed and printed at the same time, appearing inside the main report.

There are two main types of subreports:

- **Unlinked subreports**   Have no data tie-in to the main report at all—they exist completely on their own and don't typically communicate with the main report. The Company Condition report mentioned previously falls into this category. Each of the unlinked subreports stands on its own and won't change based on any controlling field in the main report.

- **Linked subreports**   Controlled by data in the main report. The subreport will "follow" the main report, returning only a certain set of records based on the main report's controlling field or fields. The previously mentioned subreport containing sales by state followed by matching credit is an example of a linked subreport. When the state group changes in the main report, the subreport will return only records for that particular state.

You can also choose when subreports are processed by the main report. *In-place* subreports process at the same time as the main report and return their results at the same time. *On-demand* subreports appear in the Preview tab only with a hyperlink placeholder and don't process until a viewer double-clicks them (or single-clicks in a web page). This improves the performance of the main report, because all the subreports don't have to be processed at the same time as the main report.

Unlinked Subreports

The most straightforward subreport is an unlinked subreport. An unlinked subreport can be thought of as a completely separate report that just shows up on the main report—there's no logical connection between them at all. The subreport has its own layout, its own database connection, and its own selection criteria. It is not affected at all by what appears on the main report.

PART I

NOTE *Crystal Reports will not create another .RPT file when you create a subreport. Even though you will see another Design tab with separate tables and record selection, the subreport definitions are all contained in the main .RPT file.*

To create an unlinked subreport, you must first create or open at least the skeleton for the main report, and then use the Insert Subreport function to create or import a subreport. Although you can insert a subreport on the report in the Preview tab, you may not be able to accurately tell where it's being placed, so it's best to display the Design tab before you add a subreport.

Start to create the subreport by clicking the Insert Subreport button on the Insert Tools toolbar, or by choosing Insert | Subreport from the pull-down menus. The Insert Subreport dialog box will appear.

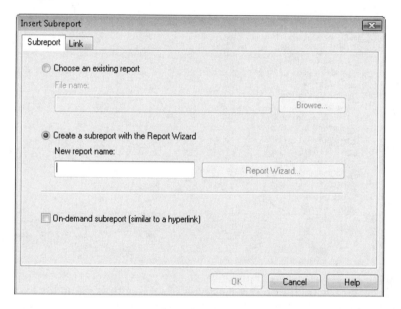

The Insert Subreport dialog box contains two tabs: Subreport and Link. The Link tab, discussed later in the chapter, is used to create a linked subreport. The Subreport tab contains two radio buttons, Choose A Report and Create A Subreport, and one check box, On-Demand Subreport (on-demand subreports are discussed later in this chapter). If you've already created another report that you would like to import as a subreport now, you can click the Choose A Report radio button and type in the path and filename of the existing report, or use the Browse button to navigate to the existing report. When you click OK, a subreport object outline will be attached to your mouse cursor. Place the subreport object in the desired location on the main report. Once you place the subreport on the main report, another Design tab will appear. If you click it, you'll find the report layout for the report you just imported.

If you wish to create a new subreport from scratch, click the Create A Subreport radio button and give the subreport a descriptive name in the Report Name text box. Remember that you are not creating a new .RPT file when you create a subreport, so the subreport name doesn't have to conform to file-naming conventions. It should be descriptive of the subreport, because the name will appear on the main report Design tab wherever the subreport object is placed. Notice that once you enter a name, the only button that becomes enabled is the Report Wizard button. The OK button at the bottom of the dialog box is still dimmed. This indicates that you must use the Report Wizard to create at least a minimal portion of your subreport. (Once you close the Report Wizard and return to the Insert Subreport dialog box, the OK button will be enabled.) When you click the Report Wizard button, the Standard Report Creation Wizard appears.

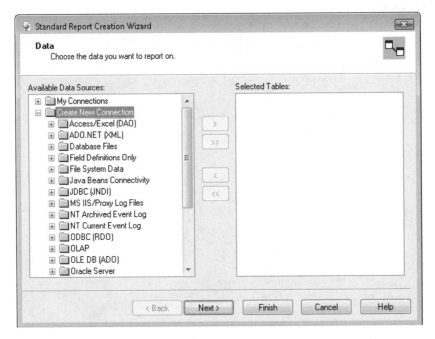

Don't forget that one of the powerful features of subreports is the ability to create reports based on entirely different databases and tables. You can select completely different databases, tables, and fields than are used on the main report. You don't have to complete any of the dialogs in the wizard in order to click Finish and place the subreport on the main report—you can have a completely empty subreport as a placeholder while you work on other things—but usually you would choose options in at least the Data and Fields dialogs. All of the same dialogs available in the Standard Report Creation Wizard when creating a main report are available when you're creating a subreport, including Grouping, Summarizing, Group Sorting (TopN), Chart, Record Selection, and Template. You can refine your subreport before you click Finish, or enter minimal information and work in the subreport Design tab directly.

When you've selected your desired options in the Wizard and clicked Finish, you'll be returned to the Insert Subreport dialog box. Notice that the OK button is now enabled, because you have created enough of a report in the Wizard. When you click OK, you will be returned to the main report Design tab, and a box-like subreport object will be attached to your mouse cursor. Drop the object by clicking in the report section of the main report where you want the subreport to appear. Choose this section carefully; it typically makes no sense for an unlinked subreport to appear more than once in the main report. For example, if you place the subreport in the details section, the same unlinked subreport will appear over and over again, once for each details record. You'll typically place an unlinked subreport in a report header or footer, unless you want it to repeat on more than one page.

TIP *Don't forget the Underlay formatting option on the Section Expert (discussed in detail in Chapter 7). You can, for example, easily create a second page header section for your subreport object and format the second page header to Underlay Following Sections. That way, your subreport will print alongside—not on top of—any data on the main report.*

When you place your subreport in the main report Design tab, it simply shows up as a box with the subreport name centered inside it. You'll also notice that another Design tab labeled with the subreport name will appear alongside existing report tabs. If you click the new tab, the subreport Design tab will appear.

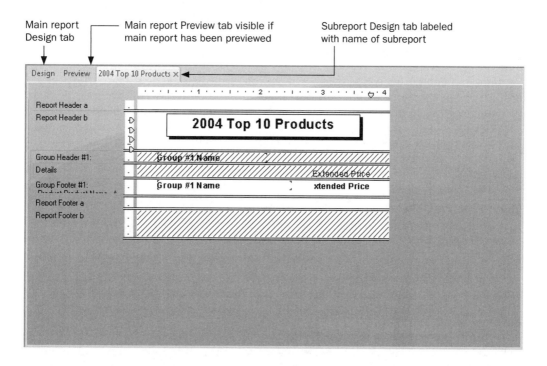

You can now move, resize, reformat, and otherwise modify objects in the subreport just as you would in the main report. The subreport will present its own Database Expert and Field Explorer, allow a separate set of formulas to be created, and allow you all the flexibility you have on the main report. However, the subreport Design tab has two limitations. First, you cannot add another subreport to it—subreports can be created only one level deep. And second, subreports don't contain page headers or footers, as the main report page header and footer will appear when the subreport is displayed in the main report Preview tab.

CAUTION *Since subreports can be only one level deep, an existing report that already contains subreports will not include those subreports when it is imported from the Insert Subreport dialog box. The report will be imported into the subreport Design tab, but the lower-level subreports won't show up. You may need to modify the imported report to make up for the empty space that appears where the subreport used to be.*

You can even preview a subreport in its own Preview tab. With the subreport Design tab displayed, preview the report using the Preview toolbar button, the Refresh button, the F5 key, or the pull-down menu options. A separate Preview tab for the subreport will appear next to the other report tabs. This tab will simply display the subreport name next to the word Preview.

When you now preview the main report, you'll see the subreport where you placed it. By default, subreports are surrounded by a border, so you'll see a box around the subreport. If you do not want to see a box around the subreport, right-click the subreport object and select Format Subreport. On the border tab, you can remove all or some of the four border lines. You can also modify border appearance with the appropriate Formatting Toolbar button after selecting the subreport.

If the subreport is not entirely visible (it may be pushed off the right side of the page, or it may be overwriting main report data if you use the Underlay Following Sections section formatting option), return to the main report Design tab and reposition or resize the subreport object. The width of the subreport design tab is based on how wide you make the subreport object in the main report. If you don't have sufficient room in the subreport Design tab to properly place objects, return to the main report Design tab and resize the subreport object.

TIP *You may save a subreport in its own .RPT file to use elsewhere or on its own. Select the subreport object in the main report Design or Preview tab and choose File | Save Subreport As, or right-click the subreport object and choose Save Subreport As from the pop-up menu.*

Drilling Down on Subreports

You have the same flexibility for drill-down reporting in subreports as you do in the main report. If you design a subreport with grouping, hidden sections, or charts, you can drill down in the subreport, too.

When you first preview the main report, the subreport will appear inside it. If you point to the subreport, you'll notice the mouse cursor change to a drill-down cursor, indicating drill-down capability. When you double-click the subreport, it will be displayed in its own Preview tab (but no actual subreport drill-down will occur). If you've designed the subreport to allow drill-down, you'll notice the mouse cursor displaying a drill-down cursor again in the subreport Preview tab. If you then double-click again, additional drill-down tabs will appear for groups you've created in the subreport.

If Crystal Reports runs out of room to display all the tabs, two small left-right arrows will appear to the right of the group of tabs. You can use the arrows to cycle through the tabs from the left or right. If you wish to close some of your drill-down tabs, click the small X in the desired tab. This will close the tab you are currently viewing and display the tab to the left. Figure 12-1 shows an unlinked subreport with more tabs than can be displayed at once.

TIP   *When you add a subreport to the main report, a Design tab for the subreport is created automatically. You can close the subreport Design tab by clicking the small X in the tab. To redisplay a subreport Design tab, display the Design tab for the main report and then double-click the subreport object. You may also select the subreport and choose Edit | Edit Subreport from the pull-down menus, or right-click the subreport object and choose Edit Subreport from the pop-up menu.*

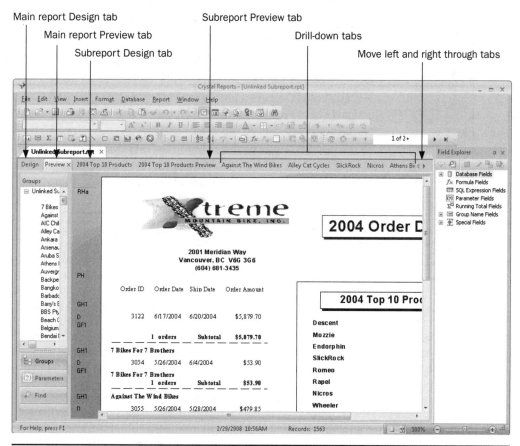

FIGURE 12-1   Unlinked subreport with Design tab, Preview tab, and drill-down tabs

Linked Subreports

A linked subreport is handy when you need to display related data elements from more
than one database table on a report, but can't tie the tables together properly for one reason
or another (such reasons are discussed in detail at the beginning of the chapter). A report
that encounters a many-to-many relationship when it attempts to show multiple sales
records in a region, followed by multiple credits in the same region, fits this category.
Linked subreports follow along with the main report.

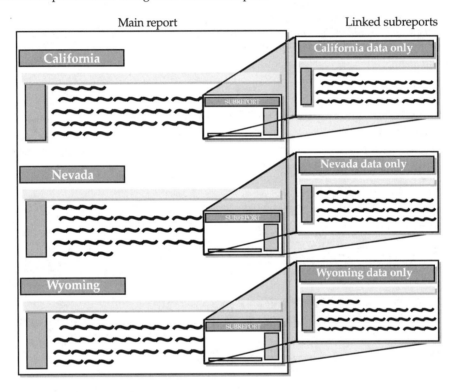

The initial steps for creating a linked subreport are the same as for creating an unlinked
subreport. Use the Insert Subreport toolbar button or menu options to create a subreport.
Then, import an existing report or create a new subreport with the Subreport Expert.
However, before you click OK in the Insert Subreport dialog box, click the Link tab. This
will display the Subreport Links dialog box, where you can choose how to link the subreport
to the main report.

If you inadvertently click OK in the Insert Subreport dialog box before linking, you can
still link the subreport after you place it on the main report. You can also choose to change
links for an existing linked subreport or link a previously unlinked subreport. Choose Edit
| Subreport Links from the pull-down menus, or right-click the subreport object and choose
Change Subreport Links from the pop-up menu. The Subreport Links dialog box is shown
in Figure 12-2.

Choose the field in the main
report that you want to link from

Choose the subreport
to set links for

Choose the parameter field in the subreport
that will hold information from the main report

Check to limit the subreport to records
that match the main report link field

Choose the
subreport field
to match to

FIGURE 12-2 Subreport Links dialog box

If you are linking directly from the Link tab on the Insert Subreport dialog box, the For Subreport drop-down list will be dimmed—you will be setting links for the subreport you are currently creating. If you are linking a subreport already on the main report, you can choose the subreport you want to set links for (don't forget—there can be more than one subreport on a main report).

The Available Fields list shows fields and formulas available in the main report. Select the field from the list you want to link from, and add it to the Field(s) To Link To list by clicking the right arrow button. If you later decide you don't want to link on that field, select it in the Field(s) To Link To list and remove it with the left arrow button.

Once you've added a main report field to link on, three additional options appear at the bottom of the Subreport Links dialog box. The Subreport Parameter Field To Use drop-down list contains any parameter fields you have created in the subreport (see Chapter 13 for information on parameter fields). In addition to any parameter fields that you may have already created in the subreport, Crystal Reports will create a parameter field consisting of the main report field prefixed with Pm-. If you want to link the subreport so that it shows only matching records for the main report field, just leave this automatically created parameter field selected.

The general approach of linked subreports is to limit the subreport to records that match the linking field from the main report. If this is the behavior you want, make sure Select Data In Subreport Based On Field is checked. Then, use the drop-down list below the check box to choose the field in the subreport that you want to use to limit records (Crystal Reports will automatically show any subreport field that has the same field name as the main report linking field). If you want to use more than one field to link the main report to the subreport, just add additional fields to the Field(s) To Link To list and match them up to the corresponding subreport fields.

Clicking OK closes the Subreport Links or Insert Subreport dialog box and creates the links between the main report and the subreport. If you're just creating the subreport, its outline will be attached to the mouse cursor. Drop it in the appropriate main report section, typically the section that matches the field you linked the subreport on. A subreport link is based on two concepts: passing data from the main report into a subreport parameter field, and creating a record-selection formula in the subreport based on the parameter field. This way, every time the main report runs the subreport, it places the value of the main report linking field in the parameter field, which is used to select records for the subreport.

Because of this method of subreport linking, whenever you try to preview a linked subreport on its own, you'll be prompted to supply a parameter field:

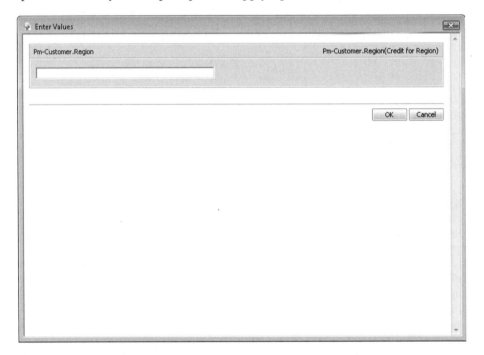

This indicates that the value for the parameter field is not being passed from the main report and you need to provide it. Type a valid value for the linked field (such as a state abbreviation, customer number, department code—whatever value is appropriate for the linked field) and click OK. The subreport Preview tab will appear showing just the records that you specified.

When you preview the main report, it will pass data to the subreport via the parameter field every time the subreport is processed; the subreport will use the parameter field in its record-selection formula and will return the limited set of resulting records to the main report. Figure 12-3 shows the customer/credit report mentioned previously, with the credit subreport appearing in the state group footer.

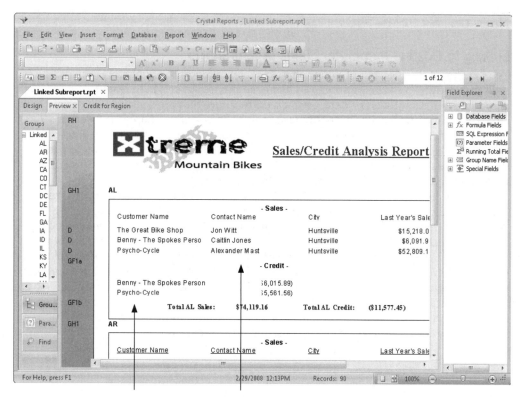

Credits (grouped & summed by customer)   Customers in main report details section
in subreport

FIGURE 12-3   Linked subreport placed in group footer

Linking Based on Formula Fields

If you use the Database Expert (discussed in Chapter 15) to link tables together in the main report, you can link only on actual database fields. This may be a problem if a field in one table doesn't exactly match the data type or organization in another table. For example, you may want to link two tables together based on a First/Last Name field because there is no other common number field or other linkable field. The problem, however, might be that the fields are separated into individual First and Last Name fields in one table, and contained in a single Name field in the other table. The link will never work in the Database Expert because of the differences in the data layout.

One of the benefits of using subreports is their ability to link based on a formula field, instead of just using database fields. By creating a subreport, you can link the two tables together. The key is to use a formula to concatenate the individual First and Last Name fields together into one combined formula field. Once you've created the formula in the report that contains the separate Name fields, the Name formula field will appear in the Subreport Links dialog box and you can choose it as a From or To linking field.

NOTE *Chapter 4 discusses concatenating string fields and other formula-creation techniques.*

Linking to Existing Parameter Fields in Subreports

You may find a situation where you wish to link a main report to a subreport via a parameter field that already exists in the subreport. For example, you may have created a subreport based on a SQL Command or database Stored Procedure that contains its own parameters (SQL Command and Stored Procedure reporting is discussed in Chapter 15). Perhaps you have already created a parameter field in the subreport to use in a calculation or formatting formula. Or, you may have created main report parameter fields that you want to pass directly to existing subreport parameter fields without creating additional subreport "?Pm-" parameter fields and additional record selection.

In these situations, you will want to pass a parameter field, database field, or formula value from the main report to the *existing* subreport parameter field, without using the standard linking procedure discussed previously of creating a parameter field and using it in record selection. When you display the Subreport Links dialog box, as described earlier in this chapter, begin by adding the main report database, formula, or parameter field you want to link from to the Field(s) To Link To list. Then, simply choose the *existing* subreport parameter field in the Subreport Parameter Field To Use drop-down list, instead of choosing the automatically generated parameter with the ?PM- prefix. By default, the Select Data check box and matching subreport field won't be selectable, indicating that no additional subreport parameter will be created and used in record selection.

Add main report field, formula, or parameter to link from

Choose existing subreport
parameter here

TIP *You also may wish to automatically create a ?PM-prefixed parameter field but not use it in subreport record selection. To do this, leave the automatically created parameter field selected, but uncheck "Select data in subreport based on field." The new parameter field will be created in the subreport but not used in record selection. Navigate to the subreport design tab and use the newly created parameter field in the desired calculation or formatting formula.*

Subreport Formatting with the Format Editor

There are a number of settings and features in the Format Editor you can use to further format and control subreport objects. On the main report Design or Preview tab, select the subreport object. Then, display the Format Editor by clicking the Format button in the Expert Tools toolbar, by choosing Format | Format Subreport from the pull-down menus, or by right-clicking the subreport object and choosing Format Subreport from the pop-up menu. The Format Editor appears with the Common tab appearing.

Some items on the Common tab may be of particular use with subreports. For example, changing the object name for the subreport will make the Report Explorer more meaningful, as well as assisting you in Report Part navigation with web reporting (discussed in more detail in Part II of the book).

CAUTION *If you are planning on passing values from a subreport to the main report (discussed later in the chapter), don't use the Suppress check box. Unlike a suppressed formula field (which will still calculate but won't display), a suppressed subreport does not process and will not generate values to pass to the main report. If you need to suppress a subreport from displaying, you will need to display the subreport Design tab and hide or suppress every section of the subreport. Then, returning to the main report, shrink the subreport object size as much as possible to reduce its height. The subreport will still run and pass values as if it were visible.*

By default, the Can Grow option is checked whenever you create a subreport. This allows the subreport to grow vertically based on the actual data returned in the subreport. You'll typically want to leave this check box on for most subreports.

Formatting options particular to subreports appear on the Format Editor Subreports tab. While most of the options on the Subreport tab apply to on-demand subreports (discussed later in this chapter), three of the options bear further discussion here: Subreport Name, Re-Import When Opening, and Suppress Blank Subreport.

If you'd like a more user-friendly name to display on the Preview and Design tabs for the subreport, you can change the Subreport Name here. The change applies as soon as you close and redisplay subreport-related tabs, and it applies to both in-place and on-demand subreports.

The Re-Import When Opening option is available only for subreports that were imported, rather than created, during the Insert Subreport dialog (this option will be dimmed if you format a subreport that you created from scratch). When you import an existing report as the subreport, Crystal Reports does not create a real-time link to the original .RPT file. The report design characteristics of the existing report are just imported into the main report and then "forgotten." If you later make changes to the original report that you imported, the changes won't be reflected here. However, Crystal Reports provides the ability to automatically or manually update (re-import) the subreport to reflect any changes to the original .RPT file.

To manually re-import a subreport that has had changes made to the original .RPT file, right-click the subreport object on the main report Design tab. Choose Re-Import Subreport on the pop-up menu. The .RPT file that was used to originally import the subreport will be read again, and any changes will now be reflected in this report.

To have Crystal Reports automatically update imported subreports every time the main report is opened, format the subreport by selecting the subreport object in the main report Design tab or Preview tab. Then either use the Format menu or right-click the subreport object and choose Format Subreport, which will display the Format Editor. On the Subreport tab, check the Re-Import When Opening check box. You may also set this option globally by choosing File | Options and then checking the Re-Import Subreports When Opening Reports option on the New Report tab.

CAUTION *The automatic re-import option will cause problems if the original .RPT file is missing, if changes have been made to it for other purposes, or if the main report/subreports have been maintained with database changes but the original subreport .RPT file hasn't. And if you re-import a subreport, any changes you made to the originally imported subreport structure will be overwritten by the updated subreport. You will be warned that your changes are going to be overwritten, and you cannot undo the import. If you realize that you've overwritten subreport changes that you wanted to keep, close the report without saving it. Then, reopen the report.*

The last option on the Subreport tab of the Format Editor is Suppress Blank Subreport. This option evaluates the subreport and suppresses its display entirely if it returns no records. However, note that the blank subreport object still takes up room in its main report section. Also, any values passed from the subreport to the main report in shared variables will not be updated (passing data from a subreport to the main report is discussed later in the chapter). The "Handling Empty Subreports" section later in this chapter describes steps to correct these display issues.

On-Demand Versus In-Place Subreports

By default, a subreport will process *in-place* as soon as Crystal Reports encounters it during main-report processing. For example, if you place a subreport in a group footer and preview the report, the subreport will process every time Crystal Reports comes to a group footer. If the report contains 75 groups and you click the last page-navigation button, 75 subreports will have to be processed before you see the page.

Depending on subreport size, database speed, or any of a number of other factors, this subreport processing may present a prohibitive performance problem. That's one reason why Crystal Reports provides the *on-demand* subreport. An on-demand subreport simply exists as a placeholder on the main report (similar to a web hyperlink), but it doesn't process as the main report progresses. Only when you click the subreport placeholder hyperlink does the subreport actually process and appear in its own Preview tab.

There are two ways to denote a subreport as on-demand versus in-place. When you first create the subreport, check the On-Demand Subreport check box in the Insert Subreport dialog box. Or, you may change the settings for the subreport on the Subreport tab of the Format Editor. Check On-Demand Subreport to make the currently selected subreport on-demand. Now, when you preview the main report, only a placeholder outline will appear where the subreport would be. When the viewer clicks the placeholder hyperlink, the on-demand subreport will process and appear in its own Preview tab.

Caution *Since data is not saved in on-demand subreports, you may wish to avoid them if you distribute a report to a viewer who doesn't have access to the database. Even if a viewer opens a report with File | Save Data With Report checked, on-demand subreports will have to connect to the database to be shown.*

There are two helpful text options that make on-demand subreports more intuitive and interactive. The On-Demand Subreport Caption and Subreport Preview Tab Caption properties also exist on the Format Editor's Subreport tab. Both of these properties are set via Conditional Formula buttons, which allow you to create a conditional string formula that determines what appears inside the subreport placeholder in the main report and in the subreport Preview tab, respectively.

Since both are conditional formulas, you can use the complete Crystal Reports formula language to create a string formula to display. This gives you the flexibility to include actual database data in the formulas. For example, to prompt the user to click a subreport placeholder to see credit information for a particular state, you could enter the following formula for the On-Demand Subreport Caption:

```
"Click to see Credit records for " & GroupName ({Customer.Region})
```

To show the state name in the Preview tab for the particular on-demand subreport that a viewer chooses, you could use the following conditional formula for the Subreport Preview Tab Caption:

```
GroupName ({Customer.Region}) & " credits"
```

Tip *The Subreport Preview Tab Caption option is available with either on-demand or in-place subreports. If you double-click on an in-place subreport, it will appear in its own Preview tab with the caption formula displayed. The On-Demand Subreport Caption option is only available if you check On-Demand Subreport.*

You can use other options on the Format Editor to choose the font face, size, and color; the border style; and the background color that appear on the placeholder hyperlink. By using these formatting options creatively, you can make an on-demand subreport placeholder look clickable. Also, when you mouse over an on-demand subreport in the Preview tab, the mouse pointer changes to the standard Windows hand, which denotes a clickable object.

You may also set Tool Tip Text in the Format Editor's Common tab to customize the tool tip that appears when you mouse over an on-demand subreport.

Figure 12-4 shows the resulting main report Preview tab. Notice that several subreports have been clicked and their Preview tabs have been customized.

CAUTION If you are passing data back to the main report from a subreport (discussed later in the chapter), making the subreport on-demand will prevent the data from being passed back when the main report runs. Since the subreports aren't processing as the main report runs, there's nothing for them to pass back.

Passing Data Between Main Reports and Subreports

In addition to passing a linking field to a subreport from a main report to limit the subreport's record selection, you may want to pass data from a main report to a subreport for other purposes. Or, you may want to pass data from a subreport back to the main report to use in summary calculations or similar functions. You can pass data to a subreport from the main report by using a parameter field, as described earlier in the chapter, under "Linking to

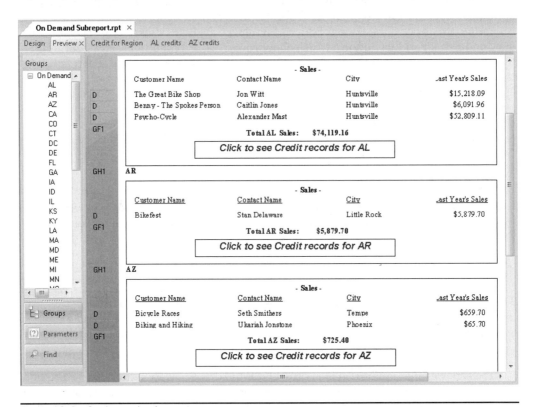

FIGURE 12-4 On-demand subreport

Existing Parameter Fields in Subreports." Crystal Reports also provides the *shared variable,* which allows you to pass data back and forth between main reports and subreports.

Passing data to a subreport from the main report without the subreport using it in record selection is fairly straightforward. Display the Subreport Links dialog box, as explained earlier in this chapter. Choose a linking field from the main report and add it to the Field(s) To Link To list. This will automatically add a parameter field prefixed with ?Pm- (all parameter fields automatically begin with a question mark) to the Subreport Parameter Field To Use drop-down list. Now, simply uncheck Select Data in Subreport Based On Field.

Uncheck to create a linked parameter field that doesn't change subreport record selection

These steps will create the Pm-parameter field in the subreport and pass data to it, but the parameter field won't be used for subreport record selection. Then, just use the parameter field in subreport formulas or place it on the subreport for display, as desired. For example, if you added a parameter for the summary field for the last year's sales by region figure in the sample report, your subreport would "know" the region's sales subtotal even though the subreport is not grouped by region. You could then add, in the footer of the subreport, a formula that compared the credit sum for the region and the sales sum for the region, and conditionally display appropriate text.

NOTE *Chapter 13 discusses how to use parameter fields in your reports.*

Using shared variables is a consistent way to pass data back and forth between the main report and one or more subreports, or even from subreport to subreport. You'll need to create formulas that declare the same shared variable in both the main report and the subreport. You can assign the variable a value in the subreport and then read the contents of the variable in the main report. Or, you can assign a value in the main report and read it in the subreport.

Here's an example of a formula in a subreport that places the sum of a currency field into a shared variable:

```
WhilePrintingRecords;
Shared CurrencyVar CreditTotal := Sum ({Credit.Amount})
```

Here's the corresponding formula in the main report that retrieves the value of the shared variable:

```
WhilePrintingRecords;
Shared CurrencyVar CreditTotal
```

An important step in using shared variables is determining if and when you need to reset the value contained in the shared variable. This may be necessary if, for example, you are passing the credit total from the subreport to the main report, and your data set includes regions that have no credit records. Should this be the case, the subreport won't encounter any data records and therefore won't evaluate the report section containing the formula that places a value in the shared variable. The variable will retain its value from the previous region that did process, resulting in incorrect calculations for the region with no credit records. To avoid this problem, create a formula to reset the shared variable to zero for each new region:

```
WhilePrintingRecords;
Shared CurrencyVar CreditTotal := 0
```

After you place this formula on the main report (in the region group header, for this example) and verify that it's producing the correct results, you can use the Format Editor to suppress it so that the zeros don't display.

For more information on assigning and using variables, and other formula topics, refer to Chapter 4.

NOTE *Because subreports process after formulas in the main report processing cycle, you must take special steps to retrieve the proper contents of a shared variable set by the subreport. For example, if you place both the subreport and a formula to retrieve the contents of a shared variable set in that subreport in a group footer, you'll notice odd behavior. Typically, you'll find that the formula returns the value of the shared variable from the previous group, instead of the current group. This is because the subreport is setting the value of the shared variable after the formula to retrieve the variable has already processed. To resolve this problem, insert an additional section (for example, a Group Footer #1 b) as described in Chapter 8. Then, place the formula that retrieves the value of the shared variable in the second section (Group Footer #1 b), while leaving the subreport in the first section (Group Footer #1 a). The formula that retrieves the contents of the shared variable will then retrieve the value from the correct subreport.*

Handling Empty Subreports

When you link subreports, there may be situations in which the subreport won't retrieve any records that match the linking field from the main report. Typically, this will just result in a subreport showing up without any details sections. If there are column headings or other information in other sections, they may appear with zeros for subtotals.

There are two graceful ways to handle empty subreports: suppress them and any related totals, or display an informational message denoting the lack of data.

If you want to suppress the blank subreport altogether, check that option on the Subreport tab of the Format Editor. For this solution to work effectively, the subreport should reside alone in its own section. You may then format the section with the Section Expert and choose

Suppress Blank Section. The entire section of the main report will then be suppressed if the subreport contains no data.

You may prefer to display an informational message instead of suppressing the blank subreport, similar to what's shown in Figure 12-5.

This is accomplished by conditionally suppressing different sections of the subreport based on the presence or absence of database records. Look at the Design tab for the subreport.

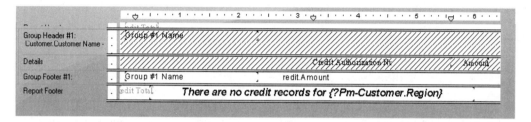

The group footer contains objects that you want to appear if the subreport actually returns records. The report footer contains the object (the text message) that you want to appear if the subreport doesn't return records. Conditional suppression of these two sections is done within the Section Expert.

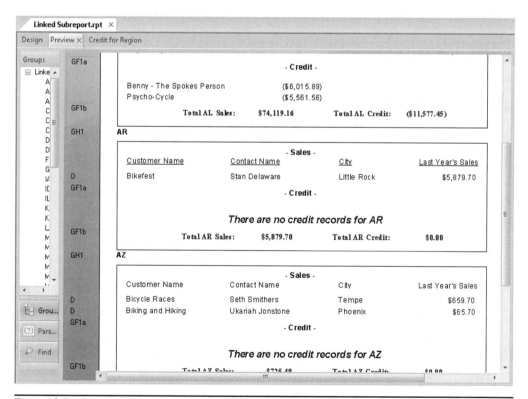

FIGURE 12-5   An empty subreport showing an informational message

Conditionally suppress the section containing the informational message by adding the following formula with the Conditional Formula button next to the Section Expert's Suppress property:

```
Not IsNull({Credit.Credit Authorization Number})
```

Then, conditionally suppress the sections that contain the actual subreport data with the following conditional formula applied to the Suppress property:

```
IsNull({Credit.Credit Authorization Number})
```

Don't forget—you are conditionally *suppressing* these sections (not displaying them), so you may need to think backward. If the subreport is empty because no records were returned based on the linked field from the main report, the Credit Authorization Number will be null. In this case, you'll want to suppress the actual subreport data but not the informational message. If data is returned, then the Credit Authorization Number will contain data and will not be null. In this case, you want to suppress the informational message but not the actual subreport data.

TIP *You can use this technique for all of your Crystal Reports, not just subreports. If you may encounter main reports that return no records, you can display an informational message in them. See Chapter 8 for more information on conditionally formatting sections.*

Performance Considerations

Subreports create potential performance problems for your reporting projects. Here are some tips to help maximize performance for your report viewer. Obviously, these considerations are more important if a viewer will be viewing a report online using Crystal Reports or as an on-demand report on the Web with BusinessObjects Enterprise/Crystal Reports Server. If a report is being printed or exported, subreports affect performance as well, but the user won't be staring at the screen waiting for them.

- Use on-demand subreports when appropriate. That way, a viewer won't have to wait for many subreports to process. Viewers can click the individual subreports they want to see when they want to see them.

- If you are creating a linked subreport, try to base the link on an indexed field in the subreport. This will cause record selection in the subreport to occur substantially faster. If the subreport is based on an ODBC or SQL database, make sure you are keeping as much of the SQL query on the server as possible (see Chapter 15 for SQL database performance considerations).

- If you are linking subreports with formula fields, try to keep the formula field in the main report and use a database field in the subreport. Using formula fields in the subreport, particularly with subreports based on SQL databases, will move part or all of the subreport query off the server, impeding performance.

Interactive Reporting with Parameter Fields

If you are designing reports to distribute to a viewer audience that may not be familiar with Crystal Reports or the Select Expert, you will soon have the need to prompt the viewer for values that affect record selection, conditional formatting, or some other ad hoc information. This becomes even more crucial when the viewer doesn't actually have a copy of Crystal Reports but wants to view a report presented in some "turnkey" fashion, such as an on-demand report run on the Web with a member of the BusinessObjects Enterprise XI 3.0 family (discussed in section II of this book). In these situations, the viewer won't have the ability to make changes with the Select Expert anyway.

The ideal solution for these types of ad hoc reporting requirements would be to present the viewer with a dialog box prompt, preferably including a choice of default values or a range of values, to help the user enter the correct values for the prompt. The response the viewer provides could then be passed to the Select Expert to customize record selection and formatting, and the values the viewer supplied could also be included on the report to indicate what data makes up the report.

This ideal solution is made possible by *parameter fields*: prompts that are presented to the viewer when he or she refreshes the report. The value the viewer provides is then passed on to the Select Expert, report formulas, or conditional-formatting formulas to customize the way the report appears, based on the viewer's response. The viewer doesn't have to know how to enter selection criteria or conditional formulas to customize the way the report behaves.

Many parameter field enhancements (such as Dynamic and Cascading pick lists) were added to version XI, the Crystal Reports version prior to version 2008. Even so, Crystal Reports 2008 adds even more flexibility, including the ability to make a parameter field optional; to include it in a saved data selection, which doesn't require the report to be refreshed against the database; or to use the new Parameter Panel, which allows interaction with parameter fields right from the Preview tab. All these new features are covered later in this chapter.

Creating a Parameter Field

Consider the following report:

RH				**Ad-Hoc Report**	

Orders placed between 1/1/2004 and 12/31/2004
Regions include AL, AR, AZ, CO, CT, DC
Customer names include *Bik*

Order ID	Order Amount	Order Date	Customer Name	Region
1188	$67.80	01/15/2004	The Great Bike Shop	AL
1192	$2,987.20	01/16/2004	The Great Bike Shop	AL
1397	$1,439.55	03/02/2004	The Great Bike Shop	AL
1487	$43.50	04/05/2004	The Great Bike Shop	AL
1632	$97.02	05/21/2004	The Great Bike Shop	AL
1660	$1,103.20	05/30/2004	The Great Bike Shop	AL
1666	$10,662.75	06/01/2004	The Great Bike Shop	AL
1703	$43.50	06/11/2004	The Great Bike Shop	AL
1765	$7,829.29	06/24/2004	The Great Bike Shop	AL
2011	$4,697.61	08/22/2004	The Great Bike Shop	AL
2020	$126.60	08/25/2004	The Great Bike Shop	AL
2117	$823.05	09/16/2004	The Great Bike Shop	AL
2120	$8,861.45	09/18/2004	The Great Bike Shop	AL
2161	$431.87	09/28/2004	The Great Bike Shop	AL
2419	$83.30	11/24/2004	The Great Bike Shop	AL
2456	$2,294.55	12/07/2004	The Great Bike Shop	AL
2527	$67.80	12/23/2004	The Great Bike Shop	AL
2552	$2,644.20	12/31/2004	The Great Bike Shop	AL
3033	$8,819.55	05/21/2004	Bikefest	AR
3034	$49.50	05/21/2004	Biking and Hiking	AZ
3036	$161.70	05/21/2004	Fred's Bikes	CO
3037	$43.50	05/21/2004	Phil's Bikes	CT
3038	$13.50	05/21/2004	Colin's Bikes	DC

This report uses three fields in record selection:

- **Order Date**   Filtered with a Between selection criterion to include orders that were placed during 2004 (between January 1 and December 31).
- **Region**   Filtered with a One Of selection criterion to include orders placed from AL, AR, AZ, CO, CT, and DC.
- **Customer Name**   Filtered with a Like selection criterion to include customer names that contain the string *Bik*.

These criteria are hard-coded into the Select Expert, and text objects appear in the report header to indicate the restrictions.

The difficulty comes when you want the person reviewing the report to be able to easily change these criteria whenever the report is refreshed. The way this report is currently designed, the viewer must have the ability to alter record selection (and know enough about its intricacies to be able to change it). That person also must be able to edit the text object that displays what records are included. Even in this case, it's time-consuming to change this information every time the viewer wants to change these options. Parameter fields are the answer.

Using parameter fields to provide flexibility in this scenario is, at minimum, a two-step process. The third step is optional:

1. Create the parameter field.

2. Use the parameter field in record selection.

3. Place the parameter field on the report, perhaps embedded in a text object, to indicate what is included on the report.

Parameter fields are created from the Field Explorer, which can be displayed when either the Design or Preview tab is selected. You can click the Field Explorer button in the Standard toolbar, or choose View | Field Explorer from the pull-down menus. Or, if you shrunk the Field Explorer with the push pin earlier, just click the push pin again to redisplay it. Then, click the plus sign next to the Parameter Fields category to show existing parameter fields, if any.

If there are parameter fields in the report already, you can edit them by selecting the desired parameter field and clicking the Edit button on the Field Explorer toolbar. You can also rename or delete existing parameter fields with the Rename and Delete buttons on the toolbar. If there are no existing parameter fields, or if you wish to create a new parameter field, ensure that the Parameter Fields category of the Field Explorer is selected (click it), then click New. You can also right-click the Parameter Fields category of the Field Explorer and choose New from the pop-up menu. The Create New Parameter dialog box appears, as shown in Figure 13-1.

Choose a name for your parameter field (presumably the "My Parameter" default name won't be appropriate in most cases). It can be the same name as other database or formula fields, because Crystal Reports distinguishes parameter fields by preceding their names with a question mark. Choose a descriptive yet reasonably short name for your parameter field.

You may want to consider changing the default descriptive message that will appear in the Enter Values dialog box when a viewer is prompted to provide the value. This is done by changing the default Prompt Text value in the Options list at the bottom of the Create New Parameter dialog box. Choose something that is easy to understand and helpful to the user, such as "Enter the state code (2 characters only) for this report." You can enter up to 254 characters of prompting text, although excessive prompting text will probably look unsightly when the parameter value is prompted for. Crystal Reports will word-wrap the prompting text when the viewer is prompted, if the prompting text won't all fit on one line.

Choose a data type for the parameter field from the Type drop-down list. This is a crucial step, as it determines how your parameter field can be used in record selection, formulas,

Type your own parameter field name   Choose data type

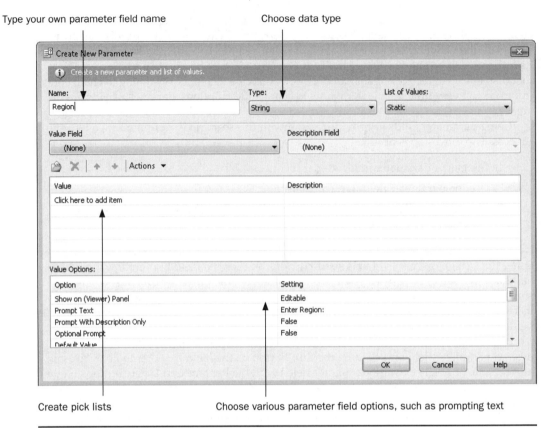

Create pick lists   Choose various parameter field options, such as prompting text

FIGURE 13-1   The Create New Parameter dialog box

and conditional formatting. For example, if you are planning on using the parameter field to compare to a string database field in the Select Expert, choose a String data type. If you are going to limit the report to a certain date range, based on a date/time field in the database, choose a DateTime data type.

These are the only items that are actually required for using a parameter field (and, changing the prompt text is optional). However, there are many features in Crystal Reports that enhance the flexibility of parameter fields.

Responding to Parameter Field Prompts

Once you've created a parameter field, you must make some use of the parameter field on the report—in record selection, in a formula, or just by placing it on the report—before you'll be prompted to supply a value (if a green check mark or question mark icon doesn't appear next to the parameter field in the Field Explorer, you have not made use of it). You will be prompted for it the first time you preview the report. The Enter Values dialog box will be displayed.

If you haven't entered any default values or created a pick list (discussed later in the chapter), the viewer will need to type their response to the prompt. If you've created a pick list, the prompt will appear as a drop-down list from which one of the predefined values can be selected. If you have created more than one parameter field for the report, only one Enter Values dialog box will appear, but each parameter field will appear in the list. Click the parameter field you want to select.

TIP   *Parameter fields will appear in the Enter Values dialog box in the order you created them. If you'd like to change the order in which they appear, either select the Parameter category of the Field Explorer or select an individual parameter within the category. Right-click and choose Set Parameter Order from the pop-up list. The Parameter Order dialog box will appear. Select the desired parameter field and click the up or down arrow to reposition the parameter field.*

When you refresh the report, the Refresh Report Data dialog box will ask whether to use the currently set parameter field values or to prompt for new values. If you use the current values, the database will be reread with the current values in the parameter fields. If you choose to prompt for new values, the Enter Values dialog box will appear again, and you may specify new values for any necessary parameter fields. Values you entered previously will reappear in the Enter Values dialog box, so you only need to change values that you wish to differ from the last report refresh.

Data Type Considerations

The data type you choose for your parameter field determines how the parameter field can be used in the rest of the report. If, for example, you need to compare a parameter field to a date database field, you'll need to use a date parameter field. The data type will also determine how the report viewer must respond to the parameter field prompt.

String and number/currency parameter fields are fairly straightforward. In the case of strings, a viewer can respond with any combination of letters, numbers, or special characters. For numbers, only characters appropriate for numeric data, such as the numbers 0 through 9 and a minus sign, can be used—other characters will result in an error message when you click OK. Using date, time, date/time, or Boolean parameter fields will introduce some new features and limitations.

TIP *Ranges and edit masks can be used to limit or format what a viewer can enter into a parameter field. These special features are discussed later in this chapter.*

Dates and Times

You'll often want to use date or time parameter fields to limit your report to certain date or time ranges. You can choose data types of Date, Time, or DateTime. When you are prompted for a date or time parameter field, a few special features are available to you:

Make the selected range inclusive of exact date/time entered; otherwise, entered values are not included

Click to see date picker (calendar)

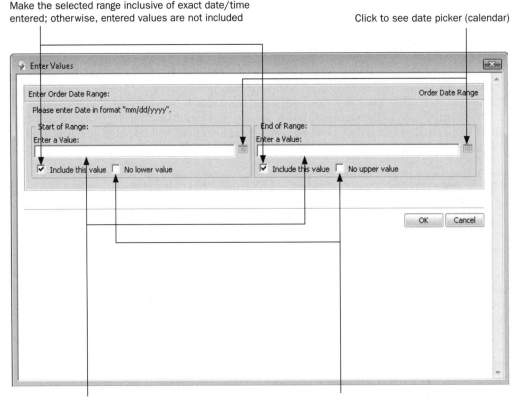

Type in date and/or time values directly, using format specified at top of box

Use only one value to limit the range (useful for "everything up to *x*" or "*x* and everything higher")

Preformatted dates and times may appear in the dialog box (perhaps from a pick list or a previous report refresh)—just type the correct date and time over any existing default value. If no pick list or default has been specified, or no previous value remains from an earlier report refresh, follow the example at the top of the box for entering date/time information. If you enter it incorrectly (for example, if you enter a date in a format not matching the sample format provided), an error message will appear when you click OK.

TIP *Parameter field date formats are determined by the Preferred Viewing Locale setting available from the View pull-down menu. The regional locale you choose will determine the format you use when supplying values to date and date/time parameter fields.*

Boolean Parameter Fields

You may find a Boolean parameter field helpful when using record selection based on a Boolean database field or when conditionally formatting according to a parameter field value. A Boolean parameter field, like a Boolean formula (discussed in Chapter 4), can contain one of only two values: true or false.

When you choose a data type of Boolean in the Parameter dialog box, you may make certain choices to accommodate the special features of a Boolean parameter field, as shown in Figure 13-2. Specify the Name of the field and the Prompt Text for the parameter field just as you would for other parameter fields. You can also choose a True or False default value, as well as typing custom descriptions for the True and False options under the Description column.

The Options section differs slightly for a Boolean parameter field. If you type a number for the Boolean Group # option, you will add this parameter field to a grouping of one or more other Boolean parameter fields. Boolean parameter field groups allow you to simulate the "radio button" behavior you see in Crystal Reports and other Windows applications. Since you can have more than one group of Boolean parameter fields, specify a unique number here for each group of Boolean parameter fields you wish to create—if, for example, you create four Boolean parameter fields with the number 1 specified here, all four will be prompted for together.

If you choose True for the Exclusive Group option, a single drop-down list consisting of all group parameters will appear when you're prompted to supply a value. The chosen field will return true, and all others will return false. If you choose False for the Exclusive Group option, two boxes will appear when you're prompted to supply a value—the box on the left will contain all parameters in the group, and the box on the right will contain parameters that you've specifically added. Each added parameter field will return true, while others will return false.

Using Parameter Fields in Record, Group, or Saved Data Selection

Probably the most common use for a parameter field is in report selection. By creating a parameter field and using it with the Select Expert or a record-selection formula, you can prompt the viewer to provide variable information when the report runs, and have the report record selection reflect the viewer's choices.

After creating the desired parameter fields, use the toolbar button or pull-down menu option to display the Select Expert. You may choose either Record, Group, or Saved Data selection (finer points of these options are described in Chapter 3). Add a selection tab for the field, formula, or summary value you want to compare to the value the viewer enters into the parameter field. In the operation drop-down list, choose the appropriate operation

Type in alternative text descriptions for True and False values

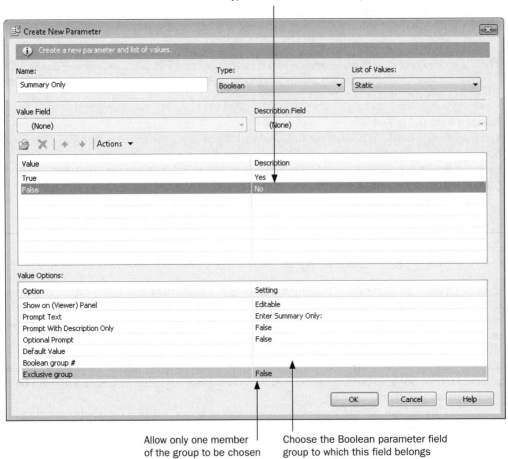

Allow only one member
of the group to be chosen

Choose the Boolean parameter field
group to which this field belongs

FIGURE 13-2 Special features of a Boolean parameter field

for the parameter action you need, such as "is equal to" for a region selection parameter, "greater than" for an order threshold parameter, or "is like" for a string-matching name parameter. Keep in mind that you may need to use a different Select Expert operation with parameter fields than you would otherwise. You'll typically use "is equal to" even if you want to allow multiple values or range values (discussed later in the chapter) to be supplied by a parameter. Even though you might be tempted to use "is between" for a range parameter or "is one of" for a multivalue parameter, you should just use "is equal". When you choose the drop-down list to see sample database values, you'll see parameter fields of the same data type in the list. Choose the correct parameter field.

CAUTION *Only parameter fields of the same data type as the database field will show up in the Select Expert. If you don't see the parameter field you expect in the Select Expert, it wasn't created with the same data type as the database field you are using. Change the data type of the parameter field and rerun the Select Expert.*

You may also use the formula portion of the Select Expert, or the Formula Editor, to edit the selection formula. In the Select Expert, you'll need to type the parameter field into the formula manually, including the left and right curly braces, and the question mark in front of the parameter field name. If you use the Formula Editor, you'll see all parameter fields (regardless of data type) in the Field Tree box. Choose the parameter field you want to use in the record-selection formula. The formula may look something like this:

```
{Customer.Region} = {?Region}
```

Make sure you choose a parameter field of the same data type, or use functions to convert the parameter field to the correct data type. If you try, for example, to compare a numeric parameter field to a string database field, you'll receive an error.

Crystal Reports 2008 Parameter Refresh Options

In previous Crystal Reports versions, every time you wished to supply a new value to one or more parameter fields (whether they were used in record selection or not), you had to refresh the report. If your report was based on a large, slow database, each report refresh could take a significant amount of time to retrieve a new set of database records, even if the parameter field value you changed didn't effect record selection at all. Crystal Reports 2008 has solved this problem.

Crystal Reports 2008 now determines whether or not your parameter field will require a database refresh, based on where you use the parameter field in the report. If you use the parameter field in record selection, in a formula that is used in record selection, for a stored procedure or SQL command parameter value, or in other similar situations where the parameter field will effect record selection, Crystal Reports will place a question-mark-with-database-barrel icon next to it in the Field Explorer. If, however, the parameter is used in saved data or group selection, in a calculation formula, in conditional formatting, or in some similar scenario that doesn't effect record selection, Crystal Reports will place a check mark next to the parameter field in the Field Explorer. If you don't use the parameter field at all on the report, nothing will appear next to the parameter field name in the Field Explorer and it won't be prompted for.

In order to take full advantage of this new feature, you must place non-refresh parameter fields in the new Parameter Panel, discussed next (you can place refresh-required parameters in the panel as well, but they will still require a database refresh if you do). Once placed in the Parameter Panel, non-refresh parameter field value changes won't require a database refresh to redisplay the report. This can provide a more responsive level of report interactivity by using non-refresh parameter fields in saved data selection, conditional formatting, and calculation formulas. Every time these parameters are changed in the Parameter Panel, the Preview tab will display a different organization of data without any extra time taken for a new query from the database.

The New Parameter Panel

In previous Crystal Reports versions, there was only one way to supply values to parameter fields—by refreshing the report. While this option remains in Crystal Reports 2008, there is an entirely new user interface that can also be used to supply parameter field values. *The Parameter Panel,* which appears as part of the new Preview Panel at the left side of the Preview tab, allows you to interact in real time with one or more parameter fields. Once you've modified the desired parameters in the panel, one mouse click will update the report with the new values (and, if only non-refresh parameters are modified, no database requery will be necessary).

When you create a parameter field, you can choose whether or not it will appear in the Parameter Panel, and if so, whether it will appear as a read-only or modifiable parameter. Make this choice in the Create Parameter dialog box when you create or edit the parameter field.

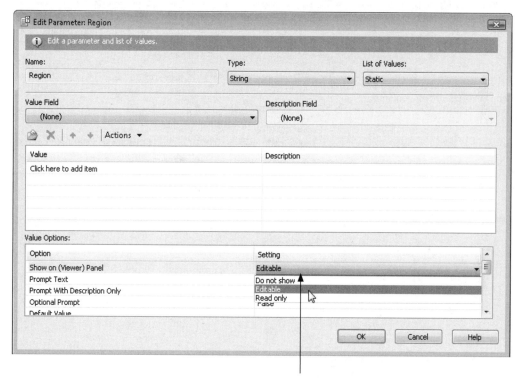

Choose Parameter Panel appearance option

Once you've chosen desired Parameter Panel view choices, preview the report (you will need to supply parameter values with the traditional Enter Values screen the first time you preview a report). If the Preview Panel is not displayed to the left of the Preview tab, display it by clicking the Preview Panel button in the Standard toolbar, or by choosing View | Preview Panel from the pull-down menus. If necessary, click the Parameters button at the bottom of the Preview Panel to display parameter fields instead of the Group Tree or Find tab.

The Parameter Panel will appear, as illustrated in Figure 13-3. Parameter fields that were provided an Editable or Read Only value in the Create Parameter dialog box's Show On Viewer Panel property will appear.

NOTE *Figure 13-3 exhibits several types of more sophisticated parameter fields, such as multiple-value parameter fields and range parameter fields. These are covered in more detail later in the chapter, under "Special Parameter Field Features."*

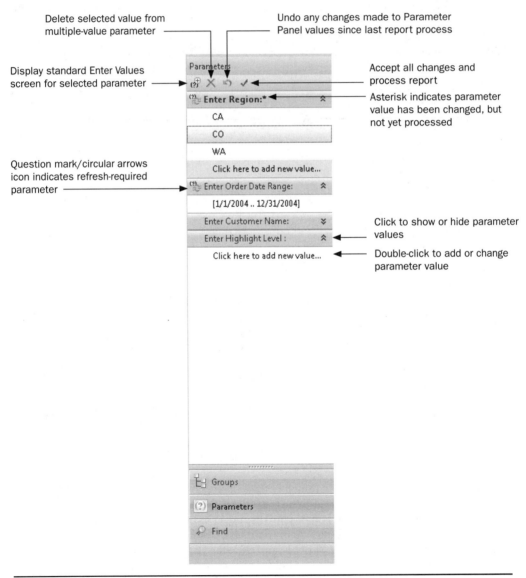

FIGURE 13-3   The Parameter Panel

To add or change a parameter value, double-click the Click Here message, or double-click an existing parameter value (you must have specified the parameter field as editable to be able to add or edit values). If the parameter field is designed to accept one or more individual values, or it uses a static pick list of available values, the Parameter Panel will display a cursor in-place to allow you to add or edit a value. If, however, the parameter field requires one or more range values to be added, or provides a dynamic pick list of available values, the traditional Enter Values dialog box will appear for this particular parameter field. If you wish to display the traditional Enter Values dialog regardless of parameter field type, click the first button in the Parameter Panel toolbar (above the first parameter field in the panel) to display the Enter Values dialog for the selected parameter field.

If multiple values appear for a particular parameter field, you may delete an individual value by selecting it and clicking the X Parameter Panel toolbar button (note that a selected value will appear with an orange shade, as opposed to the light cyan shade given to every other value in a multiple-value parameter list). The curly left arrow Parameter Panel toolbar button will allow you to undo all changes to Parameter Panel values that you have made since the report was last processed.

If you don't care to interact with a particular parameter field any longer (perhaps it contains a large list of multiple values and is taking up too much space), you may click the small double-up-arrow icon to collapse the parameter's values. To view it later, click the double-down-arrow to redisplay it.

When you are finished supplying values to the Parameter Panel, click the small check mark Parameter Panel toolbar button. If any of the parameter fields you modified in the Parameter Panel are refresh-required parameter fields (a question mark–circular arrows icon indicates these parameter fields), the database will be requeried prior to the report being displayed. The report will immediately reprocess, and the updated report will appear in the Preview tab.

NOTE *The Parameter Panel not only appears in Crystal Reports 2008, but also in new web- and Windows-based viewers available with a custom Visual Studio .NET application (covered in Chapter 19), as well as in members of the BusinessObjects Enterprise XI 3.0 family (covered in Part II of this book). This provides much improved parameter field interactivity for report viewers.*

Displaying Parameter Field Values on the Report

One of the other major benefits of using parameter fields is that you can place them on your report just like database or formula fields. Whatever value the viewer placed in them before the report ran will appear on the report. By creatively using parameter fields, you can have a customized report that changes selection and shows the values used in selection on the report.

To place a parameter field on the report, drag and drop it from the Field Explorer just as you would a database or formula field. Depending on the data type of the parameter field, you can format it using the usual Format toolbar or Format Editor features discussed elsewhere in this book. You can also combine parameter fields with other fields and literal text inside text objects (as discussed in Chapter 6). A text object combining a parameter field looks like this in the Design tab:

Orders over {?Order Level} are highlighted

and will use the value supplied by the viewer when the report runs:

> Orders over $2,500.00 are highlighted

TIP *Only single-value parameters are effectively displayed this way. To display multiple values or ranged values, you must create a formula that extracts the whole set or range of values the user has entered. Solutions for these cases are discussed later in this chapter.*

Creating Pick Lists

If you don't add any default values when you first create a parameter field, the viewer will have to type in the value for the parameter field. While this sometimes may be desirable, it requires that the viewer know enough about the parameter field and the way the report and database are designed to type the value correctly. The viewer may make a mistake by misspelling a name or entering an incorrect code for the field. By creating a pick list, you can let the viewer choose from a predefined list of default values.

NOTE *Crystal Reports documentation and dialog boxes refer to these lists variously as "Prompts" and "Lists of Values." However, the term "pick list" is used in this book, as it is a more common term to refer to a list of available options chosen from a drop-down list.*

The first choice you'll encounter when you decide to create a parameter field pick list is whether the pick list should be static or dynamic. A *static* pick list contains a list of default values that doesn't change until you modify the parameter field. The list can contain default values that you type in manually, import from a text file, or import from a database field. These lists do not change as new data is added to a database—the only way to change a static pick list is to edit the parameter field and change the list.

A *dynamic* pick list is refreshed every time a viewer is prompted to supply the parameter field value. This real-time pick list allows additional values to be added to the pick list automatically as they are added to a source database. For example, if you create a dynamic pick list based on a sales rep name in a database, the pick list will show a current list of sales reps in the database every time a sales rep parameter field is prompted for. As sales reps are added or removed from the database, their names will appear or disappear from the pick list automatically.

A variation on a dynamic pick list is called a *cascading* pick list. A cascading pick list is one of a series of related pick lists that depend on each other. While there is no practical limit to the number of related pick lists that can cascade, an example might be two dynamic pick lists that can apply to a single parameter field, or two different parameter fields. These pick lists can relate to each other such that one pick list's values are based on another. To illustrate, the previously described sales rep pick list could be used to "cascade" a customer name pick list. When a specific sales rep is chosen from the sales rep pick list, the customer name dynamic pick list will show only customers that belong to the just-chosen sales rep. Both pick lists are dynamic—their contents are refreshed from the source database in real time.

Static Pick Lists

The simplest pick list is a static pick list. In this scenario, a fixed set of values appears to the report viewer in a drop-down list when they are prompted for the parameter field in the Enter Values dialog box or in the Parameter Panel. This pick list will always be the same until you manually edit the parameter field and change the list. Static pick lists can merely be typed in manually, can be imported from a text file, can be gathered from a table and field contained in the report, or can be created with a combination of these methods.

The first step in creating a static pick list is to ensure that the Static option is chosen from the List Of Values drop-down list in the Create New Parameter or Edit Parameter dialog box. You may then perform various steps to create or import the list of values that will make up your pick list. The simplest way to add a value to the pick list is to click the File Folder button at the top of the Value/Description table or click Click Here To Add Item in the Value/ Description table. You may then manually type in a value to appear in the pick list. Repeat these steps to manually add additional list values.

Optionally, you may add descriptions for your pick list values by typing in the matching description column. This may be helpful if your parameter field requires codes or abbreviations to be provided to the report (for example, sales rep numbers instead of names), but you'd like descriptions of the codes or abbreviations to appear next to them, or in place of them, in the pick list. The Prompt With Description Only option in the Value Options portion of the dialog box controls whether the pick list will show only the descriptions you've typed in (if you set the option to true), or the values and descriptions together (if you set the option to false).

You may also populate your pick list from a field used in the report. To do this, choose the desired field in the Value Field drop-down list. Optionally, you may choose a description field from the report or choose the desired field in the Description Field drop-down list. Once you've made these choices, click the Actions button above the Value/Description table. Choose Append All Database Values from the drop-down menu. This will fill the Value/Description table with sample data from the database (adding this data to any existing non-duplicative values already in the list).

If you have a large number of default values (and potentially descriptions) that you'd like to add to your pick list, you may want to import a pick list file. When you click Actions and choose Import from the pop-up menu, you are presented with a standard File Open dialog box that asks you to select the ASCII text file containing your pick list data. When you choose the appropriate pick list text file and click OK, the Default Values list will be populated with the data from the text file (adding this data to any existing non-duplicative values already in the list). If you wish to create a pick list file from the existing values that you've already added to the list (to use in another report, for example), click Actions and choose Export from the pop-up menu. A standard File Save dialog box will appear in which you can specify the filename for the pick list file to export to.

Once you've built a static pick list using these procedures, you may later decide that you don't want some existing values to be included in the pick list. You can remove one or more specific items by selecting them in the Value/Description table with click, CTRL-click, or SHIFT-click combinations. Once you've chosen the values you wish to remove, press DEL or click the *X* button above the table. Or you can remove all the values in the pick list by choosing Clear from the drop-down menu after clicking Actions.

CAUTION *Removing individual items from a pick list or using the Clear option can't be undone. Make sure you really want to remove these pick list values before making these choices.*

You may also wish to change the order that pick list items appear in the list. For example, if you've typed several values in manually, or you've combined manually typed entries with other values from the database or a text import, you may wish to reorder some individual values. Simply select the value in the table that you wish to move and click the small up or down arrow above the Value/Description table. The value you chose will move up or down in the list. Or, you may want to sort the entire list by the value or description. To sort the entire pick list, merely click the Value or Description column name in the Value/Description table. A small arrow will appear in that column, and the pick list will be sorted by that column. An up arrow in the column heading will indicate an ascending (*a* to *z*) sort, while a down arrow in the column heading will indicate a descending (*z* to *a*) sort.

Once you create your pick list, you may wish to ensure that report viewers only pick items from the pick list. Or, you may choose to let them pick something from the list, or type in their own value. Make this choice with the Allow Custom Values option in the Value Options section of the Parameter dialog box. Choose True for this option to allow the viewer to supply their own values to the parameter field, in addition to choosing from the pick list. Choose False for this option to force the viewer to pick values only from the pick list.

Dynamic and Cascading Pick Lists

If you create a parameter field whose pick list will be based on a frequently changing database field, you'll want to create a *dynamic* pick list. This feature allows pick lists to be dynamically generated every time a report viewer is prompted to supply a parameter value. Select the Dynamic option from the List Of Values drop-down list at the top of the Create New Parameter or Edit Parameter dialog box to begin the process. The remainder of the dialog box will adjust to settings you make from this point forward.

NOTE *Steps in this chapter refer to creating dynamic and cascading pick lists with reports that are not published to a member of the BusinessObjects Enterprise XI 3.0 family. If you plan on publishing a report to these tools, dynamic and cascading pick lists are managed within the enterprise server environment using Business Views. This is covered in more detail in the "Creating and Using Business Views" chapter, available as a download from CrystalBook.com, this book's companion web site.*

If this is your first dynamic pick list in the report, and you have not connected to a BusinessObjects Enterprise system, the only available radio button in the Choose A Data Source section is New. If there are existing dynamic pick lists in this report, or you are connected to BusinessObjects Enterprise, you may click the Existing radio button and choose an existing pick list from the associated drop-down list as the source for this pick list. With the New radio button selected, click either the File Folder button or the Click Here To Add Item table entry. A drop-down list of available report fields will appear. Choose the desired report field to act as the data source for the pick list. Pick a field in the Value drop-down list to act as the data source for the pick list.

Optionally, you may choose a report field to provide descriptions for your chosen value field. This may be helpful if your parameter field requires codes or abbreviations to be provided to the report (for example, sales rep numbers instead of names), but you'd like descriptions of the codes or abbreviations to appear next to them, or in place of them, in the pick list. The Prompt With Description Only option in the Value Options section of the dialog box controls whether the pick list will show only the descriptions (if you set the option to true), or the values and descriptions together (if you set the option to false).

You may sort your dynamic pick list by the value or description field supplied. In the Value Options area of the dialog box, choose the desired ascending or descending sort choice for either the value or description field. The pick list will appear in the chosen order when the Enter Values dialog prompts for the parameter field (dynamic pick lists will not appear directly in the Parameter Panel).

Once you've defined the value and description fields for the pick list, click the "Click To Create Parameter" message under the Parameters column to assign the pick list to the parameter field itself. This will assign the value chosen from the pick list to the parameter field you are creating or editing.

TIP *While you may enter text into the Prompt Group Text box, it's not particularly beneficial with a single dynamic pick list. You may, instead, simply supply regular parameter prompting text in the Value Options section once the pick list has been defined. Prompt Group Text is more appropriate for cascading pick lists, discussed later in the chapter.*

Creating a Cascading Pick List

A *cascading* pick list is similar to a single dynamic pick list, in that data is retrieved from the database in real time when the parameter field prompt is displayed. However, a cascading pick list consists of two or more pick lists that relate to each other. For example, you can create a higher-level customer name pick list and a lower-level order number pick list that are related. Only order numbers that belong to the customer (or customers) that are chosen in the first pick list will appear in the second pick list.

Steps for creating a cascading pick list are largely the same as for a dynamic pick list (described earlier in the chapter). However, you must add additional fields to create the cascading "hierarchy." Following the customer name/order number example, you wish to create a cascading pick list to determine an order number, but you want to limit order numbers in the pick list to match a previously chosen customer name. To do this, you must first add the customer name field to the Create New Parameter dialog box. Then, add the order number below it. By creating this hierarchy, what's known as a *prompt group* (a collection of one or more dynamic pick lists treated as a single unit) will be created, displaying a customer name dynamic pick list first, and then limiting the second order number dynamic pick list to the customer chosen. Once you've defined the last pick list in the hierarchy, click the "Click To Create Parameter" message under the Parameters column to assign the last pick list to the parameter field. This will assign the value chosen from the last pick list in the hierarchy to the parameter field you are creating. If you wish to pass values from the intermediate-level pick lists to separate parameter fields, you may click the "Click To Create Parameter" entry next to the desired field in the hierarchy, which will create a new parameter field in the report. You may then make use of the new parameter field in selections, formulas, and so forth.

You may create as many levels in the cascading hierarchy as necessary. For example, you might start with a Country field, followed by a State field, followed by a City field, followed by a ZIP Code field, and finally, a Store ID field—each lower-level dynamic pick list would be limited by the pick list above it. Just select the desired fields in the proper order and assign the parameter field to the last pick list in the hierarchy.

CAUTION *When you create a cascading pick list, you will find that Crystal Reports changes the name of the parameter field you are creating, using a combination of the original name you gave the field and the report field it's connected to in the prompt group. If you wish to rename the parameter field back to its original name, return to the Field Explorer and either hold the mouse button down on the parameter name for a few seconds until it goes into edit mode or select the parameter and click the rename button in the Field Explorer toolbar. You may then return the parameter field to its original name.*

Since your prompt group contains more than one pick list, you may customize two different sets of prompting text. First, you may change the default prompt text for each individual pick list in the Prompt Text area of the Value Options portion of the dialog box. Furthermore, you can type free-form text into the Prompt Group Text text box at the top of the dialog box. The text you add here will apply to the overall prompt group, whereas the individual prompt text options you set for each pick list will appear next to the drop-down for that particular list. Using the just-discussed Customer Name/Order Number example, you might set prompt text for the Customer pick list to "Choose Customer:", prompt text for the Order Number pick list to "Choose Order Number:", and Prompt Group Text to "Choose Customer/Order Number Combination:".

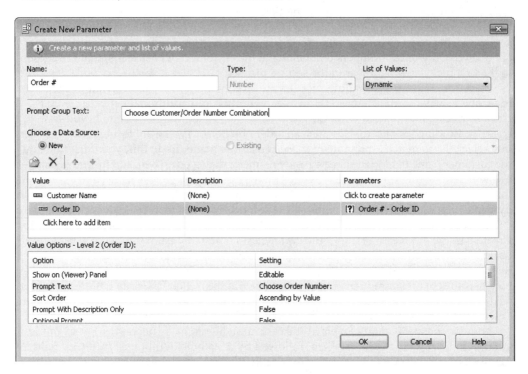

When the report is run and the parameter field using the cascading pick list is prompted for, you'll be presented with multiple pick lists, in the order of the cascading hierarchy. Pick lists lower in the hierarchy won't be enabled until you've chosen values from higher pick lists. And, lower pick lists will show limited sets of values based on choices in the higher pick lists. You'll also notice the individual pick list prompting text, as well as the prompt group text.

Using a SQL Command or Stored Procedure to Populate a Pick List

There are times when fields already included on the report may not be sufficient for dynamic pick list data sources. For example, inherent Crystal Reports limitations may not present a large enough pick list if large amounts of duplicate data are encountered in the report field you base your pick list on. A separate SQL query containing a SELECT DISTINCT clause may solve this problem. Or, you may want to base a pick list on data that comes from another database table, a stored procedure, or custom SQL that's not used in the current report. Also, even though your report may contain some sort of record selection that limits the report to a smaller set of records, this record selection is not applied to dynamic or cascading pick lists, potentially returning more pick list values than you'd like.

In these cases, you can add a database stored procedure or create a SQL Command, perhaps using a WHERE clause as a filter, to be used as a data source for your dynamic pick lists (a detailed discussion on creating SQL Commands is contained in Chapter 15). Add either of these database connections by redisplaying the Database Expert and adding a stored procedure or creating a SQL Command. These will simply appear as additional tables in the Database Expert's Selected Tables list.

Once you've added the desired stored procedure or SQL Command, just click OK to close the Database Expert. If you aren't using the stored procedure or SQL Command as part of your regular report's data, you will not need to link the stored procedure or SQL Command to other tables in the report—you may ignore the error message that indicates that this non-linking is "generally not supported." You'll also be presented with a message confirming that your report contains mixed database connections.

When you create a parameter field that contains a dynamic or cascading pick list, you'll find the SQL Command or stored procedure appearing as another table in the list of available fields. Simply choose the desired field from the stored procedure or SQL Command you wish to use to populate your pick list.

Reusing a Pick List or Prompt Group

Once you've created a dynamic pick list or prompt group, you may wish to reuse it with additional parameter fields you create later. Or, you may initially create a cascading pick list that includes several pick lists in the hierarchy, and later wish to add an additional parameter field that uses one of the higher-level pick lists in the existing prompt group. In these types of cases, you can reuse either the "data source" created with an earlier dynamic or cascading pick list or add an additional parameter field to an existing prompt group.

Create a parameter field as discussed earlier in the chapter. Choose the Dynamic List Of Values option. However, instead of clicking New under Choose A Data Source, click Existing. The drop-down list next to the Existing radio button will show existing pick lists and prompt groups belonging to other parameter fields. If you want to use the existing set of data from the pick list, but create *an additional* prompt group, choose the first entry in the existing data source list without the words "prompt group." This will create a new prompt group, including the parameter field you are creating, along with additional copies of parameter fields that existed in the initial prompt group. If, however, you merely wish to add this new parameter field so that it's part of an existing prompt group (perhaps you want to retrieve the value selected in a higher-level pick list in a cascading pick list hierarchy), choose an entry in the existing data source list that includes the words "prompt group." Then, click the "Click To Create Parameter" entry next to the field in the prompt group that you want to assign the new parameter field to (as discussed earlier, Crystal Reports will rename your parameter field to indicate the field in the pick list you are assigning it to—you may rename it in the Field Explorer if you wish).

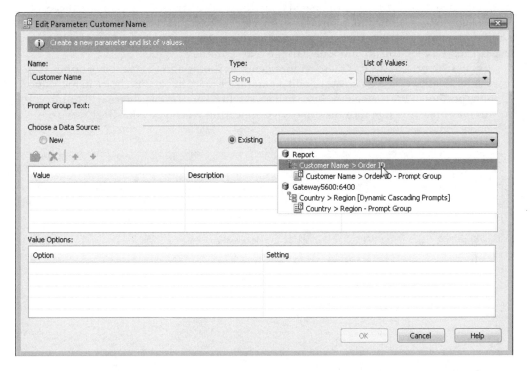

NOTE *If you are logged on to BusinessObjects Enterprise, any repository-based pick lists will also appear in the Existing data source list underneath the BusinessObjects Enterprise server name. These may also be used as pick lists for your parameter fields.*

Special Parameter Field Features

Parameter fields provide a good deal of flexibility for various prompting scenarios. For example, a viewer can choose multiple values for a single parameter field to allow one-off types of record selection. Parameter fields can be specified to include entire ranges of values, so a viewer can, for example, include all orders placed between January 1, 2004, and December 31, 2004. Also, string parameter fields can be limited to certain lengths (for example, no less than three nor more than six characters) or limited to certain formats with edit masks. And, Crystal Reports 2008 adds the ability to make a parameter field optional, allowing a report viewer to bypass entering any value for it, if the viewer so chooses.

Optional Parameter Fields

In previous Crystal Reports versions, all parameter fields on the report had to be supplied values, even if certain reporting situations didn't require them. Whenever the Enter Values parameter field dialog box appeared, leaving parameter fields empty always resulted in an error message indicating that a value had to be supplied. This sometimes required special report logic to be designed to, for example, provide a "None" default value or entry in a static or dynamic pick list. Then, report selection formulas or calculation formulas had to use If-Then-Else logic to accommodate the "None" parameter value.

Crystal Reports 2008 eases these requirements, as it now allows creation of optional parameter fields. When you create or edit a parameter field, make this choice in the Value Options portion of the dialog box. Note that specifying True for this choice will result in a "this may break existing formulas" message appearing when you click OK to save the parameter field.

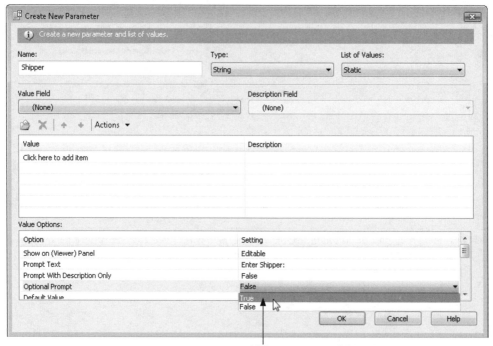

Make a parameter field optional

When a parameter field is specified as optional, no value need be entered for it in the Enter Values dialog box or the Parameter Panel. This allows report viewers to simply bypass a parameter field they don't wish to supply a value for. While this makes it easier for a report viewer to interact with parameter fields, it adds an additional layer of complexity for the report designer, as you now must specifically accommodate empty parameter fields within your report. If you use an optional parameter field in the Select Expert (covered in Chapter 2), Crystal Reports automatically makes this accommodation in the associated selection formula, as illustrated here.

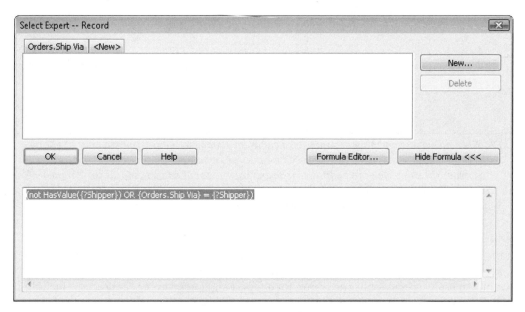

The new Crystal Reports 2008 HasValue formula function is automatically added to the underlying selection formula by the Select Expert to accommodate an optional parameter field. If, however, you initially use a non-optional parameter field in a selection, and later change it to be optional, the selection formula will not be updated with the HasValue function. Furthermore, if you use an optional parameter field in any other portion of your report and don't specifically use the HasValue function in an associated formula, Crystal Reports will return an error if the user doesn't supply a value to the optional parameter field.

To fully accommodate optional parameter fields throughout your report, ensure that you use the HasValue function to determine if an optional parameter field has been supplied a value by the report viewer. For example, you may be required to change a conditional formatting formula that initially looks like this:

```
If {Orders.Order Amount} > {?Highlight Level} Then
    crAqua
Else
    crNoColor
```

to this:

```
If HasValue({?Highlight Level}) And
{Orders.Order Amount} > {?Highlight Level} Then
    crAqua
Else
    crNoColor
```

TIP *When displaying an optional parameter field in the Parameter Panel, you may initially leave the value empty. However, if you later add a value for an optional parameter and then later wish to remove the value, you can't edit the value and backspace out its contents, as the Parameter Panel will still force you add a different value. You must, instead, select the value and click the small X in the Parameter Panel toolbar to remove the value.*

Multiple Values

Often, you may want to be able to choose more than one value for a parameter field and have the report recognize the multiple values in record selection. You may, for example, want to initially specify only one region for a report and later run the same report including ten different regions. If you're not using parameter fields, you'll need to change the Select Expert operator from Equal To to One Of and select the multiple regions.

By setting the Allow Multiple Values option to True in the Value Options section of the Create Parameter or Edit Parameter dialog box, you allow multiple entries to be added to a parameter list—you, in essence, turn the parameter field into a single object called an *array* that contains more than one value. Even if you choose an Equal To operator in the Select Expert with a multiple-value parameter field, all the values in the array will be included in record selection.

When you are prompted for a multiple-value parameter field, you select one or more values in the Available Values list of the Enter Values dialog box (CTRL-clicking will select multiple values) and click the single arrow to add them to the Selected Values list. If the parameter field is using a static pick list with the Allow Custom Values option set to True, the values that are added to the list can be either chosen from the pick list or typed in the Enter A Value text box and then added with the right arrow (dynamic and cascading pick lists only allow you to pick a value from the list). You may remove a set of selected values with the Remove button (again, CTRL-click will multiselect in the Selected Values list) or remove all values with the Remove All button.

In the Parameter Panel, you may edit an existing entry in a multivalue list by double-clicking it. To add a new entry, click the "Click Here to Add New Value" entry in the list and type in the new entry. If the parameter field includes a static pick list, you can also choose a value from the drop-down list that will appear. To delete an value, select the desired value and click the small *X* in the Parameter Panel toolbar. Dynamic pick lists can't be used in the Parameter Panel—the traditional Enter Values dialog box will appear if you attempt to add, edit, or delete values from the Parameter Panel.

CAUTION *If you simply drag a multiple-value parameter field to your report to attempt to display chosen values, only the first value will actually appear on the report, even though all values will be used by the Select Expert. Use array functions in a formula, such as the Join function, to retrieve all the values in the parameter field. The Join function is described in detail in Chapter 5.*

Range Values

Crystal Reports provides *range-value* parameter fields, which allow you to create just one parameter field that can contain both low and high values. When this parameter field is supplied to the Select Expert with the Equals operator, it effectively supplies both the low and high values and changes the operator to Between.

To create a range-value parameter field, set the Allow Range Values option to True in the Value Options section of the Parameter dialog box (this and the Allow Discrete Values option are mutually exclusive—only one of these options can be set to True). This will change the way the parameter field prompt appears when the report is refreshed.

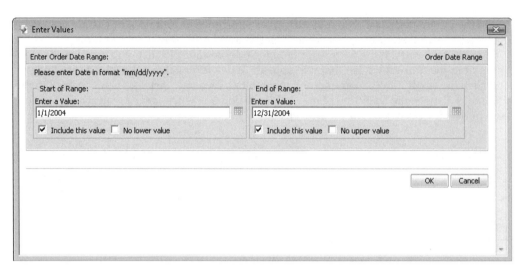

There are now two prompts for choosing or entering values: the Start Of Range prompt and the End Of Range prompt. These two prompts behave the same way a single prompt would behave, being based on pick list creation, allowing custom values, and so forth. However, when the viewer clicks OK, both prompts will be supplied to the Select Expert or selection formula, and all records between and including the selected values will be returned.

Normally, range-value parameter fields are "inclusive"; that is, the values returned to the report *include* the two values that are specified in the Enter Values dialog box. If you uncheck Include This Value, however, the chosen value *will not* be included in the range. For example, if you choose the number 300 as the Start Of Range and leave Include Value checked, any records including the number 300 will be included in the report. If you uncheck Include Value, anything over 300 will be included, but not 300 itself.

There are also No Lower Value and No Upper Value check boxes to allow you to make the range an open-ended range. If you leave both boxes unchecked (the default), the range will be limited to the finite values you enter as Start Of Range and End Of Range. If you check No Lower Value or No Upper Value (you can't select both), the corresponding range value will be discarded and the range will include only the other value. For example, if you specify a range of 100 to 1000, checking No Lower Value will discard 100 and return records where the value is simply less than 1000 (or less than and including 1000 if you leave Include This Value checked). Checking No Upper Value will return records exceeding 100 (or equal to or greater than 100 if you leave Include This Value checked).

If you drag a range-value parameter field directly on to your report to display supplied values, the parameter field will not show anything, because the parameter field is actually a range value. A *range* value is a single object (in this case, the parameter field) that actually contains the entire range of values specified by the parameter field. If you just put the object on the report by itself, Crystal Reports won't display anything, because it's not sure which value in the range you want to display. You can use range functions in the Formula Editor to return the first or last entries in the range. For example, the following formula will display the starting and ending dates of a date-range parameter field:

```
"Orders between " & Minimum({?Date Range})
& " and " & Maximum({?Date Range})
```

The Minimum and Maximum functions return the first and last entries in the range, respectively. Even though the Minimum and Maximum functions return date data types in this example, the ampersand concatenation operator (&) automatically converts them to strings.

However, when either No Lower Value or No Upper Value is selected for a date range, the corresponding Minimum or Maximum value is displayed oddly—it may appear to return a nonsensical or blank value. To display a more helpful message, you can use a formula to evaluate the date using the HasLowerBound and HasUpperBound functions and display text in place of the beginning or ending date:

```
"Orders placed between " &
IIf(HasLowerBound({?Date Range}),
     ToText(Minimum({?Date Range})),
     "beginning of time")
& " and " &
IIf(HasUpperBound({?Date Range}),
     ToText(Maximum({?Date Range})),
     "into the future")
```

NOTE *The usage of techniques used in this formula is explained more fully in Chapter 4.*

If, in addition to setting the Allow Range Values option to True, you also set the Allow Multiple Values option to True in the Parameter dialog box, the parameter field will allow entry of multiple range values, or an *array of ranges*. For example, you could choose to see orders placed between January 1, 2003, and March 31, 2003; January 1, 2004, and March 31, 2004; and January 1, 2005, and March 31, 2005. When you are prompted for a range-value parameter field that allows multiple values, a list will appear in which you can add multiple ranges.

NOTE *While Range Parameter Fields will appear in the Parameter Panel, any time you attempt to add or edit values, the traditional Edit Values dialog box will appear. The only manipulation allowed in the Parameter Panel is deleting of a range value with the small X in the Parameter Panel toolbar if the parameter field is defined to allow both range and multiple values.*

Different values can be specified in the Start Of Range and End Of Range areas and added to the list with the Add Range button. If you want to delete one or more existing ranges, select them in the Selected Values list and click Remove. You may delete all ranges with the Remove All button.

This single parameter field, when supplied to the Select Expert or record-selection formula, will effectively change the selection operator to Between *and* One Of at the same time.

CAUTION *The Minimum and Maximum array functions demonstrated earlier behave a little differently with combination range/multiple-value parameter fields and combination range and discrete-value/multiple-value parameter fields. In these cases, you may use the Minimum and Maximum functions, as well as an array subscript (a number inside square brackets after the parameter field name), to extract the beginning and ending values of different elements of the array.*

Controlling Parameter Field Data Entry

One of the issues Crystal Reports users face is how to best customize the user interface for "turnkey" report viewers—those who aren't familiar with the intricacies of Crystal Reports. In an ideal world, the user interface will contain business rules, limits, and customized formatting to guide an end user through proper choices of parameters. While this ideal world is best provided with a customized "front end" program developed, perhaps, in Visual Studio .NET, Crystal Reports still gives the report developer a fair amount of control over how end users can enter data into parameter fields.

Limiting Entry to Certain Ranges of Values

With relevant parameter field types (such as date and number), you can limit the range of entries that a viewer can supply. By supplying values to Min Value/Start, and Max Value/End, in the Value Options section of the Create Parameter or Edit Parameter dialog box, you can limit the values a report viewer can enter when prompted. When the viewer is prompted for the parameter field, they will receive an error if they enter values that are below the beginning range or above the ending range.

An added feature of range limiting is the set of values that can be added to a static pick list. When you range-limit a parameter field and choose a database table and field to help populate the static pick list, only database items that fall within the specified range will be added to the list (dynamic pick lists do not have range limiting capabilities).

Minimum and Maximum Lengths

If you create a string parameter field, the Min Length and Max Length options appear in the Options area of the Parameter dialog box. You can specify the minimum and maximum number of characters that must be supplied when responding to the parameter field's prompt. If a report viewer enters too few or too many characters, an error message will appear.

If you supply a length limit, you are also restricted from adding any default values to a static pick list that fall outside the minimum and maximum lengths.

Edit Masks

The most flexibility for controlling string parameter field entry comes from *edit masks.* An edit mask is a string of characters that controls many different aspects of data entry. One example might be an edit mask that allows only two uppercase characters to be entered (perhaps for a state abbreviation). Another example would be an edit mask that sets up the parameter field to accept data in a social security number format, accepting only number characters, and automatically adding hyphens between the third and fourth characters and between the fifth and sixth characters.

The key to using edit masks is learning the correct use of masking characters, listed in Table 13-1. Note that not only is the character you use significant, but so is the *case* of the character—uppercase and lowercase versions of the same character perform different masking functions.

Character	Usage
A	Requires entry of an alphanumeric character.
a	Allows an alphanumeric character to be entered, but doesn't require it.
0 (zero)	Requires a digit between 0 and 9 to be entered.
9	Allows a digit between 0 and 9 or a space to be entered, but doesn't require it.
#	Allows a digit, space, or plus or minus sign to be entered, but doesn't require it.
L	Requires entry of a letter between A and Z to be entered.
?	Allows a letter between A and Z to be entered, but doesn't require it.
&	Requires entry of any character or space.
C	Allows entry of any character or space, but doesn't require it.
>	Requires any subsequent characters to be typed in as uppercase characters (any resulting error message is unclear about this requirement).
<	Requires any subsequent characters to be typed in as lowercase characters (any resulting error message is unclear about this requirement).
\	Requires the next character to be typed into the parameter field in the exact position—you use this option if you want to actually include masking characters, (such as A, a, <, and so forth) in the parameter field.
. , : ; - / ( ) or any character not listed in this table	These characters must be typed into the parameter field in the same position they are placed in the mask. They will be returned in the parameter field result exactly as typed.
Password	Causes characters typed in the parameter field to be displayed with circles instead of their actual characters; the actual characters are passed to report formulas but are not displayed on the report if the parameter field is simply dragged to the report.

TABLE 13-1   Parameter Field Masking Characters

So, an edit mask of (000) 000-0000 when used with a phone number parameter field will require entry of the area code and phone number portions, including the parentheses, the space, and the hyphen. The resulting content of the {?Phone} parameter value will include the literal characters, as well as the numbers.

An edit mask of Password will replace characters typed in the parameter prompting field with circles. This is commonly used for entry of passwords or other sensitive information to prevent the information from being learned by someone looking at the screen. When the viewer clicks OK, the actual characters typed will be passed to report formulas in the parameter value. However, if you simply drag and drop a password-formatted parameter to the report, it will not display anything.

Conditional Formatting with Parameter Fields

Parameter fields can be used to customize other parts of the report, not just record selection. If a viewer wishes to highlight orders over a certain amount, they can specify the amount in a parameter field and use the parameter field to set conditional formatting. If they wish to see summary data instead of detail data, they can respond to a Boolean parameter field that is used to suppress the details section. Basically, any place you can specify formatting conditionally, you can base formatting on parameter fields just as easily as you can on database or formula fields.

Highlighting Data Based on Parameter Fields

Once a parameter field has been created, it can be used for conditional formatting just as easily as any database or formula field. As with any parameter field, you need to consider the data type used to create the parameter field. For example, you might wish to prompt the viewer for an order amount threshold to highlight orders over that amount in red. If the Order Amount field in the database is contained in a currency data type, you'll need to either create the parameter field with the currency data type or do some data-type conversion in the conditional formula.

For example, you may wish to change various formatting properties of both report objects and sections based on a parameter. A currency parameter field will prompt the viewer to enter an order amount threshold. Then, two conditional formulas can be created: one to set the background color of the details section and one to set the font color of the order amount and customer name fields. The details section background color can be formatted to display in silver if the order exceeds the parameter value, as follows:

```
If {Orders.Order Amount} > {?Order Level} Then crSilver Else crNoColor
```

Then, another conditional formula, when applied to the font color of both the order amount and customer name, will display the fields in red if the order amount exceeds the threshold:

```
If {Orders.Order Amount} > {?Order Level} Then crRed Else crBlack
```

So, supplying a value of $2,500 to the Order Level parameter will highlight sections and change the font color for orders that exceed $2,500.

| Design | Preview × |

Parameters

Enter Highlight Level: ⌃

2,500

Order ID	Order Amount	Order Date	Customer Name	Region
1121	$851.77	01/01/2004	Rough Terrain	WI
1122	$1,025.40	01/01/2004	Hooked on Helmets	MN
1123	$5,219.55	01/02/2004	Clean Air Transportation Co.	PA
1124	$59.70	01/02/2004	Off the Mountain Biking	CA
1125	$75.42	01/02/2004	Road Runners Paradise	RI
1126	$3,842.55	01/02/2004	Platou Sport	Rogaland
1127	$520.35	01/02/2004	BBS Pty	Greater London
1128	$65.70	01/02/2004	Tandem Cycle	ID
1129	$2,997.25	01/02/2004	The Bike Cellar	VA
1130	$23.50	01/03/2004	Rowdy Rims Company	CA
1131	$357.41	01/03/2004	Magazzini	Lombardia
1132	$38.98	01/04/2004	Fulcrum Cycles	VA
1133	$43.50	01/04/2004	Spokes for Folks	NJ
1134	$43.80	01/05/2004	Paris Mountain Sports	Ile de France
1135	$2,584.85	01/05/2004	Blazing Saddles	WI
1136	$3,209.53	01/05/2004	C-Gate Cycle Shoppe	VA
1137	$6,040.95	01/05/2004	Furia	Lisbon
1138	$79.62	01/05/2004	Crazy Wheels	BC
1139	$2,654.56	01/05/2004	BBS Pty	Greater London
1140	$27.00	01/06/2004	Bikes, Bikes, and More Bikes	IA
1141	$21.60	01/06/2004	Paris Mountain Sports	Ile de France
1142	$1,127.42	01/06/2004	Cycles and Sports	BC
1143	$62.33	01/06/2004	City Cyclists	MI
1144	$1,529.70	01/06/2004	Bikes, Bikes, and More Bikes	IA
1145	$27.00	01/06/2004	Pathfinders	IL
1146	$1,071.06	01/06/2004	Crazy Wheels	BC
1147	$1,830.35	01/06/2004	Cyclopath	RI
1148	$157.11	01/07/2004	Magazzini	Lombardia
1149	$329.85	01/07/2004	Mountain Madmen Bicycles	NJ
1150	$83.80	01/08/2004	Biking's It Industries	BC
1151	$5,879.70	01/08/2004	Alley Cat Cycles	MA
1152	$27.00	01/09/2004	Insane Cycle	PA
1153	$72.00	01/09/2004	Changing Gears	CA
1154	$1,709.72	01/09/2004	Blazing Saddles	WI

🔲 Groups

⟨?⟩ Parameters

🔎 Find

CAUTION *Since the Highlighting Expert allows you only to compare to actual database values to set formatting conditionally, the Highlighting Expert will not work with parameter fields. You must use the Conditional Formula buttons that appear in the Format Editor if you wish to conditionally format with parameter fields.*

Conditional Suppression Based on Parameter Fields

Use a parameter field just like a database or formula field to conditionally suppress individual objects or sections. Since the Suppress property requires a Boolean formula when being set conditionally, you can create a Boolean parameter field and supply it as the sole part of the Boolean formula, or you can create a Boolean formula by using a comparison operator with another type of parameter field.

You could, for example, create a Boolean parameter field called Summary Only that returns a true or false value based on the viewer's choice. By simply supplying the Boolean parameter field as the only item in a section or object's Suppress conditional formula, you could control whether the details section or a page header section containing column headings for the details section appears or doesn't appear.

When prompted for this parameter field, the viewer could select a True or False option for the Summary Only parameter field. You could then place this parameter field directly in the Suppress conditional formula for the details section. If the Summary Only parameter were true (indicating that the viewer wants a summary-only report), the details section would be suppressed. You could also suppress the page header section that contains column headings for the details fields.

A Password parameter can be used to conditionally format a sensitive data field, such as Salary, to suppress it if {?Password} does not equal a certain value. Since the password is masked by circles when the viewer enters it, it's protected from inadvertent "over-the-shoulder" viewing, and only people who enter it correctly will see the sensitive data. Note, however, that anyone with access to the report and to the Crystal Reports Designer can simply view the conditional formatting formula to determine the password value required, so the password edit mask is not, in itself, a security measure for sensitive data.

Using Parameter Fields with Formulas

There will be many situations in which you need to prompt for a parameter field in a certain way or choose a particular data type for a parameter field so that it will work properly with record, group, or saved data selection. However, you might want to display the parameter field on the report in a different way, perform some calculation based on the parameter field, or otherwise manipulate the parameter field in a formula. Or, you may want to provide some variable information to a formula, such as a sales tax rate. By setting up a parameter field to prompt for the tax rate, it's very easy to run the report for different states or cities that have varying sales tax rates.

When you create a parameter field, it will appear in the Formula Editor's Field Tree box under Report Fields. It can be added to a formula just like a database field or another formula. Just remember the data type you choose when creating the parameter field—you must use it correctly inside the formula to avoid type-mismatch errors. You may need to use ToText, ToNumber, or other conversion functions.

Using a Parameter Field for Partial Text Matches

A handy capability of the Select Expert is the Like operator that can be used when selecting records based on string database fields. Like allows you to supply *wildcard characters,* such as the question mark (?) and asterisk (*) to indicate single-character and partial-field matches, respectively. For example, supplying a Select Expert operator of Like with the literal *?eor?e* would return George, Jeorge, Jeorje, or Georje. Using the Like operator with an asterisk in the literal *Je** would return Jean, Jenny, Jennifer, and Jerry.

NOTE *A more complete discussion of record, group, and saved data selection is contained in Chapter 3.*

By allowing question marks and asterisks to be included in parameter fields, and by using the Like operator in the Select Expert, you give your report viewer great flexibility in choosing only the records they want to see. However, if you want a meaningful message to appear on the report indicating what the user has chosen, you'll need to use a formula to display different information than the parameter field actually supplies to the Select Expert.

Consider a parameter field called Customer Name that will prompt the viewer to add question marks or asterisks for partial-match searches:

If you wish to place a descriptive message in the page header indicating which customers have been chosen, you can create the following formula:

```
If {?Customer Name} = "*" Then
    "All Customers"
Else
    If Instr({?Customer Name},"?") > 0 or
        Instr({?Customer Name},"*") > 0 Then
        "Customers matching the pattern " + {?Customer Name}
    Else
        "Customer: " + {?Customer Name}
```

This formula simply uses the Customer Name parameter field as you would another database or formula field in an If-Then-Else statement. If the parameter field contains only an asterisk, it will return all records, so the formula returns "All Customers." Otherwise, if the parameter field contains at least one asterisk or question mark (the Instr function will return the location of the first occurrence of the character, or zero if there isn't any occurrence), the formula indicates that the report is based on a partial pattern. Finally, if there are no asterisks or question marks at all, the report will be returning an exact text match to the parameter field, and this formula indicates that.

To make it easy for the report to default to all customers without the viewer knowing or remembering to enter an asterisk in the prompt, you may wish to add it as a default value for the parameter prompt, with the description All Customers.

NOTE *If you make use of this type of parameter field in the Select Expert, remember that you'll need to use the Like operator instead of Equal To. This will ensure that record selection interprets asterisk and question mark characters properly.*

Another method of allowing an "all, one, or some" parameter field can include a combination of new Crystal Reports 2008 optional parameter fields, and the new HasValue formula function. For example, if you create a Customer Name parameter field (it can accept single or multiple values) and set the Optional Prompt value to True, you may add it to the Select Expert as you would a non-optional parameter field. Crystal Reports will automatically determine that it is optional and set the underlying selection formula to something similar to this:

```
(not HasValue({?Customer Name}) OR
{Customer.Customer Name} = {?Customer Name})
```

TIP *If you set an existing parameter field to be optional that is already used in selection, you will need to manually modify the underlying selection formula to use the HasValue function to accommodate the optional parameter field.*

You may also create a report formula that indicates the value or values supplied to the parameter field by the viewer. You may then place the formula on the report to indicate to the view what was specified for the parameter value. This formula can also accommodate the optional parameter field as follows:

```
If Not HasValue({?Customer Name}) Then
    "All Customers"
Else
    "Customer Chosen: " & {?Customer Name}
```

A variation on this formula can accommodate an optional parameter field that accepts multiple values.

```
If Not HasValue({?Customer Name}) Then
    "All Customers"
Else
    "Customers Chosen: " & Join({?Customer Name}, ", ")
```

TIP *General discussions on arrays (which is what multiple-value parameter fields are), and the Join function, can be found in Chapter 4.*

Using a Parameter Field to Change Sorting or Grouping

You may often wish to have a report viewer choose the report sorting or grouping on the fly. Since a parameter field can't actually return a database or formula-field name itself, you need to create a formula based on the parameter field, and use that formula as the sort or group field in the report.

You could, for example, create a parameter field called Group By that prompts for grouping by Country, Region, or City. These would be the only three options, as the viewer will not be allowed to enter custom values. The prompt for this parameter field would look like this in the Parameter Panel:

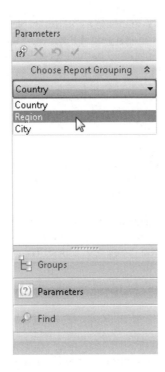

Because the parameter field will contain only the string Country, Region, or City, you can't use the parameter field directly as a sort or group field. You need to create a formula based on the parameter field and supply it as the sort or group field. Look at this formula:

```
If {?Group By} = "Region" Then {Customer.Region}
Else
If {?Group By} = "City" Then {Customer.City}
Else {Customer.Country}
```

This will actually return a different database field based on the parameter field's value. Then, this formula can be supplied as the grouping or sorting field, and the group or sort will change according to the viewer's response to the parameter field. And, as this parameter field doesn't affect record selection, it will be created as a "non-refresh" parameter field. Interacting with it in the Parameter Panel will allow on-the-fly grouping changes for your report without new database queries being required for each change.

Using a Parameter Field to Control Top N Reporting

Top N reporting (covered in more detail in Chapter 2) allows a "hard-coded" value for N. That is, if you want to see the top 5 groups, or the bottom 10 groups, you may choose Top N or Bottom N and type an actual "5" or "10" into the Group Sort Expert dialog box. You may also supply the value of N with a conditional formula. By supplying the value of a parameter field within the conditional formula, you may now allow a report viewer to specify the value of N every time the report is refreshed.

And, as with the parameter-based grouping option described earlier, setting the value of N with a parameter field will denote the parameter field as a "non-refresh" parameter field. By displaying it in the Parameter Panel, you may change the organization of your Top N or Bottom N report without requiring database refreshes for each new choice.

Tip *A sample report that demonstrates many of these features may be downloaded from the book's companion web site, CrystalBook.com. Look for "Parameter Fields.rpt."*

Exporting Reports to Different Formats

When you save a Crystal Report, your report file is saved on disk with an .RPT extension. This Crystal Reports native format can be used only with another copy of Crystal Reports, with a member of the BusinessObjects Enterprise family, with a Web-based application using a native Crystal Reports programming interface, or with a customized Windows application (customized Visual Studio .NET applications are discussed in Chapter 19). Since everyone who might ever need to view a report probably won't have their own copy of Crystal Reports, there are many ways to *export* a report to a different file format for use with such products as Microsoft Word, Microsoft Excel, Acrobat Reader, and others. You can also export your reports in HTML format for viewing in a web browser. Furthermore, you can attach these differently formatted files to e-mail messages or place them in a Lotus Domino database or a Microsoft Exchange public folder.

Although exporting is a handy way of distributing reports to non–Crystal Reports viewers, your exported reports are *static,* meaning they contain a picture of the database as it existed when the report was exported. As soon as the source database changes (perhaps the second after the report was exported), the report becomes outdated. If your viewers have their own copies of Crystal Reports, they can solve this problem by opening and refreshing the report, but this also means that they can *change* the report. This solution also assumes that your viewers know enough about Crystal Reports to be able to open and refresh a report.

If your viewers do not have their own copies of Crystal Reports and do need real-time data reporting, you may want to consider implementing a member of the BusinessObjects Enterprise XI 3.0 family to allow real-time running of reports in a web browser (see Part II of this book for more information). Or, you may develop a custom-programmed Windows or web application to integrate the report for viewing by your target audience (see Chapter 19 for more information). Also, there are third-party utility programs available to help distribute reports to viewers (the *Crystal: The Complete Toolset* portion of this book's companion web site, CrystalBook.com, features a large number of these utilities).

Most examples in this chapter are based on a report, shown in Figure 14-1, containing a bitmap image, text, an embedded Xcelsius Flash object (that is not tied to any underlying report data), and a chart placed beside the text with the Underlay feature. In addition, some of the text contains special formatting, such as drop shadows. The report also contains

Figure 14-1   Sample report for exporting

additional graphical elements, such as line and box drawing. The report also contains hyperlinks to external web site and e-mail addresses.

Exporting Reports to Office Applications

You'll often wish to convert or export a report you've designed to a popular office file format, such as Excel, Word, WordPerfect, or Acrobat Reader. With Crystal Reports, this is as simple as choosing an option from the File menu. You can also export the file to a temporary location and immediately launch the application you want to use to view the file, provided it's installed on your PC.

Exporting to Different File Formats

To export a file, first open the report you wish to export. Refresh and preview the report, if necessary, to ensure that it contains the most up-to-date data from the database. Then, click the Export button on the Standard toolbar or choose File | Export | Export Report from the pull-down menus. The Export dialog box will appear.

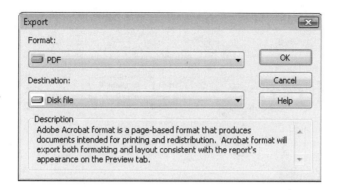

You initially have two simple choices to make for your export: the file format of the export, and the destination of the export. The Format drop-down list lets you choose from the large number of file formats to which Crystal Reports will export. You can choose from several different ASCII or "straight-text" formats, several Microsoft Excel formats, Microsoft Word, Acrobat Reader, and others.

The Destination drop-down list lets you choose how you want the report exported: to a disk file, attached to an e-mail message, placed in a Microsoft Exchange public folder, added to a Lotus Domino database, or launched in an application on your workstation. If you choose Disk File, the Choose Export File dialog box will prompt you for the folder and filename to export to. Choose a folder and type a filename, if the default folder and filename aren't sufficient.

CAUTION *If your report contains several drill-down tabs or subreport Preview tabs, ensure that the tab you want exported is selected before you begin exporting. Whatever appears in the current tab (and all pages you specify that are generated by that tab) is what will be exported by Crystal Reports.*

Page-Oriented Export Formats

Figure 14-2 shows the sample report from Figure 14-1 after it has been exported to a Microsoft Word document. Notice that it, for the most part, accurately depicts the source report with a couple of exceptions—the Xcelsius Flash object has been replaced with a static image that was supplied on the Flash tab of the Format Editor, and the drop shadow on the report title is much subtler. Both the web and e-mail hyperlinks are accurately exported. This is an example of a *page-oriented export format*, an export format that attempts to preserve as much of the original formatting of the report page as possible.

TIP *While most Crystal Reports page-based export formats exhibit accurate reproduction of original report formatting, you'll still find that some of the Crystal Reports formatting doesn't always translate to other file formats. You should export to your ultimate destination format throughout your report design process to make sure everything you want to include will be exported correctly. Certain page-based formats, such as the Editable RTF format, don't retain as much formatting as other RTF formats but make Word documents created with the Editable RTF format easier to modify.*

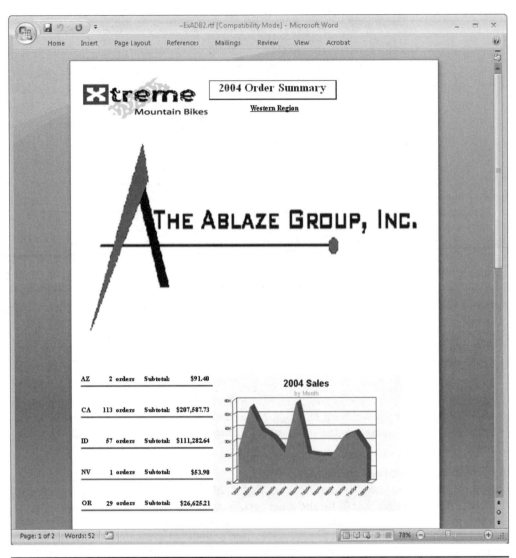

Figure 14-2 Exporting to a Word document

If you drill down on a report, a different report "view" will appear inside the drill-down tab. Only the material inside the open drill-down tab will be exported. The main Preview tab won't be included. Exporting the Idaho (ID) drill-down tab will result in a Microsoft Excel file, shown in Figure 14-3. While this still exhibits the formatting retention of a page-oriented export format, notice that there are still slight differences between the original Crystal report and the Excel sheet (the ID group name field is repeated, for example).

FIGURE 14-3   Drill-down tab exported to Excel

Depending on the file format you choose, you may receive an additional dialog box prompting you for the page range to be exported, as well as other extended information about the export. If, for example, you choose one of the Excel formats, a dialog box will allow you to choose more customized information when exporting to Excel.

TIP *Crystal Reports allows you to set default values for many options on these dialog boxes so that they will be automatically set for subsequent exports. By choosing File | Export | Report Export Options, you may set defaults for many individual export format options.*

Adobe Portable Document Format, or *PDF,* is probably the most accurate page-oriented export format. This format will faithfully export a report that contains Flash objects; and complex formatting and graphics, including underlaid sections, as shown in Figure 14-4.

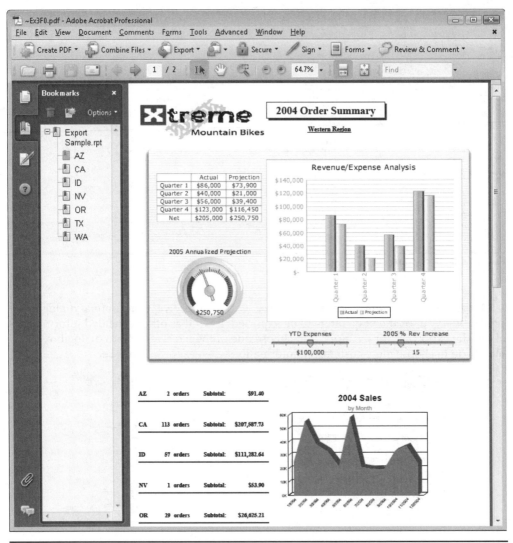

FIGURE 14-4 Exporting to an Acrobat PDF format

As PDF files are generally accepted formats for Windows, the Web, and other cross-platform applications, you'll find that its accurate formatting representation of the original report will often benefit a wide audience.

Not only will PDF exports exhibit an embedded Xcelsius Flash object, but Flash files will retain their interactivity as well—you may double-click an embedded Flash file in a PDF document to activate it. Formatting (including the drop shadow on the title text box) is accurately reproduced. Both hyperlinks are accurately passed on to the PDF file as well. And, Crystal Reports 2008 introduces the ability to include the report group tree when exporting to PDF. This makes PDF format the only export format to maintain some level of report interactivity, by allowing PDF viewers to click group tree entries in the PDF bookmarks section to navigate directly to exported report groups.

CAUTION *The initial release of Crystal Reports 2008 will only include Flash objects in a PDF export if they are not tied to report data by way of the Flash Data Expert (discussed in Chapter 11). A Flash object connected to report data will only appear as a blank placeholder, or will display a static image, if one has been specified in the Flash tab of the Format Editor. Later Crystal Reports 2008 updates, however, may support data-connected Flash object export to PDF. Use Help | Check For Updates from the pull-down menus to check for the latest update to Crystal Reports 2008.*

Data-Oriented Export Formats

Certain data file formats do not lend themselves to full page-oriented formatting. Many ASCII (a computer term indicating a standard method for representing characters internally in memory) file formats are designed to encompass data only, with no formatting information. Crystal Reports supports exporting to these *data-oriented export formats* as well. When you export to these formats, most, if not all, Crystal Reports formatting is lost, and only the underlying data within the report is formatted.

For example, consider how the main preview tab of the report exhibited in Figure 14-1 looks when exported to the regular Excel format:

Notice that Crystal Reports has attempted to maintain as much of the formatting and spacing of the original report design as possible (and, also notice that embedded Flash objects do not export to Excel format). However, if the purpose of the Excel export is to manipulate or calculate the data for what-if scenarios, you will find a great deal of effort is required to remove blank rows and columns, and move values and text to different locations to more easily enable standard Excel what-if analysis.

You may prefer a data-oriented export instead. Look at the same report exported to Excel with the Excel – Data Only export format:

Images, any embedded Flash objects, extra vertical or horizontal white space, and object formatting aren't exported. This Excel export format is immediately more palatable from a pure data-analysis perspective.

Ultimately, you'll want to plan your report design techniques to match the eventual output format for your report. You'll probably want to avoid spending lots of time designing a "pretty" report with lots of formatting, charts, and images, if the ultimate output format will be an ASCII data file that needs to be passed to a third-party vendor for processing. Rather, you should probably choose to place report data in single-line-high report sections with no extraneous vertical white space, and minimal white space appearing between fields. Formatting properties won't be exported, so there will be no need to do any extensive font or color formatting on text. Not only can this minimal formatting effort save you report design time, but it will probably result in a more accurate export to a data-oriented format as well.

NOTE *You may notice that some file formats and export destinations display a small number "1" beside them in the Export dialog box. This indicates that these formats and destinations were given an Install on first use attribute when Crystal Reports was initially installed. When you choose these formats or destinations for the first time, you'll be prompted to insert the original Crystal Reports program CD to install the necessary export drivers.*

Exporting and Launching an Application

If you choose Application in the Destination drop-down list, Crystal Reports will export the file to a temporary folder and immediately open the file in the corresponding Windows application. If you choose a file format for an application that isn't installed on your computer, you may be presented with a dialog box asking you to choose an application to open the file with. If there is an alternative application that will open that file type, choose it from the list.

NOTE *The temporary files that Crystal Reports creates will be located in the Windows temporary folder (typically, your private folder underneath the Documents and Settings folder) and may not automatically be deleted when you close the application. If you wish to periodically "clean out" your Windows temporary folder, use Disk Cleanup or another appropriate utility or measure to remove temporary files.*

Exporting to an ODBC Data Source

You can export a Crystal Report to an ODBC data source, such as a Microsoft SQL Server or Oracle database. Typically, you'll want to do this with a simple columnar details report that you might be using to transport data from one database to a another database.

To export to an ODBC data source, choose the data source you want to export to in the Format drop-down list. You'll then be asked to supply a table name, which Crystal Reports will create in the database referred to by the data source. If the data source refers to a secure database, you will be asked to supply a database logon user ID and password before the export starts. And if the data source does not contain a specific database reference, you may be asked to choose a database in addition to the table name.

Crystal Reports will create a new table in the ODBC database and define fields to hold data from the exported report. If you want to change field names or the layout of the table, you need to use a utility specific to the ODBC database that you exported to. You may also notice that the fields and data that are exported to your ODBC database may not be what you initially expect. You may need to modify the original Crystal Report to accurately export data via ODBC.

Sending Reports via E-Mail and Messaging Systems

In addition to exporting reports to office applications, you may want to create an exported report and attach it to an e-mail message, place it in a Lotus Domino database, or send it to a Microsoft Exchange public folder. You might expect to have to do this in two steps: export to your chosen file format and then run a separate e-mail package to send the file. However, Crystal Reports lets you do it all in one step.

Use the Export toolbar button or choose the File | Export menu option to display the Export dialog box. Choose the desired format from the Format drop-down list. From the

Creating a Report Definition File

When you create reports, you may want to keep documentation that details the report design, such as the tables that are included, what formulas you've created, and what objects are contained in the report sections.

The Export dialog box in Crystal Reports provides a Report Definition format in the Format drop-down list. When you choose this format, Crystal Reports will save a text file containing a great deal of helpful information about the makeup of the report. You may wish to create and keep these text files in a central location to document the design of your reports. You may also open the text files in a word processor and reformat them to look more appealing.

```
~ExABEE.txt - Notepad
File  Edit  Format  View  Help
          Crystal Report Professional v11.0 (32-bit) - Report Definition

1.0 File Information

        Report File:
        Version: 11.0

2.0 Record Sort Fields

3.0 Group Sort Fields

4.0 Formulas

4.1 Record Selection Formula
        {Customer.Region} in ["CA","WA","OR","ID","AZ","NV","TX"] and
{Orders.Order Date} in #1/1/2004# to #12/31/2004#

4.2 Group Selection Formula


4.3 Other Formulas

5.0 Sectional Information

5.1 Page Header Section
        Hidden, Keep Together

5.2 Page Footer Section
        Visible, New Page After, Keep Together, Print At Bottom of Page

5.3 Report Header Section
        Visible, New Page Before

        Subsection.1
                Visible, Keep Together

        Subsection.2
                Visible, Keep Together, Underlay

        2004 Order Summary
                String, Visible, Horizontal Centre Alignment, Top Alignment,
                Keep Together


        Western Region
                String, Visible, Horizontal Centre Alignment, Top Alignment,
                Keep Together
```

Destination drop-down list, choose the e-mail system you wish to send the report with. Choosing Lotus Domino will place a report in your Lotus Domino database; choosing Exchange Folder will add the report to a Microsoft Exchange; and choosing MAPI will use a Microsoft-compatible e-mail program, such as Microsoft Outlook, to attach the report to an e-mail message. Note that you need to have the appropriate "client" software installed on your PC for any of these options to work.

For example, if Microsoft Outlook is installed on your PC and you choose MAPI as the destination, the following dialog box will appear (you may be prompted to choose an Outlook profile first):

Specify the e-mail address or addresses you want the message to go to, along with the message you want to appear in the e-mail body. The message will be sent with the report file attached (in the format you specified).

New Crystal Reports 2008 XML Exporting

As each new Crystal Reports version is released, its flexibility to export to various forms of XML (Extensible Markup Language) increases. Crystal Reports 2008 continues in this direction by providing a simpler, yet more flexible, method to export to various XML formats, and various non-XML formats, via the XML export option. Not only is XML-formatted data increasingly becoming a standard for data interchange, but the flexibility to use Crystal Reports 2008's XML export option to create custom non-XML exports makes this new feature even more appealing.

The foundation of XML exporting is an XML *schema*, a definition for the way report data is organized when exported to an XML data file. Upon initial examination, Crystal Reports 2008 may appear to offer fewer options than previous versions, as the only initial schema available for XML exporting is the built-in Crystal Reports XML schema. While this schema may be usable when exporting data for another system that is very flexible in determining the organization of incoming XML data, its primary purpose in Crystal Reports 2008 is to act as an initial source schema for use with an XML *transform*, a process of applying an XML style sheet to describe a customized way of reformatting data initially presented in the Crystal Reports XML schema. By using a customized XML transform style sheet (often referred to as an *XSLT document*), you may completely customize the way Crystal Reports 2008 exports via the XML format. Even non-XML exports, such as formatted HTML pages, text files, comma-separated values exports, and so forth, can be accomplished. With the flexibility of Crystal Reports 2008 custom XSLT definitions, virtually any export file that consists of standard ASCII characters can be created.

NOTE   *An exhaustive discussion of XML standards, and detailed steps for creating your own custom XSLT document, are outside the scope of this Crystal Reports book. Various tools and documents, reachable via standard Internet search engines, are available to learn about and create custom XSLT transform documents.*

Initial Export via Crystal Reports XML Schema

Consider the sample report illustrated in Figure 14-5. This is a simple order listing containing a few fields that are required to ultimately be exported to a customized comma-separated value file. Notice that the report contains minimal font and color formatting. As XML is a data-oriented export format, extensive object and page formatting to make the report appear "pretty" will be ignored when exporting to XML (even if the eventual export will be reformatted by way of a transform with, for example, embedded HTML font and color formatting tags).

Just like exporting to other file formats (as discussed previously in this chapter), XML exporting is accomplished with the Export toolbar button on the Standard toolbar, or the File | Export pull-down menu option. When the export dialog box appears, choose XML

Order Date	Order ID	Customer Name	Order Amount	City	State
01/01/2004	1122	Hooked on Helmets	$1,025.40	Eden Prairie	MN
01/01/2004	1121	Rough Terrain	$851.77	Madison	WI
01/02/2004	1123	Clean Air Transportation Co.	$5,219.55	Conshohocken	PA
01/02/2004	1124	Off the Mountain Biking	$59.70	Irvine	CA
01/02/2004	1125	Road Runners Paradise	$75.42	Kingston	RI
01/02/2004	1128	Tandem Cycle	$65.70	Nampa	ID
01/02/2004	1129	The Bike Cellar	$2,997.25	Winchester	VA
01/03/2004	1130	Rowdy Rims Company	$23.50	Newbury Park	CA
01/04/2004	1132	Fulcrum Cycles	$38.98	Winchester	VA
01/04/2004	1133	Spokes for Folks	$43.50	Hightstown	NJ
01/05/2004	1135	Blazing Saddles	$2,584.85	Brown Deer	WI
01/05/2004	1136	C-Gate Cycle Shoppe	$3,209.53	Winchester	VA
01/06/2004	1144	Bikes, Bikes, and More Bikes	$1,529.70	Des Moines	IA
01/06/2004	1140	Bikes, Bikes, and More Bikes	$27.00	Des Moines	IA
01/06/2004	1143	City Cyclists	$62.33	Sterling Heights	MI
01/06/2004	1147	Cyclopath	$1,830.35	Kingston	RI
01/06/2004	1145	Pathfinders	$27.00	DeKalb	IL
01/07/2004	1149	Mountain Madmen Bicycles	$329.85	Hightstown	NJ
01/08/2004	1151	Alley Cat Cycles	$5,879.70	Concord	MA
01/09/2004	1154	Blazing Saddles	$1,709.72	Brown Deer	WI
01/09/2004	1153	Changing Gears	$72.00	Irvine	CA
01/09/2004	1152	Insane Cycle	$27.00	Conshohocken	PA
01/10/2004	1159	Insane Cycle	$8,910.95	Conshohocken	PA
01/10/2004	1155	Our Wheels Follow Us Everywhere	$5,219.55	DeKalb	IL
01/10/2004	1158	Wheels Inc.	$9.00	Des Moines	IA
01/10/2004	1157	Whistler Rentals	$31.00	Tualatin	OR
01/11/2004	1161	Rockshocks for Jocks	$1,799.70	Austin	TX
01/12/2004	1162	Crank Components	$46.50	Champaign	IL
01/12/2004	1165	Making Tracks	$3,712.60	Concord	MA
01/12/2004	1164	Road Runners Paradise	$66.99	Kingston	RI
01/12/2004	1166	Rocky Roadsters	$67.80	Conshohocken	PA
01/12/2004	1163	Wheels and Stuff	$31.00	Clearwater	FL
01/13/2004	1167	Blazing Saddles	$9,353.30	Brown Deer	WI
01/14/2004	1171	Pathfinders	$479.85	DeKalb	IL
01/14/2004	1170	Spokes for Folks	$781.35	Hightstown	NJ
01/14/2004	1172	Tyred Out	$101.70	Santa Ana	CA

FIGURE 14-5   Simple report to export with XML format

from the Format drop-down list, and the desired destination you wish the XML export to be sent to. When you click OK, the XML Export Options dialog box will appear.

If this is the first time you've performed an XML export (or, if previous exports haven't used a custom XSLT transform), you'll only be presented with one schema choice in the dialog box: the Crystal Reports XML schema. Click OK to export the report to XML with this default schema. The resulting output will be formatted based on this schema in a fairly standard XML format.

If the system that you're passing the XML-formatted data to can accept the data formatted by the default Crystal Reports XML schema, then simply import the resulting XML file into that system. However, if you wish to take full advantage of Crystal Reports 2008 XML export capabilities, you will now need to use the default XML output to define an XLST transform document to convert the standard XML output to the output format of your choice.

Using an XSLT Transform

Once you've used various tools available for creating an XSLT transform file (Windows Notepad being the simplest), you are ready to import the XSLT transform into the report and perform a custom XML export. Consider this simple XLST transform file that will be used to create a comma-delimited ASCII file, including a field name definition in the first output record, for the order listing example illustrated previously:

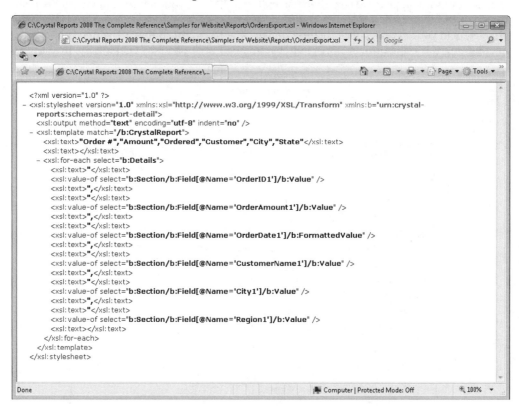

Add the transform file to the report with XML Export Options available from the pull-down menus. Choose File | Export | Manage XML Exporting Formats to display the dialog box where you can add, delete, and manage custom XSLT transforms. If no transforms have been added to the report previously, the only format that will initially appear in the dialog box is the standard Crystal Reports XML format. While you cannot delete or modify this format, you can view the schema for it by clicking the Show Schema button in the upper left-hand corner of the dialog.

NOTE *Even if you later add a custom XSLT transform and select it in this dialog box, the schema for the standard Crystal Reports XML format will be shown if you click Show Schema.*

If a custom XSLT has previously been added to the report, it will also appear in this list. If you wish to choose a custom transform as the default format to use when exporting to XML in the future, select it and click Set Viewer Default (this format will also act as the XML export format with certain web-based report viewers, such as those used in Visual Studio .NET and BusinessObjects Enterprise XI 3.0). You may make modifications to existing formats by selecting them and clicking Modify. The dialog box illustrated in Figure 14-6 will appear, where you may modify various aspects of the transform, or re-import an updated XLST transform file. To add a new custom XSLT transform document, click Add to view the Add a New XML Format dialog box, as illustrated in Figure 14-6.

Specify a name for this particular transform in the Name text box. The name you give the transform will appear the next time you export to XML. If your report contains embedded image or BLOB (binary large object) data that you wish to include as converted ASCII characters in your export, check Include Image Data In Export. If this is the first time you are defining this transform, import your custom XSLT style sheet by clicking the Import

FIGURE 14-6 Add or modify a custom XSLT transform

XML Transform button and choosing the desired .XSL file. The schema will be embedded in the report and stored in the .RPT file the next time you save the report (you will no longer need the original .XSL file at this point). If you've previously embedded a stored schema in the report, you may export it to another style sheet file by clicking the Save XML Transform As button and specifying a filename. You may change the file extension for this export by specifying a file extension in the Output File Format text box. And, any text you type in the Description of this Export text box will appear when you select the format in the XML Export Options dialog box when you perform the export.

Once you've defined the custom transform, you may perform another XML Export using the Export toolbar button or File | Export pull-down menu option. After choosing XML in the format drop-down list and choosing your desired output destination, the XML Options dialog box will appear. Notice that your custom transform now appears as a choice in this dialog box. Select it (if you didn't make it the default when you initially created it) and click OK to export using the custom transform. The report will be formatted internally using the Crystal Reports XML format, and then transformed using your custom schema, being output in the format and with the file extension you specified. In the case of the order listing example used throughout this section, the resulting export will appear as a comma-delimited text file with field names specified in the first record.

```
~XM552.TXT - Notepad
File  Edit  Format  View  Help
"order #","Amount","ordered","Customer","City","State"
"1122","1025.40","01/01/2004","Hooked on Helmets","Eden Prairie","MN"
"1121","851.77","01/01/2004","Rough Terrain","Madison","WI"
"1123","5219.55","01/02/2004","Clean Air Transportation Co.","Conshohocken","PA"
"1124","59.70","01/02/2004","off the Mountain Biking","Irvine","CA"
"1125","75.42","01/02/2004","Road Runners Paradise","Kingston","RI"
"1128","65.70","01/02/2004","Tandem Cycle","Nampa","ID"
"1129","2997.25","01/02/2004","The Bike Cellar","winchester","VA"
"1130","23.50","01/03/2004","Rowdy Rims Company","Newbury Park","CA"
"1132","38.98","01/04/2004","Fulcrum Cycles","winchester","VA"
"1133","43.50","01/04/2004","Spokes for Folks","Hightstown","NJ"
"1135","2584.85","01/05/2004","Blazing Saddles","Brown Deer","WI"
"1136","3209.53","01/05/2004","C-Gate Cycle Shoppe","winchester","VA"
"1144","1529.70","01/06/2004","Bikes, Bikes, and More Bikes","Des Moines","IA"
"1140","27.00","01/06/2004","Bikes, Bikes, and More Bikes","Des Moines","IA"
"1143","62.33","01/06/2004","City Cyclists","Sterling Heights","MI"
"1147","1830.35","01/06/2004","Cyclopath","Kingston","RI"
"1145","27.00","01/06/2004","Pathfinders","DeKalb","IL"
"1149","329.85","01/07/2004","Mountain Madmen Bicycles","Hightstown","NJ"
"1151","5879.70","01/08/2004","Alley Cat Cycles","Concord","MA"
"1154","1709.72","01/09/2004","Blazing Saddles","Brown Deer","WI"
"1153","72.00","01/09/2004","Changing Gears","Irvine","CA"
"1152","27.00","01/09/2004","Insane Cycle","Conshohocken","PA"
"1159","8910.95","01/10/2004","Insane Cycle","Conshohocken","PA"
"1155","5219.55","01/10/2004","Our wheels Follow Us Everywhere","DeKalb","IL"
"1158","9.00","01/10/2004","wheels Inc.","Des Moines","IA"
"1157","31.00","01/10/2004","Whistler Rentals","Tualatin","OR"
"1161","1799.70","01/11/2004","Rockshocks for Jocks","Austin","TX"
"1162","46.50","01/12/2004","Crank Components","Champaign","IL"
"1165","3712.60","01/12/2004","Making Tracks","Concord","MA"
"1164","66.99","01/12/2004","Road Runners Paradise","Kingston","RI"
"1166","67.80","01/12/2004","Rocky Roadsters","Conshohocken","PA"
"1163","31.00","01/12/2004","wheels and Stuff","Clearwater","FL"
"1167","9353.30","01/13/2004","Blazing Saddles","Brown Deer","WI"
"1171","479.85","01/14/2004","Pathfinders","DeKalb","IL"
"1170","781.35","01/14/2004","Spokes for Folks","Hightstown","NJ"
"1172","101.70","01/14/2004","Tyred Out","Santa Ana","CA"
"1169","664.00","01/14/2004","wheels Inc.","Des Moines","IA"
"1178","989.55","01/15/2004","Bikes and Trikes","Sterling Heights","MI"
"1189","110.30","01/15/2004","Bikes, Bikes, and More Bikes","Des Moines","IA"
"1179","329.85","01/15/2004","Cyclopath","Kingston","RI"
"1176","101.70","01/15/2004","Cyclopath","Kingston","RI"
"1184","1146.45","01/15/2004","Fulcrum Cycles","winchester","VA"
"1187","959.70","01/15/2004","Fulcrum Cycles","winchester","VA"
"1190","2478.60","01/15/2004","Hercules Mountain Bikes","DeKalb","IL"
"1183","36.00","01/15/2004","Hooked on Helmets","Eden Prairie","MN"
```

Reporting from SQL Databases

As newer leading-edge database applications are released, fewer and fewer make use of PC-style databases. The performance and capacity limitations of local PC databases often limit their usefulness for larger, performance-dependent applications. Instead, most newer applications rely on *client/server* database systems. A client/server system includes two parts: a *client,* typically a PC running software such as Crystal Reports or a data-entry application, and a *server,* typically a larger, high-end PC running a Windows server platform, a midrange, or even a mainframe computer. The server maintains the database, and the client makes requests of the server for database access. Many different client/server databases exist, with Microsoft SQL Server, Oracle, IBM DB/2, and Informix being among the more popular ones.

It's important to understand and contrast the differences between a client/server database system and a PC-style database system that is installed on a shared local area network (LAN). For reporting purposes, in particular, a LAN-based database system presents a much more serious performance hurdle than a client/server database. Figure 15-1 shows a PC reporting on two database environments. The first depicts a Microsoft Access database on a LAN server. The second depicts the same database on a SQL Server system.

The LAN-based scenario places heavy burdens on both the network and the PC making the reporting request. In this scenario, the PC must read the entire 100,000-record Access database across the network, picking and choosing the records that meet the report-selection criteria. This requires large amounts of data to be passed across the network, and the PC has to perform all the selection logic itself.

The client/server environment is much more efficient. The client PC simply makes a request to the database server via a Structured Query Language (SQL) request. The database server, presumably a larger, high-powered PC, Unix computer, or mainframe, runs database software designed to process such queries very efficiently. It directly queries the 100,000-record

PC must transfer all 100,000 records across the network, retaining only the 1,000 it needs

Local area network

PC

F:\Accounts.MDB
100,000 records

LAN
server

Client sends SQL statement to server requesting certain records

Local or wide
area network

PC

AccountsSQL
100,000 records

SQL
server

Server reads database and chooses the 1,000 requested records,
sending only them to the client

FIGURE 15-1 Retrieving 1,000 specific records from a LAN-based database vs. a client/server database

database and sends only the required 1,000 records back across the network. This places less demand on the client and the network, and the whole process typically takes less time.

Logging On to SQL Databases

The first step to creating a Crystal Report is to select the SQL database that you want to base your report on. There are three general communication methods you can use to connect to a client/server database with Crystal Reports: direct database drivers, ODBC, and OLE DB (pronounced oh-LAY-dee-bee).

Direct Database Drivers

Crystal Reports provides direct database drivers that work with many industry-standard client/server databases, including, among others, Oracle, and IBM DB2 (there is no Microsoft

SQL Server Direct Database driver, however). A direct database driver uses the native communication methods provided by the server vendor to communicate with the database server. This typically requires installing the specific client software provided by the database vendor on the PC, such as Oracle client software.

Crystal Reports will recognize the existence of these packages and provide a direct database driver to connect to the database. In addition, Crystal Reports provides other direct drivers to allow you to report from non-SQL data sources, such as Microsoft Outlook folders, Microsoft Exchange folders, Lotus Domino databases, Internet web server activity logs, and the Windows 2000/XP/2003 event log. You can even write reports based on the *local file system,* which consists of the file and directory structure of your C drive or a network drive. More details on these specialized types of reports can be found in Chapter 16.

Using direct database drivers to connect to the database server has two general advantages:

- Because fewer layers of communications protocols are being used, there may be a slight performance improvement when reporting.

- The direct database driver may allow more flexibility for creating more server-specific SQL statements or other query features for reporting.

ODBC

Although many companies standardize on database servers that Crystal Reports provides direct database drivers for, many other database systems and specialized data systems exist that you may want to report on. Some standard method of communication is needed to connect standard PC clients with the myriad specialized servers and systems that exist. Microsoft designed open database connectivity (ODBC) to accomplish this communication.

As a general rule, any server or proprietary data platform that is ODBC-compliant can be used with Crystal Reports. If the database or system vendor provides a Windows ODBC driver for its system, Crystal Reports should be able to report against that server or system. Because it has been accepted as an industry standard, ODBC is in widespread use.

TIP *Before you can use Crystal Reports to report against an ODBC-connected database, you must set up an ODBC data source. Use the ODBC Administrator from Windows Control Panel to set up the data source.*

OLE DB

Microsoft provides an additional standard, OLE DB, to extend its previous universal data connectivity method, ODBC. OLE DB provides data access in much the same manner as ODBC. A *data provider* acts as an interface between disparate client and server systems. Data providers are available not only for typical relational database systems, but also for more nontraditional data sources, such as spreadsheets, web servers, and multidimensional OLAP data sources.

Crystal Reports supports OLE DB data sources that are installed on your client PC. Various client applications, such as OLAP client software, will automatically install OLE DB data providers.

NOTE *You may also use Crystal Reports Server/BusinessObjects Enterprise Business Views or Universes as data sources. In these cases, the Business View or Universe will simply "point" to a Crystal Reports data source, such as a direct, ODBC, or OLE DB connection to the target SQL database.*

Choosing the Database

When you first start Crystal Reports, you can immediately choose and log on to a client/ server database before you open an existing report or create a new report. If you don't log on but open a report based on a client/server database, you will be prompted to log on as soon as you try to refresh the report or choose any other function that requires the database to be read.

If you want to create a new report based on a client/server database, you can use a report wizard or the Blank Report option. If you use a report wizard, the first section of the wizard will display your database connection choices.

If you choose the Blank Report option to create a new report, the Database Expert will appear immediately.

The Database Expert combines in one place all data sources, including direct database drivers, ODBC, and OLE DB. You may choose from one of these connection types from two places, depending on whether you've used data sources in the past (recently used data sources will appear in the My Connections category), or whether you're already logged into a data source from using another report (currently connected data sources also appear in the My Connections category, with a small "power code" appearing on the icon of currently connected databases).

You'll also find Data Explorer folder entries for the repository, where you can choose a SQL Command or Crystal Reports Server/BusinessObjects Enterprise Business View as a data source. (SQL Commands are covered later in this chapter, and Business Views are covered in Chapter 16 and in an extra online chapter available for download from CrystalBook.com.)

You'll also find a Universes folder, which allows reporting against Business Objects Universe data sources (covered in more detail in Chapter 16). Click the plus sign next to the either of these categories to log on to the BusinessObjects Enterprise to choose the desired SQL Command, Business View, or Universe.

If you don't see the data source you wish to connect to in either the Current Connections or Create New Connection folder, try clicking the plus sign next to the More Data Sources folder within the Create New Connection folder. This will display an additional set of database categories that you can choose from. Again, click the plus sign next to the desired category to create a connection using that connection type.

TIP *As if ODBC and OLE DB aren't enough "alphabet soup" in the Database Expert, you are also presented with the abbreviations "RDO" and "ADO" after the ODBC and OLE DB categories. These are abbreviations for yet more Microsoft standards for database connectivity. RDO (which stands for Remote Data Objects) and ADO (which stands for ActiveX Data Objects) are technical terms to describe the internal method Crystal Reports uses to connect to ODBC and OLE DB data sources.*

Clicking the plus sign next to the ODBC (or, double-clicking the "Make New Connection" entry if existing ODBC connections already exist in the category) will display a separate dialog box listing all the predefined ODBC data sources (use the ODBC Administrator from Windows Control Panel to add a data source if you don't see the desired data source here). Choose the desired data source and click the Next button in the dialog box. Depending on the data source you've chosen, as well as the database type it connects to, you'll probably see additional dialog boxes asking you to supply valid logon credentials.

Clicking the plus sign next to the OLE DB category (or, double-clicking the "Make New Connection entry if existing OLE DB connections already exist in the category) will also launch a separate OLE DB dialog box. You'll initially see a list of installed OLE DB *providers*, or database-specific connection drivers, that have been installed on your PC. Choose the provider you wish to use and click Next. As with ODBC, the remaining options in the OLE DB dialog box, such as those to choose a specific database and supply logon credentials, will vary according to the provider you choose.

If you wish to use a direct database driver, click the plus sign next to the desired driver (you may need to display the More Data Sources category to see it). As with other connection methods, these drivers will provide database-specific dialog boxes asking you to provide logon credentials.

If the entry "no items found" appears below an expected folder, or if you don't see an entry for an expected direct database driver, it may be that you haven't properly installed necessary database client software on your PC. For example, you encounter this condition if you haven't properly installed the Oracle client software on your PC.

TIP   *Not all database drivers will be installed by default when you install Crystal Reports. The first time you choose one of these data sources in the Database Expert, you may be prompted to insert the original Crystal Reports CD to install the specific driver. Also, if you add an additional data source from Crystal Reports Setup, you'll often see an additional, related category appear within the Create New Connection category.*

Once you've successfully logged on to the database, the Database Expert will expand the folder you originally selected and display a list of databases, owners, schemas, tables, views, or stored procedures available in the database (the display will vary depending on the type of database chosen). Figure 15-2 shows the Database Expert with a list of available SQL Server database tables with two tables already having been added to the report.

Select the table, stored procedure, or view that you want to include in your report, either by double-clicking it or by selecting it and clicking the single right arrow. You can also CTRL-click more than one table and add them at once with the right arrow, or you can select one or more tables and simply drag them to the Selected Tables box. And if you want to add all the tables to the report (probably not a very common occurrence), you can click the double-right arrow. As you add tables, they will appear under the Selected Tables list on the right side of the Database Expert. If you accidentally add the wrong table or tables, you may highlight them in the Selected Tables list and remove them with the left arrow. You may remove all previously added tables with the double-left arrow.

FIGURE 15-2 The Database Expert

- **Perform Grouping on Server** Choose this option to have Crystal Reports "push" as much of the subtotaling and aggregation as possible to the database server, to improve reporting performance. Certain conditions required to take full advantage of this feature are discussed later in the chapter, under "Enabling Server-Based Grouping."

- **Database Server Is Case-Insensitive** Choose this option to ignore case when doing record selection with a database (this option may not affect your particular database, as all databases cannot be made case insensitive).

- **Select Distinct Data for Browsing** This option will continuously read the database until it has retrieved the first 500 *unique* values of a field when you browse the field in the Field Explorer or Formula Editors. If you leave this option turned off, Crystal Reports reads only the first 500 records in the table, even if there are a few (or no) unique values. Although you'll have bigger browse lists with this option turned on, you may also suffer from slower performance.

- **Perform Query Asynchronously** This option allows you to stop a query from processing on the database server before database records are returned to Crystal Reports. In some cases, queries submitted to the SQL database can take minutes (sometimes hours) to run. By selecting this option, you can click the Stop button (the red *x* button in the Navigation Tools toolbar) to cancel the query on the database server. Note that this option applies only to certain databases and database drivers— not all databases and drivers support this option.

- **Verify Options** These options determine when Crystal Reports reads the database layout to determine if additional fields have been added, field names or data types have changed, and so forth. If database fields have changed, a message will appear and the Field Explorer will reflect the changes once you respond to the message. If you leave these options turned off, you must manually verify from the Crystal Reports Database pull-down menu if you want database changes to be recognized.

Changing to a Different Database

You may initially create a report based on a PC-style database, such as Microsoft Access, and then decide later to convert the report to use a similarly organized SQL database. Perhaps the Access database has been upsized to SQL Server, or you may initially be developing reports against a test database in Btrieve, but the reports will eventually have to run against an identical Oracle database. Or else you may encounter other situations in which you initially develop a report against a specific database type, such an ODBC database, which now needs to be "pointed" to an alternate ODBC database.

In any case, Crystal Reports provides a single, streamlined choice for choosing a different database. Choose Database | Set Datasource Location from the pull-down menus, which will display the Set Datasource dialog box, shown in Figure 15-4.

If you wish to replace a single table with a new table, select the particular table you wish to replace in the Current Data Source list. Or, you can replace an entire database, including all its tables, by selecting the actual database name above the Properties and individual table entries. Then, expand the database category in the Replace With list where the new database

Choose original table or database
that you wish to replace

Click Update to update the report

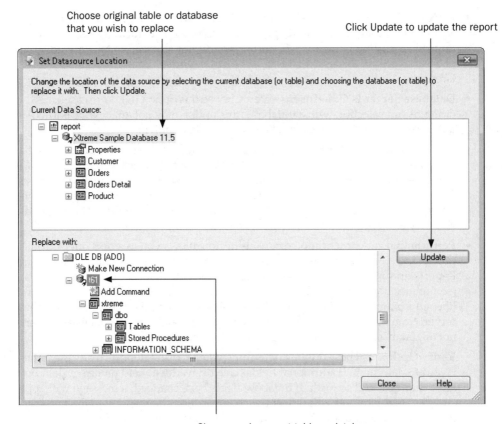

Choose replacement table or database

FIGURE 15-4 Set Datasource dialog box

or table resides. Select a like object type (if you selected the entire database above, select a database name below—if you chose a single table above, select a single table below). If you choose a database in the Replace With list that requires logon credentials, supply proper credentials. Once you've chosen the desired tables or database, click Update.

If table or field names have changed in the new database, you'll be prompted to remap old fields to their new names. This is covered in more detail later in the chapter, under "Accommodating Database Changes and Field Mapping."

Adding Additional Tables to the Report

Once you've initially chosen and linked tables and continued with report design, you will often find that you need to add and link additional tables to your report afterward. To do so, click the Database Expert toolbar button in the Expert Tools toolbar, or choose Database

| Database Expert from the pull-down menus. The Database Expert will return, where you can add additional tables from the Available Data Sources list. Once you've added the additional tables, click the Database Expert Links tab to link the tables together (linking is discussed in detail later in the chapter, under "Linking Tables").

Any tables that you've previously added to your report will already appear in the Selected Tables list. If you attempt to add one of these existing tables again, you'll be prompted to give the second occurrence of the table an *alias*, because each table used in the Database Expert Links tab must have a unique name.

TIP *You may want to intentionally add the same table to a report more than once. If, for instance, you have a common lookup table that is used with several master or transaction tables, you won't be able to retrieve lookup information by linking all the transaction or master tables to the same lookup table. You'll need to add the lookup table to the report multiple times, using a different alias each time. You can then link each transaction or master table to the different aliased versions of the lookup table.*

Removing Unused Tables from the Report

You may inadvertently add too many tables to your report, or you may no longer need tables that you used earlier in the report design process. If the Database Expert is displayed, just select the table you want to remove from the Selected Tables list and click the left arrow. If you want to remove all tables from the Selected Tables list and start table additions over from scratch, click the double-left arrow. If any of the tables you attempt to remove are in use on the report, you will be so notified and prompted to confirm their removal.

If you have proceeded to report design and are currently working in the Design or Preview tabs, redisplay the Database Expert with the toolbar button or Database menu option and delete tables from the Selected Tables list.

CAUTION *Make sure you really want to remove the table before you click the left arrows and close the Database Expert. You can't undo a table removal. Also, if you remove a table that is referenced in any formulas, the formulas will no longer work after the table is gone. If you remove a table by mistake, redisplay the Database Expert to re-add and link the table. Or if you had a known good copy of the report saved on disk, you may wish to close the existing report without saving changes and open the known good copy.*

Linking Tables

Although you may have rare instances in which you design a report based on just one database table, you usually need to use at least two, and often more, tables in your report, because most modern relational databases are *normalized*. Database normalization refers to breaking out repetitive database information into separate tables in the database for efficiency and maintenance reasons. Consider the following Employee table:

Employee Name	Department Name	Salary
Bill	Information Technology	50,000
Karen	Human Resources	32,500
Renee	Information Technology	37,500
John	Executive	85,000
Carl	Mail Room	24,000
Jim	Information Technology	48,000
Julie	Executive	87,000
Sally	Mail Room	23,500

Although this makes for a simple reporting environment, because you don't need to choose more than one table to print an employee roster or paycheck, it becomes more difficult to maintain. Notice that department names repeat several times throughout this small table. (Think about this same scenario for a 50,000-employee company!) This not only takes up a large amount of storage space, but if a department name changes, much work has to be done to make the change in this table. For example, if the Information Technology department changes its name to Information Systems, a search-and-replace function must be performed through the entire Employee table, replacing every occurrence of the old name with the new name.

Contrast this single-table layout with the following database environment:

Employee Table:

Employee Name	Department Number	Salary
Bill	25	50,000
Karen	17	32,500
Renee	25	37,500
John	8	85,000
Carl	13	24,000
Jim	25	48,000
Julie	8	87,000
Sally	13	23,500

Department Table:

Department Number	Department Name
8	Executive
13	Mail Room
17	Human Resources
25	Information Technology

Here, you can see that the database has been normalized by placing the department information in its own lookup table. In this environment, much less storage is used by the Employee table, because only a department number is stored for each employee, not the entire department name. And if the Information Technology department's name changes, only one record in the Department table has to be changed in the entire database.

Database Expert Links Tab

Using multiple tables complicates the reporting environment, because you need more than just the Employee table to print an employee roster or paycheck. In the preceding example, you not only have to include the two tables in your report, but you must also link them together with a common field. *Linking* tables (often also known as *joining* tables) consists of choosing a common field or fields that will allow the second table to follow the main table as the main table is read record by record. You link tables in Crystal Reports with the Database Expert Links tab, illustrated in Figure 15-5.

FIGURE 15-5 The Database Expert Links tab

The Database Expert Links tab appears if you initially choose two or more tables when you first create a report, or whenever you choose additional tables within the Database Expert later in the report design process. If you want to work with database links at other times, simply display the Database Expert by clicking the Database Expert toolbar button or by choosing Database | Database Expert from the pull-down menus (as discussed earlier in the chapter). Then, click the Links tab.

You are free to move the individual tables around in the Links tab if you wish to see them in a different organization. You can also resize each table window to make it taller, shorter, narrower, or wider. If you wish to have Crystal Reports automatically rearrange the tables according to the way they're linked, click Auto-Arrange. If you wish to see a sample of actual data contained in a particular field, or see the data type of a field, click the desired field in a table. Right-click, and choose Browse Field from the pop-up menu.

The Database Expert Links tab typically chooses links between the tables when you first display it. If you see lines connecting fields in the tables, the Database Expert Links tab has already automatically linked the tables for you (automatic linking is discussed later in the chapter). You may need to delete these existing links if they are incorrect, or add new links yourself.

To delete a link, click the line connecting the two tables. The link line, along with the fields it connects, will be highlighted. Click Delete Link or press the DEL key. If you want to change link options, such as the join type (discussed later in the chapter, under "Join and Link Types") or multiple-table link behavior, click Link Options, double-click the selected link, or right-click the link and choose Link Options from the pop-up menu.

To draw a new link, click a field in the table you want to link from, drag your mouse to the other table you want to link, and then drop onto the field you want to link to. A link line will be drawn between the two tables and fields.

If Crystal Reports detects no potential problems with the link you've drawn, the link line simply appears and you see no messages. If, however, Crystal Reports detects a potential problem with the link, such as mismatched field types, you'll receive a warning message and the link may not be created.

Significance of the Index Arrows

Most database systems allow database fields to be indexed by the database designer. These indexed fields are indicated by colored arrows. An *index* is a special setting that the database designer creates to speed up access to a table. Searching for specific records from that table will be much faster when the search is based on an indexed field. The different colors of the index arrows indicate that different indexes have been created by the database designer for the table. To display a key to the index arrow colors, click Index Legend. The window will appear showing the different colors and their indexes.

When linking database tables together, you may link on any field you choose—there is no requirement to link to or from an indexed field. For performance reasons, however, you may still want to try to link *to* indexed fields anyway. You may see improved record retrieval speeds.

Link Order

When you add tables to the report and then display the Links tab, Crystal Reports makes an assumption about the order in which you wish to link tables (this assumption is made only if Crystal Reports automatically links tables, which it will often do). If you are linking only two tables together, this will not be an issue, as there is only one link between two tables.

However, if you link three or more tables (tables A, B, and C in this example), Crystal Reports will link the tables in a certain order: perhaps first linking table A to table B on one field, and then linking table A to table C on another field. If the database you've used in the report is based on Structure Query Language, or SQL (discussed in more detail later in the

---

So, Which Tables and Fields Should I Link?

You'll quickly figure out that you have to be very familiar with the database you are reporting against to accurately link tables and fields. You have to know the layout of the tables and the data that the common fields contain to successfully link them. This task is complicated even further by database designers who insist on protecting their jobs by creating confusing and cryptic table and field names.

Probably the most expeditious approach is to consult reliable database documentation, or perhaps chat with someone who either designed the database or is familiar with its layout and contents. Barring that, you may be able to discern the proper tables and fields to link if they are named logically. If nothing else, you can browse individual fields in the Database Expert Links tab by right-clicking a field name and choosing Browse Field from the pop-up menu. By looking for similar data types and sample data that seems to match up in both tables, you can find good candidates for links.

Always make sure you test your report and verify that correct data is being returned once you've linked tables. It's *very easy* to create an incorrect link that displays no error message but doesn't return the correctly matched data to the report.

chapter), you'll be able to view the SQL query that Crystal Reports sends to the database and see the order in which these links will occur.

In most cases, the link order won't be significant and you won't need to change it. However, in certain situations with certain types of table structures and database systems or connection drivers, you may notice a difference in the resulting data if you choose an "an A to C, then A to B order" instead of the "A to B, then A to C order." If this is significant, you can change the order by clicking the Order Links button. Clicking this button will display the Order Links dialog box.

Select the link that you want to move up or down in the order and click the up or down arrow at the top of the dialog box. Click the Link Ordering Is Enforced check box to ensure that Crystal Reports reorders the link statements in the SQL query being sent to the database.

Using Multiple Database Types in the Same Report

Crystal Reports doesn't limit you to using just one type of database per report. You may, for example, wish to get the main transaction table for your report from a client/server database using a direct access database driver, one smaller lookup table from a Microsoft Access database on a shared LAN drive, and another lookup table from a Microsoft Excel spreadsheet on your C drive via the Access/Excel (DAO) connection.

To accomplish this, simply choose all the different tables from different categories of the Database Expert when you first create the report. Or to add additional tables (even from different database types) after you've already started designing a report, simply redisplay the Database Expert using the toolbar button or pull-down menu options discussed earlier. After choosing the additional table or tables, click the Links tab and link them appropriately.

In general, this type of mixed reporting is perfectly acceptable. However, because connections to the different database types cannot be accomplished with a single SQL query (this is because a SQL query, by its nature, can't cross database boundaries), Crystal Reports will link the tables itself internally. In limited cases, this may require you to only link on string fields. Most often, however, mixed database usage will result in a warning message that your report contains more than one database type and that you can't use SQL Expressions or server-based grouping (both topics are discussed later in this chapter).

CAUTION *While the ability to include multiple database types in a single report greatly adds to Crystal Reports flexibility, it may impair report performance. Because several different database queries have to be performed, with Crystal Reports combining them together locally, reports may take longer to process.*

Does Crystal Reports Automatic Linking Work?

When you initially add tables to a report, Crystal Reports will attempt to link the tables automatically. The result will often be link lines appearing in the Links tab when you first display it, even before you draw any manual links in yourself. This is a feature with good intentions, but it is often more trouble than it's worth. This linking automatically links fields in two adjacent tables if the fields meet these criteria:

- The field names are exactly the same.
- The data types are identical.
- In the case of string fields, the field lengths are the same.

In an ideal setting, automatic linking works perfectly. In the real world, however, things are usually quite different.

Consider, for example, a report that includes a Vendor table and a Customer table. Both tables contain fields named Address, City, State, and Zip Code. It's perfectly conceivable that these fields have identical data types and field lengths. Automatic linking will dutifully link the two tables together on all four fields. But, these aren't the proper fields with which to link these two tables together.

Another type of automatic linking that Crystal Reports will attempt is linking by key. In this scenario, Crystal Reports attempts to determine a "primary key/foreign key" relationship between tables by reading the internal database structure provided by the database driver. You must typically choose this form of automatic linking yourself by clicking the By Key radio button, and then clicking the Auto-Link button in the Link tab. If the specific set of primary key/foreign key settings can't be found by Crystal Reports, you'll receive a message indicating that key linking can't be performed and asking if you wish to link via the field name scenario.

You'll probably find that automatic linking, either by key or by field name, often results in incorrect link lines being drawn. You then are forced to delete the incorrect links and draw in the correct ones. If you find that you are spending extra time deleting automatic links, you may turn the Automatic Smart Linking feature off. Display the database options dialog box by right-clicking in the Available Data Sources portion of the Database Expert, or choose the Database tab after selecting File | Options from the pull-down menus. Uncheck Automatic Smart Linking.

Join Types, Link Types, and Join Enforcement

When you link two tables, you must consider carefully what records will be returned from both tables. Consider a slight modification to the normalized table structures illustrated earlier in this chapter.

Employee Table:

Employee Name	Department Number	Salary
Karen	17	32,500
Renee	25	37,500
John	8	85,000
Carl	13	24,000
Denise	32	125,000

Department Table:

Department Number	Department Name
8	Executive
13	Mail Room
17	Human Resources
4	Finance
25	Information Technology

A quick glance at these two tables reveals two inconsistencies: Denise has no matching record in the Department table, and the Finance department has no employees in the Employee table. These two tables are said to lack *referential integrity*—a fancy computer term that simply means the two tables don't completely match up. Fancy term or not, this will be *very* important to you as a report designer. You have to decide how you want to deal with a lack of referential integrity.

NOTE *Many databases can enforce referential integrity, so the situation described previously will never happen. If the database designer chooses to enforce referential integrity between these two tables, an employee cannot be given a department number that doesn't exist in the Department table, and a department record can't be deleted from the Department table if any Employee table records still contain that department. However, enforcing referential integrity often introduces other complexities in the database, and there are many times when the basic function of the database will not allow referential integrity to be enforced. The database designer or administrator should be consulted if you have questions about the way your database is designed.*

A situation in which you would be very concerned about referential integrity is if you were designing a report to print paychecks for employees. Consider the tables previously shown as the basis for your paychecks. If you wish to have the employee's department printed on the check stub to help in check distribution, you would need to link the Employee and Department tables together on the Department Number field. It's a fair assumption that your paycheck run would get at least this far:

The big question for you, the report designer, is "What happens to Denise?" (the last employee in the Employee table). Considering that she's a highly paid employee, at least from most viewpoints, she will probably be very interested in being paid, regardless of referential integrity. Another interesting question is "Will any checks print for the Finance department?" The answers to your questions are dependent upon which *join type* you use when linking these two tables together.

The following are the two join types that you will be concerned with most of the time:

- **Inner join (sometimes referred to as an *equal join*)** Includes records from both tables *only when the joining fields are equal.*

- **Left outer join (sometimes simply referred to as *outer join*)** Includes *all* records from the left table, and records from the right table only when the joining fields are equal.

Even though Denise probably doesn't know what a left outer join is, she probably will be much happier if you choose it. This will result in her receiving a paycheck that doesn't have just a department name printed on it. This is particularly important in Crystal Reports, because the default join type for SQL databases is an inner join.

Two other types of joins that you may use less frequently are the following:

- **Right outer join**   Includes *all* records from the right table, and records from the left table only when the joining fields are equal.

Denise would be as displeased with this choice as she would with an equal join. You would also get a wasted paycheck with the Finance department on the pay stub, but no employee or salary printed on it.

- **Full outer join**   Includes all records from *both* tables, whether the joined fields are equal or not.

Denise wouldn't mind this joint type—she'd get paid. However, you'd also have a wasted check for the Finance department with no employee information on it.

Choosing the Join and Link Type in the Database Expert Links Tab

Choose the join type in the Database Expert Links tab by double-clicking the link line between the two tables you are interested in, by right-clicking the link line and choosing Link Options from the pop-up menu, or by selecting the link and clicking Link Options. The Link Options dialog box, shown in Figure 15-6, will appear. Select the desired join type from the left side of the dialog box.

NOTE *If tables are linked by more than one field, choosing a join type for any of the links will set the same join type for all the links. You cannot have different join types for multiple links between the same tables.*

Although most typical business reporting can be accomplished with inner joins and left outer joins, you may have occasion in specialized reporting situations to use these other join types.

FIGURE 15-6   Link Options dialog box

Crystal Reports Link Types In addition to a join type, Crystal Reports provides the additional choice of a *link type* that can be chosen along with a join type.

- **Equal (=)** Returns records from the tables, matching records from the right table every time the joining field in the left table *is equal to* the joining field in the right table.

- **Greater than (>)** Returns records from the left table, matching records from the right table every time the joining field in the left table *is greater than* the joining field in the right table.

- **Greater than or equal (>=)** Returns records from the left table, matching records from the right table every time the joining field in the left table *is greater than or equal to* the joining field in the right table.

- **Less than (<)** Returns records from the left table, matching records from the right table every time the joining field in the left table *is less than* the joining field in the right table.

- **Less than or equal (<=)** Returns records from the left table, matching records from the right table every time the joining field in the left table *is less than or equal to* the joining field in the right table.

- **Not equal (!=)** Returns all combinations of records from the two tables where the joining fields *are not equal.*

Various combinations of join and link types can return very interesting combinations of data. For example, choosing an Inner Join but a Less Than link type will return a much larger set of records than an Inner Join with an Equal link type. However, it still won't return records where there is no match at all between link fields. But if you choose a Left Outer Join and a Less Than link type, you'll receive a larger number of matching records, as well as records from the left table that have no match in the right table.

You can choose Database | Show SQL Query from the pull-down menus to see how the combination of join and link types will affect the SQL Query. If you are familiar with the structure of the SQL query, you'll notice that the combination of join and link types will change different portions of the query. For example, an Inner Join with an Equal link type will create this type of query:

```
FROM   "xtreme"."dbo"."Employee" "Employee" INNER JOIN
"xtreme"."dbo"."Orders" "Orders" ON
"Employee"."Employee ID"="Orders"."Employee ID"
```

And, a Left Outer Join using a Less Than link type will return this type of query:

```
FROM   {oj "xtreme"."dbo"."Employee" "Employee" LEFT OUTER JOIN
"xtreme"."dbo"."Orders" "Orders" ON
"Employee"."Employee ID"<"Orders"."Employee ID"}
```

Of course, the exact format of the SQL query and where the joins are performed (the FROM clause in some cases, the WHERE clause in others), is dependent upon the database type and driver being used. Also, you'll see *very* different sets of returned data for the different join and link types you choose. If you aren't extensively familiar with join and link types, you'd be best advised to stick with tried and true Inner or Left Outer join types and

Equal link types. In any event, you are well advised to validate the results of your report against your original data source to ensure that all the proper data is being returned by the report once you make join and link choices.

NOTE *Some join and link types won't be available, depending on the types of databases you have chosen for your report. In those cases, the unavailable join and link types will be dimmed in the Link Options dialog box.*

Crystal Reports Join Enforcement

The Link Options dialog box (shown previously in Figure 15-6) includes the Enforce Join category. The four radio buttons in this category allow you to choose whether to include tables you've added to the Database Expert in the eventual SQL query sent to the database, even if you *haven't used any fields from the table* on the report.

By default, joins are not enforced. In this scenario, if you add several tables to the Database Expert but only include fields from one table on the report, the other tables aren't even referenced in the SQL query and any joins and links you choose in the Links tab won't take effect. The Enforce Join options give you the choice of whether to enforce the joins and links, even if fields from all tables aren't included on the report.

Consider an example of two Oracle tables—Orders and Customer—that are being used on a report (Orders is the *from* table and Customer is the *to* table). The tables are linked together on one common field (Customer_ID) using an Inner join and an Equal link. By default, the join is not enforced. The final important piece of this example is what fields are placed on the report, used in a formula or record selection, or otherwise added to the report.

Depending on the choice you make by clicking one of the Enforce Join radio buttons, you'll potentially see different database records on the report, as well as a different SQL query being sent to the Oracle server:

- **Not Enforced**   This choice does not add any extra tables to the SQL query that are not used elsewhere on the report. For example, if only the Order_ID field from the Orders table is added to the report, but no fields from the Customer table are used, the following SQL query will result:

```
SELECT "Orders"."ORDER_ID"
FROM    "XTREME"."ORDERS" "Orders"
```

  Notice that the Customer table is not included in the query and the join and link types chosen *will not* affect the set of data returned from the database.

- **Enforced From**   This choice will include the FROM table in the query, enforcing its joins and links, even if no fields in the FROM table are used on the report. For example, if only the Customer_Name field from the Customer table is added to the report, and no fields from the Orders table are added, the following SQL query will result:

```
SELECT "CUSTOMER"."CUSTOMER_NAME"
FROM    "XTREME"."ORDERS" "ORDERS", "XTREME"."CUSTOMER" "CUSTOMER"
WHERE   ("ORDERS"."CUSTOMER_ID"="CUSTOMER"."CUSTOMER_ID")
```

  Notice that the Orders table is still included in the query and the join and link types chosen *will* affect the set of data returned from the database, even though no Orders table field is used on the report. The result is the inclusion of duplicate Customer Names in order to match each order record.

- **Enforced To**   This choice will include the TO table in the query, enforcing its joins and links, even if no fields in the TO table are used on the report. For example, if only the Order_ID field from the Orders table is added to the report, and no fields from the Customer table are added, the following SQL query will result:

```
SELECT  "ORDERS"."ORDER_ID"
FROM    "XTREME"."ORDERS" "ORDERS", "XTREME"."CUSTOMER" "CUSTOMER"
WHERE   ("ORDERS"."CUSTOMER_ID"="CUSTOMER"."CUSTOMER_ID")
```

  Notice that the Customer table is still included in the query and the join and link types chosen *will* affect the set of data returned from the database, even though no Customer table field is used on the report. The result is the inclusion of only order IDs that have a matching Customer table entry (because of the Inner Join), even though no Customer information is included on the report.

- **Enforced Both**   This choice will include the FROM table and TO table in the query, enforcing their joins and links, regardless of which tables are included on the report. So, while the SELECT clause will be affected by whether you include fields from the Orders table, the Customer table, or both, the FROM and WHERE clauses will always refer to both tables:

```
FROM    "XTREME"."ORDERS" "ORDERS", "XTREME"."CUSTOMER" "CUSTOMER"
WHERE   ("ORDERS"."CUSTOMER_ID"="CUSTOMER"."CUSTOMER_ID")
```

  The results will be a combination of only orders that have a matching customer record, and repetition of customer fields for each matching order.

Which Should Be the Left ("From") Table, and Which Should Be the Right ("To") Table?

When you use the Links tab, you begin to draw a link by clicking a "from" table. You then drop the link onto the desired field in the "to" table. Initially, you may not be able to tell which table was dragged from and which table was dropped onto. In many cases, Crystal Reports won't indicate this if you are using the default Inner Join and Equal link types.

However, if you change to alternate join or link types, or you use certain databases or database drivers, you'll be able to see which table is the "from" and which is the "to" by looking carefully at the link line—the "from" side of the line will display a small block, while the "to" side will display an arrow.

This begs the question, "Does it make any difference which is the 'from' and which is the 'to' table?" The answer, again, relates to the join and link types you choose, and whether you choose to enforce joins. Generally speaking, if you select an Inner Join and an Equal link and don't enforce them, it doesn't make a great deal of difference. However, if you use any other join or link types, or enforce the joins, it makes a great deal of difference, because the "from" or left table and the "to" or right table determine how the SQL query is formed and what records are returned.

Because left-outer joins return records based on which table is the "left" table and which table is the "right" table, the order in which you join tables together becomes particularly crucial when using this join type. If you use a left-outer join but have the join logically reversed, you'll not receive the proper set of records on the report.

If you're concerned that the link may be in "reverse" order, and you'd like to switch the "from" and "to" tables, you can simply delete and redraw the link, or right-click the link and choose Reverse Link from the pop-up menu.

Viewing the SQL Query

Because Crystal Reports works with SQL databases, it must eventually translate the tables, fields, links, sorting, and grouping that you've used to design your report into SQL. You can view the SQL statements Crystal Reports creates by choosing Database | Show SQL Query from the pull-down menus.

Consider the following report Design tab that uses data from the XTREME sample database (available for download from the book's companion web site, CrystalBook.com), converted from Microsoft Access to Microsoft SQL Server, accessed via ODBC. This report uses the Orders and Customer tables, linked with a left outer join and equal link on Customer ID. The join isn't enforced, but fields from both tables are included on the report. The Select Expert is limiting the report to U.S.A. customers only. Notice the fields that have been placed in the details section. Also, notice that a group based on Customer.Region has been created.

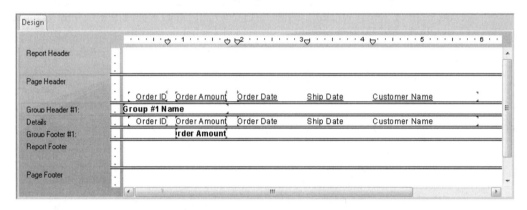

To view the SQL statement that Crystal Reports creates to query the database, select Database | Show SQL Query. You will see the dialog box illustrated here.

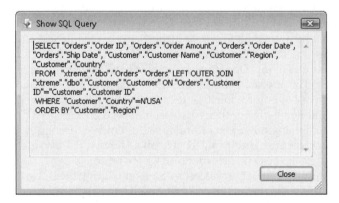

Notice the different parts, or *clauses,* of the SQL statement:

- **SELECT**   Matches the database fields that your report needs (for the details section, formulas, grouping, record selection, and so on).
- **FROM**   Chooses the tables to use and specifies the join type for table linking.
- **WHERE**   Supplies record selection to the server.
- **ORDER BY**   Requests that the SQL server sort records in Customer.Region order (for the Region group) before sending them back to the client.

The SQL syntax may change, depending on the type of database you are reporting against and whether you're using ODBC or direct database drivers to communicate with it. You'll also see different syntax for joining tables. And, you may see the actual table join appear in either the FROM or WHERE clause.

Here is the exact same Show SQL Query dialog box based on a database connection to Oracle using a native driver (notice, among other things, that the join and link is done in the WHERE clause and not the FROM clause):

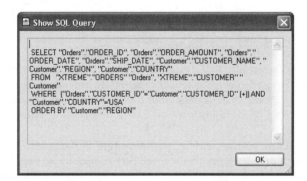

and, based on the XTREME.MDB Microsoft Access database via ODBC (this is similar to the SQL Server query, with the exception of different punctuation around field names and the missing "N" character in the WHERE clause):

Although you may not consider yourself a database expert and might not make a habit of writing huge SQL statements off the top of your head, there is one advantage to being able to see the SQL query that Crystal Reports is sending to the server: this is useful if you are experiencing performance problems or other peculiarities when running the report. In particular, you want to ensure that as much as possible, if not all, of the report's record selection is translated into a WHERE clause in the SQL query. This will maximize the work performed by the database server and minimize the amount of data and amount of processing left for Crystal Reports to deal with once data is returned from the server. More details on performance considerations can be found later in the chapter.

NOTE *If you have added tables from more than one database type to your report (as described previously, under "Using Multiple Database Types in the Same Report"), the SQL Query dialog box will show queries for all database types, including "External Link" notations. The reference to an External Link indicates that Crystal Reports will perform the link locally after all queries have processed on their respective database servers.*

Crystal Reports SQL Commands

As shown previously, you may see the SQL query created by Crystal Reports in the Show SQL Query dialog box (the SQL query in this box is for viewing only and cannot be changed). This query is designed internally by Crystal Reports according to choices you make in the Database Expert, the Select Expert, the report Design tab, and so forth. However, if you are versant in your particular database's version of the structured query language, you may find a need to create your own SQL query and base a report on it. This can be accomplished with the *SQL Command.*

SQL Commands allow you to create a "pass-through" SQL statement that performs more database-specific query processes on the database server, such as aggregate functions, UNION queries, or sub-SELECT queries. Once you've created a SQL Command, you can base a report on it (it looks like a table) or add it to the BusinessObjects Enterprise repository so that other report designers sharing the same repository can base their reports on it.

Creating the SQL Command

Before you can create a SQL Command, you must log on to the database that the command will be based on. When first creating a report, you can log on to a database from the Database Expert as described earlier in the chapter. Or if you want to create a SQL Command after you've already commenced report design, redisplay the Database Expert with the toolbar button or Database | Database Expert menu option.

Once you've logged on to a database, notice the "Add Command" option that appears above the tables, views, and stored procedure categories of the Database Expert Available Data Sources list. Double-click the Add Command option to display the Add Command To Report dialog box, shown in Figure 15-7.

Begin by typing the SQL statement you wish to use for the command in the appropriate box. Note that there is no "Expert" or "Build" functionality in this dialog box—you're on your own for typing correctly formatted SQL particular to the driver or database connection

Remove run-time parameter

Modify run-time parameter

Type SQL statement here

Add run-time parameter

FIGURE 15-7   Add Command To Report dialog box

you're using. If you are unsure of proper SQL syntax, you may wish to develop the SQL in another tool provided by your database vendor. Once you've debugged the SQL query in that tool, copy the SQL code to the Windows clipboard and paste the statement into this dialog box.

When you click OK on the Add Command To Report dialog box, Crystal Reports will submit the command to the database to be checked for proper syntax. If you have made an error, the database driver will return a message indicating the particular problem with the SQL statement submitted. The Add Command To Report dialog box will then return, where you may correct the SQL statement and click OK again. Once you've submitted a correct SQL statement, the dialog box will close and "Command" will appear as a table name on the Selected Tables side of the Database Expert. If you wish to give your SQL Command a more descriptive name, select it in the Selected Tables list and then hold your mouse button down for a few seconds. This will place the command name into edit mode, where you may replace the word "Command" with a new name (note that you cannot include spaces in the new name).

If you wish to view or edit the contents of a command you've created previously, select the command in the Selected Tables list and then right-click. Choose Edit Command or View Command from the pop-up menu. Both options will display the SQL Command in the same dialog box it was created with. If you choose View Command, the command will not be editable—Edit Command will allow the command to be changed; parameters to be added, changed, or deleted; and the command to be added to the BusinessObjects Enterprise repository.

CAUTION *To delete a command that you no longer wish to use, select the command in the Selected Tables list and click the left arrow. Be aware; this is a permanent deletion. The command won't move to the left side of the Database Expert, where you could add it back to the report. It will be permanently deleted.*

Adding a Parameter to the Command

As with reports, you may wish to have the SQL Command prompt a viewer for one or more variable pieces of information when it's submitted to the database. This will allow, for example, the SQL Command to run for a specified department, date range, or sales level threshold. You may accomplish this by creating a parameter in the Command dialog box, and then placing that parameter within the SQL statement.

To add a new parameter, click the Create button next to the parameter list. The Command Parameter dialog box will appear, as shown in Figure 15-8.

Supply desired options in this dialog box. You must, at least, choose a name for the parameter and a value type. The other three choices, prompting text, default value, and Allow multiple values, are optional. Type a name for the parameter that hasn't been used by any other parameters in the SQL Command. And, ensure you choose a data type that matches the use you have in mind for the parameter—if you are going to use it to compare to a numeric database field, choose Number as the value type for the parameter. Crystal Reports 2008 adds the ability to create a multiple-value parameter field in a SQL Command. This will allow the report view to supply more than one value for this parameter (more detail on

FIGURE 15-8 Command Parameter dialog box

multiple-value parameter fields can be found in Chapter 13). Once you've made these choices, click OK. The parameter will be added to the Parameter List.

If you later wish to modify or delete a parameter, select the parameter in the Parameter List that you wish to work with. Then, click Modify or Delete. Delete will simply remove the parameter from the list (make sure you also remove any references to the parameter from the SQL statement). Modify will redisplay the Command Parameter dialog box, where you may change any of the parameter elements.

Once you've created the parameter, you must now reference it somewhere in the SQL statement for it to have any effect. For example, if you wish to replace a hard-coded number in the WHERE clause with the parameter, edit the SQL statement and replace the hard-coded number with the name of the parameter. You can either type the parameter name in directly (including curly braces around the parameter name and a question mark preceding the name) or simply place the cursor where you want the parameter name to be placed and then double-click on the parameter in the Parameter List.

Thus, a previous WHERE clause with a hard-coded number:

```
WHERE "State" = 'CO'
```

can be replaced with a parameter-driven version:

```
WHERE "State" In {?State}
```

TIP *Depending on the syntax requirements of your database, you may need to supply single quotes around a parameter field reference, change the SQL syntax from = to In for multiple-value parameter fields, and so forth.*

Once you've added one or more parameters to the SQL Command, click OK. You will then be prompted to supply values for any parameters, and again, the command will be submitted to the database to check for proper SQL syntax. Any errors generated by adding the parameter will appear in an error message, and you'll be returned to the Add Command To Report dialog box, where you may fix the problem. If the command is syntactically correct, the Database Expert will reappear.

If you'd like to share the SQL Command with others in your organization, you may copy and paste the SQL text to a shared text or word processing file on your network. Or, if you have a member of the BusinessObjects Enterprise family installed, such as Crystal Reports Server or BusinessObjects Edge, you can store the SQL Command in the repository. Using SQL Commands with the repository is covered in Chapter 18.

Using a SQL Command in a Report

Once you've created a SQL Command, it will appear in the Selected Tables list of the Database Expert just like a "native" table from a database. Once you close the Database Expert, any fields that the SQL Command returns will appear in the Field Explorer—just drag and drop them onto the report as you would any other database field.

You can even link a SQL Command to another database table in the Database Expert before you proceed to report design. And, you can add an additional table to the report later, linking it to the existing SQL Command on one or more common fields. If you link additional tables to the SQL Command, be aware that you'll be limited in your join and link type choices, as described earlier in the chapter, under "Using Multiple Database Types in the Same Report."

Using a Parameter-Based SQL Command   If you added one or more parameters to your SQL Command, you'll find that the command will prompt you for parameter values as you create the command, and later when you refresh a report based on the command. Notice, also, that the parameter will appear in the Field Explorer as though you added it to the report (Chapter 13 discusses report-based parameter fields).

When you refresh the report, you'll be prompted to choose whether to rerun the report with existing parameter values or to specify new parameter values. If you choose to specify new, the familiar parameter prompt will appear asking for values for the SQL Command parameters. You can even place the parameters you added to the command right on the report, or use the command parameters in report formulas.

CAUTION   *While Crystal Reports 2008 now allows SQL Command–based parameter fields to receive multiple values, other advanced parameter types, such as range, are still not available. Even if you edit the resulting parameter from within the Field Explorer, you won't be able to make such choices. You can, however, create static and dynamic pick lists for SQL Command parameters, as well as use the resulting data from a SQL Command as a data source for dynamic/ cascading pick lists. See Chapter 13 for more information on these options. You can even rename a command-based parameter in the Field Explorer the same way you would rename a regular parameter field (although this won't change the name of the parameter in the SQL Command).*

Using SQL Stored Procedures

Most SQL database systems include the capability to use stored procedures. A *stored procedure* is a SQL query that has been evaluated, or "compiled," by the database server in advance and is stored on the server along with regular database tables. Because the stored procedure is compiled in advance, it often performs faster than a SQL query submitted on the fly. Stored procedures can be created by the database designer or administrator for specific queries that will be run on a frequent basis.

To enhance flexibility, stored procedures can contain one or more stored procedure *parameters* that prompt the user to enter a value. The stored procedure then uses the value to run the query. For example, if you have a stored procedure that returns several fields from linked tables, based on Country and Order Date parameters, you'll be prompted to enter a particular country and order date when the stored procedure runs. The procedure will then return a result set containing only records matching the two-parameter values you supplied.

Choosing Stored Procedures

Crystal Reports treats stored procedures almost identically to regular database tables. Stored procedures appear in the Database Expert and are used in a report just like regular database tables. The only difference is that a stored procedure may have parameters associated with it. However, you do have a choice of whether or not stored procedures will appear in the Database Expert in the first place. The quickest way to ensure that they show up is to right-click in the Available Data Sources portion of the Database Expert and choose Options from the pop-up menu. Then, ensure that the Stored Procedure check box in the Database Options dialog box is checked (shown earlier in Figure 15-3). You may also make the change permanent for all new reports in the future by checking the same option on the Database tab after choosing File | Options from the pull-down menus.

Now, when you open a SQL database, you'll see stored procedures appear along with regular database tables.

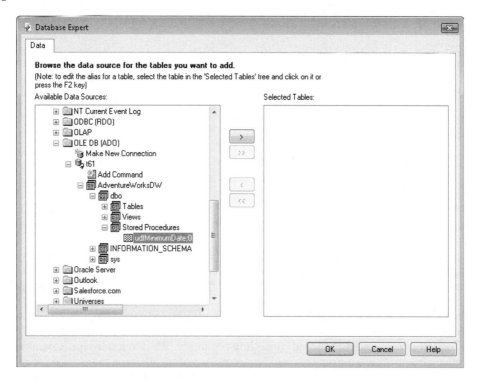

TIP   Crystal Reports allows you to link other database tables to Stored Procedures. Just be aware of limited join and link types, as well as potential performance degradation, as discussed earlier in the chapter, under "Using Multiple Database Types in the Same Report."

Working with Stored Procedure Parameters

After you choose a stored procedure to report on, you are prompted to supply any values for any stored procedure parameters in the Enter Parameter Values dialog box. This dialog box is largely identical to the one that prompts for report parameter fields, discussed in Chapter 13.

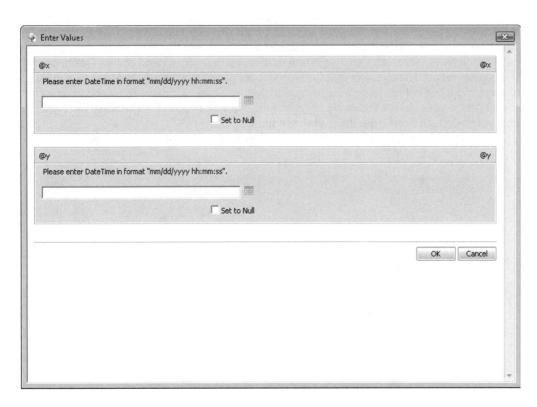

Type your desired parameter values, and click OK (if you want to supply values, you must uncheck Set To Null). You can then simply continue your report design process normally. The stored procedure will supply a list of fields you can use in your report, just like a normal database table.

Stored procedure parameters behave almost identically to Crystal Reports parameter fields. The stored procedure parameters will appear in the Parameter Fields category of the Field Explorer. You can edit a stored procedure parameter like a regular report parameter (except you cannot delete it from the Field Explorer). As with SQL Command–based parameters (discussed earlier in the chapter), you don't have the choice of certain advanced parameter types, such as range.

You can, however, create static or dynamic/cascading pick lists, set length limits or an edit mask for string parameters, or set range limits for number or date parameters. See Chapter 13 for more information on these options. You can even rename a stored procedure–based parameter in the Field Explorer the same way you would rename a regular parameter field (although this won't change the name of the parameter in the stored procedure).

When you refresh the report, you receive the same prompt as when using parameter fields.

You can choose whether to use the existing values for the stored procedure parameters or to prompt for new values. When you prompt for new values, the server will run the stored procedure with the new values and return a new result set to Crystal Reports.

Using SQL Expression Fields

Sometimes you'll want to have the database server actually perform some calculations for you, sending the already calculated field back with the database result set. This is accomplished with SQL expression fields, which can be created right from the Field Explorer. A *SQL expression* is like a formula, except that it's made up entirely of database fields and SQL functions that are supported by the language of the particular SQL server that you're working with. Sometimes there are advantages to using a SQL expression instead of a Crystal Reports formula. The expression is evaluated on the server, not by the client, which may improve performance.

A particular advantage involves calculations or other specialized functions that are used in record selection. If you use a Crystal Reports formula in record selection, the database server typically won't be able to perform the selection, because it doesn't understand the Crystal Reports formula language. However, when you create a SQL expression and use that in record selection, the SQL server will fully understand the expression, and the record selection will be performed by the database server.

Creating SQL Expressions

The first prerequisite for using SQL expressions is that you must be using a SQL or ODBC database. If you're using a PC-style database that doesn't utilize a SQL-based interface, SQL expressions don't apply and you won't even see the SQL Expression category in the Field Explorer. You also won't be able to use SQL Expressions if your report is based on one or more SQL Commands, stored procedures, Business Views, or Universes.

However, when you are using a single SQL database connection, the Field Explorer includes an additional category, labeled SQL Expression Fields. Click the Field Explorer button in the Standard toolbar, or use View | Field Explorer from the pull-down menus to display the Field Explorer (or, if you've shrunk the Field Explorer using the push pin, point to it to expand it). Then, click the SQL Expression Fields category and click the New button in the Field Explorer toolbar or right-click the SQL Expression Fields category and choose New from the pop-up menu.

TIP *Sometimes you can "fool" Crystal Reports into letting you use a SQL Expression, even if you are using mixed database types, stored procedures, and so forth. Begin by including just the database table you want to base the SQL Expression on in the report. Create the SQL Expression and use it some place on the report. Then, add and link the additional database tables from various database types that preclude SQL Expression usage. In many cases, the SQL Expression will continue to work, although you will no longer be able to see it in the Field Explorer or modify it.*

Creating a SQL expression is very similar to creating a Crystal Reports formula (discussed in detail in Chapter 4). You first are asked to give the SQL expression a name. As with formula names, you should make the SQL expression name reasonably short and easy to understand. You may include spaces as well as upper- and lowercase letters in the name. The name you give the SQL expression will also be the column heading if you place the SQL expression in the report's details section.

After you give the SQL expression a name and click OK, the SQL Expression Editor appears, as shown in Figure 15-9.

FIGURE 15-9   SQL Expression Editor

Note the similarities between the SQL Expression Editor and the other Crystal Reports formula editors. Creating SQL expressions is essentially the same as creating other formulas: you can type the expression directly into the Formula text box, or double-click in the top three boxes to help build the expression. Notice that, as when dealing with formulas, parameter fields, and running total fields, Crystal Reports appends a special character to the beginning of the SQL expression's name. The percent symbol (%) is used to denote SQL expression fields.

The functions and operators available in the SQL Expression Editor change, depending on the database and database driver in use. If you look at the Function Tree box in Figure 15-9, you'll notice a certain set of available SQL functions. This example is for a report using Microsoft SQL Server via OLE DB. If you use another method to connect to the same database, or another type of database, the SQL Expression Editor will show a completely different set of SQL functions. For this reason, you will probably have to edit or modify some SQL expressions if you change your report from one database to another using Set Location from the Database pull-down menu. To get detailed descriptions of the different built-in SQL functions for your particular database or driver, consult documentation for that database or driver.

For example, you may want a report viewer to be able to specify with just one parameter field a full or partial contact name to search for. If a customer exists whose contact matches what's entered, the customer will be included on the report. In the Customer table of the XTREME sample database used throughout this book (available for download from CrystalBook.com), the contact information is actually split into separate first and last name database fields. Without using a SQL expression, you have two choices for setting up this search:

- Create two parameter fields—one for first name and one for last name—and try to compare those to database fields.

- Create a Crystal Reports formula that combines the contact's first and last names, and compare the formula to the parameter field.

There are problems with both approaches, however. If you choose the first option, it's much harder for the viewer to simply type a full or partial contact name, such as "Chris" (to find both Christopher and Christine, for example), because some additional logic will be necessary to ignore the last name parameter field if the viewer just wants to search for full or partial first names. Or if the viewer wants to see everyone whose last name is "Jones," regardless of first name, then similar logic will have to apply for the first name parameter field. It would be much simpler for the viewer to be able to type **Chris*** or ***Jones** to search for their desired customers.

If you choose the second option, the full or partial searches mentioned in the previous paragraph will work; but because the first and last names are combined in a formula, the record selection will not take place on the database server (remember that most Crystal formulas can't be converted to SQL, so the client will perform record selection).

By using a SQL expression, you can have the best of both worlds. The first and last names can be concatenated into one object and compared to the parameter field. But because the concatenation takes place on the database server, it will still perform the record selection, sending only the resulting customers back to the client, not all customers.

The SQL expression to accomplish this is surprisingly similar to a Crystal Reports formula:

```
"Customer"."Contact First Name" + ' ' +
"Customer"."Contact Last Name"
```

Notice that a couple of differences exist, however:

- There are no French, or "curly," braces around the field names.
- The literal string that separates the first and last name fields must use apostrophes—quotation marks won't work.

Once this SQL expression has been created, it can be dropped onto the report just like a database field, formula field, or other object. It can also be used inside regular report formulas or in conditional formatting formulas. Notice the change to the SQL query (viewed with Database | Show SQL Query) after placing this SQL expression in the details section:

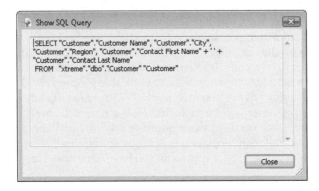

Even though the SQL expression field was given a name in the report, Crystal Reports just adds the SQL expression formula itself right into the SQL statement. The name is simply used by Crystal Reports in the Select Expert or elsewhere on the report.

To now use this SQL expression in record selection, you use the Select Expert's Like operator to allow a wildcard search on the combined first and last names of the contact. If you have already created a string parameter field called {?Contact Prompt}, the Select Expert will look like this:

When you refresh the report and are prompted for the Contact Prompt parameter field, entering the Chris* wildcard will return the following records:

Now, look at the SQL query being sent to the database server:

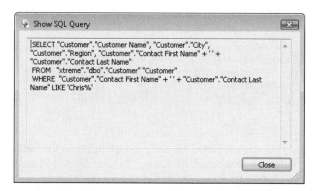

Notice that the WHERE clause includes the SQL expression formula text and a SQL comparison operator that allows wildcard searches. The end result: the flexibility of Crystal Reports formulas with the speed of server-based record selection.

Grouping on the Database Server

Another powerful feature of SQL database servers is server-side processing, or server-based grouping. *Server-based grouping* refers to the ability of the SQL server to perform aggregate calculations on groups of records, returning only subtotals, summaries, and other aggregates to the client. If you are creating a summary report (very often the case), this server capability can significantly decrease the amount of data being passed over the network. Also, the summary calculations can be performed on the server rather than on the client.

Consider the following simple Sales by Region report:

PH				
		Customer Name	Last Year's Sales	City
GH1	AL			
D		Psycho-Cycle	$52,809.11	Huntsville
D		The Great Bike Shop	$15,218.09	Huntsville
D		Benny - The Spokes Person	$6,091.96	Huntsville
GF1		**3 customers**	**Subtotal: $74,119.16**	
GH1	AR			
D		Bikefest	$5,879.70	Little Rock
GF1		**1 customers**	**Subtotal: $5,879.70**	
GH1	AZ			
D		Biking and Hiking	$65.70	Phoenix
D		Bicycle Races	$659.70	Tempe
GF1		**2 customers**	**Subtotal: $725.40**	
GH1	CA			
D		Tyred Out	$18,126.33	Santa Ana
D		Changing Gears	$26,705.65	Irvine
D		Off the Mountain Biking	$25,000.00	Irvine
D		Sporting Wheels Inc.	$85,642.56	San Diego

This is the beginning of a report that simply shows all U.S.A. customers, grouped by region, with a customer count and sales subtotal for each group. Because the details section is shown, the database server will need to send all customers in the U.S.A. to Crystal Reports. Crystal Reports is actually calculating the subtotal and count for each group on the client machine as the report processes. This is confirmed by looking at the SQL query for this report:

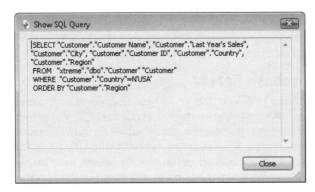

```
Show SQL Query

SELECT "Customer"."Customer Name", "Customer"."Last Year's Sales",
"Customer"."City", "Customer"."Customer ID", "Customer"."Country",
"Customer"."Region"
 FROM   "xtreme"."dbo"."Customer" "Customer"
 WHERE  "Customer"."Country"=N'USA'
 ORDER BY "Customer"."Region"

                                              Close
```

Notice that this fairly simple SQL statement just selects database fields and limits records to the U.S.A. The only server feature used here that helps with grouping is the ORDER BY clause, which presorts the result set into Region order before sending it to the client.

To create a summary report, simply hide the details section by right-clicking in the shaded details area in the left of the Design tab, and choose Hide (Drill-Down OK) from the pop-up menu. The report will now show just the summary data, with no individual customers appearing on the report.

		Customer Name	Last Year's Sales	City
GH1 GF1	AL			
		3 customers	Subtotal: $74,119.16	
GH1 GF1	AR			
		1 customers	Subtotal: $5,879.70	
GH1 GF1	AZ			
		2 customers	Subtotal: $725.40	
GH1 GF1	CA			
		6 customers	Subtotal: $211,479.24	
GH1 GF1	CO			
		1 customers	Subtotal: $7,874.25	
GH1 GF1	CT			
		1 customers	Subtotal: $27.00	
GH1 GF1	DC			
		1 customers	Subtotal: $40.50	

However, if you look at the SQL query, even after refreshing the report, you'll notice that it hasn't changed, because server-based grouping is turned off by default. The server is still sending all customers in the U.S.A. to Crystal Reports, and Crystal Reports still has to cycle through the individual customer records to calculate the customer count and sales subtotals. Database fields in the details section are hidden, but the database returns them anyway.

Enabling Server-Based Grouping

There are several ways to turn on server-based grouping:

- To turn it on for the current report only, choose Database | Perform Grouping On Server from the pull-down menus. You can also choose File | Report Options from the pull-down menus and check Perform Grouping On Server. And, you can choose the same option when you right-click in the Available Data Sources area of the Database Expert and choose Options from the pop-up menu.

- To turn it on for all new reports you create from this point forward, choose File | Options from the pull-down menus and check Perform Grouping On Server on the Database tab.

Once this option is enabled, the report should look the same. There will be some significant changes to the SQL query, however.

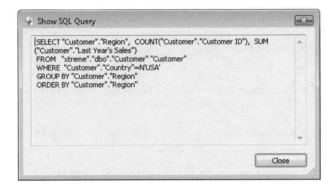

You will see that the SELECT clause now includes only the group field (in this case, Region) and two *aggregate functions* that perform the sum and count functions right on the database server before data is sent to the client. You will also see a new GROUP BY clause that you have not seen before. This new SQL function tells the server to group database records and perform the summary calculations all on the server. Only the summary totals will be sent to the client.

What's Required to Use Server-Based Grouping

Your report must meet certain criteria and be designed in a certain way to use server-based grouping. When you think about the way the server groups and summarizes records, you'll begin to realize why your report must meet these requirements, shown in Table 15-1.

Effects of Drill-Down

When Crystal Reports is performing its own grouping, the concept of report drill-down is fairly straightforward. Even though the details section or lower-level group headers and footers aren't being shown, Crystal Reports is still processing them and storing the data they create. When a viewer double-clicks to drill down on a group, Crystal Reports simply opens a new drill-down tab and displays the data it had previously not displayed.

However, when you enable server-side grouping, there is no detail data to display when a viewer drills down—only the summary data has been sent to the client! Crystal Reports still enables drill-down, however; it just sends another query to the SQL server whenever

Requirement	Reasoning
There must be at least one group on the report.	For the GROUP BY clause to be added to the SQL query, there needs to be at least one group defined on the report.
The details section must be hidden or suppressed.	If the details section is visible, no grouping will occur on the server, because the server must send down individual database records to show in the details section.
Include only the group fields or summary fields in group headers and footers.	If you include any other database fields (or formula fields that contain anything other than group fields or summary fields), the server will have to send detail data to the client to properly display the report.
Don't group or base record selection on Crystal Reports formulas.	Because most Crystal Reports formulas can't be converted to SQL, they must be calculated on the client before the report can select or group on them. Because of this requirement, the server has to send detail records to the client. This is another reason you may want to use SQL expressions as an alternative to formulas, as SQL expressions can still be used for server-based grouping.
Running totals must be based on summary fields.	If running totals (described in Chapter 4) are based on detail fields, Crystal Reports needs the detail data to calculate them as the report processes. This prevents grouping from being done on the server.
The report can only contain Sum, Maximum, Minimum, and Count summaries.	Crystal Reports can't convert other summary types to SQL. Therefore, the grouping will be performed by the client if other functions are used.
Report groups can be sorted only in ascending or descending order. Specified-order grouping won't work.	Since Crystal Reports bases specified-order grouping on its own internal logic, it needs detail records to properly evaluate what specified groups to place them in. This requires detail records to be sent by the server.

TABLE 15-1 Server-Based Grouping Requirements

a viewer drills down. This second query requests just the detail data for the group that was drilled into by adding additional criteria to the WHERE clause. This method provides the benefits of server-based grouping, while still allowing the powerful interactivity of drill-down. The price a viewer pays is the additional time the SQL server may take to process the drill-down query.

Look at the following example. Notice that a viewer has drilled down on a particular region. A new drill-down tab appears, showing detail data for that region. Notice the new SQL query that was created on the fly.

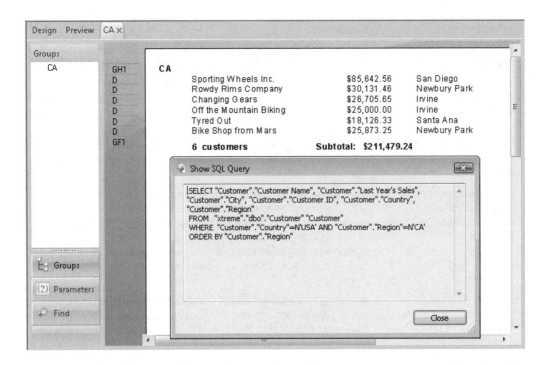

You can view drill-down SQL queries by choosing Database | Show SQL Query when viewing the drill-down tab. If you return to the main Preview tab and show the query, you'll once again notice the GROUP BY clause.

Accommodating Database Changes and Field Mapping

There are many situations in which the database you initially developed a report against will change. Perhaps the database is in a state of flux and will be changing dynamically as your report design proceeds. Or, you may develop a report against a test database and then change the report to point to a production database later. Possibly the database has been moved to a different server for network efficiency. Or you may determine that a different database driver should be used to connect to the database. For true flexibility, you need to be able to accommodate these changes easily, so that you don't have to recreate any features or functions of your report just because the database has changed.

With some of these database changes, the database designer or administrator may rename fields. When Crystal Reports detects these changes, it gives you the opportunity to change the field references inside your report, so the new field names can be automatically associated with the previous field names. This field mapping prevents you from having to add fields to the report again or modify formulas that refer to changed fields.

In addition to the Database Expert, Crystal Reports provides three functions for efficient management of database changes:

- Verifying the database
- Setting the data source location
- Mapping fields

When you use either of the first two functions, and Crystal Reports detects changes that it is unable to resolve, such as field name changes or deletions, the field mapping function is automatically displayed.

Recognizing Database Changes

If the database layout changes (field names change, data types are altered, and so forth), if the database is moved to a new location, or if you want to point your report to a different database than it was originally designed with, you need to use Crystal Reports' functions to recognize these changes.

Verify Database

If the database your report is based on changes (perhaps the database designer adds new fields, deletes old fields, or gives existing fields new names or data types), your report won't automatically recognize these changes when the report is opened. Even if you refresh the report, Crystal Reports won't detect the changes, unless a specific field used in the report no longer exists in the database (it has been removed or renamed). To detect changes to the database the report is based on, you must verify the database.

Choose Database | Verify Database from the pull-down menus. If the database has not changed, you'll see a dialog box indicating so:

However, if the database has changed, you'll receive a message like this:

When you click OK at this prompt, Crystal Reports will read the database structure and make any changes to field names and data types. When you display the Field Explorer, you'll notice the changes. And if you have previously linked tables together and table structures have changed significantly, you may need to relink tables in the Database Expert, as discussed earlier in the chapter. If field names have changed, you will see the Map Fields dialog box (discussed later in the chapter, under "Mapping Old Fields to New Names").

Verify on First Refresh   If the database changes and you don't verify the database thereafter, your report may show incorrect data if fields have been moved or renamed, or it may display an error message if tables have been removed or renamed. Be very careful when working with a database that may be changing. You'll want to verify the database often to catch any changes.

One way to accomplish this is to ensure that Verify On First Refresh is checked after selecting File | Report Options from the pull-down menus. When you check this option, Crystal Reports will verify the database the first time the report is refreshed in any given report session. The on/off state of Verify On First Refresh will be saved with the report—if it was turned on when a particular report was saved, it will be turned on when that report is opened. If you wish to change this choice for all new reports you create in the future, you may modify the same check box on the Database tab after choosing File | Options (this option is turned on by default in Crystal Reports 2008).

Using Set Datasource Location

Crystal Reports provides a single menu function for changing the connection to the database or database driver, recognizing a change to the physical location of a database or table, or changing the actual database to be used. All of these types of changes are accomplished via the Set Datasource Location function.

Choose Database | Set Datasource Location from the pull-down menus. The Set Datasource Location dialog box will appear. This dialog box contains two main sections: the Current Data Source box, and the Replace With box. Begin by choosing the existing database or table that you wish to alter—you may choose either the entire database name by choosing an entry to the right of the database barrel icon, or an individual table within the database by choosing the table name to the right of the table icon.

Then, expand the appropriate category in the Replace With box to find the new data source you wish to use in place of the selected data source in the Current Data Source box. If necessary, you'll need to provide log on credentials to the new server. Choose a replacement object similar to that selected in the Current Data Source box; if you selected an entire database in the top box, select an entire database in the bottom box. If you selected an individual table above, choose a single table below. Only if you select like object types, will the Update button be enabled.

Select current table or database
that needs to change

If necessary, update subreports

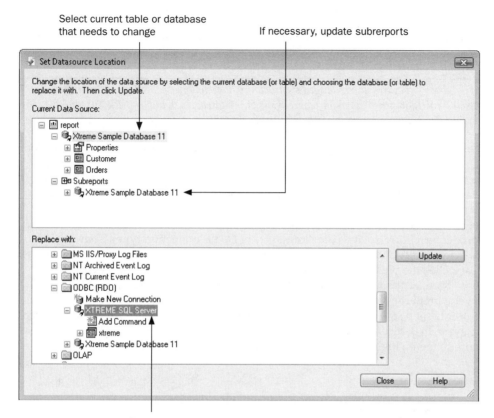

Select the table or database the report will be pointed to

When you click Update, Crystal Reports will log on to the identified replacement data source. If the database name is different on the replacement, the database will be verified (as discussed previously in this chapter), and you may see the Map Fields dialog box (discussed in the section "Mapping Old Fields to New Names" later in this chapter). But as long as the database names match, Crystal Reports assumes that the databases are the same and does not prompt for further input; it simply makes the change. The new data source is now displayed in the Current Data Source list, and you can click Close on the Set Datasource Location dialog box or make other data source location changes.

If your report contains one or more subreports, a separate category below the main report data source will appear in the Current Data Source box. Simply select the subreport data source as you did the main report data source and choose an alternate data source from the bottom list. All subreports that share the original data source will be directed to the new data source.

NOTE *If database structures have changed significantly, you may need to relink tables in the Database Expert for either the main report or affected subreports. Double-check links by displaying the Database Expert and clicking the Links tab.*

Not only can you use these steps to point your report from one database of a particular type (SQL Server, Informix, etc.) to another of the same type, but you may also change database types in the process. For example, if you've built a report based on a test Microsoft Access database, you can use Set Datasource Location to point the report to a production database hosted on Microsoft SQL Server.

Three special features in Set Datasource Location apply only to reports based on PC-style data source connections (such as the Access/Excel DAO connection type). They provide quick ways to identify and modify the name, local directory, or network path for a database. If necessary, click the plus sign to the left of the PC database name in the Current Data Source box. Then, expand the Properties category by clicking the plus sign next to it. You'll notice several properties for the chosen database, including the database type, physical file location, user ID, and so forth. While some of these properties are display-only, many of them can be changed. In particular, the Database Name property has several options you can choose from a pop-up menu. Right-click the Database Name property to see the three options:

Editing Database Name   The Edit option allows you to change the path to the PC-style database used in the report. If the location or name of the database has changed or will be different for the person to whom you are sending the report, you can change the path here. Changing the database filename in this path tells Crystal Reports to point to a database with the new name.

Same As Report Option   The Same As Report function will remove any drive letter and pathname from the PC-style database location. From that point forward, Crystal Reports will look for the database on the same disk drive and in the same folder as the report.

This allows you to create and save a report for distribution to other report viewers. The other viewers can place the report on any drive and in any folder that they choose. As long as the database the report is based on is in the same folder as the report, the report will be able to find it.

Converting to a UNC Name   The Convert To UNC function will change the hard-coded drive letter and path name for the PC-style database to a Uniform Naming Convention (UNC) name that can easily be found by any computer on the network, regardless of its drive mapping. UNC is a way of pointing to a file on a network disk drive without using a drive letter. Consider the following scenario:

Groucho\Databases mapped to drive H:
H:\Accounts.MDB

Groucho\Databases mapped to drive F:
F:\Accounts.MDB

LAN server Groucho

Databases

Accounts. MDB

The two PCs are connected to the same LAN server but use different drive letters to reach the server. If the first PC creates a report based on Accounts.mdb, the report will have the drive letter and filename H:\Accounts.mdb hard-coded into it. When the second PC opens the report, the report will fail—the database won't be found on drive H.

To avoid this kind of problem, you can use a UNC name to replace the drive letter. A UNC name appears in the following format:

\\<Server Name>\<Share Name>\<Path and Filename>

- *Server Name* is the actual name of the computer or server where the file is located (in this case, Groucho). Two backslash characters precede the server name.

- *Share Name* is a name that the LAN administrator has given to a particular group of shared files and folders on the server. When a PC maps a drive letter to a LAN server, the drive letter is mapped to a particular share name (in this case, Databases). A single backslash character separates the *Server Name* from the *Share Name.*

- *Path and Filename* are similar to path names and filenames used on a local PC hard drive, except they are located on the LAN server. In this case, the Accounts.MDB file is in the root of the Databases share name. A single backslash character separates the *Share Name* from the *Path and Filename* (and this path may contain additional backslash characters).

Based on these rules, the corresponding UNC name for the Accounts.MDB file will be as follows:

```
\\Groucho\Databases\Accounts.MDB
```

Notice that the drive letter has been removed. Now, any PC on the network can find the file based on the UNC name—the PC doesn't have to have a drive letter mapped to the LAN server.

Table Names vs. Aliases

When you first create a new report based on certain database tables, you'll notice that the actual name of the table you originally chose shows up in the Field Explorer, the Database Expert, and other places in the report. Although it may appear that Crystal Reports must refer to a database table by its physical name, this name is actually an *alias* assigned to the table. While the alias takes on the physical table name by default, it doesn't have to always keep that name. You have the flexibility to change the alias Crystal Reports uses to refer to this table.

To change the alias, display the Database Expert with the appropriate toolbar button or Database | Database Expert menu option. Choose the table you wish to assign a new alias by clicking it in the Selected Tables box on the right side of the Database Expert. Then, press the F2 key, right-click, and choose Rename from the pop-up menu, or simply hold your mouse button down on the table name for a few seconds. The table name will be placed in edit mode. Simply type a new alias name in for the table.

In some cases, Crystal Reports will add an alias for a table on its own. In particular, if you try to add the same table to a report more than once (perhaps your database contains a shared lookup table that must be added to a report multiple times), Crystal Reports will display a message indicated that duplicate table names aren't allowed. It will then add the table with a unique number appended to the end of the table name. If this new table name is not acceptable, you may supply a more appropriate table name using steps described previously.

Dealing with Table Name Changes   If a database designer or administrator changes the name of a table in the database, the next time you try to refresh your report, you will receive an error indicating that the table can't be found. Unfortunately, refreshing the report or verifying the database will not solve this problem—the message will persist and the report will not print properly.

To solve this problem, perform the following simple steps:

1. Use the Set Datasource Location function as described in this chapter to connect to the new data source (this may be as simple as contracting and re-expanding the category of the Database Expert where the original database was). Select the old table name in the Current Data Source list and the new table name in the Replace With list. Click Update. This will correctly point the report to the new table name. However, the table will still be referred to by the old name in the report.

2. If you want the new name to appear throughout the report, use the Database Expert to change the alias of the old table to the new table name as described earlier in the chapter. This will change the name of the table as well, avoiding confusion as to which physical table is actually being used.

Mapping Old Fields to New Names

Database changes can cause a mismatch of field names in your report. For example, your original report may be developed against a Microsoft Access database that includes a field named "Account Number" (note that the space between the words is significant to Crystal Reports). You may need to eventually have the same report work with a SQL Server database where the field is known as "Account_Number" (notice that the space has been replaced with an underscore).

Whenever Crystal Reports detects these kinds of database changes, it can't be sure which new database field the old report object should be associated with. By using Field Mapping, you can point the old object to the new database field. Field mapping simply allows you to change the field name that a report refers to, so that, for example, all objects that used to be associated with "Account Number" will now be associated with "Account_Number." No formulas have to be changed, no old objects have to be removed, and no new objects need to be added.

The Field Mapping function cannot be chosen from a menu. It is triggered when Crystal Reports detects any field name changes in the source database. Crystal Reports will check for these changes whenever you verify the database or use the Set Datasource Location function to change the database or data source connection. When Crystal Reports detects that fields in the report are no longer in the database, it displays the Map Fields dialog box, as shown in Figure 15-10.

The Map Fields dialog box is divided into four boxes or lists. The upper-left Unmapped Fields list shows report fields that don't match up to any field names in the new database. The upper-right list shows a choice of fields in the new database that you can map the report fields to. To map the report field to the new database field, select the report field you want to map in the upper-left box, select a matching database field in the upper-right box, and then click Map. The fields will be moved from the upper boxes to the lower boxes.

Limit the map-to list to fields of the same data type
as the selected field in the unmatched fields list

List of fields in the new database
that can be mapped to

Map the field selected in the upper-left
list to the field selected in the upper-right

List of report fields that
have no matching field
names in new database

List of report fields that
are already mapped to
the new database

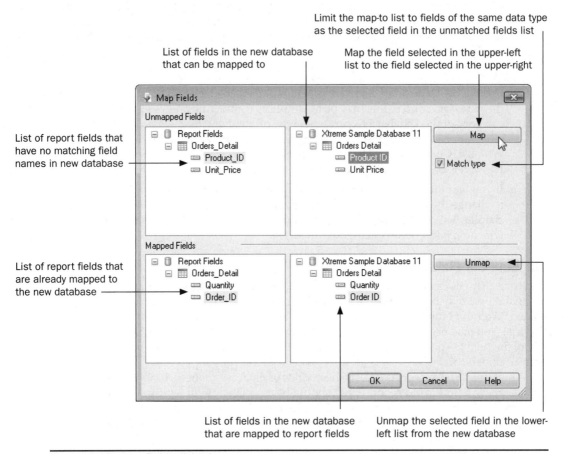

List of fields in the new database
that are mapped to report fields

Unmap the selected field in the lower-
left list from the new database

FIGURE 15-10   Map Fields dialog box

The list of database fields will change according to whether or not you click the Match Type check box on the right side of the dialog box. If the box is checked, only fields of the same data type (string, number, date, and so forth) as that of the selected report field will show up. This helps to ensure that you're making the correct match of fields, by not inadvertently mapping a string field on the report to a number or date field in the new database (although you may want to do this sometimes). There may be times that you won't see the field you want to map to in the right list, however, because of data type mismatches. For example, if you're remapping fields originally from a Microsoft Access database to a SQL Server database, you may not find any SQL Server field that matches a currency field in the Access database. In this situation, uncheck Match Type and look for the field to map to.

When the Map Fields dialog box first appears, some fields probably will already be present in the lower two Mapped Fields boxes. The lower-left list shows report fields that already have a matching field in the new database. And once you've mapped fields from the upper lists, they will be moved to the lower lists as well. If existing mapping was assumed by Crystal Reports (because of identical field names), or you mistakenly mapped fields that don't belong together, you can select a field in the lower-left or lower-right list. The mapped field will appear highlighted in the other box. You can then click Unmap to unmap the fields and move them back to the top lists.

Once you have finished mapping fields, click OK to close the Map Fields dialog box. Crystal Reports will now associate the mapped fields with the new database. The Design tab, as well as any formulas, will reflect the new field names. If additional tables have mismatched fields, you'll be presented with the Map Fields dialog box for each subsequent table.

CAUTION *Any fields that no longer exist in the source database must be remapped to new fields. If you don't map old field names to new fields, the old fields and objects they're based on will be deleted from your report.*

Performance Considerations

SQL databases (or PC-style databases accessed via ODBC) present a very different set of performance considerations than do PC-style databases. As has been discussed throughout the chapter, one of the main benefits of SQL databases over PC databases is the ability of the database server to perform record selection and grouping locally as soon as a SQL query is received from Crystal Reports. Only when the database server has performed record selection or grouping itself will it return the result set back to Crystal Reports.

Let the Server Do the Work

As a general reporting rule, you want to always have the database server perform as much of the processing as possible. Database server software is designed and tuned to perform just such operations, and server software is often placed on very high-end hardware platforms to enhance this performance even further. Any glitch that might cause the database server to send back every record in its database (million-plus-record SQL databases are not at all uncommon) to be selected or summarized locally by Crystal Reports will often result in unsatisfactory performance.

To see how much (or if any) of the query is being evaluated on the database server, view the query by choosing Database | Show SQL Query from the pull-down menus. Look at the SQL statement for the WHERE clause. If you don't see one, no selection at all will be done on the server—every record in the database will come down to the PC, to be left to Crystal Reports to sort through. This can be *very* time-consuming!

Look for an ORDER BY clause if you are sorting or grouping your report. If you see this clause, the database server will presort your data before sending it to Crystal Reports. This can speed the formatting of your report. If you don't see an ORDER BY clause but you specified grouping or sorting in your report, the server will send records to Crystal Reports unsorted, and the client will have to sort the records.

If you wish to use server-based grouping, make sure you see a GROUP BY clause in the query. This ensures that the server is grouping and aggregating data before sending it to Crystal Reports. If you don't see this clause, check back to the server-based grouping requirements in Table 15-1 earlier in this chapter.

To ensure record selection occurs on the server, Crystal Reports must convert your record-selection formula to a SQL WHERE clause. Several rules of thumb help to ensure that as much record selection as possible is converted to SQL and that it is done on the server:

- Don't base record selection on formula fields. Crystal Reports usually can't convert formulas to SQL, so most record selection based on formula fields will be passed on to Crystal Reports. Most *first-pass* formulas can be converted to SQL, while the remainder cannot. Look at the SQL query to ensure that any formulas you use in record selection are converted into WHERE clause SQL.

NOTE *See Chapter 4 for more information on what constitutes first-pass formulas.*

- Don't use the Crystal Reports formula language's built-in functions, such as ToText, in your selection criteria. Again, Crystal Reports usually can't convert these to SQL, so these parts of record selection won't be carried out on the server. You may be able to find a similar function in a SQL Expression field and use the expression in record selection.

Use Indexed Fields

In Crystal Reports, you'll typically see colored arrows in the Links tab of the Database Expert indicating fields that have been indexed by the database designer. Although you aren't typically required to link only on indexed fields, you may want to attempt links on indexed fields if possible anyway (provided the core design of the database will properly link tables if you do). Depending on the database system that you're using, linking to non-indexed fields or performing record selection on non-indexed fields can prove detrimental to the performance of your report. Most SQL database systems have indexing capabilities that the database designer probably considers when designing the database.

If at all possible, work with the database designer to ensure that indexes are created to solve not only your database application needs, but your reporting needs as well. Try to use indexed fields as much as possible as "to" fields in linking, and for record selection.

Also, it may improve performance to select records using as many fields as possible from the main or driving table. For example, you may have a main transaction table that is linked to five lookup tables, and you may want to use the descriptions from the lookup tables in record selection. Instead, consider using the fields in the *main* table for record selection (even if you have to use the codes in the main table, and not the descriptions from the lookup table). Again, if these fields in the main table are indexed, you'll probably see a performance improvement.

Reporting from Proprietary Data Types

C rystal Reports is best known as the "reporting tool of choice" for use with any standard corporate database. "Standard" databases might generally be thought to include Microsoft Access or SQL Server, Sybase, Oracle, IBM Informix and DB2, and others that are well known in the mainstream of corporate database technology.

But, what do you do if your data is contained in some other form of database or data file? Well, if the database or data file system is very proprietary and out of the mainstream, and the vendor doesn't provide an ODBC (open database connectivity) or OLE DB driver for the database, then you may be, quite simply, out of luck. However, many proprietary databases can be accessed via ODBC or OLE DB, which Crystal Reports will work with. You can also create reports against regular ASCII-delimited text files and against XML files that conform to certain standards. And, Crystal Reports supports other data types directly, without even requiring an ODBC driver. You can create reports based on Microsoft Exchange Server and Systems Management Server databases, the ubiquitous ACT! contact manager, Microsoft Outlook, Windows Server and XP event logs, Microsoft Customer Relationship Management data, and web server activity logs. And, Crystal Reports 2008 add the ability to report directly against your Salesforce.com web-based data, too.

The general approach for creating reports against these proprietary types of data sources is similar, regardless of the data source:

1. Ensure that the Crystal Reports Data Access driver you wish to report from is installed. If you're unsure, rerun Crystal Reports setup and expand the Data Access area to ensure that proper drivers have been installed. If you haven't done this in advance, you may be prompted to insert the Crystal Reports CD when you initially try to create a report based on a certain type of data.

2. Ensure that the software you want to report from (such as Microsoft Outlook), or the vendor's "client" application to access data (such as an Oracle database client), is installed on the same PC as Crystal Reports. Crystal Reports automatically detects these software packages and will list them when you choose a data source.

3. Create a new report using either the report wizards or the Blank Report option. Using either a wizard or the Blank Report option, expand the Create New Connection category of the Database Expert. Then, look for the type of data you want to report against (you may need to expand the More Data Sources folder). So, if you want to write reports against a Microsoft Exchange server, expand the More Data Sources folder from within the Create New Connection category and choose one of the Exchange data types.

4. Follow any prompts specific to the data source, such as choosing an Exchange server and profile. You'll then see a list of tables and/or fields that are specific to that data type. Use them in your report just as you would use other database tables and fields.

This chapter will focus on several commonly used data types: Microsoft Outlook, file system data (basically, the disk directory on a PC or network disk drive), the Windows event log, and standard web server activity logs.

In addition, the chapter covers enhanced XML reporting capabilities added to Crystal Reports 2008, reporting from a BusinessObjects Enterprise XI 3.0 Universe, and Salesforce.com reporting (also newly added to Crystal Reports 2008).

Reporting from Microsoft Outlook

Microsoft Outlook has become a popular standard on office desktops, because it smoothly integrates e-mail, contact management, and calendar maintenance in one package. Outlook's folder metaphor is handy for organizing your office affairs, and it's also handy for reporting.

The first requirement for creating a Crystal Report based on your Outlook folders is rather obvious—you must have Outlook installed on your PC. More specifically, you must have Outlook installed on the same computer on which you will be running Crystal Reports. Crystal Reports won't report on any other Outlook systems on the network—just your own.

To report on your Outlook data, start a new report just as you would for a standard database. You can use the report wizards or the Blank Report option. In either case, expand the Create New Connection category and then expand the Outlook folder. If you have not reported from Outlook before, or there is more than one Outlook Profile on your system, you'll be presented with the Choose Profile dialog box, and you will need to select your profile (or the default Microsoft Outlook profile) from the drop-down list and click OK. Then you'll be presented with the Choose Folder dialog box, showing the folder hierarchy of your Outlook data. Choose the folder that you want to report on, and click OK.

NOTE   *In order to use Outlook as a data source with Crystal Reports, you need to use the full version of Microsoft Outlook. Outlook Express is not available for use in Crystal Reports.*

CAUTION *You cannot report on the Notes folder. You'll receive an error message if you try to select it.*

After you choose the folder and click OK, a "table" will appear in the Available Data Sources list. Select and add the folder just as you would any database table. When you close the Database Expert or advance to the next wizard area, the list of Outlook fields you can report from will appear in the expert or in the Field Explorer.

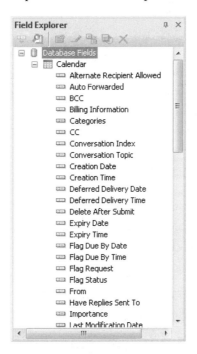

Use the Outlook fields just like other database fields to create your report. You can sort, group, and format the report as you normally would. You can also create formulas, if necessary, to calculate or modify the way Outlook material appears in the report. Figure 16-1 shows a sample report based on the Calendar folder from Outlook.

NOTE *The field names you see in the Crystal Reports Field Explorer may not always match the field names you see in Outlook. If you don't see the field you expect, look for a reasonable alternative field name. Also, you may need to add other Outlook folders (such as the Contact folder and the Inbox folder) and link the two together to get all the data you expect. Make sure you link on correct fields—Auto Linking typically won't pick the correct fields to perform an Outlook link.*

Reporting from the File System Data

You are probably familiar with Explorer, the Windows application that helps you view the hierarchy and layout of your local and network drives, as well as locate one or more

Figure 16-1 Crystal Report based on the Outlook Calendar folder

particular files you may be looking for. However, if you want a more powerful reporting-type tool to search or report on drive contents, you need another software solution.

Crystal Reports provides the file system data option, allowing you to write powerful reports against any local or network drive on your PC. By choosing a drive and folder or directory, as well as specifying some detailed criteria (if you choose), you can create reports that select and sort files and folders with the complete power and flexibility of Crystal Reports.

To report on your file system data, start a new report just as you would for a standard database. You can use the report wizards or the Blank Report option. When choosing a database, expand the File System Data folder in the Create New Connection category.

You'll be presented with the File System Data dialog box, shown in Figure 16-2. If you simply want to supply a drive or path name, you can either type it or click the ellipses button to navigate to the desired drive and directory. You may also add some additional criteria to narrow down the files and directories you want to see.

Choose whether to include all files or only
those that match wildcard pattern

Type or choose a directory
to report on

Choose whether to include all subdirectories, or only *N* levels deep
(you must uncheck Include All Subdirectories to see this)

Include directory names
even if they contain no files

Figure 16-2   The File System Data dialog box

Make your choices and click Finish. A table entry in the Database Expert Available Data
Sources list will appear, showing the directory you chose. Add it to the Selected tables list to
proceed.

The Field Explorer will expose many different fields containing information you might
not have previously been familiar with. Some fields apply only to certain types of files, such
as .EXE or .DLL files. Others apply only to files that belong to certain applications (for example,
Number of Words generally applies only to Word or other word processing documents).
Use these file system fields just like other database fields to create your report. You can sort,
group, and format the report as you normally would. You can use the fields to create flexible
selection criteria to narrow down your report. You can also create formulas, if necessary, to
calculate or modify the way file system material appears in the report. Figure 16-3 shows a
sample report based on a local C disk drive.

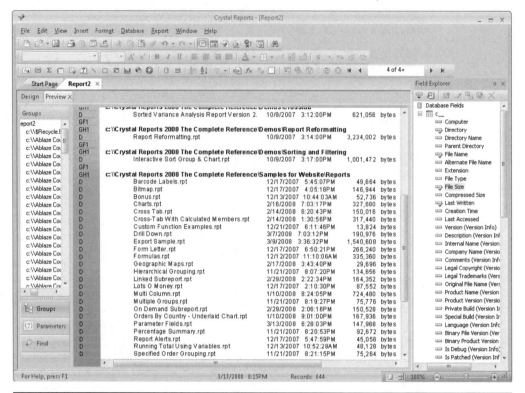

FIGURE 16-3   Crystal Report based on file system data

Reporting from the Windows Event Log

An integrated part of the original Microsoft Windows NT operating system, and its successors Windows 2000, XP, and Windows Server, is the event log. The event logs are files that document events that occur during the general operation of Windows. Several different types of event logs are available, and different types of entries are placed in the event logs as users log on and off, and programs start, stop, and operate. Crystal Reports includes the capability to create flexible reports on these event logs.

NOTE   *Although designing reports against the event logs won't harm the computer containing the log, you probably won't find the information returned to be of much use if you're not generally familiar with Windows and its components. This Crystal Reports capability will probably be most useful to system administrators and other technical personnel.*

To report on event logs, start a new report just as you would for a standard database. You can use the report wizards or the Blank Report option. In either case, expand the NT Current Event Log folder in the Create New Connection category to report on current active event logs on Windows computers. Or, you can click the NT Archived Event Log folder to display an Open File dialog box in which to search for archived (.EVT) event log files. If you use this option, upon selecting an event log you will be presented with the Select Archived Event Log dialog box, and you must identify the type of event log you selected (System, Security, or Application).

If you choose the NT Current Event Log folder, you'll see the Select Current Event Log dialog box, shown in Figure 16-4. This allows you to select an event log on a remote computer—it doesn't have to reside on the computer that you are running Crystal Reports on. You can even include event logs from more than one computer at a time in your report, if you choose.

If you know the domain and computer name, you can simply type it in the Computer(s) text box at the top of the dialog box. If you include more than one computer name, separate the names with commas. If you're not sure which computers to include, you can use the Explorer-like hierarchy to select the computers you wish to use. When you see the computer list, you can select one or more computers.

Make your choices and click OK. A new level in the Database Expert will appear for the computer you've chosen, showing the three event logs that are available as tables: Application, Security, and System.

Depending on the types of events you want your report to be based on, choose the appropriate log. If you'd like a better idea of what types of events are contained in each log, use the Event Viewer application from the Windows Control Panel to view the different event log entries. Once you've made your log choice, the list of event log fields you can report on will appear in the expert or in the Field Explorer.

FIGURE 16-4
The Select Current Event Log dialog box

Type in one or more computer names, separated by commas

Use the plus and minus signs or double-click to navigate through your network hierarchy

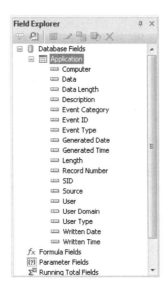

Use these event log fields just like other database fields to create your report. You can sort, group, and format the report as you normally would. The Event Viewer application can help you identify what some of the available fields contain. You can use the fields to create flexible selection criteria to narrow down your report, and you can also create formulas, if necessary, to calculate or modify the way event-log material appears in the report. Figure 16-5 shows a sample report based on a Windows NT application event log.

Reporting from Web Server Logs

It's now a given that most organizations need to document what pages web users are pointing their browsers to, as well as when and from where. Virtually all Windows and Unix/Linux web servers keep various amounts and levels of data about web site visits. What better tool to create web activity reports than Crystal Reports?

There are several types of web server logs that you may encounter, depending mostly on the web server that you are using. Most web server logs are standard delimited ASCII files (a term you don't necessarily need to be familiar with, but it is a common denominator for data-file formats). However, the layout of fields in the files and the information they contain can vary from server to server. There are several "standard" types of log files, including a file type simply known as Standard, and another known as the NCSA Standard, defined by the National Center for Supercomputing Applications for its original web server. Other web server developers have adopted both standards. In addition, if you are using Microsoft Internet Information Server (IIS), you'll find additional types of log files available, such as Microsoft's extended log format. When you configure IIS, you can choose the type of log file that is generated, as well as the fields that are kept in the log file.

As a general rule, web servers will create a new log file every day, adding statistics to the daily log file as they occur. The filenames consist of variations of the date on which they were created, with a standard file extension. For example, you may see a file named EX080302.LOG, indicating a Microsoft extended-format log for March 2, 2008. These files

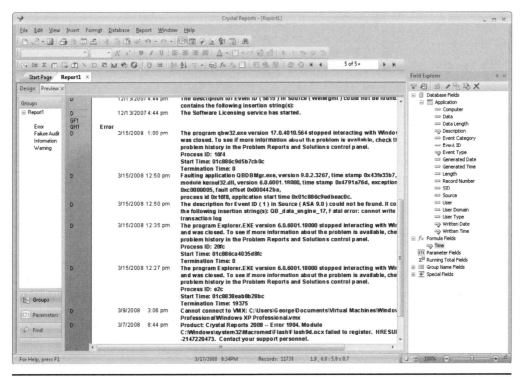

FIGURE 16-5   Crystal Report based on event log

will be located in a standard directory, such as WINDOWS\system32\LogFiles\W3SVC1 (this is the default location for Microsoft IIS versions running on Windows Server 2003).

To report on web server logs, start a new report just as you would for a standard database. You can use the report wizards or the Blank Report option. In either case, expand the Create New Connection category of the Database Expert to proceed. You'll see two categories that may interest you: MS IIS/Proxy Log Files and Web/IIS Log Files. MS IIS/ Proxy Log Files will report on "standard" formats, the various Microsoft IIS formats, and Web Proxy and Winsock Proxy formats. The Web/IIS Log Files folder will simply report on "standard" and NCSA formatted logs.

Regardless of whether you're using a wizard or the Blank Report option, the rest of the prompts will be consistent. If you choose the more generic Web Log option, you'll simply be prompted to choose a drive and directory where the standard or NCSA Web logs are located. You can type or browse to select a local or network drive and directory. If you choose the IIS option, you'll see the Select Log Files And Dates dialog box, as illustrated in Figure 16-6.

Choose the type of log file your web server uses (look for files in a standard location with the .LOG extension to help determine this). You can also choose the format your web server uses when writing log files, based on how often it creates a new log file. And, if you prefer to limit Crystal Reports to using only log files within a certain date range, make that selection as well.

Choose type of log
file to report on

Choose which log files to
include in your report

Choose directory where
log files are located

Limit to logs created
during a date range

FIGURE 16-6 IIS Select Log Files and Dates dialog box

When you're finished with your choices, click OK. A new database entry will appear in the Available Data Sources list of the Database Expert showing the directory name of the log files. Underneath this category, a table-type entry will appear, showing a somewhat cryptic entry for the log files you just chose. Add this table to your report (by double-clicking the table name, dragging it to the Selected Tables list, or selecting the table name and clicking the right arrow) and close the Database Expert. The list of web server log fields you can report from will appear in the wizard or in the Field Explorer.

NOTE *The log fields you see here will vary, depending on the web server you are using and the log settings you've chosen for that web server. If you're using Microsoft IIS with Windows 2000, XP, or 2003 Server, you can configure the server to include a variety of helpful statistical fields.*

Use these web server log fields just like other database fields when creating your report. You can sort, group, and format the report as you normally would. You can use the fields to create flexible selection criteria to narrow down your report. You can also create formulas, if necessary, to calculate or modify the way web server log material appears in the report. Figure 16-7 shows a sample report based on a Windows 2003 Server web server log.

FIGURE 16-7   Crystal Report based on IIS web server log

Crystal Reporting with XML Data Sources

As Extensible Markup Language, or *XML*, becomes more of a standard data interchange format (both in Windows and Unix/Linux environments), the need for a robust reporting tool increases as well. Crystal Reports includes flexible and comprehensive support for reporting from XML data sources.

While overall Crystal Reports 2008 XML support hasn't changed radically, improvements to web service XML compatibility have been added, allowing connection to more types of XML-based web service data sources. Crystal Reports 2008 reads XML data via a "native" XML driver that reads XML data directly (either from a data file located on a local or network drive, or from a network or Internet "stream") and processes the XML data as though it were a standard database with consistent table and field formats.

Using Local XML Data Sources

A *local* XML data source is XML-formatted data that resides on your computer's local disk, or a network-connected disk. Typically, XML-formatted data consists of two parts: the data file itself, and a *schema* file that describes the organization of the XML data file. While Crystal Reports can report on XML data only without a matching schema file, the XML data must meet very specific requirements in order for Crystal Reports to determine the organization of the XML.

Consider Figure 16-8, beginning with a sample customer XML data file. A cursory look will give you a general idea of the layout of the data in the XML file. However, most XML-compliant software programs, including Crystal Reports, will benefit from a schema file

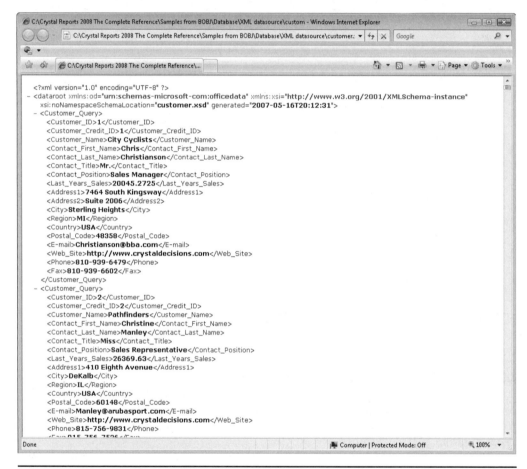

FIGURE 16-8A   Sample XML data file

that specifically defines the XML data layout. The second part of Figure 16-8 illustrates such a schema file. Crystal Reports generally requires you to specify both a data file and a schema file when reporting on local XML data sources.

To report on local XML data, start a new report just as you would for a standard database. Expand the Create New Connection section of the Available Data Sources list, and then select the XML entry. The XML dialog box will appear, where you can specify your local data and schema files.

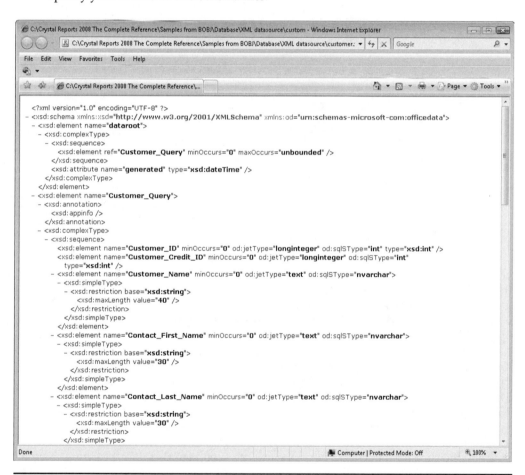

Figure 16-8b   Sample XML schema file

Select the Use Local Data Source radio button. Then, type the full path/file name for your XML data file into the box below the radio button, or click the ellipsis button to find the file from a standard Open dialog box.

Unless the XML data file is well formed, allowing Crystal Reports to determine its layout without a schema file (few "real world" XML files meet this criterion), you'll need to check Specify Schema File and provide the location for the schema file on the next portion of the XML dialog box. Checking Validate XML will force Crystal Reports to compare the XML data and schema files to ensure that they match (this option will most probably increase processing time before XML tables appear in the Database Expert). And, checking the Convert Multi-Occurs To Table check box will organize certain types of repetitive XML data into a more logical table structure.

Click Next to specify the matching schema file. If the schema file is also located on a local drive or network drive, check the Use Local Schema radio button and type the full path and filename for the schema file in the text box (you may also click the ellipses button to navigate to the schema file). If the data file happens to have a common schema file located on an intranet or Internet site, you may click Use HTTP(S) schema and type in the URL in the associated text box.

When you have specified local XML data and schema filenames and options, click Finish. The XML dialog box will close and Crystal Reports will attempt to interpret the data and schema files. When this process is complete, resulting tables will appear in the Database Expert underneath the XML data source in the Available Data Sources box. Choose the desired table or tables and move them to the Selected Tables box by dragging and dropping, double-clicking, or using the right-arrow button.

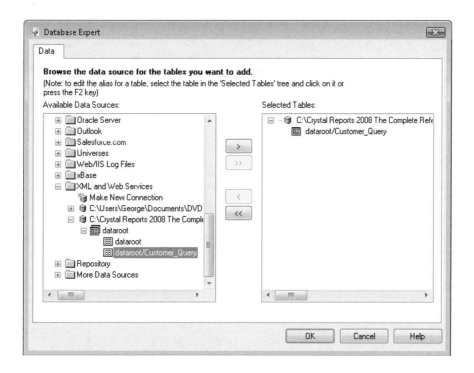

Click OK to close the Database Expert. Crystal Reports will now interpret XML data the same as it does standard database data. Field names will appear in the Field Explorer, where they may be dragged and dropped onto the Design tab, just like standard database fields. Preview the report to see the resulting XML data.

CAUTION *XML data is read by Crystal Reports sequentially from the top of the data file to the bottom. Large XML data files will typically perform slower in Crystal Reports that traditional SQL-based relational database files.*

Using Web-Based XML Data Sources

As the XML standard largely grew out of HTML, the original "language of the web," it's not surprising that a large amount of XML data that's becoming available is exposed via the Internet or a company intranet. This XML data is generally made available in two broad categories. First, individual XML data files and schema files can be served from a standard web server. And, data is also provided via XML Web Services, which provide a more robust and customizable approach to integrating web-based XML data with custom applications, as well as reporting environments, such as Crystal Reports.

Internet/Intranet-Based XML Data and Schema Files

Using XML data and schema files hosted on a web server is largely the same as using local XML files (covered earlier in the chapter under "Using Local XML Data Sources." Start a new report just as you would for a standard database. Expand the Create New Connection section of the Available Data Sources list, and then select the XML entry. The XML dialog box will appear, where you can specify your web-based data and schema files.

Click the Use HTTP(S) Data Source radio button and type in the URL to your data source in the associated text box. Precede the URL with either an HTTP:// or HTTPS:// protocol designator, depending on whether the web server you will connect to supports a secure sockets layer connection or not. As with a local XML data source, you may choose whether or not to supply a schema file, whether to have Crystal Reports validate the XML data against its schema, and how to treat multi-occurs in the underlying XML data file. Then, click Next.

If the URL you supplied for the XML Data File requires authentication, supply the proper user ID and password on the HTTP Authentication for XML File screen. If the data source is not secure, you may leave these fields blank. Click Next to advance to the Schema File Type And Location screen.

If you have a copy of the schema file for the web-based data source on your local hard drive or a network drive, click the Use Local Schema radio button and type or navigate to the schema file. If the schema is, like the XML data file, stored on a web server, click the Use HTTP(S) Schema radio button and type the URL for the schema in the associated text box, using the proper HTTP:// or HTTPS:// protocol designator. Click Next, and specify the user ID and password required to access the schema file, if it's stored on a secure server. If the URL you initially supplied for the XML data file doesn't include prompts or parameters, you may click Finish. Otherwise, click Next to supply URL parameter values.

The HTTP Parameters screen will appear, where you may supply different values for parameter portions of the URL that Crystal Reports detects (known as *HTTP Parameters*). You may supply fixed values for these, or even supply an @PROMPT formula that will create a report parameter field to prompt for a variable value every time the report is refreshed (exact argument descriptions for the @PROMPT formula can be found in online help).

Once you have finished all entries on the XML dialog box, click Finish. The dialog box will close and Crystal Reports will attempt to interpret the data and schema files. When this process is complete, resulting tables will appear in the Database Expert underneath the XML data source in the Available Data Sources box. Choose the desired table or tables and move them to the Selected Tables box by dragging and dropping, double-clicking, or using the right-arrow button.

Click OK to close the Database Expert. Crystal Reports will now interpret XML data the same as it does standard database data. Field names will appear in the Field Explorer, where they may be dragged and dropped onto the Design tab, just like standard database fields. Preview the report to see the resulting XML data.

XML Data from Web Services

A more defined and structured method of obtaining XML data from Internet and intranet sources is the *web service*. Web services provide structured XML data to custom applications (and other applications such as Crystal Reports) via standard Internet protocols, but with additional capabilities beyond the standard XML data and schema file described earlier in the chapter. Instead of a schema file to describe XML data, web services make use of a Web Service Description Language, or WSDL, file. This file describes the various data types and options the web service exposes.

The initial steps to creating a report based on a web service is the same as creating other XML-based reports. Start a new report just as you would for a standard database. Expand the Create New Connection section of the Available Data Sources list, and then select the

XML entry. The XML dialog box will appear. The only option on the first screen to consider is Convert Multi-Occurs To Table, which indicates how certain formations of XML data will be treated by Crystal Reports. The other choice is the Use Web Service Data Source, which you should click. Then, click Next.

The Web Service Location screen will appear, where you specify the location of the Web Service Description Language (WSDL) file that describes the web service. If the WSDL file is located on a local or network drive, click the Use Local WSDL radio button and type or browse to the local file. If the WSDL file is located on an Internet or intranet server, click the Use HTTP(S) WSDL radio button and type in the URL to the WSDL file in the appropriate text box. Use the required HTTP:// or HTTPS:// protocol designator, depending on whether the server supports secure sockets layer security or not. Crystal Reports 2008 introduces WS-Security support, which you may use by checking the appropriate check box and then typing or browsing to the local WS-Security specification file. Click Next.

If the web service you are going to use requires authentication, supply the proper user ID and password on the Authentication For HTTP WSDL URL screen. If the data source is not secure, you may leave these fields blank. Click Next to advance to the Web Service, Port, And Method screen.

The WSDL file will retrieve specifications for the web service that populate the values on the Web Service, Port, And Method screen. Display the drop-down lists to make desired choices for web service data. If the web service requires a user ID and password for authentication, these fields will be enabled. Enter your user ID and password.

Once you have finished all entries on the XML dialog box, click Finish. The dialog box will close and Crystal Reports will attempt to interpret the data exposed by the web service. When this process is complete, resulting tables will appear in the Database Expert underneath the XML data source in the Available Data Sources box. Choose the desired table or tables and move them to the Selected Tables box by dragging and dropping, double-clicking, or using the right-arrow button.

Click OK to close the Database Expert. Crystal Reports will now interpret XML data the same as it does standard database data. Field names will appear in the Field Explorer, where they may be dragged and dropped onto the Design tab, just like standard database fields. Preview the report to see the resulting web service data.

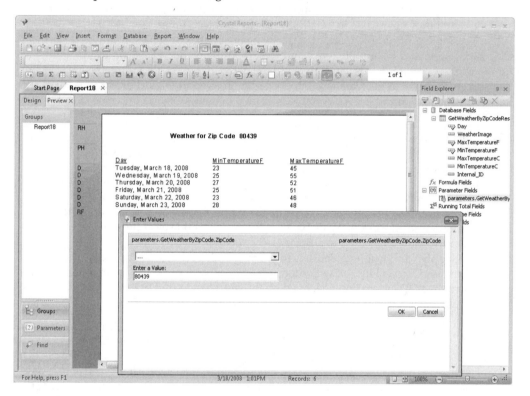

NOTE   *As many web service data sources parameterize their internal XML queries, Crystal Reports will often create automatic report parameter fields to match the web service. You'll be prompted to supply these values when initially adding the web service to the report, and when you refresh the report later on. Supply parameter values as you do for other parameterized reports (parameter fields are discussed in Chapter 13).*

BusinessObjects Enterprise Universes

Crystal Reports allows you to connect to many types of databases using different database drivers. Often, you'll find yourself designing reports directly with database tables, which often number in the hundreds. And, many databases are composed of confusing table and field names. One way to simplify database structures for query and report designers is by use of *metadata* products. These products allow a person intricately knowledgeable of database design to create a simplified "view" of the database, prejoining tables together, creating easy-to-understand table and field names, and creating formulas and calculations in advance and embedding them in the metadata. Then, the report designer can start report design right away, without having to muddle through complex database structures first.

One example of a metadata tool built into BusinessObjects Enterprise XI 3.0 is the *Universe*. While Crystal Reports is able to report directly against database tables, traditional Business Objects tools, such as Web Intelligence and Desktop Intelligence, must connect to a universe for reporting. Crystal Reports can connect to the native database, or a universe. By selecting the Universes option in the Database Expert (either in a report wizard or with the Blank Report option), you may base a Crystal Report on a Business Objects universe.

NOTE *Only universes contained within a BusinessObjects Enterprise (BOE) system may be used as a Crystal Reports data source. Older versions of universes not contained in a BusinessObjects Enterprise system are not available as Crystal Reports data sources.*

To base a report on a universe, start a new report just as you would for a standard database. You can use the report wizards or the Blank Report option. Expand the Create New Connection section of the Available Data Sources list and select the Universes category. If you are not already logged on to a BusinessObjects Enterprise system, you'll be prompted to log on. Supply valid logon credentials to connect to the desired BOE system.

The BusinessObjects Enterprise Explorer dialog box will appear, showing only universe objects from the BOE system you've logged on to. Select the desired universe and click Open. The Business Objects Query Panel will appear, as shown in Figure 16-9.

NOTE *The initial release of Crystal Reports 2008 does not include BusinessObjects Enterprise connectivity. Upgrade to Crystal Reports 2008 Service Pack 0, or a later upgrade, to enable universe capabilities. Once you've performed this upgrade, remember that you will only be able to connect to a member of the BusinessObjects Enterprise XI 3.0 family. Connecting to earlier BusinessObjects Enterprise versions isn't supported.*

If you've used other Business Objects products, you may be familiar with the Query Panel. Ultimately, you make choices in this panel to create SQL (Structured Query Language) that will be returned to the Database Expert as a SQL Command (covered in more detail in

Give query name for use in
Database Expert

Create combined UNION query
Add subquery to Filter panel
Create database ranking (Top/Botto
Click to see resulting SQL

Set detailed properties for
Universe query

Drag to Result Objects pane to include on report

Drag to Query Filters pane to create a filter
(record selection)

FIGURE 16-9   Query Panel based on universe

Chapter 15). Simply drag objects from the left-hand pane to the Result Objects pane (you may also double-click a desired object) to include the object on the report. To add a filter to limit the report to a specific set of database records, drag an object from either the object list or the Result Objects pane to the Query Filters pane. A separate dialog box will appear where

...ou may specify filter criteria (including the ability to base the filter on a prompt, as you do when creating a parameter field with a SQL Command or in a report).

More advanced Query Panel features are available with four buttons at the top of the Query Panel.

You may see the SQL that your query will produce by clicking the small SQL button. You may also combine multiple queries together (specifically, create a SQL UNION) by clicking the Combine Queries button. And, there are also buttons to create a subquery (another separate query that can be used as part of a filter), and a database ranking (the ability to set a Top N or Bottom N criteria within the database query itself). Finally, the Properties button at the bottom left of the Query Panel will present a separate dialog box where you may choose more specific properties for the Universe query.

Once you've completed work with the Query Panel, click OK to save the query and return to the Database Expert or wizard. The query you created will appear underneath the Universes category of the Available Data Sources list. Add it to the report, as you would any other database table (Crystal Reports will treat it as a SQL Command). If you wish to view the SQL that the query creates, you may right-click the query in the Selected Tables list and choose View Command from the pop-up menu. If you wish to edit the query, right-click the query in the Selected Tables list and choose Edit Command from the pop-up menu. The Query Panel will reappear, where you may make changes to the query. You may also redisplay the query panel after you've closed the Database Expert by choosing Database | Query Panel from the pull-down menus.

NOTE *The other BusinessObjects Enterprise "metalayer" tool that Crystal Reports makes use of is Business Views. An extra online chapter devoted to designing and reporting with Business Views is available on this book's companion web site, CrystalBook.com.*

Reporting with Salesforce.com Web Data

Several terms refer to the newest approach to enterprise software hosted on the web, the first being ASP (for application service provider), and more recently, "Software as a Service." However it's termed, this trend continues to appeal to organizations that would rather not provide a hardware/server environment or support for complex internal software systems. By simply using software hosted on the vendor's web servers, application implementation and upgrades are virtually seamless to the customer. Perhaps the best-known leader in this area is Salesforce.com, an early entrant into the web-based software arena with its now ubiquitous Customer Relationship Management system.

One of the immediate questions that may come to mind with this type of environment is, "How do I get to my data if it's hosted outside our organization?" For many web-based software systems, this is a valid question. However, with the expansion of web services (discussed earlier in this chapter) and other server-hosted database connection possibilities, this is becoming less of a significant issue. Crystal Reports 2008 eliminates this question as it pertains to Salesforce.com by including a Salesforce.com database driver (some previous versions of Crystal Reports could connect if you obtained a Salesforce.com add-on product). Once you've set up your Salesforce.com account, you may simply log on to it from the Crystal Reports 2008 Database Expert to create your own reports using data stored on the Salesforce.com servers.

Create a new report as you normally would with the wizards or the Blank Report option. When the Database Expert appears, expand the Create New Connection category and click the plus sign next to Salesforce.com. The Salesforce.com logon dialog box will appear, prompting for a server name, user ID, and password. Typically, the default www.salesforce. com server name will suffice (unless you are instructed by Salesforce.com to use an alternate server). Supply your standard Salesforce.com user ID and password and click OK.

CAUTION *You may be required to add the IP address of your computer to a "trusted servers" list on your Salesforce.com account before you can connect via Crystal Reports. Alternatively, you may log on to your web-based Salesforce.com account and request a Security Token, which you must append to your regular Salesforce.com password.*

Once you've successfully logged on, the Salesforce.com section of the Database Expert's Available Data Sources box will expand, showing all available Salesforce.com tables and stored procedures. Expand the desired category and add one or more tables to the Selected Tables list as you normally do. And, just as with a standard relational database, you will need to link tables together on the Links tab. When you are finished adding and linking tables, click OK to close the Database Expert.

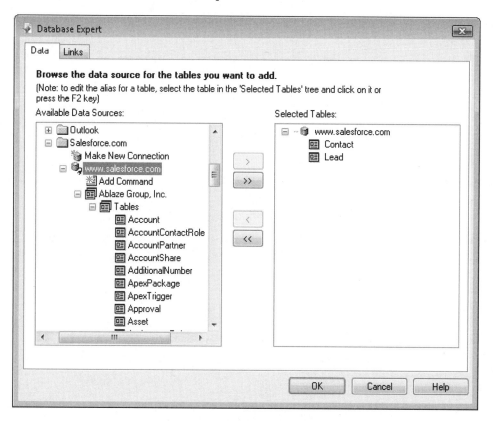

Crystal Reports will display Salesforce.com fields in the Field Explorer, just as with standard databases. Drag and drop fields to the report, create formulas, format objects, and perform other standard report design steps. When you preview the report, your Salesforce.com data will appear just as though it came from a local database.

Reporting from OLAP Cubes

Relational database systems provide the vast majority of the data analysis and reporting capabilities that most organizations need. However, a smaller segment of many organizations can benefit from more flexible and sophisticated analysis tools. In many cases, an organization's higher-level analysts are still using spreadsheet tools in combination with relational databases to make strategic company decisions.

Online analytical processing (OLAP) is a newer analysis technique that provides much more flexibility in analyzing company data. Crystal Reports supports most standard OLAP tools and enables you to create reports based on these database systems.

What Is OLAP?

Most typical company data is viewed in two dimensions, whether it is viewed by a reporting tool such as Crystal Reports or a spreadsheet program such as Microsoft Excel. In the case of a spreadsheet, the rows and columns constitute the two-dimensional analysis. You may be viewing product sales by state, salesperson volume by product category, or customer totals by demographics. In each of these cases, you typically can see only two dimensions at any one time, even though you actually may prefer to analyze a combination of three or more of these factors.

Product \ Region	USA	CAN	UK
PROD 1	534	212	231
PROD 2	45	21	12
PROD 3	321	324	112
PROD 4	204	120	40
PROD 5	78	43	31
PROD 6	32	12	2
PROD 7	786	512	49
PROD 8	123	23	17

Online analytical processing is a leading-edge analysis approach that allows data to be analyzed and viewed in multiple dimensions in real time. With a typical OLAP tool, you may initially be presented with a spreadsheet-like view that shows information using two dimensions, such as product sales dollars by state (or perhaps by country or region, allowing drill-down to the state level). This initial two-dimensional view is natural—despite the ability of OLAP tools to analyze multiple dimensions, most people still readily conceive data only in two dimensions.

Even though only two dimensions are visible, additional dimensions are available "behind the scenes" to control the two dimensions you are viewing; you can limit dollars by state by using other dimensions. Perhaps you want to see dollars by state limited to just certain sales reps, certain customer demographics, or certain product categories—you still see the original Dollars and State dimensions, but the numbers are filtered by the other dimensions. You may also want to quickly see sales by product category, demographics by state, or some other combinations of dimensions. Using an OLAP analysis tool, "slicing and dicing" through the different dimensions is typically as easy as dragging and dropping one dimension on top of another. Figure 17-1 shows the multidimensional "Adventure Works" sample database used with Microsoft SQL Server 2005 Analysis Services.

Whereas relational databases represent data in a two-dimensional, row-and-column (or field-and-record) structure, OLAP databases utilize a multidimensional structure known as a cube (which, despite its name, is capable of storing more than three dimensions of data). Often, cubes are built on the basis of regular relational database systems—the relational

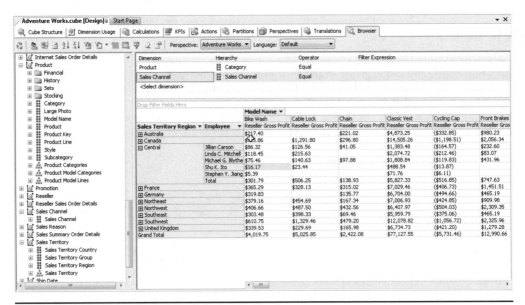

Figure 17-1 SQL Server Analysis tool viewing OLAP cube

database is populated using typical data-entry or data-import techniques, and a cube is built that is based on the relational database. Cubes can be refreshed or repopulated on a regular basis to allow multidimensional, real-time analysis of the data in the relational database.

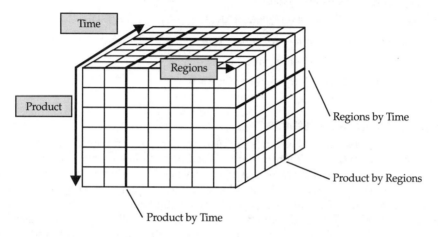

Crystal Reports OLAP Capabilities

You might ask, "Where does Crystal Reports fit into all of this?" Crystal Reports, obviously, can report on the data stored in the two-dimensional relational database. However, Crystal Reports also allows reporting against many industry-leading OLAP cubes. In fact, Crystal Reports can combine reports that are based on both relational databases and OLAP cubes, all in the same report. You have several choices:

- Create a standard report against the relational database the cube is based on.
- Create an OLAP-only report based solely on the cube.
- Create a standard report against a relational database (either the same database the cube is based on or an entirely different database) and include an OLAP report based on a cube inside the standard report.
- Create several different OLAP reports based on the same, or different, cubes. These OLAP-based reports can exist individually or be included together inside a standard report based on a relational database.

Supported OLAP Systems

While OLAP technology has been somewhat fragmented and proprietary until recently, industry standards are starting to emerge. Crystal Reports will work with leading proprietary

OLAP databases, as well as with the emerging Open OLAP standard. Thus, Crystal Reports can create OLAP reports based on the following tools:

- Hyperion Essbase and System 9
- Microsoft SQL Server 2000/2005 Analysis Services via OLE DB
- OLE DB for OLAP sources (or other "Open OLAP" sources)
- SAP BW (with the SAP Integration Kit)
- BusinessObjects OLAP Intelligence (.CAR file)

OLAP Report Creation Methods

There are several ways Crystal Reports can be used to report on your OLAP data. While all OLAP reporting in Crystal Reports will be based on the same type of object (the OLAP grid), there are several ways to create it. An OLAP grid is very similar in appearance and functionality to a cross-tab object (discussed in detail in Chapter 8). An OLAP grid displays one or more cube dimensions in rows and columns on the report. As with a cross-tab, you may format individual rows and columns to appear as you wish. You may also easily swap, or pivot, the rows and columns to change the appearance of the OLAP grid. And, you can launch the OLAP Analyzer, an interactive viewer similar to full interactive OLAP analysis products, to conduct real-time "slice and dice" analysis of your OLAP data right from within Crystal Reports.

Creating reports with OLAP cubes is straightforward and very similar to creating reports with regular relational databases. You may either use the OLAP Report Creation Wizard right from the Start page or File | New menu option, or add an OLAP grid object to a report you've already created using a standard relational database. The OLAP Report Creation Wizard leads you step-by-step through choosing the cube and dimensions you want to use in the row and column of your report. It will then create a report containing an OLAP grid. If you add an OLAP grid object to your report manually, you can make similar choices to that of the OLAP Report Creation Wizard to construct the OLAP grid (this is similar to creating a cross-tab object).

Using the OLAP Report Creation Wizard

The OLAP Report Creation Wizard is available from the Start page that appears when you start Crystal Reports. Just click the OLAP Cube Report Wizard link under the Start a New Report category. You may also choose File | New | OLAP Cube Report from the pull-down menus.

The OLAP Data dialog displays first in the Report Creation Wizard, to allow you to identify the OLAP cube you wish to base your OLAP report on.

Click the Select Cube button to display the OLAP Connection Browser, where you can choose from the OLAP cube connections available. If you wish to report on a Crystal Analysis Professional/BusinessObjects OLAP Intelligence .CAR file, you can click CAR; CAR files are found through the standard Open dialog, rather than the OLAP Connection Browser used for most OLAP connections.

Use the OLAP Connection Browser tree to navigate to the OLAP cube you want to report on, then select it and click Open, or simply double-click the OLAP cube. If you don't see the desired OLAP cube, you may need to click Add to display the Connection Properties dialog box, where you may add an additional OLAP connection.

Depending on the type of cube and location of the OLAP database, complete the fields in the Connection Properties dialog box. If you are using a Microsoft Analysis Services cube with SQL Server 2000, choose the Microsoft OLE DB Provider for OLAP Services 8.0 server type. SQL Server 2005 Analysis Services makes use of the OLE DB Provider for Analysis Services 9.0. In either case, you'll then need to specify the server name, user ID, and password in the following three fields (the user ID and password may not be required). If you have been provided with an Analysis Services local cube (.CUB) file, select the Local Cube file radio button and type in or navigate to the .CUB file. Or, if you've been instructed to connect to the Analysis Services server via HTTP (the standard Internet protocol), select the HTTP Cube radio button and type in the URL to the server, along with your user name and password.

If you choose other OLAP Server Types, appropriate options will appear in the Connection Properties dialog box for connecting to the associated cube. If you are unsure of how to connect to your particular cube type, consult with the administrator of your OLAP database.

TIP   *If your OLAP server doesn't appear in the Server Type drop-down list, you may need to install client software specific to your particular OLAP system, such as a cube-viewing application, on your PC. After you install this software, restart Crystal Reports and try creating the report again.*

Once you've successfully logged on to and connected to the proper cube, you'll be returned to the OLAP Connection Browser and the cube will appear in the OLAP Cubes list—you won't have to go through the Add process again, as the cube will remain in the list from this point on. If you made errors in the connection process in the Connection Properties dialog box and the cube can't be connected to, select the cube definition in the list and click the Edit button in the OLAP Connection Browser (you can also right-click on the cube definition and choose Edit from the pop-up menu). The Connection Properties dialog box will reappear, where you may make necessary changes.

Depending on the OLAP database you connected to, you may be prompted to select the initial dimensions you wish to add to your OLAP report. Select the desired dimensions from the list. Once you've made choices in the OLAP Connection Browser and, if necessary, the Select Dimensions dialog box, the Data dialog of the Report Creation Wizard redisplays, and the Cube, Type, and Server fields on the Data tab of the Expert will be filled in. Again, depending on the database you chose, you may now see a Select Dimensions button to reselect dimensions, if you so choose.

After you make these choices, click Next to show the Rows/Columns section, shown in Figure 17-2, to choose the dimension or dimensions you want to include in the rows and columns of your report.

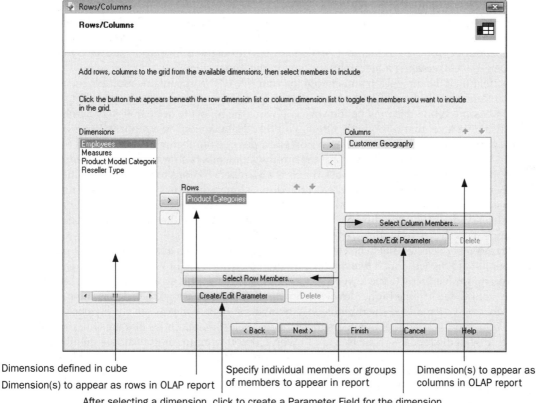

FIGURE 17-2   The OLAP Report Creation Wizard Rows/Columns section

If the default dimensions already in the Rows and Columns lists aren't correct, choose from the Dimensions list the dimension that you want to appear as the row in your OLAP report. Then, simply drag and drop it into the Rows box or click the right arrow next to the Rows box.

Use the same drag-and-drop method to add to the Columns box the dimension you want to appear as the column in your OLAP report. Or, select a dimension and click the right arrow next to the Rows or Columns list.

You aren't limited to placing just one dimension in the Rows and Columns boxes. If you add multiple dimensions, Crystal Reports will "group" the dimensions in the OLAP report. For example, if you add a State dimension, followed by a Customer dimension, Crystal Reports will print states and show customers broken down within each state. If you place the dimensions in the Rows or Columns box in the wrong order, you can simply drag and drop the dimensions into the correct order within the Rows or Columns box. Alternatively, you can select the dimension you want to move, and use the up and down arrows above the Rows and Columns boxes.

If you wish to remove a dimension from the Rows or Columns box, drag the dimension back to the Dimensions list. Or, you can select the desired dimension and click the left arrow (you won't be allowed to leave a row or column empty).

Depending on the cube you choose for your report, you may find dimensions that contain many levels or members. A member (sometimes referred to as a generation) is a lower level of information that breaks down the higher level above it. For example, a Products dimension could contain several members: product type, product name within product type, and size within product name. Each member further breaks down the information shown by the member above it, creating a hierarchy for data in the dimension.

By default, if the dimension you choose for your OLAP report contains multiple members, Crystal Reports will show only the highest member in a group hierarchy when it displays the dimension. While this may be the way you want the report to appear, it may actually display a data level that is too high. Often, you'll add dimensions to a report's Rows and Columns boxes, only to have the OLAP report show just one number at the intersection of one row and column. If you need to increase the number of members shown inside a dimension that appears on the report, you can use the Select Members buttons to select the additional members that you want to see. First select the dimension in the Rows or Columns list that you wish to work with and then click Select Row Members or Select Column Members. You may also just double-click a dimension in the list. When you do either, the Member Selector will appear, as shown in Figure 17-3.

The Member Selector dialog box shows the dimension members in a hierarchy, with pluses and minuses to the left, much like the display of folders and files in Windows Explorer. You can expand the hierarchy to see lower members by clicking the plus signs next to the members. If you want to see just the higher-level members, click the minus sign to collapse them.

Once you've expanded the dimension's members sufficiently, you can simply click the check box next to individual members to select or deselect them. Those that are checked will be included in the report—those that aren't won't. If you want to select multiple members at the same time, you may CTRL-click or SHIFT-click on multiple member names to highlight them (multiselect or range-select respectively), and then click one check box. All the members that are highlighted will be selected.

If you want to be more systematic in member selection, particularly for very large hierarchies, click the down arrow attached to the Select button in the Member Selector's

FIGURE 17-3   The Member Selector

toolbar to display a pull-down menu (you can also right-click a member name to get a similar set of choices). You'll see various options for selecting groups of members (such as all, none, all members at a certain level, and so forth). Notice that once you choose one of the options in the select menu, the Select button will display an icon similar to the choice you made from the menu. By just clicking Select, you can repeat that selection without displaying the drop-down menu again.

You can also control other aspects of the Member Selector by choosing other toolbar buttons:

- Select Display Mode will change from viewing members in a hierarchy to sorting them in ascending or descending order.

- Select Hierarchy will provide additional options if the particular dimension you've chosen encompasses more than one hierarchy.

- New Favorite Group will add an additional category underneath the Favorites folder where you may drag "favorite" members.

- Display Members Using chooses between displaying dimension captions, names, or both (if your cube makes a distinction).

- Search displays a dialog box to allow you to search for members using text searches. You can either use a simple search or click the Advanced tab to create a more complex Boolean search. When the search is complete, you can search again from the resulting list of members, add the selected members to those already selected, or replace selected members with this list.

After you choose the members you want included in the report, click OK. You won't notice any difference in the Rows/Columns tab—you'll need to double-click the dimension or click Select Member again to see what members you've chosen.

You may also create a parameter field to allow the viewer to choose members to include in the OLAP grid whenever the report is refreshed. Click either the row or column dimension you wish to parameterize and click Create/Edit Parameter. The Create Parameter Field dialog box will appear. Steps for creating an OLAP parameter are similar to those for a regular report parameter, except that you must set default values before you save the parameter field (and, there are no dynamic or cascading pick lists available when you create an OLAP parameter). When you click Default Values, the Set Default Values dialog box will appear. Within this dialog box, clicking Select Default Values will again display the Member Selector, where you can choose members to add to the parameter's pick list.

NOTE *More information on parameter field creation is available in Chapter 13.*

Once you've chosen dimensions and members, click Next to advance to the Slice/Page section, shown in Figure 17-4, to determine how the remaining dimensions included in the cube will affect your OLAP report.

In the Slice/Page section, you'll see all the other dimensions in the cube that you didn't include in the Rows or Columns boxes. You can use these dimensions to either slice or page your OLAP report. Slicing (similar to filtering) the OLAP report limits the report to certain occurrences of data in these dimensions. Paging the OLAP report is very similar to setting up report grouping. Like the grouping of other reports, discussed in Chapter 2, this creates a new section of the OLAP report showing a different OLAP grid every time the value of the chosen dimension changes. Each resulting OLAP report section will contain data just for that one member.

Limit view to particular member of dimension   Dimensions not included in row or column

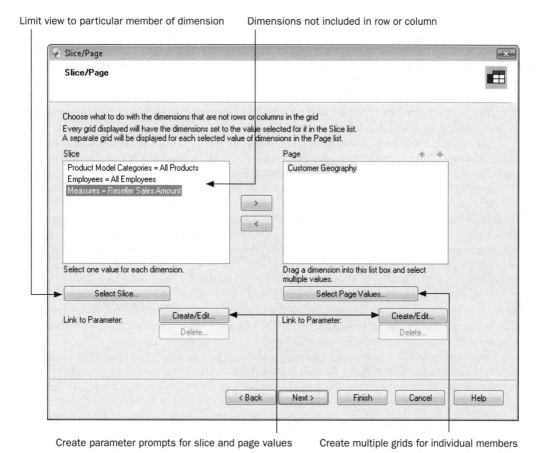

Create parameter prompts for slice and page values   Create multiple grids for individual members

FIGURE 17-4   The Slice/Page section

To slice the report according to a dimension, look at the Slice part of the dialog box. You'll notice that each dimension displays a filter criterion, such as Store = All Stores. Typically, this default value will be either All or a particular general value that was set as the default when the OLAP cube was defined. Either double-click the dimension you want to slice, or select the dimension and click Select Slice. The Member Selector dialog box, described earlier, will appear, in which you can choose a particular value to limit the OLAP report. After you make your choice and click OK, the criterion in the Filter list will change to indicate the value you picked. The OLAP report will now be limited to only values that are included in the dimension you chose.

TIP   *Unlike in the previous example with the Member Selector dialog box, you can choose only one value in the box here. Selecting a new value deselects the preceding value.*

To page the OLAP report according to a dimension, select the desired dimension in the Slice list and either drag it to the Page list or click the right arrow. Once again, the Member Selector dialog box appears, in which you can again select any combination of members (using options from the Select menus, if you'd like). After you make your choices, click OK to close the Member Selector dialog box. The dimension you chose for paging will appear in the Page list at the right of the Slice/Page section. If you wish to later change the members you chose to page the report, return to the Slice/Page section and double-click the dimension in the Page list, or select the dimension and click Select Page Values.

You can add more than one dimension to the Page list. If you do so, you can change the order in which Crystal Reports will group the OLAP report, by selecting one of the dimensions and clicking the up or down arrow. If you want to remove one of the Page dimensions, select it in the Page list and click the left arrow button or drag the dimension back to the Slice list.

As with the previous section of the wizard, you can base pages on parameter fields. To do this, select the slice or page dimension that you want to create a parameter field for and click Create/Edit. The Create Parameter Field dialog box will appear, where you may choose options to prompt the report viewer when the OLAP report is refreshed. Then, the value that the viewer supplies to the parameter field will be passed to the slice or page dimension to control how the OLAP report appears. Once you've added a parameter to a dimension, you'll notice the parameter field to the right of the equal sign in the Slice or Page list. If you later want to edit the parameter field, click the desired dimension and then Create/Edit. To delete the parameter and return to a fixed value or values chosen in the Member Selector, choose the desired dimension and click Delete.

Once you've made any slicing and paging choices, you're ready to display the OLAP report if you're satisfied with the default formatting Crystal Reports will apply. Click Finish if you're ready to view the report. However, you have additional choices in the OLAP Report Creation Wizard if you wish to choose them. You may choose from a set of preformatted styles for the OLAP report, as well as adding charts to show data plotted in your OLAP report.

To customize the formatting of the OLAP grid objects the wizard will create (very similar to the cross-tab object discussed in Chapter 8), click Next to display the Style section of the wizard. Choose from one of the predefined grid styles to apply to the OLAP report.

You may then click Finish to display the report, or click Next to create a chart based on your OLAP data. There is a minimal set of charting choices on this section (more detail on charting on OLAP grids is discussed in Chapter 9).

Click Finish in the OLAP Report Creation Wizard to run the report and show it in the Preview tab. Depending on any page dimensions you chose, you'll see a few simple objects on the report, such as the print date and page number. You'll also see one or more OLAP grid objects, plus any report sections and groups that were created to accommodate the page dimensions.

If you need to make changes to the Rows/Columns or Slice/Page values in the OLAP cube, you can rerun the Report Creation Wizard by clicking the OLAP Design Wizard button in the Expert Tools toolbar or by choosing Report | OLAP Design Wizard from the pull-down menus.

Alternatively, to display the full OLAP Expert with all possible options (discussed in the next section, "Adding an OLAP Grid to an Existing Report"), you can select the OLAP grid object by clicking in the blank area of the object's upper-left corner (if there is more than one, select the particular one you want to change). Then, right-click and select OLAP Grid Expert from the pop-up menu.

Adding an OLAP Grid to an Existing Report

You probably will encounter situations in which you want to create a standard database report that includes one or more OLAP grids. By choosing the Blank Report option or other wizards from the Start page or File | New menu, you have more flexibility in creating this type of report. Simply create the base report using the techniques discussed elsewhere in the book.

You may even find it useful to base the main report on some fields from your OLAP database. To use the OLAP database for the main report, choose the OLAP entry under the Create New Connection category of the Database Expert. The OLAP Connection Browser (shown earlier in the chapter) will appear, where you can choose an OLAP cube. You can add as many of these cubes or tables as necessary for the report. Depending on the type of OLAP database you've chosen, the Field Explorer will show the dimensions and members for your chosen cubes, or the fields in the chosen tables. You can add these fields to your main report as you would a regular database field. You may need to try some experimentation to determine which dimensions or fields can be used—OLAP data often doesn't behave the same as relational database data. Once the main part of your report is finished, you can add the necessary OLAP grid objects.

CAUTION *Even though you can access the OLAP cube by using the Blank Report option, you won't be able to actually include any cube values in any report sections. You'll only be able to include and manipulate dimension names. The only way to actually include the numeric values from the cube is to create an OLAP grid object.*

Adding an OLAP Grid Object

To create an OLAP grid on an existing report, click the OLAP grid toolbar button in the Insert Tools toolbar or choose Insert | OLAP Grid from the pull-down menus. The OLAP Expert appears.

OLAP Expert

OLAP Data | Rows/Columns | Slice/Page | Style | Customize Style | Labels

Choose the data to be your On Line Analytical Processing (OLAP) source

Choose an OLAP Server type then select the Cube that contains the data.

[Select Cube...]

Cube:
Type:
Server:

[OK] [Cancel] [Help]

The tabs in the OLAP Expert behave almost identically to the same sections in the OLAP Report Creation Wizard, described earlier in the chapter. Follow the same steps for the Data and Rows/Columns tabs to choose the cube and dimensions for your OLAP grid. You may also use the Style and Customize Style tabs to format the OLAP grid, similar to formatting a cross-tab object (covered in detail in Chapter 8). Three of the tabs deserve more discussion, however: the Slice/Page tab, the Customize Style tab, and the Labels tab.

Slice/Page Tab

Notice that the Page dimension list and the Parameter field buttons that appear with the OLAP Report Creation Wizard are unavailable here, and a note suggests that you use the Wizard if you want to use these features. If you want to have several cubes work as pages, you can either recreate the report using the Wizard or add multiple OLAP grids to your report, specifying a different slice for each grid to mimic the Paged dimension process discussed in the Wizard portion of this chapter.

Customize Style Tab

This tab is identical to the same tab used to format cross-tab objects (see more information on this tab in Chapter 8). Options you choose on this tab change formatting options, such as background color, grid line formatting, and "Alias for Formulas," which lets you give a shorter, more meaningful name to a column or row for use in conditional formatting.

OLAP Labels

Many OLAP cubes of even moderate complexity often contain many dimensions. However, unlike a "slice and dice" OLAP analysis tool, the OLAP grid object that initially appears in the Preview tab or appears when you print or export the report doesn't offer a high level of interactivity (although the Cube View, discussed later in the chapter, under "The OLAP Worksheet," does provide high interactivity). Accordingly, you'll probably use only a few (if not just one) dimensions for a row and column. The remainder of the dimensions not actually appearing as a row or column (often called qualified dimensions) can simply be ignored, used as Slice dimensions, or used as Page dimensions. Of particular interest is how the report viewer will know what settings have been made for Slice dimensions: if the OLAP grid is limited to just one year, one sales manager, and one product type, how will this be known? The answer is OLAP labels.

When you create an OLAP grid object either with the OLAP Wizard or by inserting an OLAP grid manually, OLAP labels are added to the OLAP grid by default, as shown here:

Reseller Sales A All Resellers   All Sales Channels   CY 2002
All   All Source Currencies All Customers   All Employees

		⊟ All				
			⊞ Accessories	⊞ Bikes	⊞ Clothing	⊞ Components
⊟ All Sales Territories		24,144,429.65	92,735.35	19,956,014.67	485,587.15	3,610,092.47
	⊞ Europe	1,698,880.94	8,976.30	1,300,926.54	52,003.83	336,974.26
	⊞ NA					
	⊞ North America	22,445,548.71	83,759.05	18,655,088.13	433,583.32	3,273,118.21
	⊞ Pacific					

Notice that any Filter dimensions, such as CY 2002, are listed. Otherwise, the All designations appear. This indicates to the report viewer what limits have been placed on the OLAP grid. You may choose to limit the set of OLAP labels that appear—perhaps to just the ones that are used as a Filter dimension. Or, you may want to otherwise customize the way the OLAP labels appear. To do this, click the Labels tab, shown in Figure 17-5.

By default, all qualified dimensions (those that are in the cube, but not included as a row or column on the grid) are placed in the right Labeled Dimensions box. You can change the order in which they will appear next to the OLAP grid by selecting a label and using the small arrows above the box to move it up or down in the list. If you don't want a particular label to appear with the grid, select it and click the left arrow to move it to the Unlabeled Dimensions box.

You can also customize the amount of white space Crystal Reports will place between the labels by specifying a new value in the Vertical Gap and Horizontal Gap text boxes. You can choose to place the entire set of labels on the top or left side of the OLAP grid (or not have the labels show up at all). And finally, you can check the Display Dimension Name check box to replace the "All <value>" label with "<Dimension> = <value>" for labels.

After you make your desired choices in the OLAP Expert, click OK. An outline of the OLAP grid object will be attached to the mouse cursor. Drop the object in the desired section of the report.

FIGURE 17-5   The Labels tab

You may make changes or additions to the OLAP grid object by selecting it and then formatting the OLAP grid by using pull-down menu options, the Format button in the Expert Tools toolbar, or format options from the right-click pop-up menu. You can also format individual parts of the OLAP grid, as discussed later in the chapter, under "Controlling OLAP Grid Appearance."

Changing the OLAP Database Location

An OLAP grid "points" to a specific OLAP cube location on a server. If that location changes, or if you want to report on a different cube without redesigning the entire OLAP grid, you need to change the location of the OLAP database that the grid refers to.

Select the OLAP grid you want to change by clicking its upper-left corner. Right-click and choose Set OLAP Cube Location from the pop-up menu, or choose Database | Set OLAP Cube Location from the pull-down menus. The Set OLAP Cube Location dialog box appears.

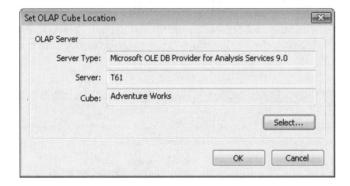

Click Select to choose the new OLAP cube or new server location for the associated OLAP database. Then click OK.

Controlling OLAP Grid Appearance

An OLAP grid organizes cube information in a row-and-column format, much as a cross-tab object does. In fact, formatting and changing OLAP grid appearance is essentially identical to formatting a cross-tab object:

- Make choices on the Style or Customize Style tab in the OLAP Expert. You can choose from built-in formatting styles on the Style tab or perform more detailed formatting of individual elements on the Customize Style tab.

- Select individual fields that make up the OLAP grid, and resize or format them individually. When you resize an individual field, the row or column that the field is in will change accordingly. You can change field font face, font size, and color. And if you're formatting numeric information, such as the OLAP grid value fields, you can choose rounding, decimal places, currency symbols, and other formatting that applies to the type of field you're formatting.

- Perform conditional formatting on values in the OLAP grid, using the actual numeric data contained in the cells (such as CurrentFieldValue), or using various Grid functions to determine the row or column location of the cell. You can also use the Highlighting Expert.

- Format OLAP Grid labels, either individually or as a group. Select an individual label and use typical formatting options. Or, you may click on the edge of the label area and select all the labels as a group (you'll see OLAP Grid Labels appear in the status bar at the bottom of the screen). You actually have selected the border around all the labels, and you can add a border, drop shadow, or other "border-oriented" formatting options. You can also suppress the labels on the Format Editor common tab if you don't want to see them (this can be done conditionally, as opposed to making as similar choice in the OLAP Labels tab of the OLAP Expert).

TIP *Formatting OLAP grids is virtually identical to formatting cross-tab objects. Refer to Chapter 8 for a thorough discussion.*

Virtual Page Formatting Options

Crystal Reports deals with OLAP grids that span multiple pages in an inconsistent manner between the Preview tab and what actually is printed or exported from the finished report. If an OLAP grid contains a sufficient number of columns that it exceeds the chosen Crystal Reports page width, it simply expands the Preview tab horizontally and shows the OLAP grid across a single page. However, when you print or export the report, the OLAP grid will actually be broken into multiple pages that print one after the other.

Crystal Reports provides specialized formatting options that make OLAP grids that span pages easier to view. A formatting option in the Format Editor, as well as a page number special field, are designed to enhance OLAP grid appearance.

The Repeat on Horizontal Pages formatting option appears on the Format Editor Common tab. You may select this formatting property for virtually all Crystal Reports object types, such as database fields, bitmap graphics, text objects, and so forth. Any object that you apply this formatting option to will repeat on each subsequent page that a OLAP grid object appears on, whether in the Preview tab or on a printed or exported report.

The other feature that's helpful with multipage OLAP grids is the Horizontal Page Number special field. Available along with other special fields in the Field Explorer, Horizontal Page Number will increment as OLAP grids span multiple pages, whereas the standard Page Number special field won't. Simply drag and drop the Horizontal Page Number special field onto the report as you would any other field. The page numbers will increment as OLAP grids span pages.

Figure 17-6 illustrates these features. Notice that the text object title appears on multiple horizontal pages displayed in the Preview tab. Also, notice that the Horizontal Page Number special field automatically increments when the OLAP grid spans multiple pages.

Interacting with the OLAP Grid

Although you don't have quite the "slice and dice" flexibility with Crystal Reports that you may have with your particular OLAP analysis tool, you might be surprised by how easy it is to rearrange the appearance of an OLAP grid object. When you first create the OLAP grid, you choose which dimensions you want to use as rows and which you want to use as columns. If you choose multiple row or column dimensions, the order in which you add them determines the grouping order for the rows or columns.

FIGURE 17-6 Multipage OLAP grid

You may want to change the order of the OLAP grid's row or column grouping, or you may want to swap or pivot the rows and columns, drill down on higher-level dimensions, and so forth. There are a large number of manipulation choices in Crystal Reports (many of these options are only available when viewing the OLAP grid in the Preview tab—limited options exist in the Design tab):

- **Pivot the rows and columns** Select the OLAP grid. Then, right-click and choose Pivot OLAP Grid from the pop-up menu. You can also choose Format | Pivot OLAP Grid from the pull-down menus.

- **Reorder dimensions** Simply click the row or column heading of the dimension you want to reorder. As you hold down the mouse button, you will notice a little "piece of paper" icon appear on the mouse pointer. This indicates that the dimension can be dragged and dropped below or above another dimension to reorder the dimensions. You can even drag and drop a dimension from a row to a column, or vice versa, provided that at least one dimension will be left in the row or column of the OLAP grid.

- **Add or remove dimensions** Select a visible label above the OLAP grid. As you hold down the mouse button, you will notice a little "piece of paper" icon appear on the mouse pointer. This indicates that the dimension can be dragged and dropped below or above another dimension on the grid. If you wish to remove an existing dimension from the grid, select the desired row or column heading and drag it to the labels area (you won't be able to drag a dimension if it's the only dimension in the row or column).

- **Drill down and drill up** Double-click a higher-level member, or click the plus sign next to the member (the plus sign will not appear if you've suppressed drill-down indicators from the Grid Options pop-up menu). This, in essence, is the same as rerunning the OLAP Expert and using the Select Row Members option to show the next level of the hierarchy. You can then drill down on the lower levels that you just exposed, until there are no more lower levels to show. To drill up (hide the lower levels you already showed), just double-click the higher-level member again or click the minus sign next to the member (the plus sign will not appear if you've suppressed drill-down indicators from the Grid Options pop-up menu)—the lower-level members will disappear. You can also select the member name, right-click, and choose Expand Member or Collapse Member from the pop-up menu.

- **Total columns or rows**   Select any row or column member (you can't total when you've selected an individual number "cell") and right-click. Choose Automatic Totals from the pop-up menu. A submenu will appear giving you totaling choices.

- **Add custom calculations**   You may add one or more additional rows or columns (members) based on a calculation. These additional calculated members can consist of such calculations as contribution, growth, ranking, variance, or other statistical calculations that you can create using the MDX query language derived from Microsoft Analysis Services.

To create the calculated member, select the member row or column heading that you want to use as the basis for your calculation. Right-click, and choose Add Calculated Member from the pop-up menu. The Calculated Members dialog box will appear.

There are three choices: the Calculation Expert tab, the Data Analysis Expert tab, and the Calculation tab. You can create a calculation using one of the three tabs, depending on the type of calculation you want to create.

The Calculation Expert tab allows calculations using contribution, growth, ranking, and variance. The Data Analysis tab allows calculations using trend line, moving average, and linear regression. And, the Calculation tab allows you to create a more complex calculation from scratch using the MDX calculation language.

Once you've finished your calculation, an additional member will appear in the grid showing your calculation. To edit or delete the calculated member, select the member name at the left or top of the grid, right-click, and choose Edit or Delete options from the pop-up menu.

NOTE *For more in-depth coverage of OLAP calculations and MDX calculations, consult Crystal Reports online help, or documentation with your online OLAP analysis tool, such as Microsoft Analysis Services books online.*

- **To create "on-the-fly" filters** Even though you may have limited your OLAP grid by using a Slice, you can further filter the OLAP grid interactively while you're viewing it. Your filter, based on the "numbers" rather than on the member hierarchy, can consist of a comparison to the numbers, or a top or bottom "N" or percentage.

To add a filter, select the member name column or row that you want to use as a filter (you can't click a number in a cell—it has to be at the edge of a column or row, and only a member name that shows some "filter-able" numbers—not all rows or columns can be filtered), and right-click. Choose Add Filter from the pop-up menu. The Define Filter dialog box will appear.

Once you've applied your filter, you'll see a reduced set of rows or columns in the grid, with the filter limiting what appears. You'll know you've added a filter to a row or column if you point to it and your mouse pointer changes to an X. If you want to modify or remove the filter, right-click on the column or row again and choose Edit Filter or Remove Filter from the pop-up menu.

- **Sort the rows or columns by numeric values** Normally, rows and columns are ordered according to the member name at the top of the column or the left of the row. However, you can sort the rows or columns by "the numbers" if you choose. To do this, select the row or column member name you want to sort (you can't click a number, and the row or column you choose must be "sort-able"—not all columns or rows will offer the option), right-click, and choose Add First Sort from the pop-up menu. A submenu will appear with sorting options. Choose your desired sort option. Notice that the selected row or column is now sorted by the numbers. Also notice that you'll see a double-arrow cursor appear when you point to the row or column member name, indicating that a sort exists.

If you have duplicate values in a row or column and you wish to add a second level of sorting, click the next column or row member name that you want to sort, right-click, and choose Add Next Sort. Choose similar options.

To change or remove an existing sort, select a row or column member name (one with the double-arrow cursor, indicating an existing sort), right-click, and choose Change Direction Of Sort or Remove Sort.

The OLAP Worksheet

If the interactivity options discussed previously in the chapter aren't enough, Crystal Reports includes even more OLAP interactivity with the OLAP Worksheet, which provides a great deal of "slice, dice, swap, and analyze" interactivity right in Crystal Reports.

To display the OLAP Worksheet, select the desired OLAP grid object in the Preview tab (you can't launch the OLAP Worksheet in the Design tab). Then, right-click and choose View Cube from the pop-up menu. The OLAP grid will be displayed in an additional tab in Crystal Reports labeled Cube View, as shown in Figure 17-7.

Once you've launched the OLAP Worksheet, you may return to the report's regular Design or Preview tab by just clicking it, and then return to the Cube View tab by clicking it. To close the Cube View tab and return to a regular report view, click the x on the Cube View tab.

Interactivity in the OLAP Worksheet is somewhat similar to that of the OLAP grid in the preview tab discussed earlier in the report. There is also additional functionality to swap and nest dimensions.

These are among the highlights of OLAP Worksheet interactivity:

- Click plus or minus signs to drill down or drill up (expand or compact members).

- To "drill through" to base relational database data that makes up an individual cell number, right-click on the cell and choose Drill Through from the pop-up menu (only limited OLAP cube servers provide this functionality, so this option may not be available).

- Right-click a member name (row or column name) to choose options from the pop-up menu. Many of these options are similar to those discussed earlier in the chapter relating to the OLAP grid. Some notable additions to the pop-up menu include formatting options, including the Highlighting Exceptions option, which will color cells that fall within selected numeric ranges.

- Click down arrows next to a dimension to launch the Member Selector (Figure 17-3 earlier in the chapter) where you can choose to display individual members of the

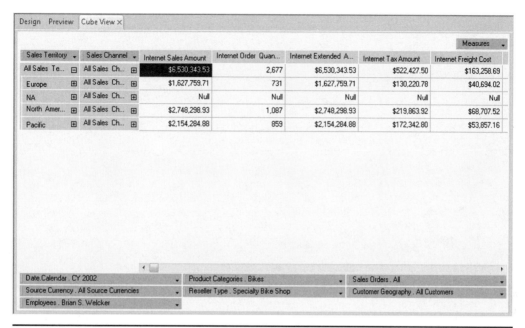

FIGURE 17-7   OLAP Worksheet Cube View tab

hierarchy in the grid, or slice the grid (if you choose a dimension at the bottom of the grid).

- To swap a row or column dimension with another row or column dimension, or a filter dimension (at the bottom of the Cube View tab), click the dimension name that you wish to swap. Then, drag the dimension to the other dimension that you wish to swap with. When you see the double-arrow, release the mouse button.

- To nest or "stack" dimensions (add an additional row or column dimension within another dimension), click the dimension name that you wish to nest. Then, drag the dimension to the existing row or column dimension that you wish to nest it under. Look very carefully for the single arrow. When you see it, release the mouse button.

- To move a dimension back to the bottom of the Cube View tab (there must be at least two or more nested dimensions to move one of them to the bottom), click the dimension name that you want to move. Drag the dimension to the bottom of the Cube View tab between the rows or columns of existing dimensions. Look very carefully for the single arrow (a double arrow will swap the dimensions). When you see it, release the mouse button.

Sharing Report Items with the Repository

One of the most frequently heard questions asked by Crystal Reports users (especially users in larger organizations) is "Can I share parts of this report with other users or other reports?" It would be convenient to be able to store a shared company logo, some sort of shared text, formula logic, or parameter field pick lists, so that all your reports could access them. And, these shared items would be available to your colleagues as well.

This is the benefit of using the repository. The repository allows several types of report objects to be stored in a central database for sharing among other reports and other users. Not only does this greatly reduce the need for repetitive report design steps, it also affords a simple, centralized way of automatically updating common portions of shared reports.

The repository in Crystal Reports 2008 is only available if you are using a member of the matching BusinessObjects Enterprise XI 3.0 product family (abbreviated in this book as *BOE*), as the repository is stored in the BOE Central Management Server database. This arrangement provides for tight integration with the enterprise reporting environment, including full support for the integrated BOE security model.

NOTE *The initial release of Crystal Reports 2008 shipped prior to availability of the matching version of BusinessObjects Enterprise XI 3.0. As such, the initial Crystal Reports 2008 version does not provide support for connecting to BusinessObjects Enterprise. In this initial version, any attempt to connect to Enterprise results in a dialog box indicating that the feature is unavailable. Use the Crystal Reports update feature (Help | Check For Updates from the pull-down menus) to download the appropriate Service Pack or update to enable BusinessObjects Enterprise XI 3.0 connectivity. Note that, even after this update, you will only be able to connect to members of the BusinessObjects Enterprise XI 3.0 family. Connection to earlier versions of Enterprise is not supported.*

The Repository Defined

Simply put, the Crystal Reports *repository* is a common place where report objects can be stored. Once you store a report object in the repository, it's available to be added to other reports you create. If you connect to your BOE-shared repository that other users in your organization also share, objects you add to the repository are available to other Crystal Reports users, and objects they add are available to you.

The repository stores all of its items in the BOE Central Management Server database. Any Crystal Reports user who has a valid user ID and connectivity to your BOE system will be able to connect to the repository. Even if you have just a few report designers who share a common repository, the benefits of shared report design and automatically updated report objects will soon become evident.

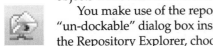 You make use of the repository in Crystal Reports with the *Repository Explorer,* a separate "un-dockable" dialog box inside the report designer, similar to the Field Explorer. To display the Repository Explorer, choose View | Repository Explorer from the pull-down menus, or click the Repository Explorer toolbar button in the Standard toolbar.

The Repository Explorer window will appear. If this is the first time you've displayed the Repository Explorer since you started Crystal Reports (and, you haven't already logged into BusinessObjects Enterprise), the Repository Explorer won't display any contents. Click the Logon button in the Repository Explorer toolbar to log on to BOE. Once you've supplied proper logon credentials, the Repository Explorer will display the repository contents in a folder structure.

After you've used the repository, you may wish to log off Enterprise (perhaps to release your user license). Simply click the Logoff toolbar button in the Repository Explorer toolbar, or right-click the BOE server name at the top of the Repository Explorer and choose Logoff Server from the pop-up menu. You'll be logged off BOE, and the repository folder structure will disappear. Click the Logon button again to redisplay the logon dialog box. Enter desired credentials to again log on to BOE. You may also log on as a different user without logging off first by just clicking the Logon button in the Repository Explorer toolbar again.

As with other "explorer" windows in Crystal Reports, you may dock the Repository Explorer to the side of the Crystal Reports designer, may undock the window so that it floats free, or may dock the window, but shrink it, by clicking the push-pin icon in the upper right-hand corner. You may also close the Repository Explorer completely by clicking the small x in the upper right-hand corner. If you close the Repository Explorer, simply use the toolbar button or View | Repository Explorer menu option to redisplay it.

Notice that the Repository Explorer breaks down items stored in the BusinessObjects Enterprise system into several folders: the Repository Items folder, the Enterprise Items folder, and Corporate and Personal category entries.

The Repository Explorer Enterprise Items Folder

The Enterprise Items folder contains a list of BOE object folders and subfolders, as well as objects within the folders and subfolders. This folder structure is where various BusinessObjects Enterprise documents are kept, including Crystal Reports documents and report packages. Click the plus sign next to a folder to open it and see its subfolders and objects. You may also right-click a folder within the Enterprise Items folder and choose Expand All from the pop-up menu. This will expand all subfolders within the selected folder, showing all available objects in them.

NOTE *Although all objects stored in the Enterprise Folders category (such as PDF files, hyperlinks, and so forth) will appear in the Repository Explorer, only Crystal Report objects are usable from within the Crystal Reports Repository Explorer. You'll note the "piece of paper with the green and blue arrow" icon that denotes an available Crystal Report object. You'll also notice report "instances" that were previously scheduled underneath the associated report object.*

Report objects (original reports added to Enterprise that have not been scheduled) can be opened and modified right from the Repository Explorer. And, report instances that show a Complete status can be opened as well, although they cannot be directly modified (instances that are not noted "Complete," such as recurring instances, can't be opened). To open the desired report object or instance, just double-click it. You may also right-click the desired report and choose Open Report from the pop-up menu. The report will appear inside the Crystal Report designer, where you may refresh and modify it. If you opened an object, you may use the Save toolbar button or File menu option to update the BOE version (provided your BOE user ID has sufficient rights). The File | Save As option may be used to save either a modified object or instance to your local hard drive or a network drive.

The Repository Explorer Categories Folders

In addition to organizing reports in folders and subfolders, BusinessObjects Enterprise can categorize reports in one or more categories. This allows a subset of reports that may be scattered across a variety of Enterprise folders and subfolders to all be consolidated in a single place. Personal categories are assigned to you alone, whereas Corporate categories are shared among all Enterprise users. Regardless, the steps to view and work with reports in a category are the same: expand the desired category in the Repository Explorer and choose the desired report object or instance.

As with Enterprise folder-based reports, you may open both report objects and instances by double-clicking them. You may also right-click a report within a category and choose Open Report from the pop-up menu (as with reports located in the Enterprise Folders section of the Repository Explorer, only report objects and "Complete" instances can be opened). Any modifications you make to a report object can be saved back to the Enterprise server by simply using the Save toolbar button or File menu option. The File | Save As option may be used to save either a modified object or instance to your local hard drive or a network drive.

The Repository Explorer Repository Items Folder

The portion of the repository that contains "sharable" objects is displayed as the Repository Items category. The Repository Explorer shows this section categorized into folders. Although the sample repository that ships with BusinessObjects Enterprise shows folders for specific types of objects (text objects, bitmaps, SQL commands), you don't have to organize folders this way—you may put any type of object that the repository supports into any folder. You may add any of the objects in the repository to appropriate areas of your report.

The repository supports several types of Crystal Reports objects:

- **Text objects**   Standard text objects containing static text (no embedded fields)
- **Bitmaps (pictures)**   Bitmap pictures, such as logos, photos, and signatures
- **Custom functions**   Functions or "subroutines" that can be used inside report formulas. Note that repository custom functions appear only in the Formula Workshop, not in the Repository Explorer
- **SQL commands/queries**   Server-based SQL commands that reports can be based upon
- **Business Views**   BusinessObjects Enterprise–based metalayer "views" of database connectivity that reports can be based upon (Using Business Views as report data sources is discussed in more detail in Chapter 16.)
- **Lists of Values**   Portions of new Crystal Reports dynamic/cascading parameters that display real-time values in a pick list
- **Prompt Groups**   Portions of Crystal Reports dynamic/cascading parameters that organize one or more Lists of Values in a group

Text objects and bitmaps can simply be dragged from the Repository Explorer onto the report, just as you would drag and drop fields from the Field Explorer. Repository custom functions must be added to report formulas from within the Formula Workshop (covered in Chapter 4). Repository SQL commands and Business Views must be added to the report from within the Database Expert (SQL commands are covered in more detail in Chapter 15, and reporting with Business Views is covered in Chapter 16). And, Lists of Values and Prompt Groups are used when creating parameter fields (see Chapter 13 for more information).

TIP *You can install sample objects into your BusinessObjects Enterprise repository by using the Business View Manager's Tools | Install Repository Samples menu option. More information on using the Business View Manager is discussed later in this chapter, as well as in a supplementary document available for download from the book's companion web site, CrystalBook.com.*

The Repository Explorer toolbar contains four buttons, besides the Logon and Logoff buttons: Change View Settings, Advanced Filtering, Delete, and Add Folder. The Delete and Add Folder buttons, described later in the chapter, perform fairly self-explanatory functions. The Change View Settings and Advanced Filtering buttons allow you to customize what appears in the Repository Explorer.

Clicking the Change View Settings button, or right-clicking anywhere inside the Repository Explorer and choosing Change View Settings from the pop-up menu, will display the View Settings dialog box. By un-checking any of the repository object types, you can eliminate them from appearing in the Repository Explorer. For example, you may prefer not to see SQL commands (since you can't add them to the report from the Repository Explorer anyway). Just un-check Report Command to eliminate them from the Repository Explorer. You can also sort repository objects by name or type by clicking the desired radio button.

If you click Advanced Filter, or right-click anywhere inside the Repository Explorer and choose Advanced Filtering from the pop-up menu, the Repository Explorer will expand to show two filter text boxes and an Apply button. Type in a combination of full or partial object name in the "Show items with this text in the name" box and full author name in the "Show items by this author" box. Then, just click Apply or just press ENTER. The Repository Explorer will redisplay showing just repository objects matching the criteria you typed. To remove the criteria, just delete the text on the filter boxes and click Apply or press ENTER. If you no longer wish to see the filter text boxes, just click the Advanced Filtering toolbar button again, or right-click and choose the Advanced Filtering pop-up menu option.

NOTE *Even though folders may show plus signs next to them after setting filters, nothing will appear inside the folder if it doesn't meet the filter requirements.*

Adding To/Updating the Repository

Once you've installed your initial BusinessObjects Enterprise system with its default database, you'll need to begin to populate it with your shared objects. And while it's not required, you'll probably gain more usability with the repository if you organize the repository into folders.

NOTE *The ability to add, change, and delete repository objects and folders is based on BusinessObjects Enterprise security. If your BOE user ID hasn't been granted these rights, you'll receive errors when you attempt these operations. Steps to control these rights are discussed later in this chapter, under "Controlling Repository Rights."*

Creating Folders and Categories

You may create as many folders in the repository as you like. You may create folders within either the Enterprise Items or Repository Items folders. And you're not limited to creating a single level of folders—you may create subfolders within other folders to build a hierarchy for report objects or repository objects. You may also create new categories within the existing Personal or Corporate category folders (provided you have proper rights set up in BOE).

Once folders have been created in the Enterprise Items folder, you may save reports to the new folder with the Save toolbar button, or File | Save pull-down menu options. Folders created within the Repository Items folder can now be used to store text objects, bitmap graphics, or SQL commands (custom functions are placed in a separate part of the repository reserved just for themselves—they won't appear in the Repository Explorer). And, while you can create new categories and subcategories from within the Repository Explorer, objects can only be assigned to them in other Enterprise tools, such as InfoView or the Central Management Console (discussed in Part II of this book).

From within Crystal Reports, you can create, delete, or modify folders and categories from the Repository Explorer. You may create a top-level folder that appears directly underneath the Enterprise Items or Repository Items category, or a subfolder that exists within another folder. You may create new categories, or subcategories that exist within either Personal or Corporate categories. If you wish to create a top-level folder, ensure that you've selected the desired Enterprise Items or Repository Items folder first. Click the folder button in the Repository Explorer toolbar, or right-click the selected folder and choose New Folder from the pop-up menu. A folder will be added to the repository with the default name of "New Folder," and you'll be placed immediately into edit mode, where you can type your own name for the folder. Type the new folder name and press ENTER or click elsewhere with your mouse.

Create categories within the Corporate and Personal category folders using the same steps. First, select the high-level category (Corporate or your User ID within the Personal category) that you wish to create a subcategory within. Then, click the folder button in the Repository Explorer toolbar, or right-click the high-level category and choose New Category from the pop-up menu. A new category will be added with the default name of "New Category," and you'll be placed immediately into edit mode, where you can type your own name for the category. Type the new category name and press ENTER, or click elsewhere with your mouse.

If you wish to create additional folders or categories, you may repeat the previous steps (just make sure you've selected the desired Enterprise Items folder, Repository Items folder, or Corporate or Personal category prior to clicking the folder toolbar button). If you wish to create a subfolder below an existing folder, or a subcategory below an existing category, select the higher-level folder or category first. Then, click the folder button in the Repository Explorer toolbar or right-click and choose the New option from the pop-up menu. You'll see a lower-level folder or category within the higher-level item you right-clicked, again with the default New name, which you can rename immediately.

If you wish to rename a folder or category you've already added, select the item you wish to rename and then hold the mouse button down for a few seconds. You may also select the item and press F2, or right-click the desired item and choose Rename from the pop-up menu. In all cases, the item name will go into edit mode and you can type a new name for the folder or category.

Deleting folders or categories is similarly straightforward. In the case of Repository or Enterprise folders, you must ensure that all subfolders and objects within the folder have been deleted, as you cannot delete a folder that contains any subfolders of objects. Select the folder or category you wish to delete and simply press the DEL key. Or, you may click the X button in the Repository Explorer toolbar or right-click the desired item and choose Delete from the pop-up menu. You'll be prompted to confirm the deletion.

Steps are similar for deleting Categories. The slight difference, however, is that Corporate categories can be deleted even if they contain objects (as deleting a category won't delete related objects). Personal subcategories can be deleted, but the top-level Personal category tied to your Enterprise user ID cannot.

CAUTION *Deleting folders and categories, like deleting individual objects in the repository, cannot be undone. Make sure the object or folder you want to delete is no longer needed before you delete it.*

Adding and Deleting Repository Item Objects

You may add report objects to the repository at any time, even if you haven't yet created any folder structure (moving objects into or among folders will be discussed later in the chapter). The method for adding an object to the repository is dependent on the type of object you wish to add, and there is more than one way to add different types of items.

Text Objects or Bitmap Graphics

A text object or bitmap graphic can be added to the repository by simply dragging and dropping it from the Design or Preview tab of the report into the Repository Explorer. You may add the object at the very top level by dropping it on the Repository Items folder. If you wish to place the object into a particular folder, drag and drop the text object or bitmap on top of the folder you wish to add it to. You may also add a text object or bitmap by right-clicking the desired object and choosing Add To Repository from the pop-up menu.

Specify a name for the object to appear in the repository. Make sure you don't use a name already used for another repository object of the same type in the same folder (you'll be warned if you do this and will overwrite the repository object with the same name if you proceed). You can, however, add a repository object with the same name into a different folder, or an object with the same name, but of a different type, in the same folder.

Although they are not required, you can also add an author name and description for your entry. If you choose the pop-up menu method to add the object, the contents of the Repository Items folder will appear within the Add Item dialog box. If you wish to place the object in a folder, choose the folder where you want to place the new object. If you select the name of the BOE server instead of a folder, the object will be placed directly in the top level (the Repository Items folder) in the Repository Explorer. Click OK when you've specified all information to add the object to the repository.

If you wish to rename an object you added to the repository previously, you may simply select the object inside the Repository Explorer and then hold the mouse button down for a few seconds. You may also select the object and press the F2 key, or right-click the object and choose Rename from the pop-up menu. The object will go into edit mode, where you can type in a new name and press ENTER or click away from the object name. The object will be renamed (you'll receive an error if you try to use a name of another object of the same type and name in the same folder).

If you initially place an object in a particular folder (or in no folder, but right within the Repository Items folder itself), you may move or copy it to another location with a simple drag-and-drop operation. Select the object you wish to move and hold your mouse button down. Then, drag the object on top of its new preferred location (a folder if you wish to move the object to that folder, or the Repository Items folder if you wish to move the object out of a folder and place it in the repository top level). When you drop the object in its new location, it will then appear where you dropped it. Holding the CTRL key down while dragging will copy the object to its new location, also leaving the object in its original location. If there is already an object with the same name in the destination folder, you will be warned that it will be overwritten.

NOTE *You cannot drag and drop any repository items to any Enterprise Items folder, or to a Corporate or Personal category, from within the Repository Explorer. You'll receive a "no-drop cursor" (a circle with a line through it) if you attempt to drop into these portions of the Repository Explorer.*

Deleting a text object or bitmap from the repository is similar to deleting folders. Just select the object you want to delete and press the DEL key. You may alternatively click the X button in the Repository Explorer toolbar or right-click the object and choose Delete from the pop-up menu. And as with folders, deleting text objects or bitmaps can't be undone. Make sure you really want to delete the object from the repository before proceeding. Note that deleting an object from the repository won't delete it from reports that had originally made use of it. It will still remain in those reports, but it won't be available to add to any new reports.

While you can't add a SQL command to the report from the Repository Explorer (you must do this in the Database Expert), you can rename or delete it from there. And, although you must add Lists of Values or Prompt Groups to the repository from the Business View Manager (or by publishing a report with a Dynamic/Cascading Pick List to BOE), you may rename them from the Repository Explorer. Use the same steps mentioned previously for deleting or renaming text objects and bitmaps to delete or rename SQL commands, or to rename Lists of Values or Prompt Groups.

NOTE *If you delete an object from the repository that may be part of existing reports, users will receive an error message when they open the report and attempt to "Update Repository Objects." The object on the report will then appear as it did when the report was last saved.*

Custom Functions

Add custom functions to the repository from the Formula Workshop. With the Formula Workshop displayed, select the report custom function you wish to add to the repository and click Add To Repository. You may also right-click the custom function name and choose Add To Repository from the pop-up menu. And you may also simply drag the custom function name from the Report Custom Functions category of the Formula Workshop to the Repository Custom Functions category.

NOTE *You won't be prompted for a folder to place the custom function in. The folder structure discussed earlier doesn't apply to custom functions, which are placed in a separate area of the repository just for them. If you assigned categories to your custom functions when you created them, the categories will be retained when you place the custom function in the repository. Chapter 5 discusses how to categorize custom functions.*

Deleting a custom function from the repository is quite straightforward. Simply expand the Repository Custom Functions category of the Formula Workshop, select the custom function that you wish to delete, and press the DEL key. You may alternatively right-click the custom function name and choose Delete from the pop-up menu. In either case, you'll be warned that deleting a custom function from the repository can't be undone. Confirm that you want to delete the function and it will be permanently removed from the repository. Note that deleting an object from the repository won't delete it from reports that had originally made use of it. It will still remain in those reports, but it won't be available to add to any new reports.

TIP *The sample repository shipped with BusinessObjects Enterprise contains a few sample text objects, SQL commands, and bitmaps. These are for demonstration only and will be of little or no use to you when designing your own reports. There are, however, some useful custom functions supplied with the BOE repository that you may find of use in your own reporting tasks.*

SQL Commands

Add SQL commands to the repository in the Database Expert (creating SQL commands is discussed in more detail in Chapter 15). First, create the SQL command so that it appears in the Selected Tables list of the Database Expert. Then, right-click and choose Add To Repository from the pop-up menu.

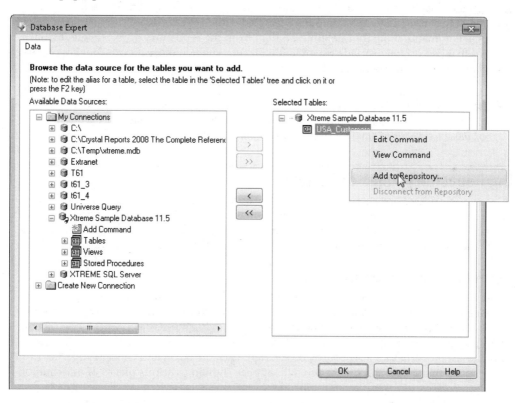

If you haven't previously logged on to BOE, you'll be prompted to do so. You'll be presented with a dialog box similar to previously described dialogs prompting you to name the object and choose a location in the repository for the object (SQL commands can be stored in the same folder structure you set up in the Repository Explorer). You may optionally specify the author, as well as changing the description for the SQL command to something other than the SQL statement that makes up the command (which is placed in the description text box by default). When you click OK, the SQL command will be added to the repository. It will then appear in the Repository section of the Database Expert.

NOTE *You'll also be able to see SQL commands in the Repository Explorer alongside text objects and bitmaps—they'll just be displayed with a different icon. However, you won't be able to just drag and drop them to the report as you can text objects or bitmaps. You can, however, rename and delete SQL commands from the Repository Explorer using the same techniques described for other items.*

Renaming or deleting a SQL command from the repository must be done in the Repository Explorer—you cannot rename or delete a SQL command from the repository in the Database Expert. Once you've closed the Database Expert and have arrived at the report Design tab, display the Repository Explorer. Navigate the folder structure to find the desired SQL command. Use techniques described earlier in the chapter to rename or delete the SQL command. Note that deleting an item from the repository won't delete it from reports that had originally made use of it. It will still remain in those reports, but it won't be available to add to any new reports.

NOTE *BOE Business Views are also stored and managed in the repository. Complete details on how to maintain repository-based Business Views are available in a supplementary document available for download from this book's companion web site, CrystalBook.com.*

Adding Repository Items to Reports

Once you've added objects to the repository as outlined earlier in the chapter, you, along with other users sharing the same repository, will want to add the items to reports. Repository versions of text objects, bitmap graphics, custom functions, SQL commands, dynamic pick lists, and Business Views are added in different places throughout Crystal Reports.

Text Objects or Bitmap Graphics

Add these items to your report from the Repository Explorer (which can be displayed by clicking the Repository Explorer button in the Standard toolbar or with the View | Repository Explorer pull-down menu item). If necessary, log on to BusinessObjects Enterprise. Then, simply expand any folders to reveal the text objects and bitmaps that are available. If you want to see properties for a repository object, right-click the object and choose Properties from the pop-up menu. A small dialog box will appear showing various pieces of information about the object.

To add the object to the report, simply drag it from the Repository Explorer to the report. As when dragging and dropping fields from the Field Explorer, an outline will appear as you drag. When you've reached the desired position for the object, release your mouse button. The text object or bitmap graphic will be placed on the report.

TIP   *Don't be alarmed when you are unable to format or resize objects you add to the report from the repository. These objects are "connected" to the repository and can't be edited, resized, or formatted until they have been "disconnected." This is discussed later in the chapter.*

Custom Functions

Make use of repository custom functions in the Formula Workshop. You may add a custom function to the report from the repository directly, which will place it in the Formula Editor's function tree for use like built-in Crystal Reports functions. Alternatively, you can use the Formula Expert to create a formula based on a custom function from the repository.

To add a custom function to the report directly, so that it appears in the Formula Editor's function tree, begin by displaying the Formula Workshop. You may do this by clicking the Formula Workshop button in the Expert Tools toolbar, or by choosing Report | Formula Workshop from the pull-down menus.

Expand the Repository Custom Functions category of the Formula Workshop until you find the custom function that you wish to use (you may need to log on to BusinessObjects Enterprise if you haven't previously). Select the function you wish to add and click the Add To Report toolbar button in the Formula Workshop toolbar. You can also right-click the function name in the Formula Workshop tree and choose Add To Report from the pop-up menu. And finally, you may simply drag the custom function you wish to add to the report from the Repository Custom Functions category to the Report Custom Functions category of the Formula Workshop tree.

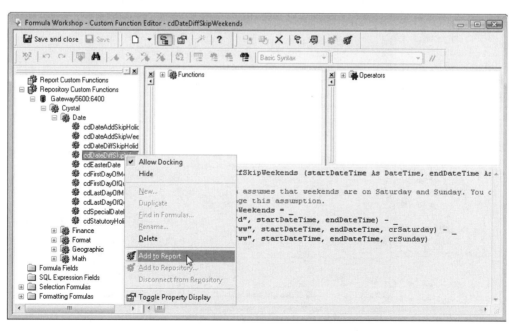

Since a repository custom function can potentially call other custom functions within the repository, you may be asked to confirm the addition to the report of other custom functions. Once you do this, all custom functions you've added from the repository will now appear in the Custom Functions category of the function tree for you to add to formulas.

TIP *More details on creating formulas with the Formula Expert and using custom functions in formulas can be found in Chapters 4 and 5.*

SQL Commands and Business Views

Add repository-based SQL commands and Business Views to your report from the Database Expert, the Set Location dialog box, or another data-related dialog box that you typically use to add database tables to the report. In these dialog boxes, you'll see a Repository folder within the Create New Connection folder. When you click it, you may be prompted to log on to BOE. Then, the BusinessObjects Enterprise Explorer dialog box will appear, showing the repository folder structure. Expand the folders to reveal SQL commands or Business Views that are located in the repository. An example of the BusinessObjects Enterprise Explorer from the Database Expert is shown here:

Choose the SQL command or Business View that you want to add to the repository. Then, double-click the item, or select it and click Open. The BusinessObjects Enterprise Explorer will close, and the original dialog box will reappear with the item you chose added to the Repository folder. Select the desired item and click the right arrow to add it to the report, right-click the item and choose Add To Report from the pop-up menu, or just drag it from the left side of the Database Expert to the right side. Similar procedures will add SQL commands and Business View "tables" to the report from the repository in other data-related dialog boxes.

Changing Repository Items on Your Report

As indicated earlier in the chapter, you may become confused once you add an object from the repository to your report. This might occur if you attempt to change the format of a text object you added from the repository, resize a bitmap graphic you added from the repository, or change the text of a SQL command or custom function that's been added to the repository. In all these cases, you'll discover that the objects are "locked" or set to a read-only status—you won't be able to make these kinds of changes.

This behavior is by design. In order to ensure that the repository controls the appearance and behavior of these objects, they remain *connected* to the repository once you've added them to the report. As long as they're connected, the repository will control their appearance and size (in the case of text objects and bitmap graphics), or their text (in the case of SQL commands and custom functions). Probably the most obvious clue that an object is connected is the inability to change it. However, in some dialog boxes, you'll also notice a small vertical-bar-with-link icon next to the object's name, which will indicated that the object is connected to the repository.

The main benefit of leaving objects connected to the repository is to allow them to be updated automatically if anybody else makes changes to the repository. For example, if you have added a common company logo and slogan to your report using a repository-connected bitmap graphic and text object, you'll probably want all reports using those objects to automatically reflect changes to the repository should your logo or slogan change. In order to ensure consistency with this behavior, individual changes to the objects once they've been added to reports shouldn't be allowed.

TIP *To ensure connected objects will be updated when you initially open your reports, you must make one of two choices. By choosing File | Options from the pull-down menus and checking the Update Connected Repository Objects On Open option on the Reporting tab, you ensure all reports automatically update connected objects when opened. If you only want to update connected objects on a report-by-report basis, leave this global option off and instead check the Update Repository Objects check box on the Open File dialog box when opening a Crystal Report.*

To change this behavior and manually make changes to objects you've added from the repository, you must *disconnect* them from the repository. Begin by right-clicking the object. In the case of text objects or bitmap graphics, right-click directly on the object in the Design or Preview tabs. For SQL commands or custom functions, right-click the command or function name in their respective dialog boxes. From the pop-up menu, choose Disconnect From Repository. Notice that you may now resize or reformat text objects or bitmap graphics, as well as changing the contents of SQL commands or custom functions. Also, you'll notice the previously mentioned vertical bar "connected" icon is no longer visible.

Be aware, though, that these objects will now behave as though you just added them to the report—they won't be automatically updated by the repository any more. Using the company logo and slogan example mentioned previously, if you disconnect the objects from the repository and save the report, they won't reflect any repository changes the next time you open the report.

Updating Repository Versions of Objects

Continuing with the company logo and slogan examples referred to previously in this chapter; what if you are in charge of updating the repository copies of the company logo and slogan? Or you may have a company-wide custom function that requires changing for a new fiscal year or a new bonus program. In these situations, you must add the object from the repository to your report, make changes, and update the repository with the changed object.

As mentioned previously, you can't edit or modify an object that's connected to the repository. This may cause confusion if you are required to update the repository copy of an object. To get around this confusion, consider the steps required to update the repository copy of an object:

1. Add the object to a report from the repository.

2. Disconnect the object from the repository.

3. Make necessary changes to the object.

4. Save the object back to the repository in the same folder and with the same name as the original object.

Step 4 will exhibit behavior that is slightly different than the first time you added the object to the repository. When you attempt to add an object to the repository in the same folder with the same name, you will be warned that an object already exists and given the opportunity to update the version in the repository with the version that you're saving. If you choose to do this, the old repository object will be replaced with the updated version.

Once you've performed these steps, note that the updated object you just added back to the repository will once again be connected—you won't be able to change formatting or contents. To make future changes to the object, you must once again disconnect it from the repository.

NOTE *Business Views, including parameter field dynamic pick list objects, are modified using the BusinessObjects Enterprise Business View Manager—you cannot update Business Views from inside Crystal Reports. The Business View Manager is discussed in detail in a supplementary chapter available for download from the book's companion web site, CrystalBook.com.*

Controlling Repository Rights

With a shared repository, as with company database connections and network resources, you may wish to limit the ability to update or delete repository objects to a certain set of key users, while permitting the rest of those sharing the repository to just add existing repository items to their reports. As the Crystal Reports repository is managed by BusinessObjects Enterprise, you make use of BOE user and group permissions to accomplish this.

While typical BusinessObjects Enterprise user and group right assignment is accomplished in the Central Management Console (more detail on BusinessObjects Enterprise architecture and management is discussed in Part II of the book), repository rights are maintained in the BOE Business View Manager. If you don't already have access to the Business View Manager in an existing BusinessObjects Enterprise installation, you must specifically install the Business View Manager on a Windows computer from the BOE product CD. And, needless to say, since the repository is part of BusinessObjects Enterprise, you must have a functional member of the BusinessObjects Enterprise XI 3.0 system in place to make use of the Business View Manager.

NOTE *Other Business View capabilities of the Business View Manager not relating to repository rights are covered in an online chapter available from this book's companion web site, CrystalBook.com.*

Start the Business View Manager from your Windows start menu. You will be prompted to log on to BusinessObjects Enterprise. Ensure that you use a BOE user ID (initially, the Administrator ID or a member of the Administrators group will be required) that provides sufficient rights to change repository security. The Business View Manager will appear. If necessary, display the Repository Explorer within the Business View Manager by choosing View | Repository Explorer from the pull-down menus. This window, similar in appearance to the Repository Explorer in Crystal Reports, may be "undocked" and moved around as a free-floating window.

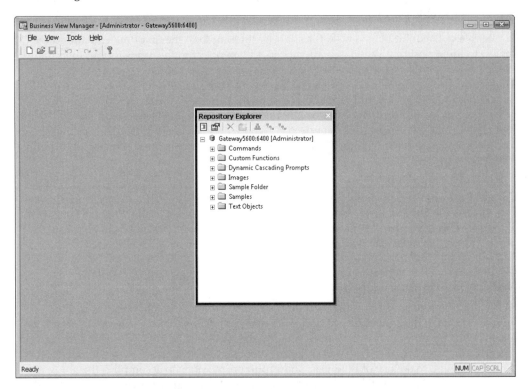

Notice that the folder structure of the repository is exposed in the Repository Explorer: your BOE Central Management Server name appears at the top of the folder hierarchy, with top-level folders appearing below them. If you click the plus sign next to a folder, it expands to show any subfolder or repository objects within it. The initial difference between the Repository Explorer contained in the Business View Manager and that contained within Crystal Reports is the lack of the Enterprise Items and Repository Items folders, and of the Corporate and Personal categories in the Business View Manager version. Here, only repository items are shown—no report objects or categories are visible.

Notice an additional folder labeled Custom Functions that you may not have seen before in other versions of the Repository Explorer or Formula Workshop. This is the dedicated folder within the repository where all custom functions are contained. As you can't specify a folder name in the Formula Workshop when adding a custom function, they will all be placed in this single repository folder.

Consider this repository folder and object hierarchy carefully when planning your repository security plan. If you simply want to supply a single set of repository rights for the entire repository (perhaps you want Administrators to have full repository rights, but everyone else to have only read rights), you may set repository rights at the *Central Management Server level.* However, if you want to provide more granular rights (perhaps you want a

Sales group to have full rights to the entire Sales repository folder or just certain objects or subfolders within the Sales folder), then you may set rights at the *folder and object level*.

Furthermore, you will want to consider the concept of *rights inheritance*, the capability to set rights at a higher level in the repository (perhaps on the Central Management Server or a top-level folder) and have the rights automatically *inherited* by folders, subfolders, and objects at lower levels. By creative use of different levels of rights and inheritance, you have very tight control (perhaps more than you'll need) over repository rights.

Controlling Rights at the Central Management Server Level

Begin by considering the overall set of rights you want to give to the repository as a whole; these will be the rights you set at the Central Management Server level. All folders, subfolders, and objects in the repository will inherit the rights you set here. If, as discussed previously, you only wish to have a single set of rights apply to the entire repository, you need only set rights at this level.

Begin by selecting the top-level Central Management Server name in the Repository Explorer. Then, right-click and choose Edit Rights from the pop-up menu. The Edit Rights dialog box will appear, as illustrated in Figure 18-1.

You'll see a list of BusinessObjects Enterprise groups and users that have already been granted or denied rights at the Central Management Server level (a freshly installed Central Management Server will initially show the Administrators and Everyone groups here). Note the three different rights that can be set for each user or group:

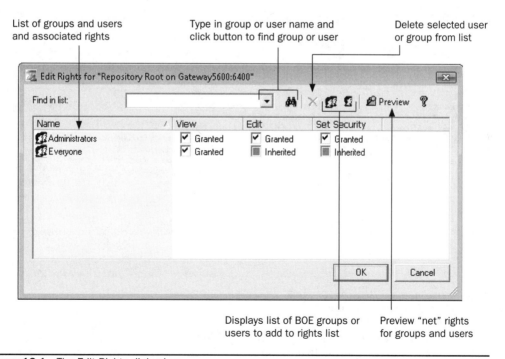

FIGURE 18-1   The Edit Rights dialog box

- **View**   The ability to add objects in the repository to reports
- **Edit**   The ability to add new objects to the repository, or update and delete existing objects in the repository
- **Set Security**   The ability to change repository security settings for others

Further, if you cycle through the available options for each right by clicking the check box, you'll notice that a right can be granted, denied, or inherited. *Granting* the right explicitly gives that right to the chosen group or user. *Denying* the right explicitly takes the right away from the chosen group or user. And, allowing the right to be *inherited* will grant or deny the right on the basis of higher-level security settings (at the Central Management Server level, inherited rights apply only to the Administrators group, which is automatically granted all rights to the repository).

If you wish to specifically grant or deny rights to additional groups or users, you'll need to add the group or user to the list by clicking the Add Groups or Add Users button in the Edit Rights dialog box toolbar. These buttons will display and additional Add Groups or Add User dialog box showing all BusinessObjects Enterprise groups or users (to actually create additional BOE groups or users, you must use other BOE administrative tools, such as the Central Management Console—you can't add these here). Use this dialog box to choose additional groups or users to add to the Edit Rights dialog box.

Filter the list of groups or users by criteria   Clear any filter to show all users or groups

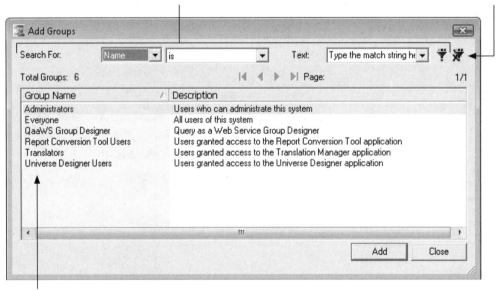

Double-click a group or user or click
Add to add it to the Edit Rights dialog

Once the additional groups or users you've added appear in the Edit Rights dialog box, you can grant or deny rights to that group or user by clicking the appropriate check boxes. The next time you set rights for the Central Management Server, the new groups and users you added will reappear with the specific rights you granted or denied appearing next to them. If you wish to remove a group or user that you previously set rights for, select the user or group and click the Delete toolbar button (the X).

Although it's not as relevant at the Central Management Server level, you may still want to see what the ultimate or *net* set of rights is for each group or user. Do this by clicking the Preview button in the Edit Rights dialog box toolbar. The list of users and groups will change, showing the actual combination of rights that result from explicit settings and inheritance. If you need to change any rights, click Preview again to return the list to its "editable" state.

Once you've set rights for all necessary groups and users, just click OK to close the Edit Rights dialog box. The rights you set will be saved on the BusinessObjects Enterprise system and will take effect immediately for all repository users. The rights you set at the Central Management Server level will automatically be inherited by all folders and objects in the repository.

CAUTION *Be careful when denying rights at the Central Management Server level. If you deny a right to a group or user at this level, that user or group won't have the right anywhere in the repository, even if you explicitly grant it at a lower level. Because of the repository's inheritance rules, denial of rights takes precedence over granting of rights when rights are inherited.*

Controlling Rights at the Folder and Object Level

If you wish to take advantage of BusinessObjects Enterprise's folder- and object-level repository security, perform similar steps to those discussed previously for setting repository security at the Central Management Server level. However, prior to choosing the Edit Rights option from the pop-up menu, ensure that you've selected the desired folder, subfolder, or object in the Repository Explorer that you want the rights to apply to. The same Edit Rights dialog box will appear.

If you've granted or denied rights for groups or users at a higher level, you'll already see the group or user listed in the Edit Rights dialog box. You may either change rights that may be inherited by clicking the check boxes for existing groups or add additional groups or users to the Edit Rights dialog box by clicking the Add Groups or Add Users button in the Edit Rights dialog box toolbar.

The important thing to consider when setting rights at this level is inheritance. If a right has already been granted or denied at a higher level (the Central Management Server or a higher-level folder), that right will be inherited at this lower level. Specifically, if a right has been denied at a higher level, even granting it at this lower level won't give the group or user the right. If a right hasn't been granted or denied at all, granting at this level will enable the right for the group or user. If a right has never been specifically granted (either at this or a higher level), then the user won't have the right.

Once you've specified rights at the lower level, click Preview to see the set of net rights granted to users and groups. This net rights display takes into account inherited rights from higher-level folder and the Central Management Server, as well as rights specifically granted and denied at this level. By using the Preview button, you can see what each group and user will ultimately be able to do within this folder or to this object. If you need to modify rights after viewing net rights, click Preview again to return the list of groups and users to an "editable" state.

NOTE *Preventing users from updating or deleting repository objects will still allow them to "detach" objects from the repository and change them once they've been placed on the report. However, if they make any changes to such objects, they still won't be able to update the repository with their updated versions.*

Creating Crystal Reports Applications with Visual Studio .NET

N ow in its latest, "2008" version, Microsoft's cornerstone development tool, Visual Studio .NET, continues its close association with Crystal Reports. Visual Studio .NET (abbreviated as VS.NET in much of this chapter) not only includes its own version of Crystal Reports out of the box, but provides additional capabilities if you install Crystal Reports 2008 after VS.NET installation. With this powerful combination of application creation and report design, you may create complex and intricate reporting applications by embedding reports right inside your VS.NET Windows or web applications. While minimal coding is required to integrate a report, a complete set of object models exists to allow incredibly precise control of your reports at run time.

Crystal Reports 2008 Integration with Visual Studio 6 and Java

While Business Objects continued to provide support for both the COM-based Visual Studio 6 and Visual Studio .NET in previous Crystal Reports Developer's Editions, Visual Studio 6 COM integration with the Report Designer Component has been deprecated as of Crystal Reports 2008. As most organizations have moved toward the myriad versions of VS.NET, Visual Studio 6 development has slowed significantly. As such, Business Objects has elected to only support the VS.NET environment moving forward.

If you still require Visual Studio 6 COM support to integrate Crystal Reports, Business Objects recommends that you use Crystal Reports XI, the Crystal Reports version released prior to version 2008. In particular, Crystal Reports XI Developer Edition provides full COM support with the Report Designer Component for COM-based Windows applications and Active Server Pages web systems. Full coverage of this integration method can be found in *Crystal Reports XI: The Complete Reference*, also published by McGraw-Hill.

Crystal Reports integration with custom Java applications is provided by *Crystal Reports 2008 for Eclipse*. This integration option consists of a free download available from the Business Objects web site. Crystal Reports 2008 for Eclipse integrates with open-source Eclipse development environments, providing a Java integration option for custom Crystal Reports applications.

Crystal/VS.NET Bundle Options

Crystal Reports has played a prominent role in Microsoft development environments for many years. Not only was Crystal Reports bundled with earlier versions of Visual Basic (Microsoft's original COM-oriented development tool), but every Professional or higher edition of VS.NET, up to and including Visual Studio 2008, includes an option to install Crystal Reports as well (Crystal Reports support isn't available in VS.NET Express editions, or Visual Studio .NET 2003 Standard Edition). These "included in the box" versions of Crystal Reports have been referred to using various terminologies in different VS.NET versions. The latest bundled Crystal Reports version, included with Visual Studio 2008, has been named *Crystal Reports Basic*, to provide a clear delineation between it and the full Crystal Reports version, such as Crystal Reports 2008.

When you initially install VS.NET, you'll find a Crystal Reports option as part of the standard installation screen. Selecting this option installs the .NET-bundled version of Crystal Reports Basic, consisting of the Crystal help collection added to the combined VS.NET help collection; and necessary assemblies for designing a report within the VS.NET IDE, integrating the report with a Windows or web application, and creating a Crystal Report web service. This *will not* install a stand-alone copy of Crystal Reports that allows you to design reports outside of the VS.NET IDE.

As such, one of the first decisions you'll need to make as a Visual Studio .NET developer is whether or not the Crystal Reports Basic edition bundled with VS.NET is sufficient for your integration needs. While the bundled Crystal Reports versions provide varying capabilities (generally, the newer the version of VS.NET, the more capable the bundled version of Crystal Reports), Business Objects "incentivizes" developers to upgrade to the full version of Crystal Reports by providing additional features when the full version is installed on a computer already containing a bundled VS.NET Crystal Reports version.

The full version of Crystal Reports 2008 continues this tradition. When you install Crystal Reports 2008 on a computer already containing Microsoft Visual Studio 2003, 2005, or 2008 (Crystal Reports 2008 will not work with VS.NET versions earlier than 2003), you'll see additional developer tool options in the installation screen. Choosing this option will install updated VS.NET assemblies, and additional online help, for the full version of Crystal Reports 2008. Many of the new features described elsewhere in this book, such as the interactive Parameter Panel, optional parameter fields, interactive sorting, saved data selection, and Flash/Xcelsius integration, are provided by installing the full version of Crystal Reports 2008 alongside Visual Studio .NET.

PART I

CAUTION *Make sure you install VS.NET before Crystal Reports, or the VS.NET integration options won't appear in the Crystal Reports installation screen and the extra features won't be available in your VS.NET development environment. You may double-check that you've properly installed extra Crystal Reports 2008 features by using Visual Studio's Help | About pull-down menu option. Look for a Crystal Reports 2008 entry in the installed products list, particularly denoting your Crystal Reports 2008 installation keycode. If you don't see a specific reference to Crystal Reports 2008, you will not be able to use the extra features of Crystal Reports 2008 in your custom applications. In this event, you must re-run Crystal Reports 2008 installation and select the Visual Studio add-on options from the installation screen.*

Also, a full Crystal Reports 2008 installation will add the ReportClientDocument object model. The additional coding interface works with an embedded version of the Report Application Server, which is also part of the full Crystal Reports 2008 version. These two additions provide the ability to actually create and modify *new* report objects from within your custom applications. These code-designed report objects can be displayed and manipulated within your application just like report objects designed within the VS.NET IDE or stand-alone Crystal Reports, or they may be saved as external .RPT files for use in other reporting applications.

Not only are there increased integration capabilities with a full installation of Crystal Reports 2008, but report design can be performed with the stand-alone Crystal Reports designer, instead of just within the VS.NET Integrated Development Environment (IDE).

While later versions of Crystal Reports Basic have improved design capabilities within the IDE (in particular, later versions include the ability to preview report output within the VS.NET IDE without actually running the application), you may still find it preferable to create reports with the full version of Crystal Reports 2008, instead of the report designer embedded in the IDE. The resulting .RPT file can then simply be imported into your VS.NET application for integration. Also, you may design stand-alone reports with the full version that can run outside of a Visual Studio application, if your organization requires this capability.

> **NOTE** *Crystal Reports versions prior to 2008 only provided VS.NET integration capabilities if you purchased the Developer Edition of the software. Crystal Reports 2008 has been simplified, in that only one software edition is available. As such, VS.NET integration capabilities are available without regard for any special edition of Crystal Reports 2008.*

Crystal Reports Windows and Web Forms Viewer Control Objects

The first concept you will want to become familiar with when integrating a Crystal report into a Windows or web application with VS.NET is the separation between the actual report itself (the .RPT file you either create within the VS.NET IDE or add to it after creating it in the Crystal Reports designer) and the viewer that actually shows the report to the user in the application. It's important to distinguish these two separate, but related, objects. If you only wish to include a report in the application for the purpose of exporting to an external file (perhaps placing the exported report on the web server for later download or sharing somewhere else within the web server's network), or printing a report on an attached printer, then you may not even need to present the report visually to the user.

However, for most applications you'll need to determine how to present the report to the user within your Windows or web form. For this, VS.NET includes separate versions of the *CrystalReportViewer* control for both Windows and web forms. By dropping the CrystalReportViewer object onto a Windows or web form, you can immediately display a Crystal report, including all embedded formatting. This viewer also supports all typical Crystal Reports interaction, including page-on-demand viewing, group tree navigation, report group drill-down, on-demand subreport interactivity, and report exporting and printing. And, if you've installed the full version of Crystal Reports 2008 (examples and illustrations in this chapter assume you have), then new version 2008 features, such as the Parameter Panel, will also be visible and usable within these viewer controls.

> **NOTE** *Throughout this chapter, most of the techniques apply equally to Windows and web applications. When there are differences, they will be noted.*

Your First Application: Viewing a Report

After creating a Windows application or a web application (the language you use to create it is irrelevant—Crystal Reports is entirely language independent in VS.NET), add a viewer to the desired form by dragging it from the appropriate section of the Toolbox (in Visual Studio 2008, the control is located in the toolbox Reporting section). An outline will initially appear inside the form, and a set of properties specific to the viewer will appear in the Properties box. This is shown in Figure 19-1.

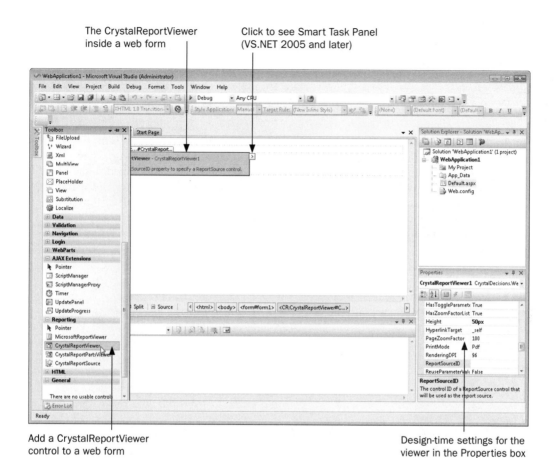

The CrystalReportViewer inside a web form

Click to see Smart Task Panel (VS.NET 2005 and later)

Add a CrystalReportViewer control to a web form

Design-time settings for the viewer in the Properties box

FIGURE 19-1   CrystalReportViewer control in a Web Form

However, merely adding a viewer to a form won't display anything when the application is run. This is because you must tie or *bind* an actual Crystal Report object to the viewer so that there's an actual report to view.

There are numerous ways to bind reports to the viewer. The option you choose depends largely on the way your application is designed—whether your reports are "external" to your application (located at a specific file location or elsewhere on the network connection), designed within the VS.NET IDE, or contained in a Report Component (discussed later); whether you want to use the web-only report caching feature (also discussed later); and so forth.

Probably the simplest way to bind a report to the viewer is to specify the full pathname and filename of an .RPT file located on local or network drive with one line of code. The report can be bound at run time by specifying the viewer's ReportSource property. For example, if you display the code window for the form containing the viewer (perhaps the Page_Load event), specify the viewer's ReportSource property as follows:

```
Protected Sub Page_Load(ByVal sender As Object, ByVal e As EventArgs) Handles
Me.Load
        CrystalReportViewer1.ReportSource = "C:\Temp\Sample Report.rpt"
End Sub
```

In this particular scenario, the viewer will retain its smaller footprint with no report display inside the form at design time, as illustrated in Figure 19-1. However, when you run the application, the form will display the report. If the report contains saved data, it will simply be displayed with the saved data and the report will not be refreshed. If the report does not contain saved data, you may be prompted for database credentials or parameter values before the report displays. If you wish to refresh the report before it displays even if it has saved data, add one more line of code below the assignment of the ReportSource property.

```
CrystalReportViewer1.RefreshReport()
```

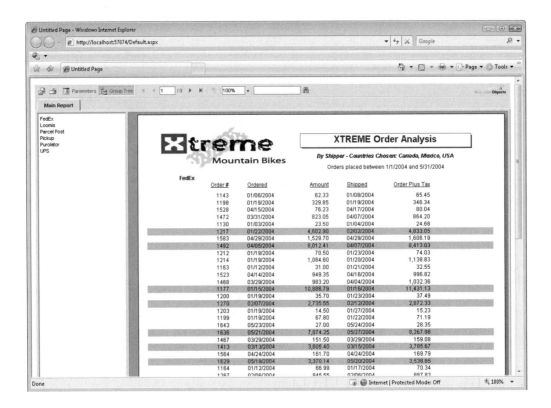

Although there are few differences between the Windows and web versions of the CrystalReportViewer control, you will see a slight difference when you create the same simple viewing application as a Windows application. While the process of adding a CrystalReportViewer control to a Windows form is identical to that for a web form, the VS.NET properties box actually displays a ReportSource property for the CrystalReportViewer control in a Windows form. This allows you to specify an .RPT file to bind to the control at design time (the web version only presents a ReportSourceID property, which is different). By selecting this property and clicking the ellipses button, you'll be presented with a File Open dialog box. Select an .RPT file to bind to the viewer control.

The other immediate difference you will notice is the Design-Time Preview feature. While this is also available with web applications when you use a different method of binding a report to the viewer control, the Windows viewer will display a preview of the report in VS.NET design view once you've supplied the report filename to the ReportSource property in the properties box.

CrystalReportViewer control will display chosen report in VS.NET design view

Specify report filename with ReportSource design-time property

Once you've added the CrystalReportViewer control to a Windows form and bound an .RPT file, run the application to display the report in the Windows form. Report viewing behavior will be the same as with a web application. If the report contains saved data, it will simply appear. If the report doesn't contain saved data, or you add a line of code executing the viewer control's Refresh method, the CrystalReportViewer will prompt for any necessary database credentials or parameter values before refreshing the report against the database.

TIP *You may notice an additional Crystal Reports viewer choice when you create a web application. The CrystalReportPartsViewer, also available in the Toolbox within web applications, will display only certain objects on a report, instead of the entire report. The initial object displayed by the CrystalReportPartsViewer can be specified on the Options dialog box, available by using Report | Options from the stand-alone Crystal Reports pull-down menus, or from the right-click Report | Report Options menu in the embedded report designer in the VS.NET IDE.*

Crystal Report Object Types

The method of calling an external report file demonstrated previously in this section is referred to as using a *non-embedded report*. A non-embedded report is simply an .RPT file that you've created with the stand-alone version of Crystal Reports 2008 (or, perhaps saved as an .RPT file from within the VS.NET IDE report designer, described later in the chapter). The external .RPT file is not directly contained within your VS.NET project file, doesn't appear in the Solution Explorer, and won't be contained in the final project when it is built. There are advantages and disadvantages of using non-embedded reports with VS.NET projects. Advantages include the ability to modify the .RPT file should changes be required without recompiling or redistributing your application. Disadvantages include the ability for the .RPT file to be inadvertently moved or deleted, causing the application to fail when the report is called. Also, one of the just-mentioned benefits could also be a disadvantage, if you prefer that uncontrolled modifications not be made to external reports.

The other major Crystal Reports integration approach in VS.NET is the *embedded report* object (embedded reports were referred to as "strongly typed" reports in earlier Crystal Reports versions). An embedded report is a report that actually exists as part of your VS.NET project and appears in the Solution Explorer. Embedded reports can be added to your project via a number of Add New Item and Add Existing Item methods, as well as using the CrystalReportSource .NET control from the Toolbox. Embedded reports not only offer tighter integration when controlling report behavior at run time with custom code (a class is added to your project for an embedded report), but they can also be edited right in the VS.NET IDE with the built-in Crystal Report designer (discussed later in the chapter, under "Integrated Report Designer"). Surprisingly, though, if you attempt to set the viewer's ReportSource property to the .RPT filename (via the Smart Panel in VS.NET 2005 or later, or the Property Box in earlier versions), you won't find the file in the drop-down list of available options.

NOTE *In previous versions of Crystal Reports in VS.NET applications, reports could only be embedded in Windows applications. However, Crystal Reports 2008 now allows embedded reports to be compiled into web application assemblies as well.*

An embedded report can be bound using a single line of code in the form's Page_Load event. By setting the viewer's ReportSource property to a new instance of the desired report class (sans the .RPT extension), you can bind the viewer to the report included in the project. The following examples assume that "Sample Report.RPT" has been added to your project by way of either Add Existing Item or Add New Item.

```
'Binds embedded Sample Report.RPT file from Solution Explorer
CrystalReportViewer1.ReportSource = New Sample_Report
```

In web applications, you can also bind the viewer to a cached version of the embedded report. By caching the report, you may improve performance when multiple users access the same web page that contains the report viewer. Whenever you add an embedded report to a web project, a cached class of the same report is also created, which can be bound to the Web Forms Viewer.

```
'Binds cached Sample Report.RPT file from Solution Explorer
CrystalReportViewer1.ReportSource = New CachedSample_Report
```

NOTE *Cached reports are only supported in ASP.NET web applications (not Windows applications). By caching a report, you can potentially improve performance by storing recently viewed report data on the web server for additional users that access the same web form within the prescribed cache time. If, however, you are using a very fluid transactional database that changes frequently, you may choose not to use cached reports to ensure that the user will always see the most current set of data.*

You may also wish to bind a report to the viewer via the *CrystalReportSource .NET Control.* In this situation, you add an additional component to the form from the Toolbox and choose an existing embedded report already in the project, an external .RPT file to embed within the project, or a new report to design immediately inside the VS.NET IDE. In all cases, the chosen report will be hosted by the CrystalReportSource control, which can be extensively controlled with code at run time, as well as being passed as a report source to the CrystalReportViewer control.

There are two ways to add a CrystalReportSource control to your project, and then supplying it as the report source for a CrystalReportViewer control. While the following steps refer to Crystal Reports tools in web applications, steps in Windows applications are very similar (in some Windows controls, however, embedded reports are still referenced as "typed" reports).

- Drag the CrystalReportSource control from the Reports area of the Toolbox to the form. Once you've dropped it on the form, click the Configure Report Source option on the Smart Panel (in VS.NET 2005 or later). The Configure Report Source dialog box will appear. Click the drop-down list and choose the desired report (you'll see any embedded reports you've already added to your project, the ability to browse for an external .RPT file to add to the project and tie to the control, or the option to create a new report right in the VS.NET IDE and tie to the control). Then, click the CrystalReportViewer control and select the just-added CrystalReportSource control as the report source, using either the Smart Panel Choose Report Source or Properties Box ReportSourceID drop-down list.

- Select the existing CrystalReportViewer control on the form (or, add one from the Toolbox if necessary). From the Smart Panel (in VS.NET 2005 or late), select New Report Source in the Choose Report Source drop-down list. You can also choose New Report Source from the ReportSourceID drop-down list in the Properties Box. The Create Report Source dialog box will appear. You may leave the default report source object name as-is, or change it to a more meaningful name. Then, click the drop-down list and choose the desired report (you'll see any embedded reports you've already added to your project, the ability to browse for an external .RPT file to add to the project and tie to the control, or the option to create a new report right in the VS.NET IDE and tie to the control).

Both of the just-described methods of binding a report to both CrystalReportSource and CrystalReportViewer controls provide several benefits:

1. No code whatsoever must be written to choose and display a report in a custom application.

2. If you do wish to customize report behavior with custom coding, a more robust object model is available for the CrystalReportSource control.

3. The report will be embedded in the application and will not be modifiable or "lose-able" by the end user.

4. The CrystalReportViewer control will show a representative view of the finished report via the Design-Time Preview capability of Crystal Reports 2008.

TIP *There are yet additional ways of binding reports to viewers. A complete discussion of all viewer binding options can be found in the Crystal Reports 2008 .NET Developer Guide. This guide is available in the VS.NET help collection when a full version of Crystal Reports 2008 is installed. The Developer Guide, along with sample code demonstrating many report integration techniques, can also be obtained from Business Objects' Diamond Developer community at Diamond. BusinessObjects.com.*

Integrated Report Designer

One of the more exciting integration benefits of Crystal Reports and Microsoft development environments is the *Integrated Report Designer.* This feature was originally introduced with the Report Designer Component and Visual Basic 6. As Microsoft continued to support Crystal Reports as an integrated reporting tool in Visual Studio .NET, this capability has remained in all recent versions of the VS.NET environment as well (with the exception of VS.NET Express editions). With this design tool built in to the VS.NET IDE, you can perform complex report design tasks, such as adding and joining tables, adding fields, grouping records, and formatting objects, much the same way as you can with the full Crystal Reports designer in an off-the-shelf version of Crystal Reports. When you are finished, the .RPT file you've created or modified will exist within the project as an embedded report.

NOTE *One of the initial decisions you'll be making is whether to create reports in the VS.NET IDE or in stand-alone Crystal Reports. While VS.NET allows you to create reports without buying a stand-alone copy of Crystal Reports, your report design choices are more limited in the Integrated Report Designer. This, and other differences discussed earlier in the chapter, under "Crystal/ VS.NET Bundle Options," may lead you to actually do most of your report design in a stand-alone copy of Crystal Reports and then add the .RPT file to your project with Add Existing Item.*

If you've already worked on another report (perhaps with the full stand-alone copy of Crystal Reports or another VS.NET application), you can add it to your existing project. Simply right-click the project name in the Solution Explorer and choose Add | Existing Item from the pop-up menu. An open file dialog box will appear. If you wish to only view Crystal Report files in the dialog, add a wildcard filename of *.RPT (or, choose that file extension if your particular version of VS.NET offers it). Then, only .RPT files will appear in the dialog box. Navigate to the location for your desired report and open it. It will be added to the Solution Explorer. To edit the report, simply double-click it in the Solution Explorer window. The report will appear in its own tab in the VS.NET IDE inside the Integrated Report Designer.

NOTE *Adding an existing report to your project will make a copy of the report in your project folder. Any modifications you make to this report in the Integrated Report Designer won't affect the original report you chose when you added the item.*

If you wish to create a new report from scratch for design in the Integrated Report Designer, begin by selecting the project name in the Solution Explorer. Right-click and choose Add | New Item from the pop-up menu. The Add New Item dialog box will appear. If necessary, scroll through the available items until you find the Crystal Report icon, or choose the Reporting item category (depending on the VS.NET version you are using). Once you select it, a default filename will appear at the bottom of the dialog box. Either accept it or type the desired filename in before clicking Add.

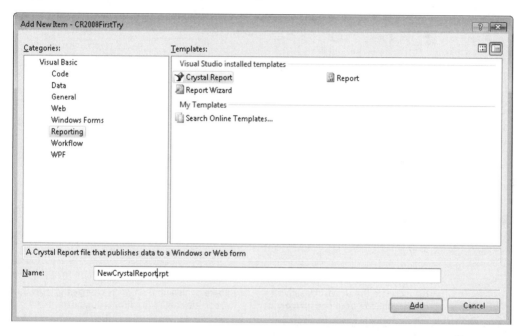

A new tab will appear in the VS.NET IDE for the new Crystal Report, and the Crystal Report Gallery will appear, which will allow three initial choices, Using The Report Wizard, As A Blank Report, and From An Existing Report.

Leaving the Using the Report Wizard radio button chosen and selecting one of the report wizards will display the step-by-step report design dialogs discussed briefly in Chapter 1 of this book. If you choose As A Blank Report, an empty report canvas will appear in VS.NET (the Database Expert won't appear automatically, as it does when using the Blank Report option in stand-alone Crystal Reports). And, if you choose the From An Existing Report choice, an open file dialog will appear where you can navigate to an existing .RPT file to import into the VS.NET Integrated Report Designer.

Once you've made your choices (and, in the case of a report wizard, proceeded through the necessary steps), your report will appear in the Integrated Report Designer inside the VS.NET IDE, as shown in Figure 19-2.

Use the Field Explorer to add fields, create formulas, create parameter fields, and so forth

Use Crystal Reports toolbars, much as you would in stand-alone Crystal Reports

Right-click in the Report Designer to choose options from pop-up menus

Make design-time property changes to individual report objects in the Properties box

FIGURE 19-2   Integrated Report Designer in VS.NET IDE

NOTE *If you are using Windows Vista with Visual Studio, the Integrated Report Designer may not appear, or you may receive an error message when you attempt to display it. This may be a side effect of Vista's Data Execution Prevention (DEP) feature. If you experience inconsistent behavior, turn off DEP in a Vista command prompt, reboot your computer, and try again.*

Choosing a Data Source

If you are creating a new report from scratch in the Integrated Report Designer, you'll initially be presented with a blank design screen when you first create the report. As with most report design scenarios, the first step will be to choose a data source to base your report on.

As with stand-alone Crystal Reports, this is done with the Database Expert. However, unlike stand-alone Crystal Reports, the Database Expert doesn't automatically appear when you first create a new report—you need to display it by using a pop-up menu option. Ensure no existing report objects are selected and right-click in the report design area. Choose

Database | Database Expert from the pop-up menu (you may also click the Database Expert toolbar button). The Database Expert will appear.

Choose the desired data source category from the list. Note that the choice of categories (and choice of available data source types) may vary, depending on whether you've installed full version of Crystal Reports 2008—additional data sources are made available when you do this. Also note that some data sources available in the stand-alone version of Crystal Reports, such as BusinessObjects Enterprise–based repository objects and Universes, won't be available in VS.NET. You will find a Project Data category, however, that will allow you to connect a report to an existing "project" data source, as an ADO.NET dataset, that has already been defined in your project.

Choose the data source (or data sources) that you wish to use for your report. You may be required to supply logon credentials to a server to make a connection. Expand the various data source categories once you've connected to choose individual tables, views, stored procedures, and so forth that you wish to use in your report. Add each desired table, view, or stored procedure to the Selected Tables list.

If you add more than one item to the Selected Tables list, the Links tab will appear in the Database Expert. Click it and link tables as described in Chapter 15. Once you've correctly added and linked tables, close the Database Expert by clicking OK.

Selecting Records and Adding Field Objects

Once you've added and linked tables or other data sources, you're ready to add field objects to the actual report canvas. You should also add either record, group, or saved data selection criteria to ensure that your report will be limited to a meaningful set of data records.

To limit the report to a certain set of records, use the Select Expert or the selection formulas. The Select Expert is displayed by right-clicking on a blank area of the report design canvas and choosing Report | Select Expert from the pop-up menu. You can also click the Select Expert toolbar button in the Crystal Reports toolbar within the VS.NET IDE. You may choose either record, group, or saved data selection with either option. If you prefer to edit the selection formula using the Crystal formula language directly, choose Report | Selection Formulas from the same pop-up menu as the Select Expert, and choose which selection formula you wish to edit. The Formula Editor will appear, where you can create or edit the selection formula. Selection is covered in detail in Chapter 3.

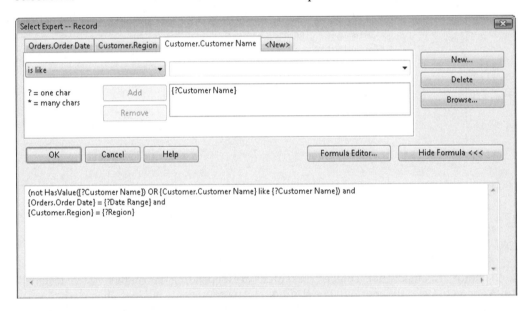

Add field objects to your report from the Field Explorer, which is initially docked at the left side of the report design window. These fields can consist of fields directly from your data source, formulas that you create, parameter fields that prompt the report viewer for a value, and so forth. Expand the desired Field Explorer category and drag the desired field to the appropriate report section. You may also right-click a Field Explorer category, or an individual field, and choose options from the pop-up menu.

You can use the Field Explorer to create report formulas, parameter fields, and SQL Expressions (all are discussed in various chapters in Part I of this book). You can also drag and drop Special Fields, such as page numbers, print date and time, and so forth, to the report from the Special Fields category. The Unbound Fields category is unique to the VS.NET Integrated Report Designer. Opening this category will reveal a field type for each supported Crystal Reports data type (String, Currency, Date, and so forth). By dragging an unbound field to the report, you are merely adding a "placeholder" object that you'll need to fill with data programmatically at run time with a project data source, such as an ADO. NET dataset.

Once you've added some initial fields to the report design canvas, you may preview the report to get a more accurate idea of how it will look when it's eventually displayed in a viewer. Visual Studio .NET 2005 and later, when combined with Crystal Reports 2008, provides the report preview capability that, previously, was only available with the stand-alone version of Crystal Reports. Notice the Main Report Design and Main Report Preview tabs at the bottom of the report design canvas. By clicking the Main Report Preview tab, the report will actually be refreshed from the chosen data source and the first page will appear. You may click the Refresh toolbar button at the top of the Preview view to run the refresh the report again (and, prompt for any necessary parameter values, if the report is designed with parameter fields).

Refresh the report

Click to switch between integrated report design and preview views

---

TIP *If you plan to modify your report's behavior at run time (almost a given, since you are most probably integrating a Crystal report with a custom application that will control report behavior from your own UI), you should consider using Parameter Fields to control various aspects of report behavior. By using Parameter Fields when you design your report to control record selection, report formulas, section or object formatting, and so forth, you can control report behavior at run time by passing different values to the parameter fields from within your VS.NET code. These run-time modification techniques are discussed later in this chapter.*

Formatting Objects and Sections

Crystal Reports provides default formatting for individual report objects (fields, formulas, and so forth) and report sections (page header, details, group footer 1, and so forth) when you initially create a report. However, as Crystal Reports is a complete Windows- and web-oriented design tool, you have complete control over a wide variety of properties that affect field and report section appearance.

Format individual report objects by selecting them. Then, make choices from the formatting portion of the Crystal Reports toolbars at the top of the VS.NET IDE. You may also right-click the desired object or objects and choose Format options from the pop-up menu. And, you can also select an object and make choices in the VS.NET Properties box. You'll notice some formatting options change appearance of the report right in the Integrated Report Designer. Other options, however, will only be apparent when you actually preview the report within the VS.NET IDE, or run your application and see the report in a report viewer.

Format entire report sections (such as the Details section, Page Header, and so forth) by clicking the gray section title, right-clicking, and choosing options from the pop-up menu. In particular, you can perform all available section formatting by choosing Section Expert from the pop-up menu. This will display the Section Expert dialog box, which allows control of suppression, page breaks, section background colors, and much more. Make desired choices and click OK. As mentioned previously, some of these changes (especially conditional formatting formulas that you may supply) won't be visible until you preview the report or run your application and see the report in a viewer.

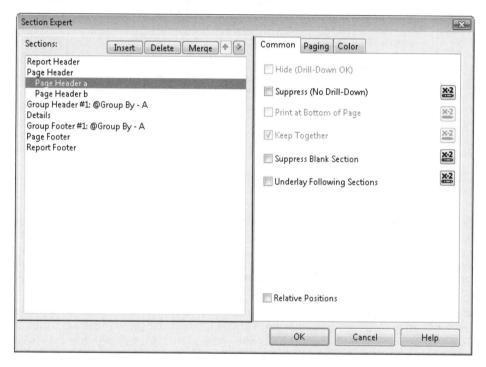

TIP *Formatting report objects is covered in Chapter 6. And, section formatting is covered in Chapters 6 and 7. Refer to these chapters for detailed information on report formatting techniques.*

Sorting and Grouping

While you can just display data records one after the other in the order the database supplies them, your reports become much more powerful if you at least sort the records in a meaningful fashion by one or more relevant fields. Do this by right-clicking on a blank area of the report designer and choosing Report | Record Sort Expert from the pop-up menu. You can also click the Sort Order button in the Crystal Reports toolbar in the VS.NET IDE. The Record Sort Expert dialog box will appear.

Select a desired sort field from the Available Fields list and click the right arrow to add it to the Sort Fields list. By default, the report will be sorted in ascending (A to Z) order. To change this order, select the desired field in the Sort Fields list and click the Descending radio button at the bottom of the dialog box. The report will be sorted by the chosen field in descending (Z to A) order. You are not limited to sorting the report on a single field—add additional fields in the desired order, choosing ascending or descending sorts for each. If you need to change the priority of fields in the Sort Fields list, simply select the desired field and click the up or down arrow above the Sort Fields list to change the field's priority.

However, you may find that simply sorting the report doesn't provide sufficient flexibility for your needs. In many cases, report grouping is preferable to (or at least helpful in addition to) sorting. By creating report groups, you create "level breaks" that allow placement of summaries and subtotals at the end of each group. Furthermore, these grouping concepts, when used in concert with section formatting (typically, the hiding of report sections), become the basis for sophisticated drill-down reports that maximize the interactive capabilities of Crystal Reports placed in VS.NET applications.

To create a report group, right-click on a blank area of the report designer and choose Insert | Group from the pop-up menu. You can also click the Insert Group toolbar button in the Crystal toolbars in the VS.NET IDE. The Insert Group dialog box will appear.

PART I

Insert Group ▣

Common | Options

When the report is printed, the records will be sorted and
grouped by:

▭ Customer.Country   ▾

in ascending order.   ▾

☐ Use a Formula as Group Sort Order   ⌘·2

The section will be printed on any change of:
Customer.Country

OK   Cancel   Help

Choose the desired field on which you wish to group the report from the first drop-down
list. Then, choose the order in which you want report groups to appear from the second
drop-down list. If you wish to set additional group options, click the Options tab of the
Insert Group dialog box and make choices. When you're finished, click OK to close the
Insert Group dialog box and add the group to the report. You'll notice that group header
and group footer sections appear in the report for your chosen group.

TIP *Complete details on sorting and grouping are provided in Chapter 2.*

Once you've created necessary report groups, you can insert summary and subtotal
fields in the group footers for the groups (as well as grand totals in the Report Header or
Report Footer). To insert a summary, you may optionally select the field in the Details
section you wish to summarize (although you don't have to). Then, right-click the field
you've selected and choose Insert | Summary from the pop-up menu. You can also click the
Insert Summary toolbar button from the Crystal Reports toolbar in the VS.NET IDE (this
button can be used even if you haven't selected a details field first). The Insert Summary
dialog box will appear.

If necessary, choose the field you wish to summarize in the first drop-down list (the proper field should already appear in this list if you selected it first). Then, choose the desired type of summary (sum, average, count, and so forth) from the second drop-down list. In the third drop-down list, choose where you want the summary to be placed. Available options will be a grand total (placed in the report footer), or a subtotal placed in the desired group footer. If you wish to use a Percentage Summary Field or summarize across hierarchical groups (described in Chapter 2), check the appropriate boxes. When you click OK, the summary will be placed in the group footer or report footer.

While the user interface in the Integrated Report Designer differs somewhat from that in stand-alone Crystal Reports 2008, the general techniques used to design reports are similar. While this chapter covers very general techniques for report design, Part I of this book covers report design techniques in much greater detail. Refer to chapters in Part I for information on various report design steps that also apply to reports designed with the VS.NET Integrated Report Designer.

NOTE *Many new Crystal Reports 2008 features, such as optional parameter fields, the Parameter Panel, interactive sorting, and integrated Xcelsius/Flash objects (as long as they aren't connected to report data), are only available in Visual Studio .NET if you install the full version of Crystal Reports 2008 after you install VS.NET. While some of these additional features will appear in the Integrated Report Designer, many of these capabilities, such as interactive sorting and Xcelsius/ Flash integration, must be added to a report with the stand-alone Crystal Reports 2008 designer. Then, the finished .RPT file must be embedded in your project, or called as a non-embedded report, for the new features to be exposed by the finished application.*

VS.NET Report Customization Object Models

While your application may not require any additional capabilities than are provided by a simple report bound to a viewer, there's a good possibility that you'll need to customize one or more aspects of the report at run time from within your application. These customizations can be as simple as supplying the user ID and password for a report's database connection from within your code (so that the user doesn't have to log on to the report's database again, after they've already logged in to your application). Or, they may require more complex code that changes several report groups, formulas, parameter fields, formatting, or the report's record selection formula all on the fly based on other elements of your application.

Crystal Reports has always been the favorite of developers because of its flexible programming interfaces. And, the versions of Crystal Reports integrated with Visual Studio .NET carry on that tradition by providing rich object models that can control many aspects of report behavior at run time. Installing the full version of Crystal Reports 2008 after you've installed VS.NET will improve on this programming flexibility even further.

There are two general ways of customizing your report at run time regardless of your VS.NET installation: using the Crystal Windows or Web Forms Viewer (CrystalReportViewer) object model, and using the Crystal Reports Engine (ReportDocument) object model. If you install the full version of Crystal Reports 2008, a third object model becomes available, the in-process (or *in-proc*) Report Application Server (or *RAS*) object model, referred to as the ReportClientDocument object model.

The first two object models will probably be appropriate for the vast majority of your custom reporting applications, as they provide complete flexibility for changing behavior of *existing* reports at run time. The third object model (ReportClientDocument) allows creation of *entirely new* report objects from within your code. Using this object model, you are able to build a new report entirely within code, including defining database connections, adding and formatting fields, and so forth. You may then display the resulting report in a viewer, or even programmatically save the report as an .RPT file for other uses.

For the vast majority of applications that just provide existing report run-time customization and viewing, the decision of whether to use the CrystalReportViewer object model or the ReportDocument object model is determined by your application requirements. Business Objects documentation discourages mixing object model usage—particularly when changing the same properties in both object models. For example, you will probably encounter confusion (and, possibly application instability) if you change a parameter field using the ReportDocument object model, and then change the parameter again using the CrystalReportViewer object model before displaying the report in a viewer.

As you read the remainder of this chapter, and explore both object models, you'll notice that the viewer object model provides a fair amount of report behavior customization capability at run time. It's quite possible that this object model will provide all the necessary customization you need. However, certain complex reporting requirements that require more involved section formatting or run-time addition or removal of fields, groups, and so forth will not be satisfied with the CrystalReportViewer object model. These will require use of the ReportDocument object model, which can make significant run-time modifications to a report object *before* it is passed to a report viewer.

Run-Time Customization with the CrystalReportViewer Object

Some of the most obvious run-time customization that you may wish to perform with the viewer is basic viewer appearance. You can, for example, control viewer properties at run time that you see in the Properties box at design time. In addition, commonly used report options, such as the report's record selection formula and parameter field values, can be changed at run time only with calls to the CrystalReportViewer object model.

These CrystalReportViewer object model choices are provided by assemblies installed with VS.NET and Crystal Reports 2008. In particular, the *CrystalDecisions.Windows.Forms* or *CrystalDecisions.Web* namespace is added as a reference to your project automatically when you add the respective viewer. This namespace exposes the object model available when using the viewer. When you install the full version of Crystal Reports 2008 on an existing computer containing Visual Studio .NET, this namespace is updated with additional version 2008 capabilities.

Some initial customization you may wish to perform at run time simply involves viewer behavior, such as visibility of the group tree, appearance of individual toolbar buttons on the viewer toolbar, or complete invisibility of the entire toolbar. VS.NET "intellisense" technology will automatically show you available properties once you type the report viewer class, followed by a period. You can navigate through the various properties and, if necessary, see available arguments for available properties and methods.

For example, the following code will completely hide the group tree/Parameter Panel in the viewer:

```
CrystalReportViewer1.ToolPanelView = _
CrystalDecisions.Web.ToolPanelViewType.None
```

whereas

```
CrystalReportViewer1.ToolPanelView = _
CrystalDecisions.Web.ToolPanelViewType.ParameterPanel
```

will display the Parameter Panel initially, still allowing the report user to click the Group Tree button to see the group tree in place of the Parameter Panel (presuming that the HasToggleGroupTreeButton and HasToggleParameterParameterPanelButton properties have not been set to False). These object exposures are an example of the improved model that comes with installation of the full version of Crystal Reports 2008.

And, more involved run-time customization to the viewer can involve instantiating additional objects, setting object properties, and passing the object to a viewer property to change viewer behavior. The following code will result in a group tree displaying an aqua background color and group tree entries in a bold coral color:

```
Dim GroupTreeStyle As New CrystalDecisions.Shared.GroupTreeStyle
With GroupTreeStyle
  .BackColor = System.Drawing.Color.Aqua
  .ForeColor = System.Drawing.Color.Coral
  .Font.Bold = True
End With
CrystalReportViewer1.GroupTreeStyle = GroupTreeStyle
```

Notice the declaration of the GroupTreeStyle class, taken from the *CrystalDecisions.Shared* namespace. This namespace, also added to your project automatically when you add a viewer, provides an object model that exposes common objects and properties that can be used in both Crystal Windows and web applications.

NOTE *The preceding example shows an object declaration with the fully qualified namespace. If you choose to add an Imports statement to import the namespace, then you would only need to declare the object using its class name without the need to precede it with "CrystalDecisions.Shared".*

Other report properties not related to appearance can also be set by using various portions of the CrystalReportViewer object model. Some of the most obvious are described in the sections that follow.

Specifying Database Credentials

If the report bound to the viewer is based on a secure database, the viewer will prompt for proper database credentials before displaying the report. If you have already gathered security information elsewhere in your application, you probably won't want your user to be prompted again. You can supply these credentials via the CrystalReportViewer object model as follows:

```
'Provide database credentials via Viewer object model
Dim Counter As Integer
For Counter = 1 To CrystalReportViewer1.LogOnInfo.Count
   With CrystalReportViewer1.LogOnInfo(Counter - 1).ConnectionInfo
     .ServerName = "SQLServer1"
     .DatabaseName = "xtreme"
     .UserID = "sa"
     .Password = "password"
   End With
Next Counter
```

This code loops through the individual ConnectionInfo objects within the report viewer's LogonInfo class, setting credentials for each. All database connections, regardless of original data source, as well as subreport connection objects, will be included in the LogonInfo class. Accordingly, you'll need to take extra steps to properly assign values if the source tables in your main report or subreports come from different databases.

Modifying the Record Selection Formula

This is a very common requirement of report integration applications. You may wish to control report record selection based on some other control on a form or another element of your embedded application logic. This is accomplished by setting the viewer's RecordSelectionFormula property.

```
'Set record selection via Viewer object model
If Countries = "USA Only" Then
   CrystalReportViewer1.SelectionFormula = _
        "{Customer.Country} = 'USA'"
Else
   CrystalReportViewer1.SelectionFormula = ""
End If 'Countries = "USA Only"
```

Make sure you pass a valid record selection formula, using Crystal Reports Crystal Formula Syntax, to this property. Don't forget to include proper punctuation, such as French braces around field names and apostrophes around string literals. You may find discussions in Chapters 3 and 4 helpful in working with record selection formulas.

Supplying Parameter Field Values

In many cases, you may actually base your report's record selection on a parameter field. Or, perhaps you have created formulas based on parameter fields that change report grouping or formatting. In these cases, the ability to pass values to parameter fields at run time is crucial. Here's an example of passing a value to a single-value (or "discrete") numeric parameter field:

```
'Set parameter via Viewer object model
Dim Parameters As New ParameterFields
Dim Parameter As New ParameterField
```

```
Dim ParamValue As New ParameterDiscreteValue

Parameter.ParameterFieldName = "Tax Rate"
ParamValue.Value = CDbl(5.25)
Parameter.CurrentValues.Add(ParamValue)

Parameters.Add(Parameter)

CrystalReportViewer1.ParameterFieldInfo = Parameters
```

Note that additional objects are instantiated to hold a parameters collection, a parameter field, and a parameter field discrete value (the preceding code assumes that you have IMPORTed the CrystalDecisions.Shared namespace in the code-behind page). The parameter field name is supplied, using the parameter field's name in the underlying report. The actual discrete value for a 5 ¼ percent tax rate is supplied, including a cast to ensure proper data type matching. The discrete value object is added to the parameter's CurrentValues collection. The parameter is added to a parameters collection. And finally, the viewer's ParameterFieldInfo property is set to the parameter's collection. When the report application is run, any parameter fields you have supplied values to within code will not be prompted for, as their values are being supplied by your code.

Report Viewer Events

Not only can you set report viewer properties at run time, but you can also trap report viewer events. As Crystal Reports blends into the entire .NET framework and .NET event processing, you can trap viewer events in the viewer and add code based on them. By selecting the desired viewer in the Class Name list in the code window, you'll then be able to see a list of events that the viewer fires in the Method Name list.

You may, for example, add code that traps a viewer drill-down event and performs some action based on the group that is drilled into.

```
Private Sub CrystalReportViewer1_Drill(ByVal source As Object, _
     ByVal e As CrystalDecisions.Web.DrillEventArgs) _
     Handles CrystalReportViewer1.Drill
  If e.NewGroupName = "USA" Then
     e.Handled = True
  End If
End Sub
```

In this example, the event class exposes DrillEventArgs from the CrystalDecisions.Web namespace, including various properties to indicate what is being drilled into. Here, the code checks to see if the USA group is being drilled into. If so, the drill-down is canceled by setting the class's Handled property to True.

Run-Time Customization with the Crystal Reports Engine (ReportDocument)

So far, this chapter has concentrated entirely on run-time customization with the CrystalReportViewer object model (with classes exposed by the CrystalDecisions.Windows. Forms or CrystalDecisions.Web namespace) and the shared object model (with classes exposed by the CrystalDecisions.Shared namespace). There's still yet another object model/ namespace that exposes classes you can use to customize report behavior at run time.

By using the ReportDocument object model, you can customize report behavior at run time using techniques similar to those discussed previously in the chapter. However, this object model (exposed by the CrystalDecisions.CrystalReports.Engine namespace) offers properties, methods, and events that are strictly limited to the core report object you are integrating in your application, independent of any viewer you may have added to your application. Also, a much larger number of customization options are available with the Report Engine. In addition to setting parameter field values, supplying database credentials, and setting the report's record selection formula, the Report Engine offers the ability to control object formatting, supply new formula contents, export the report to various file formats, and much more.

Any customization you perform here typically takes place *before* you bind a report to a viewer (or, in situations where you don't even add a viewer to your project). Once you've made these customizations to the report object, they will take effect when the report is bound to the viewer (or, in the case of a non-viewing application, whenever you execute a report method to ultimately output the report to a printer, exported file format, and so forth).

As discussed earlier in the chapter, you'll find properties and methods in the Report Engine that duplicate those found in the CrystalReportViewer object model. For example, you can supply database credentials, set the record selection formula, and supply parameter field values via either object model. The decision as to which object model to use is dependent upon your application particulars and how detailed your integration requirements are. Again, Business Objects recommends that you avoid duplicate calls from different object models in the same application. So, as you develop your application, look at which object model provides the best combination of simplicity and functionality, depending on your requirements.

To make use of the ReportDocument object model, you must ensure that the CrystalDecisions.CrystalReports.Engine namespace is being referenced in your project. In most cases, you'll also need references to the CrystalDecisions.Shared namespace. Typically, if you add a CrystalReportViewer or a CrystalReportSource .NET control to a form from the Toolbox, these namespaces will automatically be added. If, however, you are designing an application that does not make use of a web or Windows viewer, or a CrystalReportSource object (perhaps you are only referring to external non-embedded reports), you'll need to use the VS.NET Add Reference option to add these namespaces to your project (if you have several versions of Crystal Reports installed, make sure you choose the correct version, and consistently use the same version if you add more than one reference). Also, you'll need to declare references to several classes from these namespaces in your code and may prefer to use the Imports statement to allow class references without the fully qualified namespace name.

One of the first requirements of using the Report Engine is instantiation of a report object. As discussions earlier in the chapter indicate, there are several ways of adding reports to your project. And, there are several types of reports (non-embedded, embedded, and so forth) that can be added. As an example, you may have added an embedded report to your project, either by using Add | Existing Item with an existing .RPT file or by using Add | New Item and designing a new Crystal report. You then must declare an object to refer to the embedded report and expose the Report Engine's object model. Here's an example:

```
Dim Report As New Interactive_Sorting
'refers to embedded Interactive Sorting.rpt in project
```

Once you've declared this object, you will notice many of the Report Engine properties and methods available via VS.NET's "Intellisense" technology.

Some of the more common run-time customizations you can make with the Report Engine (but, by no means, an exhaustive list) are described next.

Supplying Database Credentials

If your report is based on a secure database, you will probably prefer that your application code provide database credentials to prevent your report viewer from being prompted, or from your application failing if your report is not bound to a viewer. There are several ways for the Report Engine to supply these credentials. Examine the following:

```
'Provide database credentials via ReportDocument object model
Report.SetDatabaseLogon("sa", "password")
```

This single line of code supplies a user ID and password to every data source in the report, including those contained in subreports. The SetDatabaseLogon method greatly simplifies supplying database credentials if your report is based entirely on a single database connection.

A second permutation of SetDatabaseLogon accepts four arguments:

```
Report.SetDatabaseLogon("sa", "password", "SQLServer1", "xtreme")
```

This allows a database server and database name to also be specified, in case you've made use of several different connections in your report.

If you need a more granular way of supplying database credentials for individual table objects in your main report and subreports, you've got a little more coding ahead of you. Examine the following:

```
Dim Logon As New TableLogOnInfo
Dim Tbl As Table
For Each Tbl In Report.Database.Tables
    Logon = Tbl.LogOnInfo
    Logon.ConnectionInfo.ServerName = "SQLServer1"
    Logon.ConnectionInfo.DatabaseName = "xtreme"
    Logon.ConnectionInfo.UserID = "sa"
    Logon.ConnectionInfo.Password = "password"
    Tbl.ApplyLogOnInfo(Logon)
Next Tbl

'Provide database credentials to subreports
Dim Subreport As ReportDocument
For Each Subreport In Report.Subreports
    For Each Tbl In Subreport.Database.Tables
        Logon = Tbl.LogOnInfo
        Logon.ConnectionInfo.ServerName = "SQLServer1"
        Logon.ConnectionInfo.DatabaseName = "xtreme"
        Logon.ConnectionInfo.UserID = "sa"
        Logon.ConnectionInfo.Password = "password"
        Tbl.ApplyLogOnInfo(Logon)
    Next 'Tbl
Next 'Subreport
```

In the preceding code fragment, a TableLogonInfo class (from the CrystalDecisions.Shared namespace) and Table class (from the CrystalDecisions.CrystalReports.Engine namespace) are instantiated. Then, each table in the main report is cycled through, supplying database credentials via the ConnectionInfo property.

To accommodate subreports, a ReportDocument class is instantiated (this comes from CrystalDecisions.CrystalReports.Engine), which is used to cycle through the main report's Subreports collection. For each subreport, similar loops through the Database.Tables collection are made to supply database credentials.

While the preceding code will work with Crystal Reports 10 and greater, earlier versions (including Crystal Reports included with early versions of VS.NET) do not expose a Subreports collection. In this situation, code to deal with subreports must be even more granular, as the following example shows.

```
crSections = Report.ReportDefinition.Sections

For Each crSection In crSections
    crReportObjects = crSection.ReportObjects

    For Each crReportObject In crReportObjects
      If crReportObject.Kind = ReportObjectKind.SubreportObject Then
        crSubreportObject = CType(crReportObject, SubreportObject)
        subrpt = _
           crSubreportObject.OpenSubreport(crSubreportObject.SubreportName)
        For Each subtbl In subReport.Database.Tables
            str &= subReport.Name & "-" & subtbl.Name & " - "
            objTableLogonInfo = subtbl.LogOnInfo
            objTableLogonInfo.ConnectionInfo = objConnInfo
            subtbl.ApplyLogOnInfo(objTableLogonInfo)
            subtbl.Location = _
             subtbl.Location.Substring(subtbl.Location.LastIndexOf(".") + 1)
            str &= subtbl.TestConnectivity() & vbCrLf
        Next
      End If
    Next
  Next
Next
```

Setting Record Selection and Saved Data Selection

As with the viewer object model, you can set the report's record selection formula at run time via a simple property setting in the ReportDocument object model. You will probably want to do this based on values obtained from other controls or conditions in your application. For example,

```
Report.RecordSelectionFormula = "{Customer.Country} = 'USA'"
```

will return records where the country is USA. Ensure that you pass a syntactically correct formula using the Crystal Reports Crystal Syntax, including French braces around field names and apostrophes surrounding string literals. Discussions on record selection and formula syntax can be found in Chapters 3 and 4 in this book.

Crystal Reports 2008 introduces the saved data selection formula as well. While setting the record selection formula from within code will force a database refresh when the report is processed, setting the saved data selection formula will not force a database refresh. It will simply apply the selection formula to the existing set of saved data in the report and redisplay the report (if it is hosted in a CrystalReportViewer control). While the record selection formula property is derived directly from the report object, the saved data selection formula is derived from the report's DataDefinition object.

```
Report.DataDefinition.SavedDataSelectionFormula = _
"{Customer.Region} = 'CA'"
```

TIP Another method of modifying selection at run time makes use of parameter fields. You may define a report parameter field, reference it in the desired selection formula, and set the parameter field's contents in code.

Modifying Existing Formula Contents

One area of report customization that can only be accomplished with the ReportDocument object model is run-time report formula modification. For example, you may wish to change some sort of calculation or string customization contained in a report formula based on a user control or other element of your custom application. By modifying a report formula at run time, you can change report calculations or customized fields based on your application elements. For example,

```
If GroupBy = "Country" Then
    Report.DataDefinition.FormulaFields("Group Field").Text = _
        "{Customer.Country}"
Else
    Report.DataDefinition.FormulaFields("Group Field").Text = _
        "{Customer.Region}"
End If 'GroupBy = "Country"
```

You may navigate directly to the FormulaFields collection of the report's DataDefinition object. Notice that the particular collection member can be retrieved by name, in addition to numeric index. By setting the formula's Text property, you can change the formula contents at run time. In this example, a variable is examined indicating the user's grouping choice. Report grouping is being controlled via a formula that is set to the database field corresponding to the user's choice. Note that you must supply a formula of proper syntax when setting the Text property. Chapter 4 discusses report formulas in greater detail.

Providing Parameter Field Values

A very common requirement of run-time report modification is dealing with parameter fields. As many report customizations can be accomplished by designing reports with parameter fields, you may find this one of the most common run-time modifications you'll be required to perform. While the viewer object model can change parameter field values at run time, you may prefer (or be required) to use the ReportDocument model to supply parameter values at run time. The report object's SetParameterValue method is a simple way to supply a value to a parameter field:

```
'Set parameter via ReportDocument object model
Report.SetParameterValue("Tax Rate", TaxRate)
```

The SetParameterValue method demonstrated here accepts two arguments: the parameter field to supply a value to (which can be specified either by name or by index), and the value to pass to the parameter field (in this instance, a variable that has been cast elsewhere in the code to match the data type of the parameter field).

The SetParameterValue method is fairly flexible in the data types and parameter field types (such as multivalue parameter fields) that it can accommodate. It can also be used to supply parameter values to subreports. The Crystal Reports help collection contains complete details.

If you have more complex parameter requirements that may not be accommodated by the SetParameterValue method, you may modify parameters via an additional object. Here's an example that sets a simple, single-value parameter field:

```
Dim ParamValue As New ParameterDiscreteValue
'CrystalDecisions.Shared.ParameterDiscreteValue if no Imports
ParamValue.Value = TaxRate
Report.ParameterFields("Tax Rate").CurrentValues.Add(ParamValue)
```

A discrete parameter class is instantiated to hold a single-value (discrete) parameter field. The object's Value property is set to a variable (again, properly cast earlier in the code). And, finally, the parameter object is added to the existing parameter field's CurrentValues collection (which, for a single-value parameter field, will contain only one member). The parameter field can be obtained from the report's ParameterFields collection, either by name or by numeric index.

Once values have been supplied to parameter fields within code, they will not be prompted for when the report is displayed on a web or Windows viewer. However, if some parameter fields are supplied values from within code while others are not, those that are not supplied values will still be prompted for when the report is viewed. While this may afford some flexibility in report design, one of the benefits of being able to programmatically supply parameter field values is to provide for more robust user interface elements than the fairly rudimentary report viewer parameter prompt screens. As such, you'll probably want to provide most, if not all, parameter field values from within code.

TIP *In previous versions of Crystal Reports, parameter field values could only be set from within code, or supplied by the report user via the CrystalReportViewer control prompt screens before the report was refreshed against the database. If you install the full version of Crystal Reports 2008, saved data selection, optional parameter fields, and the Parameter Panel will be available in your custom applications. These new features allow you to design more interactive reports that permit report users to change parameter values and, by use of parameters in saved data selection, modify the set of records viewed in the report without a database refresh. This interactivity can be exposed to your application entirely with report design techniques and the Parameter Panel, requiring no custom coding at all.*

Supplying Text Object Text

While there are several ways to display a custom string or "message" on a report (perhaps you wish to display various run-time options chosen by the report viewer on the report itself), one way is to set the actual text displayed by a text object at run time. This capability is provided by the ReportDocument object only and cannot be accomplished by using any of the CrystalReportViewer object model calls. Here's an example:

```
'Set text object via ReportDocument object model
Dim SelectionText As TextObject
'CrystalDecisions.CrystalReports.Engine.TextObject if no Imports
SelectionText = Report.ReportDefinition.ReportObjects("SelectionText")
SelectionText.Text = strSelection
```

Instantiate a TextObject object (supplied by the CrystalDecisions.CrystalReports.Engine namespace). Set it to proper text object in the report by navigating through the report's ReportObjects collection from the ReportDefinition object (if you choose to access the text object member by name instead of index, the Object Name value provided in the Format Editor or Properties Box can be used). Then, set the text object's Text property to change the actual text contained in the text object on the report.

Exporting Reports in Windows and Web Applications

While viewing reports in a web or Windows viewer is no doubt a large part of many custom applications, the ability to export reports into a variety of other file formats will also come in handy within your application. Exporting can be accomplished in a variety of ways; interactively with the Export toolbar button in a CrystalReportViewer control, or programmatically from within the ReportDocument object model.

The first, and simplest, method for exporting a report is to use the Export toolbar button on the CrystalReportViewer control in a web or Windows form. Although the full complement of export formats and options from the stand-alone Crystal Report designer isn't available from the CrystalReportViewer, most common formats are still available when exporting in a VS.NET application. This exporting method will simply display a Save As dialog box when exporting with a Windows viewer, where you may specify the location , filename, and file type. Exporting from a web viewer will allow you to choose a report page range, followed by downloading the file to the browser (with the commensurate View or Save As option appearing in most standard browsers).

While the viewer includes an Export toolbar button that allows the user to export the viewed report to various file formats, you may wish to do this programmatically. You may, for example, prefer to limit the formats that the report may be exported to and not allow the user to export with the toolbar button. You might, then, disable the export button in the viewer and export the file to a specified format within code. Examine the following:

```
CrystalReportViewer1.HasExportButton = False
Report.ExportToHttpResponse(ExportFormatType.PortableDocFormat, _
        Response, False, "")
```

Initially, the viewer's export toolbar button is hidden. Then, the report object's ExportToHttpResponse method is used to export the file via the Response object in Acrobat

PDF format. There are several versions of this method with arguments documented in the Crystal Reports 2008 help collection.

Here's an example of the more involved exporting in a Windows application that attaches a file to an e-mail message:

```
Dim ExportOptions As New ExportOptions
Dim EMailOptions As New MicrosoftMailDestinationOptions
ExportOptions.ExportFormatType = ExportFormatType.PortableDocFormat
ExportOptions.ExportDestinationType = ExportDestinationType.MicrosoftMail
EMailOptions.MailToList = strEMailAddress
EMailOptions.MailSubject = "XTEME Orders Report"
EMailOptions.MailMessage = _
  "The XTREME Orders report is attached in PDF format"
ExportOptions.ExportDestinationOptions = EMailOptions
Report.Export(ExportOptions)
```

In this example, both ExportOptions and MicrosoftMailDestinationOptions objects are instantiated (both classes are exposed by the CrystalDecisions.Shared namespace). The ExportOptions export format type is set to Adobe Acrobat Portable Document Format (PDF), and the export destination type is set to Microsoft Mail. Various properties of the MicrosoftMailDestinationOptions object are used to set the e-mail's To address, subject, and message text. The ExportOptions ExportDestinationOptions property is set to the MicrosoftMailDestinationOptions object. And, finally, the report object's Export method is executed, with the ExportOptions object being supplied as an argument.

New Crystal Reports 2008 XML Export Support

Crystal Reports 2008 expands on previous versions' report exporting capabilities from within a custom VS.NET application. Probably the most notable exporting benefit derived from installing the full copy of Crystal Reports 2008 is new XML exporting capabilities. As discussed in Chapter 14, XML exporting can be extensively customized via an XSL/XSLT transform style sheet. While Crystal Reports Basic, bundled with VS.NET, doesn't support the new XML exporting capabilities, VS.NET will be upgraded to support them when full Crystal Reports 2008 is installed.

Making use of new XML export options requires some special considerations. First, you must set export options, including specification of one or more custom XML formats via XSL/XSLT transforms, in the stand-alone Crystal Reports 2008 designer (XML export formats can't be defined in the VS.NET embedded report designer). A particularly important setting when specifying XML export options is the default XML format. If you don't specifically change the default choice, the Crystal XML Schema will be used when exporting to XML with a CrystalReportViewer control. If you wish to use a different XML schema when exporting from a CrystalReportViewer control, you must *specify the desired format as the default* in stand-alone Crystal Reports 2008's Manage XML Exporting Formats dialog box. Once the custom schema has been imported and set as the default, the report must be saved and referenced as a non-embedded or embedded report in your VS.NET project. The default format will be used when the XML format is chosen from the viewer control's export button.

And, the upgraded Crystal Reports 2008 ReportDocument object model also includes support for XML exporting. Exporting to XML from within custom code gives you additional options not available when exporting manually from the viewer. Not only can you export to the default XML format set in the report, but you can also cycle through the collection of saved XML formats, extracting pertinent information from each member, such as the name, description, and file extension specified for each format. Furthermore, you can programmatically choose an XML format other than the default to export the report to. For example,

```
Dim xmlExportOptions As New ExportOptions
Dim xmlExportFormatOptions As XmlExportFormatOptions = _
    ExportOptions.CreateXmlExportFormatOptions
Dim DiskFileDestinationOptions As New DiskFileDestinationOptions

xmlExportOptions.ExportDestinationType = ExportDestinationType.DiskFile
xmlExportOptions.ExportFormatType = ExportFormatType.Xml
xmlExportFormatOptions.ExportSelection = 1  'Second XML Export format
DiskFileDestinationOptions.DiskFileName = "C:\Temp\XML Export Sample." & _
    Report.SavedXmlExportFormats(1).FileExtension
xmlExportOptions.ExportDestinationOptions = DiskFileDestinationOptions
xmlExportOptions.ExportFormatOptions = xmlExportFormatOptions
Report.Export(xmlExportOptions)
```

defines several objects pertinent to XML exporting, selects the second saved XML export option in the report, extracts the stored file extension for the second stored format (both using a zero-based collection, hence the index of 1), and exports the report.

The Report Application Server and ReportClientDocument Object Model

Current, as well as past, versions of the Crystal and BusinessObjects Enterprise family include the Report Application Server (RAS for short), as one of the many components that make up the Enterprise software system (more information on BusinessObjects XI 3.0 can be found in Part II of this book). Specifically, the RAS is charged with processing certain Crystal Report requests from the Enterprise system, particularly relating to on-demand report generation. While this on-demand report generation capabilities of the RAS have largely been relegated to custom Crystal and BusinessObjects Enterprise .NET applications, a smaller version of the RAS (known as the in-process RAS, or *InProc RAS*) is now available when you install the full version of Crystal Reports 2008 alongside Visual Studio .NET.

An enhanced object model, the *ReportClientDocument* model, exposes additional capabilities provided by the RAS to actually create entire new reports, as well as modify existing report objects, from within your VS.NET code. The ReportClientDocument object model then allows reports to be saved as stand-alone .RPT files from within your code as well.

A separate help file providing namespaces, object model diagrams, sample code, and an API reference is installed in the combined VS.NET help system when you install a full version of Crystal Reports 2008. Look for the *Report Application Server 12 .NET SDK*.

Distributing Crystal Reports Visual Studio .NET Applications

Custom applications developed in Visual Studio .NET may often need to be prepared for distribution to end users if the application will not be used solely in your organization's environment, or won't be located on the same computer environment it was developed with. While Visual Studio .NET provides standard features for application distribution, there may be some special considerations you'll still want to make for Crystal Reports–based applications.

As versions of Visual Studio .NET have advanced, so have the choices for application deployment. The latest version of Visual Studio .NET, Visual Studio 2008 (as well as version 2005), provides three ways to deploy custom Windows or web applications that use integrated Crystal Reports (earlier versions of VS.NET support fewer, but similar, options). Your choice of deployment options will depend not only on your individual application particulars and your end-user audience, but potentially on Crystal Reports integration considerations as well. The deployment options, and their Crystal Reports considerations are:

- **ClickOnce Deployment**   This deployment option, only appropriate for VS.NET Windows applications, places an installer package on a centralized web server where Windows clients can receive central access to an installation package. Not only can the installation package be retrieved from the central web server, but VS.NET applications can be designed to regularly check the central ClickOnce site for updates to the application.

This will allow Crystal Reports run-time files to be designated as an application prerequisite, only requiring installation with the initial application. When subsequent updates to the application are deployed, Crystal Reports run-time installation will not need to be repeated. This option, however, installs the complete Crystal Reports run-time package, including all database and export drivers, which involves a slightly larger footprint and longer installation time.

- **Windows Installer Deployment**   Available for both Windows and web deployments, this option creates a separate, stand-alone .MSI (Microsoft Installer) installation file that installs the Crystal Reports run-time components, along with another .MSI package for the application. These installations can be performed separately, or included in one overall installation script.

  This approach allows the Crystal Reports run-time files to be installed separately from the application, which, among other things, allows Crystal Reports updates or fixes to be installed without re-installing the entire application, while still allowing initial "silent" installation to be performed in an overall installation script. This method installs the entire set of database and export drivers and requires the end user to specify a valid keycode, or for the keycode to be included in a silent installation script. Business Objects generally recommends this as the most flexible option for redistributing Crystal Reports run-time files.

- **Merge Modules Deployment**   This option (the original VS.NET deployment option), creates a single SETUP program that includes not only application-specific files, but those supporting Crystal Reports run time as well. The setup program is run on either a web server or an end-user Windows computer to install the application. When you create a deployment package using merge modules, you must obtain Crystal Reports merge modules in advance and reference them in your setup project (the latest merge modules can be downloaded from Support.BusinessObjects.com/ MergeModules). Merge modules give you the advantage of being able to optionally pick and choose the database and export drivers that you embed in the resulting SETUP file. You also must specify a valid keycode as part of a merge module–based setup project. While no Business Objects or Crystal Reports branding appears in the resulting setup package, you must rebuild and redistribute the entire setup package if any Crystal Reports run-time modules change. And, if you distribute multiple merge module–based SETUP files, the Crystal Reports run-time files will be distributed in each separate occurrence.

General Concepts

Regardless of the deployment method you use, there are several general concepts that you should take into account as part of your deployment strategy.

- **There's no need for any special deployment on a development web server**   If you happen to provide production access to the same web server where you are developing VS.NET/Crystal Reports applications, no additional deployment will be required. However, if you wish to host a Crystal Reports .NET application on an alternate web server, you must either deploy the application using one of the three

VS.NET deployment scenarios, or install an identical development environment on the additional web server.

- **Don't forget about non-embedded report files**   If you integrate .RPT files into your Windows or web application via a non-embedded method (you simply reference them with a report object LOAD method and don't add them to your project), you'll need to distribute them with the application, or ensure that they are located in a central location where the application will be able to find them when run.

- **The target machine must contain the .NET Framework**   Depending on how you create your setup project, you may not include the .NET Framework files in the setup routines. Because Crystal Reports for VS.NET fully integrates with the .NET Framework, you'll need to ensure it is installed on the web server before installing your Crystal web application.

- **Keep track of a keycode**   Whether you use the version of Crystal Reports bundled with Visual Studio.NET, or install a full copy of Crystal Reports 2008 after installing VS.NET, you are using a Crystal Reports copy that's enabled with a software keycode. While the keycode is automatically specified with the bundled version of Crystal Reports, you must specify it when installing the full version of Crystal Reports. In either case, you may need it when it comes time to deploy a custom application. If you installed the stand-alone version of Crystal Reports, the keycode you originally used to install the software can be used for deployment. If you are using the bundled version of Crystal Reports, you can obtain the automatically specified keycode by choosing Help | About Microsoft Development Environment from the VS.NET menus. Note the keycode that appears next to the Crystal Reports entry in the list. Depending on your deployment method, you may need to either embed the keycode in a merge module or supply the keycode to your end user for specification when a Microsoft Installer installation is done.

Crystal Reports
Enterprise Reporting

PART

Crystal Reports Web Alternatives

S o far, this book has discussed many techniques for creating sophisticated reports with the Crystal Reports 2008 designer. Chapter 19 discusses methods for integrating those reports into your custom web and Windows applications using custom programming tools with Visual Studio .NET. But, as both large and small business organizations are moving even more to web-based technology for both internal corporate intranets and the Internet, ways to display your Crystal reports in a web browser without custom programming is crucial.

Various alternatives to get your reports on the Web are available, depending on your particular web environment and your budget (many options require upgrades or additional licenses). From simple HTML exports, to third-party utilities, to a multitier, multiserver enterprise-wide implementation of BusinessObjects Enterprise XI 3.0, you have many choices to consider when looking toward web distribution and customization of Crystal Reports.

These different options give you many ways to place a Crystal Report on the Web—either on your internal corporate intranet or on the entire Internet. Some require custom programming (covered in Chapter 19), and others are out-of-the-box solutions:

- **Export Static Reports to HTML Format (covered in this chapter)** In this case, you just export your report to one of several different HTML formats, much as you would export a Word or Excel file. Viewers can simply open the HTML file in their browser, or the file can be placed on a web server for viewing.

- **Use Visual Studio .NET with Web Forms (covered in Chapter 19)** Visual Studio .NET (VS.NET) incorporates a special version of Crystal Reports as its included reporting tool. The VS.NET object model exposes Crystal Reports functionality, allowing complete control of reports at run time in a web browser. Crystal Reports 2008 expands on VS.NET functionality by adding additional capabilities and features to the base VS.NET Crystal Report functionality.

- **Using Crystal Reports for Eclipse** This free download from the Business Objects web site allows you to create custom web applications using the open-source Eclipse Java development environment.

- **Using Third-Party Tools for Web-Based Reporting** Several third-party software developers have created tools that allow Crystal Reports to be placed in various web-based environments. This book's companion web site (CrystalBook.com) includes *Crystal: The Complete Toolset,* a web portal constantly updated with the latest available Crystal Reports utilities.

- **Using a Member of the BusinessObjects Enterprise XI 3.0 Family (covered in this chapter, as well as Chapters 21 and 22)** BusinessObjects Enterprise XI 3.0 (abbreviated as BOE in much of this book) provides a rich, multitier/multiserver method of hosting real-time and automatically scheduled Crystal Reports on the Web. You can use the standard out-of-the-box user interface provided by BOE, or you may completely customize the user interface using various custom development technologies.

Exporting to Static HTML

More and more, organizations are looking to distribute Crystal Reports to a large audience in a web format, through a company intranet or the Internet. To provide this capability, you need to convert your report to Hypertext Markup Language (HTML) format—the "markup language" understood by web browsers. If you've decided to provide only static, non-interactive reports in a web browser, you simply need to export the report from Crystal Reports, just as you'd export to a Word document or an Excel spreadsheet.

Simply start Crystal Reports and open or create the report you want to export to HTML. Remember that whatever is visible on your screen is what will be exported to HTML. If you want to export the main report, make sure the Preview tab is clicked. If you want to export just a drill-down tab, select the correct drill-down tab before exporting. Then, choose File | Export from the pull-down menus, or click the Export button in the Standard toolbar. Figure 20-1 shows a sample report, consisting of several complex report objects (including an embedded Xcelsius Flash file), and complicated formatting (such as a title surrounded by a border on all four sides and a drop shadow, and a chart placed alongside data with the "underlay" section formatting option).

When you choose the Export command, the resulting dialog box allows you to choose the format and destination of your report. You'll be concerned with the two HTML format options available in the Format drop-down list: HTML 3.2 and HTML 4.0. The different versions refer to the different extensions of the HTML language that Crystal Reports can use. To determine which version of HTML you want to use, experiment with your own exports and the browsers that your report viewers will use. Typically, version 4 (dynamic HTML) will better represent the actual formatting of the report in the web browser. However, significantly older versions of a web browser (Internet Explorer or Netscape Navigator/ Communicator versions prior to 4) may not be able to properly interpret DHTML. If you're using an older version of these browsers, you may see better results with HTML 3.2.

NOTE *Some export drivers are not installed by default when you install Crystal Reports. If you see a small number 1 beside the desired HTML export format (indicating "install on first use"), you'll be prompted to insert the Crystal Reports program CD the first time you export to HTML.*

No matter what destination you ultimately choose from the Destination drop-down list, Crystal Reports must write the HTML code and any associated graphics files (for charts,

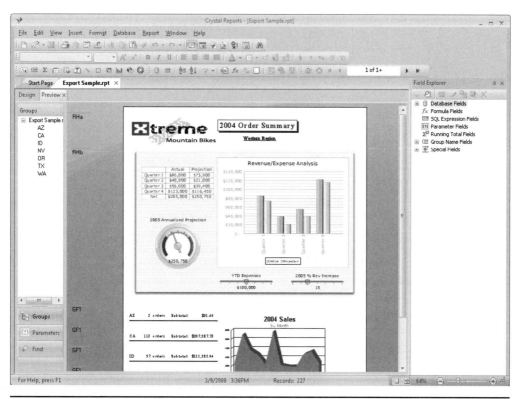

FIGURE 20-1   Sample report with special formatting features

maps, and bitmaps) to a disk folder. You will be asked to make several choices about how and where you want your report exported, as illustrated in Figure 20-2.

Crystal Reports will create a whole new directory to contain the HTML and graphics files that will make up your report. The drive and folder boxes will let you choose an existing directory *under which* a new directory will be created. Type the name of the new directory in the Directory Name box (Crystal Reports will name the new directory HTML by default). If you wish to place the HTML in a specific folder referred to by a web "home" page, make sure you export to the predetermined folder on the web server referred to by the page. Crystal Reports will place the name of the report into the Base File Name box by default. You may want to change this filename to something your web server expects (for example, DEFAULT.HTM), if you are exporting to a web server folder.

You may also use the Page Navigator and Separate HTML Pages check boxes (which typically are helpful only with reports that are more than one page in length). If you check Separate HTML Pages, Crystal Reports will export sequentially numbered HTML pages, one for each page in the report. For example, if you're exporting a drill-down tab that consists of four pages, and you chose DEFAULT.HTM as the base filename, the first page of the report will be exported to DEFAULT1.HTM, the second to DEFAULT2.HTM, the third to

Type name of new folder to create
inside chosen existing folder

Type filename for initial report page

Choose drive and existing folder
for new folder creation

Choose page range to
export to HTML

Choose whether or not to create
separate page files and page navigation
controls on each page

FIGURE 20-2 Select Export File dialog box

DEFAULT3.HTM, and the fourth to DEFAULT4.HTM. If you don't check this box, all three report pages will be combined into one larger DEFAULT.HTM.

CAUTION *This numbering behavior when using the page navigator may cause unintended results by appending numbers onto each HTML file. Keep this behavior in mind if your web server expects a default filename, such as DEFAULT.HTM. You may wish to actually export your report with a different filename and create a DEFAULT.HTM file that immediately redirects the viewer to the "number 1" exported filename.*

If you check Page Navigator, Crystal Reports will place First, Next, Previous, and Last navigation hyperlinks at the bottom of each page that is exported. If you export to separate HTML pages, these links will navigate to the proper separate HTML page. If you don't export to separate HTML pages, the navigation links will still appear inside the one large HTML page, simply moving the viewer to different locations within the one HTML page.

Once you've specified all export options, click OK. If the folder you specified doesn't exist, Crystal Reports will automatically create it. If the folder already exists and contains an HTML file with the same name as you specified, you'll be prompted to overwrite the existing file. In addition to the HTML report file, Crystal Reports will create uniquely numbered .PNG graphics files—one for each bitmap, chart, or map contained in the report.

When you point your browser to the folder and view the HTML file, you'll see the exported report in the browser window. Figures 20-3 and 20-4 illustrate the same report, with Figure 20-3 showing the HTML 3.2 version, and the HTML 4.0 version shown in Figure 20-4.

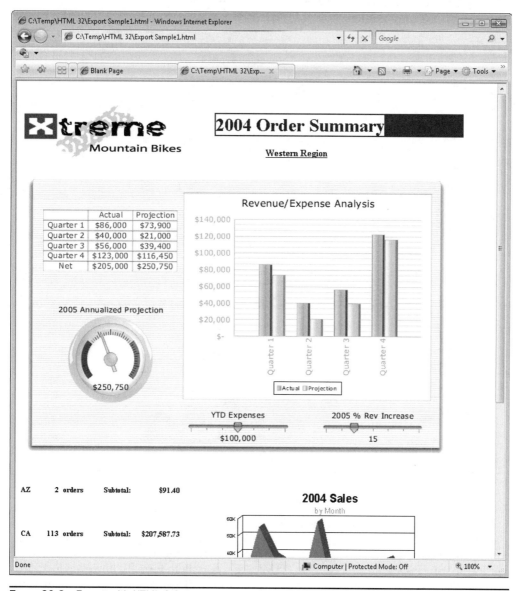

FIGURE 20-3   Export with HTML 3.2

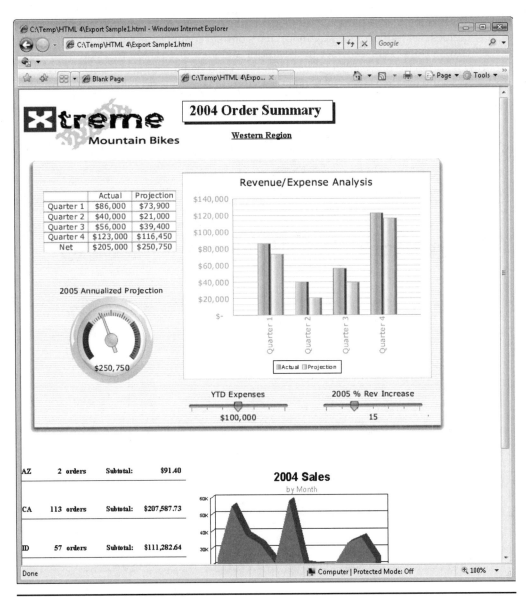

FIGURE 20-4 Export with HTML 4.0

Notice the difference between the HTML 3.2 and 4.0 exports. HTML 3.2, for example, didn't display the report title properly and didn't include the horizontal lines between state totals. And, even though the displayed chart appeared beside text, there were significant vertical spacing issues introduced in an HTML 3.2 export. Both formats, however, included the embedded Xcelsius/Flash object. Even HTML 4.0 doesn't always perform perfect exports, but you'll often find much better rendition of your original report formatting. It's a good idea to try sample exports as you're developing your report, to make sure you don't depend on any features that may not export properly. If your organization has standardized on Adobe Acrobat format files, you can also export to .PDF in the same manner. You'll typically find that Acrobat files exhibit a very accurate representation of your original report formatting.

NOTE *Remember that with HTML, particularly HTML 3.2, some "fancy" report formatting (such as drop shadows or special fonts) may not export to HTML properly. You'll want to try some test exports and view the resulting reports in the web browser that will be used by the majority of your report viewers. That way, you can see what your reports will ultimately look like.*

Don't forget that reports exported to HTML or PDF are static. They will simply show database information as it existed when the report was exported. The only way to update the exported reports is to refresh the report in Crystal Reports and export again. Also, drilling down and using group trees won't work with exported HTML, although a PDF report export can be provided a Table of Contents that mimics the group tree. If you want viewers to be able to refresh reports on their own, as well as interact with the report by drilling down and using the group tree, use other Crystal Reports web options, such as a custom Visual Studio .NET application, available third-party utilities, or a member of the BusinessObjects Enterprise XI 3.0 family. And, giving web users the ability to print reports on their local printers with accurate pagination also becomes a challenge. The options that best provide this capability are PDF export, or web or Windows report viewers available in custom Visual Studio .NET applications, some third-party utilities, and BOE.

Hyperlink Capabilities

Crystal Reports provides hyperlink capabilities so that you can build hyperlinks into your reports. Virtually any objects on your report, such as text objects, database fields, charts, maps, or bitmap objects, can be linked to web pages, e-mail addresses, other Crystal Reports, or other Windows programs. When you point to an object with an attached hyperlink, your mouse cursor turns into the now-familiar pointing finger. Click, and your web browser will launch the web site, your e-mail program will launch a new message window, or the Windows program or file that is specified will be launched.

Hyperlinks are created right in the Crystal Reports designer. In either the Design or Preview tab, select the object you want to create the hyperlink for. Then, choose Format | Hyperlink from the pull-down menus, right-click, and choose Format Field (or a similar format option) from the pop-up menu, or click the Hyperlink toolbar button from the Expert Tools toolbar. The Format Editor will appear. If it's not already selected, click the Hyperlink tab, shown in Figure 20-5.

Choose the type of hyperlink you'd like to create:

- **No Hyperlink**   If a hyperlink has already been assigned to this object, clicking this radio button will clear the hyperlink.

- **An E-Mail Address**   Click this radio button and add the e-mail address you want the hyperlink to send e-mail to in the Hyperlink Information text box after the mailto: text. If you'd like to create a conditional string formula to customize the hyperlink according to a database field or conditional value, click the conditional formula button next to the text box.

FIGURE 20-5   The Format Editor Hyperlink tab

- **A Website on the Internet**   Click this radio button and add the web site URL you want the hyperlink to launch in the Hyperlink Information text box after the http:// text. If you'd like to create a conditional string formula to customize the hyperlink according to a database field or conditional value, click the conditional formula button next to the text box. You may also click the Create Enterprise Hyperlink button, new in Crystal Reports 2008, to build a hyperlink to an existing object in a BOE XI 3.0 system (this feature is described in more detail later in the chapter).

- **A File**   Click this radio button and add the path and filename of the file you want the hyperlink to launch or the command you want to execute in the Hyperlink Information text box. Type the same command or path/filename you'd type after choosing Start | Run in Windows. If you'd like to create a conditional string formula to customize the hyperlink according to a database field or conditional value, click the conditional formula button next to the text box.

- **Current Website Field Value/Current E-mail Field Value**   These options are available only if you've chosen a string database or summary field on the report. In this case, the hyperlink will simply be the value of text from the database. To correctly use this option, the database field must return a complete web site URL (including the http:// prefix), or an e-mail address, depending on which option you've chosen.

NOTE *The "DHTML Viewer Only" options in this dialog box are used to control Guided Navigation and Report Part viewing. More details can be found later in this chapter.*

To further benefit the report viewer, you may wish to click the Common tab on the Format Editor and add a tool tip indicating what the hyperlink does. Either type the tool tip into the tool tip text box directly, or click the conditional formula button next to the text box and enter a string formula that will display when the viewer moves his or her mouse over the object.

Once you've specified all necessary information, click OK to close the Format Editor. When you preview the report in Crystal Reports, you'll see the mouse cursor change to a familiar pointing finger hyperlink cursor when you point to the object. If you added a tool tip, it will appear in a small yellow box. When you click your mouse button, the hyperlink will launch the web page, e-mail Send dialog box, or Windows file.

After you create a hyperlink, follow the same steps you used to create it to modify or remove it. If you are modifying your report in the Preview tab, you may find it difficult to select an object that you've defined a hyperlink for. If you point to it with your mouse, your mouse cursor will change to a hyperlink cursor and you'll actually execute the hyperlink if you click. If you need to select an object in the Preview tab that has a hyperlink associated with it, SHIFT-click or right-click the object to select it.

TIP *Hyperlinks aren't applicable only to reports exported or viewed on the Web. When you view reports in the Crystal Reports Preview tab or view a report integrated with a custom program, hyperlinks will work as you expect. Just remember that a viewer who is using Crystal Reports needs a network connection to your corporate intranet or the Internet to successfully use web or e-mail hyperlinks.*

New Crystal Reports 2008 Enterprise Hyperlink Feature

If you select the A Website On The Internet radio button on the Format Editor Hyperlink tab, the Create Enterprise Hyperlink button appears below the Website Address text box. This button, new in Crystal Reports 2008, will launch a dialog box prompting for information about a particular Crystal Report, Web Intelligence document, or other target object located on a member of the BusinessObjects Enterprise XI 3.0 family, as illustrated in Figure 20-6.

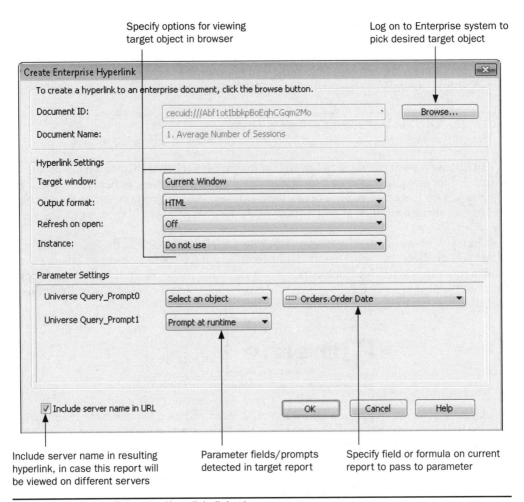

Specify options for viewing
target object in browser

Log on to Enterprise system to
pick desired target object

Include server name in resulting
hyperlink, in case this report will
be viewed on different servers

Parameter fields/prompts
detected in target report

Specify field or formula on current
report to pass to parameter

FIGURE 20-6   Create Enterprise Hyperlink dialog box

Click the Browse button to display a list of predefined BusinessObjects Enterprise
connections (you may also directly log on to a BOE system, as well as create a new predefined
connection). Select the desired connection and supply valid logon credentials. Then, navigate
through the resulting BOE folder hierarchy to find the desired target Crystal Report, Web
Intelligence document, or other object. When you select a particular document you wish
to hyperlink to, the internal Enterprise document ID and name will appear in the Create
Enterprise Hyperlink dialog box.

Choose desired options from the Hyperlink Settings portion of the dialog box to determine
how the target object will appear in a browser. Choices include whether the object will
appear in the same browser window or a new browser window; what format the object will

appear in; and whether to view a currently refreshed version of the object or a previously scheduled object "instance." If the chosen object contains parameter fields or prompts, they will be displayed in the Parameter Settings portion of the dialog box. Choose whether to prompt for values when the object is viewed, whether to supply a constant value, or whether to supply a report field or formula. If you choose a constant value or field or formula, that value will be passed to the commensurate parameter field when the object is viewed.

After you have specified all options on the dialog box, click OK. Crystal Reports 2008 will create a conditional string formula for the web site address, using the BusinessObjects Enterprise OpenDocument function. You can view, or modify, the resulting formula by clicking the conditional formula button to the right of the Website Address text box in the Format Editor Hyperlink tab.

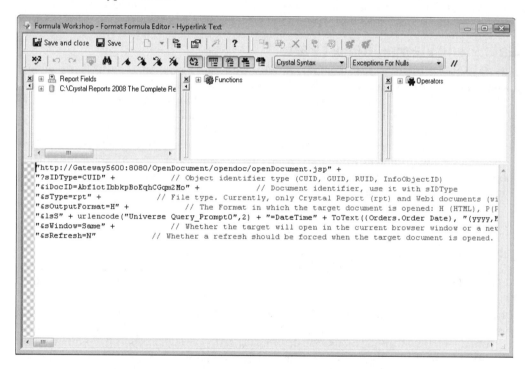

NOTE *The initial release of Crystal Reports 2008 does not include the ability to connect to BusinessObjects Enterprise XI 3.0. Download the latest Crystal Reports 2008 service pack to enable this capability. Use the Crystal Reports Help | Check For Updates option from the pull-down menus to download updated versions.*

Cascading Style Sheet Support

If you are a web developer, an option on the Format Editor Common tab may catch your eye. The CSS Class Name text box/conditional button allows you to specify a Cascading

Style Sheet (CSS) class name for most any object on the report (boxes and lines are notable exceptions). By specifying a CSS class name for the object, you can control formatting "globally" from a style sheet in an HTML document that includes the report.

Either type a CSS class name directly into the text box, or click the conditional formula button. A conditional formula editor will appear, where you may type in a string formula that can dynamically set the CSS class name according to database fields, formula functions, and so forth.

NOTE *CSS class names specified in the Format Editor will be exposed in the "native" HTML report viewers used with Crystal Reports integration tools and BusinessObjects Enterprise, but not when reports are simply exported to HTML as outlined earlier in the chapter.*

Navigating and Viewing Report Parts

Crystal Reports includes features that enhance web-based reporting, particularly when using BusinessObjects Enterprise or a custom web application designed with Visual Studio .NET. Crystal Reports "online" web viewers used with custom application environments, as well as with BusinessObjects Enterprise, support standard Crystal Reports drill-down capabilities (discussed in detail in Chapters 2 and 7). Also, they support hyperlinks to standard "web" items, such as web pages and e-mail addresses. These standard drill-down capabilities allow drilling down within groups in the same report, provide for using other non–Crystal Report web resources as hyperlink targets, and support navigation throughout BusinessObjects Enterprise XI 3.0 systems with the new Enterprise hyperlink capability. However, there are two additional features that provide additional flexibility for drill-down and navigation.

The first feature is known as Guided Navigation (or just *Navigation* for short). Navigation allows you to designate certain objects on your report, such as charts, summary fields, and so forth, to act as hyperlinks to *other* objects on a report—either the same report where the original object resides, or an entirely separate report. The second feature is *Report Parts*, the ability to display just certain portions of a report in a web page, rather than the entire page of a report. Navigation gives you additional flexibility to navigate through reports—you are not limited to hyperlinking to web pages or e-mail addresses. And by using report parts, you can develop web applications that show just specific parts of a report that you may be interested in, such as a single chart or a single grand total in a portal application (report parts can often make web-based Crystal Reports more useful on handheld devices with small screens).

Using Navigation

The first requirement for using Navigation is that your reports must be used in a member of the BusinessObjects Enterprise XI 3.0 family. Navigation can be used in several ways in the DHTML-based report viewers available with these systems (you cannot use the feature in other viewers, such as the ActiveX or Java viewer). By using navigation, you can set up two types of hyperlinks:

- **Report Part Drilldown** A hyperlink to another part of the same report. Only the object or objects that you choose as the destination of your hyperlink will appear when you drill down—not the entire report. Only available when using the Report Part viewer, this option is discussed later in the chapter, in the section "Displaying Report Parts."

- **Another Report Object** A hyperlink to another report object, either in the same report as the calling object, or in a completely separate report. If you use this option with the Report Part viewer, only the object or objects you choose as the destination of your hyperlink will appear when you click. If you use one of the page-oriented DHTML viewers, the entire report will appear when you click, but the object you choose as the destination will be navigated to and highlighted.

First, if you will be hyperlinking from one report to another, it's helpful to begin the process by opening *both* reports in the Crystal Reports designer. This comes in handy when you need to reference the destination object in the Format Editor Hyperlink tab of the source object. If you are only hyperlinking within the same report, you need only have one report open.

1. Select the object that you wish to be the destination of the hyperlink. For example, if you wish to click a group name field in one report to display related detail data from another report, select the object in the detail report that you wish to navigate to.

2. Right-click the destination object and choose Copy from the pop-up menu. While you will actually be able to paste a copy of the object onto the Design tab if you choose, if you "paste" the object into the Hyperlink tab of the Format Editor, a *reference* to the object will be pasted.

3. If you are working with multiple reports, use the Window menu to choose the report that will contain the original hyperlink. If you are hyperlinking from the same report, you can obviously skip this step.

4. Select the object that you wish to act as the hyperlink. Click the Insert Hyperlink toolbar button in the Expert Tools toolbar, or choose Format | Hyperlink from the pull-down menus.

5. The Format Editor Hyperlink tab will appear. Click the Another Report Object radio button in the DHTML Viewer Only section.

6. Click the Paste Link button. You may also click the down arrow next to the Paste Link button to choose from available "contexts" (options in this drop-down list will vary, depending on what type of object you copied in Step 2).

PART II

Several (if not all) of the text boxes will be populated based on the object you originally copied.

- **Select From** will show the name of the report that the copied object resided in. If you opened the "source" report from within BusinessObjects Enterprise, an Enterprise "identifier" will appear in this box. While you cannot type over what is placed in this box, you can click the conditional formula button to the right of the box to create a string formula that sets this value.

- **Report Title** will display the value placed in the Report Title field of the Summary Info dialog box (displayed with File | Summary Info) when the source report was created. If this field was not filled, the filename of the report will appear here. You cannot type over what is placed in this box.

- **Object Name** will contain the name of the object that will appear and be highlighted when you click the hyperlink. This object name can be set in the source report by typing a name into the Object Name text box on the Format Editor common tab. You may wish to give relevant objects more logical names (TopProductsChart instead of Chart1) when preparing them to act as hyperlink targets. You may also find it helpful to use the Report Explorer (discussed in Chapter 1) to determine object names. If you want to navigate to and highlight additional objects beyond what you had originally copied in the source report, type a semicolon after the existing object name and type in additional object names. You will also want to specify multiple object names here if you are only displaying report parts via the Report Part viewer (discussed later in the chapter).

- **Data Context** indicates the location in the destination report that will initially be displayed. For example, if you preview a report and, in the Preview tab, click a group name field displaying "1/2004", you'll notice a data context string similar to /Order Date[1/2004] when you paste the object reference into the Hyperlink tab. Data Context strings require some getting used to. The best approach is to experiment with various permutations of "copy and paste" operations to see the resulting Data Context strings. These context strings will vary (or may not even appear), depending on whether you copied the source object when displaying the Design tab or Preview tab, and what choice you make from the Paste Link button drop-down list. You may either type over what has already been placed in this box or click the conditional formula button to the right of the box to create a string formula that sets the context.

Displaying Report Parts

By default, reports are always displayed a full page at a time when viewed in the various Crystal "native" web viewers. While the "page on demand" architecture that's familiar to most Crystal Reports users is very effective at displaying only the currently required page of the report, an entire page is always displayed. However, there is an additional choice available to those who use Crystal Reports Server/BusinessObjects Enterprise as their web reporting method. The *Report Part Viewer* allows individual objects on a particular report page (such as charts, summary fields, cross-tabs, text objects, and so forth) to be specifically chosen as report part targets. When you use the Report Part Viewer, only those objects specifically chosen as Report Part hyperlink targets will be shown in the viewer.

The general idea in using report parts is to show only limited sets of report objects in a web browser (perhaps inside a larger web application, such as a portal or on a mobile device) and allow those limited sets of objects to act as hyperlinks to other limited sets of objects. The stark difference between the Report Part Viewer and the other DHTML viewers is that the other viewers all maintain the "whole report page at a time" approach, whereas the Report Part Viewer can now display just individual objects on a report.

NOTE *The Report Part Viewer can be used in a custom Visual Studio .NET or Crystal Reports for Eclipse web application, as well as in BusinessObjects Enterprise XI 3.0. In BOE, the Report Part Viewer is used with the My InfoView dashboard, or must be implemented with custom programming web code. More information on using the Report Part Viewer within a My InfoView dashboard can be found in Chapter 21.*

Initial Report Part Setting

The first step in setting up a report to use the Report Part viewer is selecting initial report part settings. These indicate what specific object or objects will initially appear when you view a report in the Report Part viewer. If you don't specify these, the report will appear as an empty web page when you attempt to view it. Initial report part settings are chosen in the Report Options dialog box. Choose File | Report Options from the pull-down menus to display this dialog box.

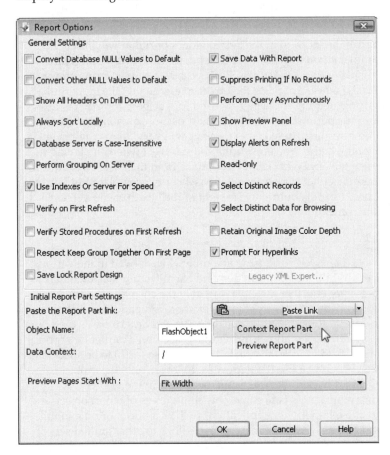

Complete the Object Name and Data Context fields with appropriate report object names and data context strings (discussed earlier in the chapter). You'll probably want to use the same "copy and paste" approach to place an object reference in these fields. If you wish to initially display more than one object in the Report Part Viewer (perhaps a chart along with a text object describing the chart or multiple summaries and text objects), either CTRL-click the objects before copying or type in each separate object name in the Object Name field, separating them with semicolons. As discussed previously, you may find it helpful to give report objects more meaningful names in the Format Editor before using them, as well as using the Report Explorer to locate specific objects.

NOTE *It's important to remember that you can only display objects in the same report section when working with the Report Part Viewer. For example, if you want to display a chart and a text object side by side in the Report Part Viewer, they must be in the same section of the originating report—the chart can't, for example, be in the report header if the text object is in a group header. This limitation also pertains to Report Part Drilldown, discussed in the following section.*

Report Part Drilldown

While showing an initial limited set of objects in the Report Part Viewer may be sufficient for simple applications, the drill-down capabilities of the Report Part Viewer give you tremendous flexibility in controlling how end users navigate through your report. While the page-oriented viewers use the grouping hierarchy of your report to determine drill-down logic, you can more closely control individual objects that appear when you drill down with the Report Part viewer.

This is accomplished by setting up a specific drill-down "path" in your report. For example, you may choose to have a group chart contained in the report header be the initial report part object that appears when you first view the report. If a viewer then clicks on a particular pie wedge or bar in that chart, your drill-down path will take them to a lower-level summary field or advanced chart that appears in a lower group level. In this situation, you are mimicking the regular drill-down capabilities of the page viewer, but you are completely controlling the specific objects that appear when the user drills down. You can go a step further and combine report parts and Navigation (discussed earlier in the chapter) to drill down to a predetermined set of objects in *another* report.

Once you've defined your initial report part object or objects, you may then further define your path by creating a Report Part Drilldown hyperlink for these objects. For example, you may want to select a group name field as your initial report part object and then click the Hyperlink toolbar button to set up the report part drilldown. Click the Report Part Drilldown radio button in the DHTML Viewer Only section. The Format Editor will expand, showing available report sections, and fields within it, that can be drilled down on (only sections and objects in a logical report section just below your selected object will appear).

NOTE *Report Part Drilldown is only available if you've chosen a group chart or map or a summary field in a group header or footer. Other objects will not allow a Report Part Drilldown to be chosen.*

Choose the field or fields you'd like to appear when the report viewer drills down. You may click on one field, or CTRL-click to choose multiple fields, clicking the right arrow to add them to the Fields To Display list. Or, click the double-arrow to add all fields. The order the fields are displayed in the Fields To Display list is the order the fields will appear when a viewer drills down. If you need to change the order of the fields, select a desired field and click the up or down arrows above the Fields To Display list to change the order.

When you view the report in a custom application using the Report Part Viewer, you'll see that the initial report view shows only the object or objects that you chose in the initial report part settings. If you then click the initial object (assuming you've defined a Report Part Drilldown for the object), only the resulting objects for that Report Part Drilldown will appear in the browser.

Introduction to BusinessObjects Enterprise XI 3.0

Over the years as Crystal Reports has migrated from vendor to vendor, and version to version, various companion enterprise distribution systems have followed it. From the original Windows-based Crystal Info product, to various versions of Crystal Enterprise and BusinessObjects Enterprise, there has typically been a companion product to host, schedule, and distribute Crystal Reports on a larger scale. Crystal Reports 2008 continues that tradition with the latest edition of BusinessObjects Enterprise, known as BusinessObjects Enterprise XI 3.0.

> **NOTE** *At the time of this writing, the initial release of BusinessObjects Enterprise XI 3.0 was available. However, other members of this product family, such a matching version of Crystal Reports Server or BusinessObjects Edge, had not been announced. It is safe to assume, however, that concepts described in this book will apply equally to any subsequent releases of the BusinessObjects Enterprise XI 3.0 family that include a Crystal Report component.*

BusinessObjects Enterprise Defined

As the World Wide Web has become not only a more integral part of consumer computing, but an important consideration for business computing platforms as well, Crystal Reports has continued to offer more and more web-based reporting solutions as each new version is released. Simply exporting a report to HTML format (as described earlier in this chapter) and posting the exported files to a web server is one approach. Various web-based programming interfaces have existed with many recent versions of Crystal Reports, including the currently available Visual Studio .NET and Crystal Reports for Eclipse options as well. All of these options allow end users who wish to view reports to do so from within their web browsers. A stand-alone copy of Crystal Reports or a custom Windows application integrating Crystal Reports is not required on each of the workstations. And, the workstations don't all have to have connectivity to the corporate database.

However, these options are sometimes constrained with no interactivity (in the case of a report exported to HTML format), or limited capacity (with custom Visual Studio .NET or Java applications). As such, there is a demand for more enterprise-oriented, high-capacity web reporting capabilities. As larger organizations look more and more toward web-based solutions, options need to be made available that offer alternatives to the limited-user, web-server-centric tools just described. Some organizations need a reporting solution that will scale to potentially support hundreds, or even thousands, of web-based report viewers.

While the earlier Crystal Info/Seagate Info multitier reporting tool eventually offered a web-based interface that could be used in place of its typical Windows front end, the direction in enterprise solutions was clearly web based. Crystal Enterprise 8, introduced alongside Crystal Reports 8.5, was the first entry in the next generation of unified, enterprise-oriented reporting and analysis tools.

The Two-Tier Web Reporting Method

A Visual Studio .NET or Java custom web application is considered a limited web server–based reporting system that can be described as *two-tier architecture.* The basic premise of this architecture is to route the report viewing audience through a web browser and a web server, rather than placing an individual copy of Crystal Reports or a Crystal Reports–based custom application on each user PC. Only the web server requires connectivity to the corporate database for ad hoc reporting. This architecture is illustrated in Figure 20-7.

NOTE *Yes, the argument could be made that the architecture being described here is in fact a three-tier architecture—web browser to web server to database. However, by basically moving all of the previous client-based processing to the web server and transforming clients to simple viewer status, the previous two-tier client/server architecture is just being moved around. It can still be argued that in the typical database/query client/server model, the web server has become the client and the database remains the server.*

By centralizing this approach via the web, much reduced software maintenance on client-side computers is required. New versions of reports or reporting systems do not require any new software to be installed on individual client computers—only the web pages that compose the application need to be updated on the web server. As long as a compatible web browser can be used, Crystal Reports can be viewed on a computer or workstation.

The Multitier Reporting Method
While the existing architecture just described is an overall improvement beyond the classic client/server computing model of an application on a client with a network connection to a

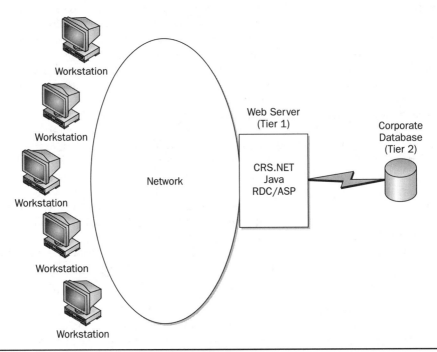

FIGURE 20-7 The existing two-tier processing architecture

server, there are still bottlenecks and disadvantages that limit this architecture's capacity for large reporting environments. In particular,

- The web server suddenly becomes a concentrated reporting and query client instead of the web page distribution server it's designed to be. Every request for an ad hoc report requires the web server to send a query to the database, wait for a result set, and format the result set before sending the report back to a web browser.

- The network connection between the web server and the database can become overloaded, depending on the types of queries and reports that the web server submits to the database and the size of the return result sets.

- There is limited sharing or caching of report requests (particularly for ad hoc real-time reports). If 25 users request the same report (particularly if there are parameter fields or different database user IDs involved), the web server oftentimes will have to submit the report's query to the database 25 times.

- The simpler Crystal Reports web systems do not allow reports to be automatically scheduled to run at regular intervals, such as once per day, once per month, and so on.

The answer to these inherent limitations of existing Crystal web reporting alternatives lies in the BusinessObjects Enterprise multitier report processing architecture, as illustrated in Figure 20-8. This multitier structure allows report distribution scalability far greater than the previously described "classic" two-tier architecture. By creating multiple software

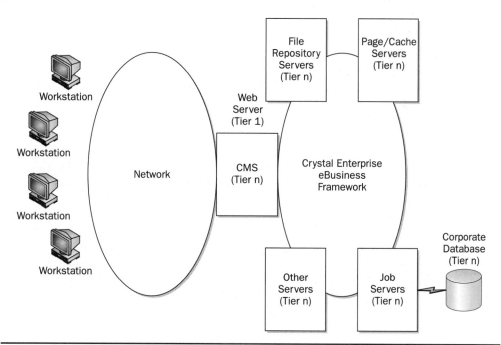

Figure 20-8   BusinessObjects Enterprise multitier processing architecture

functions and creating the ability for them to be rolled out or "scaled" to multiple processors, BusinessObjects Enterprise immediately offers a dramatic improvement in reliability, load capability, and fault tolerance. The web server can return to its core requirement to serve up web pages. Additional components now work together to run ad hoc report and query requests, schedule automatically recurring reports, convert completed reports pages to "page-on-demand" viewing files, handle security, and cache recently reviewed report pages for delivery to the next report viewer. The result is a completely scalable multitier structure that dramatically improves the capabilities and capacity of web-based reporting.

NOTE   *A complete BusinessObjects Enterprise XI 3.0 system supports many document and object types besides Crystal Reports. However, this book will only cover BOE features that are relevant to designing, publishing, and viewing Crystal Report document types.*

BusinessObjects Enterprise Licensing

Various versions of the BusinessObjects Enterprise XI 3.0 family include various licensing scenarios. There are three different types of possible licenses, depending on the member of the BOE family you are using, and the types of licenses your organization has purchased. In some cases, a particular BOE implementation will only consist of one license type (for example, processor licenses cannot typically be mixed with other license types). In other cases, mixed license types may reside on the same BOE implementation (for example, some versions support a combination of named and concurrent licenses).

- A *named user license* (sometimes abbreviated as NUL) allows one specific user to log on, and that license is reserved for that particular user. You may only create as many user IDs in a BOE system as there are named user licenses. Any attempt to add additional user IDs beyond the named user license count will result in an error message.

- A *concurrent access license* (sometimes abbreviated as CAL) allows any user to log on using the license, but that license is not reserved for any particular user. Concurrent access licenses allow for an unlimited number of potential users (you may create as many user IDs as you wish), provided that the total number of users logged on at any one time doesn't exceed the concurrent access license limit. A user attempting to log on will receive an error message if they would exceed the number of licenses.

- A *processor license* allows as many user IDs as possible to be added to a BOE system, and for unlimited number of users to be logged on simultaneously. However, a separate processor license must be purchased for each CPU used in an Enterprise system.

BusinessObjects Enterprise XI 3.0 New Features

While there are many features that are new overall to BusinessObjects Enterprise XI 3.0 (including significant architecture changes and administrative enhancements), several are of particular interest to Crystal Reports designers and viewers.

- **An entirely new look and feel**   Both InfoView (the BOE web-based end-user interface), and the Central Management Console (the web-based BOE administration interface) have been completely redesigned. InfoView is covered in detail in Chapter 21, and the Central Management Console is covered in detail in Chapter 22.

- **Support for new Crystal Reports 2008 features**   Most new Crystal Reports 2008 features, such as Flash/Xcelsius integration, optional parameter fields, the parameter panel, enhanced cross-tabs, and so forth, are fully supported in BOE XI 3.0 (note that you must upgrade your version of Crystal Reports 2008 to Service Pack 0 or later to work with BOE).

- **Report bursting and distribution**   This impressive new feature allows you to set up a single Crystal Report to be broken in to different portions aimed at different users (sometimes called *bursting*) for automatic distribution to multiple recipients, both inside the BOE system, as well as external to your organization.

BusinessObjects Enterprise XI 3.0 Architecture

BusinessObjects Enterprise is a significant departure from the traditional two-tier web server–based approach to report processing. As discussed previously in this chapter, one of the huge benefits of BusinessObjects Enterprise over earlier tools is its multitier, multiserver approach to web reporting. By spreading the processing load over multiple software and hardware layers, it enables much higher numbers of users and much better sustained performance.

If you are an end user of BusinessObjects Enterprise, there are several software components that you may encounter as you view reports. Depending on your particular BusinessObjects Enterprise implementation, you may also be required to design, publish, and schedule reports as well. You'll want to be familiar with the different components that are required to use BusinessObjects Enterprise in these various ways. If you are an administrator who is responsible for installing, maintaining, and supporting BusinessObjects Enterprise, you'll want to be familiar with not only the end-user tools available to your user community, but also the particular server components, communications methods, and administrative tools available for your use.

NOTE *More detailed information about end-user components and their usage can be found in Chapter 21. Chapter 22 contains more technical discussions and coverage of administrative tools and processes.*

End-User Components for Reporting

As a web-based reporting tool, BusinessObjects Enterprise provides interaction almost entirely within a web browser. If you are using a Windows PC, an Apple Macintosh, or a Unix/Linux workstation, all you need to work with the majority of BusinessObjects Enterprise features is a standard web browser (a newer browser that supports HTML Version 4 and JavaScript is required). The only exception to the web browser rule is for designing reports in the stand-alone Crystal Reports product—Crystal Reports 2008 is used to design reports and must run in a Windows environment. And, there are several ways of publishing reports to BusinessObjects Enterprise. One way, the Crystal-supplied Publishing Wizard, is also a Windows-only program.

As an end user, you'll normally start using BusinessObjects Enterprise from InfoView. InfoView is a web interface that can be viewed by pointing your browser to a standard location specified by your BusinessObjects Enterprise administrator. But because BusinessObjects Enterprise is web-based, it's entirely possible to customize the web interface to the BusinessObjects Enterprise system. Your organization may still use the standard locations for BusinessObjects Enterprise pages (but may have customized the pages), or it may have created an entirely customized interface (such as an internal intranet or portal) that interfaces with BusinessObjects Enterprise.

If you wish to add newly designed Crystal reports to InfoView, you can save them directly to BusinessObjects Enterprise folders from Crystal Reports 2008, use InfoView itself, use the web-based Central Management Console, or add one or more reports en masse with the Windows-based Publishing Wizard.

InfoView   InfoView is the out-of-the-box end user interface to BOE. The vast bulk of end-user navigation, report viewing, scheduling, and day-to-day BOE usage will take place through InfoView. You may also use InfoView to add new reports to BOE, remove reports you no longer use, and organize folders and categories used to logically organize reports (all these capabilities are determined by security rights set up by your BOE administrator).

If you wish to run InfoView from a main BOE server, or if your administrator has set up a shortcut to InfoView on your computer, you may select the appropriate InfoView choice from the Start menu. More likely, a standard hyperlink from your corporate intranet will be provided, or you will be provided with a specific web site location (known in web parlance as a Universal Resource Locator, or URL) to navigate to InfoView.

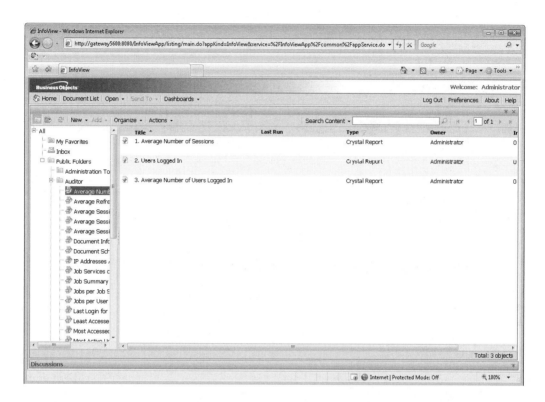

From InfoView you can log on as a different user; navigate through and create folders; add new reports; view reports, report alerts, PDF documents, Word documents, and so forth; and schedule reports, packages, or programs to run on a recurring basis. (InfoView will most likely appear identical to the preceding illustration, but it may have been modified to more closely align with your organization's standard web look and feel.)

Customized Web Interface   InfoView is a Business Objects–designed interface to BusinessObjects Enterprise. Based on a standard programming interfaces (initially Java, with Microsoft .NET support slated for a later BOE XI 3.0 release), all InfoView source code is provided for perusal and modification. Experienced developers may modify the existing InfoView to more closely match your standard web interface, or create a completely new set of web pages to expose BusinessObjects Enterprise features. If a customized intranet page or portal has been created, your administrator may give you a completely different URL to launch your BusinessObjects Enterprise system.

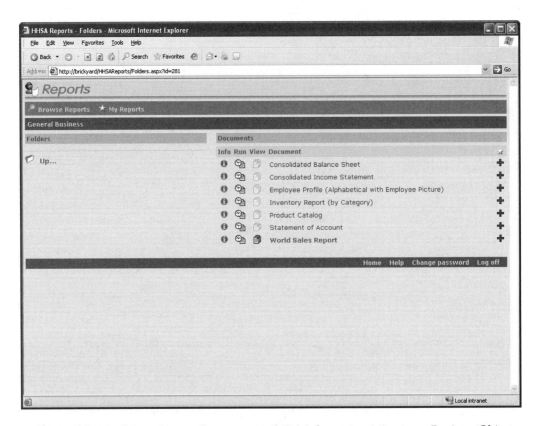

Publishing Wizard Depending on how responsibilities for maintaining your BusinessObjects Enterprise system are divided within your organization, you may need the ability to post reports you've designed with Crystal Reports 2008 to your BusinessObjects Enterprise system. There are several ways to accomplish this: using InfoView (covered in Chapter 21), or with the Central Management Console and the Publishing Wizard (both discussed in Chapter 22).

The Publishing Wizard provides certain advantages over the Central Management Console and is designed to be easier to use overall. This is a Windows program that does require installation on your individual computer from a Windows Setup routine.

You may also edit existing BusinessObjects Enterprise reports or add new reports right from Crystal Reports 2008. When you choose File | Open or File | Save As from the Crystal Reports 2008 pull-down menus, the file dialog box will contain extra icons labeled Enterprise

Folders and My Connections. Click either of these icons to log on to either a newly specified or previously defined Enterprise system. If the rights assigned to your user ID allow editing or adding, you'll be able to open existing BOE reports for modification, or add new reports directly to the Central Management Server.

NOTE *You must update the initial version of Crystal Reports 2008 to Service Pack 0 or later to connect to a BOE XI 3.0 system.*

Server and Maintenance Components for Administrators

While end users will probably stick close to the InfoView (and, perhaps to Crystal Reports 2008 or the Publishing Wizard if they are in charge of maintaining reports), administrative personnel will find additional items that they can use to administer and maintain the BusinessObjects Enterprise system.

Central Management Console   The Central Management Console (often abbreviated to CMC) is the administrator's entry point into the BusinessObjects Enterprise system. Because the Central Management Console is web-based, you can run it on any computer on the network that has a web browser. You don't need to run it on any of the physical components that make up BusinessObjects Enterprise. You can even run it in a remote location from the Internet, provided your internal network security allows an outside browser to navigate to the proper location.

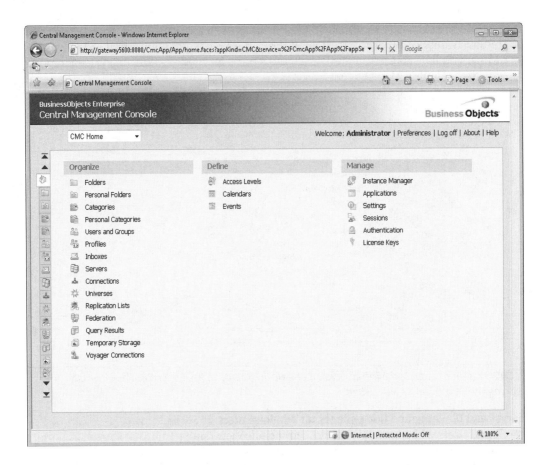

Here, administrative personnel can add and edit user IDs; organize users into user groups; change passwords and grant and deny rights to users; manage back-end servers; add, remove, and modify folders to logically organize reports; and add and remove reports in existing folders.

TIP *More detailed information about Crystal Management Console functions and capabilities can be found in Chapter 22.*

Import Wizard If you are a user of an earlier version of BusinessObjects Enterprise or Crystal Enterprise, you may need to migrate the earlier system to BusinessObjects Enterprise XI 3.0. Or, you may have set up an initial test version of BusinessObjects Enterprise but wish to copy the existing set of user IDs, the same report and folder structure, and other characteristics to a newer production system.

To prevent an administrator from having to manually reenter all Enterprise information into a new BusinessObjects Enterprise system, Business Objects supplies the Import Wizard.

The Import Wizard reads the contents of an existing Crystal Enterprise or BusinessObjects Enterprise system and copies it into your BusinessObjects Enterprise XI 3.0 system.

In the process, an administrator can choose which users, user groups, folders, and reports to automatically transfer to a new BusinessObjects Enterprise system. When completed, the Import Wizard will have created a new BOE system that closely mirrors that of the previous system.

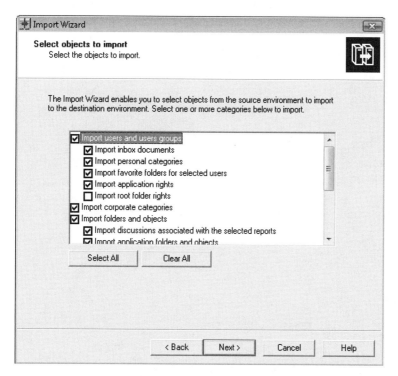

NOTE *For complete information on the Import Wizard, including descriptions of how users and reports may be affected by a migration, consult the online Administrator's Guide.*

Using InfoView

As versions of Crystal Enterprise and BusinessObjects Enterprise have progressed, so has the web-based end user interface that connects to it. The Enterprise version that matches Crystal Reports 2008, BusinessObjects Enterprise XI 3.0, continues that trend. This "out-of-the-box" user interface, called *InfoView,* provides capabilities to perform virtually all day-to-day activity required to work with BusinessObjects Enterprise XI 3.0 (abbreviated BOE throughout this book).

While you could accomplish many tasks in previous versions of the BOE InfoView, version XI 3.0 improves on this even more. While some administrative tasks (such as adding, removing, and maintaining user accounts) are still relegated to other tools, most Crystal Reports–related BOE maintenance can be done entirely with InfoView. These tasks can include viewing reports, adding new reports, organizing the BOE folder and category structure, and scheduling reports for recurring processing. And, version XI 3.0 also introduces an entirely revamped user interface, providing more capabilities than the previous version in a streamlined organization.

NOTE *As of this writing, the only Enterprise XI 3.0 product available is the full release of BusinessObjects Enterprise XI 3.0. However, Business Objects has stated a future direction to provide versions for Crystal Reports–only organizations, such as the previously released Crystal Reports Server XI. Although it is assumed that future products in the BusinessObjects XI 3.0 family will generally share the same functionality and look and feel as the full BOE XI 3.0 product demonstrated in this chapter, you may notice some reduced features or options. As such, some items demonstrated in this chapter may not be visible or available.*

Connecting to InfoView

Your intranet may already have a link that launches BOE InfoView. If so, merely click the link. However, you may need to navigate directly by typing a specific web address into your browser. In this case, point your browser directly to the URL provided by your administrator. By default, you can navigate directly to InfoView by browsing to

```
http://<web server>:<port>/InfoViewApp
```

where *<web server>* is the name of the web server where BOE is installed, and *<port>* is the web server port designated for the BOE web server (the port specification is optional and should only be added if specified by your administrator).

NOTE *As BusinessObjects Enterprise can be heavily customized, it's possible that your organization has implemented a unique version that will not use the default URL. Check with your BusinessObjects Enterprise administrator if you are unsure of the proper URL to use.*

If your BOE administrator has enabled single sign-on, you may be taken directly to the InfoView homepage (the same user ID and password you logged on to your network with will be used to connect you to BOE). If single sign-on isn't enabled, you'll be presented with the Log On To InfoView screen. Fill in the user name and password fields with the values provided by your administrator. If your administrator also provided you with special values for the System and Authentication fields, supply them (otherwise, these fields may be left alone). You may also be able to log on using a guest account, provided that the administrator hasn't disabled it. In this case, merely leave the user ID and password field blanks, leave the

Authentication choice set to Enterprise, and click Log On. Once you've successfully logged on to BOE, you'll see the initial InfoView screen, as illustrated in Figure 21-1.

InfoView consists of two major areas: the Header Panel and the Workspace Panel. The *Header Panel* (at the top of the InfoView screen) looks and behaves much like a toolbar, with a series of buttons and drop-down lists that remain constant, regardless of what options you've chosen in InfoView. The *Workspace Panel,* comprising the large bottom portion of InfoView, is where various folder displays, object dialog boxes, content-related toolbars, and viewed reports will appear.

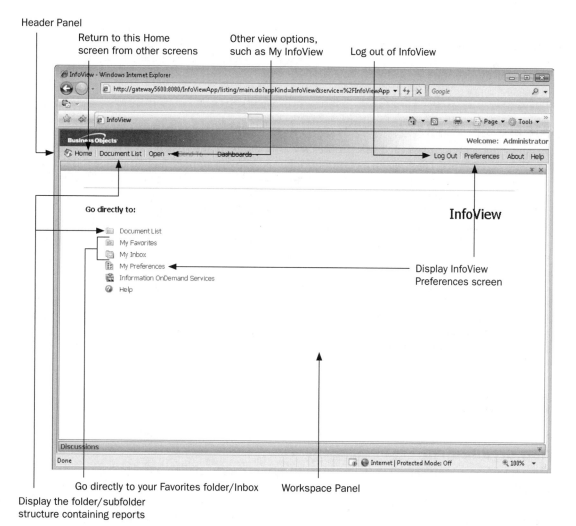

Header Panel

Return to this Home screen from other screens

Other view options, such as My InfoView

Log out of InfoView

Display InfoView Preferences screen

Go directly to your Favorites folder/Inbox

Workspace Panel

Display the folder/subfolder structure containing reports

FIGURE 21-1   InfoView home page

The Most Important BOE Component: The CMS

The Central Management Server, or *CMS*, is the heart of BusinessObjects Enterprise. Every other component communicates through the CMS—other servers won't know about each other without the CMS. The CMS also acts as the central security point for BusinessObjects Enterprise logon—all user IDs, passwords, and rights lists are maintained on the CMS. And, the CMS also keeps track of report scheduling. If a report is scheduled to automatically run every day at midnight, the CMS sets the report processing cycle in motion at the prescribed time.

While a substantial number of different software components go into making BOE work, the one you'll be concerned with as a regular report viewer or scheduler is the CMS. You must first log on to the CMS when you start to use BOE. If the CMS isn't working, you won't be able to use BusinessObjects Enterprise (and neither will anybody else, for that matter).

BOE Security Model

BusinessObjects Enterprise includes a robust security model that works behind the scenes in InfoView to control what you can or cannot do. For example, you may find you have the ability to schedule a report and view the resulting "saved instance," but not run the report in real time. Or, you may find the opposite—you may be able to run a report in real time, but not schedule it. Or, you may have the even higher restriction of being allowed to view only a report instance that another user has scheduled—you will not be able to schedule your own reports nor view a report on demand. And, your administrator can grant or deny you other rights, such as the ability to create, rename, or delete folders, or to add or remove reports.

This security is quite granular. It can be assigned to an individual user or to a group of users (such as the Accounting group, the Finance group, the Power Users group, or the Administrators group). And, you may have a combination of rights granted or denied you by being a member of more than one group. In addition to this group- and user-based security, certain security settings can also be applied to certain folders or individual reports.

Suffice it to say that you may find a variety of capabilities provided to you, depending on various settings and configurations of your particular BOE system. Your BOE administrator is your source of information on your current security model. Contact him or her if you wish to have additional capabilities provided to you.

InfoView Organization

Since InfoView can potentially provide access to a large variety of different objects (Crystal Reports is but one type of document that can be stored in BOE), there are several available approaches to make InfoView organization more logical. You get an idea of the various organizational choices when you display the InfoView homepage—such as the Document List, My Favorites, My Inbox, and so forth. Some of these organizational elements apply to you only—no one else (save for BOE administrators) will be able to see their contents. Other organization elements are shared by all BOE users, while yet more are shared by a subset of BOE users. Through a series of folders, subfolders, categories, an inbox, third-party documents, report and program objects, and report and program instances, you can find a particular object, run it on demand for a refreshed view of your data, view a report with saved data, or view a recent instance of the report or program that resulted from a schedule.

In addition to standard Crystal Reports, BusinessObjects Enterprise XI 3.0 also allows you to view many "third-party" documents, such as Word documents, .PDF files, and PowerPoint presentations, from within InfoView. And, while you will notice a certain "look and feel" of InfoView when it is first installed, you have the capability of customizing several behavioral characteristics of InfoView to your own liking.

NOTE   *As BOE hosts more than just Crystal Reports, the generic term object can apply to a Crystal report, a third-party document (such as a .PDF file, Word document, or Excel spreadsheet), or a program object that performs some sort of logic or script. You'll see the term "object" used generically throughout this chapter to refer to any of these types of documents.*

My Favorites and My Inbox

Two immediate choices you'll find on the InfoView homepage are My Favorites and My Inbox. *My Favorites* is a folder (more discussion about InfoView folders follows) that belongs just to you—no other BOE user (except for administrators) can see its contents. Generally, objects that are only relevant to you, such as custom reports that only you choose to run, or third-party documents that only you need to see, will appear here. Generally, you will have full rights to control what appears in your Favorites folder—you'll be able to create subfolders; add, remove, and rename objects; and so forth. Clicking the My Favorites link on the home page will redisplay the Workspace Panel, showing you the contents of your Favorites folder on the right side of the screen.

Your other personal choice is My Inbox. Your *Inbox*, as the name might suggest, is similar to the inbox you probably use with an e-mail program. It is designed as a placeholder for new objects or instances that may be placed there by you, by the administrator or another authorized user, or automatically by a report schedule. You'll probably want to designate the Inbox as a single place to hold new report instances that you want to see as soon as they have run. If you schedule them to appear in your Inbox, all new report instances will be viewable in a single location, regardless of the original location of the report. Clicking the My Inbox link on the home page will redisplay the Workspace Panel, showing you the contents of your Inbox on the right side of the screen.

You are, in fact, displaying a subset of the full Document List (described next) when you click My Favorites or My Inbox. The Workspace Panel will show you chosen private content, but will also show the full BOE folder hierarchy in the left side of the Workspace Panel, as well as the content-specific toolbar at the top of the Workspace Panel, just below the Header Panel.

The Document List

While you may want to work with objects in My Favorites and My Inbox that pertain just to you, you'll almost certainly need to view objects that are shared among all BOE users. These objects are stored in another organizational layer, called the Document List. The *Document List* will display public BOE objects in either a folder/subfolder hierarchy or a category hierarchy (you may choose which you wish to view). To view the Document List, click the

Document List link on the InfoView home page. The Workspace Panel will show you the full BOE folder hierarchy in the left side of the Workspace Panel, as well as the content-specific toolbar at the top of the Workspace Panel, just below the Header Panel.

Navigating Folders and Subfolders

Initially, you'll see the series of folders and subfolders on the left side of InfoView in the Tree Panel. Top-level folders are the first levels you see in the Tree Panel when logging on to InfoView (you'll also see My Favorites and Inbox on the same level as top-level folders). You can either click a folder name directly to see objects within the folder (if any) or click the plus sign next to a folder to expand the Tree Panel to show subfolders. Subfolders can contain other subfolders and objects as well. To see more subfolders within a subfolder, expand the Tree Panel again with the plus sign. Or, click a subfolder name directly to see any objects in the subfolder. Once you click a folder or subfolder, a list of objects in that folder will appear in the right side of the Workspace Panel. You'll also see another toolbar (in addition to the Header Panel toolbar) at the top of the Workspace Panel. This toolbar provides functions appropriate to the folder/object view now displayed in the Workspace Panel.

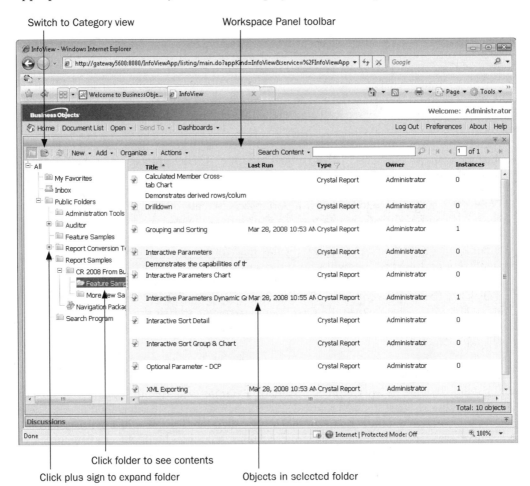

Switch to Category view   Workspace Panel toolbar

Click folder to see contents

Click plus sign to expand folder   Objects in selected folder

Categories

While a BOE object must be placed in a folder (and, it can only reside in a single folder), BusinessObjects Enterprise provides an alternative way of organizing objects: categories. Unlike folders, *categories* are optional. Also unlike folders, an object can be assigned one or more categories at the same time. To display categories, switch the Tree Panel to category view by clicking the Switch To Categories toolbar button in the Workspace Panel toolbar. A category view will appear that behaves similarly to the folder view discussed previously— click the plus sign to expand a category to see subcategories, and click a category itself to fill the objects area with objects assigned to that category.

There are two initial "top-level" categories: *personal categories* and *corporate categories*. Personal categories are those that you create and that only you can see. Corporate categories are created by the BOE administrator (or other users, provided they have sufficient rights) and are available for all users of BOE.

Switch to folder view

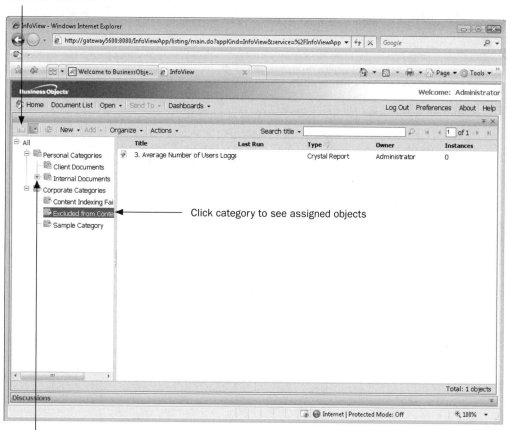

Click category to see assigned objects

Click plus sign to expand category

Objects and Instances

Obviously, just seeing folders and subfolders does you little good if you're trying to make business decisions. Your ultimate goal is to view a report or document within one of the folders. Reports inside InfoView can actually take on two different forms: a report object or a report instance. Likewise, BOE program objects (such as executable programs, Java programs, or scripts) can also appear as objects or instances. And, while other "third-party" objects, such as Word documents, PDF files, and Excel spreadsheets, can be stored on BOE, they will only appear as objects—there will never be a third-party instance.

- A *report object* is a report "template" or design—it may or may not contain saved data (*saved data* is data that was saved with the .RPT file from the last time it was refreshed against the database before being added to BOE).

- A *report instance* appears only after a report has been scheduled. An instance is one of the occurrences of a scheduled report.

- A *program object* is a "pointer" to an executable program, Java program, or script file (JScript or VBScript) that can perform some sort of administrative or functional operation, such as updating a data warehouse. The object will perform its task when it is scheduled.

- A *program instance* appears only after a program object has been scheduled. An instance shows the output of the particular "run" of the program object. In particular, the "standard" and "error" output from the program object will be shown when you view the instance.

- A *third-party object* is simply a static document, such as an Acrobat PDF file, Word document, or PowerPoint .PPT file, that you can view in your web browser. It cannot be scheduled. For this reason, no instances will ever appear for a third-party object.

When a report or program object is first added to InfoView, only an object will be available. Only after the report or program has been scheduled at least once, will any instances of that object be available.

Third-party object, which will
never contain instances

Crystal Report that has
not been scheduled

Crystal Report with multiple instances

NOTE *The folders, subfolders, and objects that are available to you will most likely vary according to BusinessObjects Enterprise security. You may, for example, see a completely different set of folders, subfolders, and objects than a coworker sees. Or, you may see some items in common with others in your organization, but everyone may not see the same set of items.*

Viewing Reports: On Demand or Instance

Your ultimate goal in using InfoView will no doubt be to view output from various types of objects. In particular, you'll almost certainly want to view reporting results in your web browser. There are three general ways to view reports in InfoView: on demand with saved data, on demand with no saved data, or as a report instance.

- Viewing a report *on demand with saved data* will view the last set of data saved with the report before it was added to BusinessObjects Enterprise. The age of the data shown in the report will depend on how recently the report was refreshed before it was added to BOE (saved data is discussed in more detail in Chapter 1). If the data in the viewed report appears to be stale, you may *refresh the report,* which will then load the report you are viewing into one of the BOE servers and run it against the database immediately—you'll see the most current view of the data (the refresh data right must be granted to you to do this).

- Viewing a report *on demand without saved data* will actually load the report object into one of the BOE servers and run it against the database at the time you request it—you'll see the most current view of the data (the refresh data right must be granted to you to do this).

- Viewing a *report instance* requires the corresponding report object to have been previously run at least once via a schedule. One of the occurrences of that scheduled report will be viewed, showing the view of the data as of that point in time.

There are advantages and disadvantages to each method. For the most current view of the data, you'll probably want to view the report on demand without saved data, or perhaps refresh a report with saved data—especially if the database the report is based on is fluid and changes rapidly. However, the load on the database and network can be heavily impacted if a large number of BOE users are viewing reports on demand without saved data, or refreshing reports. And, if the report requires a large database query or lots of report processing, viewing on demand can be slow.

Viewing report objects with saved data, or viewing report instances, greatly reduces demand on the database. These views show you a set of "saved data" current as of the time the object was added to BOE (in the case of viewing reports with saved data), or current as of the time the instance was run. Because the report has already run by the time you view, viewing objects with saved data and report instances is typically faster than viewing without saved data or refreshing—sometimes by a huge factor. By use of objects with saved data and instances, a single database query can populate a report that can then be viewed by hundreds or thousands of viewers. Of course, any changes to the underlying database won't be reflected in these cases. However, if the database changes infrequently or up-to-the-minute analysis of the database isn't required, saved-data objects and instances can provide accurate data views without impacting the network or database with repetitive queries.

View a report object or instance by performing several simple steps:

1. After logging on to InfoView, choose a folder, a category, or your Inbox that contains reports you want to view. Select the report object that you wish to view.

2. To view the report with or without saved data, double-click the report, choose View from the Actions drop-down toolbar button in the Workspace Panel toolbar, or right-click the report and choose View from the pop-up menu. If the report contains saved data, you'll be presented the saved data in the Workspace Panel. If the report doesn't contain saved data, it will be run in real time and displayed with a current set of data.

3. To view the latest report instance (the report that ran on a schedule most recently), choose View Latest Instance from the Actions drop-down toolbar button in the Workspace Panel toolbar, or right-click the report and choose View Latest Instance from the pop-up menu. The most recent instance of the report will appear in the Workspace Panel.

4. If you want to examine all report instances that have run, including information on instances that may run in the future, you'll need to view the History List. Choose History from the Actions drop-down toolbar button in the Workspace Panel toolbar, or right-click the report and choose History from the pop-up menu. A separate window will appear in the Workspace Panel showing all instances of that report:

PART II

Status of instance (success, failed, recurring, running, and so forth)

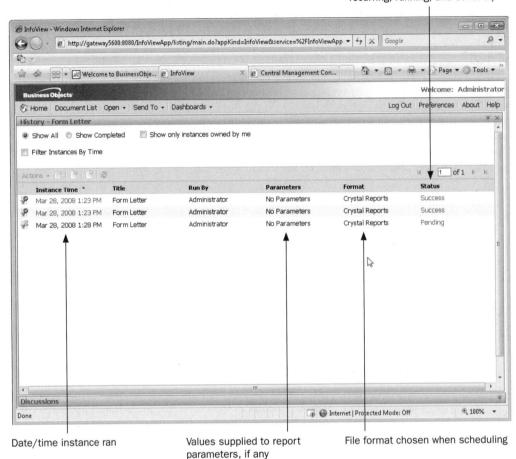

Date/time instance ran

Values supplied to report parameters, if any

File format chosen when scheduling

5. To get details on the status of an instance (perhaps you wish to find out more information on a failed instance), click the status value (Success, Failed, and so forth) of the instance you want more information about.

6. To view the instance itself, click the date/time of the desired instance.

NOTE *Your right to view reports on demand or view instances is controlled by BOE security. You may not have the right to view reports on demand—you may only be able to view instances. Or, you may be able to view some reports on demand, but not others. In some cases, these rights may result in non-availability of options on menus. In others, you may encounter "no right to refresh" error messages when attempting to view or refresh reports. If you have questions about your on-demand versus instance capabilities, check with your BOE administrator.*

Viewing Third-Party Objects

BusinessObjects Enterprise XI 3.0 allows additional document types (beyond Crystal Reports documents) to be added to InfoView. These document types, known as *third-party objects,* include standard office documents (such as Word, Excel, and PowerPoint documents), text files, Rich Text Format documents, and Adobe PDF files. You'll notice an appropriate icon appearing next to a third-party object indicating the type of document that the object represents.

Viewing third-party objects is a very straightforward process. Simply double-click the name of the document that you wish to view (you may also choose View from the Actions drop-down toolbar button in the Workspace Panel toolbar, or right-click the object and choose View from the pop-up menu), which will download the document to your web browser as though you were downloading it from a regular web site. Depending on what viewers or office software packages are loaded on your computer, the document may immediately be displayed in Workspace Panel. If not, you may be prompted with several options, such as saving the document to disk.

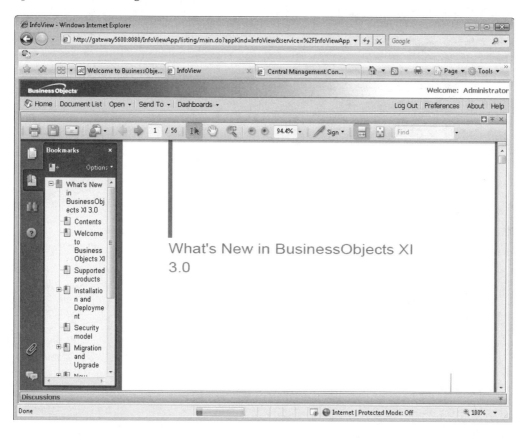

TIP *Viewing program object instances is similar to viewing report instances. However, there is no equivalent to an on-demand program object. As such, program objects must be scheduled before any output can be viewed at all. Scheduling is covered in more detail later in this chapter.*

Setting InfoView Preferences

InfoView is installed with a default look and feel, default color set, and default report viewer. You, however, can change quite a few of these features to match your own particular preferences. Choose your own InfoView preferences by clicking the Preferences button in the upper right-hand corner of the InfoView screen (the Header Panel toolbar). You can also click the My Preferences link in the Workspace Panel when the InfoView homepage appears. The Preferences screen will appear, with the General section expanded. Make desired settings on the General section, or expand other preferences sections (such as those for Crystal Reports) by clicking the small left-arrow icon next to the category you wish to expand. If you no longer wish to see a particular category, click the small down-arrow icon next to the category to collapse it.

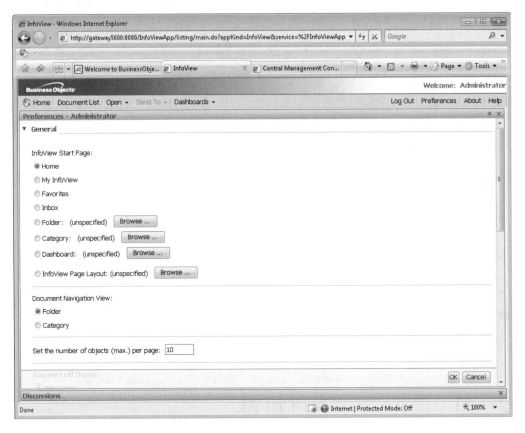

General Preferences

The General area is one of several applicable preferences sections (Change Password and Crystal Reports being the others). Preferences you set here are general in nature, applying to InfoView overall. Make any desired changes to items on this screen. When finished, click OK to save your changes and return to InfoView. Available General Preferences options follow.

InfoView Start Page

This option determines the initial InfoView organization you see in the Workspace Panel when you log on.

- **Home** This will show the InfoView home page, consisting of a short list of "Go Directly To" hyperlinks. If BOE security limits your user ID to seeing a certain set of top-level folders, this setting will show them.

- **My InfoView** This will show the current customized "dashboard" view you have set up using the My InfoView option (described later in the chapter).

- **Favorites** The Favorites view will show your Favorites folder (more information on customizing your Favorites folder can be found later in this chapter).

- **Inbox** This will display the Inbox (discussed earlier in the chapter) where report objects and instances specifically scheduled or copied to your private Inbox will appear.

- **Folder** Click the Browse button to choose a specific folder or subfolder to display immediately upon logging on to InfoView.

- **Category** Click the Browse button to choose a specific category or subcategory to display immediately upon logging on to InfoView.

- **InfoView Page Layout** Click the Browse button to explore the BOE folder structure for saved My InfoView saved views, selecting the one you wish to appear when you first log on to BOE (My InfoView is discussed later in this chapter).

Document Navigation View

Choose whether you wish InfoView object listings to be displayed according to the BOE folder hierarchy, or by category. This setting may not apply, depending on choices you make in the InfoView Start Page area.

Set the Number Of Objects (max.) Per Page

Specify a value indicating the number of report or third-party objects to display on a single page when you open a folder, a category, or your Inbox. If more objects are available than you specify here, you may use the page navigation buttons on the right of the Workspace Panel toolbar to move through the available pages of objects.

Document List Display

Check options in this section to indicate which report properties you wish to see in the InfoView objects area.

Document Viewing

Choose how reports and objects should be displayed. You may display them within the "InfoView Portal," which will show report or object output entirely within the Workspace Panel in a single InfoView window. Choosing Single Fullscreen Browser Window, One Document at a Time will launch a separate window for a report or object view, separate from the InfoView window (and, BOE will make the new browser window the entire size of your screen)—any new views you launch will replace the previous view in the single separate window. Choosing Multiple Fullscreen Browser Windows, One Window for Each Document will launch a separate window for each report or object view, separate from the InfoView window and other existing view windows (and, BOE will make each new browser window the entire size of your screen).

Product Locale

Choose available options from the drop-down list to designate what language you would like InfoView menus and dialog boxes to display in. The default, Use Browser Locale, ties a locale set by your local operating system or browser to BOE. If your desired language choice isn't in the drop-down list, either it isn't an available BOE option or your administrator must install additional BOE language packs.

Current Time Zone

This determines the time zone that your current web browser session is operating in. The default, Local To Web Server, assumes that you and the web server are located in the same time zone. If, however, you are in an enterprise environment where the web server is in a different time zone, you'll want to choose your specific time zone from the drop-down list.

This setting ensures that any reports or program objects you schedule will execute at the time you choose. For example, if you are several time zones away from the web server and you don't change the default time zone setting, scheduled jobs will run according the web server time zone, not your time zone.

Preferred Viewing Locale

Choose available options from the drop-down list to designate what locale you would like to use to determine region-specific settings, such as currency symbols and date formatting (this setting won't affect the actual language of InfoView menus and dialog boxes). The default, Use Browser Locale, ties a locale set by your local operating system or browser to BOE.

Change Password

Expand the Change Password section to change your existing password (provided you aren't using an integrated security method, such as Windows Active Directory or LDAP). Type your existing password, followed by the new password you wish to assign to your BOE user ID. You will need to type the new password twice. Provided your new password meets any minimum password requirements set by your BOE administrator (perhaps you need a minimum number of characters, and so forth), your password will be changed.

Crystal Reports Preferences

Expand the Crystal Reports section to expose options that apply only to Crystal Reports views in InfoView. Available Crystal Reports preferences are:

Select a Default View Format

Since Crystal Reports can create highly formatted reports (including such features as various fonts, foreground/background color schemes, bitmap graphics, line and box drawing, drop shadows, and so forth), displaying all possible formatting options in a web page is often a challenge. Also, printing reports with their original formatting and pagination intact can also be challenging. As such, several ways of viewing and printing reports are available. This choice determines how reports are viewed within your web browser.

- **Web**   This is the default choice when InfoView is initially installed. This choice converts the Crystal Report to Dynamic Hypertext Markup Language (DHTML)—the language used to format web pages. When you use DHTML, no extra controls or objects need to be downloaded to your web browser—the report can be displayed in the browser's native "language." However, some formatting compromises may be made in certain rare situations. Also, if you click the Print button in your web browser toolbar or choose Print from your web browser menu, only what's currently showing in the browser window will print—not an entire paginated and formatted report (two "native" printing options are discussed later in this section, under "Select Printing Control").

- **Web ActiveX (ActiveX required)**   This choice will download a small ActiveX control to your browser (Internet Explorer is typically the only browser that supports ActiveX controls). The ActiveX report viewer shows report formatting almost exactly as it was originally created, as well as allowing you to print a perfectly formatted report on your local printer.

- **Web Java (Java required)**   This viewer will use the built-in "Java Virtual Machine" from your web browser (different browsers and operating system installations contain various forms of Java Virtual Machine support). The Java "applet" or control that will appear in your browser shows report formatting almost exactly as it was originally created, as well as allowing you to print a perfectly formatted report on your local printer.

Select Printing Control (for Web)

This setting allows you to choose how to print reports from the Web (DHTML) report viewer. While the ActiveX and Java viewers include their own "native" Print button, pure HTML reports cannot be printed in their native form by using just the Print button from your browser. This choice determines what happens when you click the Print button contained in the Web viewer toolbar.

- **PDF (Adobe Acrobat required)**   This choice will cause the report to be downloaded to your browser as an exactly formatted Acrobat .PDF document. Assuming you have a properly configured Acrobat viewer installed on your computer, you'll then be able to print the report using the Acrobat viewer's Print button.

- **ActiveX One-Click Printing (ActiveX required)**   This choice will download a small ActiveX control that displays a Print dialog box (the first time you use this, you may be prompted to accept the ActiveX control). Choose desired options for printing, such as a page range or number of copies. The ActiveX print control will then stream the Crystal Report in its native format to the chosen printer.

Select a Rendering Resolution (for Web)

Choose a resolution (in dots per inch, or DPI) for BOE to use when rendering text and images in the Web viewer. The optional 120 DPI setting may result in higher-resolution images and text, but it will cause the overall report to appear larger on the screen and may require slightly more time to be downloaded and formatted.

Select a Default Measuring Unit

Choose whether to have BOE display any associated report measurements (if any) in inches or millimeters. You may wish to customize this setting to match the generally accepted unit of measurement in your locale.

Searching InfoView Objects and Instances

It's not uncommon for larger organizations to implement BusinessObjects Enterprise systems composed of hundreds, if not thousands, of objects and instances. In these larger environments, logical folder or category organization may not be enough to allow users to quickly find the object or instance they want. Also, with many possible sources of a desired report or data item, object-by-object or instance-by-instance searching is not the most efficient method to find data. To help alleviate this problem, Business Objects has improved the search capabilities for BusinessObjects Enterprise XI 3.0 in several areas.

You may search for objects or instances in InfoView via two broad approaches: object-level search and content search. *Object-level search* will return a set of objects that contain search terms in combinations of their title, keywords, owner name, description, and date/time added to the BOE system. Object-level searches can be performed with a simple string search, or a more advanced search screen where more precise search criteria may be specified. *Content search* provides capabilities similar to those available in a typical Internet search engine, such as Google. Content search will search actual content within reports with saved data and report instances, as well as third-party documents. If you're searching Crystal Report document types, when you select a resulting "hit" from the search, BOE will even display the object or instance with the search terms highlighted.

Object-Level Search

Begin by selecting the folder or category you wish to search in Document List view. If you want to search the entire system, select Public Folders in folder view. Otherwise, select a subfolder in folder view, or a category or subcategory in category view (the search process will search through the selected folder or category, and all subfolders or categories below them). Type in your search term in the Search text box in the Workspace Panel toolbar. Then, choose the type of object search you wish to perform from the Search drop-down button to the left of the Search text box. "Search title" will search for the term in object titles only, "search keywords" will search object keywords, and "search all fields" will search both title and keywords. Then, click the Search button (the magnifying glass button) to the right of the Search text box.

InfoView will search all objects in the chosen folder/subfolder or category/subcategory, displaying search "hits" in the Workspace Panel. A new Search Result category will appear in the Tree Panel on the left side of InfoView (this category will delineate the displayed objects as being a search result, as opposed to a regular folder or category). If you wish to perform a subsearch *within* the existing search results, leave the Search Result category selected and type an additional search term into the Search text box. Again, choose whether to search title, keywords, or all fields and click the Search button. The reduced set of search results will appear in the Workspace Panel and a Search Refinement subcategory will appear underneath the original search result category. You may continue to perform subsearches as you wish until you narrow down your search to the desired set of objects. Then, select the desired object and perform typical viewing or maintenance activities as discussed elsewhere in this chapter.

TIP *The search result and search refinement categories will remain in the panel tree until you either log off InfoView or select another main folder or category and begin a new search.*

Advanced Object-Level Search

If you wish to perform a more granular search on report objects, choose the Advanced Search entry from the Search drop-down button to the left of the Search text box (there's no need to type in any search text first). The Advanced Search screen will appear inside InfoView. Make various selections to perform a more granular search (such as choosing the types of locations where you want to perform the search, provide search terms for additional types of searches beyond title and keyword, specify a date/time range indicating when the objects were added to BOE, and so forth). When you've finished your specifications, click Search.

The Advanced Search screen will be replaced by a search results screen showing just objects that match the advanced search criteria. Unlike a simple object search, the panel tree won't appear with a Search Result category, and you can't perform any subsearches on advanced search results. If you wish to narrow down an advanced search, simply choose the Advanced Search option again from the drop-down button and specify more restrictive search criteria.

When the advanced search results screen displays the desired object, select it and perform typical viewing or maintenance activities as discussed elsewhere in this chapter. To close the advanced search screen and return to the original folder or category view, click the small *x* button to the right of the search button in the Workspace Panel toolbar, or the small *x* Close Document button above and to the right of the Workspace Panel toolbar.

Content Search

BusinessObjects Enterprise XI 3.0 adds new powerful search engine–like capabilities that can assist you in searching the vast array of data in saved data reports and report instances.

This is accomplished via a background indexing routine that BOE performs on saved-data reports and instances on a regular basis (if content search doesn't appear to be operating properly, contact your BOE administrator and ask that he or she check content search indexing).

Steps used to perform content search are almost identical to those used to perform object-level search: type a search term in the Search text box, choose Content Search from the drop-down button to the left of the Search text box, and click the magnifying glass Search button. However, content search differs from object search in the way you create search terms. Use search term techniques similar to those you may be familiar with for standard Internet search engine searches: surround the search term with quotation marks to perform an exact match search, separate words with spaces to perform an "all terms must appear" search, add OR between words to perform an "either term may appear" search, and so forth.

Content search will search virtually all text in many document types; including Crystal Report objects with saved data; Crystal Reports instances; Microsoft Excel and Word documents; and RTF, TXT, and PDF third-party documents. The results screen will appear showing objects and instances that meet the search criteria. Double-click the desired object or instance to display it in the Workspace Panel. If the result is a Crystal Report, the report will be displayed in the Web viewer with the first occasion of the search item visible (similar display/navigation capabilities don't exist in the ActiveX or Java report viewers).

NOTE *Content search capabilities are provided by an executable program object (program objects are discussed later in this chapter and in Chapter 22) that only runs on an occasional basis. If you add new objects to BOE or schedule new instances to run, they won't appear in a Content Search until the search program object has run and indexed the new objects or instances. Check with your BOE administrator to determine how often the Content Search index program runs.*

Viewing, Printing, and Exporting Reports

Often when you choose to view a report on demand (or schedule a report, for that matter), you need to supply additional information before the report will run properly. In many cases, the report will need to connect to a secure database as its data source—this database will typically require a user ID and password for proper access.

Also, many reports of moderate to high sophistication will be based on Crystal Reports parameters. A parameter will prompt the viewer for customized information each time the report is run on demand (the exception being new Crystal Reports 2008 optional parameter fields). This information, such as one or more departments, a date range, a region, one or more salespeople—the list can go on and on—is used to limit or customize the report to the chosen parameter items.

Supplying Database Credentials and Parameters

If a report that doesn't contain saved data is based on a secure database, you'll probably need to supply one or more database credentials, such as user ID, password, server name, or database name, when you view the report or schedule the report (scheduling is covered later in this chapter, under "Scheduling Objects"). If the report does have saved data, you'll be prompted for database credentials if you attempt to refresh it. If you don't supply a proper set of credentials, the report will be unable to connect to the database. The set of database credentials required in your particular organization can vary, depending on what database system your reports connect to. If you have a variety of different databases that reports can be based on (for example, some reports are based on Microsoft SQL Server, while others are based on Oracle and yet others are based on Informix), you may find that different sets of credentials are required for different reports.

If any Crystal Reports parameter fields have been added to a report without saved data, you will probably be prompted to supply one or more parameter values when you run a report on demand or schedule it (reports with saved data will prompt for values if they are refreshed). Parameter fields may ask for a variety of values, such as one or more regions, a salesperson number, or a date range (with the exception being new Crystal Report 2008 optional parameter fields).

NOTE *Default values for database credentials and parameter fields can be set in the Central Management Console, negating the need for them to be entered when scheduling or viewing certain reports. Information on this process is covered in Chapter 22.*

Parameter fields can vary widely in data type (text, dates, numbers, and so forth) and parameter type (multiple value, range, and so forth). For example, a single text parameter may be required to specify the country to be used in the report. In this case, you might supply "USA" as the value for the parameter. Another parameter might request one or more salesperson numbers. You, therefore, might supply just salesperson number 5. Or, you might want to see the report for several salespeople—you would then supply salesperson numbers 5, 10, 15, and 17. Or, you might encounter another parameter that needs a date range to be supplied. You would, for example, supply dates between January 1, 2008, and May 31, 2008. In each case, InfoView will prompt you differently for each parameter. For the most part, experimenting and experience will help you supply parameter values properly.

To respond to InfoView prompts for database credentials or parameter values, when viewing reports on demand, follow some simple steps:

1. Select the desired folder or category where the report resides. Select the report in the right side of the Workspace Panel.

2. Double-click the report name, choose View from the Action drop-down button in the Workspace Panel toolbar, or right-click on the report and choose View from the pop-up menu.

3. InfoView will prompt for database credentials and/or parameter values (depending on how the report is designed) before showing the report.

4. Type in any necessary values for database user ID, password, and so forth. If parameter values are requested, add necessary values to customize the report for this particular view, clicking OK after each prompt.

5. The report will be viewed with the supplied values.

NOTE *The format of values you supply to Date or Time parameter values can vary, according to locale settings in Preferences (discussed earlier in the chapter). For example, if you wish to supply a date of October 1, 2007, you can type "10/1/2007" if your InfoView preferred viewing locale (via either the browser default locale or a specifically selected locale) is English - United States. However, if your locale is English - Canada, you must type the date as "1/10/2007." The parameter field prompt screen will indicate the format you must use. Also, note the "date picker" icon that appears when prompting for a date parameter. If you click this icon and specify a date in the corresponding calendar box, the properly formatted value will be filled in for you.*

Using the Report Viewer

When you view a report, InfoView will display the report either in the Workspace Panel or in a new browser window (depending on the choice made in Preferences). The report will appear in the Web, ActiveX, or Java viewer, again depending on your Preferences choice. The report viewer contains many features that enhance your ability to navigate through the report and perform other useful functions, such as re-sorting the report with new interactive sorting options, interacting with the new Parameter Panel, searching the report, exporting the report to another file format, and so forth. Viewer toolbars and buttons will vary, depending on the report viewer you are using. An example of a report displayed in the default Web viewer is illustrated in Figure 21-2.

NOTE *While there may be times that the ActiveX or Java viewer is more appropriate for your particular environment, the increasingly rich capabilities of the Web viewer, as well as complete compatibility with most standard web browsers, makes it a strong choice for viewing Crystal Reports. For this reason, the remainder of this chapter will assume usage of the Web viewer.*

Toolbar buttons available in the Web report viewer consists of the following:

- **Export** You have the option to export a report from the viewer to several different file formats, as described in more detail later, under "Exporting and E-Mailing Reports."

- **Print** Print the report currently displayed in the viewer on a printer configured on your computer. If you are using the ActiveX or Java viewers, or the ActiveX print control in one of the DHTML viewers, a print dialog box will appear where you may choose page range, number of copies, and so forth. If you are using the Acrobat PDF print option with one of the DHTML viewers, the report will be downloaded as an Acrobat .PDF file. Use the Acrobat Viewer's Print button to actually print the report.

- **Parameter** Displays the Parameter Panel in the left Preview Panel portion of the viewer (discussed later in the chapter, under "Using the New Parameter Panel." If the group tree was displayed previously, the Parameter Panel will replace it. If the

Narrow or widen Preview Panel   Report Viewer toolbar

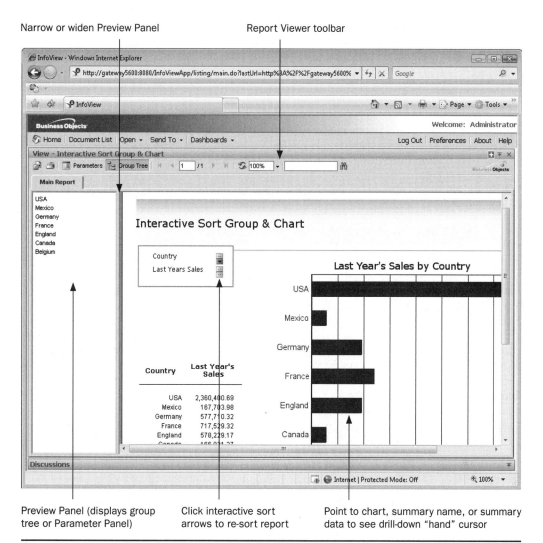

Preview Panel (displays group   Click interactive sort   Point to chart, summary name, or summary
tree or Parameter Panel)   arrows to re-sort report   data to see drill-down "hand" cursor

FIGURE 21-2   Crystal Report displayed in Web viewer

Parameter Panel was already displayed, the entire Preview Panel will be turned off
and the report will fill the entire viewer screen.

- **Group Tree**   Displays the group tree in the left Preview Panel portion of the viewer.
  The group tree is a powerful navigation tool that shows you an outline of the grouping
  levels on the report and allows you to click directly to an item and display that page.
  If the Parameter Panel was displayed previously, the group tree will replace it. If the
  group tree was already displayed, the entire Preview Panel will be turned off and
  the report will fill the entire viewer screen.

- **Page Navigation** Click the arrow buttons to navigate to the first page, previous page, next page, or last page. You may also type a page number directly into the page number text box and press ENTER to navigate directly to that page.

- **Refresh** Refresh an older instance or a recent view to reflect the latest data. Note that your BOE administrator may deny you the refresh right. If you try to refresh it without this right, you will receive an error message in the browser.

- **Zoom** Choose various report window zoom levels from the zoom drop-down list. You may also type your own zoom level percentage directly into the text box next to the zoom drop-down arrow and press ENTER to zoom the report to that specific percentage.

- **Find** Search the report for certain text or data content. Type in the desired search text and click the Find button.

- **Drill Down** If the report has further detail supporting some of the data on the report, you may be able to drill down to the detail by clicking the summary information on the report or on a chart element (such as a pie wedge or bar). The cursor will change when it is rolled over clickable areas, just as it does when rolled over a link on a web page. When you click on a drill-down area, a drill-down page opens in the browser with its own drill-down tab (similar to the way drill-down tabs appear in Crystal Reports). You can then toggle between the main report page and any open drill-down pages by clicking the desired drill-down tab. You may also close an open drill-down page by clicking the small x button on the drill-down tab you wish to close.

Using the New Parameter Panel

Crystal Reports 2008 introduces interactive and optional parameter fields. To derive full benefit of these new features, a report viewer may use the Parameter Panel (complete discussions on how to create optional parameter fields, and how to place them in the Parameter Panel, can be found in Chapter 13). BusinessObjects Enterprise XI 3.0 fully supports the Parameter Panel in the report viewer.

Display the Parameter Panel by clicking the Parameters toolbar button in the viewer toolbar. The Parameter Panel will appear, as illustrated in Figure 21-3. There may be several types of parameter fields in the panel:

- **Data Refresh parameters** A small question mark/circular arrows indicator on a parameter field indicates that changes to this parameter field will require the report to be refreshed against the database if the parameter value is changed. This is important to an InfoView user for two reasons: the user may not have the refresh right, in which case the report will not be able to use the new parameter; and, refreshing the report may take a long time, depending on report design and database speed factors.

- **Non–Data Refresh parameters** A parameter without the question mark/circular arrows indicator can be freely modified without the need to refresh the report. This not only allows a new parameter value to be supplied without need for the refresh right to be specified in BOE security, but the report will only need to be reformatted to encompass the new value, which requires minimal processing resources.

- **Optional parameters**   An (Optional) indicator means that no value need be specified for this parameter field. If you desire to provide a value, you may do so. However, the report has been specifically designed to run without a value being specified for this parameter. If you supply a value for an optional parameter field, and you later wish to remove it, select the existing value and click the Delete button at the top of the Parameter Panel.

- **Range parameters**   Some parameter fields accept both beginning and ending range values (date ranges often use these types of parameter fields). Range parameter fields cannot be edited "in place" on the Parameter Panel. Click the small Edit icon to the right of the parameter field to display a separate dialog box where you may specify your beginning and ending range values.

- **Multivalue parameters**   Some parameter fields accept more than one value. Multivalue parameter fields appear as a list in the Parameter Panel, with each of the multiple values appearing on its own line. You may change an existing multivalue entry by clicking the desired line and specifying a new value. You may remove one of the values by selecting it and clicking the Delete button at the top of the Parameter Panel. Adding a new value can be done by clicking the Click To Add entry at the bottom of the list. You may also manipulate multivalue parameter fields by selecting one of the parameter values and clicking the small Edit icon to the right.

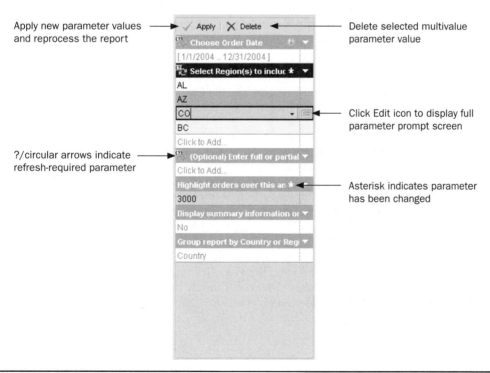

FIGURE 21-3   The Parameter Panel

Once you've made desired changes to the Parameter Panel, click the Apply button at the top of the panel. The report will be re-processed (if necessary, it will be refreshed against the database) and will redisplay based on the new parameter values. You may continue to change Parameter Panel values and Apply again as often as you like.

Exporting and E-Mailing Reports

You may wish to save a copy of a report from InfoView to your own local computer. Perhaps you wish to include it in a Word document, perform some more unique analysis in Microsoft Excel, or attach an Adobe Acrobat file to an e-mail to send to a colleague who doesn't have access to InfoView. All of this can be accomplished by exporting reports from a report viewer:

1. View the report or instance you wish to export.

2. Click the Export button in the viewer toolbar. The Export dialog box will appear.

3. Choose the desired export format from the drop-down list of formats and the page range you wish to export. Then, click OK to start downloading the report to your browser.

4. Depending on your browser, you may need to respond to a security prompt to download the file. Also, you may be prompted to view the file, or save the file to your local computer. If you choose the option to view, the file will appear in a browser window. If you choose to save, a File Save dialog box will appear, where you may specify the filename and location. The file will be saved on your local hard disk.

5. If you wish to e-mail the file to a colleague, attach the file you just downloaded to an e-mail message using typical steps to send e-mail attachments.

NOTE *BusinessObjects Enterprise XI 3.0 supports the new Crystal Reports 2008 XML exporting formats. The XML schema used when exporting from InfoView is the default schema chosen in XML options in the Crystal Reports designer (XML Exporting is covered in detail in Chapter 14).*

Printing Reports on Your Local Printer

Often, you'll want to print a full or partial copy of the report you're viewing on a locally attached printer. And, you'll most probably want it printed with the original formatting and pagination that was used when the report was designed. While the ActiveX and Java report viewers (available in the Crystal Report section of InfoView Preferences) will print directly to an attached printer, there are two ways of printing with the Web viewer print toolbar button (don't use your browser print button, as it will only print the contents of the current browser window, not a formatted report).

As discussed earlier in the chapter, the Crystal Reports section of InfoView Preferences gives you two options for printing from the Web viewer: Adobe Acrobat format, or the ActiveX print control. Adobe Acrobat format will simply download the fully paginated and formatted report in .PDF format to your browser. You may print the report from the Acrobat Reader that displays the report.

NOTE *You must have the Adobe Acrobat Reader installed on your computer for this method of local printing to work. If you don't have the application installed, you will simply be prompted to save the .PDF file on disk, which won't ultimately accomplish your print requirement. Check with your Information Technology department, or visit www.adobe.com to get a copy of the Acrobat Reader for your particular computer and operating system.*

If you've chosen the ActiveX print control, a small ActiveX control will be downloaded to your browser the first time you print a report from the Web viewer (typically, you can only make use of ActiveX controls if you are using Microsoft Internet Explorer as your browser). You may be prompted to accept this control when it is first downloaded (or, you may be notified that it can't be downloaded if your browser's security settings prohibit ActiveX control download). Once the control is downloaded, it will simply display a standard print dialog where you can specify print settings, such as page range and number of copies. The report will then be streamed to your printer with all original pagination and formatting.

Scheduling Objects

One of the many benefits of using BusinessObjects Enterprise for managing your organization's reporting and analysis infrastructure is its ability to schedule reports. This allows automatic running of reports on a daily, weekly, or monthly basis, or on other regular schedules that suit your particular environment. In addition to reports, BOE also includes program objects (executable programs, Java programs, or scripts) that can also be scheduled on a regular basis. And, Object Packages, consisting of groups of related reports or program objects, can be scheduled as well.

NOTE *The majority of scheduling discussions in this section pertain to reports. Program object scheduling options are generally limited to specifying the frequency of the schedule, any command-line arguments supplied when run, and the destination of the program's output text. The remaining scheduling options apply to reports only.*

When you schedule a report or program object, you are setting a time to run it—either once or on a recurring schedule. You can schedule a report to run immediately, if desired; the difference between doing this and viewing on demand is that BusinessObjects Enterprise saves the "instance" of the report when it is run, and makes it available to other users. Unlike the temporary copy that's available only to you for a little while after you view a report, the Schedule action adds the report instance to a historical list of instances, where it may be available for a much longer time. Scheduling of program objects allows an executable program or script (such as a data warehouse update or BOE administrative task done with JScript or VBScript) to be run on a regular recurring basis. The "instance," in the case of a scheduled program object, is a text view of the standard and error output from the program object when it runs.

Using scheduled reports has several advantages:

- Scheduling instances can optimize database and network performance by avoiding excess network and database requests.
- The scheduling function provides the ability to enter embedded parameter values, database logon, report format, and/or selection criteria, so that viewers aren't prompted for these values.
- Scheduling instances can significantly reduce the time it takes to support a large group of users requesting reports.

So, scheduled instances are flexible and informative while still protecting databases from uncontrolled access, protecting the database servers from unnecessary repetitive queries, and maximizing sharing of common reports.

NOTE *The ability to schedule objects is controlled by BOE security. Your BOE administrator may not have granted you this right for some or all objects. If you don't see the Schedule option for some (or all) objects in InfoView, check with your BOE administrator to see if you have this right.*

Scheduling Options

When you schedule an object in InfoView, there are several sets of options you must choose from to customize your schedule. These options may vary, depending on whether you're scheduling a report or program object, how the report you're scheduling is designed (reports based on secure databases or with parameter fields must have database credentials or parameter values supplied when scheduling), what output destination you want the object sent to, and so forth. And, you have several other scheduling options, such as how many times and when the report should run.

To schedule a report or program object (remember that third-party objects cannot be scheduled), navigate to the desired folder or category where the object appears. Select the desired object and choose Schedule from the Actions drop-down button in the workspace area toolbar. You can also right-click the object and choose Schedule from the pop-up menu. The Workspace Panel will be replaced with a schedule screen, consisting of a list of scheduling properties on the left, and options for the selected property on the right.

CAUTION   *Make sure you specify all necessary scheduling options from the various choices in the schedule dialog before you click the Schedule button. If you don't specify all necessary items, the instance will fail or return incorrect results when it is run prematurely.*

Instance Title

By default, instances will retain the same title given to the report or program object when it was added to BOE. However, if you prefer to delineate a certain instance or set of instances from others within the same object, you may specify a unique instance title with this option. Just select the Instance Title property and type the new instance title in the text box.

Recurrence

This property determines how often and at what time a report instance will be created or a program object will execute. The default option is "Now," meaning the object will run immediately. The second option, "Once," means it will run only once—at the date and time specified. It defaults to the current date and time, so accepting the defaults provides an immediate run. The other options run the object regularly at the time specified or based on a calendar that your administrator has defined.

Other options include Hourly, Daily, Weekly, Monthly, Nth Day of the Month, 1st Monday of the Month, Last Day of the Month, X Day of Nth Week of the Month, and Calendar. Once you've chosen one of the options from the Run Object drop-down list, the remainder of the recurrence screen will change, depending on the first choice you made. Depending on the choice you make, you may have additional flexibility in scheduling. For example, if you choose Weekly scheduling, you'll also be able to choose which days of the week to run the object.

Fill in necessary items for the chosen scheduling interval. Note that you'll typically be prompted to specify both starting and ending dates and times. While specifying an end date makes logical sense in most situations, specifying an end time still is valuable. This comes into play if an object, for some reason, doesn't run at the exact time you specify (perhaps a BOE component is down at that time, the object initially fails and needs to be retried, and so forth). By specifying an end time, you ensure that any such schedules will not occur after a "point of no return" time during the day.

Scheduling Based on a Calendar   BusinessObjects Enterprise XI 3.0 also provides for calendar-based scheduling. With this feature, you may simply choose to run an object on specific days defined in one of any number of calendars defined by your BusinessObjects Enterprise administrator. For example, you may find that your particular organization's payroll processing is on a somewhat irregular schedule that the built-in scheduling periods don't quite fit. In these cases, calendars can be defined that identify specific pay days, regardless of holidays, two- or three-payday months, and so forth.

To schedule according to a calendar, choose Calendar from the Run Object drop-down list. A list of predefined calendars will appear (creating calendars is covered in Chapter 22). Choose the desired calendar. The screen will redraw once again, showing several months in advance with days identified in green acting as days the object will run. Make any desired adjustments to start and end dates and times to customize the schedule within the calendar.

Database Logon

Depending on the database, or databases, the report you are scheduling is based on, you must specify database credentials as part of the scheduling process (this is not required when scheduling program objects). If proper credentials aren't provided, or a prestored set of database credentials haven't been set by the BOE administrator, the instances will fail when they attempt to connect to the database.

Items you may need to specify include the data source name (an ODBC data source, server name, etc.), the database you wish to connect to, the user ID, and password. If there is more than one database, you'll be able to make these choices for each database included in the report.

Parameters

If the report you are scheduling uses Crystal Reports parameter fields, you'll need to supply parameter values in order for an instance to run successfully, unless the parameter fields have been defined as optional, or default parameter values have been set in the report or set in advance by the BOE administrator. In either of these situations, you won't have to change them before scheduling the report. However, if you need different values for this instance, you'll need to supply the new values you wish the instance to use every time it runs.

Click the Parameters proper in the Schedule dialog box to display report parameter fields. If default values are already specified, they will appear next to the associated parameter name. If no default is specified, the parameter will indicate such. Click the default value or "No Value" hyperlinks, or the Edit button, to assign a new value. The parameters displayed will vary, depending on what types of parameters exist on the report you're scheduling. Generally, you'll see each parameter listed with its user prompt, and beneath that you'll see an area for adding values for that parameter. You may be able to choose from a set of possible values from a "pick list"—a drop-down list that will show all available values. BOE dynamic and cascading pick lists may appear here too.

NOTE *If you are scheduling a program object, the Parameters entry will display a single text box where you may specify command-line arguments for the program object.*

Filters

Most reports contain a record selection formula that you may wish to modify when scheduling (program objects do not make use of a Filters option). A record selection formula is a Crystal Reports–specific statement that filters database records so that a limited set of data will be included on the report.

You can also modify a group selection formula. A group selection formula is similar to a record selection formula, except that it uses subtotal or summary functions at the end of report groups to limit the report to only groups that contain certain values.

You can modify any existing selection formula this instance uses (either record selection or group selection), as well as adding additional criteria to the formulas. Make sure you supply proper Crystal Reports formula syntax in the selection formula (Record and Group Selection formulas are covered in Chapters 3 and 4).

NOTE *If the report's existing record or group selection formulas are based on parameter fields, you need not modify the selection formulas themselves—the parameter fields will take care of customizing report filtering for you. However, if you do need to modify the selection formulas manually, be careful. Your formulas must strictly adhere to Crystal Reports formula language syntax or the instances will fail.*

Format

You have a choice of file format when scheduling a report (format choices aren't available for program objects). Rather than saving the report in Crystal Reports' proprietary .RPT file format, you have a number of format choices, including two Excel formats, Word, Acrobat, various text formats, and Crystal Reports 2008's new XML format.

Depending on your format choice, the dialog box will change with prompts for various format-related options, such as page range or how to convert report formatting to spreadsheet formatting.

TIP *Choosing a format other than "Crystal Report" when using the Default destination will cause different behavior when you attempt to view an instance with a report viewer. Rather than launching the report viewer chosen in Crystal Report Preferences, BOE will download the instance in the file format chosen in the Format drop-down list. If a matching application (such as Excel or the Adobe Acrobat Viewer) is installed on your PC, the application will be launched and the instance displayed in that application. Otherwise, you'll be prompted to save the file to disk.*

Destination

By default, InfoView will run a scheduled report against the database, save the set of data returned from the database with the instance, and allow it to be viewed online in one of the report viewers. And, a scheduled program object's standard and error output is saved as a text file, which can be viewed online after the object has run.

However, in the case of report output, you may prefer to have the instance attached to an e-mail message in a different file format (such as Adobe Acrobat format). Or, you might want to save the instance as an Excel .XLS file to a specific location on a LAN server. Or, you might want to send the instance as a Word document to another site via the File Transfer Protocol (FTP). You may prefer to route the report instance to one or more BusinessObjects Enterprise inboxes. Finally, you may simply want the report printed on a printer whenever the instance runs.

If you are in charge of several program objects that, perhaps, perform data warehouse updates or other administrative functions, you may want the standard and error output of the program objects to be e-mailed to you whenever the object runs. Or, you may prefer that the text comprising the object's output be placed in a fixed location on your corporate LAN so that, at any given time, the output from the latest instance of the program object can always be found.

The Destination drop-down allows you to choose various destinations, including the Inbox, a file location, an FTP server, and e-mail. The Default Enterprise Location indicates that the instance will be automatically saved on a BOE server with a filename managed by BOE. Whenever you view the instance, BOE automatically knows where to find the right files for online viewing. The remaining destination choices all produce a set of additional options related to that particular destination, such as inbox choice, e-mail address, or specific file location and filename. Consult your BusinessObjects Enterprise administrator for more specific instructions on which destinations are configured on your BOE system and what choices you may make for them.

Print Settings

If you are scheduling a report, you may desire that the report simply print on a printer configured on the BOE server (for example, you may migrate mainframe-based production reporting to BusinessObjects Enterprise and wish regular printing jobs, such as invoices and accounts payable checks, to be scheduled by BOE).

Regardless of the Destination and Format settings you make, you can choose to print a copy of the report in Crystal Reports format on a printer when the report is run (Print Settings don't apply to program objects). If you check Print Crystal Reports, the dialog will redraw with additional options, such as a page range and number of copies. You may allow the BOE server to use its default printer, or you may specify a printer name (the name you supply must be properly configured or recognized on the BOE server—check with your BOE administrator if you're unsure of what printer name to use).

Events

Basing a scheduled instance on an event allows it to run only when one or more conditions are met (a complete discussion of different events, how to set them up, and how they affect processing can be found in Chapter 22). You may also specify an event that will be triggered when this instance has finished running. The Events screen shows these two types of events: events that this instance will wait for before it runs (in the Available Events/Events To Wait For section), and events that this instance will trigger when it finishes processing (in the Available Schedule Events/Events To Trigger On Completion section).

You may specify one or more events for this instance to wait for before it runs. Select the event, or events, in the Available Events list and add them to the Events To Wait For box with the arrow button. You may also choose one or more Available Schedule Events list entries to trigger when this instance has finished running. Again, add the desired entries to the Events To Trigger On Completion list with the right arrow.

Scheduling Server Group

If the BOE administrator has defined multiple job servers (the particular BOE server that processes Crystal Reports or program objects), then you may choose which of these servers processes this particular instance. Other than the default "Use The First Available Server," you may choose to give preference to a specific group of servers, or force only a specific group of servers to be used.

Once you're satisfied with all your various scheduling choices, click the Schedule button. The instance will be submitted to the CMS for scheduling.

The History screen will appear showing the newly scheduled instance. Click the Refresh button in the History dialog toolbar to update the status of any scheduled or processing instances. The History dialog box initially shows instances sorted by date/time run in ascending (oldest to newest) time. You may alternatively sort instances in descending date/time order, or in ascending or descending order by other columns in the list (except Title). Simply click the column heading of the desired sort item—an "up arrow" or "down arrow" will appear next to the column heading, indicating which column instances are currently sorted by, and in what order.

Choose options for selected instances from
Actions drop-down button or toolbar buttons

Choose a subset of
instances to display

Highlight one or more instances
with click, CTRL-click, or SHIFT-click

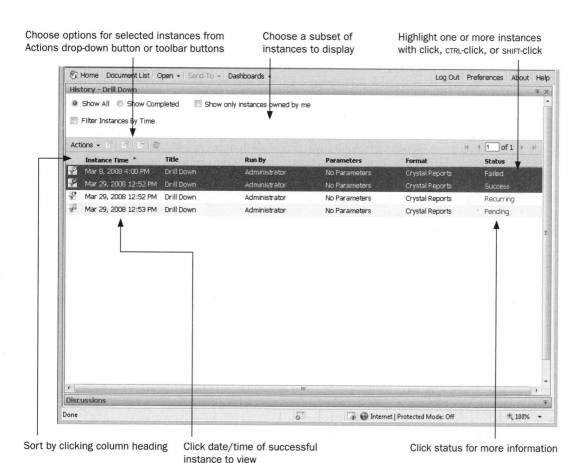

Sort by clicking column heading

Click date/time of successful
instance to view

Click status for more information

The History dialog will show several different status entries that you may notice:

- **Recurring**   The instance is set up to run on a regular basis, such as every day. When the recurring instance's next run time approaches, BOE will copy the recurring instance to a new Running instance. By clicking the Recurring status, you can see what the instance's recurrence pattern is and when the next instance is scheduled to run.

- **Paused** A recurring or pending instance has been "paused" so that it will not run on its schedule for the time being. These instances can be paused by highlighting a recurring instance and clicking the Pause toolbar button, or choosing Pause in the Actions drop-down button. To resume a paused instance, select the paused instance and click the Resume toolbar button, or choose Resume in the Actions drop-down button. The original status will reappear.

- **Pending** The instance is scheduled to run at some point in the future, or is waiting for an event to be triggered (events are discussed in more detail earlier in the chapter and in Chapter 22). Clicking the Pending status will show you the time the instance is scheduled to run, as well an indicator if the instance is waiting on an event.

- **Running** The instance is being processed by the BOE server at this time. Clicking the Refresh icon in the History screen toolbar will update the running status as the instance processing progresses.

- **Success** The instance has completed successfully. By clicking the Success status, you can find out more information about the completed instance.

- **Failed** The instance failed when it attempted to run. Failed instances can occur for many reasons, such as lack of proper database credentials, failure to supply parameter fields, or incorrect database connectivity on the BOE server. By clicking the Failed status, you'll find out more information on the failed instance, including a description of the reason for the failure (sometimes helpful and descriptive, sometimes not).

To view a successful instance, simply click the date/time entry for the instance. The instance will be displayed in the format chosen when the report was scheduled (to view the latest instance, you can simply choose the View Latest Instance option after originally selecting the object—you needn't even display the History list first). You may also pause, resume, or delete one or more instances by highlighting the desired instance or instances and clicking various toolbar buttons, or choosing options from the Actions drop-down button. Note that rights to pause, resume, and delete instances may be denied to you by the BOE administrator.

Scheduling Reports Containing Alerts

Crystal Reports can be designed to make use of report alerts. *Report alerts* are settings in a report that trigger a "red flag" when certain conditions are met. Examples would be alerts that would be triggered if sales exceeded a certain goal, customer support calls exceeded a critical level, and so forth (designing Crystal Reports with alerts is discussed in Chapter 6).

When you view a report containing alerts on demand (that is, you simply click the report name in the objects area), the report runs just like any other report and alerts *are not* triggered. However, reports containing alerts behave a little differently when scheduled.

Reports containing alerts will display a special icon in the History list if alerts were triggered when the report ran (you'll notice a small yellow exclamation point added to the report's icon). However, viewing report instances from the History list still will show the entire report, without any indication of what alerts were triggered or what report records triggered them.

However, reports containing alerts will provide an additional Alerts option in the Actions drop-down button, or in the right-click pop-up menu when you select the object in the Workspace Panel. Choose these options to see any report instances that have run that contain triggered report alerts. A list of instances that triggered alerts will appear. The original report name, the report's folder or category, the date and time the instance completed, as well as the defined alert or alerts that were triggered will appear. Clicking the report name will simply display the report instance, just as if you would have clicked it in the History list—no alert information will be displayed. However, clicking an alert name will display the report instance showing *only* report records that conform to the alert.

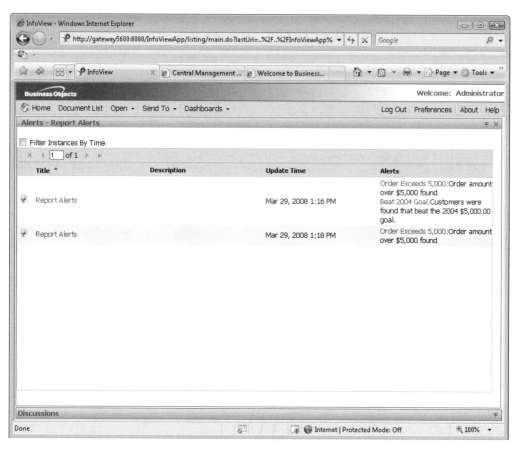

TIP *BusinessObjects Enterprise can also be configured to send an e-mail when a report alert is triggered. This is discussed in Chapter 22.*

Rescheduling Existing Instances

You will probably find situations where you wish to change some aspect of an already-scheduled report or program object. Perhaps you need to extend the end date of the report to run it for a longer period of time. Or, perhaps you need to add or remove e-mail addresses you specified in the Destinations property. And, you'd rather not delete the existing instance and add a completely new scheduled instance to make these small changes. The ability to change some aspect of an existing scheduled object, or else to copy an existing scheduled object to another scheduled instance with changes, is a handy feature of BOE.

First, display the History List by selecting the desired object in the Workspace Panel and choosing History from the Actions drop-down button or the right-click pop-up menu. Then, highlight the existing instance that you want to change or copy. Choose Reschedule from the Actions drop-down button in the History List toolbar. The Workspace Panel will display a schedule screen that's similar (but not identical) to the original screen you used when scheduling the instance. Instead of selecting properties on the left side of the schedule screen, you'll need to click small arrow icons to display and hide the various scheduling properties.

If the instance can still run in the future (it's a Pending or Recurring instance, for example), a Replace property will appear providing two choices: Replace Existing Schedule and Create New Schedule From Existing Schedule. Choose the Replace Existing Schedule option to change some aspect of the original schedule (such as the end date and time or the destination options) that will affect any future instances that run. Choose the Create New Schedule option to copy this instance to a new instance with the changes you make elsewhere in the dialog box. The original instance will remain unchanged. If the original instance you choose to reschedule has already completed its scheduling cycle (for example, it has failed or run successfully), the Replace property won't appear and you'll only be able to copy the changed instance to a new instance.

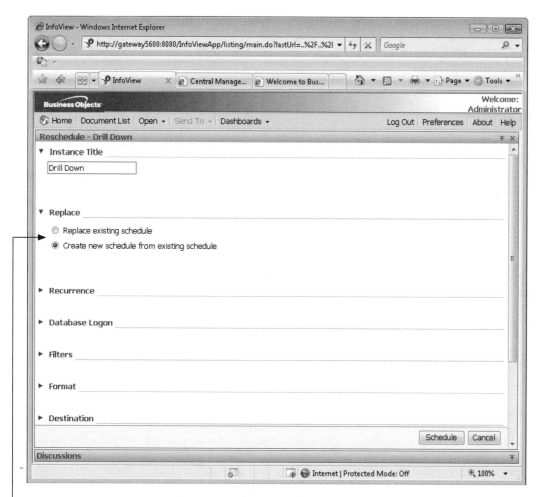

Choose whether to modify existing schedule or copy updated scheduling information to a new instance

Make any desired changes to scheduling options (such as Recurrence, Destination, or Parameters), and click the Schedule button. Either the existing instance will be updated to reflect the new scheduling options, or the copied instance with your new options will appear in the History List.

Using Discussions

If you spend any time on the web, you've probably encountered one or more "discussion groups," where those with similar interests or common requirements can post messages that others can read. BusinessObjects Enterprise provides this feature as an integral part of the software. *Discussions* allow BOE users to enter text comments that are attached to any object within BOE. "Threaded" discussion capabilities indicate the ability to respond to a specific initial comment, with another response to that response, and so forth, creating a *thread* of related messages. This discussion technique is common to many web-based support applications.

NOTE *The ability to add notes to discussion threads can be denied by the BOE administrator. If you are unable to post messages, check with the administrator to see if you have proper rights.*

Begin by selecting the object you wish to "discuss." This can be any type of BOE object, including a report, program object, or third-party object. You may view either the object itself or any associated instance (remember, however, that a discussion thread will apply to the object and all instances—separate threads can't be created for individual instances of the same object). Once the desired object is selected, click the small "Show Discussions" arrow icon on the Discussions Panel at the bottom of InfoView. The panel will expand upward. The Discussions Panel is illustrated in Figure 21-4.

Any existing message threads will appear in the left side of the Discussions Panel. You'll notice the hierarchy of messages—initial messages in a thread will appear at the top, replies will appear underneath with plus signs, replies to replies will also appear with plus signs, and so forth. Expand the hierarchy by clicking the plus signs or contract them by clicking minus signs. Any messages you have not yet read will appear in a bold font. Click a message title to display the message in the right side of the Discussions Panel.

To create a new thread (this can be done whether any existing threads appear or not), click the New Message button at the top of the Discussions Panel. A new top-level thread message will be created on the left side of the panel, with the subject and message fields appearing on the right side of the panel. An automatic subject will be created based on your BOE user ID and the date you create the thread. You may leave the default subject as-is or type a different subject in the field. Then, type the message you wish to add in the message field. If you wish to assign the message a high or low priority, click either the high priority or low priority button at the top of the Discussions Panel. A similar high- or low-priority icon will be added to the message you are creating.

Once you are satisfied with the subject and message, click the Post button below the message field on the right side of the panel. The message will be posted to the BOE database. Once the message is posted, other users who view the same object and who also expand the Discussions Panel will see the message you created.

Create new thread for chosen object

Create public reply to selected message

Create reply to selected message that only message originator will see

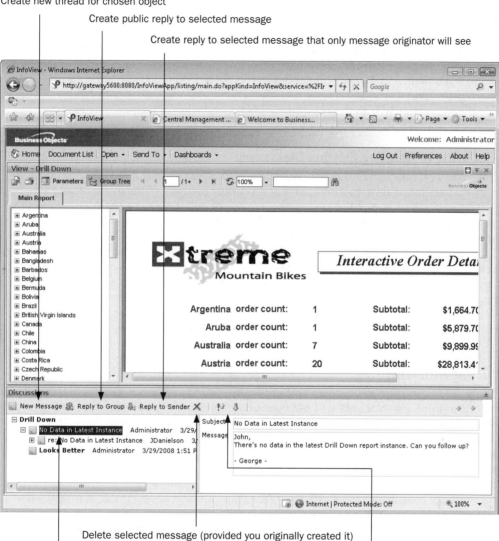

Delete selected message (provided you originally created it)

Series of messages known as "thread"

Flag message with high or low importance

Figure 21-4   Discussions Panel

CAUTION   *It's easy to add a new message and click some other item in InfoView without actually posting the message. If you do this, the message will not be saved. Make sure to click the Post button when you are satisfied with your message to actually save it.*

If you wish to reply to an existing message, select the message that you wish to reply to. Then, click either the Reply To Group or Reply To Sender button at the top of the Discussions Panel. Reply To Group will cause your message to be visible to all users who view the thread, while Reply To Sender will cause your message to be visible only to the user who created the original message you are replying to. Once you click either button, a new message will be created indented underneath the message you are replying to. If you are not satisfied with the default subject, you may change it in the subject field. You may also assign the message a high or low priority with the appropriate button at the top of the panel. Then, type your reply in the Message field and click the Post button to add your new message to the thread.

Modifying or Deleting Existing Messages

After you've created a message, you may desire to change the text or subject of the message, or perhaps delete it entirely. Provided that you originally created the message, and provided that it has not been responded to, you may change or delete the message. Merely select the message in the thread hierarchy that you wish to change. The subject and message will appear on the right side of the Discussions Panel.

If the message can be edited, you'll be able to change entries in the subject and message fields, you'll be able to assign a high or low priority, and the Post button will appear. Make any changes to the subject or message, assign a priority if you wish, and click the Post button to post the changed message to the Central Management Server database. To delete the message, click the X button at the top of the Discussion Panel toolbar. You'll be prompted to confirm the deletion. Once you confirm the deletion, the message will be deleted.

Organizing InfoView

There are many ways to organize and view folders and categories and their associated objects in InfoView. Not only will BOE security determine what folders, categories, and objects you can and cannot see, but there are different ways of displaying those folders and objects that you can see (such as by category, by folder, in the Favorites folder, and your Inbox). BusinessObjects Enterprise XI 3.0 provides additional features as well, including the ability to assign categories to objects and to add your own objects directly to InfoView without having to use other methods.

You may consider sticking with the folder/category and object/instance organization undertaken by your BOE administrator (in fact, the administrator may require this, not allowing you much leeway in organizational capabilities by limiting your right to add and move things). However, if you are given the freedom to organize InfoView, you will need to know the various ways of accomplishing this. In any case, you will probably be given free reign to at least your own personal Favorites folder and categories, so you'll still benefit from the ability to create subfolders and categories within it, as well as moving or copying objects and instances to the Favorites folder, creating shortcuts in your Favorites folder, and creating and assigning personal categories.

NOTE *Your BOE administrator may have limited the right to create, modify, or delete folders or objects in BusinessObjects Enterprise. If you are unable to perform actions that you need, contact the administrator for assistance.*

Working with Folders and Categories

Most organizational tasks revolving around folders and categories are undertaken by clicking Workspace Panel toolbar buttons, or choosing right-click pop-up menu choices, when the main Document List is displayed. If necessary, redisplay the Document List by clicking the Document List button in the top Header Panel toolbar.

Creating New Folders

While the existing set of folders you encounter when logging on to BusinessObjects Enterprise may be adequate, you may find that you'll benefit from additional folders that don't currently exist. In particular, you may want to create additional folders within the My Favorites folder to further organize reports or other objects that are stored in My Favorites.

Before you can create a folder, you must ensure that the Tree Panel is displaying BOE folders (instead of categories). If necessary, click the Switch To Folders toolbar button in the Workspace Panel toolbar. This will display the initial My Favorites and Public Folders top-level folders. Click plus signs next to these top-level folders to view subfolders within them. Whether you create a folder within your Favorites folder, or a folder within the Public Folders category, the initial step is the same: select the existing folder that you wish the new folder to reside in. For example, if you want the new folder to be a subfolder of the My Favorites folder, select the My Favorites folder first. If you want the new folder to be located directly underneath the top-level Public Folders area, click the Public Folders item in the Tree Panel.

To create a new folder, either choose Folder from the New drop-down button in the Workspace Panel toolbar or right-click the existing folder and choose New | Folder from the pop-up menu. The Create Folder dialog box will appear. Type the name for your new folder in the new folder name field (note that you cannot use the same name as an existing folder already in the same location) and click OK. The new folder will be created and will appear in the proper location within the folder hierarchy.

If you wish to rename the folder, or add a description or keywords for the folder, select the new folder and choose Properties from the Actions drop-down button in the Workspace Panel toolbar. You may also right-click the folder and choose Properties from the pop-up menu. The properties dialog box will appear, where you can type a new name in for the folder, add or change a description for the folder, and add keywords. Once the folder property changes have been made, click OK to save the changes. You may need to refresh InfoView with the Refresh toolbar button in the Workspace Panel toolbar for the folder changes to appear in InfoView.

Moving, Copying, and Deleting Folders

Before you can move, copy, or delete a folder, you must ensure that the Tree Panel is displaying BOE folders (instead of categories). If necessary, click the Switch To Folders toolbar button in the Workspace Panel toolbar. This will display the initial My Favorites and Public Folders top-level folders. Click plus signs next to these top-level folders to view subfolders within them. Once you've found the folder you wish to delete or move, select it.

Moving a folder to a new location will move the folder and its contents (objects and instances) to the new location. To move the selected folder, you must actually perform two steps: initially Cut the chosen folder, and then Paste the folder to its new location. Cut the selected folder by selecting Cut from the Organize drop-down button in the Workspace Panel toolbar. You can also right-click the selected folder and choose Organize | Cut from the pop-up menu. Then, select the new folder where you wish to paste the just-cut folder (you may select the Public Folders top-level folder, the My Favorites folder, or a subfolder). Once you've selected the new folder, choose Paste from the Organize drop-down button in the Workspace Panel toolbar. You may also right-click the destination folder and choose Organize | Paste from the pop-up menu.

Copying a folder to a new location will leave the original folder and its contents (objects and instances) unchanged, while making a copy of the folder and its contents in the new location (only objects will be copied to the new locations—no instances will be copied). The initial step is the same: ensure the folder you want to copy is selected within the Tree Panel. Then, select Copy from the Organize drop-down button in the Workspace Panel toolbar. You can also right-click the selected folder and choose Organize | Copy from the pop-up menu. Then, select the new folder where you wish to paste the just-copied folder (you may select the Public Folders top-level folder, the My Favorites folder, or a subfolder). Once you've selected the new folder, choose Paste from the Organize drop-down button in the Workspace Panel toolbar. You may also right-click the destination folder and choose Organize | Paste from the pop-up menu.

Deleting a folder will remove the folder and all its contents (objects and instances) from BOE. The initial step is the same: ensure that the folder you want to delete is selected within the Tree Panel. Then, select Delete from the Organize drop-down button in the Workspace Panel toolbar. You can also right-click the selected folder and choose Organize | Delete from the pop-up menu. You'll be prompted to confirm the folder deletion. If you reply Yes, the folder and its contents will be removed.

CAUTION *Deleting folders is a permanent operation—there is no Undo capability. Make sure you really want to delete a folder and its contents before you undertake these steps. You may wish to check with your BOE administrator to see if he or she has a regular backup procedure in place before you delete valuable folders.*

Creating New Categories

Before you can create a new category, you must ensure that the Tree Panel is displaying BOE categories (instead of folders). If necessary, click the Switch To Categories toolbar button in the Workspace Panel toolbar. This will display the initial Personal Categories and Corporate Categories top-level categories. Click plus signs next to these top-level categories to view subcategories within them. Whether you create a category within your Personal Categories, or a category within Corporate Categories, the initial step is the same: select the existing category that you wish the new category to reside in. For example, if you want the new category to be a subcategory of your Personal Categories, select the Personal Categories category first. If you want the new category to be located directly underneath the top-level Corporate Categories category, click the Corporate Categories item in the Tree Panel.

Create a new category by either choosing Category from the New drop-down button in the Workspace Panel toolbar, or right-click the existing category and choose New | Category from the pop-up menu. The Create Category dialog box will appear. Type the name for your new category in the new category name field (note that you cannot use the same name as an existing category already in the same location) and click OK. The new category will be created and will appear in the proper location within the category hierarchy.

If you wish to rename the category, or add a description or keywords for the category, select the new category and choose Properties from the Actions drop-down button in the Workspace Panel toolbar. You may also right-click the category and choose Properties from the pop-up menu. The properties dialog box will appear, where you can type a new name in for the category, add or change a description for the category, and add keywords. Once the category property changes have been made, click OK to save the changes. You may need to refresh InfoView with the Refresh toolbar button in the Workspace Panel toolbar for the category changes to appear in InfoView.

Moving or Deleting Categories

Before you can move or delete a category, you must ensure that the Tree Panel is displaying BOE categories (instead of folders). If necessary, click the Switch To Categories toolbar button in the Workspace Panel toolbar. This will display the initial Personal Categories and Corporate Categories top-level categories. Click plus signs next to these top-level categories to view subcategories within them. Once you've found the category that you wish to delete or move, select it.

Moving a category, in essence, relocates it within another top-level category or subcategory. For example, if you initially have a category defined directly underneath the Corporate Categories high-level category and wish to make it a subcategory of another category directly underneath Corporate Categories, you may move it to the other category. To move the selected category, you must actually perform two steps: initially Cut the chosen category, and then Paste the category to its new location. Cut the selected category by selecting Cut from the Organize drop-down button in the Workspace Panel toolbar. You can also right-click the selected category and choose Organize | Cut from the pop-up menu. Then, select the new category where you wish to paste the just-cut category. Once you've selected the new category, choose Paste from the Organize drop-down button in the Workspace Panel toolbar. You may also right-click the destination category and choose Organize | Paste from the pop-up menu.

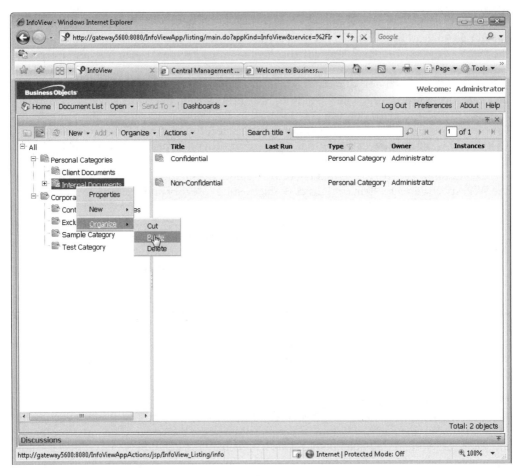

NOTE *There are a few restrictions on moving categories: you may not move your top-level personal category or the top-level corporate category, and you may only move categories to another location within their existing "level" (in other words, you can't move a personal category to a corporate category or vice versa).*

Deleting a category will remove the category from BOE. Unlike removing folders, removing a category will not remove any objects. However, objects that were assigned to the category will obviously no longer be assigned to it once it is deleted. The initial step is the same: ensure that the category you want to delete is selected within the Tree Panel. Then, select Delete from the Organize drop-down button in the Workspace Panel toolbar. You can also right-click the selected category and choose Organize | Delete from the pop-up menu. You'll be prompted to confirm the deletion. If you reply Yes, the category will be removed.

Organizing Objects and Instances

Once you've created folders and categories to your liking, you'll probably want to place desired reports, program objects, and third-party objects in the folders and assign them desired categories. You may wish to delete objects that you no longer need. Or, you may wish to copy or move objects from one folder to another. And, you may find creating Shortcuts to be helpful if a single report needs to be accessed from more than one folder.

NOTE *The ability to add and delete objects is controlled by BOE security. You may, for example, have sufficient rights to add objects to, or delete objects from, My Favorites, instead of public folders. If you're unsure of your ability to add or delete objects, check with your BOE administrator.*

Adding New Objects

Once you've created reports with Crystal Reports 2008, you will probably want to post them to BusinessObjects Enterprise XI 3.0 for scheduling or distribution. Don't forget that BOE also supports third-party objects (such as Acrobat PDF files, Word documents, PowerPoint presentations, Excel spreadsheets, and more) that you can add directly to InfoView. The only object that still must be added by other means is a program object (executable program, JavaScript, and so forth). Steps to add program objects to BOE are covered in Chapter 22.

The first step in adding an object is to display the Document List, ensure that the folder view is displayed, and select the folder in the left Tree Panel where you want the object to be copied. For example, if you are only permitted to add objects to My Favorites folder, select it in the Tree Panel before you attempt to add the object. Then, click the Add drop-down button in the Workspace Panel toolbar, or right-click the selected folder and click Add from the pop-up menu. Two choices will appear: Crystal Reports, and Local Document. Choose Crystal Reports to add an existing .RPT file to BOE. The Crystal Reports screen will appear in the Workspace Panel.

Use description saved in Summary Info portion of report, or type your own

Existing report title
(can be overtyped)

Type full path/filename to report,
or Browse to find file

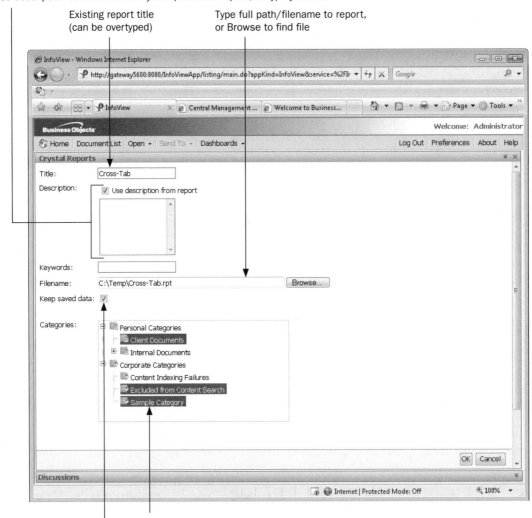

Click or CTRL-click to assign one or more optional categories

If report contains saved data, retain it on BOE

Specify the file path and name of the document you wish to upload to BusinessObjects Enterprise in the Filename field. If you prefer, you may click the Browse button to launch a standard File Open dialog box. Locate the desired file in this dialog box and click Open. The full path and filename will be filled in the Filename field for you. The Title field will be filled with either the report filename (without the .RPT extension) or the value supplied in the report's Summary Info dialog box. If the report also contains a description from Summary Info, you may automatically import it by checking Use Description From Report. If you wish to type a description in manually, uncheck Use Description From Report and type the description in. You may also type descriptive keywords (keywords can be helpful when conducting document searches, as described earlier in the chapter). If the report contains saved data, you may retain it on BOE by checking Keep Saved Data. This will allow the report to be viewed in InfoView without immediately requiring a database refresh (it will also potentially show older report data). Optionally, you may also assign one or more categories to the report in BOE. Expand entries in the categories list and highlight desired categories (you may highlight as many categories as you'd like).

Once you've made the desired choices, click OK. The report will be uploaded to BusinessObjects Enterprise (be patient—this may take some time, depending on the size of the file). The Workspace Panel will reappear with your new object now appearing in the object list.

Steps to add third-party objects, such as Acrobat files, Word documents, and so forth, are almost identical to those for adding a Crystal Report. First, select the folder where you'd like to add the object in the Tree Panel. Then choose the Local Document option from the Add drop-down button in the Workspace Panel toolbar, or the right-click pop-up menu. The Select Document screen will appear in the Workspace Panel.

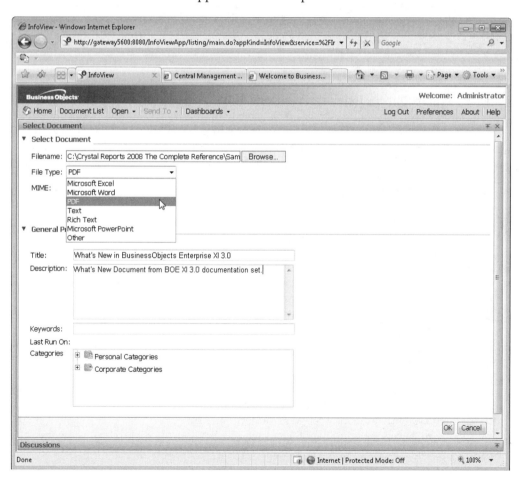

As with a Crystal Report, you may type the full path/filename for the document into the field, or click the Browse button to navigate to the file. If the file extension of your chosen file matches one of the standard BOE-supported third-party document types, the File Type drop-down list will automatically be set. If the file type cannot be determined, choose the desired file type from the File Type drop-down list. If the file you are adding does not match any of the standard file types (BOE refers to this as an *agnostic* file), choose Other as the file type and type in the specific web server MIME type required to properly display the file (if you are unsure of the MIME type to specify, check with your web administrator or search the Internet for standard web MIME types).

You may expand the General Properties area of the screen by clicking the small arrow icon to the left of General Properties. Here, you may type the title and description for the object, as well as specifying any keywords (keywords can be helpful when conducting document searches, as described earlier in the chapter). You may optionally specify one or more categories to assign to the object, as described earlier in the chapter. When finished, click OK to upload the file to BOE.

TIP *You can also add a hyperlink to another web page to a selected folder. Instead of choosing the Add drop-down button or pop-up menu option, choose New. The Hyperlink option will appear. Choose it and specify the web page you wish to hyperlink to.*

Adding Reports Directly from Crystal Reports 2008

The ability to add Crystal Reports to BOE directly in InfoView is handy, especially if the report was created in an earlier version of Crystal Reports (earlier versions of Crystal Reports will not connect to version XI 3.0 as described in the rest of this box). However, adding reports in InfoView does required that you have already created the report in Crystal Reports and saved the .RPT file to a known location. You may prefer to add reports directly to BusinessObjects Enterprise XI 3.0 from Crystal Reports 2008, providing a more direct path from report design to posting.

First, ensure you have updated your copy of Crystal Reports 2008 to Service Pack 0 or greater, as the initial release of Crystal Reports 2008 didn't provide Enterprise connectivity. Then open an existing report or design a new report using techniques described in Part I of this book. When you are ready to save the report to BOE XI 3.0, choose File | Save As from the pull-down menus, as though you were going to save the report with a new filename on your local drive. However, note the Enterprise and My Connections icons in the left of the Save As dialog box. These are the keys to Enterprise XI 3.0 connectivity.

The Enterprise option will simply prompt you to log on to Enterprise. Supply the proper user ID and password (and, if necessary, specify your Enterprise CMS server name and authentication type, as provided by your BOE administrator). If you regularly connect to a standard BOE system in your organization, you may predefine the connection by using the My Connections icon. You may create this definition, as well as connect to the defined system, by clicking the My Connections icon.

Once you've connected to the BOE system, the Save As dialog box will show the Enterprise folder structure. Simply select the folder or subfolder you wish to save the report to and type the desired object name in the File Name text box (you can remove the .RPT extension). If the report contains objects from the BOE repository (covered in Chapter 17) and you wish the report to look for updated repository objects when it is "refreshed" in BOE, check the appropriate check box. Click Save to upload the report to the chosen BOE folder.

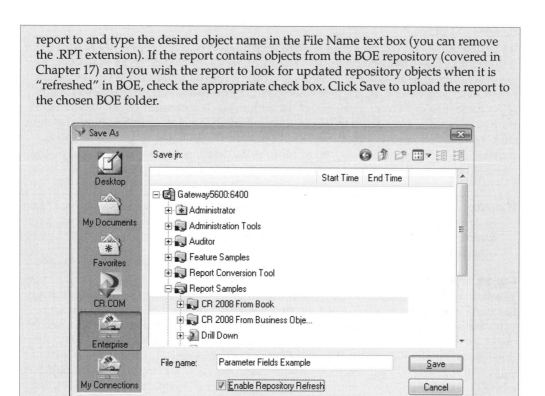

Modifying Existing Objects and Assigning Categories

Once you have added a Crystal Report or third-party document to BOE, you may wish to change some aspect of it, such as the title, comments, or keywords (perhaps you save a report directly from Crystal Reports 2008 and were unable to specify these items when the report was saved to BOE). You may also wish to assign different categories to the object than were initially assigned, assign categories for the first time, or remove all category assignment (assigning one or more categories to an object is optional). These steps are all performed by changing the properties for an already-posted object.

Begin by navigating through the folder or category structure until you find the object you want to modify. Then, select the object in the object list on the right side of the Workspace Panel. Choose Properties from the Actions drop-down button in the Workspace Panel toolbar. You may also right-click the object and choose Properties from the pop-up menu. The Properties screen will appear in the Workspace Panel. Make any desired changes to the title, description, or keywords fields. You may also expand the category structure and deselect any existing category assignments, or assign one or more new categories by clicking on desired categories. When you are finished with your changes, click OK to save the new properties.

Deleting Objects

If you determine that you no longer wish to keep a report or other object, you may delete it. If the report or program object contains instances, they will be deleted as well. Begin by navigating through the folder or category structure until you find the object you want to delete. Once you've selected the desired object or objects that you wish to delete (you may select more than one object in the object list with CTRL-click or SHIFT-click), choose Delete from the Organize drop-down button in the Workspace Panel toolbar. You may also right-click the selected object or objects and choose Delete from the Organize pop-up menu. A dialog box will display asking you to confirm the deletion. Once you respond Yes, the object (and any associated instances) will be permanently deleted.

CAUTION *Deleting objects is a permanent operation—there is no Undo capability. Make sure you really want to delete an object and its instances before you undertake these steps. You may wish to check with your BOE administrator to see if he or she has a regular backup procedure in place before you delete valuable objects.*

Copying or Moving Objects

You may wish to copy or move one or more objects to another folder. First, navigate through the folder or category structure until you find the object you want to copy or move. Once you've selected the desired object or objects (you may select more than one object in the object list with CTRL-click or SHIFT-click), choose the desired option from the Organize drop-down button in the Workspace Panel toolbar, or the Organize right-click pop-up menu. Copy will copy the selected objects for a later Paste operation, leaving the original objects where they now are. Cut will copy the selected objects for a later paste operation, deleting them from their current location (once the paste operation has been completed).

Once you have copied or cut the desired object or objects, navigate to the folder where you wish to place them. You may either select the folder itself in the Tree Panel, or any object within the folder. Then, choose Paste from either the Organize drop-down button in the Workspace Panel toolbar, or the Organize right-click pop-up menu. The objects will be moved or copied to their new location (objects will have a number appended to their name if objects with the same name already exist in the destination folder).

NOTE *The difference between copying and moving an object is based on whether the object remains in its original location and whether instances are moved to the new location. If you move an object, it will not remain in the original location, and any related instances will be placed in the new location along with the object. Copying an object will leave it intact in its original location with no instances copied to the new location.*

Creating Shortcuts

One issue that may face you is how to deal with a report or other object that you wish to be available in multiple folders. While you could copy the object to multiple folders, as described earlier, BOE makes separate copies of reports or objects in each folder. Thereafter, if you want to modify the original report or object, the modification will only be made to the particular object you select—the others that were copied to other folders will remain unchanged. And, if you schedule one of the copied objects, the instances will only be available within the one folder—other folders won't include the instances.

BusinessObjects Enterprise provides a way to deal with this situation. The Shortcut option creates a shortcut, or link, to the original object. When you schedule the shortcut, the instances you create are accessible in the History lists in the original folder where the object is located. And when other users schedule the object, you will see those instances in the History list within all folders where shortcuts are placed. Much as with Windows itself, an InfoView shortcut is merely a "pointer" to the source object in another location.

First, navigate through the folder or category structure until you find the object you want to create a shortcut for. Once you've selected the desired object or objects (you may select more than one object in the object list with CTRL-click or SHIFT-click), choose Create Shortcut from the Organize drop-down button in the Workspace Panel toolbar, or the Organize right-click pop-up menu. Then, navigate to the folder where you wish to place the shortcut or shortcuts. You may either select the folder itself in the Tree Panel, or any object within the folder. Then, choose Paste Shortcut from either the Organize drop-down button in the Workspace Panel toolbar, or the Organize right-click pop-up menu. Shortcuts will appear in their new locations with a Shortcut designation under the type column, and a small arrow/paper icon to the left of their name. Shortcuts can be viewed, scheduled, and manipulated similarly to the main objects themselves.

The My InfoView Custom Layout

So far, this chapter has discussed viewing the standard InfoView Document List either via the folder hierarchy or in category view. While you can navigate fairly quickly among various folders and categories, and while you can store your most frequently used objects in My Favorites, you still may wish for an even more streamlined or consolidated view of a set of key reports, web sites, or third-party objects that you are most interested in. This consolidated view may even comprise a simple *dashboard*, loosely described as a series of separate high-level presentations that appear on the same physical screen.

BusinessObjects Enterprise provides the *My InfoView* customized layout as a way of presenting several key object view on a single screen. You may create a custom My InfoView layout, which will be stored in the My Favorites folder. Any time you wish to view the My InfoView layout, just double-click it. The Workspace Panel will be replaced with the custom My InfoView layout.

To begin working with My InfoView, choose My InfoView from the Open drop-down button in the Header Panel toolbar. If the default My InfoView layout has already been defined, it will appear in the Workspace Panel. Click on any pane to further interact (a pane can consist of a Crystal report, web page, or third-party document). If My InfoView has yet to be defined, the Define Content screen will appear, initially showing a single pane available for customization.

Creating a My InfoView Layout

The My InfoView custom layout consists of a series of "panes," or subwindows, which can each contain a full or partial Crystal Report, a third-party document (such as an Excel spreadsheet, a Word document, or an Acrobat PDF file), a web page, and a header and footer (consisting of text or a web page link). Initially, a single pane will appear when you first start customizing My InfoView. You may either add panes manually one at a time or choose a predefined pane layout by clicking one of the Choose Template buttons at the top of the My InfoView window. For example, if you click the third Choose Template button (the three-pane vertical layout button), the screen will be divided into three vertically organized panes. This is illustrated in Figure 21-5.

If you wish to manually lay out your set of My InfoView panes, you may begin by splitting the single initial pane horizontally or vertically. Click the Split Vertically or Split Horizontally button in the upper right-hand corner of the pane. The pane will be split in half horizontally or vertically with another pane appearing. The new pane will contain the same set of buttons so that it, as just discussed, can also be split horizontally or vertically. If you wish to resize a pane, point to the right or bottom border (you can't resize a pane from the top or left). Your

FIGURE 21-5   My InfoView with three-pane layout

mouse cursor will change to a double-arrow cursor—drag to resize the pane, adjusting adjacent panes to fit.

If you wish to delete a pane that you've already created and sized (whether or not you've defined content for it yet), click the small *X* close button at the top of the pane. After a confirmation message, the pane will be deleted, with other panes resizing to fill the space. This process of splitting and resizing existing panes and deleting unwanted panes is how you define the layout of My InfoView. You may also use the same techniques to modify a layout that resulted from clicking one of the predefined template buttons.

To define the content that will appear in each pane, click either the Define Content link or the Properties button at the top of the pane. The Dashboard Properties dialog box will appear, as illustrated in Figure 21-6. Choose either a web address or BusinessObjects Enterprise

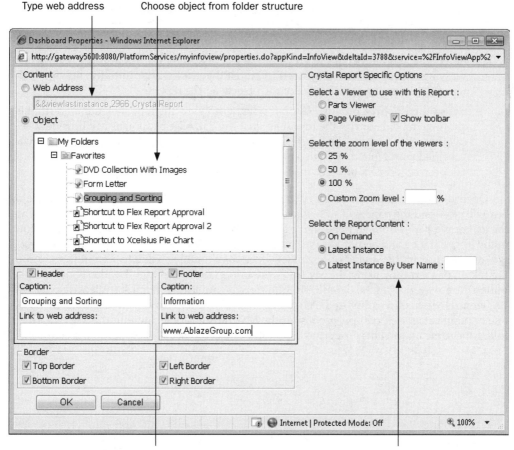

FIGURE 21-6   The Dashboard Properties dialog box

object to appear in the pane. Click the appropriate radio button and either type the web address in directly or choose the desired object from the BOE folder structure.

In addition to the choice of web address or BOE object, you may specify a header and a footer for the pane. Text can be typed that will appear at the top and bottom of the pane. Optionally, if you supply a web address for the header or footer, the text you type will become a hyperlink to the web address you supply.

If you choose a Crystal Report object from the folder list, the Dashboard Properties dialog box will expand to show an additional set of choices to display the Crystal Report.

- **Select a Viewer to use with this Report**   Choose the report viewer to display the report within the pane. The Page Viewer will display the entire report within the pane, while the Parts Viewer will display the initially defined report part in the pane (defining report parts is covered in Chapter 20). In either event, any report part navigation or drill-down defined in the report can be used from within the pane. Checking Show Toolbar will display the report viewer toolbar within the pane, where the report alone will be displayed if this is unchecked.

- **Select the zoom level of the viewers**   Select or specify the initial zoom level when viewing the report. You may need to adjust this choice after initially viewing the report to accommodate the size of the objects on the report.

- **Select the Report Content**   Choose whether to view the report on demand (that is, show saved data or run the report against the database as soon as My InfoView is displayed) or to show the latest instance overall, or else the latest instance run by a specified user. Note that if you specify a latest instance option and the report has not yet been scheduled, an error message will appear within the pane.

Once you've specified all necessary properties, click OK. The Dashboard Properties dialog box will close and the pane will show the contents just specified. Continue to specify contents for remaining panes until all panes have been supplied with content. Click the Save button in the upper right-hand corner to save the default My InfoView layout. The default layout will now appear in the My Favorites folder—you may double-click it to view it from within the folder, or view it by using the My InfoView option from the Open Header Panel toolbar button. You may also set the default My InfoView layout as the initial InfoView display with Preferences (discussed earlier in the chapter). And, if you wish to assign My InfoView to one or more categories, edit properties for the My InfoView object within the My Favorites folder the same as you edit properties for another object (discussed earlier in the chapter).

CAUTION *Make sure to click the Save button after you've defined content. If you fail to save the dashboard definition and click an alternative object in the Tree Panel, you'll lose your layout definition.*

Modifying the Default Layout

Once you've defined the initial My InfoView default layout, you'll no doubt wish to make changes at some point in the near or far future. You may simply want to change the zoom level of a Crystal Report viewer. Or, you may wish to delete the entire My InfoView definition and start over. To delete the default My InfoView layout, simply select it in the My Favorites folder and choose Delete from the Organize drop-down toolbar button or right-click pop-up menu. To edit the default layout, select it in My Favorites and choose Modify My InfoView from the Actions drop-down button in the Workspace Panel toolbar. You may also right-click the object and choose Modify My InfoView from the pop-up menu. You may also view the My InfoView layout and click the Edit link in the upper right-hand corner.

Once you are editing the My InfoView layout, just click the Properties button at the top of the pane you wish to modify. The Dashboard Properties dialog box will reappear. You may also delete panes, split panes, and add new panes as desired. Once you finalized your changes, click the small Save link in the upper right-hand corner to save the default layout.

You may save additional My InfoView layouts by starting with the default layout. Edit the default layout as just described and make desired changes (delete panes, add new panes, edit dashboard properties, and so forth). However, instead of clicking the small Save link in the upper right-hand corner, click Save As. A properties screen will appear where you can provide the new My InfoView layout with a name, as well as specifying the folder to place the object in. Optionally, you may also expand the Categories area of the dialog box and select one or more categories to assign to the layout. When you click OK, the layout will be saved in the selected folder. To view the new layout, navigate to the folder and just double-click the layout name. You may also choose the layout as the initial thing you see when starting InfoView by using Preferences.

Administering Enterprise Reporting Systems

The BusinessObjects Enterprise family (abbreviated BOE throughout this chapter) presents a fairly complex approach to web-based report automation and distribution. Its ability to schedule reports to run on a regular basis, and then make those reports available to viewers in a variety of ways, has made BOE an increasingly popular method for automating corporate reporting. The Enterprise version that matches Crystal Reports 2008, BusinessObjects Enterprise XI 3.0, fully supports new Crystal Reports 2008 features, such as enhanced cross-tab objects, Xcelsius/Flash integration, the Parameter Panel, and so forth. Architecturally, it has also improved over previous versions by more tightly consolidating administrative functions and reducing the steps required to troubleshoot and administer various BOE components.

NOTE *As of this writing, the only Enterprise XI 3.0 product available is the full release of BusinessObjects Enterprise XI 3.0. However, Business Objects has stated a future direction to provide versions for Crystal Reports–only organizations, such as the previously released Crystal Reports Server XI. Although it is assumed that future products in the BusinessObjects XI 3.0 family will generally share the same functionality and look and feel as the full BOE XI 3.0 product demonstrated in this chapter, you may notice some reduced features or options. As such, some items demonstrated in this chapter may not be visible or available.*

As is usually the case, the more flexible and capable a software system is, the more complex its infrastructure becomes. BusinessObjects Enterprise is no exception. Its scalable, flexible, feature-rich foundation for information automation and dissemination results in a more complex and complicated hardware and software combination in the "back end." Part of the initial process of implementing BOE, as well as a continuing requirement of organizations that put it in place, is BOE administration.

This chapter, while not covering every possible combination of BOE implementations and administrative tasks, will give those tasked with implementing, troubleshooting, and maintaining their BOE systems good background on common administrative tasks. BOE administrators work with various software components, user management, and server configuration, among other common tasks.

NOTE *The full version of BusinessObjects Enterprise XI 3.0 includes support for document types other than Crystal Reports. However, this chapter will cover and concentrate on only those components and steps required to support Crystal Reports document types and third-party documents.*

Introducing the Central Management Console

Virtually all the administration work in BusinessObjects Enterprise is performed in the Central Management Console, or *CMC*. This is a web-based application may be accessed from any computer that has access to the BOE network. For example, you may access the CMC directly from the main computer that BOE is installed on, as well as other computers on the same subnet (provided no firewall rules block access). You may also access the CMC from other computers on your main organization's network, or even the Internet (again, providing that firewall rules allow access to the particular IP address or DNS name, and port, that BOE is running on).

If you happen to be using the main computer that BusinessObjects Enterprise is installed on, you may access the CMC directly from the appropriate Windows Start menu. Otherwise, you may launch a web browser and type in the URL to navigate to the CMC. In this case, navigate directly to

```
http://<web server/IP address>:<port>/CmcApp
```

The *<web server/IP address>* portion is determined by the name or IP address of the application server BOE is installed on. *<Port>* is also determined by the application server. (Port 8080 is used by default when installing BOE on the bundled Apache Tomcat server.)

You'll be prompted to log on to BusinessObjects Enterprise. Complete the User Name and Password fields (a newly installed BOE system will provide an Administrator user ID with a blank password). Optionally, you may need to specify a Central Management Server name in the System field (typically, this is filled in by default). And, if you've implemented an integrated security method, such as Windows Active Directory (discussed later in the chapter), specify that method in the Authentication drop-down list. Click Log On to display the CMC main menu.

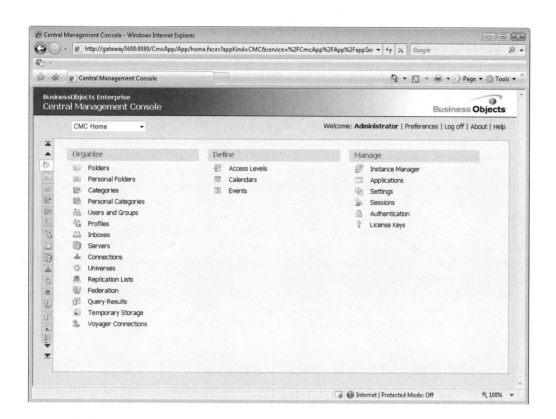

NOTE *Most BOE components are available for both Windows and various Unix/Linux platforms. However, this book will concentrate only on the Windows implementation of BOE.*

In addition to clicking a desired menu option under one of the three main categories of menu options (Organize, Define, and Manage), you may navigate directly to management tasks using two other approaches: tabs on the left side of the CMC screen (you may need to use the up- or down-arrow buttons to expose all available tabs), and options from the navigation drop-down list at the upper left of the CMC. These tabs and drop-down list will always appear in the CMC, regardless of the particular administrative task you are conducting at the time.

Managing Users and Groups

BusinessObjects Enterprise contains its own security system, separate from the operating system underneath. Maintained by the core software server in BOE, the Central Management Server (abbreviated CMS, and discussed in detail later in the chapter, under "BusinessObjects Enterprise Architecture"), this allows the BOE administrator to build a unique security model to control access to the reports in the system. Your security model system can be as simple or as complex as needed, providing complete flexibility for the system architect and administrator.

BusinessObjects Enterprise security is designed to closely mimic many security models, with the security model in Windows Server being particularly close. There are individual user accounts that include a user name and password. Those user accounts may be placed into one or more groups that incorporate similar users. For example, all sales users can be placed in a National Sales group. Groups can also be placed within other groups to create a parent/child relationship between groups. For example, all Western Region Sales users can be placed in a Western Region Sales subgroup, contained within the National Sales main group. This allows the administrator to define a hierarchical setup for easier application of security rights across the system.

Users are not limited to being placed in one group. If a user crosses multiple group boundaries, such as being assigned a BOE administrative position, while also being employed in the Sales department, the user can be placed in both the Administrators and National Sales groups.

Adding, Modifying, and Deleting User Accounts

Two user accounts are created automatically when BusinessObjects Enterprise is installed: Administrator and Guest. The Administrator account is used as the "all access" account for managing your BOE system. The Guest account, which is disabled by default, is available for general use for users that don't have a specific account. If you enable the Guest account, a user who leaves both the User ID and Password fields blank will be able to log on to BOE. Both of these accounts are set to use Enterprise authentication.

NOTE *Various authentication types are covered later in this chapter.*

To add a new user account, click the Users And Groups menu option within the Organize category of the CMC home page. You may also click the Users And Groups tab on the left side of the CMC, or choose Users And Groups from the navigation drop-down list. The user and group listing will appear, with the Group Hierarchy displayed by default. You may choose to view the basic user list by clicking the User List entry in the Tree Panel to the left. However, you may add a new user directly without first displaying the user list. To do this, click the Create New User button in the upper-left corner of the user and group listing. You may also choose New | New User from the Manage drop-down button above the listing. The New User screen will appear.

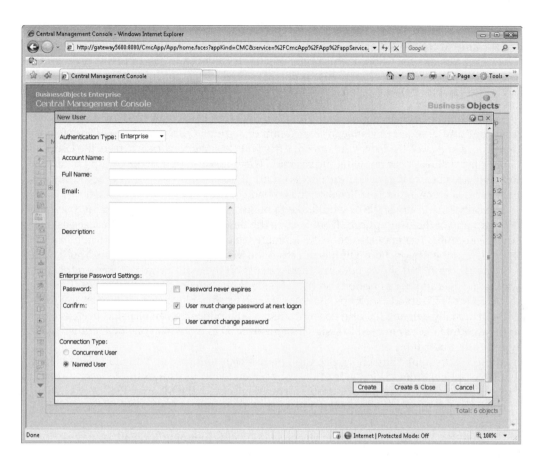

Most fields on the user screen are self-explanatory, and some are optional. Some fields or options may be of particular concern:

- **Password Settings** While entries you choose here may conflict with overall password requirements set in the Enterprise Authentication screen (available from the Authentication link from the Manage area of the main CMC screen), the CMC will generally allow them to be ignored. For example, if you have set requirements for mixed-case passwords, or passwords of a minimum length in the Authentication screen, you'll be able to set initial passwords for users that fall outside of these requirements. The users, however, will need to adhere to the password requirements when they change their own password.

- **Connection Type**   Depending on the licenses you have purchased, you may be able to choose either a Concurrent or Named license (or perhaps both) for this particular user. Choose which type of license you wish to assign to this user with the proper radio button (a discussion of named versus concurrent licenses appears in Chapter 20).

When finished specifying user information, click Create to create the new account and leave the New User screen visible to create another account. Or, click Create & Close to create the account and close the New User screen. After you close the New User screen, the Users and Groups list will reappear, showing the selection (User List, Group List, or Group Hierarchy) that appeared before you added the new account. If you wish to see the new account, click the User List entry in the Tree Panel on the left side of the Users and Groups list.

If you've made a mistake or would like to make a change to the user account, you may now edit any of the user options. Double-click the desired user account in the User list to edit the account. You may also click the Manage Object Properties toolbar button in the upper left of the list, or choose Properties from the Manage drop-down button. You'll notice a different screen that shows both additional items on the main properties screen for the user, as well as additional options on the left side of the screen. For example, you'll notice the Account Is Disabled check box that may be used to disable a user account at any time without actually deleting the user account. Also, you'll notice that an alias has been assigned to the account (aliases are used to assign a single user ID to more than one BOE authentication type or other user ID).

If necessary, make any changes on the main Properties screen. You may also click available options from the left side of the user screen to change, for example, user rights (with the User Security option) or group membership (with the Member Of option). Once you've made changes, click the desired Save or Close button at the bottom of the screen to save changes.

To delete a user account, use the Users And Groups menu option, tab, or navigation drop-down list option. Select either the User list or the Group Hierarchy to navigate to the user account you wish to delete. Select the desired account (you may select more than one user account with CTRL-click or SHIFT-click). Then, choose Delete from the Manage drop-down button above the user list. Note that some users will result in a dimmed Delete option. The Administrator and Guest accounts can't be deleted. And, any accounts provided by other authentication methods (Windows NT, Active Directory, or LDAP) must be deleted in their original locations—they cannot be deleted here.

NOTE *The preceding steps assume you are using Enterprise authentication and will be adding and maintaining users directly in BusinessObjects Enterprise. If you prefer to use an existing Windows NT, Windows Active Directory, or LDAP system to authenticate users, create users and groups in these systems and use steps described later in the chapter to integrate BOE with your existing security system.*

Password Settings

As noted earlier, each individual user account has its own password and several check boxes that affect that password. But, there are also global password settings for user accounts based on Enterprise authentication that affect password behavior overall. To edit the global settings, click Authentication in the Manage section of the CMC home page. You may also click the Authentication tab in the left tab list, or choose Authentication from the navigation drop-down list. The Authentication screen will appear, displaying the various security authentication methods BOE supports. Double-click the Enterprise entry to view or change Enterprise password settings.

Password Restrictions allow the administrator to force a mixed-case password, as well as a password of a certain character length. User Restrictions allow the administrator to force users to change their passwords every so often, as well as require a series of different passwords. And, Logon Restrictions allow the administrator to shut down the account if a number of unsuccessful logons are attempted. You may use any combination of these choices to enforce password standards and practices for an organization.

Adding Groups

BusinessObjects Enterprise groups can be created to organize users together. Users can be placed in one or more groups. Groups can also be made subgroups of other groups. Access rights in BOE can be assigned to groups, in addition to individual users. Users inherit rights from their group membership, which often makes group organization and security key to a good security model with minimal effort. If you use an external authentication method (Windows NT, Active Directory, LDAP), user groups will also be imported into BOE. You may merely accept these existing imported groups, or create additional groups within BOE itself to group all users.

Based on the version of BOE you install, several default groups are created automatically (at minimum, Administrators and Everyone). These groups are integral to the overall BOE system and can't be deleted. You'll find the Administrator user in the Administrators group and all users in the Everyone group. Place users that will need to perform administrative tasks into the Administrators group—these users will be able to perform most administrative tasks automatically. By default, every user of BusinessObjects Enterprise will be placed in the Everyone group (and, you can't remove this group or take a user out of this group)— you'll set the most basic set of rights for this group.

While the groups that are created by default when BOE is installed are convenient for certain basic security tasks, they are probably not sufficient for even mildly sophisticated security models. As the administrator, you'll want to think about the best way to group your users for security purposes. For example, some organizations group users by their job functions, with groups such as Sales, Executive, and Human Resources. Other organizations group the users by region, such as East Coast, Midwest, and West Coast. Or, organizations may use a combination of both, or other similar scenarios. There is no right or wrong way to group users, but well-thought-out grouping can make applying access rights much, much easier.

To add a new group, click the Users And Groups menu option within the Organize category of the CMC home page. You may also click the Users And Groups tab on the left side of the CMC, or choose Users And Groups from the navigation drop-down list. The user and group listing will appear, with the Group Hierarchy displayed by default (if you don't expand the Group Hierarchy, both it and the Group list will show the same set of groups). Click the Create New Group button in the upper-left corner of the user and group listing. You may also choose New | New Group from the Manage drop-down button above the listing. The Create New User Group screen will appear.

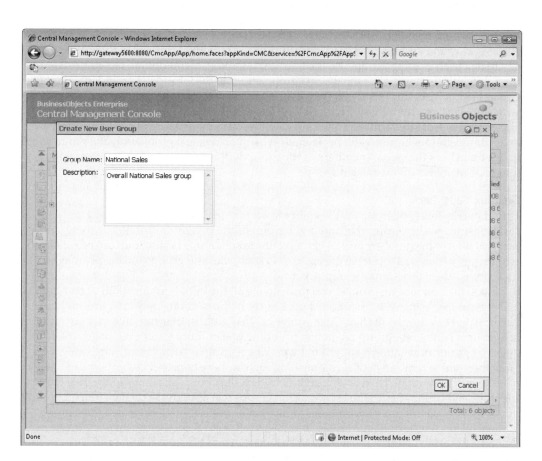

Type a name and optional description for the group and click OK to create the group. The User and Group list will be displayed, showing the new group in the list (if a group option is chosen). To change some aspect of a group, click the Group List entry in the Tree Panel (you can't edit groups if the Group Hierarchy is displayed). Double-click the desired group in the list to edit it. You may also click the Manage Object Properties toolbar button in the upper left of the list, or choose Properties from the Manage drop-down button. You'll notice a different screen that shows both additional items on the main properties screen for the group, as well as additional options on the left side of the screen. If necessary, make any changes on the main Properties screen. You may also click available options from the left side of the group screen to change, for example, group rights (with the User Security option)

or users that are members of the group (with the Member Of option). Once you've made changes, click the desired Save or Close button at the bottom of the screen to save changes.

To delete an existing group, use the Users And Groups menu option, tab, or navigation drop-down list option. Select the desired group either in the Group list or underneath the Group Hierarchy in the Tree Panel (you may select more than one group in the Group list with CTRL-click or SHIFT-click). Then, choose Delete from the Manage drop-down button above the list. Note that some groups will result in a dimmed Delete option. The Everyone and Administrators groups can't be deleted. When you delete a group, only the group itself is deleted. Users that were members of the group will not be removed, but they will no longer be members of the deleted group.

Creating Subgroups

Part of the flexibility of groups is the ability to set up hierarchies, whereby one group can reside inside another group (become a subgroup of the parent group). While there's no practical limit to the numbers and levels of groups to subgroups (a subgroup can be contained within a subgroup or a top-level group, and so forth), nesting groups too deeply may not make for a reasonably simple group structure.

If you plan on nesting groups, you must create all the initial groups (both parent groups and subgroups) using steps mentioned previously in this section. Only after groups have been created can they be nested. Once you've created groups, there are two main ways of setting up a parent/subgroup relationship: adding one or more groups as subgroups of a "parent" group, or creating a subgroup by making a group a "member of" a parent group. And, there are several ways of accomplishing each of these approaches.

The quickest way to create subgroups is to click the Group List entry in the Tree Panel of the Users and Groups list. In the list of existing groups that appears, select the group or groups you want to make subgroups of another group. For example, if you've created three groups—National Sales, Western Region Sales, and Eastern Region Sales—and you want Western Region Sales and Eastern Region Sales to be subgroups of National Sales, CTRL-click on both Western Region Sales and Eastern Region Sales to select them. Then, click the Add Member To User Group toolbar button in the upper left-hand corner of the Users and Groups list, or choose Join Group from the Actions drop-down button. The Choose A Destination Group screen will appear.

Select one or more groups you would like to make the group or groups you selected subgroups of. You may select more than one group with CTRL-click or SHIFT-click. Then, click the right-arrow button to add the selected group or groups to the Destination Group(s) list. If you accidentally add too many groups, you may select one or more groups in the Destination Group(s) list and click the left-arrow button to remove them. Click OK when finished to create the group hierarchy. You can then expand the Group Hierarchy entry in the Tree Panel to ensure that the groups are now a subgroup of your chosen group.

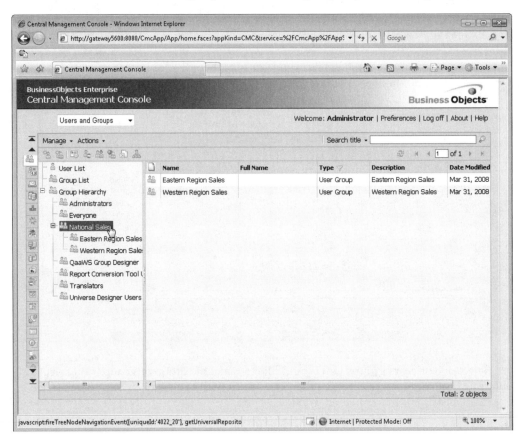

Another option is to initially display the Users and Groups list and select the top-level group you wish to add subgroups to (note that this step only allows one group to be selected—selecting multiple groups will disable the appropriate option). Then, click the Add Members To Parent Group toolbar button, or choose Add from the Actions drop-down button. The Available Users/Groups screen will appear. Select one or more groups you wish to become subgroups of the group you just selected (you may CTRL-click or SHIFT-click to choose more than one group). Click the right-arrow button to add the selections to the Selected Users/Groups list. If you add too many groups, select the desired group or groups in the Selected Users/Groups list and click the left-arrow button to remove them. When you're finished selecting groups, click OK to make the selected group subgroups of the group you initially selected. Again, viewing the Group Hierarchy will confirm that you properly created your group/subgroup hierarchy.

If you later decide you wish to remove a subgroup from a parent group, there are, again, several ways to accomplish the removal. Probably the most straightforward is to expand the Group Hierarchy entry in the panel tree and navigate to the parent group you wish to remove subgroups from. Click the parent group name in the Tree Panel. All subgroups will appear on the right side of the Users and Groups list. Select one or more groups you wish to remove from the parent group and click the Remove User Or Group From User Group toolbar button, or choose Remove from the Actions drop-down button. Respond Yes to the confirmation prompt. The selected groups will then no longer be subgroups of the originally selected parent group.

TIP *Yet another option for creating a group hierarchy is selecting an existing group that you want to make a subgroup. Double-click the desired group in the Users and Groups list. Then, click the Member Of option in the left side of the group screen. From the resulting Member Of list, you may click the Join button to select a parent group, or select existing parent groups and click Remove to remove the selected group from the parent group.*

Placing Users in Groups

Once you've created groups and subgroups, you'll want to add users to the groups. There are two general approaches to placing users in one or more groups: selecting one or more users and choosing the group or groups you want to add them to, or selecting a group and choosing the user or users you want to add to the group. Begin by ensuring that the Users and Groups list is displayed in the CMC by using main menu, toolbar, or navigation drop-down list choices.

To select users you wish to add to a group or groups, click the User List entry in the Tree Panel to display the user list. Select the user or users you wish to add to a group (CTRL- or SHIFT-click will select more than one user). Then, click the Add Member To User Group toolbar button, or choose Join Group from the Actions drop-down button. The Choose A Destination Group dialog box will appear. Add the group or groups you want to assign to the Destination Group(s) list with the right-arrow button. You may also remove already-added groups with the left-arrow button. Click OK when finished to assign users to the selected groups.

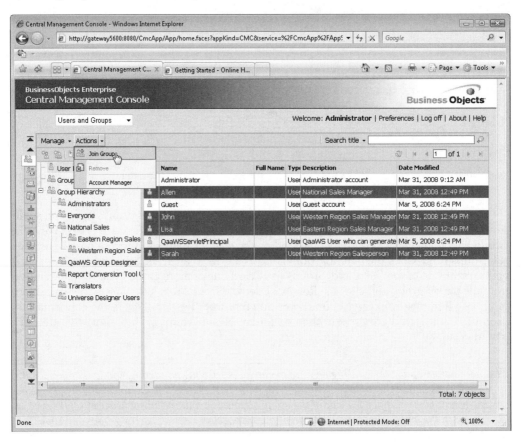

Another way to add users to a group is to select the group first. Click the Group List entry in the Tree Panel, or expand the Group Hierarchy in the Tree Panel and select the single group you want to add users to (you can't multiselect groups for this process). Then, click the Add Members To Parent Group toolbar button, or choose Add from the Actions drop-down button. The Available Users/Groups list will appear. Select one or more users you wish to add to the selected group and move them to the Selected Users/Groups list with the right-arrow button. Any users you later decide you don't want in the group can be removed from the Users/Groups list with the left-arrow button. Click OK when finished to add the users to the selected group.

While there are several ways to delete users from a group, probably the most straightforward method is to view the Group Hierarchy in the Tree Panel, navigating to the group or subgroup you want to remove users from. Once you've selected the desired group or subgroup in the Tree Panel, users in that group will appear on the right side of the list. Select one or more users that you want to remove from the group. Then, click the Remove User Or Group From User Group toolbar button, or select Remove from the Actions drop-down button. Respond Yes to the confirmation prompt. This will remove the users from the selected group, *but will not remove them from BOE* (you'll need to select users in the Users list to remove them from BOE).

You may also find the Member Of option handy for manipulating group membership. Select User List in the Tree Panel to show all BOE users. Double-click the desired account, which will display the user screen for the selected user. Click the Member Of link in the left side of the screen. The group or groups that the user is a member of will appear. You may remove the user from a group by select the desired group or groups and clicking the Remove button (you will be unable to remove a user from the Everyone group). Conversely, you can click the Join Group button and pick a group or groups that you wish to have the selected user join.

Once you've created your group/subgroup hierarchy, and added users to desired groups/subgroups, the Group Hierarchy entry in the Users and Groups list Tree Panel is a handy way to double-check that you've probably organized your user, group/subgroup model. Selecting a group within the group hierarchy will display its "members" in the right-side list. Subgroups within the selected group will appear with a "two-head" icon and a User Group type, whereas users within the selected group will appear with a "one-head" icon and a User type.

Expand Group Hierarchy to see
group/subgroup relationship

Click group in Tree Panel to see
subgroups and users in group

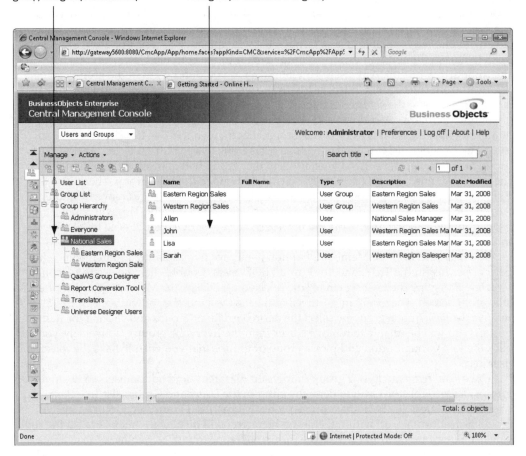

NOTE *Even if you integrate BOE with an outside authentication method (Windows NT, Active Directory, or LDAP), you may create and manipulate additional groups within the CMC, beyond those that are imported from the outside server.*

Integrating BusinessObjects Enterprise with Existing Security Environments

So far, everything previously discussed is part of Enterprise Authentication, which is BusinessObjects Enterprise's native stand-alone security system. However, if you prefer to integrate BOE security with another authentication system already in place in your organization, you have three additional authentication methods: Windows NT, Windows Active Directory, and LDAP.

You may use the built-in security model that's part BOE, and/or if you already have a security system in place within your organization, you may tie BOE to it, provided you are using one of the three standard security models. As such, you have four overall security/authentication choices:

- **Enterprise authentication** In this scenario, you manage all users and groups entirely within BusinessObjects Enterprise—no external security system is used. This is separate from any existing network or server security you may already have in place. Enterprise authentication is discussed earlier in this chapter.

- **Windows NT authentication** Existing Windows Server local or domain groups can be used to populate your BOE security model. Members of these groups are automatically granted access to BOE, and users supply their existing network credentials to log on to BOE.

- **Windows Active Directory** If you've set up Active Directory (AD) security with a Windows Server environment, you can use AD groups and users to authenticate BOE users. AD members are automatically granted access to BOE, and users supply their existing network credentials to log on to BOE.

- **LDAP** If your organization's security model is based on the open LDAP (Lightweight Directory Access Protocol), you can integrate users maintained by your existing LDAP server into BOE. LDAP members are automatically granted access to BOE, and users supply their existing network credentials to log on to BOE.

NOTE *You are not limited to choosing just one authentication method. You may use more than one method (or all four methods) to build your total complement of BOE users and groups.*

Windows NT

In some BusinessObjects Enterprise environments, it may be easiest to use the same users and groups that are already defined in your Windows Server environment (assuming Active Directory has not been implemented). BOE supports this by "mapping" those users and groups into the Enterprise security system. There are two basic methods for this: add the desired NT users or groups into the BusinessObjects NT Users group inside of Windows NT, or map the desired NT groups into BOE from within the CMC.

CAUTION *The initial release of BusinessObjects Enterprise XI 3.0 is only available on Java application servers, such as the bundled version of Apache Tomcat. In a Java environment, Windows NT Authentication is not supported. Therefore, this option (and this portion of the book) will only apply if a .NET version of BOE is released later in the product cycle.*

By default, when you install BusinessObjects Enterprise onto a Windows computer, a local NT group called BusinessObjects NT Users is created. To map NT users in the BusinessObjects NT Users group, run the Windows NT User Manager (or other similar tool, depending on your operating system). Select the BusinessObjects NT Users group. Click Properties, then Add, and then select the users and/or groups to be added. Click OK to add the selected users and groups, and then click OK to complete the process. Once the new

accounts are added, the users can log on with the user name format of *NTDomain*\
NTUserName and their standard NT password. They'll need to ensure they select the Windows
NT authentication method when they log on.

To map existing NT groups into the BOE system, click Authentication in the Manage
category of the CMC home page. You may also click the Authentication tab on the left side
of the CMC, or choose Authentication from the navigation drop-down list at the top of the
CMC. The list of available authentication types will appear. Double-click the Windows NT
entry to display the Windows NT authentication screen. Confirm that NT Authentication Is
Enabled is checked. Add the Default NT Domain shown to allow users to simply supply their
user ID and password without full machine name/domain qualification if they're in the
default domain. If you need to change the default domain, click it and specify a new default
domain when prompted.

Enter the path to the NT group you wish to add in the Add NT Group text box. For global
groups, use the format *NTDomain**NTGroup*. For local groups, use the format *Machine*\
Group. Click Add to add that group. Enter as many NT groups as desired to the list box in
this manner. If you later wish to delete an existing domain, select it in the list of existing
domains and click Delete.

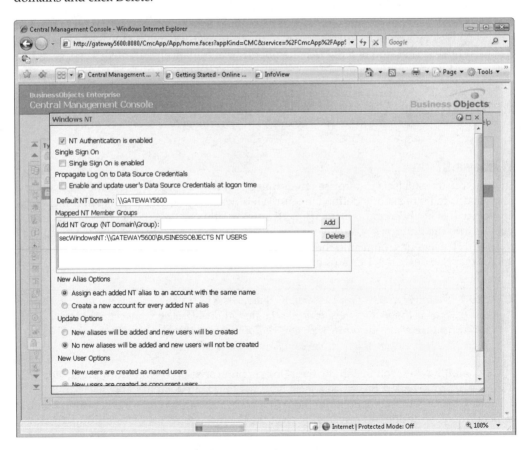

Select various radio button options for dealing with New Alias, Update, and New User options:

- **New Alias Options**   If you choose the first option, BOE will assign an "alias" to any existing BOE accounts that have the same name as an account being imported from the security server. If an imported account does not duplicate an existing account, a new account will be created. If you choose the second option, new accounts will be created even if an existing account with the same name already exists. In the case of duplicate account names, a sequential number will be added to the new account name to distinguish it from the existing account.

- **Update Options**   If you choose the first option, BOE will create a new account (or assign an alias based on your choice in New Alias Options) for every account contained in the groups being imported. This may create a large number of users if the imported groups contain large numbers of users. If you choose the second option, users in the imported groups will be created in BOE once they log on to BOE for the first time. If they never log on, their account will never actually be created in BOE.

- **New User Options**   When new user accounts are created from imported groups, this choice determines which license type they use by default. Note that you must have enough licenses of the chosen type for all users that will be created by the import. If you don't, not all user accounts will be created. If you later decide you want to change the license type for certain imported users, you may select the individual users from the Users link and change their license type.

Once you've made all desired choices, click Update to complete the process. If you chose to immediately create users and groups from the imported groups, you can now navigate to user and group lists to see the newly added users and groups.

Windows Active Directory

Similar to Windows NT authentication is Windows Active Directory (AD) authentication. AD authentication can connect using "native" AD protocols (NT authentication can use AD "mixed mode") to connect to existing Windows Server Active Directory security models.

To map existing AD groups into the BOE system, click Authentication in the Manage category of the CMC home page. You may also click the Authentication tab on the left side of the CMC, or choose Authentication from the navigation drop-down list at the top of the CMC. The list of available authentication types will appear. Double-click the Windows AD entry to display the Windows AD authentication screen.

Confirm that Windows Active Directory Authentication Is Enabled is checked. Click the double quotes to specify an AD administrator name and password for BOE to use when authenticating AD users and groups. Also, click the double quotes to specify a default AD domain. You won't have to fully qualify groups in this domain when adding them. And, users in that domain won't have to provide a fully qualified user ID when signing on to BOE.

Enter the path to the AD group you wish to add in the Add AD Group text box. Click Add to add that group. Enter as many AD groups as desired to the list box in this manner. If you later wish to delete an existing group, select it in the list of existing groups and click Delete.

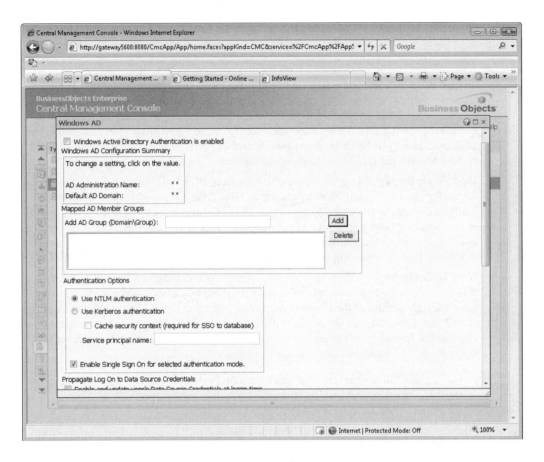

Select various radio button options for dealing with New Alias, Update, and New User options:

- **New Alias Options** If you choose the first option, BOE will assign an "alias" to any existing BOE accounts that have the same name as an account being imported from the security server. If an imported account does not duplicate an existing account, a new account will be created. If you choose the second option, new accounts will be created even if an existing account with the same name already exists. In the case of duplicate account names, a sequential number will be added to the new account name to distinguish it from the existing account.

- **Update Options** If you choose the first option, BOE will create a new account (or assign an alias based on your choice in New Alias Options) for every account contained in the groups being imported. This may create a large number of users if the imported groups contain large numbers of users. If you choose the second option, users in the imported groups will be created in BOE once they log on to BOE for the first time. If they never log on, their account will never actually be created in BOE.

- **New User Options**   When new user accounts are created from imported groups, this choice determines which license type they use by default. Note that you must have enough licenses of the chosen type for all users that will be created by the import. If you don't, not all user accounts will be created. If you later decide you want to change the license type for certain imported users, you may select the individual users from the Users link and change their license type.

Once you've made all desired choices, click Update to complete the process. If you chose to immediately create users and groups from the imported groups, you can now navigate to user and group lists to see the newly added users and groups.

CAUTION *The initial release of BusinessObjects Enterprise XI 3.0 is available only on Java application servers, such as the bundled version of Apache Tomcat. In a Java environment, Windows AD Authentication with NTLM is not supported. You must use AD Kerberos Authentication. NTLM authentication will apply only if a .NET version of BOE is released later in the product cycle. Steps to configuration AD Authentication with a Java application server, as well as discussions on enabling single sign-on in this environment, are discussed in the BusinessObjects Enterprise Administrator's Guide. This guide is available with the initial installation of BOE, as well as being available for download from the Business Objects web site.*

LDAP

Another authentication method supported by BusinessObjects Enterprise is via Lightweight Directory Access Protocol, or LDAP. LDAP users and groups maintained in your organization's LDAP server are mapped to BOE, with LDAP user accounts being used either to create a new BOE account or to map to an existing BOE account.

The first step in enabling LDAP authentication is to be sure your LDAP directory is set up and operating properly. Then, click Authentication in the Manage category of the CMC home page. You may also click the Authentication tab on the left side of the CMC, or choose Authentication from the navigation drop-down list at the top of the CMC. The list of available authentication types will appear. Double-click the LDAP entry to display the LDAP authentication screen. If you have not previously set up LDAP authentication, a message indicating such will appear with a button to start the LDAP Configuration Wizard. Click the button.

The wizard will proceed through various screens asking for specific information relating to your particular LDAP server. These screens allow you to supply the hostname (or hostnames, if you want to add failover LDAP servers), the server type, the base LDAP distinguished name, the ID and password the CMS should use when querying the server, the type of secure connection to use, and the same BOE account and licensing options specified when using NT or AD authentication. Details on LDAP server settings can be found in the online Administrator's Guide, and details on the BOE account and licensing options are described in the previous NT and AD authentication sections.

Once you've successfully specified all wizard options, click Finished. The wizard will gather necessary information from your LDAP server and display the LDAP summary page in the LDAP tab. Now, you can specify existing LDAP groups to map to BOE. Enter the name of the LDAP group you wish to add in the Add LDAP Group text box. Click Add to add that group. Enter as many groups as desired to the list box in this manner. If you later wish to delete an existing group, select it in the list of existing groups and click Delete.

Once you've made all desired choices, click Update to complete the process. If you chose to immediately create users and groups from the imported groups, you can now navigate to user and group lists to see the newly added users and groups.

Managing Folders, Crystal Reports, and Third-Party Objects

The BusinessObjects Enterprise environment uses the tried-and-true hierarchical folder method of organization similar to Windows and other operating systems. Reports and other BOE objects may be placed in these folders to organize the objects into logical groups and simplify navigation for the users. Also, the folder structure can be set up to intelligently apply rights settings using folder inheritance to ease security maintenance. While some sample folders and objects are installed as part of BOE, you'll certainly want to add your own folders and objects, as well as potentially remove the sample folders and objects that are installed with BOE.

Generally speaking, when you are building a new BOE system structure, you'll create a set of folders and subfolders logically organized to ease navigation by your report viewers. Once a basic set of folders is created, you can then add Crystal Reports and third-party objects (such as Word documents, Acrobat files, PowerPoint presentations, and so forth) to the existing folders. If you initially create a minimal folder structure and add a large number of objects, you'll find it tedious to later add additional folders or rearrange existing folders, and then be required to move the existing objects to new locations. As such, it's a good idea to plan your overall folder structure before you add a large number of objects to BOE. Not only can a folder/subfolder hierarchy make it easy for report viewers to navigate the BOE system, but it may ease security settings by administrators. Security rights (discussed later in the chapter) can be set at the folder and subfolder level.

NOTE *This section discusses how to add, delete, and move folders and objects in the CMC. Complete folder and object management (with the exception of adding Program objects) can also be accomplished in InfoView, as discussed in Chapter 21.*

BusinessObjects Enterprise contains two main types of folders: *public folders* that are available to various users and groups of users in BOE (subject to rights that are set for the folders), and *personal folders* that are visible only to each individual user (as well as Administrators). While public folders can be created, manipulated, and deleted by system administrators (as well as regular BOE users, provided they have a Create Folder right assigned), a personal folder is created only when a new user is added to BOE. This folder cannot be moved or deleted, although subfolders can be created within it. When a user account is deleted, the matching personal folder is deleted as well.

Managing Public Folders and Subfolders

 To create, move, and delete public folders, click Folders under the Organize area of the CMC. You may also click the Folders tab in the left portion of the CMC, or choose Folders from the navigation drop-down list at the top of the CMC. The Folders and Objects list will appear with two entries in the Tree Panel on the left: Objects List and All Folders (All Folders will be selected by default). Folder manipulation can take place when the All Folders Tree Panel entry is selected or expanded.

When you select or expand the All Folders entry in the Tree Panel, you will see a set of BOE top-level folders. A *top-level folder* is a folder that will initially appear directly in the Public Folders section of InfoView when a BOE user views the Document list. You'll generally want to create top-level folders that broadly organize your Crystal Reports and objects, such as folders relating to your organizational departments or functional structure.

If a top-level folder appears next to a plus sign, it contains one or more subfolders. A *subfolder* is a folder within another folder. Subfolders can be created either directly within a top-level folder, or within another subfolder.

NOTE *Object packages, which consist of a set of related Crystal Reports or program objects, can also appear within a folder or a subfolder. An object package will be indicated by an "open box with paper" icon.*

Expand or contract folders/
subfolders with plus/minus signs

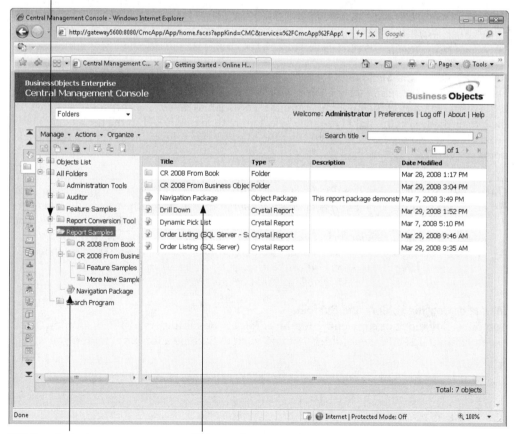

Object packages are
designated with open-box icons

List area shows contents
of selected folder/subfolder

Creating New Folders and Subfolders

To create a new top-level folder, select the All Folders entry in the Tree Panel. Then, click the Folder toolbar button above the Tree Panel, or choose New | Folder from the Manage drop-down button. You may also right-click the All Folders entry and choose Manage | New | Folder from the pop-up menu. The Folder Name dialog box will appear. Type in the folder name, ensuring the name is not already assigned to an existing top-level folder. Click OK to create the new folder. The Tree Panel will refresh with the new top-level folder appearing in alphabetical order within other top-level folders.

To create a new subfolder, you must first select the folder under which the new subfolder will be created (you may select the existing folder in either the Tree Panel or object list). Then, click the same New Folder option on the toolbar, from the drop-down Manage button, or from the Manage right-click pop-up menu. Again, a New Folder dialog box will appear. Type in the name for the subfolder and click OK to create it. You may create subfolders as many levels deep as you prefer.

NOTE *If a user does not have the rights to a particular folder or object, that folder or object is not displayed as the user browses the BOE system. Once folders and objects have been added, you may need to adjust rights to determine who can and cannot perform various actions on the folder or object. Assigning folder and object rights is discussed later in the chapter, under "Controlling Access Using Rights."*

Deleting Folders and Subfolders

Deleting a folder or subfolder is a fairly simple process. Make sure the Folders and Objects list is displayed. Select the folder or subfolder you wish to delete in either the Tree Panel on the left, or the list on the right (you may select more than one folder in the list by CTRL- or SHIFT-clicking). Choose Delete from either the Manage drop-down button or the right-click pop-up menu.

CAUTION *Deleting a folder or subfolder will delete the folder, all subfolders, and all the objects and instances contained within it. As this action cannot be undone, make sure you really want to delete a folder before you do so. If you are in charge of administering your BOE system, you may want to undertake a regular backup procedure to archive both the Central Management Server database and the File Repository Server data stores (more information on these server components can be found later in the chapter, under "BusinessObjects Enterprise Architecture" and "Managing Servers"). You may be able to restore critical objects from this backup, if necessary.*

Moving or Copying Folders and Subfolders

You can easily move or copy entire top-level folders or subfolders to a new location. For example, if you created a subfolder that you wish to become a top-level folder, you may move it. Or, if you created a top-level folder that you wish to copy to another folder as a subfolder, you may also do this. You may also choose a public folder or subfolder and move or copy it as a subfolder within a user's personal folder (personal folders are discussed next).

Make sure the Folders and Objects list is displayed. Select the folder or subfolder you wish to move or copy in either the Tree Panel on the left or the list on the right (you may select more than one folder in the list by CTRL- or SHIFT-clicking). You may choose either Copy or Move from the drop-down toolbar button, the drop-down Organize button, or the Organize right-click pop-up menu. The Select Destinations screen will appear, showing both the Personal Folder and Public Folders hierarchy. To move or copy the just-selected folder as a top-level folder, click the Public Folders entry under the Title list and click the right-arrow button to add Public Folders to the Destinations box. To move or copy the just-selected folder as a subfolder, select the upper-level folder you want to place it in from either the folder hierarchy or under the Title list. Then, click the right-arrow button to add the folder to the Destinations box. If you are copying a folder, you may select more than one folder to add to the Destinations box with the right-arrow button.

When you have selected the destination folder or folders, click Move or Copy to move or copy the folder. The Folders and Objects list will redraw, showing the new folder structure in the Tree Panel.

Managing Personal Subfolders

As discussed earlier, a personal folder is created for each BOE user when their account is created (the folder appears as My Favorites in InfoView). Although you cannot create or delete personal folders in the CMC, you can create subfolders within personal folders. You can also copy and move other folders (both personal and public) as subfolders to personal folders, as well as copying personal folders or subfolders to other locations.

To manage personal folders, click Personal Folders under the Organize area of the CMC. You may also click the Personal Folders tab in the left portion of the CMC, or choose Personal Folders from the navigation drop-down list at the top of the CMC. The Personal Folders list will appear with the Personal Folders entry appearing in the Tree Panel, and all personal folders appearing in the list. You may expand the Personal Folders entry in the Tree Panel to see all personal folders, as well as any subfolders already existing within them (plus signs next to personal folders will indicate that they contain subfolders).

To create a subfolder within a personal folder, select the desired personal folder in either the Tree Panel or the list. Then, click the Folder toolbar button above the Tree Panel, or choose New | Folder from the Manage drop-down button. You may also right-click the personal folder and choose Manage | New | Folder from the pop-up menu. The Folder Name dialog box will appear. Type in the subfolder name, ensuring the name is not already assigned to an existing subfolder. Click OK to create the subfolder. The Tree Panel will refresh showing the new subfolder within the personal folder.

You may create subfolders as many levels deep as you wish within personal folders. Also, you may use the same techniques described earlier, under "Managing Public Folders and Subfolders," to delete, move, or copy personal folders and subfolders. While you can copy a personal folder or subfolder to another location, you cannot move or delete the personal folder itself—it will only be deleted when the matching BOE user account is removed.

NOTE *When moving or copying folders among the Public and Personal folders area, already-assigned rights may or may not go along with the folder. Generally speaking, when moving folders, rights assigned to the folder will move with the folder. However, when copying folders, the new folders will take on the inherited rights of their parent folders, not the rights they had before they were copied.*

Adding Reports

One of the main reasons BusinessObjects Enterprise exists, of course, is to manage reports. Therefore, one of the most common and important tasks is to add reports to the system. There are several ways to accomplish this task: with InfoView (covered in Chapter 21), with the CMC, directly from Crystal Reports 2008, and by using the Publishing Wizard.

Adding Reports with the CMC

You may add new reports to BOE one at a time via the CMC. Reports are added in the Folders and Objects list, where public folders are also managed. Display this list by clicking Folders under the Organize area of the CMC. You may also click the Folders tab in the left portion of the CMC, or choose Folders from the navigation drop-down list at the top of the CMC. The Folders and Objects list will appear with two entries in the Tree Panel on the left: Objects List and All Folders (All Folders will be selected by default).

Although existing reports will appear under the Objects List entry in the Tree Panel, you must select a folder within the All Folders category before you can add a new report (the exception to this rule is if you want to add a report to an existing object package that appears within the object list—in that case select the desired object package first). Expand the All Folders category and select the folder where you want to add the new report (you can't add reports to a folder selected in the list to the right). Then, choose Add | Crystal Reports from the Manage drop-down button, or right-click the folder in the Tree Panel and choose Manage | Add | Crystal Reports from the pop-up menu. The Crystal Reports screen will appear.

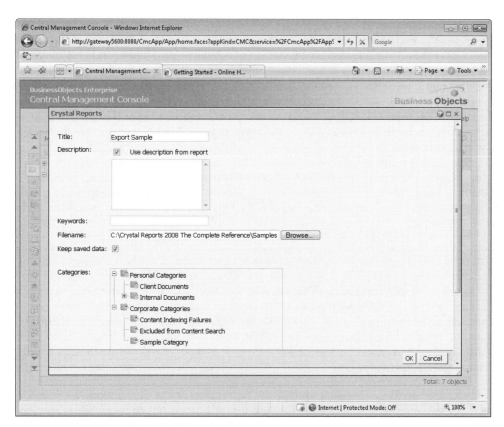

Specify the file path and name of the document you wish to upload to BusinessObjects Enterprise in the Filename field. If you prefer, you may click Browse to launch a standard File Open dialog box. Locate the desired file in this dialog box and click Open. The full path and filename will be filled in the Filename field for you. The Title field will be filled with either the report filename (without the .RPT extension) or the value supplied in the report's Summary Info dialog box. If the report also contains a description from Summary Info, you may automatically import it by checking Use Description From Report. If you wish to type a description in manually, uncheck Use Description From Report and type the description in. You may also type descriptive keywords (keywords can be helpful when conducting document searches). If the report contains saved data, you may retain it on BOE by checking Keep Saved Data. This will allow the report to be viewed without immediately requiring a database refresh (it will also potentially show older report data). Optionally, you may also assign one or more categories to the report in BOE. Expand entries in the categories list and highlight desired categories (you may highlight as many categories as you'd like). Categories are discussed later in this chapter.

Once you've made the desired choices, click OK. The report will be uploaded to BusinessObjects Enterprise (be patient—this may take some time, depending on the size of the file). The Folders and Objects list will reappear with the new report appearing within the selected folder (you can also now expand the Objects List entry in the Tree Panel and find the report).

CAUTION *Don't forget that adding a report to BOE copies the .RPT file from the source location to the Input File Repository Server (server architecture is discussed later in the chapter, under "BusinessObjects Enterprise Architecture"). Any changes you make to the original report in its source location will not be reflected in BOE. If you wish to change an already-published report, you must open the report through the Enterprise Folders option of Crystal Reports 2008. Alternatively, you may change the report in its source location, delete the original report from BOE, and post the updated report. Note that if you delete and repost a report, all report instances will be deleted along with the original report.*

If you later decide you wish to change the report title, report description, keywords, or category assignments, you may redisplay the report's properties to make these changes. Select the report in the right-hand list when the report's folder is selected, or in the Objects list. Double-click the report, click the Manage Object Properties toolbar button, choose Properties from the drop-down Manage button, or right-click the report and choose Properties from the Manage pop-up menu. The report's properties screen will appear, where you can change the title, description, keywords, and category assignments. Other options appearing on the left side of the screen, such as Default Settings, Schedule, History, and so forth, are used to control other BOE behavior with the report (these other functions are discussed in other relevant areas of this chapter).

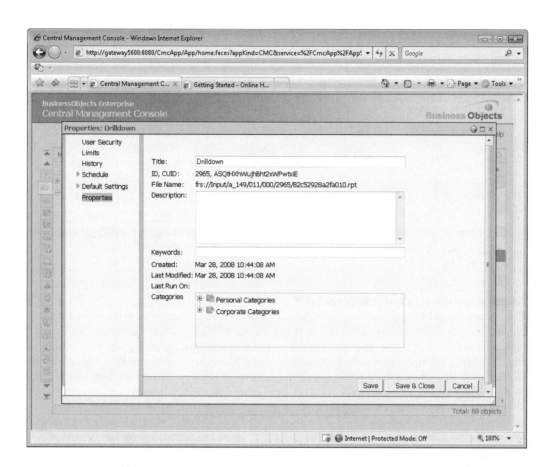

Deleting, Copying, and Moving Reports and Other Objects

Once you've added new Crystal Reports or third-party objects, you may find a need to move or copy them around the BOE folder structure. Or, if an object is no longer needed, you may wish to delete it, as well as its associated scheduled instances. Steps for deleting, copying, and moving objects are virtually identical to those for managing folders.

First, select the desired object in either the Folder list or the Object list in the Folders and Objects list. Then, use the Manage or Organize toolbar, drop-down button, or right-click pop-up menu options to delete, copy, or move the object. If you copy or move an object, the Select Destination dialog box will appear, where you may choose the destination folder where you want the object moved or copied (more than one folder may be added if you are copying an object). The difference between copying and moving an object is based on whether the object remains in its original location and whether instances are moved to the new location. If you move an object, it will not remain in the original location, and any related instances will be placed in the new location along with the object. Copying an object will leave it intact in its original location with no instances copied to the new location.

CAUTION *Deleting objects is a permanent operation—there is no Undo capability. Make sure you really want to delete an object and its instances before you undertake these steps.*

Adding Reports from Crystal Reports 2008

The ability to add Crystal Reports within the CMS is handy, especially if the report was created in an earlier version of Crystal Reports (earlier versions of Crystal Reports will not connect to version XI 3.0 as described in the rest of this section). However, adding reports in the CMC does require that you have already created the report in Crystal Reports and saved the .RPT file to a known location. You may prefer to add reports directly to BusinessObjects Enterprise XI 3.0 from Crystal Reports 2008, providing a more direct path from report design to posting.

First, ensure you have updated your copy of Crystal Reports 2008 to Service Pack 0 or greater, as the initial release of Crystal Reports 2008 didn't provide Enterprise connectivity. Then open an existing report or design a new report using techniques described in Part I of this book. When you are ready to save the report to BOE XI 3.0, choose File | Save As from the pull-down menus, as though you were going to save the report with a new filename on your local drive. However, note the Enterprise and My Connections icons in the left of the Save As dialog box. These are the keys to Enterprise XI 3.0 connectivity.

The Enterprise option will simply prompt you to log on to Enterprise. Supply the proper user ID and password (and, if necessary, specify your Enterprise CMS server name and authentication type, as provided by your BOE administrator). If you regularly connect to a standard BOE system in your organization, you may predefine the connection by using the My Connections icon. You may create this definition, as well as connect to the defined system, by clicking the My Connections icon.

Once you've connected to the BOE system, the Save As dialog box will show the Enterprise folder structure. Simply select the folder or subfolder you wish to save the report to and type the desired object name in the File Name text box (you can remove the .RPT extension). If the report contains objects from the BOE repository (covered in Chapter 17) and you wish the report to look for updated repository objects when it is "refreshed" in BOE, check the appropriate check box. Click Save to upload the report to the chosen BOE folder.

NOTE *Remember that when you save a report directly to the BOE system from Crystal Reports, you may have to still use the CMC later to set additional information (default database logon information, default parameters, rights, and so forth) required for the report.*

Adding Reports with the Publishing Wizard

The Publishing Wizard is a stand-alone Windows application designed with one purpose in mind: to publish reports and third-party objects (such as Word documents, PDF files, and so forth) into a BusinessObjects Enterprise system en masse. It works in standard "wizard fashion," taking you from one dialog to the next, showing only those dialogs that are necessary to complete the task at hand. It is most useful when you are adding multiple reports and objects to the system, including objects from multiple folders. In fact, you can even preserve the folder structure from the original source location when you publish objects with the Publishing Wizard. Another benefit of the wizard is that it prompts for much of the "extra" information for a report, such as parameter fields and database logon and scheduling information.

Because the wizard is a stand-alone Windows application, you must specifically install it from the BOE program CD if you want to run it on a computer that doesn't already contain a full BOE installation. You will then launch the wizard directly from the appropriate program group in the Start menu. Once you've started the wizard, simply follow the instructions from screen to screen. There are many steps, and some portions and steps are optional.

Here are some of the more common steps used in publishing reports and objects once you've started the Publishing Wizard.

1. Click Next to proceed past the welcome screen.

2. Log on to BOE with an appropriate account that has publish rights. Click Next.

3. Click the appropriate button to add files or a folder. The Add Files button allows you to add one or more individual files (.RPT, .DOC, .PDF, and so forth). The Add

Folder button will add all files in a folder on a disk drive (optionally including files in subfolders below the chosen folder).

4. If you click Add Files, a file dialog box will appear. Choose one or more files to add (you may CTRL-click or SHIFT-click to choose multiple files). If you wish to change the type of file shown in the dialog (instead of .RPT, perhaps you would like to choose .PDF), make your choice from the Files Of Type drop-down list. Files you choose will appear in the file list once you close the file dialog. You may click the Add Files button as many times as necessary to add additional sets of files to the list.

5. If you click Add Folder, a folder dialog will appear where you may choose a specific folder. If you would like to publish files in subfolders below the chosen folder, check Include Subfolders. And, you may also choose the type of file you'd like to publish (.RPT, .PDF, .DOC, and so forth) from the drop-down list. You may click the Add Folder button more than once if you wish to add additional folders.

6. Once you've clicked the Add Files and/or Add Folders buttons as necessary, a complete list of files that are ready to be published will appear. Delete excess files you don't want to publish by selecting them individually or CTRL-clicking or SHIFT-clicking to select multiple files. Then, click Remove Files.

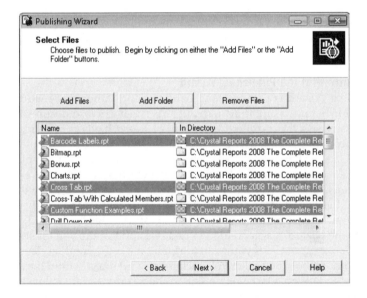

7. Once you've chosen the right set of files you want to publish, click Next. The Publishing Wizard will read the various files to obtain information it needs to continue. It will then present the Folder Hierarchy screen, indicating the set of folders contained in BOE.

8. Select the BOE folder where the objects are to be added (select the BOE server name to add the reports to the root folder or to begin your folder creation at the root folder). You may create new folders directly in this dialog box if so desired. You may also create an object package by clicking the appropriate icon. Once you've chosen the desired destination folder, click Next.

9. If the reports you added from your local drive were stored in more than one directory, you'll be asked if you wish to preserve the folder hierarchy on BOE. If you wish to preserve the folder names that the original source files come from, select Duplicate Folder Hierarchy. The same folder structure will be created on BOE within the folder you selected when files are published. If you select Put Files in the Same Location, all the files chosen in the previous step will be published in the same BOE folder. Click Next.

10. The Location Preview screen shows you where the objects you are publishing will appear within the BOE server. If you chose to preserve the original source folder hierarchy, you'll see the source folder names here, with objects contained in them. You may use this screen to move objects into other folders, create additional folders, and so forth. You may select an object and use the up and down arrows to move it, or you may simply drag the object and drop it "into" the desired folder. The Show File Names/Show Titles button will toggle between displaying source filenames and the title that will appear once the objects are published to BOE. When satisfied with the location of your published files, click Next.

NOTE   *You will only be able to delete folders and object packages that you have previously added with the wizard (these will be denoted with a green folder icon). You won't be able to delete any folders that existed on the CMS before you started the wizard.*

11. The Specify Categories screen will now appear. This optional step lets you assign one or more categories to each report you are publishing. The File drop-down list will contain all reports that will be published—select the report you wish to categorize in this list. Then, choose the category you want to place the report in and click the plus sign (Insert File) button to add the selected report to the category. You may remove a report from a category by selecting the report in the category list and clicking the X delete button. And, you can create either new corporate or personal categories and subcategories by selecting the desired location for the new category and clicking the New Category button (categories are discussed in more detail later in the chapter). If you don't wish to assign categories, or you have made your category selections, click Next.

12. The Specify Schedule screen will now appear, provided you are publishing at least one Crystal Reports .RPT file. Select one or more reports that you wish to set scheduling options for. You have the option to specify limited scheduling options for the reports. Let Users Update The Object will simply publish the report object with no scheduling options. Run Once Only will create a single instance of each new report. Run On A Recurring Schedule will allow additional limited scheduling options to be chosen. Make these choices by clicking the Set Recurrence button and choosing options from the resulting dialog. Once you've made desired choices, click Next.

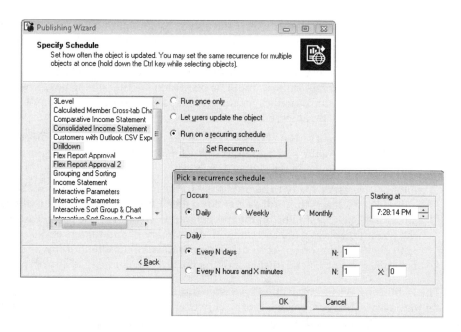

13. The Specify Repository Refresh screen will appear, provided you've published at least one report. Choose reports from the list that contain BOE repository objects that you'd like refreshed. Then, check Use Object Repository When Refreshing Report. You may also select the option for all or no reports by clicking the Enable All or Disable All button respectively. Click Next.

14. The Specify Keep Saved Data screen will appear, provided you've published at least one report. Choose reports from the list that have saved data that you'd like retained in BOE (BOE XI 3.0 now will view a report's saved data if it exists, not requiring a database refresh). Then, check Keep Saved Data When Publishing Report. You may also select the option for all or no reports by clicking the Enable All or Disable All button respectively. Click Next.

15. The Change Default Values screen gives you the choice to modify additional items for any reports that you may be publishing. If you choose to Publish Without Modifying Properties, you won't have the chance to specify the report title, comments, parameter values, database logons, and so forth, for selected reports. You'll proceed immediately to Step 20. If you do want to edit these items, choose Review Or Modify Properties. Click Next.

16. The Review Object Properties screen allows you to alter the title and description of each report. To edit the values, select a report from the list box on the left and change the information in the text boxes on the right. Click Next.

17. The Specify Database Credentials screen allows you to alter the database logon information for each report. To change the information, select a report in the list box, click the plus sign to the left of the report to expose database connections, select a database from that report, and then change the logon information. Continue for each report and database before moving on. Click Next.

18. The Set Report Parameters screen allows you to alter parameter field information for each report that contains at least one parameter field. In this dialog, reports appear in the left list box. When you select a report, the individual report parameters are listed in the right list box. To edit the parameter information, select a parameter and click the Edit Prompt button. You'll be presented another dialog box, where you may supply a value or values for the chosen parameter field. Once you've specified all parameter field values, click Next.

19. The Specify Format screen allows you to set the output format for scheduled instances of each report. Again, select a report in the left list box and set that report's format with the drop-down on the right. Click Next.

20. Finally, objects are ready to be published to BusinessObjects Enterprise. You'll see a final list of objects that will be copied to the BOE server and added to the folder structure. Click Next to begin the publishing process. After the objects are added, the wizard displays a final screen with a summary of add folders and objects. You may click a folder or object to display an indication of whether it was properly published or not. Click Finish to exit the wizard and complete the process.

The Publishing Wizard may initially seem tedious when compared to quick publishing capabilities of the CMC or Crystal Reports. However, using the wizard can be considerably more efficient if you are adding multiple objects to the system, especially if reports share similar characteristics or you wish to maintain the folder structure when publishing.

Adding Program Objects

A *program object* is an executable program (for example, a program with a .COM, .EXE, .BAT, or similar file extension) that can be run from a command line, a Java program, or a file containing executable script, such as VBScript or JScript. This feature allows you to schedule executable programs and scripts on a regular basis the same way you schedule reports on a regular basis. This feature greatly expands the flexibility of BusinessObjects Enterprise beyond just a report scheduling tool, allowing you to schedule such tasks as data warehouse updates, server or database maintenance tasks, or other regularly required processing tasks.

When you schedule a program object to run, the Input File Repository Server transfers the files that make up the program object to the Program Job Server, which actually runs the program object in a shell process. The Program Job Server captures the error and output streams from the process and passes them on to the Output File Repository Server to store as a program instance (server architecture is discussed in detail later in the chapter). Therefore, you can actually view instances for program objects much as you would for a report. However, what will be shown when you view the program instance is the output and error streams from the particular execution of the program object.

NOTE *When initially installed, BOE is only set to allow Java program object execution. If you wish to schedule other types of program objects, they will initially fail. To enable program object execution for all program object types, set Program Object Rights for the CMC after choosing the Applications option from the Manage area of the CMC main menu, from the Applications tab on the left side of the CMC, or after choosing Applications from the navigation drop-down list at the top of the CMC.*

Steps for adding program objects in the CMC are virtually the same as those for adding Crystal Reports (refer to "Adding Reports with the CMC" earlier in the chapter for details). However, instead of choosing Crystal Reports from the Add option, choose Program File. The Program File dialog box will appear.

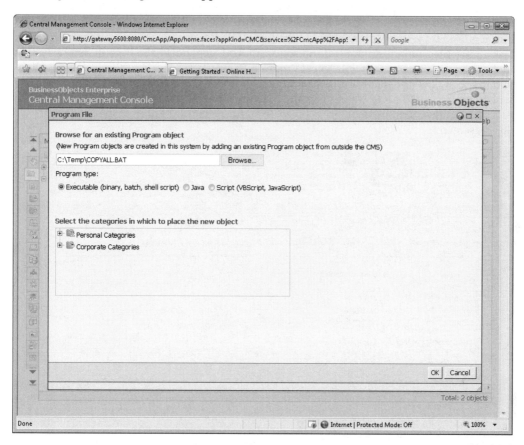

If you know the full pathname/filename of the program object (.BAT file, .EXE file, VBScript, Java program, and so forth) that you want to add, type the full pathname/filename into the text box. You can also click the Browse button to search for the file via a file dialog box. Choose the type of object you are adding by selecting the desired radio button. Click OK to copy the object to the Input File Repository Server.

The Folders and Objects list will reappear with the program object appearing within the selected folder (you can also now expand the Objects List entry in the Tree Panel and find the program object). As with a Crystal Report, the program object is copied to the BOE server from its original location—any changes you make to the original program object won't be reflected in BOE unless you re-post the program object after changes are made.

If you later decide you wish to change the program object properties, such as title, program object description, keywords, or category assignments, you may redisplay the program object's properties to make these changes. Use the same techniques as described earlier to locate the program object in the Folders and Objects list and view its Properties screen.

The new program object's properties page will appear. Make any desired changes to the object's title, description, keywords, or category assignments. Two unique sets of options for program objects can be set here as well: Associated Files, and Program Parameters. By clicking Associated Files in the program object screen, you will be able to copy additional files required by your program object to the Input File Repository Server (perhaps dynamic link library files, initialization files, and so forth). And, expanding the Default Settings entry in the program object screen will reveal Program Parameters. Clicking this option will allow you to specify default values for items unique to scheduled program objects, as opposed to scheduled Crystal Reports. Values you specify in this screen will appear as defaults when you eventually schedule the program object from the Schedule section of the program objects screen.

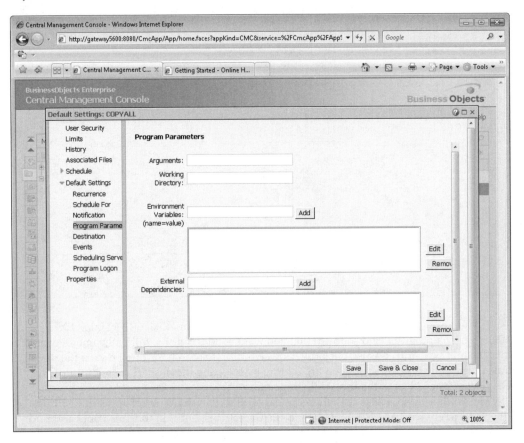

NOTE   *There are many fine points to providing specific information to various program objects, such as environment variables, supplementary files, and such. Get complete information on these finer program object points by viewing CMC online help or the BOE Administrator's Guide.*

Adding Third-Party Objects and Hyperlinks

While you may primarily be interested in BusinessObjects Enterprise's Crystal Reports capabilities, other types of documents can be added to a desired folder. In addition to program objects (discussed earlier in the chapter), you can add common office-type documents, including Acrobat PDF files, Microsoft Word documents, Excel spreadsheet files, Microsoft PowerPoint documents, Rich Text files, and standard text files, as well as hyperlinks to other web pages. These additional object types, sometimes referred to as *third-party objects,* can be added to a folder, where they will be available for viewing by anyone using BOE (provided they have rights to the object).

Initial steps to add a third-party object or hyperlink are virtually the same as those for adding Crystal Reports (refer to "Adding Reports with the CMC" earlier in the chapter for details). However, to add a third-party object, instead of choosing Crystal Reports from the Add option, choose Local Document. If you are adding a hyperlink, choose New | Hyperlink from the Manage toolbar or drop-down buttons, or the Manage right-click pop-up menu. Either the Hyperlink or Local Document dialog box will appear.

For a hyperlink, you may type in a title, optional description, and optional keywords. If you so desire, you may also assign the hyperlink to one or more categories. Then, type in the address of the desired web site in the URL box. For third-party documents, if you know the full pathname/filename of the document that you want to add, type the full pathname/ filename into the Filename text box. You can also click the Browse button to search for the file via a file dialog box. Choose the type of object you are adding by choices from the File Type drop-down list. Then, expand the General Properties area by clicking the small arrow. You may type in a title, an optional description, and optional keywords. If you so desire, you may also assign the document to one or more categories. Click OK to copy the object or add the hyperlink to the BOE. Remember that any documents you add to BOE will be copied to the Input File Repository Server (server architecture is discussed later in the chapter). As such, any changes you make to the original document you copied won't be reflected on BOE. If you change the original document, you'll need to re-post it using these same steps.

The Folders and Objects list will reappear with the hyperlink or third-party object appearing within the selected folder (you can also now expand the Objects List entry in the Tree Panel and find it). If you later decide you wish to change the hyperlink or document's properties, such as title, description, keywords, category assignments, or the hyperlink URL, you may redisplay the object's properties to make these changes. Use the same techniques as described earlier to locate the object in the Folders and Objects list and view its Properties screen.

NOTE *In essence, viewing a third-party object from BOE is identical to viewing or downloading a similar document from a web page. You should ensure that your user community has appropriate client software (such as Microsoft Office or Acrobat Reader) installed on their computers for the types of third-party objects you add to BOE.*

Working with Categories

The Categories feature provides an additional method for organizing reports and other objects in customized ways. In essence, you can use Categories to create an unlimited number of "virtual" folder structures. While an object added to BOE in the CMC must be assigned a folder, category assignment is completely optional. You may choose to categorize some, but not all, objects. And, while an object can only be assigned to a single folder or subfolder, multiple categories can be assigned to a single object.

There are two types of categories: Corporate Categories and Personal Categories. Corporate Categories are created by system administrators, while Personal Categories (as the name might suggest) are created by individual users (administrators can also manipulate personal categories). Administrators can use Corporate Categories to provide alternate groupings or create easier browsing for their entire audience of users. And as with folders, administrators can set rights for Corporate Categories to restrict access. Individual users can use Personal Categories to create their own custom organization of reports and other objects, perhaps to assemble and group the set of reports that are specific to their particular job function. Personal Categories can only be accessed by that specific user.

Why Categories? An Example

You may be thinking "Why would I need to use Categories if I already have Folders?" That's a good question, and sometimes the answer may be "You don't need to use Categories." However, consider the following example.

A company decided to create their BusinessObjects Enterprise folder structure to mimic their organization. Sales reports went in a Sales folder, HR reports went in an HR folder, etc. Some of the departments have a few subfolders, while others have an entire hierarchy of subfolders under the main folder. Wisely, this folder structure was created in conjunction with appropriate groups to simplify the application of security rights.

For many users (such as the Director of West Coast Sales), the folder structure works just fine for browsing reports and accessing other documents. The reports that are relevant to their job function are found in the same folder or at least the same section of the hierarchy. However, there are some users (such as the Chief Operating Officer) that need to access reports from many different folders in the hierarchy. Because the reports are so spread out (especially in a system with a large hierarchy and/or a large number of reports), browsing to them is tedious and time-consuming.

> To help alleviate this issue (especially for the COO), the BOE administrator created a Corporate Category called "Executive Reports." Shortcuts to reports from various locations in the folder structure were placed in the category. Now, the executive staff can go to a single location and find all of the reports they typically need to view. Those reports are still stored in their original folder locations, and they are still governed by the security rights assigned using those folders, but the executive staff can get to them with a minimum of clicking and in a lot less time.
>
> The Director of Web Coast Sales likes to start each morning by taking stock of a piece of the business, and viewing a series of reports is a great way to do that. Various sales reports are viewed, of course, but the Director also likes to see an inventory status report, a manufacturing status report, and several financial reports. So the Director created a Personal Category called "Daily Morning Reports" and put shortcuts to all of those reports in the category. Now the Director can go to a single place for all the reports, making the morning routine easier and less error-prone.

Manipulating Categories

As an administrator, you can create both Corporate Categories and Personal Categories, and the process for each is nearly identical. One difference is that you can create new top-level Corporate Categories, but you cannot create new top-level Personal Categories. Top-level Personal Categories are automatically created by the system for each user when that user is created (and all other Personal Categories are created as subcategories of that top-level category).

While categories are an alternative to folders for organizing BOE, the concepts are similar: multiple top-level categories can be created, as can subcategories that reside in top-level categories. And, creating, editing, moving, and deleting categories is also very similar to the corresponding operations on their folder counterparts. As with folders, there are two separate screens in the CMC to work with categories: a Corporate Categories screen and a Personal Categories screen. Each is available with the commensurate CMC main menu option, tabs at the left of the CMC, and navigation drop-down list at the top of the CMC.

As with folders, the corporate or personal category hierarchy will appear in the Tree Panel at the left, with the resulting set of subcategories or objects assigned to the category appearing in the list to the right. You may use similar menu options as with folder manipulation to create, edit, move, and delete categories. Note that you cannot copy a category, only move it. Also, you cannot move a personal category to a corporate category or vice versa.

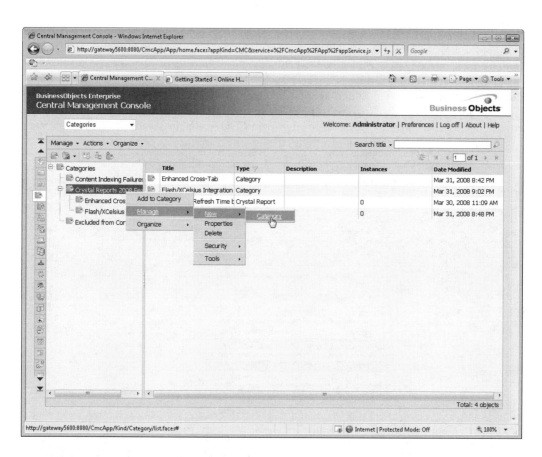

Assigning Categories to Reports and Other Objects

There are two ways to assign reports and other objects to categories: 1) assign categories to reports and objects when you add them to BOE, or after you add them by displaying their properties screen, or 2) assign objects to a category from the Corporate Categories or Personal Categories screens.

Assigning categories to objects when you add them to BOE, or after you add them with their properties screens, has been discussed and illustrated earlier in the chapter. However, the alternative approach to assigning objects to categories, using the Corporate or Personal Category screen, bears explanation. Display either category screen with CMC main menu options, tabs, or navigation pull-down list choices. Then, select the category you wish to assign objects to in either the Tree Panel on the left or the list on the right (categories will be denoted with an "expanded folder" icon). Click the Add To Category toolbar button, choose Add To Category from the Actions drop-down button, or right-click the desired category and choose Add To Category from the pop-up menu. The Available Objects screen will appear.

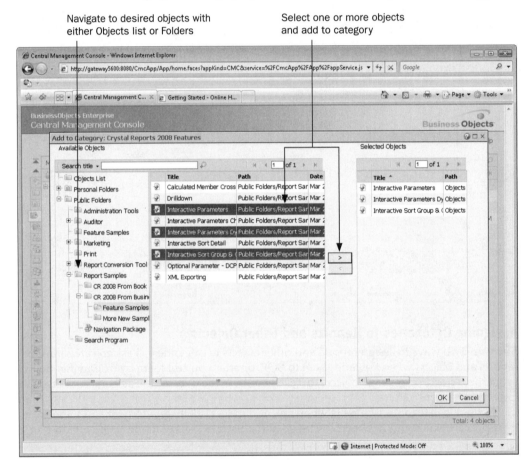

Using the Objects list, Personal Folders, or Public Folders options in the Tree Panel, find the object or objects you want to assign to the just-selected category. You may select some objects from one area of the Tree Panel, add them to the Selected Objects list, and then navigate to another area via the Tree Panel and select more objects. You may CTRL-click or SHIFT-click to select multiple objects before clicking the right-arrow button to add them to the Selected Objects list. When all objects have been added, click OK to assign them to the category.

The Corporate or Personal Categories screen will reappear, with the objects that were assigned to the category now appearing in the right side of the category list when the appropriate category is selected in the Tree Panel. If you wish to remove objects from an already-assigned category, select one or more objects in the right-side object list. Then, choose Remove from Category from the Actions drop-down button, or from the right-click pop-up menu. The selected objects will be unassigned from the category.

CAUTION *When selecting a category to view its encompassed objects, take care if you want to remove an object from a category. Ensure you select the Remove From Category option and not the Delete option from the menu. Even if you are viewing an object in Category view, Delete will delete it from BOE, which may very well not be the desired action.*

Controlling Access Using Rights

The BusinessObjects Enterprise security model includes a series of rights that control a user's access to the various BOE objects such as folders and reports. For example, a user may be able to view a report and schedule it to run at a particular time, but may not be able to refresh the data or delete report instances. As another example, you may imagine a BOE system where company executives have access to all folders, the sales team has access only to the Sales and Inventory folders, and the head of the Human Resources department is the only non-executive with access to the Salary and Compensation Reports folder.

NOTE *This chapter discusses rights from a report and folder perspective. Separate rights exist for objects in the BusinessObjects Enterprise repository, as well as for the BOE Business Views feature. Repository details can be found in Chapter 18. Business Views are covered in detail in an extra chapter available for download from the book's companion web site, CrystalBook.com.*

Before you undertake an extensive examination of all the ways that BOE security can affect users, groups, folders, objects, and administration, it's helpful to understand some fundamental terms and concepts with BusinessObjects Enterprise XI 3.0 security:

- **Rights are assigned to objects, not users**   You select folders, subfolders, categories, subcategories, and objects within these folders and categories and then assign rights to these items based on users or groups. You do not initially select users and groups and assign a list of folders, categories, and objects that the user or group has access to. This concept may be further confused by the ability to assign security in the Users and Groups list. However, rights assigned in the Users and Groups list apply to delegating administrative tasks, not assigning rights to folders, categories, and objects.

- **Rights can be assigned by group, or individual user**   In either case, a group or user is termed a *principal* in BusinessObjects Enterprise XI 3.0. You may select a folder, category, object, and so forth, and "Add Principal" to choose a user or group to assign rights relating to the object.

- **There is a relationship among three high-level permissions**   As a general rule, one of three permissions may be assigned to individual rights in BOE: Explicitly Granted, Explicitly Denied, or Not Specified. If a permission is explicitly granted, then the right is allowed. If the permission is explicitly denied, then the right is not allowed. If the permission is not specified, then the right is not allowed. However, when more than one set of permissions are assigned to a resource by combined user/group membership, or by folder/subfolder or category/subcategory inheritance, a set of combined rights/permissions results. In this case, if a permission is not specified in one area but explicitly granted in another, the right is allowed. However, if a permission is explicitly granted in one area and explicitly denied in another, the right is not allowed (deny takes precedence over grant).

- **Rights generally "trickle down" the user/group or folder/category hierarchy**   One of the major benefits of BOE user and group structure (users are members of one or more groups, and groups can be subgroups of other groups), and of the folder/ subfolder or category/subcategory hierarchy, is the concept of *rights inheritance*. As a general rule, rights assigned to a group apply to users within the group. Rights assigned to a top-level folder or category apply to subfolders/subcategories within the top-level folder/category. And, objects within a folder/subfolder or category/ subcategory hierarchy inherit rights assigned to the upper level. As with most everything in BOE security, there are exceptions (inheritance can be turned off, and rights explicitly assigned to lower-level objects that countermand upper-level object rights take precedence). However, by minimizing exceptions, you can create a fairly robust security model that's easy to maintain by applying security only to upper-level objects and letting inheritance take care of what falls below.

- **The "trickle down" rights approach can cause trouble**   The just-described inheritance method can cause potential difficulty when attempting to granulate your security model. For example, if you have a certain set of top-level folders you want only the Marketing department to see, not the HR department; and another set of folders for the HR department that Marketing shouldn't see, you may be tempted to grant a view right for each department to its respective folders, while not specifying any rights to either department at the CMS root level. This is flawed, as rights inheritance will prevent either group from seeing anything, since both top-level folders are contained within the CMS root level. This is because of a basic BOE inheritance premise: if a group or user doesn't have view rights to an upper-level resource, they won't be able to see any objects within that resource even if the objects within the resource have more liberal rights set. Instead, you'll need to grant both departments View rights to the CMS root level, and then explicitly deny rights to top-level folders you don't want the departments to see. This issue requires you to make a certain number of adjustments to the Everyone group at the *CMS root-folder level* (CMS stands for Central Management Server, the core server component in BOE) to allow access to your BOE folder structure.

- **You can take advantage of new BOE XI 3.0 Access Levels**   With the large number of individual rights that can be given grant/deny/not specified permissions, it will be very difficult to manage security on even a small BOE security model if you must assign individual rights to each group, folder, and so forth (even if inheritance is taken into account). So, BOE combines a set of related rights together into *access levels*. While previous versions of BOE included five predefined access levels that you could not modify, version XI 3.0 includes these predefined levels and allows you to add your own access levels. Now, you may choose a custom set of rights and permissions and assign them to a user-specified access level. You may then specify the access level when assigning rights. You may create as many custom access levels as you need.

And, when you modify the rights set in an access level, all objects with that access level assignment will immediately behave according to the new rights.

NOTE *After looking through various security options in the CMC, you may conclude that "BusinessObjects Enterprise security is very flexible, and also very confusing." It will be difficult to argue with this conclusion. While an exhaustive discussion of every BOE security permutation and option is beyond the scope of this Crystal Reports book, several resources provide more information. In addition to CMC online help, the BusinessObjects Enterprise Administrators Guide includes detailed explanations of various security models and permutations. Even with the resources available to you, you are best advised to thoroughly test your security model by logging on to InfoView with a variety of user IDs that will be affected by security. Ensure that you experience no unintended consequences (a fairly common occurrence even with mildly sophisticated security models). If necessary, open two browser tabs or windows with the CMC visible in one and InfoView visible in the other. Make modifications to your security model in the CMC and then log off and log on to InfoView with your test user ID to check the ramifications of your changes.*

Setting Folder and Object Rights

BusinessObjects Enterprise rights can be set at two high levels within BOE: at the very top of all public folders (this level is sometimes known as the CMS root folder), and at the folder/ subfolder/object level. You don't have to set rights at either level; you may set rights at one level or the other, or at both levels. Just remember the rules of inheritance: top-level folder rights are inherited from the CMS root folder, subfolder rights are inherited from top-level folders, and report object rights are inherited from the folders or subfolders in which they reside.

Setting Root Folder Rights

When you initially install BusinessObjects Enterprise, a set of group-level rights are already applied for the Everyone and Administrators groups at the highest (sometimes referred to as "Root Folder") level. These rights can be inherited throughout the rest of the folder and object levels within the CMS. You will probably need to make at least a basic set of changes to these rights, as users not in the Administrators group will probably be unable to see any top-level folders in BOE with the default installation settings applied (as discussed at the beginning of this section, testing with various user IDs is the best way to ensure a correct security model).

Setting rights for the root folder (and, all other folders and objects, for that matter), is conducted in the Folders and Objects list. Display this list by choosing Folders from the CMC main menu, clicking the Folders tab in the left part of the screen, or choosing Folders from the navigation drop-down list at the top of the CMC.

To set root folder rights, you may take two general approaches in this list. You may select the All Folders entry in the Tree Panel on the left of the Folders and Objects list and set User Security or All Folders Security. Or, you can select any other folder in the list and set All Folders Security. If you've selected the All Folders Tree Panel entry, choose Security | User Security or Security | All Folders Security from the Manage drop-down button. You can also click the User Security toolbar button above the Tree Panel, as well as right-clicking the All Folders entry and choosing Manage | Security | User Security from the pop-up menu. If you've selected any other folder, you can only use the Manage drop-down button Security

| All Folders Security option (toolbar button and right-click pop-up menu options will only allow you to set rights for the selected folder, not the root-level folder).

The User Security screen will appear for the root folder, as illustrated in Figure 22-1. You'll notice the Administrators and Everyone user groups that are placed at the root folder by default, both indicating Advanced rights.

The initial security screen for the Root folder will show the two default groups, Everyone and Administrators, assigned rights to the folder by BOE. You'll notice that Advanced Access is set for the two groups by default—this indicates that a predefined set of rights, or an *access level*, has not been set for the root folder. Four buttons appear at the top of the dialog: Add Principals, which will let you add additional users or groups (known as *principals* in BOE security) for assigning rights; Remove, which will remove an existing principal and associated set of rights from the folder (note that you can remove Administrators or Everyone from the root folder); View Security, which will show the set of rights assigned to the selected principal; and Assign Security, which will let you modify rights for the selected principal.

You'll need to assign security for the Everyone group. Ensure this group is selected, and click the Assign Security button. The Assign Security screen will appear, as illustrated in Figure 22-2.

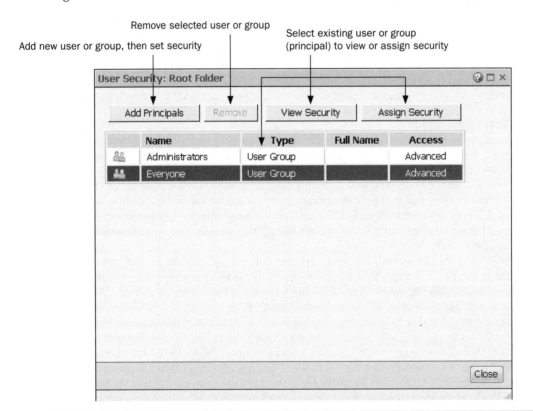

FIGURE 22-1 Root Folder security screen

Enable or disable inheritance

Set advanced rights

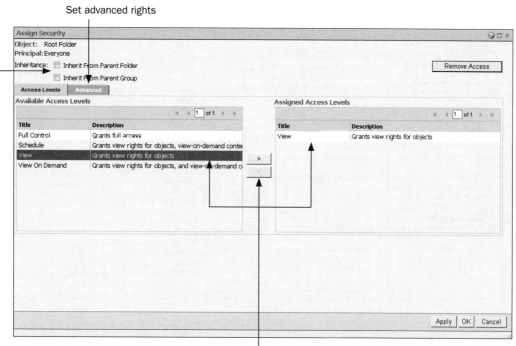

Assign or remove predefined or custom access levels

FIGURE 22-2   Assign Security screen

The initial Assign Security screen shows available access levels (both the default levels that come with BOE and any custom levels you have created). As a general rule, it's easier to use and maintain access levels instead of setting individual rights. If one of the access levels is adequate, select it and add it to the Assigned Access Level list with the right-arrow button. You may add more than one access level, with the resulting rights being combined (for example, if one access level provides an unspecified permission for a right, while another access level provides an explicitly granted permission, the right will be granted). You may remove any existing access levels by selecting them in the Assigned Access Levels list and clicking the left-arrow button. You may also specify inheritance rules for both folders and user groups with check boxes at the top of the screen (folder inheritance doesn't apply at the root folder level, but group inheritance may).

If the rights granted by an access level aren't sufficient, you may set advanced rights. Click the Advanced tab to replace the Access Level view with the Advanced view. If any existing advanced rights are set, they will be displayed in the view. To add or remove specific rights, click the Add/Remove Rights link above the list. The Add/Remove Rights screen will appear, showing a large selection of available rights that permit selecting the previously discussed Granted, Denied, and Not Specified permissions.

Add/Remove Rights

Object: Root Folder
Principal: Everyone
▼General
  General
▼Content
  Adobe Acrobat
  Agnostic
  Crystal Report
  Desktop Intelligence Report
  Desktop Intelligence Report Addin
  Desktop Intelligence Template
  Flash
  Folder
  Hyperlink
  Microsoft Excel
  Microsoft PowerPoint
  Microsoft Word
  My InfoView
  Note
  Object Package
  Program
  Publication
  Rich Text
  Shortcut
  Text
  Voyager Workspace
  Web Intelligence Report
  Xcelsius

▼General Global Rights General	Implicit Value	Granted	Denied	Not Specified	Apply to Object	Apply to Sub Object
Add objects to folders that the user owns	Not Specified	○	○	◉	☑	☑
Add objects to the folder	Not Specified	○	○	◉	☑	☑
Copy objects that the user owns to another folder	Not Specified	○	○	◉	☑	☑
Copy objects to another folder	Not Specified	○	○	◉	☑	☑
Define server groups to process jobs	Not Specified	○	○	◉	☑	☑
Define server groups to process jobs for objects that the user owns	Not Specified	○	○	◉	☑	☑
Delete instances	Not Specified	○	○	◉	☑	☑
Delete instances that the user owns	Not Specified	○	○	◉	☑	☑
Delete objects	Not Specified	○	◉	○	☑	☐
Delete objects that the user owns	Not Specified	○	○	◉	☑	☑
Edit objects	Not Specified	○	○	◉	☑	☑
Edit objects that the user owns	Not Specified	○	○	◉	☑	☑
Modify the rights users have to objects	Not Specified	○	○	◉	☑	☑

Apply   OK   Cancel

The sets of individual rights are categorized on the left side of the Add/Remove Rights screen. Click either the General section, or an appropriate Content section (in particular, content options for Crystal Reports third-party document types will be appropriate) to see the rights that are available for that section. Select appropriate granted, denied, or not specified permissions for the desired right. When you have finished specifying individual rights, click OK to save the rights and return to the Assign Security screen. Click OK to save your new advanced settings. The User Security screen will reappear, indicating that Advanced access is specified. Close the User Security screen.

Setting Folder, Category, and Object Rights

After you've set initial root folder rights, the most important aspect of setting up your BOE system is assigning rights to various folders, categories, and objects. This is the key to displaying only desired folders for certain users and groups; allowing only certain reports to be viewed or scheduled; preventing unauthorized deletion of folders, objects, and instances; and so forth. The process for setting rights for folders, subfolders, categories, subcategories, and objects is similar to setting rights for the root-level folder: select the desired object in either the Folders and Objects list or the Categories list. Then, click the Manage User Security toolbar button, choose Security | User Security from the Manage drop-down button, or right-click and choose Security | User Security from the Manage pop-up menu.

The same User Security screen demonstrated in Figure 22-1 will appear, where you may add or remove principals to assign rights to. Then, select the desired principal and click the Assign Security button to display the Assign Security screen illustrated in Figure 22-2. Steps for assigning access levels or advanced rights are the same as described previously. However, your rights settings will only apply to the folder, subfolder, category, subcategory, or object you selected before setting rights.

> **TIP** *As you assign rights, keep inheritance concepts in mind. By maximizing inheritance, you can specify rights at a few top-level folders and not have to worry about subfolders or objects within them.*

Setting Access Rights for CMC Functions

As the CMC is a web-based administration interface, you may be concerned that any user who discovers the CMC URL can suddenly administer the entire BOE system. Or, perhaps you wish to *delegate administration*, whereby certain key users in IT or user departments are given a subset of full administrative capabilities that apply only to their users/groups or folders/subfolders. Both these situations can be accommodated by setting access rights for various CMC functions and capabilities. With these rights properly assigned, even if unauthorized users discover the CMC URL, few, if any, options will appear on the CMC main menu when they log in. Those users that have been granted rights will see a limited set of menu options that apply to them. And, when users choose a CMC function, only authorized users, groups, folders, subfolders, and objects will be available to them.

Setting rights for different CMC functions is similar to setting rights for folders and objects, as discussed previously. For example, to limit who is able to work with user and group assignment, you would select the Users And Groups entry in the CMC main menu, with the appropriate tab on the left side of the CMC, or with the Users And Groups entry in the navigation drop-down list. When the Users and Groups list appears, choose options from the Manage | Security drop-down button. By adding principles and setting rights, you can control who is able to maintain users and groups, and which users and groups they are able to maintain. Similar options exist on all pertinent portions of the CMC.

> **TIP** *As with setting folder and object rights, you'll want to test your CMC security settings with appropriate user IDs to ensure that only those users authorized to change CMC settings can do so.*

Defining Custom Access Levels

Previous versions of BusinessObjects Enterprise included a set of default access levels (an *access level* is a set of predetermined rights that can be assigned as a group). While these default access levels were applicable in many situations, you were unable to modify them, nor could you create your own access levels. As such, if you needed to "tweak" an access level in previous versions, setting advanced rights was your own choice. BOE XI 3.0 introduces the ability to create custom access levels. Now, you can copy one of the default access levels to your own custom level and tweak to your heart's content (you can also create a new custom access level from scratch without copying). The newly created custom access level can then be used throughout the CMC to assign rights.

 To manage access levels, click the Access Levels entry in the Define category of the CMC main menu. You may also click the Access Levels tab on the left of the CMC, or choose Access Levels from the navigation drop-down list at the top of the CMC. The Access Levels screen will appear.

The four default access levels installed with BOE (Full Control, Schedule, View, and View On Demand) will appear in the list, along with any custom levels that have been created. If this is your first time working with access levels, probably the best place to start is examining the rights that are assigned by the four default levels. To see properties for an

PART II

existing access level, double-click the desired access level, select the desired level and click the Manage Object Properties toolbar button, or select the desired level and choose the Properties option from the Manage drop-down button. The Properties screen for the access level will appear. You may modify the title and description for the level if you choose (you can modify titles and descriptions for the default access levels, but you can't change their rights). To see rights for the selected level, click the Included Rights link in the left side of the Properties screen (you can also navigate directly to the included rights by selecting the desired access level and clicking the Included Rights option from the Actions drop-down button).

To create your own access level, you can either copy an existing access level (most probably the preferred method), or create a new access level from scratch. To copy an existing access level, select the level that you wish to copy and choose Copy from the Organize drop-down button. The level will be copied to the Access Levels list with a sequential number added on to the original name of the level you copied. You may create a new level by clicking the Create a New Access Level toolbar button, or choosing New | Create Access Level from the Manage drop-down button.

If you create a new level, specify a name for the access level and add optional comments. Once you click OK, you'll then be able to click the Included Rights link at the left of the screen to see rights, as well as add and remove rights. If you copied a level, double-click the copied level to change the name or comments. You may also click the Included Rights link on the left of the screen to see rights, as well as add and remove rights. Clicking Add/Remove Rights will display the Included Rights screen.

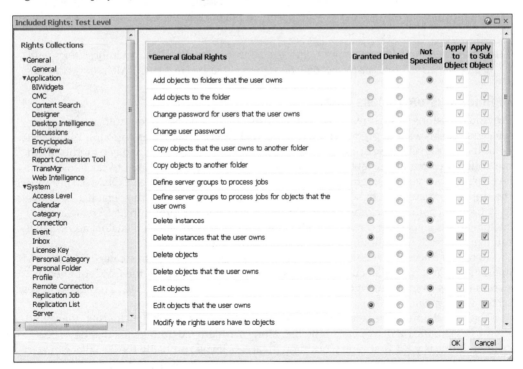

This screen will allow the complete granular setting of rights. Click entries on the left side of the screen to see various rights that apply to general BOE operation, as well as to specific document types stored in your BOE system. Then, choose the desired Granted, Denied, or Not Specified permission for each right. When finished, click OK to save the new set of rights to the access level. The Included Rights screen will reappear, showing the new set of selected rights. Click Close to save the access level. You may now use the custom access level when assigning rights to other parts of BOE.

NOTE *Be careful when modifying access levels. Security settings on the Manage drop-down button and right-click pop-up menus will not change the access level rights. Instead, these options determine who can and cannot create or modify the access levels themselves, as described earlier under "Setting Access Rights for CMC Functions."*

BusinessObjects Enterprise Architecture

While administrative and maintenance tasks described up to this point require little knowledge of core BusinessObjects Enterprise architecture, many more detailed administrative and troubleshooting requirements will benefit from a more detailed understanding of BOE architecture. Various tasks, such as server management, output destination configuration, and troubleshooting, depend on a certain level of architectural knowledge.

BusinessObjects Enterprise's multitier architecture lends itself to a much more flexible, higher-capacity system for web reporting. It also lends itself to more complexity when it comes to initial setup, operation, and administration. This increased complexity comes, in large part, from the increased number of components that make up the server portion (or "back end") of the system. While a BOE end user simply sees web pages that allow scheduling and viewing of reports, there are many separate software server components working together to provide this capability to the user. These various individual software components that make up BOE share its overall processing requirements, passing information among themselves as required.

Administrators of previous BOE family members, such as Crystal Reports Server XI and the BusinessObjects Edge XI series, will see moderate changes in the XI 3.0 family (namely, simplified server structure and an entirely new look and feel to both end-user and administrative web components). However, if you are in charge of administering BOE and this is your first experience with its multiserver environment, there is much to learn about how all these different software server components work together and pass information back and forth.

Probably the most obvious architectural change in the BOE XI 3.0 series, when compared to previous versions, is the core software structure at the operating system level. While previous BusinessObjects Enterprise versions consisted of many "back end" servers, each acting as an individual Windows NT "service," the BOE XI 3.0 family consolidates all these previous NT service components into a single NT service called the Server Intelligence Agent (SIA for short). *Server Intelligence,* the new BOE XI 3.0 approach to consolidated server management, consolidates all "internal" BOE software servers into a single external service (the SIA) visible to the operating system. You can see the SIA by displaying the Windows Control Panel Services applet from the Administrative Tools folder. You can also launch BOE's own Central Configuration Manager (the CCM for short) from the appropriate program group to see and manage the SIA (the BOE-related web/application server will also be visible in the CCM).

Part of the benefit of Server Intelligence is a more consolidated way to configure, manage, and troubleshoot the various software server components that make up BOE. In previous versions, the CCM displayed all software servers and was one of two possible administration points. In XI 3.0, you will perform virtually all configuration, troubleshooting, and maintenance in the web-based Central Management Console (or CMC for short).

While the single "physical" SIA simplifies the core server component at the operating system level, there are still many "logical" software servers that work with the SIA to carry out the different tasks that BOE performs. These logical servers are managed within the CMC. Click the Servers main menu item or the Servers tab on the left of the CMC, or choose Servers from the navigation drop-down list. The Servers list will appear.

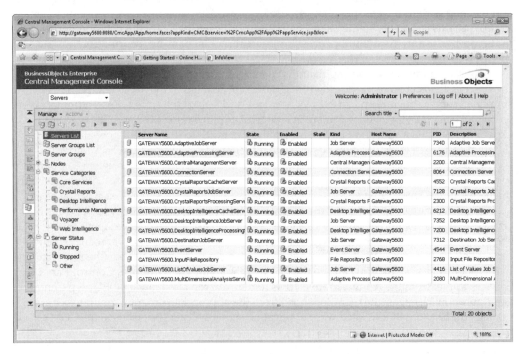

You may click different categories in the Tree Panel on the left of the Servers list to see subsets of all BOE servers. For example, to see just servers that pertain to Crystal Reports processing, select the Crystal Reports entry within the Service Categories entry. All servers can be displayed by clicking the main Servers List entry at the top of the Tree Panel. If the number of servers won't appear within a single list page, click page navigation buttons at the upper right-hand corner of the Servers list to see more servers.

NOTE *Not all servers in the Servers list will necessarily apply to the member of the BusinessObjects Enterprise XI 3.0 family that you are using. For example, if you are using a Crystal Reports–only solution, servers related to non–Crystal Reports document types may not be visible or enabled.*

Central Management Server (CMS)

The Central Management Server, or *CMS*, is the heart of BusinessObjects Enterprise. Every other component communicates through the CMS (the CMS acts as a name server, keeping track of the locations and statuses of the other server components). The CMS also acts as the central security point for BusinessObjects Enterprise logon—all user IDs, passwords, and rights lists are maintained on the CMS. And, the CMS also keeps track of report scheduling. If a report is scheduled to automatically run every day at midnight, the CMS sets the report processing cycle in motion at the prescribed time.

Because the CMS is so critical to the operation of BusinessObjects Enterprise (the entire system is completely "dead in the water" without it), certain full editions of BOE provide for fault tolerance and increased processing capacity with *CMS clustering*. With CMS clustering, multiple physical computers can run as CMS servers. Sharing a common system database hosted on a standard server platform, such as Microsoft SQL Server or Oracle, all CMS machines appear as one *logical* CMS to the entire BusinessObjects Enterprise system. They share the processing load, sending processing requests to the least-busy machine in the cluster. If one machine should fail, the remaining CMS machines pick up the load and continue to operate—the end user will not even know that one of the CMS machines has failed.

File Repository Servers

As BusinessObjects Enterprise reporting is based on Crystal Reports, procedures for handling the Crystal .RPT files that are published, scheduled, and viewed must be established. Also, BOE program objects and third-party objects (.PDF files, .DOC and .XLS files, executables, Java programs, and script) must be managed for scheduling and viewing. This is where the file repository servers come in. These servers store .RPT files that can be viewed on demand and .RPT files that are to be scheduled on a regular basis (perhaps every night, every week, and so on), as well as the finished copies of scheduled reports—the .RPT files with saved data that can be viewed after they've successfully run. They also manage stored copies of third-party files, such as Word and Excel documents and PDF files, as well as script and program files.

There are actually two different file repository servers. The *Input File Repository Server* (or Input FRS) is where Crystal Reports .RPT files, third-party files, and executable/script files are stored after they've been published with Crystal Reports 2008, the Publishing Wizard, the Central Management Console, or the Import Wizard. In the case of Crystal Reports, these "not-yet-run" reports are known as BusinessObjects Enterprise report *objects*.

When a request is received to view a published report on demand, or when the CMS runs a scheduled report on a regular basis, the Input FRS is queried for a copy of the .RPT file to run. Also, when a shared third-party object, such as a Word document, Excel spreadsheet, or Adobe PDF file, is requested for viewing, the Input FRS provides access to the file. And, when program objects are scheduled to be executed, the object is supplied by the Input FRS.

The *Output File Repository Server* (or Output FRS) keeps all the finished .RPT files with saved data (known as *report instances*) that result from reports that are scheduled by the CMS on a regular basis. When an end user wishes to view a report instance, the other BusinessObjects Enterprise components query the CMS, which keeps track of report instances in the Output File Repository Server. The .RPT file with saved data is transferred from this server to other components for caching and HTML formatting, eventually appearing in the end user's web browser. The Output FRS also keeps track of the status of scheduled program objects, such as text files containing the output from the executable or script object that was run. These *program instances* can be viewed much the same way as report instances are.

Crystal Reports Processing Server

The Crystal Reports Processing Server (known as the Page Server in previous versions) is dedicated to two tasks: creating EPF files and running on-demand .RPT files. This first task comes into play whenever an end user requests to view a completed report. The Processing Server communicates with the Crystal Reports Cache Server and may be asked to create individual page image files (known as encapsulated page files, or EPF files) that are stored by the Cache Server and delivered to the end user one page at a time. This "page-on-demand" architecture has been a cornerstone of Crystal Reports performance for several versions. This way, if a report actually encompasses several hundred pages, only the page requested by the viewer will be sent across to the web browser.

The other task given to the Processing Server is the processing of *on-demand* reports. On-demand reports differ from reports scheduled by the CMS on a regular basis, which are handled by the Crystal Reports Job Server. While the automatic scheduling of reports is a very powerful feature of BusinessObjects Enterprise, certain reporting environments require near-instantaneous access to a current set of data. In these situations, the Processing Server is used to run reports against the database in real time whenever a user requests them. By utilizing both on-demand and scheduled reports (and by dedicating servers to each), BusinessObjects Enterprise can satisfy a broad mix of regular production reporting needs as well as on-demand ad hoc reporting needs.

Because the Processing Server may need to connect to production databases in real time to run on-demand reports, the Processing Server is one of the BusinessObjects Enterprise back-end servers that may require special configuration. For example, you'll need to ensure that all possible ODBC data sources and necessary database client software packages are installed on the computer running the SIA that the Processing Server software is part of. Also, the SIA matched to the Processing Server may need to be modified to use something other than the default NT System account in order to provide necessary network security credentials. If, for example, a file-based Microsoft Access database is contained on a network share somewhere in your network, the NT System account probably won't have rights to the shared folder where the Access database is located. You'll need to assign the SIA NT Service an alternate account that exposes the desired network share.

Crystal Reports Job Server

While the Processing Server can run on-demand reports, another server may also end up running Crystal Reports, depending on how you want the report to run. The Crystal Reports Job Server is dedicated to running reports that are scheduled by the CMS. Only reports that run on a regular basis (every day, every week, the first day of the month, and so forth) and create report instances are submitted to the Crystal Reports Job Server. When the CMS needs to schedule a report to run, it passes the request on to the Crystal Reports Job Server. The Crystal Reports Job Server obtains the .RPT file to run from the Input FRS, actually connects to the database to run the report, and sends the completed report instance (an .RPT file with saved data) to the Output FRS.

Because the Job Server may need to connect to production databases to run a report, it may require special configuration. For example, you'll need to ensure that all possible ODBC data sources and necessary database client software are installed on the computer running the SIA that the Crystal Reports Job Server software is part of. Also, the SIA matched to the Crystal Reports Job Server may need to be modified to use something other than the default NT System account in order to provide necessary network security credentials. If, for example, a file-based Microsoft Access database is contained on a network share somewhere in your network, the NT System account probably won't have rights to the shared folder where the Access database is located. You'll need to assign the SIA NT Service an alternate account that exposes the desired network share.

NOTE *Another server you'll see in the server list is the Report Application Server (or RAS for short). While still available in BOE XI 3.0, the RAS is only used by custom applications that call core BOE services. This server is designed not only to run reports on demand when needed, but to handle report design tasks that are undertaken in custom applications. For example, the RAS ReportClientDocument object model can be used with a custom Visual Studio .NET or Java application to allow report design tasks to be carried out within custom code. However, the RAS is not used for any out-of-the-box Crystal Reports functions in the CMC or InfoView.*

Program Job Server

BusinessObjects Enterprise has the ability to schedule program objects, as well as report objects, on a regular basis (every day, the first day of the week, once a month, and so on). Program objects (consisting of executable programs, Java programs, and JScript or VBScript code) allow you to run maintenance tasks, data warehouse imports, or anything else that can be custom-coded, within the BusinessObjects Enterprise environment.

The Program Job Server is responsible for running program objects that are scheduled by the CMS. Much as with the Crystal Reports Job Server, the Program Job Server intercepts requests for program object schedules from the CMS. It then queries the Input FRS for the necessary program object files, runs the program object, and sends the standard and error output from the program object to the Output FRS, where it is stored as a program instance.

Destination Job Server

The Destination Job Server is used when objects are sent to certain destinations when scheduled in BusinessObjects Enterprise. It does not actually run reports but rather simply manages the sending of the report objects or instances. Users may send existing reports and report instances to other users via e-mail, to other users' Inboxes, to an FTP server, or to a file location on an accessible drive.

Crystal Reports Cache Server

As discussed earlier in the chapter, one of the benefits of BusinessObjects Enterprise (and of several versions of Crystal Reports before it) is the page-on-demand architecture. This approach to delivering report pages to the end user's web browser significantly improves performance, especially with larger reports that comprise many pages. The page-on-demand process will deliver only the page of a report that a viewer currently needs to see. When a report is first viewed, only page 1 is delivered to the viewer. If, for example, the viewer then clicks an entry in the group tree that requires page 210 of the report to be delivered, only page 210 is sent to the browser—pages 2 through 209 are ignored.

As discussed previously, part of this page-on-demand process is the creation of EPFs, which is handled by the Crystal Reports Processing Server. The other very important part of this process, however, is storing already-viewed EPFs for later reuse (known as "caching"). This process is handled by the Crystal Reports Cache Server. The Cache Server keeps track of pages that may have already been viewed (and that are already cached). When a page is requested from the Cache Server, the Cache Server checks to see if the page already exists in its cache. If the Cache Server can find an already-generated EPF, it simply sends it for viewing. If the Cache Server needs the EPF to be generated (a user, for example, has asked for a report page that hasn't been viewed previously), it asks the Processing Server to generate the EPF, which it then caches and sends for viewing.

Event Server

When you schedule a report or program object to run, you may choose to base the schedule on an event. This event might be triggered by the successful completion or failure of another report or program object. Or, the event may by triggered by the creation of a certain file somewhere on your network. While the first type of event is managed entirely by the CMS, a separate server is used to manage file-based events.

The Event Server manages file-based events. When a job is scheduled on the basis of a file event, the Event Server is charged with looking on the network in a specified location for the existence of the file (the contents of the file are irrelevant—the Event Server is only concerned with whether the file exists or not). If the file exists, the Event Server notifies the CMS and the dependent job is processed.

Because of the need to navigate various folders and file structures on your network, the SIA that's tied to the Event Server may be required to use something other than the default NT System account. If, for example, a file that will be used as a trigger for a file event is contained on a network share somewhere in your network, the NT System account probably won't have rights to the shared folder where the file is located. You'll need to assign the Event Server's related SIA NT Service an alternate account that exposes the desired network share.

List of Values Job Server

One of the important features of Crystal Reports is the ability to create dynamic pick lists for the parameter value entry. BusinessObjects Enterprise also has features to support and extend this capability. Using the Business View Manager, users can now create dynamic Lists of Values, which are stored in the repository.

When a Crystal report using a dynamic List of Values from the repository is run, the pick list may be created on the fly. However, depending on the nature of the pick list, this may be a slow process, and it may also be inefficient if many different users are requesting the same pick list. The List of Values Job Server exists to schedule the creation of dynamic pick lists, which in turn eliminates the time lags and inefficiency.

Defining Output Destinations

When you schedule a report or program object to run at a later time or on a recurring basis (third-party objects cannot be scheduled), the report instance or output of the program object is saved to the Output FRS by default. When you then view the instance, the file from the Output FRS is passed on for viewing. However, you may prefer to distribute reports to alternative destinations such as an FTP server, attach them to an e-mail message in an alternate file format, or write them to a specific file location somewhere on your network. You may also prefer to have a program object's output and error streams distributed the same way. This requires you to set destination settings on either the Crystal Reports Job Server (for report instances) and the Program Job Server (for program object instances).

As these destinations are not configured when BOE is first installed, you must add the destinations and set specific parameters to configure each output destination. Begin by clicking the Servers main menu item or the Servers tab on the left of the CMC, or choose Servers from the navigation drop-down list. The Servers list will appear. Double-click either the Program Job Server (to configure destinations for program objects) or the Crystal Reports Job Server (to configure destinations for reports). The properties screen will appear for the chosen server. Click the Destinations link at the left.

Choose the desired destination in the Destination drop-down list and click Add to enable the destination. You must also configure specific settings for each destination type. Do this by selecting the destination name in the added destination list. A specific screen will appear for each destination type.

- **Email**   This destination is for automatically e-mailing instances. Options include the SMTP server information, the default e-mail field values, and file naming conventions for the attached files.

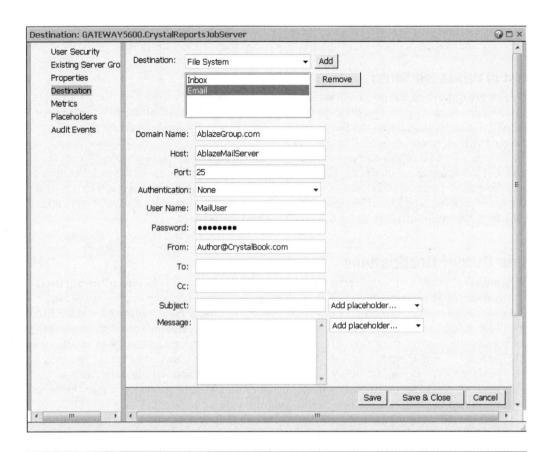

TIP *BusinessObjects Enterprise supports e-mail servers that adhere to the Internet-TCP/IP SMTP standard. If you are using a proprietary e-mail system, such as Microsoft Exchange or Novell GroupWise, you'll need to use SMTP gateway products that allow your e-mail system to send e-mails via the SMTP protocol.*

- **FTP**   This destination is for automatically sending instances to an FTP server. Options include the FTP account and logon information, the target directory, and file naming conventions.

- **Inbox** This destination is for automatically sending instances to users' Inboxes inside of BOE. Options include sending the instance as a shortcut or a copy, and the default list of recipients.

- **File System**   This destination is for saving report or program object output to hard drive files outside of the Output FRS. Options include the target directory, file naming conventions, and logon credentials for the service.

Creating Calendars

While the regular scheduling intervals provided in BOE (daily, weekly, hourly, first day of month, etc.) provide a good deal of flexibility in choosing recurring schedules, allowing reports and program objects to be scheduled according to a particular user-defined calendar expands this flexibility even further. This is handy for scheduling by your own organization's specific processing cycles, such as pay days, accounting periods, and so forth.

The first step in allowing calendar-based scheduling is to define your particular calendars to reflect your individual processing cycles. Begin this process by clicking Calendars from the Define area of the main CMC screen. You may also click the appropriate tab in the left part of the screen, or the Calendars entry from the drop-down navigation list.

The Calendars list will appear, showing any existing calendars you have already created (just column headings will appear if no calendars have yet been created). Click the Create New Calendar toolbar button or choose New | New Calendar from the Manage drop-down button to create a new calendar. The New Calendar screen will appear.

Give the calendar a meaningful name (such as Pay Days), as well as an optional description. Then, click OK to actually create the calendar definition. The Calendars list will reappear with the new calendar in it. To choose dates for the calendar, double-click the desired calendar, select the calendar and click the Manage Object Properties toolbar button, or select the calendar and choose Properties from the Manage drop-down button. Click the Select Dates link in the left side of the calendar screen.

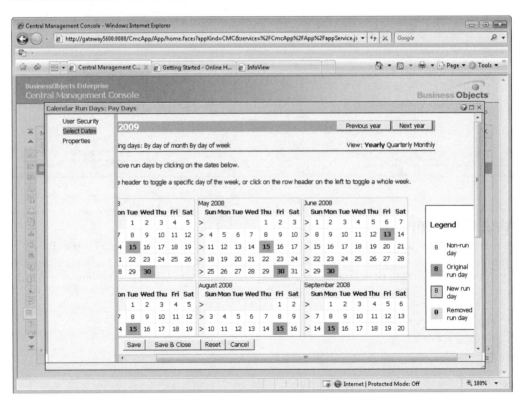

The Dates screen will initially show a yearly view of months, which can be changed by clicking the Yearly/Quarterly/Monthly View links in the upper right. Choose the desired display options, or just click one of the displayed months to set run days for that particular month. You may also specify a recurring day or month or day of week pattern by clicking the Day of Month or Day of Week "Add Recurring Days" link at the top of the screen.

Once the desired specific period (or a generic month by day of week or day of month) is displayed, simply click the days you wish objects to run. The day will be shaded in a "New Run Day" color. If you are modifying an existing calendar, you can click original run days to deselect the day from future schedules (a different color will indicate that the day has been removed). As necessary, click Next and Previous buttons to display different periods to select or deselect additional days. When finished, click the Save or Save & Close button to save the calendar to the CMS.

Once you've created your desired calendar or calendars in the CMC, you may schedule reports and program based on them. This is carried out in the Folders and Objects list in the CMC, or when scheduling in InfoView (covered in Chapter 21).

Using Events

A powerful feature of BusinessObjects Enterprise is the ability to base report and program object scheduling on events. An *event* consists of one of three different general occurrences: the existence of a file somewhere on a drive, the completion of another scheduled job (either just the completion, or specifically the success or failure of the job), or a simple "trigger" that an administrator can initiate from within the CMC. Events allow very powerful control of scheduling from within BOE. For example, you could potentially schedule a program object to execute a custom data warehouse update program, which writes data extracts to a specific file location. Reports based on the new data warehouse files will run after a specific file is detected in that location. And, given the successful completion of the reports, another program object could run a batch file that deletes the data warehouse files.

Before they can be used for scheduling, events must be defined in the Central Management Console. Begin by clicking Events in the Define area of the main CMC screen. You may also use the Events tab at the left, or choose Events from the drop-down navigation list at the top of the CMC. The Events screen will appear showing any existing events that have already been defined (just column headings will appear if no events are yet defined).

Click the Create New Event button in the toolbar, or choose New | New Event from the Manage drop-down button. The New Event screen will appear. Select the type of event you wish to create from the Type drop-down list and supply an event name (the description is optional). Depending on the type of event you select, the screen will change to allow additional specifications appropriate for the type of event.

- **File** Specify a descriptive name and optional description for the file-based event. If your BOE system includes more than one Event Server, choose the server you wish to look for the existence of the file from the Server drop-down list. Then, type the full pathname and filename of the file that the Event Server will look for to trigger the event. Remember that the filename will be used by the Event Server, not necessarily the computer you are accessing the CMC from. So, if you specify a C: drive, the file will need to reside on the chosen Event Server's C drive in order for the event to be triggered. Click OK to save the event when you're finished.

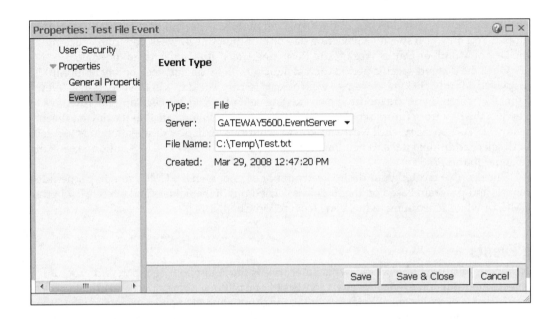

- **Custom**   Specify a descriptive name and optional description for the custom event. No other specifications are necessary. Once you click OK, the event will be saved and the screen will reappear with a Trigger This Event button displayed below the event description. Any time you wish to trigger the custom event, you need merely select the event from the CMC Events link and click the Trigger This Event button.

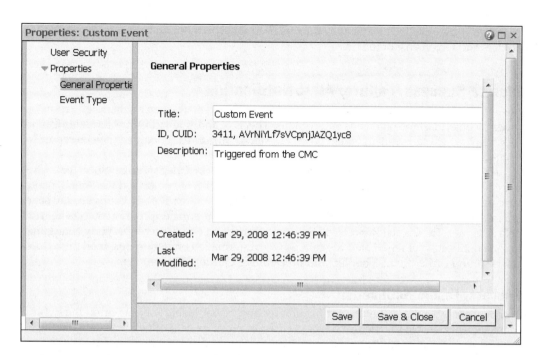

- **Schedule**   Specify a descriptive name and optional description for the scheduled event. Then, choose whether the event will be triggered only if the "source" job runs to success, fails, or simply completes in success or failure. Click OK to save the event.

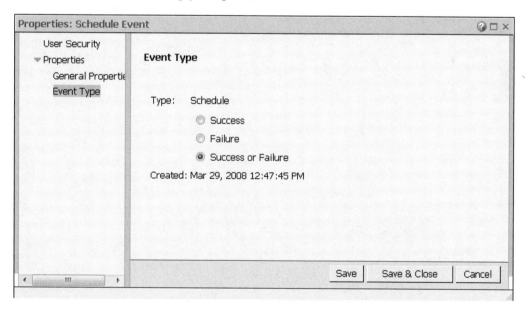

Once you've created events, they may be used for scheduling in both InfoView and the Folders and Objects list of the CMC.

Configuring Success/Failure/Alert Notification

BusinessObjects Enterprise can be configured to send an e-mail when a scheduled report or program object instance succeeds and/or fails. This is in addition to BOE's Alert Notification capability, which can send an e-mail when an Alert defined in a scheduled Crystal report is trigged.

There are one or two prerequisites for notification to work, depending on how you want to be notified of success/failures or report alerts. If you wish to be notified via e-mail, make sure the Crystal Reports Job Server and Program Job Server are properly configured to send e-mail, as they send success or failure notifications when reports or program objects are run on a schedule. The Crystal Reports Job Server must have an e-mail server properly configured to send notification of report alert triggers, as well. Information on setting up e-mail procedures can be found earlier in this chapter, under "Defining Output Destinations."

Success/Failure Notification

You may control success/failure notification for any "schedulable" object within the Central Management Console's Folders and Objects list. Once you've determined how you want to be notified, any instances for the configured object that succeed or fail may be noted via e-mail.

Begin by navigating to the object you want to set notification information for. Find the object either in the Objects list or folder hierarchy of the Folders and Objects list. Double-click the desired object. The Properties screen will appear. Expand the Default Settings category on the left side of the screen and click the Notification link. The Set Notification screen will appear.

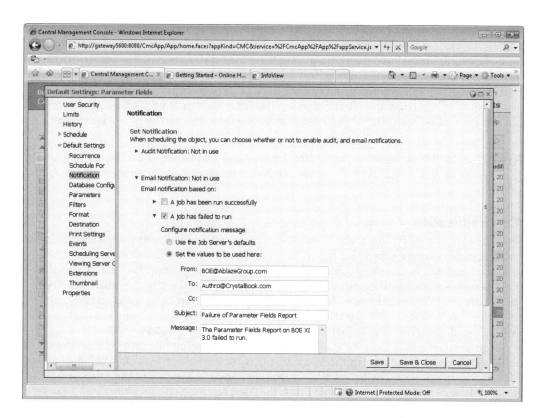

If no previous notification settings have been made for the object, both e-mail and audit notification will indicate "not in use." Click the plus signs next to Email Notification to enable it. You may then select to notify on success and/or failure.

Notifying via e-mail requires specifying more detailed e-mail information, such as from address, to address, e-mail subject, and message body. You may choose to use default settings for these values you set up when configuring the e-mail destination on the server, or specify settings individually here.

Once you've made desired settings, click Save or Save & Close to save the notification information. When you schedule the object in the future (either from the CMC or InfoView), notification will be enabled. For example, a failed job may result in an e-mail being sent.

NOTE *The Audit Notification area of the Notification screen may or may not be applicable to you, as Auditing is only available with certain members of the BusinessObjects Enterprise family based on licensing.*

Alert Notification

If you have designed reports that contain alerts, BusinessObjects Enterprise can send e-mail notification any time a scheduled report triggers the alert (creating reports with alerts is discussed in detail in Chapter 6). For example, if you've built a report that triggers an alert if a customer service representative's open call numbers exceed a predetermined level, you may notify the Customer Service Manager of the alert when the report runs on its regular schedule. Furthermore, you can place a hyperlink in the e-mail that, when clicked, will display the alerting report with just the records that triggered the alert.

Begin by navigating to the object you want to set notification information for. Find the object either in the Objects list or the folder hierarchy of the Folders and Objects list. Double-click the desired object. The Properties screen will appear. Expand the Default Settings category on the left side of the screen and click the Alert Notification link (only Crystal Reports that contain one or more Report Alerts will display an Alert Notification link). The Set Alert Notification screen will appear.

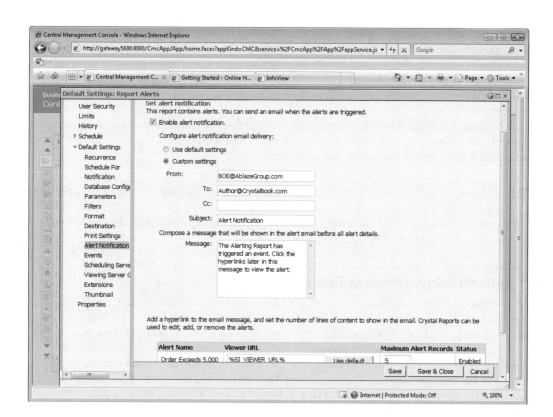

Check Enable Alert Notification. Then, specify detailed e-mail information, such as from address, to address, e-mail subject, and message body. You may choose to use default settings for these values you set up when configuring the e-mail destination on the server, or specify settings individually here. You may also designate a URL to include in the e-mail that will direct the recipient directly to the report that triggered the alerts, showing only the record in the report that triggered the alert. Typically, you'll want to click the Use Default button to add a mnemonic to the URL that will resolve to the default location from the CMS for the alert report.

Once you've made desired settings, click Save or Save & Close to save the notification information. When you schedule the object in the future (either from the CMC or InfoView), an e-mail will be sent if the report triggers alerts.

TIP   *You must set up the default viewer URL (typically, you'll at least need to specify your web server name) for the Use Default button to work properly when adding a URL to an alert e-mail. You can set the default URL by choosing Applications from the CMC main menu, tab, or navigation drop-down list and editing CMC properties.*

Other General Administrative Tasks

In addition to steps discussed previously in this chapter, other administrative tasks of a general nature will probably be required. For example, you may need to add additional license keys to the CMS to allow additional users or features to be enabled. You may choose to view metrics indicating how many users are currently logged on to the CMS. You may need to set limits on the number of report or program object instances that are retained by the CMS. Or, you may desire to change some default behavior of InfoView, which is the primary user interface for non-administrative users who view and schedule reports (InfoView is covered in detail in Chapter 21).

NOTE   *As a BusinessObjects Enterprise Administrator, you may also be responsible for maintaining the repository or Business Views. While both of these features are also maintained in the Central Management Server database, they are not administered with the Central Management Console. Instead, you must use the Business View Manager Windows application. Business Views are discussed in detail in an extra online chapter available for download from this book's companion web site, CrystalBook.com. Using the Business View Manager to work with the repository is discussed in detail in Chapter 18.*

Adding Additional Licenses

When you first install BusinessObjects Enterprise, you are prompted to supply a single keycode by the BOE Setup. That keycode will provide the initial set of licensing options available to you. However, should you ever buy additional licenses (to add more named or concurrent users), you will merely need to supply replacement or additional keycodes—no re-installation will be required.

You specify additional keycodes in the Central Management Console. Click License Keys from the Manage area of the main CMC screen. You may also click the License Key tab in the left of the CMC, or choose License Keys from the Navigation drop-down list at the top of the screen. The License Keys screen will appear.

The initial keycode you used when you installed BusinessObjects Enterprise will appear here. You may click the existing keycode in the list to display the type of keycode and number of licenses it provides in the Selected Key column below. To delete a keycode, select the existing keycode and click Delete. To add a replacement or additional keycode, type it in the Add Key box (include the dashes) and click Add.

CAUTION   In some instances, you may need to replace an initially specified keycode with another keycode (when upgrading from a trial to fully functional version, for example). In this situation, you will need to remove the first keycode before adding the replacement keycode. Otherwise, you may receive an error that you are attempting to add a conflicting keycode.

Setting Instance Limits

As you might imagine, an even moderately "busy" BusinessObjects Enterprise system can use up disk resources rapidly if many reports and program objects are being scheduled on a frequent basis. If you recall architecture discussions earlier in the chapter, you remember that the Output File Repository Server is charged with keeping all report instances that have been scheduled, as well as the text output from all scheduled program object instances. If reports and program objects are scheduled on a frequent basis, the number of instance files can grow rapidly, as can usage of Output FRS disk space. Furthermore, a report object may not be particularly useful if hundreds of saved instances appear in the History list when a user views it.

The CMS includes the capability to automatically purge report and program object instances when they exceed either a certain age or a certain quantity. Once these settings are made, the CMS will automatically purge instances from the Output FRS and its own database once instances exceed the defined age or quantity. These instance limits can be set globally at the CMS root folder level, as well as at both the folder and object levels. For example, you may choose to set a folder limit of 25 retained instances but allow a certain report that runs every hour to retain 50 instances. Furthermore, these settings can be specified for individual users and user groups.

Instance limits are set in the Folders and Objects list. Once this list is displayed, select either the All Folders entry in the Tree Panel to set instance limits for the CMS root folder. Otherwise, select the folder, subfolder, or individual object you want to set instance limits for. Then, click the Set Limit On Number of Instances Saved toolbar button, choose Limits from the Actions drop-down button, or right-click and choose Limits from the pop-up menu. The Limits screen will appear.

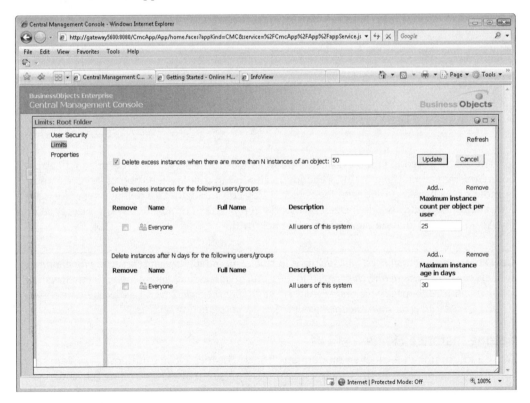

The overall number of instances retained for a folder or object can be set by checking the Delete Excess Instances check box and typing in the number of instances to retain in the text box that follows. If you do nothing else, this will set an instance limit for all objects in the folder. You may either leave this unchecked and specify individual quantity and age limits by user or group, or set a global instance limit and specify more restrictive limits by user and group.

To specify either a quantity or an age limit by user or group, click the Add link for either the Delete Excess Instances or Delete Instances After N Days section. A list of groups will appear. Choose one or more groups that you want to set limits for and click the right-arrow button to add the groups to the chosen list. If you want to set limits for individual users, choose Add Users from the top drop-down list. You can then either pick one or more users directly or use the Find feature to locate a specific user.

Once you've finished choosing users and/or groups, click OK. The Limits screen will reappear with the groups and users you chose now appearing. Set the instance quantity or time limits by typing numbers in the appropriate Maximum Instance Count or Maximum Instance Age text boxes. When finished, click Update in the upper right-hand corner to save your settings.

NOTE *An instance will be deleted if it meets any one of the criteria. So, for example, if you set an overall instance limit of 50, an instance limit for the Administrators group of 25, and a 10-day limit for the Everyone group, any instance over 10 days will be deleted, regardless of who owns it and how many instances there are overall. Administrator-owned instances will be deleted if they exceed a total of 25, and all other users will see their instances deleted if they exceed 50. Also, if you set instance limits at the object level, they will take precedence.*

Specifying Default InfoView Settings

The out-of-the-box user interface for BusinessObjects Enterprise, InfoView, contains a default look and feel when initially installed (InfoView is covered in Chapter 21). While each user can customize their InfoView appearance, you may want to control some more specific InfoView items, such as whether or not to show the Business Objects logo, what custom colors to use for headers, and so forth.

To customize InfoView, click Applications from the Manage area of the CMC main menu. You may use equivalent tabs at the left, and navigation drop-down list options. InfoView is among the application options that will appear. Select the InfoView item and then click the Manage Object Properties toolbar button, or choose Properties from the Manage drop-down button. Choose from the available choices for appearance and behavior. When finished, click Save or Save & Close to save the changes.

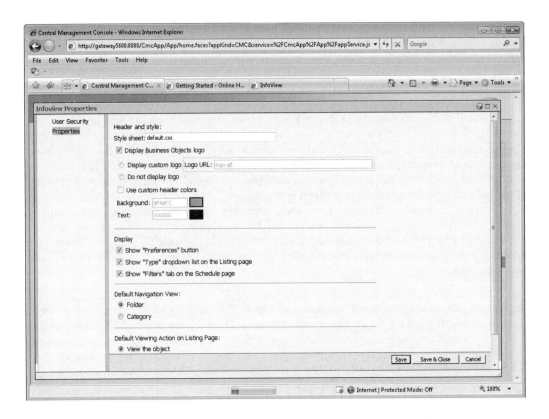

Using Instance Manager

In previous versions of BOE, various administrative "extras" were available from a supplementary Administrative Launchpad web page. In BOE XI 3.0, most administrative tools have been concentrated in the CMC. One of the new features allows a flexible way of searching for, and managing, report or program object instances. This tool will come in handy for dealing with failed, pending, or recurring instances that you may wish to search for across folders, users, and so forth.

Display the Instance Manager by clicking the Instance Manager item in the Manage area of the CMC main menu. You may also click the associated tab in the left of the CMC, or choose Instance Manager from the navigation drop-down list at the top of the screen. The Instance Manager will appear.

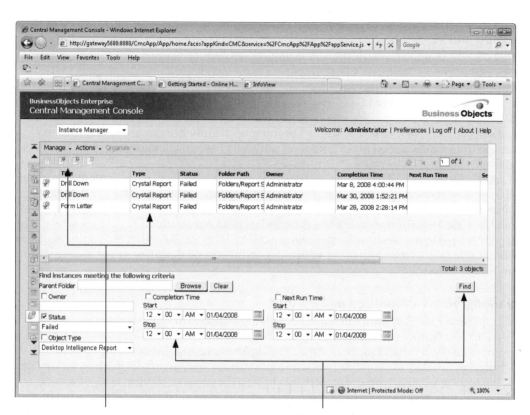

Select one or more retrieved instances and use
menu options or toolbar buttons to manage them

Provide various search criteria
to narrow down instances

Specify various search requirements at the bottom of the screen. For example, you can specify a combination of instance statuses (failed, pending, etc.), instance dates and times, "owner" (the user who initially added the object that's being schedule), and so forth, before clicking the Find button. The list of instances meeting the criteria will appear at the top of the screen. You may navigate from page to page (if there is more than one). You can see instance properties, pause instances that are recurring or pending, delete instances, and reschedule instances by selecting one or more instances in the list and using toolbar buttons or drop-down button options.

Managing Servers

Part of your administrative duties will include managing the various server components that make up your BusinessObjects Enterprise system (look earlier in the chapter, under "BusinessObjects Enterprise Architecture," for a complete overview of all BOE server components). Management tasks may merely mean making sure all servers are running after you reboot the BOE computer or restart the SIA. Or, you may need to migrate the CMS database to a different database server. Or, you may identify performance issues that may benefit from manipulation of certain server settings. These all fall under the realm of server management.

With the release of BusinessObjects Enterprise XI 3.0, virtually all your server management tasks will be conducted in the Servers list area of the CMC. While used for a certain amount of server management in earlier BOE versions, the Central Configuration Manager, or CCM (and, yes, the two acronyms are often confused) is used minimally in XI 3.0 for maintenance largely related to the Server Intelligence Agent (SIA). With the exception of a short discussion of the CCM later in the chapter, the remainder of this section discusses server maintenance in the web-based CMC.

Viewing Server Properties and Metrics

Various server metrics, properties, and settings are available from the Servers list, and the Sessions and Settings options. Settings and Sessions are both available from the CMC main menu, the left-hand toolbar, or the drop-down navigation list at the top of the CMC. Displaying Settings, for example, will show you various system metrics, such as the version of BusinessObjects Enterprise installed, including indications of service packs of version dates. You may also see how many users are currently logged on to the system, what license complements are currently being used, and so forth. If you'd like more specific information about who the currently logged-on users are, view the Sessions screen.

Other server metrics and most individual server properties can be viewed and set from the Servers list. Display the Servers list in the CMC by clicking the Servers main menu item or the Servers tab on the left of the CMC, or choose Servers from the navigation drop-down list. The Servers list will appear.

You may click different categories in the Tree Panel on the left of the Servers list to see subsets of all BOE servers. For example, to see just servers that pertain to Crystal Reports processing, select the Crystal Reports entry within the Service Categories entry. All servers can be displayed by clicking the main Servers List entry at the top of the Tree Panel. If the number of servers won't appear within a single list page, click page navigation buttons at the upper right-hand corner of the Servers list to see more servers.

NOTE *Not all servers in the Servers list will necessarily apply to the member of the BusinessObjects Enterprise XI 3.0 family that you are using. For example, if you are using a Crystal Reports–only solution, servers related to non–Crystal Reports document types may not be visible or enabled.*

To see various properties, metrics, and settings for a server, double-click the server name. Click available hyperlinks in the left side of the server screen to see or modify various server-related items (available options will differ, depending on the type of server you are viewing).

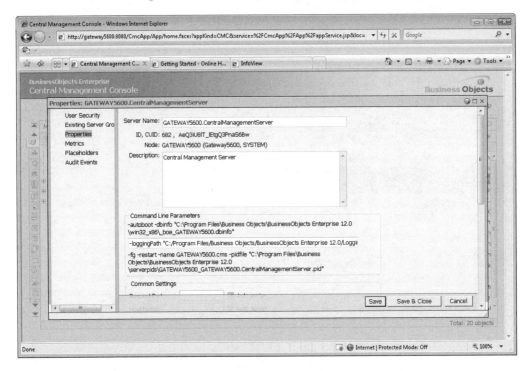

NOTE *Specific information on various options and settings in servers can be found in online help and the BusinessObjects Enterprise XI 3.0 Administrator's Guide.*

Making Sure Servers Are Running and Enabled

If you discover that some portion of BOE isn't functioning properly (perhaps users are unable to log on to the CMS, they receive a "server isn't available message," or scheduled reports are failing and instances indicate "no server available" errors), the first thing to check is that all applicable servers are both running and enabled. This can be accomplished from the Servers list.

Use toolbar buttons or drop-down buttons to start, stop, restart, enable, or disable servers

Running/enabled status columns

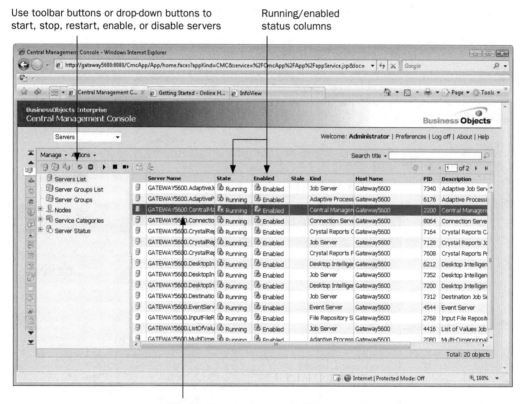

Select one or more servers in list

A quick glance at the State and Enabled columns in the Servers list will indicate whether key servers are not enabled or running. If you find a disabled or stopped server, you may select the desired server and use toolbar buttons and drop-down button options to restart or enable the server. Or, if you want to make an orderly shutdown of your BOE system for an upgrade or maintenance, you may wish to disable key servers for a short period of time before actually stopping them, or stopping the SIA with the CCM (discussed next). By disabling a server, you give the server time to purge memory cache and finish up processing tasks that it may be currently involved in before it is shut down.

The Server Intelligence Agent and the CCM

With the introduction of BOE XI 3.0, the vast majority of server maintenance is accomplished in the web-based CMC. However, the software servers that divide up various BOE processes are all managed and "virtualized" by a new XI 3.0 architecture called Server Intelligence. The Server Intelligence Agent, or SIA, performs these tasks at the operating system level. SIA configuration must be performed with the Central Configuration Manager (CCM), a stand-alone Windows application installed on the physical CMS computer.

The CCM is available from the appropriate BusinessObjects Enterprise program group on the physical CMS computer. When you initially start it, it shows the SIA (as well as any related application servers, such as Apache Tomcat), their status, version, and description. You may start, stop, or restart the SIA from the CCM (make sure no one is actively using BOE when you do this, as the SIA controls all software servers that make up BOE). If, for some reason, you are not able to access the individual software servers in the CMC (perhaps you stopped the CMS within the CMC by mistake), you may also click the Manage Servers button in the CCM to start or stop the individual "logical" BOE servers.

There may be times when you need to stop, start, or restart the SIA (perhaps your entire BOE system has become unstable, or you wish to perform a "clean start" to see if issues can be resolved). Or, you may need to perform SIA configuration (such as changing some properties, altering the Windows user ID that the SIA uses, and so forth). While you may view all SIA settings from the CCM while the SIA is running, you must stop it before changing any settings. Before you do this, ensure that all BOE users are aware that the system will be brought down—you may wish to view Session or Settings from the CMC to

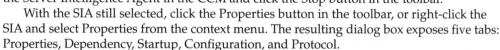

see which users are still logged on. Once you are sure that you may safely stop the SIA, select the Server Intelligence Agent in the CCM and click the Stop button in the toolbar.

With the SIA still selected, click the Properties button in the toolbar, or right-click the SIA and select Properties from the context menu. The resulting dialog box exposes five tabs: Properties, Dependency, Startup, Configuration, and Protocol.

The Properties tab contains general information about the SIA, including the display name, command, and startup type. One possibility is to alter command-line parameters in the SIA startup command (details on available command-line parameters are provided in CCM online help). By default, the SIA is assigned the Windows Server System account and is set to automatically start when the computer boots. These items may be changed here in the CCM, as well as in the Windows Services applet from the Control Panel.

The Dependency tab contains a list of the services that the SIA is dependent upon. The dependency relationship indicates that the services listed here must be running in order for the SIA to run. These services will vary depending on the type of database system that is used for the SIA database. You may add and/or remove services from the dependency list, but it is highly unlikely that you will ever need to do so.

The Startup tab contains options to customize the way the SIA's associated CMS communicates through firewall ports, whether it starts when the SIA starts, and so forth. There are also settings to allow the SIA to communicate with other remote CMS systems (these options may not be applicable to single-server implementations of members of the BOE XI 3.0 family).

The Configuration tab contains some very important parameters. First, the Port Number may be changed, if necessary, to work with firewalls and the SIA. Be sure to work closely with the network administrator if you change this number. Second, the SIA Datasource may be changed should you desire to migrate the SIA database to another server.

The Protocol tab allows configuration of the Secure Sockets Layer (SSL) for all network communication in the BOE environment. For more information on configuring the SSL, see the Administrator's Guide.

Migrating the System Database to a New Server

If you choose default settings when you initially install the BusinessObjects Enterprise SIA, a local version of the MySQL database is installed to host the BOE database. While MySQL is often perfectly acceptable for stand-alone, simple BOE installations, some system architects make the decision to migrate the database to another database system for improved performance, ease of maintenance, backup simplicity, staff knowledge, or other reasons.

NOTE *The following procedure assumes that you are copying an existing BOE SIA database to a new, fresh database in another database system. Upgrading from a previous version of BOE involves a different process that is detailed later in this chapter.*

As with most operations of this magnitude, the initial step in the process is to back up the current environment. First, back up the current SIA database just in case you need to restore it later. By default, the MySQL database is located in *C:\Program Files\Business Objects\ MySQL5\data*. Then, back up the entire Input and Output File Repository Server directory structures. By default, these are located in *C:\Program Files\Business Objects\BusinessObjects Enterprise 12.0\FileStore.*

The next step is to prepare the new destination database. First, define a new database in the destination database system. Do not create any new tables, as this will be done automatically by BOE when the SIA database is migrated. Ensure a database user ID and password combination exists that allows Create, Update, and Delete privileges. Then, create an ODBC data source for the new database on the SIA machine (note that certain databases, such as Oracle and DB/2, can be accessed via native drivers and don't require an ODBC connection). Finally, be sure that you can connect using the appropriate account and data source from the SIA machine.

Then, open the CCM and follow these steps:

1. Select the SIA and stop the SIA server.

2. With the SIA still selected, click the Specify CMS Data Source button in the toolbar. You can also select the Configuration tab in the Server Intelligence Agent Properties dialog box and click the Specify button in the CMS System Database Connection category. The CMS Database Setup dialog box will appear.

3. Select Copy Data From Another Data Source and click OK. The Specify Data Source dialog box will appear.

4. Select either Autodetect or BusinessObjects Enterprise XI Release 3 from the Source Contains Data From Version drop-down list.

5. Click the Specify button next to the Get Data From text box and specify your current data source (you may need to choose the database your current SIA data source uses before you pick the actual data source). You may need to enter logon information to complete this step.

6. Click the Browse button next to Copy To The Following Data Source to specify your new destination data source. You will be given a choice of database connection methods, and then given the choice of a new data source name. Again, you may need to enter logon information to complete this step.

7. Click OK, and then click Yes for the confirmation.

8. When the migration is complete, click OK.

After migration, it is best to check for a migration log file to see if any errors or other messages were written. If you installed BOE to the default directories, you will find the log file in *C:\Program Files\Business Objects\BusinessObjects Enterprise 12.0\Logging*.

Next use the CCM to start and enable the SIA server. Log on to the BOE system via the CMC. In the License Keys section, check to make sure all of the BOE license keys were transferred properly. Then, if necessary, return to the Servers list to start and enable all of the other BOE servers. Because the BOE file system has not changed locations, all server configurations should remain as they were before migration.

At this point, the BOE system should be fully migrated to the new database system. Test the system in a variety of ways to be sure that everything is functioning properly. For example, view a report, view an instance of a different report, and schedule yet another report to be run in the near future.

NOTE *The database configuration just described actually applies to the Central Management Server "logical" component of BusinessObjects Enterprise. However, with the introduction of Server Intelligence in the BOE XI 3.0 family, most notations in the CCM relate the database to the Server Intelligence Agent.*

Upgrading from an Earlier BusinessObjects Enterprise/Crystal Enterprise Version

Often, you will not want to just install a clean BOE system. Instead, you will want to upgrade or migrate an earlier version. In some cases, you may be able to perform an "upgrade install" in the same computer as the older version and the older version will be automatically migrated to XI 3.0. However, in many cases, you may wish to build a "test" XI 3.0 system for user acceptance testing. Once you are ready to put the new system into production, you may want to migrate an older production system to the new system. BOE provides a stand-alone Windows application called the *Import Wizard* to handle the task.

The wizard consists of two main processes: specifying the source and target environments, and specifying the objects to be imported. First, make sure you have administrator privileges for both the source and destination environments. Then, as with most wizards, simply proceed through the series of dialogs.

1. Start the Import Wizard from the appropriate BusinessObjects Enterprise program group (you may use the Import Wizard that's installed by default on the BOE computer, or can install a separate copy from the BOE installation media on a separate Windows computer). Specify your desired language and click Next to get through the intro screen.

2. Specify the source environment, including the version, the older CMS/APS name, and the logon credentials.

3. Specify the destination environment, including the CMS name and the logon credentials.

4. Using the check boxes, choose the objects to import. Depending on the version you are importing from, you will have various choices of objects and rights for import.

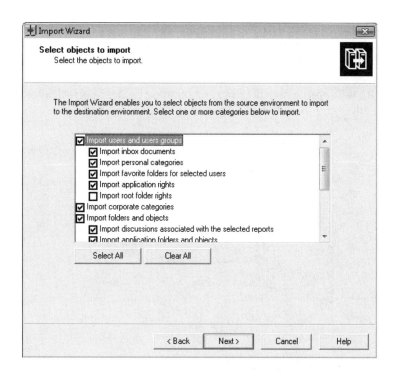

5. You will be given a choice as to how you want to accommodate situations where objects in the source and target systems may have the same names. Consider how you want to deal with potential duplicate objects and make the desire choice. Click Next.

6. Again, depending on the version you are importing from, you may see an Incremental Import screen that allows you to choose how you want to overwrite certain object types in the target system. Make desired choices and click Next.

7. You may be given several warning screens regarding server groups, indicating that importing objects with rights requires that users/groups associated with those also will need to be imported, and so forth. Click Next on each screen.

8. If you chose to import users and groups, choose which users and groups to import with the appropriate check boxes. You may use the Select All and Clear All buttons to select groups and users en masse.

9. If the version of Enterprise you are importing from supports categories, a commensurate screen will appear allowing you to choose which categories you wish to import. Make desired selections and click Next.

10. You'll be given a choice of folders/subfolders/objects that you wish to import. If you chose to import folders and objects, choose which folders and objects to import with the appropriate check boxes. You may expand and contract folders with the plus/minus signs. You may also use the Select All and Clear All buttons to select reports and folders en masse. To import existing instances (both complete and recurring), check the Import All Instances check box.

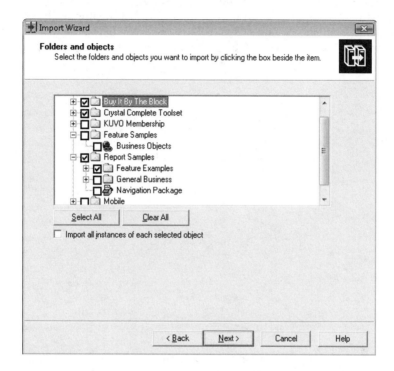

11. Depending on the version of your source system, you may be prompted to choose Application Folders you wish to import, as well as Universes and Universe connections you wish to import. Choose desired options and click Next.

12. If the source system includes supports a Crystal Reports repository, you'll be prompted how you want to import repository objects. You also may see a screen prompting for Profile and Publication import options. Make the desired choice and click Next.

13. When the Ready To Import screen appears, click Finish to begin the import.

When the import is complete, simply click Done to complete the process. If errors were noted, click View Detail Log to see the log file. The log is also written to the hard drive in a file consisting of "ImportWiz", followed by the date of the import. By default, this file is located in *Program Files\Business Objects\BusinessObjects Enterprise 12.0\Logging*.

Check the integrity of your BOE system, comparing to your just-imported system.

Formula Language Reference

This appendix provides detailed information for each Crystal Reports formula language function and operator. Functions and operators are categorized by usage (string, numeric, financial, and so forth). The purpose of each function or operator is discussed, along with explanations of various function arguments. An example of each function and operator is provided.

Consider the following points when making use of this reference:

- Crystal Syntax is used in this reference. With very few exceptions, Basic Syntax is not covered, as Visual Basic and Visual Basic for Applications (which Basic Syntax is based on) are commonly documented languages. In many cases, the Basic Syntax version of the function or operator is identical or very similar to the Crystal Syntax version documented here.

- Some more esoteric functions, such as statistical and financial functions, may not be explained in great detail. It is assumed that report designers who need to use these specialized functions will already possess a basic understanding of their usage.

- Although most of the examples in this appendix use "literal" arguments, you may easily substitute database fields, other formulas, and so forth, for function arguments.

- Formatting in examples that follow each function or operator assumes that English (United States) is chosen as the report viewing locale. If you've changed this setting, your default output formatting may be different.

Functions: Additional Functions

This category of the Function tree exposes functions that are provided to Crystal Reports by a set of external dynamic link libraries (DLLs). These DLLs, known as User Function Libraries (UFLs) within Crystal Reports, can be developed in a Windows or Java programming language to provide extensible functions to the Crystal Reports formula language. UFL functions are categorized by their UFL DLL filename.

NOTE *If you have upgraded from previous versions of Crystal Reports, or you have downloaded additional User Function Libraries from Business Objects (or other sources), you'll find additional entries in the Additional Functions category of the Function tree.*

ByteToText

Converts a number to a descriptive string indicating disk or memory storage used.

ByteToText is useful when reporting on the Local File System (or other data source that requires amounts of computer storage to be included on the report). Values less than 1,204 are returned in bytes, values between 1,204 and 1,048,576 are abbreviated to "KB", and values above 1,048,576 are abbreviated to "MB".

ByteToText (n)

n – numeric value.

```
ByteToText(1000)
```

returns "1000 bytes".

```
ByteToText(10000000)
```

returns "9 MB".

DateTimeTo2000

Converts a date-time value that may not be year 2000–compliant to a year 2000–compliant date-time with a four-digit year.

DateTimeTo2000 is "left over" from previous versions of Crystal Reports that may not have dealt with date-time values properly. It is largely not required with current versions, unless you may be dealing with older databases that don't return full four-digit years in date-time fields.

DateTimeTo2000 (dt, n)

dt – date-time value with a two- or four-digit year.
n – numeric value to act as a "sliding scale" year window.

```
DateTimeTo2000(DateTimeValue("1/1/90 1:03 pm"), 95)
```

returns 1/1/2090 1:03:00 PM.

DateTimeToDate

Returns only the date portion of a date-time value.

This function is "left over" from previous versions of Crystal Reports and has been replaced by the CDate and DateValue functions. See **DateValue** for details.

DateTimeToSeconds

Extracts the number of seconds that have passed since midnight.

DateTimeToSeconds evaluates the time portion of the supplied date-time value and returns the number of seconds that have passed since midnight.

DateTimeToSeconds (dt)

dt – date-time value.

```
DateTimeToSeconds(CurrentDateTime)
```

returns 49,980 for a current date-time value that includes the time 1:53:00 P.M.

DateTimeToTime

Returns only the time portion of a date-time value.
This function is "left over" from previous versions of Crystal Reports and has been replaced by the CTime and TimeValue functions. See **TimeValue** for details.

DateTo2000

Converts a date value that may not be year 2000–compliant to a year 2000–compliant date with a four-digit year.
DateTo2000 is "left over" from previous versions of Crystal Reports that may not have dealt with date values properly. It is largely not required with current versions, unless you may be dealing with older databases that don't return full four-digit years in date fields.

DateTo2000 (d, n)

d – date value with a two- or four-digit year.
n – numeric value to act as a "sliding scale" year window.

```
DateTo2000(#1/1/90#, 95)
```

returns 1/1/2090.

DTSTo2000

Returns a string value from a date string or date-time string with a two- or four-digit year.
DTSTo2000 will convert a string formatted in a specific year-month-day-hour-minute-second format to another string with a four-digit year. This function includes a sliding-scale year argument to ready two-digit dates for year-2000 compliance.

DTSTo2000 (s, n)

s – string containing a date in the format "yyyy/mm/dd" or "yy/mm/dd" or date-time in the format "yyyy/mm/dd hh:mm:ss.00" or "yy/mm/dd hh:mm:ss.00".
n – numeric value to act as a "sliding scale" year window.

```
DTSTo2000("90/10/01",95)
```

returns the string "2090/10/01".

DTSToDate

Converts a string formatted in a specific date-time format to a true date value.
DTSToDate is functionally equivalent to CDate and DateValue. See **DateValue** for more information.

DTSToDateTime

Converts a string formatted in a specific date-time format to a true date-time value.
DTSToDateTime is functionally equivalent to CDateTime and DateTimeValue. See **DateTimeValue** for more information.

DTSToSeconds

Extracts the number of seconds that have passed since midnight.
DTSToSeconds evaluates the time portion of the supplied date-time string and returns the number of seconds that have passed since midnight.

DTSToSeconds (s)

s – string containing a date-time in the format "yyyy/mm/dd hh:mm:ss.00" or "yy/mm/dd hh:mm:ss.00".

```
DTSToSeconds("2003/05/28 13:53:00.00")
```

returns 49,980 (the number of seconds between midnight and 1:53 P.M.).

DTSToTimeField

Converts a string formatted in a specific date-time format to a true time value.
DTSToTimeField is functionally equivalent to CTime and TimeValue. See **TimeValue** for more information.

DTSToTimeString

Returns a string containing just the time portion of a date-time string.
DTSToTimeString simply extracts the text after the eleventh character of a string (which does not actually have to be formatted as a date-time string).

DTSToTimeString (s)

s – string containing a date-time in the format "yyyy/mm/dd hh:mm:ss.00".

```
DTSToTimeString("1998/05/28 13:53:00.00")
```

returns the string "13:53:00.00".

NOTE *The preceding series of date-time string (DTS) functions are "left over" from previous versions of Crystal Reports that may not have dealt with date-time values properly. For example, Crystal Reports 6 did not properly recognize a true date or date-time value from a database but returned these values as string fields in a certain format. While you can still make the choice to convert date or date-time values to strings, these DTS functions are generally not required with current Crystal Reports versions.*

EventNumber

Returns a text description of a Microsoft Exchange event number.
EventNumber is helpful when reporting from Microsoft Exchange data sources. Certain supplied event numbers are significant (for example, 1,000 indicates local delivery). Those that aren't recognized will return "unknown event" results.

EventNumber (n)

n – numeric value representing a Microsoft Exchange event number.

```
EventNumber(1000)
```

returns "Local Delivery".

ExchGetId

Extracts the e-mail address from an X400- or X500-formatted string.

ExchGetID is helpful when reporting from Microsoft Exchange data sources. These data sources return certain e-mail address strings that can be passed to ExchGetID to return just the e-mail address.

ExchGetId (s)

s – string containing an X400- or X500-formatted address.

```
ExchGetID("c=US; a= ;p=Ablaze Group;
o=AblazeServer;dda:smtp=Info@AblazeGroup.com")
```

returns "Author@CrystalBook.com".

ExchGetOrganization

Extracts the organization string from an X400- or X500-formatted string.

ExchGetOrganization is helpful when reporting from Microsoft Exchange data sources. These data sources return certain organization strings that can be passed to ExchGetOrganization to return just the organization.

ExchGetOrganization (s)

s – string containing an X400- or X500-formatted address.

```
ExchGetOrganization("c=US; a= ;p=Ablaze Group;
o=AblazeServer;dda:smtp=Info@AblazeGroup.com")
```

returns "Ablaze Group".

ExchGetPath

Extracts the destination path string from an X400- or X500-formatted string.

ExchGetPath is helpful when reporting from Microsoft Exchange data sources. These data sources return certain destination strings that can be passed to ExchGetPath to return just the destination path.

ExchGetPath (s)

s – string containing an X400- or X500-formatted address.

```
ExchGetPath("c=US;a= ;p=Ablaze Group;ou1=Info;
ou2=Ablaze Group;o=AblazeServer;dda:smtp=Info@AblazeGroup.com")
```

will return "OU1=INFO; OU2=ABLAZE GROUP;".

ExchGetSite
Extracts the site string from an X400- or X500-formatted string.

ExchGetSite is helpful when reporting from Microsoft Exchange data sources. These data sources return certain site strings that can be passed to ExchGetSite to return just the site.

ExchGetSite (s)

s – string containing an X400- or X500-formatted address.

```
ExchGetSite("c=US;a= ;p=Ablaze Group;ou1=Info;ou2=Ablaze Group;
o=AblazeServer;dda:smtp=Info@AblazeGroup.com")
```

will return "AblazeServer".

ExtractString
Extracts the portion of a string that appears between two other strings.

ExtractString will search a string, returning the portion that falls between two other search strings. If the first search string is not found, ExtractString returns an empty string. If the second search string is not found, ExtractString will return the entire portion of the source string after the first search string.

ExtractString (s1, s2, s3)

s1 – source string to be searched.
s2 – first string to search for.
s3 – second string to search for.

```
ExtractString("The rain in Spain falls on the plain",
"rain", "plain")
```

returns "in Spain falls on the".

FRAccRecTurnover
Returns the average turnover of accounts receivable in numeric days.

FRAccRecTurnover calculates the average "turnover" of accounts receivable by dividing accounts receivable by sales, and multiplying the result by the number of days in the year.

FRAccRecTurnover (n1, n2, n3)

n1 – numeric value of total accounts receivable.
n2 – numeric value of total sales.
n3 – numeric value indicating the number of days in a year (default is 360).

```
FRAccRecTurnover(10000,100000,360)
```

returns 36 days.

FRCashFlowVsTotalDebt
Returns the ratio between cash flow and total debt.

FRCashFlowVsTotalDebt determines the ratio of cash flow to debt by dividing cash flow by total debt.

FRCashFlowVsTotalDebt (n1, n2)

n1 – numeric value indicating total cash flow.
n2 – numeric value indicating total debt.

```
FRCashFlowVsTotalDebt(100000,10000)
```

returns a cash flow–to–debt ratio of 10.

FRCurrentRatio

Returns the ratio between current assets and current liabilities.

  FRCurrentRatio determines the ratio of current assets to current liabilities by dividing assets by liabilities.

FRCurrentRatio (n1, n2)

n1 – numeric value indicating total current assets.
n2 – numeric value indicating total current liabilities.

```
FRCurrentRatio(100000,10000)
```

returns an asset-to-liability ratio of 10.

FRDebtEquityRatio

Returns the ratio between total liabilities and total equity.

  FRDebtEquityRatio determines the ratio of total liabilities to total equity by dividing liabilities by equity.

FRDebtEquityRatio (n1, n2)

n1 – numeric value indicating total liabilities.
n2 – numeric value indicating total equity.

```
FRDebtEquityRatio(10000,100000)
```

returns a liability-to-equity ratio of .1.

FRDividendYield

Returns the ratio between dividend and market price.

  FRDividendYield determines the ratio of dividend to market price by dividing dividend by market price.

FRDividendYield (n1, n2)

n1 – numeric value indicating dividend amount.
n2 – numeric value indicating share market price.

```
FRDividendYield(10,50)
```

returns a dividend–to–market price ratio of .2.

FREarningsPerCommonShare

Returns the ratio of net profit distributable to shareholders to the number of shares.

FREarningsPerCommonShare determines the ratio of net profit to number of shares by subtracting the preferred dividend amount from net profit, and dividing the result by the number of common shares.

FREarningsPerCommonShare (n1, n2, n3)

n1 – numeric value indicating net profit.
n2 – numeric value indicating dividend paid to preferred shareholders.
n3 – numeric value indicating number of issued common shares.

```
FREarningsPerCommonShare (100000, 10, 10000)
```

returns a profit-to-share ratio of 10.

FREquityVsTotalAssets

Returns the ratio between total equity and total assets.

FREquityVsTotalAssets determines the ratio of total equity to total assets by dividing equity by assets.

FREquityVsTotalAssets (n1, n2)

n1 – numeric value indicating total equity.
n2 – numeric value indicating total assets.

```
FREquityVsTotalAssets(100000,500000)
```

returns a equity-to-assets ratio of .2.

FRGrossProfitMargin

Returns the ratio between gross profit and sales.

FRGrossProfitMargin determines the ratio of gross profit to sales by dividing gross profit by sales.

FRGrossProfitMargin (n1, n2)

n1 – numeric value indicating gross profit.
n2 – numeric value indicating sales.

```
FRGrossProfitMargin(10000,100000)
```

returns a profit-to-sales ratio of .1.

FRInterestCoverage

Returns the ratio between cash flow and interest expense.

FRInterestCoverage determines the ratio of cash flow to interest expense by dividing cash flow by interest expense.

FRInterestCoverage (n1, n2)

n1 – numeric value indicating cash flow.
n2 – numeric value indicating interest expense.

```
FRInterestCoverage(100000,2500)
```

returns a cash flow–to–interest expense ratio of 25.

FRInventoryTurnover

Returns the average turnover of inventory in numeric days.

FRInventoryTurnover calculates the average "turnover" of inventory by dividing inventory by sales, and multiplying the result by the number of days in the year.

FRInventoryTurnover (n1, n2, n3)

n1 – numeric value of total inventory.
n2 – numeric value of total sales.
n3 – numeric value indicating the number of days in a year (default is 360).

```
FRInventoryTurnover(10000,100000,360)
```

returns 36 days.

FRNetProfitMargin

Returns the ratio between net profit and sales.

FRNetProfitMargin determines the ratio of net profit to sales by dividing net profit by sales.

FRNetProfitMargin (n1, n2)

n1 – numeric value indicating net profit.
n2 – numeric value indicating sales.

```
FRNetProfitMargin(10000,100000)
```

returns a profit-to-sales ratio of .1.

FROperatingProfitMargin

Returns the ratio between operating profit and sales.

FROperatingProfitMargin determines the ratio of operating profit to sales by dividing operating profit by sales.

FROperatingProfitMargin (n1, n2)

n1 – numeric value indicating operating profit.
n2 – numeric value indicating sales.

```
FROperatingProfitMargin(10000,100000)
```

returns a profit-to-sales ratio of .1.

FRPriceEarningsRatio

Returns the ratio between share market price and earnings per share.

FRPriceEarningsRatio determines the ratio of share market price to earnings by dividing share market price by earnings per share.

FRPriceEarningsRatio (n1, n2)

n1 – numeric value indicating share market price.
n2 – numeric value indicating earnings per share.

```
FRPriceEarningsRatio (10,100)
```

returns a price-to-earnings ratio of .1.

FRQuickRatio

Returns the ratio between current assets (less inventory) and current liabilities.

FRQuickRatio determines the ratio of current assets (less inventory) to current liabilities by subtracting inventory from assets and dividing the results by liabilities.

FRQuickRatio (n1, n2, n3)

n1 – numeric value indicating current assets.
n2 – numeric value indicating inventory.
n3 – numeric value indicating current liabilities.

```
FRQuickRatio (100000, 10000, 5000)
```

returns a quick ratio of 18.

FRReturnOnCommonEquity

Returns the ratio between net profit and common equity.

FRReturnOnCommonEquity determines the ratio of net profit to common equity by subtracting the dividend amount from net profit, and dividing the result by common equity.

FRReturnOnCommonEquity (n1, n2, n3)

n1 – numeric value indicating net profit.
n2 – numeric value indicating the total preferred dividend amount.
n3 – numeric value indicating common equity.

```
FRReturnOnCommonEquity (10000, 15, 100000)
```

returns a return on common equity ratio of .1.

FRReturnOnEquity

Returns the ratio between net profit and total equity.

FRReturnOnEquity determines the ratio of net profit to total equity by dividing net profit by equity.

FRReturnOnEquity (n1, n2)

n1 – numeric value indicating net profit.
n2 – numeric value indicating total equity.

```
FRReturnOnEquity (10000,100000)
```

returns a profit-to-equity ratio of .1.

FRReturnOnInvestedCapital

Returns the ratio between net profit and invested capital.
   FRReturnOnInvestedCapital determines the ratio between net profit and invested capital by dividing net profit by the sum of bank debt and equity.

FRReturnOnInvestedCapital (n1, n2, n3)

n1 – a numeric value indicating net profit.
n2 – a numeric value indicating total bank debt.
n3 – a numeric value indicating total equity.

```
FRReturnOnInvestedCapital (10000,5000,100000)
```

returns a return on invested capital ratio of .1.

FRReturnOnNetFixedAssets

Returns the ratio between net profit and net fixed assets.
   FRReturnOnNetFixedAssets determines the ratio of net profit to fixed assets by dividing net profit by fixed assets.

FRReturnOnNetFixedAssets (n1, n2)

n1 – numeric value indicating net profit.
n2 – numeric value indicating net fixed assets.

```
FRReturnOnNetFixedAssets (10000,100000)
```

returns a profit-to-assets ratio of .1.

FRReturnOnTotalAssets

Returns the ratio between net profit and total assets.
   FRReturnOnTotalAssets determines the ratio of net profit to total assets by dividing net profit by total assets.

FRReturnOnTotalAssets (n1, n2)

n1 – numeric value indicating net profit.
n2 – numeric value indicating total assets.

```
FRReturnOnTotalAssets (10000,75000)
```

returns a profit-to-assets ratio of .13.

LooksLike

Returns a Boolean (true or false) value based on whether the "mask" is found in the source string.

LooksLike uses DOS-style "wildcards" (the asterisk and question mark) to determine if the source string contains the characters specified in the wildcard-based mask. This is helpful for checking for partial text matches.

LooksLike (s1, s2)

s1 – the source string to be searched.
s2 – the mask string to search against. The mask can include a question-mark wildcard to indicate a single-character substitution and/or an asterisk to indicate a multiple-character substitution.

```
LooksLike("George Peck", "G?orge*")
```

returns True.

Now

Returns the current time from the system clock as a text string.

This function is "left over" from previous versions of Crystal Reports and is similar to the CurrentTime function. The only difference between Now and CurrentTime is the data type returned. CurrentTime returns a time data type, while Now returns a string data type.

Picture

Formats a string based on the supplied formatting "mask" string.

Picture reformats a string value, inserting literal characters supplied within the "mask" formatting string. Picture is helpful for adding characters to an existing string, such as parentheses and hyphens to string database phone numbers without such punctuation.

Picture (s1, s2)

s1 – source string to format.
s2 – string "mask" to base formatting on. Any occurrence of an *x* character in the mask will substitute a single character from the source string. Any character other than *x* will simply be added to the output string.

```
Picture("8007733472", "Phone: (xxx) xxx-xxxx")
```

returns "Phone: (800) 773-3472".

Soundex

Returns a four-character string indicating how the source string "sounds".

Soundex uses a character-based algorithm to assign a "sound" to the source string. Similar-sounding strings, such as "George" and "gorge", will return the same four-character Soundex result. You may use Soundex in If-Then-Else statements, or similar constructs, where you want to compare the sound of two or more strings.

Soundex (s)

s – a string value to perform the Soundex algorithm on.

```
Soundex("George")
```

returns the string "G620".

```
If Soundex("George") = Soundex("gorge") Then
    "Sound the same"
Else
    "Different sound"
```

returns "Sound the same".

NOTE *An involved description of the Soundex algorithm can be found in Crystal Reports online help.*

Functions: Alerts

This set of functions exposes Crystal Reports Alerts to formulas.

AlertMessage

Returns a string containing the message portion of an alert.

AlertMessage returns the message portion of an alert when a particular report record has triggered the alert. If the record has not triggered the alert, AlertMessage returns an empty string.

AlertMessage (s)

s – a string value indicating the name of the alert.

```
AlertMessage("Order Over 5K")
```

returns "Orders over $5,000 exist" (the message for the Order Over 5K alert) if the report record has triggered the Order Over 5K alert.

AlertNames

Shows the name of each alert included in the report.

The AlertNames category of the Function tree (within the Alerts category) will show the names of each alert that has been created on the report. These alert names can be supplied as arguments to other Alert functions (described later in this section). If no alerts have been created, this function category won't appear in the Function tree.

IsAlertEnabled

Returns a Boolean (true or false) value indicating whether or not the "Enabled" check box is checked for the specified alert.

IsAlertEnabled tests to see if an alert will "fire" if records meet its criteria. An alert can be enabled or disabled when the alert is edited.

PART II

IsAlertEnabled (s)

s – a string value indicating the name of the alert.

```
If IsAlertEnabled("Order Over 5K") Then
    "Over 5K orders will be tested for"
```

returns "Over 5K orders will be tested for" if the enabled check box is checked in the Order Over 5K alert dialog box.

IsAlertTriggered

Returns a Boolean (true or false) value indicating whether or not an alert is triggered.

IsAlertTriggered is used within a formula to see if a particular alert has "fired" for the current record. The formula can base the remainder of its logic on whether or not the record has triggered the alert.

IsAlertTriggered (s)

s – a string value indicating the name of the alert.

```
If IsAlertTriggered ("Order Over 5K") Then
    "Congratulations--Great Order!"
```

returns "Congratulations—Great Order!" if the Order Over 5K alert is triggered when the formula evaluates.

Functions: Arrays

This category of functions applies to arrays. An *array* is a collection of data items stored in a single "bucket," such as a single variable. If an array contains 15 items, it is said to have 15 *elements*. Arrays can contain any supported Crystal Reports data type, such as number, string, date-time, and so forth.

Average

Returns a number containing the average of the numeric elements in the array.

Average (a)

a – an array. The array must be numeric.

```
Average([1,5,10,20,10])
```

returns 9.2.

Count

Returns a number containing the number of elements in the array.

Count is helpful when performing looping logic through an array. By using Count, you can determine how many array elements to loop through.

Count (a)

a – an array. The array can be of any data type.

```
Count([1,5,10,20,10])
```

returns 5.

NOTE *Count is functionally equivalent to UBound when dealing with arrays.*

DistinctCount

Returns a number containing the number of unique entries in the array.

DistinctCount is different from Count in that a duplicated entry in the array (for example, a second occurrence of the same element) will not increment the count when using DistinctCount, whereas it will with Count.

DistinctCount (a)

a – an array. The array can be of any data type.

```
DistinctCount(["George","Paul","George","John","Ringo","John"])
```

returns 4.

MakeArray

Creates an array.

MakeArray will create an array of values. It can be used to assign an array to a variable or pass a "literal" array to another array-based function. Supplying array elements within square brackets is the equivalent of MakeArray.

MakeArray (v1, v2...)

[v1, v2...]

v1 and v2 – literal values, separated by commas, that become array elements. The literal values can be any Crystal Reports data type, as long as they are all of the same data type. An array can contain, at maximum, 1,000 elements.

```
StringVar Array Beatles :=
    MakeArray("George","Paul","John","Ringo");
Beatles[3]
```

returns "John".

```
StringVar Array Beatles :=
    ["George","Paul","John","Ringo"];
Beatles[3]
```

returns "John".

NOTE *Basic syntax contains the Array function in addition to MakeArray. Array and MakeArray are functionally equivalent in Basic syntax.*

Maximum

Returns the last entry in an array.

Maximum will return the "last" entry in an array. What constitutes the "last" entry is based on the type of data in the array. Maximum will return the highest number in a numeric array, the last string value alphabetically in a string array, and so forth.

Maximum (a)

a – an array. The array can be of any data type.

```
Maximum([#1/1/1990#,#12/15/85#,#5/13/03#,#7/4/2000#])
```

will return 5/13/2003 12:00:00 A.M. as a date-time value.

Minimum

Returns the first entry in an array.

Minimum will return the "first" entry in an array. What constitutes the "first" entry is based on the type of data in the array. Minimum will return the lowest number in a numeric array, the first string value alphabetically in a string array, and so forth.

Minimum (a)

a – an array. The array can be of any data type.

```
Minimum(["Paul","George","John","Ringo"])
```

will return "George".

PopulationStdDev

Returns a number containing the population standard deviation of an array.

PopulationStdDev (a)

a – an array. The array must be numeric.

```
PopulationStdDev([1,10,15,20,25])
```

returns 8.28 (rounded to two decimal places).

PopulationVariance

Returns a number containing the population variance of an array.

PopulationVariance (a)

a – an array. The array must be numeric.

```
PopulationVariance([1,10,15,20,25])
```

returns 68.56 (rounded to two decimal places).

StdDev

Returns a number containing the standard deviation of an array.

StdDev (a)

a – an array. The array must be numeric.

```
StdDev([1,10,15,20,25])
```

returns 9.26 (rounded to two decimal places).

Sum

Returns a number containing the sum of array elements.

Sum (a)

a – an array. The array must be numeric.

```
Sum([1,10,15,20,25])
```

returns 71.

UBound

Returns the number of elements in the array.

UBound is helpful when performing looping logic through an array. By using UBound, you can determine how many array elements to loop through.

UBound (a)

a – an array. The array can be of any data type.

```
UBound([1,5,10,20,10])
```

returns 5.

NOTE *UBound is functionally equivalent to Count when dealing with arrays.*

Variance

Returns a number containing the variance of an array.

Variance (a)

a – an array. The array must be numeric.

```
Variance([1,10,15,20,25])
```

returns 85.70 (rounded to two decimal places).

Functions: Conditional Formatting

This category of functions appears in the Function tree only when you display the Format Formula Editor by clicking a Conditional Formatting Formula button from another Crystal Reports dialog box. Some of these functions will appear only in the proper "context"—for example, the Color or RGB functions will be available only when you are setting a color property conditionally.

Color

Returns a specific red-green-blue color combination.

Color allows you to specify intricate color values for font color, background color, and so forth. Rather than choosing from the limited set of default colors (such as crRed, crAqua, and so forth), you may specify any combination of red-green-blue colors with this function.

Color (n1, n2, n3)

n1 – a numeric value specifying the amount of red. The value must be between 0 and 255.
n2 – a numeric value specifying the amount of green. The value must be between 0 and 255.
n3 – a numeric value specifying the amount of blue. The value must be between 0 and 255.

```
If {Orders.Order Amount} > 5000 Then crRed Else Color(10,100,244)
```

will set the font color to a light blue shade (consisting of a red value of 10, green value of 100, and blue value of 244) if the order amount is not over 5,000.

NOTE *The RGB function is functionally equivalent to Color. RGB also accepts three arguments and may be used interchangeably with Color.*

CurrentFieldValue

Returns the contents of the field being formatted.

CurrentFieldValue will return the value contained in the field being formatted. The data type can vary, depending on the field being formatted. CurrentFieldValue is particular valuable when conditionally formatting Cross-Tab or OLAP grid cells, as the cells themselves cannot be directly referred to in a formatting formula.

CurrentFieldValue

```
If CurrentFieldValue > 5000 Then crRed Else crBlack
```

will set the color property to red if the value of the object being formatted is greater than 5,000.

DefaultAttribute

Returns the setting of the formatting property from the originating dialog box.

DefaultAttribute returns the value set in the calling dialog box. For example, if you set the "absolute" font color to aqua but then click the Conditional Formatting Formula button, you will be able to recall the aqua value in the formatting formula by using DefaultAttribute.

DefaultAttribute

```
If {Orders.Order Amount} > 5000 Then crRed Else DefaultAttribute
```

will set the font color to that selected in the absolute font color property of the Format Editor if the order amount is not greater than 5,000.

Functions: Date and Time

This set of functions deal with date and time manipulation, including extracting the current date and time from your computer's internal clock, performing date-time math, converting date-time functions to other data types, and so forth.

CurrentDate

Returns a date value with the current date from your computer's internal clock.

CurrentDate

```
CurrentDate
```

returns 5/30/2003 if the current date is May 30, 2003.

CurrentDateTime

Returns a date-time value with the current date and time from your computer's internal clock.

CurrentDateTime

```
CurrentDateTime
```

returns 5/30/2003 2:48:32PM if the current date is May 30, 2003, and the current time is 2:48 P.M.

CurrentTime

Returns a time value with the current time from your computer's internal clock.

CurrentTime

```
CurrentTime
```

returns 2:48:32PM if the current time is 2:48 in the afternoon.

Date

Returns a date value when supplied with various other data types.

Date is functionally equivalent to DateValue (with the exception of its availability only in Crystal Syntax) . See **DateValue** for details.

DateAdd

Returns a date-time value in the past or future, depending on supplied arguments.

DateAdd is handy for calculating dates in the past or future, based on a certain number of days, weeks, years, and so forth. DateAdd automatically handles leap years, months with less than 31 days, and so forth.

DateAdd (s, n, dt)

s – string value indicating interval type (days, weeks, and so forth). See **Interval Types** later in this section for recognized values.

n – a numeric value indicating number of intervals to add to the source date-time. This can be a negative or positive number.

dt – a date or date-time value indicating the source date-time to add intervals to.

```
DateAdd("d",5,CurrentDate)
```

returns 6/4/2003 12:00:00AM if the current date is May 30, 2003.

```
DateAdd("m",-2,#1/1/2003 10:00AM#)
```

returns 11/1/2002 10:00:00AM.

DateDiff

Returns a number indicating the number of "intervals" between two dates.

DateDiff is helpful in determining a specified amount of time that has elapsed between two date or date-time values. DateDiff can return the number of years, months, days, minutes, and so forth.

DateDiff (s, dt1, dt2)

s – string value indicating interval type (days, weeks, and so forth). See **Interval Types** later in this section for recognized values.

dt1 – a date, date-time, or time value indicating the start date-time to compare.

dt2 – a date, date-time, or time value indicating the end date-time to compare.

```
DateDiff ("h",#5/2/2003 10:00 AM#,#5/3/2003 2:00 PM#)
```

returns 28.

DateDiff (s, dt1, dt2, n)

s – string value indicating interval type (days, weeks, and so forth). See **Interval Types** later in this section for recognized values.

dt1 – a date, date-time, or time value indicating the start date-time to compare.

dt2 – a date, date-time, or time value indicating the end date-time to compare.

n – a numeric value or constant indicating the first day of the week. If not supplied, Sunday is assumed to be the first day of the week. See **First Day of Week Constants** later in this section for recognized constants or numbers for this argument.

```
DateDiff ("ww",#5/1/2003#,#6/1/2003#,crMonday)
```

returns 4.

DatePart

Returns a number indicating the individual "part" (month, hour, year, and so forth) of a date, date-time, or time value.

DatePart will return just the year, month, day, hour, minute, or second of a supplied date-time value. Other functions that work similarly to DatePart are Year, Month, Day, Hour, Minute, and Second.

DatePart (s, dt)

s – string value indicating interval type (day, week, hour, and so forth). See **Interval Types** later in this section for recognized values.
dt – a date, date-time, or time value to extract the interval from.

```
DatePart ("m",CurrentDate)
```

returns 5, if the current date is May 30, 2003.

DatePart (s, dt, n)

s – string value indicating interval type (day, week, hour, and so forth). See **Interval Types** later in this section for recognized values.
dt – a date, date-time, or time value to extract the interval from.
n – a numeric value or constant indicating the first day of the week. If not supplied, Sunday is assumed to be the first day of the week. See **First Day of Week Constants** later in this section for recognized constants or numbers for this argument.

```
DatePart ("w",#May 30, 2003#,crMonday)
```

returns 5, considering that May 30, 2003, is a Friday.

DatePart (s, dt, n1, n2)

s – string value indicating interval type (day, week, hour, and so forth). See **Interval Types** later in this section for recognized values.
dt – a date, date-time, or time value to extract the interval from.
n1 – a numeric value or constant indicating the first day of the week. If not supplied, Sunday is assumed to be the first day of the week. See **First Day of Week Constants** later in this section for recognized constants or numbers for this argument.
n2 – a numeric value or constant indicating the first week of year. If not supplied, the week containing January 1 is assumed to be the first week of the year. See **First Week of Year Constants** later in this section for recognized constants or numbers for this argument.

```
DatePart ("ww",#6/1/2003#,crSunday,crFirstJan1)
```

returns 23.

DateSerial

Returns a date value based on year, month, and day arguments.

DateSerial provides similar functionality to a specific usage of CDate, Date, and DateValue. DateSerial differs from these other functions in one significant way: the arguments supplied do not have to fall into a strict "month between 1 and 12, day between 1 and 31" requirement.

By supplying other values, such as negative numbers, calculations, and so forth, arguments will be evaluated "relatively."

DateSerial (n1, n2, n3)

n1 – a numeric value indicating the year.
n2 – a numeric value indicating the month.
n3 – a numeric value indicating the day.

```
DateSerial(2003, 6, 1)
```

returns 6/1/2003.

```
DateSerial(2003, 6-10, 1-30)
```

returns 7/2/2002 (10 months before June—which equates to August 1, 2002, and 30 days before the first day of the month, which equates to July 2, 2002).

DateTime

Returns a date-time value based on one of several sets and types of arguments.

DateTime is functionally equivalent to CDateTime and DateTimeValue. See **DateTimeValue** for more information.

DateTimeValue

Returns a date-time value based on one of several sets and types of arguments.

DateTimeValue can accept a wide variety of arguments that will be converted to a date-time. DateTimeValue comes in handy when you need to convert other data types to date-time, such as database fields from older systems that stored dates as strings. DateTimeValue is functionally equivalent to DateTime and CDateTime.

DateTimeValue (d)

d – a date value that will be converted to a date-time value with midnight as the time.

```
DateTimeValue(CurrentDate)
```

returns 5/30/2003 12:00:00AM if today's date is May 30, 2003 (in essence, converting the CurrentDate date-only value to a date-time value).

DateTimeValue (d, t)

d – a date value that will become the date portion of the resulting date-time value.
t – a time value that will become the time portion of the resulting date-time value.

```
DateTimeValue(CurrentDate, Time(#10:30 am#))
```

returns 5/30/2003 10:30:00AM if today's date is May 30, 2003.

DateTimeValue (n)

n – a numeric value indicating the number of days since December 30, 1899.

```
DateTimeValue(35000)
```

returns 10/28/1995 12:00:00AM (35,000 days from December 30, 1899).

DateTimeValue (s)

s – a string value that will be evaluated for particular date and time equivalents.

```
DateTimeValue("January 1, 2003 15:50")
```

returns 1/1/2003 3:50:00PM.

DateTimeValue (n1, n2, n3)

n1 – a numeric value indicating the year.
n2 – a numeric value between 1 and 12 indicating the month.
n3 – a numeric value between 1 and 31 indicating the day of month.

```
DateTimeValue(2002,10,15)
```

returns 10/15/2002 12:00:00AM.

DateTimeValue (n1, n2, n3, n4, n5, n6)

n1 – a numeric value indicating the year.
n2 – a numeric value between 1 and 12 indicating the month.
n3 – a numeric value between 1 and 31 indicating the day of month.
n4 – a numeric value between 0 and 23 indicating the hour of day.
n5 – a numeric value between 0 and 59 indicating the minute.
n6 – a numeric value between 0 and 59 indicating the second.

```
DateTimeValue(2002,10,15,14,35,50)
```

returns 10/15/2002 2:35:50PM.

DateValue

Returns a date value based on one of several sets and types of arguments.

DateValue can accept a wide variety of arguments that will be converted to a date. DateValue comes in handy when you need to convert other data types to date, such as database fields from older systems that stored dates as strings. DateValue is functionally equivalent to Date and CDate.

DateValue (dt)

dt – a date-time value that you wish to strip the time portion away from.

```
DateValue(CurrentDateTime)
```

returns 5/30/2002 if the current date is May 30, 2003, regardless of what time of day.

DateValue (n)

n – a numeric value indicating the number of days since December 30, 1899.

```
DateValue(35000)
```

returns 10/28/1995 (35,000 days from December 30, 1899).

DateValue (s)

s – a string value that will be evaluated for particular date equivalents.

```
DateValue("January 1, 2003")
```

returns 1/1/2003.

DateValue (n1, n2, n3)

n1 – a numeric value indicating the year.
n2 – a numeric value between 1 and 12 indicating the month.
n3 – a numeric value between 1 and 31 indicating the day of month.

```
DateValue(2002,10,15)
```

returns 10/15/2002.

Day

Returns a numeric value indicating the day of the month.

Day (dt)

dt – a date or date-time value.

```
Day(CurrentDate)
```

returns 30 if the current date is May 30, 2003.

DayOfWeek

Returns a numeric value indicating the day of the week.

DayOfWeek returns the day of the week. By default, DayOfWeek assumes Sunday is equal to 1. However, you may provide an extra argument to DayOfWeek indicating a different starting day. DayOfWeek is functionally equivalent to WeekDay.

DayOfWeek (dt)

dt – a date or date-time value.

```
DayOfWeek(CurrentDate)
```

returns 6 if the current date falls on a Friday.

DayOfWeek (dt, n)

dt – a date or date-time value.
n – a numeric value or constant indicating the first day of the week. If not supplied, Sunday is assumed to be the first day of the week. See **First Day of Week Constants** later in this section for recognized constants or numbers for this argument.

```
DayOfWeek(CurrentDate, crMonday)
```

returns 5 if the current date falls on a Friday.

Hour

Returns a numeric value indicating the hour of the supplied time or date-time in military time.

Hour (dt)

dt – a date-time or time value.

```
Hour(CurrentTime)
```

returns 17 if the current time is in the 5 P.M. hour.

IsDate

Returns a Boolean (true of false) value indicating whether or not the supplied number or string can be converted to a date value.

IsDate is helpful in determining if a supplied string or numeric value can be converted to a date with the DateValue (or similar) function. Because these other conversion functions will fail with a run-time error if an invalid value is supplied to them, using IsDate with an If-Then-Else statement can prevent run-time errors.

IsDate (s)

s – a string value to be evaluated for conversion to a date.

IsDate (n)

n – a numeric value to be evaluated as the number of days since December 30, 1899.

```
If IsDate({FromMainframe.OrderDateAsString}) Then
    DateValue({FromMainframe.OrderDateAsString})
Else
    DateValue(0,0,0)
```

returns a true order date if it can be converted, or 0/0/0 if it can't.

IsDateTime

Returns a Boolean (true of false) value indicating whether or not the supplied number or string can be converted to a date-time value.

IsDateTime is helpful in determining if a supplied string or numeric value can be converted to a date-time with the DateTimeValue (or similar) function. Because these other conversion functions will fail with a run-time error if an invalid value is supplied to them, using IsDateTime with an If-Then-Else statement can prevent run-time errors.

IsDateTime (s)

s – a string value to be evaluated for conversion to a date-time.

PART II

IsDateTime (n)

n – a numeric value to be evaluated as the number of days since December 30, 1899.

```
If IsDateTime({FromMainframe.IncidentDateTimeAsString}) Then
    DateTimeValue({FromMainframe.IncidentDateTimeAsString})
Else
    DateTimeValue(0,0,0,0,0,0)
```

returns a true incident date-time if it can be converted, or 0/0/0 at midnight if it can't.

IsTime

Returns a Boolean (true of false) value indicating whether or not the supplied number or string can be converted to a time value.

IsTime is helpful in determining if a supplied string or numeric value can be converted to a time with the TimeValue (or similar) function. Because these other conversion functions will fail with a run-time error if an invalid value is supplied to them, using IsTime with an If-Then-Else statement can prevent run-time errors.

IsTime (s)

s – a string value to be evaluated for conversion to a time.

IsTime (n)

n – a numeric value to be evaluated as the number of "24-hour units".

```
If IsTime({FromMainframe.IncidentTimeAsString}) Then
    TimeValue({FromMainframe.IncidentTimeAsString})
Else
    TimeValue(0,0,0)
```

returns a true incident time if it can be converted, or midnight if it can't.

Minute

Returns a numeric value indicating the minute of the supplied time or date-time.

Minute (dt)

dt – a date-time or time value.

```
Minute(CurrentTime)
```

returns 43 if the current time is 5:43 P.M.

Month

Returns a numeric value indicating the month.

Month (dt)

dt – a date or date-time value.

```
Month(CurrentDate)
```

returns 5 if the current date is May 30, 2003.

MonthName

Returns a string value indicating the spelled-out month of the supplied numeric argument.

MonthName (n)

n – a numeric value between 1 and 12 indicating the number of the month.

MonthName (n, b)

n – a numeric value between 1 and 12 indicating the number of the month.
b – a Boolean (true or false) value, indicating whether to abbreviate the month.

```
MonthName (3, True)
```

returns "Mar".

Second

Returns a numeric value indicating the second of the supplied time or date-time.

Second (dt)

dt – a date-time or time value.

```
Second(CurrentTime)
```

returns 45 if the current time is 5:43:45 P.M.

ShiftDateTime

Returns a date/time value in a new time zone.

ShiftDateTime (dt, s1, s2)

dt – the date/time value to be converted to a new time zone.
s1 – a string representing the time zone that *dt* is currently in.
s2 – a string representing the new time zone to convert *dt* to.

The *s1* and *s2* time zone strings that are supplied to ShiftDateTime can appear to be quite complex. However, the only relevant portion of a time zone string is the *offset* (the number of minutes that the relevant time zone is offset from Greenwich Mean Time/ Coordinated Universal Time). While any other portions of the time zone string that you include must appear with proper data types and within appropriate range limits (for example, the month number portion of the time zone string must be numeric and must be between 1 and 12), these remaining portions of the time zone string are optional and don't affect the actual ShiftDateTime calculation.

To illustrate, compare this usage of ShiftDateTime:

```
ShiftDateTime (CurrentDateTime,
"Mountain Standard Time,420,Mountain Daylight Time,-60;4.1.0/02:00,10.5.0/02:00",
"Pacific Standard Time,480,Pacific Daylight Time,-60;4.1.0/02:00,10.5.0/02:00")
```

with this one:

```
ShiftDateTime (CurrentDateTime, ",420", ",480")
```

Both return "5/14/2005 8:30:00AM" if your current computer date/time is May 14, 2005, at 9:30 A.M. in the Mountain time zone. Note that the only significant portions of the time zone string are the offsets—the remaining portions are ignored when ShiftDateTime calculates the new date and time.

A more typical use of ShiftDateTime might be:

```
ShiftDateTime(CurrentDateTime, PrintTimeZone, CurrentCEUserTimeZone)
```

which displays the current date and time set on your computer adjusted to the time zone of the BusinessObjects Enterprise or Crystal Reports Server system you are currently logged into. For example, if your computer's current date/time is May 14, 2005, at 9:03:10 A.M. in the Pacific time zone and the BusinessObjects Enterprise or Crystal Reports Server system you're logged into is located in the Mountain time zone, this formula will return "5/14/2005 10:03:10AM".

Time Zone Strings

The following table describes the various portions of a time zone string that you can supply to ShiftDateTime, or that is returned by various other functions that return time zone strings (such as CECurrentTimeZone, DataTimeZone, and PrintTimeZone). Each portion is separated from the next by a comma. If you are supplying a time zone string to ShiftDateTime, you may supply an empty string to signify the local time zone to your computer. Or, if you supply a time zone string, the only required portion is the offset preceded by a comma.

Standard Time Zone	A string description of the standard time zone.
Standard Time Offset	A number indicating the number of minutes that this standard time zone is offset from Greenwich Mean Time/Coordinated Universal Time. This number will be positive for time zones west of Greenwich, England and negative for those east of Greenwich, England.
Daylight Saving Time Zone	A string description of the daylight saving time zone. If the time zone does not utilize daylight saving time, this string won't appear.
Daylight Saving Time Offset	A number indicating the number of minutes that daylight saving time in this time zone is offset from the standard time offset (the second portion of the time zone string). By default, this value is adjusted 60 minutes from the standard time zone offset. If this time zone does not utilize daylight saving time, this number won't appear.
Daylight Saving Start	A string, in the form of m.w.d/hh:mm, indicating the month, week, day, and time that daylight saving time goes into effect for this time zone. The month number, between 1 and 12, indicates the month; the week number, between 1 and 5, indicates the week during the month; and the day number, between 0 and 6, indicates the day of the week (0 being Sunday). Optionally, the month, week, and day will be followed by a slash and a time indicating the hour that daylight saving time starts. The time consists of a two-character hour, a colon, and a two-character minute (in 24-hour time format). The default is 2 a.m. (02:00).

Daylight Saving End	A string, in the form of m.w.d/hh:mm, indicating the month, week, day, and time that daylight saving time ends for this time zone. The month number, between 1 and 12, indicates the month; the week number, between 1 and 5, indicates the week during the month; and the day number, between 0 and 6, indicates the day of the week (0 being Sunday). Optionally, the month, week, and day will be followed by a slash and a time indicating the hour that daylight saving time ends. The time consists of a two-character hour, a colon, and a two-character minute (in 24-hour time format). The default is 2 a.m. (02:00).

Time

Returns a time value when supplied with various other data types.

Time is functionally equivalent to TimeValue. See **TimeValue** for details.

Timer

Returns the number of seconds since midnight.

Timer may be useful as a "seed" for the Rnd (random number) function.

Timer

```
Timer
```

returns 64,917 at 6:01:57 P.M.

TimeSerial

Returns a time value based on hour, minute, and second arguments.

TimeSerial provides similar functionality to a specific usage of CTime, Time, and TimeValue. TimeSerial differs from these other functions in one significant way: the arguments supplied do not have to fall into a strict "hour between 0 and 24, minute between 0 and 59" requirement. By supplying other values, such as negative numbers, calculations, and so forth, arguments will be evaluated "relatively."

TimeSerial (n1, n2, n3)

n1 – a numeric value indicating the hour.
n2 – a numeric value indicating the minute.
n3 – a numeric value indicating the second.

```
TimeSerial(17,30,15)
```

returns 5:30:15PM.

```
TimeSerial(17,30-40,15+25)
```

returns 4:50:40PM.

TimeValue
Returns a time value based on one of several sets and types of arguments.

TimeValue can accept a wide variety of arguments that will be converted to a time. TimeValue comes in handy when you need to convert other data types to time, such as database fields from older systems that stored times as strings. TimeValue is functionally equivalent to Time and CTime.

TimeValue (dt)
dt – a date-time value that you wish to strip the time portion away from.

```
TimeValue(CurrentDateTime)
```

returns 6:23:19PM if the current time is 6:23 P.M., regardless of what day.

TimeValue (n)
n – a numeric value to be evaluated as the number of "24-hour units."

```
TimeValue(.25)
```

returns 6:00:00AM.

TimeValue (s)
s – a string value that will be evaluated for particular time equivalents.

```
TimeValue("17:15")
```

returns 5:15:00PM.

TimeValue (n1, n2, n3)
n1 – a numeric value between 0 and 23 indicating the hour.
n2 – a numeric value between 0 and 59 indicating the minute.
n3 – a numeric value between 0 and 59 indicating the second.

```
TimeValue(14,12,0)
```

returns 2:12:00PM.

WeekdayName
Returns a string value containing a spelled-out name of the week.

WeekdayName will spell the name of the weekday ("Monday", etc.), based on a supplied numeric value.

WeekdayName (n)
n – numeric value between 1 and 7.

WeekdayName (n, b)
n – numeric value between 1 and 7.
b – a Boolean (true or false) value indicating whether to abbreviate the weekday name.

WeekdayName (n1, b, n2)

n1 – numeric value between 1 and 7.

b – Boolean (true or false) value indicating whether to abbreviate the weekday name.

n – numeric value or constant indicating the first day of the week. If not supplied, Sunday is assumed to be the first day of the week. See **First Day of Week Constants** later in this section for recognized constants or numbers for this argument.

```
WeekdayName (3, True, crMonday)
```

returns "Wed".

Year

Returns a numeric value indicating the year.

Year (dt)

dt – a date or date-time value.

```
Year(CurrentDate)
```

returns 2,003 if the current date is May 30, 2003.

Interval Types

The following interval types can be used with various date functions, such as DateAdd and DateDiff.

m	Month
d	Day (functionally equivalent to y)
yyyy	Year
y	Day of Year (functionally equivalent to d)
w	Weekday or Number of Weeks
ww	Week or Number of FirstDayOfWeeks
q	Quarter
h	Hour
m	Minute
s	Second

PART II

First Day of Week Constants

The following first-day-of-week values can be supplied to various functions that change output based on the first day of the week. Either the numeric value or the constant can be supplied.

crUseSystem	0 (default from Windows)
crSunday	1
crMonday	2
crTuesday	3
crWednesday	4
crThursday	5
crFriday	6
crSaturday	7

First Week of Year Constants

The following first-week-of-year values can be supplied to various functions that change output based on the first week of the year. Either the numeric value or the constant can be supplied.

crUseSystem	0 (default from Windows)
crFirstJan1	1
crFirstFourDays	2
crFirstFullWeek	3

Functions: Date Ranges

The following functions return date ranges based on the current date from the computer's clock. For point-in-time reporting purposes, you may change these ranges to be based on something other than the current date by using Report | Set Print Date/Time. All these functions return range values and must be used with a range operator, such as In.

Aged0To30Days

Returns a range in the last 30 days.

Aged0To30Days

```
If {AR.Due Date} In Aged0To30Days Then {AR.Amount Due}
```

returns the AR Amount due if the due date is in the past 30 days. Otherwise, 0 is returned.

Aged31To60Days

Returns a range between 31 and 60 days in the past.

Aged31To60Days

```
If {AR.Due Date} In Aged31To60Days Then {AR.Amount Due}
```

returns the AR Amount due if the due date is within 31 to 60 days past. Otherwise, 0 is returned.

Aged61To90Days
Returns a range between 61 and 90 days in the past.

Aged61To90Days

```
If {AR.Due Date} In Aged61To90Days Then {AR.Amount Due}
```

returns the AR Amount due if the due date is within 61 to 90 days past. Otherwise, 0 is returned.

AllDatesFromToday
Returns a range from today into the future (including today).

AllDatesFromToday

```
If {Shipments.Ship Date} In AllDatesFromToday Then
    "Product still needs to ship"
Else
    "Product has already shipped"
```

returns the appropriate string, depending on whether the ship date is in the future or the past.

AllDatesFromTomorrow
Returns a range from tomorrow into the future (including tomorrow).

AllDatesFromTomorrow

```
If {Shipments.Ship Date} In AllDatesFromTomorrow Then
    "Product ships tomorrow or thereafter"
Else
    "Product has already shipped"
```

returns the appropriate string, depending on whether the ship date is tomorrow or later.

AllDatesToToday
Returns a range up to, and including, today.

AllDatesToToday

```
If {Shipments.Ship Date} In AllDatesToToday Then
    "Product has been shipped"
Else
    "Product ships later"
```

returns the appropriate string, depending on whether the product shipped today or earlier.

AllDatesToYesterday

Returns a range up to, and including, yesterday.

AllDatesToYesterday

```
If {Shipments.Ship Date} In AllDatesToYesterday Then
    "Product yesterday or before"
Else
    "Product ships today or later"
```

returns the appropriate string, depending on whether the product shipped yesterday or earlier.

Calendar1stHalf

Returns a range including January 1 to June 30 of the current year.

Calendar1stHalf

```
If {Sales.Sale Date} In Calendar1stHalf Then
    "Group 1: Jan 1 - Jun 30"
Else
    "Group 2: Jul 1 - Dec 31"
```

returns one of two appropriate values, depending on whether the sale took place in the first or second half of the year.

Calendar2ndHalf

Returns a range including July 1 to December 31 of the current year.

Calendar2ndHalf

```
If {Sales.Sale Date} In Calendar2ndHalf Then
    "Group 1: Jul 1 - Dec 31"
Else
    "Group 2: Jan 1 - Jun 30"
```

returns one of two appropriate values, depending on whether the sale took place in the first or second half of the year.

Calendar1stQtr

Returns a range including January 1 to March 31 of the current year.

Calendar1stQtr

```
CurrencyVar Q1Total;
If {Sales.Sale Date} In Calendar1stQtr Then
    Q1Total := Q1Total + {Sales.Amount}
```

increments a variable with a sales amount only if the sale took place in the first calendar quarter.

Calendar2ndQtr

Returns a range including April 1 to June 30 of the current year.

Calendar2ndQtr

```
CurrencyVar Q2Total;
If {Sales.Sale Date} In Calendar2ndQtr Then
    Q2Total := Q2Total + {Sales.Amount}
```

increments a variable with a sales amount only if the sale took place in the second calendar quarter.

Calendar3rdQtr

Returns a range including July 1 to September 30 of the current year.

Calendar3rdQtr

```
CurrencyVar Q3Total;
If {Sales.Sale Date} In Calendar3rdQtr Then
    Q3Total := Q3Total + {Sales.Amount}
```

increments a variable with a sales amount only if the sale took place in the third calendar quarter.

Calendar4thQtr

Returns a range including October 1 to December 31 of the current year.

Calendar4thQtr

```
CurrencyVar Q4Total;
If {Sales.Sale Date} In Calendar4thQtr Then
    Q4Total := Q4Total + {Sales.Amount}
```

increments a variable with a sales amount only if the sale took place in the fourth calendar quarter.

Last4WeeksToSun

Returns a range including the four weeks prior to, and including, the most recent Sunday.

Last4WeeksToSun, unlike some other date and date range functions, considers a week to start on Monday and end on Sunday.

Last4WeeksToSun

```
If {AR.Invoice Date} In Last4WeeksToSun Then
    "Current"
Else
    "Past Due"
```

returns a string indicating the status of an account receivable based on the last four weeks.

Last7Days

Returns a range consisting of the last seven days, including today.

Last7Days

```
If {Sales.Sale Date} In Last7Days Then
    "Eligible for Price Protection"
Else
    "Not Eligible for Price Protection"
```

returns a string indicating if a sale is eligible for price protection because it took place within the last seven days.

LastFullMonth

Returns a range including the first day of last month to the last day of last month.

LastFullMonth

```
If {Sales.Sale Date} In LastFullMonth Then
    "Eligible for Price Protection"
Else
    "Not Eligible for Price Protection"
```

returns a string indicating if a sale is eligible for price protection because it took place within the last month.

LastFullWeek

Returns a range including Sunday through Saturday of the previous week.

LastFullWeek

```
If {Sales.Sale Date} In LastFullWeek Then
    "Eligible for Price Protection"
Else
    "Not Eligible for Price Protection"
```

returns a string indicating if a sale is eligible for price protection because it took place within the previous Sunday through Saturday.

LastYearMTD

Returns a range including the first day of this month last year through today's date last year.

LastYearMTD

```
CurrencyVar LastYearMTDSales;
If {Sales.Sale Date}In LastYearMTD Then
    LastYearMTDSales := LastYearMTDSales + {Sales.Amount}
```

accumulates a sales amount in a variable if the sale took place this month-to-date last year.

LastYearYTD
Returns a range including January 1 last year through today's date last year.

LastYearYTD

```
CurrencyVar LastYearYTDSales;
If {Sales.Sale Date}In LastYearYTD Then
    LastYearYTDSales := LastYearYTDSales + {Sales.Amount}
```

accumulates a sales amount in a variable if the sale took place this year-to-date last year.

MonthToDate
Returns a range including the first day of this month through today.

MonthToDate

```
CurrencyVar MTDSales;
If {Sales.Sale Date}In MonthToDate Then
    MTDSales := MTDSales + {Sales.Amount}
```

accumulates a sales amount in a variable if the sale took place from the first of this month through today.

Next30Days
Returns a range in the next 30 days.

Next30Days

```
If {Shipments.Ship Date} In Next30Days Then
"High Priority - shipping within the month"
```

returns the string value if the shipment date is in the next 30 days. Otherwise, an empty string is returned.

Next31To60Days
Returns a range between 31 and 60 days in the future.

Next31To60Days

```
If {Shipments.Ship Date} In Next31To60Days Then
"Medium Priority - shipping 2 months from now"
```

returns the string value if the shipment date is between 31 and 60 days in the future. Otherwise, an empty string is returned.

Next61To90Days
Returns a range between 61 and 90 days in the future.

PART II

Next61To90Days

```
If {Shipments.Ship Date} In Next61To90Days Then
"Low Priority - shipping 3 months from now"
```

returns the string value if the shipment date is between 61 and 90 days in the future. Otherwise, an empty string is returned.

Next91To365Days

Returns a range between 91 and 365 days in the future.

Next91To365Days

```
If {Shipments.Ship Date} In Next91To365Days Then
"No Concern - shipping over 3 months from now"
```

returns the string value if the shipment date is between 91 and 365 days in the future. Otherwise, an empty string is returned.

Over90Days

Returns a range from 90 days in the past and beyond.

Over90Days

```
If {AR.Due Date} In Over90Days Then {AR.Amount Due}
```

returns the AR Amount due if the due date is over 90 days past the current date. Otherwise, 0 is returned.

WeekToDateFromSun

Returns a range starting the previous Sunday through today.

WeekToDateFromSun

```
If {Sales.Sale Date} In WeekToDateFromSun Then
    "Eligible for Price Protection"
Else
    "Not Eligible for Price Protection"
```

returns a string indicating if a sale is eligible for price protection because it took place between this past Sunday and today.

YearToDate

Returns a range including January 1 through today's date.

YearToDate

```
CurrencyVar ThisYearYTDSales;
If {Sales.Sale Date}In YearToDate Then
    ThisYearYTDSales := ThisYearYTDSales + {Sales.Amount}
```

accumulates a sales amount in a variable if the sale took place this year-to-date.

Functions: Document Properties

This category of functions duplicates many of the Special Fields available from the Field Explorer. By making these values available to formulas, you may base formulas on various properties of the report, such as the page number that's currently printing, whether a group header is being repeated, and so forth.

ContentLocale

Returns a string indicating the chosen Preferred Viewing Locale set on the View menu.

ContentLocale

```
"Currently-selected viewing language: " & ContentLocale
```

returns "Currently-selected viewing language: en_US" if the Preferred Viewing Locale chosen in the View menu is English (United States). The same value will appear on your report if you insert the ContentLocale special field from the Field Explorer.

CurrentCEUserID

Returns a numeric value indicating the internal ID maintained by BusinessObjects Enterprise/Crystal Reports Server for the currently logged-on user.

CECurrentUserID helps identify who is viewing the report after it has been published to BusinessObjects Enterprise/Crystal Reports Server. While you may find some value in the numeric value this function returns, you'll probably find more value in the actual user name returned by the CurrentCEUserName function. This function returns a numeric zero if the report is not being displayed from within BusinessObjects Enterprise/Crystal Reports Server (if used in stand-alone Crystal Reports, for example).

CECurrentUserID

```
CECurrentUserID
```

returns the number 12.00 if the currently logged on user's internal ID number is 12. The function returns 0.00 if the report is not being displayed in BusinessObjects Enterprise/ Crystal Reports Server.

CurrentCEUserName

Returns a string value indicating the user name for the currently logged-on user.

CECurrentUserName helps identify who is viewing the report after it has been published to BusinessObjects Enterprise/Crystal Reports Server. You may use this function to change report logic according to who is viewing the report in BusinessObjects Enterprise/Crystal Reports Server. This may be helpful for creating certain limitations (similar to row and column security) based on the user. This function returns an empty string if the report is not being displayed from within BusinessObjects Enterprise/Crystal Reports Server (if used in stand-alone Crystal Reports, for example).

CECurrentUserName

```
If CECurrentUserName = "" Then
   "Not logged in to BusinessObjects Enterprise/Crystal Reports Server"
Else
   CECurrentUserName
```

returns the user name of the current BusinessObjects Enterprise/Crystal Reports Server user. If the report is being viewed outside BusinessObjects Enterprise/Crystal Reports Server (for example, in the stand-alone Crystal Reports designer), the formula returns "Not logged in to BusinessObjects Enterprise/Crystal Reports Server".

CurrentCEUserTimeZone

Returns a time zone string indicating the time zone of the BusinessObjects Enterprise/ Crystal Reports Server system you are currently logged in to.

CurrentCEUserTimeZone

```
CurrentCEUserTimeZone
```

returns "Mountain Standard Time,420,Mountain Daylight Time,-60;4.1.0/02:00,10.5.0/02:00 " if the BusinessObjects Enterprise/Crystal Reports Server system you are currently logged in to is in the Mountain time zone. Inserting the CurrentCEUserTimeZone special field from the Field Explorer will display the same information (and, the function and the special field both return an empty string if you are not logged in).

NOTE *A detailed description of all the portions of a time zone string can be found in this appendix under ShiftDateTime.*

DataDate

Returns a date value indicating the last date that data on the report was refreshed from the database.

DataDate will be the same date that appears to the left of the page navigation controls in the Preview tab. Click Report | Refresh Report Data (or use the appropriate toolbar button or keyboard shortcut) to refresh the database and update this value to the current date.

DataDate

```
"Data current as of " & ToText(DataDate)
```

returns the string "Data current as of 5/31/2003" if the report was refreshed on May 31, 2003.

DataTime

Returns a time value indicating the last time that data on the report was refreshed from the database.

DataTime will be the same time that appears to the left of the page navigation controls in the Preview tab. Click Report | Refresh Report Data (or use the appropriate toolbar button or keyboard shortcut) to refresh the database and update this value to the current time.

DataTime

```
"Data current as of " & ToText(DataTime)
```

returns the string "Data current as of 6:15:21PM" if the report was refreshed at 6:15 P.M.

DataTimeZone

Returns a time zone string indicating the time zone of the Data Date and Time (typically, the time zone of the computer running the report).

DataTimeZone

```
DataTimeZone
```

returns "Mountain Standard Time,420,Mountain Daylight Time,-60;4.1.0/02:00,10.5.0/02:00 " if the computer running the report is in the Mountain time zone. Inserting the DataTimeZone special field from the Field Explorer will display the same information.

NOTE   *A detailed description of all the portions of a time zone string can be found in this appendix under ShiftDateTime.*

FileAuthor

Returns a string value from the Author field in the File | Summary Info dialog box.

FileAuthor

```
"Report written by " & FileAuthor
```

returns "Report written by George Peck", if "George Peck" has been placed in the Author field in the Summary Info dialog box.

FileCreationDate

Returns a date value indicating the date that the report file was first created.
    This value will not change if the report is later opened, modified, and resaved.

FileCreationDate

```
"Report first created " & ToText(FileCreationDate)
```

will return "Report first created 5/30/2003" if the report was initially created on May 30, 2003.

FileName

Returns a string value containing the file path and filename of the report stored on disk.

FileName

```
"Report location: " & FileName
```

returns "Report location: C:\Reports\Sales Analysis.rpt" if the report is stored as C:\ Reports\Sales Analysis.rpt.

GroupingLevel

Returns a numeric value indicating a group's location in the grouping hierarchy.

This function is typically used in combination with the HierarchyLevel function to determine where in a hierarchy a particular group resides (see **HierarchyLevel** elsewhere in this appendix). If the field supplied to GroupingLevel is not used in a report group, GroupingLevel will return 0.

GroupingLevel (f)

f – any database field, formula, or SQL Expression.

```
GroupingLevel ({Customer.Country})
```

returns 1.00 if Country is the first group on the report.

```
GroupingLevel ({@Grouping Field})
```

returns 3.00 if the third group on the report is based on the Grouping Field formula.

```
GroupingLevel ({Customer.City})
```

returns 0.00 if there is no City grouping on the report.

ModificationDate

Returns a date value indicating the date that the report file was last modified.

This value will change any time the report is opened, modified, and resaved.

ModificationDate

```
"Report last modified on " & ToText(ModificationDate)
```

will return "Report last modified on 5/31/2003" if the report was changed on May 31, 2003.

ModificationTime

Returns a time value indicating the time that the report file was last modified.

This value will change any time the report is opened, modified, and resaved.

ModificationTime

```
"Report last modified at " & ToText(ModificationTime)
```

will return "Report last modified at 6:33:20PM" if the report was saved at 6:33 P.M.

PrintDate

Returns a date value indicating the date that the report is formatted or printed.

By default, this value is taken from your computer's system clock. You may change it to another value by choosing Report | Set Print Date And Time from the pull-down menus.

PrintDate

```
"Report printed on " & ToText(PrintDate)
```

will return "Report printed on 5/31/2003" if the report is printed or formatted on May 31, 2003.

PrintTime

Returns a time value indicating the time that the report is formatted or printed.

By default, this value is taken from your computer's system clock. You may change it to another value by choosing Report | Set Print Date And Time from the pull-down menus.

PrintTime

```
"Report printed at " & ToText(PrintTime)
```

will return "Report printed at 6:38:33PM" if the report is printed or formatted at 6:38 P.M.

PrintTimeZone

Returns a time zone string indicating the time zone of the Print Date and Time (typically, the time zone of the computer running the report).

PrintTimeZone

```
PrintTimeZone
```

returns "Mountain Standard Time,420,Mountain Daylight Time,-60;4.1.0/02:00,10.5.0/02:00 " if the computer running the report is in the Mountain time zone. Inserting the PrintTimeZone special field from the Field Explorer will display the same information.

NOTE *A detailed description of all the portions of a time zone string can be found in this appendix under ShiftDateTime.*

ReportComments

Returns a string value from the Comments field in the File | Summary Info dialog box.

ReportComments

```
"Report Information: " & ReportComments
```

returns "Report Information: Ablaze Group, Version 1, May 2003", taking the text from the Comments field in the Summary Info dialog box.

ReportTitle

Returns a string value from the Title field in the File | Summary Info dialog box.

ReportTitle

```
"Report Title: " & ReportTitle
```

returns "Report Title: Sales Analysis", taking the text from the Title field in the Summary Info dialog box.

SelectionLocale

Returns a string indicating the Preferred Viewing Locale that was set on the View menu the last time the report was refreshed.

SelectionLocale

```
"Viewing language when report was refreshed: " & SelectionLocale
```

returns "Viewing language when report was refreshed: en_US" if the Preferred Viewing Locale chosen in the View menu the last time the report was refreshed was English (United States). The value returned by this function may not be the same as the current Preferred Viewing Locale if the report was created on a different computer, or if the viewing locale was changed since the report was last refreshed.

Functions: Evaluation Time

This category of functions is used to force a formula to evaluate during one of Crystal Reports' three available report "passes."

By default, formulas evaluate during a certain pass based on their contents. For example, a formula that makes no reference to database fields, such as

```
"Report printed on " & PrintDate
```

prints in the BeforeReadingRecords (or preread) pass by default.

A formula that makes reference to one or more database fields, such as

```
{Orders.Order Amount} * 1.10
```

prints in the WhileReadingRecords (or first) pass by default.

And, any formula that makes reference to summary functions, report alerts, and various other "second-pass" functions, such as

```
{Orders.Order Amount} %
Sum({Orders.Order Amount}, {Employee. Last Name})
```

prints in the WhilePrintingRecords (or second) pass by default.

While you cannot force a formula to an earlier report pass than its default, you can force it to a later pass. In particular, when using variables in formulas, you'll often need to force formulas that use the same variable to the same report pass to ensure consistent results.

BeforeReadingRecords

Forces a formula to evaluate in the "preread," BeforeReadingRecords, report pass.

BeforeReadingRecords

```
BeforeReadingRecords;
NumberVar Array RegionTotals := [0,0,0,0,0,0,0,0,0,0];
0
```

will create an array variable and fill it with zeros before the report reads records from the database.

EvaluateAfter

Forces a formula to evaluate after another formula has been evaluated.

EvaluateAfter is required when you place two formulas in the same report section that evaluate in the same report pass. In this case, it's not predictable which formula will evaluate first. If both formulas, for example, refer to the same variable, you may get unintended results if one formula doesn't evaluate after the other formula.

EvaluateAfter (f)

f – the name of another report formula.

```
EvaluateAfter({@Show Count});
NumberVar BonusCount := 0
```

resets the BonusCount variable to zero after the @Show Count formula has already processed.

WhilePrintingRecords

Forces a formula to evaluate during the second, WhilePrintingRecords, pass.

WhilePrintingRecords

```
WhilePrintingRecords;
NumberVar GroupBonusCount := 0
```

resets the GroupBonusCount variable to zero during the WhilePrintingRecords pass (presumably because other WhilePrintingRecords formulas make use of GroupBonusCount).

WhileReadingRecords

Forces a formula to evaluate during the first, WhileReadingRecords, pass.

WhileReadingRecords

```
WhileReadingRecords;
StringVar GroupField
```

forces the contents of the GroupField variable to be displayed during the WhileReadingRecords pass. This may be helpful if you wish to create report groups based on this formula.

PART II

Functions: Financial

This category of functions supplies many standard financial calculations and algorithms. Many of these functions behave similarly to those available in Microsoft Excel.

ACCRINT

Returns a numeric value indicating total accrued interest for a security.

ACCRINT (d1, d2, d3, n1, n2, n3)

d1 – a date or date-time value indicating the issue date.
d2 – a date or date-time value indicating the date of first interest payment.
d3 – a date or date-time value indicating the date the security was purchased.
n1 – a numeric value indicating the annual interest rate.
n2 – a numeric value indicating the par value.
n3 – a numeric value indicating the number of payments per year: 1 = annual,
2 = semiannual, 4 = quarterly.

ACCRINT (d1, d2, d3, n1, n2, n3, n4)

d1 – a date or date-time value indicating the issue date.
d2 – a date or date-time value indicating the date of first interest payment.
d3 – a date or date-time value indicating the date the security was purchased.
n1 – a numeric value indicating the annual interest rate.
n2 – a numeric value indicating the par value.
n3 – a numeric value indicating the number of payments per year: 1 = annual,
2 = semiannual, 4 = quarterly.
n4 – a numeric value indicating the day basis system: 0 = US (NASD) 30/360, 1 = actual/
actual, 2 = actual/360, 3 = actual/365, 4 = European 30/360.

```
ACCRINT(#1/1/1995#, #1/1/1996#, #6/1/1995#, .065, 100000, 4, 3)
```

returns 2,711.30.

ACCRINTM

Returns a numeric value indicating total accrued interest for a security that pays interest when it matures.

ACCRINTM (d1, d2, n1, n2)

d1 – a date or date-time value indicating the issue date.
d2 – a date or date-time value indicating the maturity date.
n1 – a numeric value indicating the annual interest rate.
n2 – a numeric value indicating the par value.

ACCRINTM (d1, d2, n1, n2, n3)

d1 – a date or date-time value indicating the issue date.
d2 – a date or date-time value indicating the maturity date.
n1 – a numeric value indicating the annual interest rate.
n2 – a numeric value indicating the par value.

n3 – a numeric value indicating the day basis system: 0 = US (NASD) 30/360, 1 = actual/actual, 2 = actual/360, 3 = actual/365, 4 = European 30/360.

```
ACCRINTM(#1/1/1995#, #1/1/2005#, .065, 100000, 3)
```

returns 65,053.42.

AmorDEGRC

Returns a numeric value indicating depreciation of an asset.

AmorDEGRC (n1, d1, d2, n2, n3, n4)
n1 – a numeric value indicating the asset's initial cost.
d1 – a date or date-time value indicating the asset's purchase date.
d2 – a date or date-time value indicating the end of the first period.
n2 – a numeric value indicating the asset's salvage value.
n3 – a numeric value indicating the period to calculate the depreciation for.
n4 – a numeric value indicating the depreciation rate.

AmorDEGRC (n1, d1, d2, n2, n3, n4, n5)
n1 – a numeric value indicating the asset's initial cost.
d1 – a date or date-time value indicating the asset's purchase date.
d2 – a date or date-time value indicating the end of the first period.
n2 – a numeric value indicating the asset's salvage value.
n3 – a numeric value indicating the period to calculate the depreciation for.
n4 – a numeric value indicating the depreciation rate.
n5 – a numeric value indicating the day basis system: 0 = US (NASD) 30/360, 1 = actual/actual, 2 = actual/360, 3 = actual/365, 4 = European 30/360.

```
AmorDEGRC (35000,#5/1/2000#,#1/1/2001#,15000,1,.1)
```

returns 7,292.00.

AmorLINC

Returns a numeric value indication linear depreciation of an asset.

AmorLINC (n1, d1, d2, n2, n3, n4)
n1 – a numeric value indicating the asset's initial cost.
d1 – a date or date-time value indicating the asset's purchase date.
d2 – a date or date-time value indicating the end of the first period.
n2 – a numeric value indicating the asset's salvage value.
n3 – a numeric value indicating the period to calculate the depreciation for.
n4 – a numeric value indicating the depreciation rate.

AmorLINC (n1, d1, d2, n2, n3, n4, n5)
n1 – a numeric value indicating the asset's initial cost.
d1 – a date or date-time value indicating the asset's purchase date.
d2 – a date or date-time value indicating the end of the first period.

n2 – a numeric value indicating the asset's salvage value.
n3 – a numeric value indicating the period to calculate the depreciation for.
n4 – a numeric value indicating the depreciation rate.
n5 – a numeric value indicating the day basis system: 0 = US (NASD) 30/360, 1 = actual/
actual, 2 = actual/360, 3 = actual/365, 4 = European 30/360.

```
AmorLINC (35000,#5/1/2000#,#1/1/2001#,15000,1,.1)
```

returns 3,500.00.

CoupDayBS

Returns a numeric value indicating the days between the last coupon date and the settlement date.

CoupDayBS (d1, d2, n)
d1 – a date or date-time value indicating the purchase date.
d2 – a date or date-time value indicating the maturity date.
n – a numeric value indicating the number of payments (coupons) per year: 1 = annual,
2 = semiannual, 4 = quarterly.

CoupDayBS (d1, d2, n1, n2)
d1 – a date or date-time value indicating the purchase date.
d2 – a date or date-time value indicating the maturity date.
n1 – a numeric value indicating the number of payments (coupons) per year: 1 = annual,
2 = semiannual, 4 = quarterly.
n2 – a numeric value indicating the day basis system: 0 = US (NASD) 30/360, 1 = actual/
actual, 2 = actual/360, 3 = actual/365, 4 = European 30/360.

```
CoupDayBS (#1/1/2000#, #5/31/2004#, 2, 3)
```

returns 32.

CoupDays

Returns a numeric value indicating the number of days in the coupon period that includes settlement.

CoupDays (d1, d2, n)
d1 – a date or date-time value indicating the purchase date.
d2 – a date or date-time value indicating the maturity date.
n – a numeric value indicating the number of payments (coupons) per year: 1 = annual,
2 = semiannual, 4 = quarterly.

CoupDays (d1, d2, n1, n2)
d1 – a date or date-time value indicating the purchase date.
d2 – a date or date-time value indicating the maturity date.
n1 – a numeric value indicating the number of payments (coupons) per year: 1 = annual,
2 = semiannual, 4 = quarterly.

n2 – a numeric value indicating the day basis system: 0 = US (NASD) 30/360, 1 = actual/actual, 2 = actual/360, 3 = actual/365, 4 = European 30/360.

```
CoupDays (#1/1/2000#, #5/31/2004#, 2, 3)
```

returns 182.5.

CoupDaysNC

Returns a numeric value indicating the number of days between the settlement date and the next coupon date.

CoupDaysNC (d1, d2, n)

d1 – a date or date-time value indicating the purchase date.
d2 – a date or date-time value indicating the maturity date.
n – a numeric value indicating the number of payments (coupons) per year: 1 = annual, 2 = semiannual, 4 = quarterly.

CoupDaysNC (d1, d2, n1, n2)

d1 – a date or date-time value indicating the purchase date.
d2 – a date or date-time value indicating the maturity date.
n1 – a numeric value indicating the number of payments (coupons) per year: 1 = annual, 2 = semiannual, 4 = quarterly.
n2 – a numeric value indicating the day basis system: 0 = US (NASD) 30/360, 1 = actual/actual, 2 = actual/360, 3 = actual/365, 4 = European 30/360.

```
CoupDaysNC (#1/1/2000#, #5/31/2004#, 2, 3)
```

returns 151.

CoupNCD

Returns a date value indicating the next coupon date after settlement.

CoupNCD (d1, d2, n)

d1 – a date or date-time value indicating the purchase date.
d2 – a date or date-time value indicating the maturity date.
n – a numeric value indicating the number of payments (coupons) per year: 1 = annual, 2 = semiannual, 4 = quarterly.

```
CoupNCD (#1/1/2000#, #5/31/2004#, 2)
```

returns 5/31/2000.

CoupNum

Returns a numeric value indicating the number of coupon periods between settlement and maturity.

CoupNum (d1, d2, n)

d1 – a date or date-time value indicating the purchase date.

d2 – a date or date-time value indicating the maturity date.
n – a numeric value indicating the number of payments (coupons) per year: 1 = annual,
2 = semiannual, 4 = quarterly.

```
CoupNum (#1/1/2000#, #5/31/2004#, 2)
```

returns 9.

CoupPCD

Returns a date value indicating the last coupon date before settlement.

CoupPCD (d1, d2, n)

d1 – a date or date-time value indicating the purchase date.
d2 – a date or date-time value indicating the maturity date.
n – a numeric value indicating the number of payments (coupons) per year: 1 = annual,
2 = semiannual, 4 = quarterly.

```
CoupPCD (#1/1/2000#, #5/31/2004#, 2)
```

returns 11/30/1999.

CumIPMT

Returns a numeric value indicating cumulative interest paid on a loan.

CumIPMT (n1, n2, n3, n4, n5, n6)

n1 – a numeric value indicating the interest rate, which must be provided on a per-period
basis.
n2 – a numeric value indicating the total number of payment periods, which must be
provided on a per-period basis.
n3 – a numeric value indicating the loan's total or "present" value of the loan.
n4 – a numeric value indicating the first period to include in the calculation.
n5 – a numeric value indicating the last period to include in the calculation.
n6 – a numeric value indicating the type of payment: 0 = end of payment period,
1 = beginning of payment period.

```
CumIPMT (.09/12, 60, 45000, 1, 30, 1)
```

returns –7,640.28.

CumPrinc

Returns a numeric value indicating cumulative principal paid on a loan.

CumPrinc (n1, n2, n3, n4, n5, n6)

n1 – a numeric value indicating the interest rate, which must be provided on a per-period
basis.
n2 – a numeric value indicating the total number of payment periods, which must be
provided on a per-period basis.

n3 – a numeric value indicating the loan's total or "present" value of the loan.
n4 – a numeric value indicating the first period to include in the calculation.
n5 – a numeric value indicating the last period to include in the calculation.
n6 – a numeric value indicating the type of payment: 0 = end of payment period, 1 = beginning of payment period.

```
CumPrinc (.09/12, 60, 45000, 1, 30, 1)
```

returns –20,174.89.

Days360

Returns a numeric value indicating the number of days between two dates using a 30-day-per-month/360-day-per-year financial calendar.

Days360 (d1, d2)
d1 – a date or date-time value indicating start date.
d2 – a date or date-time value indicating end date.

Days360 (d1, d2, b)
d1 – a date or date-time value indicating start date.
d2 – a date or date-time value indicating end date.
b – a Boolean (true or false) value indicating the basis for the calculation: False indicates US (NASD) 30/360; True indicates European 30/360.

```
Days360(#1/1/2003#, #12/31/2003#)
```

returns 360.

DB

Returns a numeric value indicating depreciation of an asset using the declining balance method.

DB (n1, n2, n3, n4)
n1 – a numeric value indicating the asset's initial cost.
n2 – a numeric value indicating the asset's salvage value.
n3 – a numeric value indicating the useful life of the asset.
n4 – a numeric value indicating the period to calculate the depreciation for.

DB (n1, n2, n3, n4, n5)
n1 – a numeric value indicating the asset's initial cost.
n2 – a numeric value indicating the asset's salvage value.
n3 – a numeric value indicating the useful life of the asset.
n4 – a numeric value indicating the period to calculate the depreciation for.
n5 – a numeric value indicating the number of months in the first year.

```
DB(35000,15000,7,5)
```

returns 2,458.71.

PART II

DDB

Returns a numeric value indicating depreciation of an asset using the double-declining balance method.

DDB (n1, n2, n3, n4)
n1 – a numeric value indicating the asset's initial cost.
n2 – a numeric value indicating the asset's salvage value.
n3 – a numeric value indicating the useful life of the asset.
n4 – a numeric value indicating the period to calculate the depreciation for.

DDB (n1, n2, n3, n4, n5)
n1 – a numeric value indicating the asset's initial cost.
n2 – a numeric value indicating the asset's salvage value.
n3 – a numeric value indicating the useful life of the asset.
n4 – a numeric value indicating the period to calculate the depreciation for.
n5 – a numeric value indicating the factor at which the rate declines; 2 indicates double-declining.

```
DDB(35000,5000,7,5)
```

returns 2,603.08.

DISC

Returns a numeric value indicating the discount rate for a security.

DISC (d1, d2, n1, n2)
d1 – a date or date-time value indicating the date the security was purchased.
d2 – a date or date-time value indicating the date of maturity.
n1 – a numeric value indicating the security's value when purchased.
n2 – a numeric value indicating the security's value at maturity.

DISC (d1, d2, n1, n2, n3)
d1 – a date or date-time value indicating the date the security was purchased.
d2 – a date or date-time value indicating the date of maturity.
n1 – a numeric value indicating the security's value when purchased.
n2 – a numeric value indicating the security's value at maturity.
n3 – a numeric value indicating the day basis system: 0 = US (NASD) 30/360, 1 = actual/actual, 2 = actual/360, 3 = actual/365, 4 = European 30/360.

```
DISC(#1/1/2000#,#12/31/2005#,10000,14000)
```

returns .05.

DollarDE

Returns a number indicating the true fractional value of a financial fractional "representation."
      This function is helpful for calculating actual decimal values of such terms as "Five and seven eighths."

DollarDE (n1, n2)

n1 – a numeric value representing the number to be converted (such as 5.7 for "five and seven").
n2 – a numeric value representing the base of n1 (such as 8 for "eighths").

```
DollarDE (5.7, 8)
```

returns 5.88 (5.875 rounded to two decimal places).

DollarFR

Returns a number indicating the financial fractional "representation" of a true fractional value.

This function is helpful for converting actual decimal values into such terms as "Five and seven eighths."

DollarFR (n1, n2)

n1 – a numeric value representing the true fractional number to be converted (such as 5.875).
n2 – a numeric value representing the base of to convert n1 to (such as 8 for "eighths").

```
DollarFR (5.875, 8)
```

returns 5.70 (indicating "five and seven eighths").

Duration

Returns a number indicating the duration of a bond (sometimes known as the "Macauley duration").

Duration (d1, d2, n1, n2, n3)

d1 – a date or date-time value indicating the bond's purchase date.
d2 – a date or date-time value indicating the bond's maturity date.
n1 – a numeric value indicating the bond's interest rate.
n2 – a numeric value indicating the bond's yield.
n3 – a numeric value indicating the number of payments per year; 1 = annual,
2 = semiannual, 4 = quarterly.

Duration (d1, d2, n1, n2, n3, n4)

d1 – a date or date-time value indicating the bond's purchase date.
d2 – a date or date-time value indicating the bond's maturity date.
n1 – a numeric value indicating the bond's interest rate.
n2 – a numeric value indicating the bond's yield.
n3 – a numeric value indicating the number of payments per year: 1 = annual,
2 = semiannual, 4 = quarterly.
n4 – a numeric value indicating the day basis system: 0 = US (NASD) 30/360, 1 = actual/
actual, 2 = actual/360, 3 = actual/365, 4 = European 30/360.

```
Duration(#1/1/2000#,#1/1/2030#,.08,.09,1)
```

returns 11.37 years.

Effect
Returns a numeric value indicating the effective annual interest rate.

Effect (n1, n2)
n1 – a numeric value indicating the annual interest rate.
n2 – a numeric value indicating the number of compounding periods.

```
Effect(.1,12)
```

returns 0.10471 (when formatted to show five decimal places).

FV
Returns a numeric value indicating the future value of an annuity.

FV (n1, n2, n3)
n1 – a numeric value indicating the interest rate (must be adjusted to a per-period rate).
n2 – a numeric value indicating the number of annuity payments.
n3 – a numeric value indicating the payment amount.

FV (n1, n2, n3, n4)
n1 – a numeric value indicating the interest rate (must be adjusted to a per-period rate).
n2 – a numeric value indicating the number of annuity payments.
n3 – a numeric value indicating the payment amount.
n4 – a numeric value indicating the present value (the total amount that a series of future payments is worth now).

FV (n1, n2, n3, n4, n5)
n1 – a numeric value indicating the interest rate (must be adjusted to a per-period rate).
n2 – a numeric value indicating the number of annuity payments.
n3 – a numeric value indicating the payment amount (a negative amount indicating paying money "out").
n4 – a numeric value indicating the present value (the total amount that a series of future payments is worth now).
n5 – a numeric value indicating the type of payment: 0 = end of payment period, 1 = beginning of payment period.

```
FV (.04/12, 60, -500)
```

returns 33,149.49.

FVSchedule
Returns a number indicating the future value of an annuity with several compounded interest rates.

FVSchedule (n, a)
n – a numeric value indicating the present value of the annuity.
a – a numeric array containing one or more interest rates.

```
FVSchedule (10000,[.04,.0475,.05])
```

returns 11,438.70.

IntRate

Returns a numeric value indicating the interest rate for a security.

IntRate (d1, d2, n1, n2)

d1 – a date or date-time value indicating the security purchase date.
d2 – a date or date-time value indicating the security maturity date.
n1 – a numeric value indicating the original security value.
n2 – a numeric value indicating the value at maturity.

IntRate (d1, d2, n1, n2, n3)

d1 – a date or date-time value indicating the security purchase date.
d2 – a date or date-time value indicating the security maturity date.
n1 – a numeric value indicating the original security value.
n2 – a numeric value indicating the value at maturity.
n3 – a numeric value indicating the day basis system: 0 = US (NASD) 30/360,
1 = actual/actual, 2 = actual/360, 3 = actual/365, 4 = European 30/360.

```
IntRate(#1/1/2000#,#1/1/2005#,10000,13000)
```

returns .06.

IPmt

Returns a numeric value indicating an interest payment based on fixed payments and interest rate.

IPmt (n1, n2, n3, n4)

n1 – a numeric value indicating the interest rate (must be adjusted to a per-period rate).
n2 – a numeric value indicating the payment period.
n3 – a numeric value indicating the total number of payments.
n4 – a numeric value indicating the present value.

IPmt (n1, n2, n3, n4, n5)

n1 – a numeric value indicating the interest rate (must be adjusted to a per-period rate).
n2 – a numeric value indicating the payment period.
n3 – a numeric value indicating the total number of payments.
n4 – a numeric value indicating the present value.
n5 – a numeric value indicating the future value after the last payment.

IPmt (n1, n2, n3, n4, n5, n6)

n1 – a numeric value indicating the interest rate (must be adjusted to a per-period rate).
n2 – a numeric value indicating the payment period.
n3 – a numeric value indicating the total number of payments.
n4 – a numeric value indicating the present value.
n5 – a numeric value indicating the future value after the last payment.
n6 – a numeric value indicating the type of payment: 0 = end of payment period,
1 = beginning of payment period.

```
IPmt(.09/12,30,60,30000)
```

returns –128.76.

IRR

Returns a numeric value indicating the internal rate of return for a series of payments and receipts.

IRR (a)

a – a numeric array indicating the series of payments and receipts (there must be at least one negative and one positive number in the array). An IRR of 10 percent (.1) is assumed.

IRR (a, n)

a – a numeric array indicating the series of payments and receipts (there must be at least one negative and one positive number in the array).
n – a numeric value indicating the "guess" of IRR.

```
IRR([-1000,-500,2000])
```

returns .19.

ISPMT

Returns a numeric value indicating interest paid during a period (assuming equal installments).

ISPMT (n1, n2, n3, n4)

n1 – a numeric value indicating the interest rate (must be adjusted to a per-period rate).
n2 – a numeric value indicating the period to calculate interest for.
n3 – a numeric value indicating the number of payment periods.
n4 – a numeric value indicating the present value.

```
ISPMT(.09/12,30,60,30000)
```

returns –112.50.

MDuration

Returns a number indicating the modified duration of a bond (sometimes known as the modified "Macauley duration").

MDuration (d1, d2, n1, n2, n3)

d1 – a date or date-time value indicating the bond's purchase date.
d2 – a date or date-time value indicating the bond's maturity date.
n1 – a numeric value indicating the bond's interest rate.
n2 – a numeric value indicating the bond's yield.
n3 – a numeric value indicating the number of payments per year; 1 = annual, 2 = semiannual, 4 = quarterly.

MDuration (d1, d2, n1, n2, n3, n4)

d1 – a date or date-time value indicating the bond's purchase date.
d2 – a date or date-time value indicating the bond's maturity date.
n1 – a numeric value indicating the bond's interest rate.

n2 – a numeric value indicating the bond's yield.
n3 – a numeric value indicating the number of payments per year: 1 = annual, 2 = semiannual, 4 = quarterly.
n4 – a numeric value indicating the day basis system: 0 = US (NASD) 30/360, 1 = actual/actual, 2 = actual/360, 3 = actual/365, 4 = European 30/360.

```
MDuration(#1/1/2000#,#1/1/2030#,.08,.09,1)
```

returns 10.43 years.

MIRR

Returns a numeric value indicating the modified internal rate of return for a series of payments and receipts.

MIRR (a, n1, n2)

a – a numeric array indicating the series of payments and receipts (there must be at least one negative and one positive number in the array).
n1 – a numeric value indicating interest rate cost.
n2 – a numeric value indicating interest rate return.

```
MIRR([-1000,-500,2000], .9, .6)
```

returns .26.

Nominal

Returns a numeric value indicating the nominal annual interest rate.

Nominal (n1, n2)

n1 – a numeric value indicating effective rate.
n2 – a numeric value indicating number of compounding periods.

```
Nominal(.08,12)
```

returns .07721 (when formatted with five decimal places).

NPer

Returns a numeric value indicating the number of payments, based on a fixed number of payments and interest rate.

NPer (n1, n2, n3)

n1 – a numeric value indicating the interest rate (must be adjusted to a per-period value).
n2 – a numeric value indicating the combined principal/interest payment.
n3 – a numeric value indicating the present value of the loan.

NPer (n1, n2, n3, n4)

n1 – a numeric value indicating the interest rate (must be adjusted to a per-period value).
n2 – a numeric value indicating the combined principal/interest payment.
n3 – a numeric value indicating the present value of the loan.
n4 – a numeric value indicating the future value of the loan after final payment.

PART II

NPer (n1, n2, n3, n4, n5)

n1 – a numeric value indicating the interest rate (must be adjusted to a per-period value).
n2 – a numeric value indicating the combined principal/interest payment.
n3 – a numeric value indicating the present value of the loan.
n4 – a numeric value indicating the future value of the loan after final payment.
n5 – a numeric value indicating the type of payment: 0 = end of payment period,
1 = beginning of payment period.

```
NPer(.09/12,-750,40000)
```

returns 68.37 (indicating months).

NPV

Returns a numeric value indicating the net present value of an investment.

NPV (n, a)

n – a numeric value indicating the discount rate.
a – a numeric array indicating payments/receipts.

```
NPV(.05,[1000,2000,1500,1750])
```

returns 5,501.93.

OddFPrice

Returns a numeric value indicating the price of a security that pays interest with regularity, with the exception of a short or long (odd) first period.

OddFPrice (d1, d2, d3, d4, n1, n2, n3, n4)

d1 – a date or date-time value indicating the purchase date.
d2 – a date or date-time value indicating the date of maturity.
d3 – a date or date-time value indicating the issue date.
d4 – a date or date-time value indicating the date of first interest payment.
n1 – a numeric value indicating the interest rate.
n2 – a numeric value indicating the annual yield of the security.
n3 – a numeric value indicating the security redemption value (per $100 face value).
n4 – a numeric value indicating the number of payments per year: 1 = annual,
2 = semiannual, 4 = quarterly.

OddFPrice (d1, d2, d3, d4, n1, n2, n3, n4, n5)

d1 – a date or date-time value indicating the purchase date.
d2 – a date or date-time value indicating the date of maturity.
d3 – a date or date-time value indicating the issue date.
d4 – a date or date-time value indicating the date of first interest payment.
n1 – a numeric value indicating the interest rate.
n2 – a numeric value indicating the annual yield of the security.
n3 – a numeric value indicating the security redemption value (per $100 face value).

n4 – a numeric value indicating the number of payments per year: 1 = annual, 2 = semiannual, 4 = quarterly.
n5 – a numeric value indicating the day basis system: 0 = US (NASD) 30/360, 1 = actual/actual, 2 = actual/360, 3 = actual/365, 4 = European 30/360.

```
OddFPrice (#2/1/2000#,#1/1/2030#,#1/1/2000#,
   #1/1/2001#,.05,.055,75,1)
```

returns 87.69.

OddFYield

Returns a numeric value indicating the yield of a security that pays interest with regularity, with the exception of a short or long (odd) first period.

OddFYield (d1, d2, d3, d4, n1, n2, n3, n4)

d1 – a date or date-time value indicating the purchase date.
d2 – a date or date-time value indicating the date of maturity.
d3 – a date or date-time value indicating the issue date.
d4 – a date or date-time value indicating the date of first interest payment.
n1 – a numeric value indicating the interest rate.
n2 – a numeric value indicating the purchase price (per $100 face value).
n3 – a numeric value indicating the security redemption value (per $100 face value).
n4 – a numeric value indicating the number of payments per year: 1 = annual, 2 = semiannual, 4 = quarterly.

OddFYield (d1, d2, d3, d4, n1, n2, n3, n4, n5)

d1 – a date or date-time value indicating the purchase date.
d2 – a date or date-time value indicating the date of maturity.
d3 – a date or date-time value indicating the issue date.
d4 – a date or date-time value indicating the date of first interest payment.
n1 – a numeric value indicating the interest rate.
n2 – a numeric value indicating the purchase price (per $100 face value).
n3 – a numeric value indicating the security redemption value (per $100 face value).
n4 – a numeric value indicating the number of payments per year: 1 = annual, 2 = semiannual, 4 = quarterly.
n5 – a numeric value indicating the day basis system: 0 = US (NASD) 30/360, 1 = actual/actual, 2 = actual/360, 3 = actual/365, 4 = European 30/360.

```
OddFPrice (#2/1/2000#,#1/1/2030#,#1/1/2000#,
   #1/1/2001#,.05,13.23,75,1)
```

returns .0549 (formatted with four decimal places).

OddLPrice

Returns a numeric value indicating the price of a security that pays interest with regularity, with the exception of a short or long (odd) last period.

OddLPrice (d1, d2, d3, n1, n2, n3, n4)

d1 – a date or date-time value indicating the purchase date.
d2 – a date or date-time value indicating the date of maturity.
d3 – a date or date-time value indicating the security's last coupon date.
n1 – a numeric value indicating the interest rate.
n2 – a numeric value indicating the annual yield of the security.
n3 – a numeric value indicating the security redemption value (per $100 face value).
n4 – a numeric value indicating the number of payments per year: 1 = annual,
2 = semiannual, 4 = quarterly.

OddLPrice (d1, d2, d3, n1, n2, n3, n4, n5)

d1 – a date or date-time value indicating the purchase date.
d2 – a date or date-time value indicating the date of maturity.
d3 – a date or date-time value indicating the security's last coupon date.
n1 – a numeric value indicating the interest rate.
n2 – a numeric value indicating the annual yield of the security.
n3 – a numeric value indicating the security redemption value (per $100 face value).
n4 – a numeric value indicating the number of payments per year: 1 = annual,
2 = semiannual, 4 = quarterly.
n5 – a numeric value indicating the day basis system: 0 = US (NASD) 30/360,
1 = actual/actual, 2 = actual/360, 3 = actual/365, 4 = European 30/360.

```
OddLPrice(#2/1/2000#,#1/1/2030#,#1/1/2000#,.05,.055,75,1)
```
returns 84.64.

OddLYield

**Returns a numeric value indicating the yield of a security that pays interest with
regularity, with the exception of a short or long (odd) last period.**

OddLYield (d1, d2, d3, n1, n2, n3, n4)

d1 – a date or date-time value indicating the purchase date.
d2 – a date or date-time value indicating the date of maturity.
d3 – a date or date-time value indicating the security's last coupon date.
n1 – a numeric value indicating the interest rate.
n2 – a numeric value indicating the purchase price (per $100 face value).
n3 – a numeric value indicating the security redemption value (per $100 face value).
n4 – a numeric value indicating the number of payments per year: 1 = annual,
2 = semiannual, 4 = quarterly.

OddLYield (d1, d2, d3, n1, n2, n3, n4, n5)

d1 – a date or date-time value indicating the purchase date.
d2 – a date or date-time value indicating the date of maturity.
d3 – a date or date-time value indicating the security's last coupon date.
n1 – a numeric value indicating the interest rate.
n2 – a numeric value indicating the purchase price (per $100 face value).
n3 – a numeric value indicating the security redemption value (per $100 face value).
n4 – a numeric value indicating the number of payments per year: 1 = annual,
2 = semiannual, 4 = quarterly.

$n5$ – a numeric value indicating the day basis system: 0 = US (NASD) 30/360, 1 = actual/actual, 2 = actual/360, 3 = actual/365, 4 = European 30/360.

```
OddLYield (#2/1/2000#,#1/1/2030#,#1/1/2000#,.05,84.64,75,1)
```

returns .055 (formatted with three decimal places).

Pmt

Returns a numeric value indicating the payment for an annuity with fixed payments and interest rate.

Pmt (n1, n2, n3)

$n1$ – a numeric value indicating the interest rate (must be adjusted to a per-period rate).
$n2$ – a numeric value indicating the number of payment periods.
$n3$ – a numeric value indicating the principal/present value of the annuity.

Pmt (n1, n2, n3, n4)

$n1$ – a numeric value indicating the interest rate (must be adjusted to a per-period rate).
$n2$ – a numeric value indicating the number of payment periods.
$n3$ – a numeric value indicating the principal/present value of the annuity.
$n4$ – a numeric value indicating the desired future value/balance after the final payment.

Pmt (n1, n2, n3, n4, n5)

$n1$ – a numeric value indicating the interest rate (must be adjusted to a per-period rate).
$n2$ – a numeric value indicating the number of payment periods.
$n3$ – a numeric value indicating the principal/present value of the annuity.
$n4$ – a numeric value indicating the desired future value/balance after the final payment.
$n5$ – a numeric value indicating the type of payment: 0 = end of payment period, 1 = beginning of payment period.

```
Pmt(.05/12,36,10000)
```

returns –299.71.

PPmt

Returns a numeric value indicating the principal payment for a specific period of an annuity with fixed payments and interest rate.

PPmt (n1, n2, n3, n4)

$n1$ – a numeric value indicating the interest rate (must be adjusted to a per-period rate).
$n2$ – a numeric value indicating the specific period to calculate the principal for.
$n3$ – a numeric value indicating the number of payment periods.
$n4$ – a numeric value indicating the present value.

PPmt (n1, n2, n3, n4, n5)

$n1$ – a numeric value indicating the interest rate (must be adjusted to a per-period rate).
$n2$ – a numeric value indicating the specific period to calculate the principal for.
$n3$ – a numeric value indicating the number of payment periods.
$n4$ – a numeric value indicating the present value.
$n5$ – a numeric value indicating the desired future value/balance after the final payment.

PART II

PPmt (n1, n2, n3, n4, n5, n6)

n1 – a numeric value indicating the interest rate (must be adjusted to a per-period rate).
n2 – a numeric value indicating the specific period to calculate the principal for.
n3 – a numeric value indicating the number of payment periods.
n4 – a numeric value indicating the present value.
n5 – a numeric value indicating the desired future value/balance after the final payment.
n6 – a numeric value indicating the type of payment: 0 = end of payment period,
1 = beginning of payment period.

```
PPmt(.09/12,24,60,35000)
```

returns –551.05.

Price

Returns a numeric value indicating the price of a security (per $100 face value) that pays periodic interest.

Price (d1, d2, n1, n2, n3, n4)

d1 – a date or date-time value indicating the purchase date.
d2 – a date or date-time value indicating the date of maturity.
n1 – a numeric value indicating the interest rate.
n2 – a numeric value indicating the annual yield of the security.
n3 – a numeric value indicating the security redemption value (per $100 face value).
n4 – a numeric value indicating the number of payments per year: 1 = annual,
2 = semiannual, 4 = quarterly.

Price (d1, d2, n1, n2, n3, n4, n5)

d1 – a date or date-time value indicating the purchase date.
d2 – a date or date-time value indicating the date of maturity.
n1 – a numeric value indicating the interest rate.
n2 – a numeric value indicating the annual yield of the security.
n3 – a numeric value indicating the security redemption value (per $100 face value).
n4 – a numeric value indicating the number of payments per year: 1 = annual,
2 = semiannual, 4 = quarterly.
n5 – a numeric value indicating the day basis system: 0 = US (NASD) 30/360,
1 = actual/actual, 2 = actual/360, 3 = actual/365, 4 = European 30/360.

```
Price (#1/1/2000#,#1/1/2005#,.055,.05,50,1)
```

returns 62.99.

PriceDisc

Returns a numeric value indicating the discounted price of a security (per $100 face value).

PriceDisc (d1, d2, n1, n2)

d1 – a date or date-time value indicating the purchase date.

d2 – a date or date-time value indicating the date of maturity.
n1 – a numeric value indicating the discount rate.
n2 – a numeric value indicating the security redemption value (per $100 face value).

PriceDisc (d1, d2, n1, n2, n3)
d1 – a date or date-time value indicating the purchase date.
d2 – a date or date-time value indicating the date of maturity.
n1 – a numeric value indicating the discount rate.
n2 – a numeric value indicating the security redemption value (per $100 face value).
n3 – a numeric value indicating the day basis system: 0 = US (NASD) 30/360,
1 = actual/actual, 2 = actual/360, 3 = actual/365, 4 = European 30/360.

```
PriceDisc (#1/1/2000#,#1/1/2005#,.055,50)
```

returns 36.25.

PriceMat

Returns a numeric value indicating the price of a security (per $100 face value) that pays interest only at maturity.

PriceMat (d1, d2, d3, n1, n2)
d1 – a date or date-time value indicating the purchase date.
d2 – a date or date-time value indicating the date of maturity.
d3 – a date or date-time value indicating the issue date.
n1 – a numeric value indicating the interest rate.
n2 – a numeric value indicating the security's yield.

PriceMat (d1, d2, d3, n1, n2, n3)
d1 – a date or date-time value indicating the purchase date.
d2 – a date or date-time value indicating the date of maturity.
d3 – a date or date-time value indicating the issue date.
n1 – a numeric value indicating the interest rate.
n2 – a numeric value indicating the security's yield.
n3 – a numeric value indicating the day basis system: 0 = US (NASD) 30/360,
1 = actual/actual, 2 = actual/360, 3 = actual/365, 4 = European 30/360.

```
PriceMat(#3/1/2000#,#3/1/2005#,#1/1/2000#,.055,.05)
```

returns 101.82.

PV

Returns a numeric value indicating the present value of an annuity.

PV (n1, n2, n3)
n1 – a numeric value indicating the interest rate (must be adjusted to a per-period rate).
n2 – a numeric value indicating the number of annuity payments.
n3 – a numeric value indicating the payment amount.

PV (n1, n2, n3, n4)

n1 – a numeric value indicating the interest rate (must be adjusted to a per-period rate).
n2 – a numeric value indicating the number of annuity payments.
n3 – a numeric value indicating the payment amount.
n4 – a numeric value indicating the future value/balance after final payment.

PV (n1, n2, n3, n4, n5)

n1 – a numeric value indicating the interest rate (must be adjusted to a per-period rate).
n2 – a numeric value indicating the number of annuity payments.
n3 – a numeric value indicating the payment amount.
n4 – a numeric value indicating the future value/balance after final payment.
n5 – a numeric value indicating the type of payment: 0 = end of payment period,
1 = beginning of payment period.

```
PV (.04/12, 60, -500)
```

returns 27,149.53.

Rate

Returns a numeric value indicating per-period interest for an annuity.

Rate (n1, n2, n3)

n1 – a numeric value indicating the number of annuity payments.
n2 – a numeric value indicating the payment amount.
n3 – a numeric value indicating the annuity's present value.

Rate (n1, n2, n3, n4)

n1 – a numeric value indicating the number of annuity payments.
n2 – a numeric value indicating the payment amount.
n3 – a numeric value indicating the annuity's present value.
n4 – a numeric value indicating the future value/balance after final payment.

Rate (n1, n2, n3, n4, n5)

n1 – a numeric value indicating the number of annuity payments.
n2 – a numeric value indicating the payment amount.
n3 – a numeric value indicating the annuity's present value.
n4 – a numeric value indicating the future value/balance after final payment.
n5 – a numeric value indicating the type of payment: 0 = end of payment period,
1 = beginning of payment period.

Rate (n1, n2, n3, n4, n5, n6)

n1 – a numeric value indicating the number of annuity payments.
n2 – a numeric value indicating the payment amount.
n3 – a numeric value indicating the annuity's present value.
n4 – a numeric value indicating the future value/balance after final payment.
n5 – a numeric value indicating the type of payment: 0 = end of payment period,
1 = beginning of payment period.

n6 – a numeric value indicating your "guess" of the return to use as a starting point for the calculation. If you omit this argument, 10 percent (.1) is assumed.

```
Rate(36, -750, 35000)
```

returns .0134 (when formatted to four decimal places).

Received

Returns a numeric value indicating the amount received at maturity for a fully invested security.

Received (d1, d2, n1, n2)

d1 – a date or date-time value indicating the purchase date.
d2 – a date or date-time value indicating the date of maturity.
n1 – a numeric value indicating the investment amount.
n2 – a numeric value indicating the discount rate.

Received (d1, d2, n1, n2, n3)

d1 – a date or date-time value indicating the purchase date.
d2 – a date or date-time value indicating the date of maturity.
n1 – a numeric value indicating the investment amount.
n2 – a numeric value indicating the discount rate.
n3 – a numeric value indicating the day basis system: 0 = US (NASD) 30/360, 1 = actual/actual, 2 = actual/360, 3 = actual/365, 4 = European 30/360.

```
Received(#1/1/2000#,#1/1/2005#,10000,.075)
```

returns 16,000.00.

SLN

Returns a numeric value indicating straight-line depreciation of an asset.

SLN (n1, n2, n3)

n1 – a numeric value indicating original cost of the asset.
n2 – a numeric value indicating the salvage of the asset at the end of its life.
n3 – a numeric value indicating the life of the asset.

```
SLN(35000,7500,7)
```

returns a per-year depreciation of 3,928.57.

SYD

Returns a numeric value indicating sum-of-years-digits depreciation of an asset.

SYD (n1, n2, n3, n4)

n1 – a numeric value indicating original cost of the asset.
n2 – a numeric value indicating the salvage of the asset at the end of its life.
n3 – a numeric value indicating the life of the asset.

n4 – a numeric value indicating the period to calculate depreciation for.

```
SYD(35000,7500,7,2)
```

returns a second-year depreciation of 5,892.86.

TBillEq

Returns a numeric value indicating the bond-equivalent yield for a Treasury bill.

TBillEq (d1, d2, n)

d1 – a date or date-time value indicating the purchase date.
d2 – a date or date-time value indicating the date of maturity.
n – a numeric value indicating the discount rate.

```
TBillEq(#1/1/2000#,#12/31/2000#,.08)
```

returns .0864 (8.64%) when formatted with four decimal places.

TBillPrice

Returns a numeric value indicating the price for a Treasury bill (per $100 face value).

TBillPrice (d1, d2, n)

d1 – a date or date-time value indicating the purchase date.
d2 – a date or date-time value indicating the date of maturity.
n – a numeric value indicating the discount rate.

```
TBillPrice(#1/1/2000#,#12/31/2000#,.08)
```

returns 91.89.

TBillYield

Returns a numeric value indicating the yield for a Treasury bill.

TBillYield (d1, d2, n)

d1 – a date or date-time value indicating the purchase date.
d2 – a date or date-time value indicating the date of maturity.
n – a numeric value indicating the price per $100 face value.

```
TBillYield(#1/1/2000#,#12/31/2000#,91.89)
```

returns .087 (8.7%) when formatted with three decimal places.

VDB

Returns the variable declining balance for an asset.
    VDB supports various depreciation options, such as double-declining balance or other method and partial depreciation periods.

VDB (n1, n2, n3, n4, n5)

n1 – a numeric value indicating the asset's initial cost.
n2 – a numeric value indicating the asset's salvage value.
n3 – a numeric value indicating the useful life of the asset.
n4 – a numeric value indicating the start period to calculate depreciation for.
n5 – a numeric value indicating the end period to calculate depreciation for.

VDB (n1, n2, n3, n4, n5, n6)

n1 – a numeric value indicating the asset's initial cost.
n2 – a numeric value indicating the asset's salvage value.
n3 – a numeric value indicating the useful life of the asset.
n4 – a numeric value indicating the start period to calculate depreciation for.
n5 – a numeric value indicating the end period to calculate depreciation for.
n6 – a numeric value indicating the factor at which the rate declines – 2 indicates double-declining.

VDB (n1, n2, n3, n4, n5, n6)

n1 – a numeric value indicating the asset's initial cost.
n2 – a numeric value indicating the asset's salvage value.
n3 – a numeric value indicating the useful life of the asset.
n4 – a numeric value indicating the start period to calculate depreciation for.
n5 – a numeric value indicating the end period to calculate depreciation for.
n6 – a Boolean (true/false) value indicating whether to switch from declining-balance to straight-line if declining-balance is less. True will always use declining-balance. False will switch to straight-line if declining-balance is less.

VDB (n1, n2, n3, n4, n5, n6, n7)

n1 – a numeric value indicating the asset's initial cost.
n2 – a numeric value indicating the asset's salvage value.
n3 – a numeric value indicating the useful life of the asset.
n4 – a numeric value indicating the start period to calculate depreciation for.
n5 – a numeric value indicating the end period to calculate depreciation for.
n6 – a numeric value indicating the factor at which the rate declines – 2 indicates double-declining.
n7 – a Boolean (true/false) value indicating whether to switch from declining-balance to straight-line if declining-balance is less. True will always use declining-balance. False will switch to straight-line if declining-balance is less.

```
VDB(50000,15000,7,2,5)
```

returns 10,510.20 depreciation for years two through five.

XIRR

Returns a numeric value indicating the internal rate of return for a series of payments and receipts.

XIRR differs from IRR in that it calculates internal rate of return for payments/receipts that aren't necessarily periodic.

XIRR (na, da)

na – a numeric array indicating the series of payments and receipts (there must be at least one negative and one positive number in the array).
da – an array of date or date-time values indicating the matching dates for the numeric array. There must be one entry in this array for each entry in the numeric array.

XIRR (na, da, n)

na – a numeric array indicating the series of payments and receipts (there must be at least one negative and one positive number in the array).
da – an array of date or date-time values indicating the matching dates for the numeric array. There must be one entry in this array for each entry in the numeric array.
n – a numeric value indicating the "guess" of IRR.

```
XIRR([-1000,-500,2000],[#1/1/2000#,#5/1/2000#,#6/30/2000#])
```

returns 1.08.

XNPV

Returns a numeric value indicating the net present value of an investment.

XNPV differs from NPV in that it calculates net present value for payments/receipts that aren't necessarily periodic.

XNPV (n, na, da)

n – a numeric value indicating the discount rate.
na – a numeric array indicating payments/receipts.
da – an array of date or date-time values that correspond to the numeric array. There must be one entry in the date array for each entry in the numeric array.

```
XNPV(.05,[1000,2000,1500,1750],
[#1/1/2000#,#5/1/2000#,#6/30/2000#,#12/31/2000#])
```

returns 6,098.72.

YearFrac

Returns a numeric value indicating what fraction of the year is represented by two dates.

YearFrac (d1, d2)

d1 – a date or date-time value indicating the first date in the year.
d2 – a date or date-time value indicating the second date in the year.

YearFrac (d1, d2, n)

d1 – a date or date-time value indicating the first date in the year.
d2 – a date or date-time value indicating the second date in the year.
n – a numeric value indicating the day basis system: 0 = US (NASD) 30/360,
1 = actual/actual, 2 = actual/360, 3 = actual/365, 4 = European 30/360.

```
YearFrac(#1/1/2003#,#3/31/2003#)
```

returns .25.

Yield

Returns a numeric value indicating the yield of a security that pays periodic interest.

Yield (d1, d2, n1, n2, n3, n4)

d1 – a date or date-time value indicating the purchase date.
d2 – a date or date-time value indicating the date of maturity.
n1 – a numeric value indicating the interest rate.
n2 – a numeric value indicating the purchase price of the security (per $100 face value).
n3 – a numeric value indicating the security redemption value (per $100 face value).
n4 – a numeric value indicating the number of payments per year: 1 = annual,
2 = semiannual, 4 = quarterly.

Yield (d1, d2, n1, n2, n3, n4, n5)

d1 – a date or date-time value indicating the purchase date.
d2 – a date or date-time value indicating the date of maturity.
n1 – a numeric value indicating the interest rate.
n2 – a numeric value indicating the purchase price of the security (per $100 face value).
n3 – a numeric value indicating the security redemption value (per $100 face value).
n4 – a numeric value indicating the number of payments per year: 1 = annual,
2 = semiannual, 4 = quarterly.
n5 – a numeric value indicating the day basis system: 0 = US (NASD) 30/360,
1 = actual/actual, 2 = actual/360, 3 = actual/365, 4 = European 30/360.

```
Yield (#1/1/2000#,#1/1/2005#,.055,62.99,50,1)
```

returns .087 (formatted with three decimal places).

YieldDisc

Returns a numeric value indicating the yield of a discounted security.

YieldDisc (d1, d2, n1, n2)

d1 – a date or date-time value indicating the purchase date.
d2 – a date or date-time value indicating the date of maturity.
n1 – a numeric value indicating purchase price (per $100 face value).
n2 – a numeric value indicating the security redemption value (per $100 face value).

YieldDisc (d1, d2, n1, n2, n3)

d1 – a date or date-time value indicating the purchase date.
d2 – a date or date-time value indicating the date of maturity.
n1 – a numeric value indicating purchase price (per $100 face value).
n2 – a numeric value indicating the security redemption value (per $100 face value).
n3 – a numeric value indicating the day basis system: 0 = US (NASD) 30/360,
1 = actual/actual, 2 = actual/360, 3 = actual/365, 4 = European 30/360.

```
YieldDisc(#1/1/2000#,#1/1/2005#,36.25,50)
```

returns .0759 (when formatted with four decimal places).

YieldMat

Returns a numeric value indicating the yield of a security that pays interest only at maturity.

YieldMat (d1, d2, d3, n1, n2)

d1 – a date or date-time value indicating the purchase date.
d2 – a date or date-time value indicating the date of maturity.
d3 – a date or date-time value indicating the issue date.
n1 – a numeric value indicating the interest rate.
n2 – a numeric value indicating purchase price (per $100 face value).

YieldMat (d1, d2, d3, n1, n2, n3)

d1 – a date or date-time value indicating the purchase date.
d2 – a date or date-time value indicating the date of maturity.
d3 – a date or date-time value indicating the issue date.
n1 – a numeric value indicating the interest rate.
n2 – a numeric value indicating purchase price (per $100 face value).
n3 – a numeric value indicating the day basis system: 0 = US (NASD) 30/360, 1 = actual/actual, 2 = actual/360, 3 = actual/365, 4 = European 30/360.

```
YieldMat(#3/1/2000#,#3/1/2005#,#1/1/2000#,.055,101.82)
```

returns .05.

Functions: Grid Value

This set of functions retrieves values from a grid object, such as a cross-tab or OLAP grid. In particular, these functions may be used to conditionally format values in a grid object and create custom values and calculations in cross-tab Calculated Members and Embedded Summaries.

CurrentColumnIndex

Returns the number of the current column in a grid object.
CurrentColumnIndex is zero-based (the first column is zero, not one). Also, columns containing total values increment CurrentColumnIndex.

CurrentColumnIndex

```
CurrentColumnIndex
```

returns 0.00 in the first column, 2.00 in the first total column if there are two data columns to the left of it, and 11.00 in the last column of a 12-column grid object.

CurrentRowIndex

Returns the number of the current row in a grid object.
CurrentRowIndex is zero-based (the first row is zero, not one). Also, rows containing total values increment CurrentRowIndex.

CurrentRowIndex

```
CurrentRowIndex
```

returns 0.00 in the first row, 6.00 in the first total row if there are six data rows above it, and 42.00 in the last row of a 43-row grid object.

CurrentSummaryIndex

Returns the position of the current summary or "cell" (either a summarized field or Embedded Summary) among all summaries.

   CurrentSummaryIndex is zero-based (the first summary is zero, not one).

CurrentSummaryIndex

```
CurrentSummaryIndex
```

returns 0.00 if the summary is the only summary in the grid object or is in the first position in the group of summaries. Returns 3.00 if the summary is in the fourth position in the group of summaries.

GetColumnGroupIndexOf

Returns the position of the column within a column grouping hierarchy.

   GetColumnGroupIndexOf is generally only useful if a grid object contains two or more nested columns.

GetColumnGroupIndexOf (n)

n – a numeric value, generally provided by another Grid Value function.

```
GetColumnGroupIndexOf(CurrentColumnIndex)
```

returns 2.00 when evaluated in the second column within a two-column hierarchy (for example, the Quarter column in a Year/Quarter column hierarchy). Returns 1.00 when evaluated in the year total column in the same Year/Quarter column hierarchy. Returns 0.00 when evaluated in the grand total column.

GetColumnPathIndexOf

Returns the column position of the specified column or grand total column.

   GetColumnPathIndexOf returns a zero-based value. If no match can be found, the result is –1.

GetColumnPathIndexOf

```
GetColumnPathIndexOf
```

returns 3.00 in a four-column grid object, indicating the zero-based index of the grand-total column.

GetColumnPathIndexOf (v1, v2, ...)

v1, v2, ... – one or more values matching the data type of fields forming the column hierarchy. You may specify any number of arguments between one and the total number of column fields making up the column group hierarchy.

```
GetColumnPathIndexOf("UPS")
```

returns 5.00 when UPS is the value in the sixth column of a single-column cross-tab, or the UPS total appears in the sixth column in cross-tab based on multiple column fields where UPS appears in the top group level.

```
GetColumnPathIndexOf(3, "Parcel Post")
```

returns 9.00 in a cross-tab containing a Ship Via column nested within an Employee ID column, where the tenth column in the cross-tab contains the Parcel Post value within Employee #3.

GetIndexOf

Returns the row or column number of a row or column matching the specified row/ column name and value.

GetIndexOf returns a zero-based value. If no rows or columns match the search, the result is –1.

GetIndexOf (s, v)

s – the row or column name to search (available from the Row or Column Names section of the function tree).
v – the value to search for. The data type of *v* must match that of the row or column field specified in *s*.

```
GetIndexOf ("Orders.Ship Via","Parcel Post")
```

returns 2.00 if "Parcel Post" is the third column based on the Orders.Ship via field.

GetIndexOf (s, v, n)

s – the row or column name to search (available from the Row or Column Names section of the function tree).
v – the value to search for. The data type of *v* must match that of the row or column field specified in *s*.
n – a numeric value indicating the row or column number to start the search from. The first matching row or column number after *n* will be returned.

```
GetIndexOf ("Employee.Last Name","King",3)
```

returns 9.00, if a row based on the Employee.Last Name field exposes "King" in the third and tenth rows.

GetNumColumnGroups

Returns the number of nested column groups.

GetNumColumnGroups

```
GetNumColumnGroups
```

returns 2.00 if a cross-tab includes two fields added to create its column hierarchy.

GetNumRowGroups

Returns the number of nested row groups.

GetNumRowGroups

```
GetNumRowGroups
```

returns 3.00 for a cross-tab consisting of, for example, a Date row field, followed by a nested Salesperson row field, followed by a nested Region row field.

GetNumRows

Returns the number of rows in the grid object.
GetNumRows will return the total number of rows, including suppressed subtotal or grand total rows.

GetNumRows

```
GetNumRows
```

returns 22.00 for a cross-tab containing 22 rows. If inner-row subtotals and the outer row grand total are suppressed, the value returned is still 22.00, even though only 18 rows appear in the cross-tab.

GetNumSummaries

Returns the number of summary fields, including Embedded Summaries, that appear in the Summarized Fields box of a cross-tab.

GetNumSummaries

```
GetNumSummaries
```

returns 4.00, if the cross-tab contains three summarized database fields, and one Embedded Summary, in the Summarized Fields box.

GetRowGroupIndexOf

Returns the position of the row within a row grouping hierarchy.
GetRowGroupIndexOf is generally only useful if a grid object contains two or more nested rows.

GetRowGroupIndexOf (n)

n – a numeric value, generally provided by another Grid Value function.

```
GetRowGroupIndexOf(CurrentRowIndex)
```

returns 2.00 when evaluated in the second row within a two-row hierarchy (for example, the Quarter row in a Year/Quarter row hierarchy). Returns 1.00 when evaluated in the year total row in the same Year/Quarter row hierarchy. Returns 0.00 when evaluated in the grand total row.

GetRowPathIndexOf

Returns the row position of the specified row or grand total row.

GetRowPathIndexOf returns a zero-based value. If no match can be found, the result is −1.

GetRowPathIndexOf

```
GetRowPathIndexOf
```

returns 8.00 in a nine-row grid object, indicating the zero-based index of the grand-total row.

GetRowPathIndexOf (v1, v2, ...)

v1, v2, ... – one or more values matching the data type of fields forming the row hierarchy. You may specify any number of arguments between one and the total number of row fields making up the row group hierarchy.

```
GetRowPathIndexOf("UPS")
```

returns 5.00 when UPS is the value in the sixth row of a cross-tab based on a single row field, or the UPS total appears in the sixth row in cross-tab based on multiple row fields where UPS appears in the top group level.

```
GetRowPathIndexOf(3, "Parcel Post")
```

returns 9.00 in a cross-tab containing a Ship Via row nested within an Employee ID row, where the tenth row in the cross-tab contains the Parcel Post value within Employee #3.

GetTotalValueFor

Returns the total value for an upper-level row or column group.

GetTotalValueFor is only applicable to cross-tabs with a two-or-more-field nested row or column group.

GetTotalValueFor (s)

s – the row or column name below the row or column to total.

```
GetTotalValueFor("Customer.Region")
```

returns $25,346.25, the total in the upper-level Country row or column group (the group Customer.Region is nested within).

GetTotalValueFor (s, n)

s – the row or column name below the row or column to total.

n – the summary index to retrieve the value from the upper-level group.

```
If (GetRowGroupIndexOf(CurrentRowIndex) = 0) Then
    100
Else If (GetRowGroupIndexOf(CurrentRowIndex) = 1) Then
    GridValueAt(CurrentRowIndex, CurrentColumnIndex, 0) %
        GetTotalValueFor("Country", 0)
Else If (GetRowGroupIndexOf(CurrentRowIndex) = 2) Then
    GridValueAt(CurrentRowIndex, CurrentColumnIndex, 0) %
        GetTotalValueFor("Region", 0)
```

calculates the percentage of the higher-level Country or Region total that the current nested cell accounts for. In this example, the GetRowGroupIndex function is used to prevent GetTotalValueOf from evaluating in a grand total row or column (which will return an error).

GridLabelAt

Returns the row or column field heading for the specified row or column number.

GridLabelAt (s, n)

s – the row or column name to search.

n – the row or column number to retrieve the field heading from.

```
GridLabelAt ("Customer.Country",3)
```

returns "Austria," if the cross-tab column is based on Customer.Country and the third column is for Austria.

GridRowColumnValue

Returns the value of the row or column name in a cross-tab or OLAP grid object.

GridRowColumnValue will return the contents of a "title" cell of a row or column in a cross-tab or OLAP grid object. By using this function, you may determine which row or column is currently formatting and change formatting logic accordingly.

GridRowColumnValue (s)

s – string value indicating row or column name to query.

```
If GridRowColumnValue ("Orders.Employee ID") = 3 Then
    crRed
Else
    crBlack
```

will determine if the Employee ID row in a cross-tab contain employee number 3. If so, the cell will be formatted in a red color.

PART II

GridValueAt

Returns a specific "cell" value.

GridValueAt is zero-based. Specify the first row, first column, or first summary field with 0, not 1.

GridValueAt (n1, n2, n3)

n1 – a numeric value indicating the row index.
n2 – a numeric value indicating the column index.
n3 – a numeric value indicating the summary index.

```
GridValueAt(1, 2, 0)
```

returns $140,253.75, the cell value in the second row, third column, and first (or only) summary.

Row Or Column Names

Names of the rows or columns in a cross-tab or OLAP grid object.

This category of the Function tree will appear only when you are editing a cross-tab Calculated Member or Embedded Summary formula, or when you are conditionally formatting a cross-tab or OLAP grid object. The category will contain the names given to rows or columns in the cross-tab or OLAP grid. You may use these values within various other Grid Value functions to refer to a specific row or column, or to determine which row or column the formula is currently evaluating in.

Functions: Math

This set of functions performs standard math, algebraic, and geometrical calculations.

Abs

Returns a numeric value indicating the absolute value of a number.

Abs (n)

n – a numeric value to return the absolute value for.

```
Abs(-27.3)
```

returns 27.30.

Atn

Returns a numeric value (in radians) indicating the arctangent of the source number.

Atn (n)

n – a numeric value to return the arctangent of.

```
Atn(45)
```

returns 1.55.

Ceiling

Returns a numeric value rounded up to the nearest multiple (for positive numbers) or down to the nearest multiple (for negative numbers).

Ceiling (n)

n – a numeric value to round.

```
Ceiling(2.18)
```

returns 3.00.

```
Ceiling(-214.83481)
```

returns –215.00.

In the preceding examples, Ceiling rounds up (for positive numbers) or down (for negative numbers) to the nearest multiple of 1 (the next whole number up or down).

Ceiling (n1, n2)

n1 – a numeric value to round.
n2 – a whole or fractional value indicating the multiple to round *n1* to.

```
Ceiling (2.18, 2)
```

returns 4.00, as the next multiple of 2 above 2.18 is 4.

```
Ceiling(-214.83481, -.05)
```

returns –214.85, as the nearest multiple of .05 below a negative .83481 is negative .85. Note that a sign on *n2* is ignored, applying the multiple as an unsigned value.

Cos

Returns a numeric value indicating the cosine of the source number.

Cos (n)

n – a numeric value, in radians, to return the cosine of.

```
Cos(45)
```

returns .53.

Exp

Returns a numeric value indicating *e* (the base of the natural logarithm) raised to a power.

Exp (n)

n – a numeric value indicating the power to raise *e* to.

```
Exp(10)
```

returns 22,026.47 (*e* raised to the power of 10).

Floor

Returns a numeric value rounded down to the nearest multiple (for positive numbers) or up to the nearest multiple (for negative numbers).

Floor (n)

n – a numeric value to round.

```
Floor(2.18)
```

returns 2.00.

```
Floor(-214.83481)
```

returns –214.00.

In the preceding examples, Floor rounds down (for positive numbers) or up (for negative numbers) to the nearest multiple of 1 (the next whole number down or up).

Floor (n1, n2)

n1 – a numeric value to round.
n2 – a whole or fractional value indicating the multiple to round *n1* to.

```
Floor (2.18, 2)
```

returns 2.00, as the next multiple of 2 below 2.18 is 2.

```
Floor(-214.83481, -.05)
```

returns –214.80, as the nearest multiple of .05 above a negative .83481 is negative .80. Note that a sign on *n2* is ignored, applying the multiple as an unsigned value.

Int

Returns a numeric value indicating the integer portion of the supplied number.

Int (n)

n – a numeric value that you want to extract the integer portion of.

```
Int(3.574)
```

returns 3.00.

Log

Returns a numeric value indicating the logarithm of the supplied number.

Log (n)

n – a numeric value to return the logarithm of.

```
Log(22026.47)
```

returns 10.

MRound

Returns a numeric value rounded down to the nearest multiple (for positive numbers) or up to the nearest multiple (for negative numbers).

MRound (n)

n – a numeric value to round.

```
MRound (2.18)
```

returns 2.00.

```
MRound (-214.83481)
```

returns –215.00.

In the preceding examples, MRound rounds to the nearest multiple of 1 (the nearest whole number). In this one-argument permutation, MRound is identical to Round.

MRound (n1, n2)

n1 – a numeric value to round.
n2 – a whole or fractional value indicating the multiple to round *n1* to.

```
MRound (1.4, 3)
```

returns 0.00, as the nearest multiple of 3 to 1.4 is 0.

```
MRound (1.6, -3)
```

returns 3, as the nearest multiple of 3 to 1.6 is 3. Note that a sign on *n2* is ignored, applying the multiple as an unsigned value.

Pi

Returns the value of Pi (approximately 3.142).

Although this function appears as "Pi" in the Function tree, "crPi" will appear when you double-click the function name. If you type in the function yourself, type it as "crPi".

crPi

```
crPi
```

returns 3.142 (when formatted to show three decimal places).

Remainder

Returns a numeric value indicating the remainder of a division operation (not the quotient).

The Remainder function operates similar to the Mod arithmetic operator. Among other things, Remainder can be used with the RecordNumber function to shade every other line of a report in alternating colors.

Remainder (n1, n2)

n1 – a numeric value indicating the numerator of the division.
n2 – a numeric value indicating the denominator of the division.

```
Remainder (10,3)
```

returns 1.00 (the remainder of dividing 10 by 3).

```
If Remainder (RecordNumber, 2) = 0 Then
    crSilver
Else
    crNoColor
```

will shade every other details section silver if used as a conditional formatting formula for the details sections background color.

Rnd

Returns a numeric value between 0 and 1 represented as a random number.

Rnd may be helpful in situations where you wish to add a certain "randomness" to portions of your report. By multiplying Rnd by a larger number (10, 100, and so forth), you may get larger numbers that may appropriate for other uses.

Rnd

Rnd (n)

n – a number to act as a "seed" to generate the random number.

```
Rnd
```

returns a different fractional number within each record and report refresh.

```
Rnd(Timer)
```

uses the Timer function to generate a "seed" number to increase "randomness" of the numbers returned.

Round

Returns a numeric value rounded to a specified number of decimal places.

Round (n)

n – a numeric value to be rounded to the nearest whole number.

Round (n1, n2)

n1 – a numeric value to be rounded.
n2 – a numeric value indicating the number of decimal places to round *n1* to.

```
Round (1.7821, 1)
```

returns 1.80.

RoundUp

Returns a numeric value rounded up to the next highest positive number, or next lowest negative number.

RoundUp is similar to Round, with the exception of always rounding up for positive numbers and down for negative numbers, regardless of how close to a lower number the number to be rounded may be. Also, when supplying a negative value as the second argument to RoundUp, rounding to the left of the decimal occurs.

RoundUp (n)

n – a numeric value to be rounded to the nearest whole number.

```
RoundUp (100.3)
```

returns 101.00.

```
RoundUp (-7.2)
```

returns –8.00.

RoundUp (n1, n2)

n1 – a numeric value to be rounded.
n2 – a numeric value indicating the number of decimal places to round *n1* to.

```
RoundUp (100.2512, 2)
```

returns 100.26.

```
RoundUp (100.2512, -3)
```

returns 1,000.00, as a negative number supplied to *n2* will round to the left of the decimal.

Sgn

Returns a numeric value indicating the sign of the supplied number.

Sgn returns –1 if the source number is negative, 0 if the source number is zero, and 1 if the source number is positive.

Sgn (n)

n – a numeric value to determine the sign of.

```
Sgn (-25)
```

returns –1.00.

Sin

Returns a numeric value indicating the sine of the supplied angle.

PART II

Sin (n)

n – a numeric value indicating the angle to calculate the sine of (in radians).

```
Sin(45)
```

returns .85.

Sqr

Returns a numeric value indicating the square root of the source number.

Sqr (n)

n – a numeric value to return the square root of.

```
Sqr (25)
```

returns 5.00.

Tan

Returns a numeric value indicating the tangent of the supplied angle.

Tan (n)

n – a numeric value indicating an angle (in radians).

```
Tan(45)
```

returns 1.62.

Truncate

Returns a numeric value indicating the source number truncated to a specified number of decimal places.

Truncate is similar to Round in that it removes decimal places. However, Truncate doesn't round the source number in the process—it simply removes the decimal places.

Truncate (n)

n – a numeric value to be truncated to zero decimal places.

Truncate (n1, n2)

n1 – a numeric value to be truncated.
n2 – a numeric value indicating the number of decimal places to truncate.

```
Truncate (1.489,1)
```

returns 1.40.

Functions: Print State

This category of functions exposes a variety of functions that generally pertain to the current state of the report when being formatted or printed. Some of these functions duplicate items found in the Special Fields category of the Field Explorer.

CountHierarchicalChildren

Returns a numeric value indicating how many hierarchical "children" groups appear directly below the hierarchy level being evaluated.

This function, when used in combination with the GroupingLevel function (described elsewhere in this appendix) is helpful in determining how many groups appear just below a hierarchical group. "Grand-children" groups more than one level below the currently evaluated group are not included, and this function returns –1 if the group is not organized hierarchically.

CountHierarchicalChildren (n)

n – a numeric value indicating the number of the group that is organized hierarchically.

```
CountHierarchicalChildren (GroupingLevel ({Employee.Employee ID}))
```

returns 7.00 if the currently printing hierarchical group has seven children groups. This result would apply, for example, if a report is hierarchically organized by a supervisor/employee relationship, and the supervisor at the current level has seven employees that report to him/her. If the employee has no subordinates, this function would return 0.00. The result would be –1.00 if the group was not organized hierarchically.

CurrentPageOrientation

Indicates whether the current report page is printing in portrait or landscape orientation.

This function is largely intended for use in conditional page margin formulas in the Page Setup dialog box. This function will only return a value if a specific Portrait or Landscape designation is made (not a Default designation) in the Section Expert.

CurrentPageOrientation

```
If CurrentPageOrientation = crPortrait Then 720 Else 1440
```

sets a page margin to 1/2 inch if the current page is printing in portrait orientation or 1 inch if the page is printing in landscape orientation (1,440 twips equal one inch).

Page Orientation Constants

The following page orientation constants are available for use with CurrentPageOrientation. Either the numeric value or constant may be used.

crPortrait	1
crLandscape	2

DrillDownGroupLevel

Returns a numeric value indicating how many group levels a viewer has drilled down into when viewing the report online (0 is returned if a viewer has not drilled down).

This function is very helpful when you need to determine where a viewer is in a drill-down hierarchy. You may use this function, for example, to suppress a group header if a viewer has drilled down to the group's first level (showing the series of just group headers and footers for the group). You will see a different DrillDownGroupLevel result and be able to show the group header when the viewer drills down to the next level where they're seeing details sections and just a single group header and footer.

DrillDownGroupLevel

```
DrillDownGroupLevel
```

returns 2.00 if the viewer has drilled into the second group.

```
DrillDownGroupLevel = 1
```

will suppress Group Header #1 when a viewer first drills down when placed in a conditional suppression formula for Group Header #1.

GroupNumber

Returns a numeric value indicating the sequential number of the group that is currently being displayed.

GroupNumber is helpful in various conditional formatting situations, such as conditionally setting a New Page Before property, or shading every other group footer. This function returns the same value as the GroupNumber special field.

GroupNumber

```
GroupNumber > 1
```

when used as a conditional New Page Before formula for Group Header #1, will not start a new page before the report's first group.

GroupSelection

Returns a string value indicating the Group Selection Formula.

This function returns the same information as the Group Selection Formula special field.

GroupSelection

```
GroupSelection
```

returns "Sum ({Orders.Order Amount}, {Orders.Customer ID}) > $15000.00" if a group selection formula is limited groups on the report.

HasValue

Returns a Boolean (true/false) value indicating if the supplied optional parameter field contains a value.

HasValue(f)

f – a parameter field defined in the report.

```
If HasValue({?Country Prompt}) Then
    {Customer.Country} = {?Country Prompt}
Else
    {Customer.Country = "USA"
```

when used as a record selection formula, returns the country supplied by the report viewer in the Country Prompt optional parameter field if the viewer has supplied a value. If the viewer hasn't supplied a value, returns records where the country field is "USA."

HierarchyLevel

Returns a numeric value indicating the hierarchy or "indentation" level of a hierarchical group.

HierarchyLevel, when used in conjunction with the GroupingLevel function (described elsewhere in this appendix), is helpful when controlling your own indentation with a formula-driven X position in the Object Size and Position dialog box.

HierarchyLevel (n)

n – a numeric value indicating the number of the group that is organized hierarchically.

```
HierarchyLevel(GroupingLevel({Employee.Employee ID}))
```

returns 1.00 when the highest hierarchical group "indentation" is printing, returns 2.00 when the second hierarchical group "indentation" is printing, and so forth. This assumes that a hierarchical group based on Employee.Employee ID exists on the report.

InRepeatedGroupHeader

Returns a Boolean (true/false) value indicating whether or not the report is currently exposing a repeated group header.

InRepeatedGroupHeader is helpful when you wish to avoid resetting variables in a repeated group header, when you want to add a "continued" message, or similar conditional behavior.

InRepeatedGroupHeader

```
If Not InRepeatedGroupHeader Then
    NumberVar GroupTotal := 0
```

will reset the GroupTotal variable to 0 only if this is the first group header for the group.

IsNull

Returns a Boolean (true/false) value indicating if the supplied field contains a null value.

Null database values may not appear with all databases. Also, the setting of the Convert Null Database Fields To Default option (from File | Report Options or File | Options) affects whether null database values will exist or not.

IsNull (f)

f – any field name from a database table.

```
If IsNull ({Sales.Cust}) Then
    "No customer for this sale"
Else
    {Sales.Cust}
```

returns the string "No customer for this sale" if the field is null. Otherwise, it returns the field's value.

Next (Crystal Syntax only)

Returns the contents of the supplied field for the next database record.

Next (f)

f – any field name from a database table.

```
If {Sales.Cust} = Next({Sales.Cust}) Then
    {Sales.Cust} & " continues on next page"
```

compares the current customer name to the next customer name. If they're the same, the formula returns a "continues on next page" message.

NextIsNull

Returns a Boolean (true/false) value indicating if the supplied field in the next record contains a null value.

Null database values may not appear with all databases. Also, the setting of the Convert Null Database Fields To Default option (from File | Report Options or File | Options) affects whether null database values will exist or not.

NextIsNull (f)

f – any field name from a database table.

```
If NextIsNull ({Sales.Cust}) Then
    "Last order for " & {Sales.Cust}
```

returns a "last order" string if the next record's customer field is null (this assumes that the report is sorted on {Sales.Cust}).

NextValue (Basic Syntax only)

Returns the contents of the supplied field for the next database record.

This function is equivalent to Next. See **Next** for more information.

OnFirstRecord

Returns a Boolean (true/false) value indicating if the current record is the first record on the report.
OnFirstRecord is helpful for some conditional formatting requirements.

OnFirstRecord

```
Not OnFirstRecord
```

when used as a conditional formula for Group Header #1's New Page Before property, avoids a page break before the first group header on the report.

OnLastRecord

Returns a Boolean (true/false) value indicating if the current record is the last record on the report.
OnLastRecord is helpful for some conditional formatting requirements.

OnLastRecord

```
Not OnLastRecord
```

when used as a conditional formula for Group Footer #1's New Page After property, avoids a page break after the last group footer on the report.

PageNofM

Returns a string value indicating the current page number, followed by " of ", followed by the total number of report pages.
PageNofM returns the same string as the Page N of M special field.

PageNofM

```
PageNofM
```

returns "Page 3 of 20" if the current page being formatted is page 3 of a 20-page report.

PageNumber

Returns a numeric value indicating the current page being formatted or printed on the report.
PageNumber returns the same value as the Page Number special field.

PageNumber

```
PageNumber = 1
```

when supplied as a conditional formula for the Page Header Suppress property, will prevent the Page Header from being printed on the first page of the report.

Previous (Crystal Syntax only)

Returns the contents of the supplied field for the previous database record.

Previous (f)

f – any field name from a database table.

```
If {Sales.Cust} = Previous({Sales.Cust}) Then
    {Sales.Cust} & " continued from previous page"
```

compares the current customer name to the previous customer name. If they're the same, the formula returns a "continued from previous page" message.

PreviousIsNull

Returns a Boolean (true/false) value indicating if the supplied field in the previous record contains a null value.

Null database values may not appear with all databases. Also, the setting of the Convert Null Database Fields To Default option (from File | Report Options or File | Options) affects whether null database values will exist or not.

PreviousIsNull (f)

f – any field name from a database table.

```
If PreviousIsNull ({Sales.Cust}) Then
    "First order for " & {Sales.Cust}
```

returns a "first order" string if the previous record's customer field is null (this assumes that the report is sorted on {Sales.Cust}).

PreviousValue (Basic Syntax only)

Returns the contents of the supplied field for the previous database record.

This function is equivalent to Previous. See **Previous** for more information.

RecordNumber

Returns a numeric value indicating the sequential number of the current record.

RecordNumber can be used for certain conditional formatting situations. RecordNumber returns the same value as the Record Number special field.

RecordNumber

```
If RecordNumber Mod 2 = 0 Then
    crSilver
Else
    crNoColor
```

when supplied as a conditional formula to the Details section background color property, shades every other details section silver.

RecordSelection

Returns a string value containing the report's record selection formula.
RecordSelection returns the same value as the Record Selection Formula special field.

RecordSelection

```
RecordSelection
```

returns "{Sales.State} in ["MT", "ID", "WY", "CO"]" if a record selection formula has been created limiting the report to several states.

TotalPageCount

Returns a numeric value indicating the total number of pages on the report.
TotalPageCount returns the same value as the Total Page Count special field.

TotalPageCount

```
If PageNumber < TotalPageCount Then "report continues on next page"
```

prints a "report continues on next page" message of the report is not printing the last page.

Functions: Programming Shortcuts

This category of functions supplies shortcuts for other, more involved programming constructs (such as If-Then-Else or Select-Case).

Choose

Returns a value (the data type depends on function arguments) from the list of "choices."

Choose (n, c1, c2...)

n – a numeric value indicating which entry in the "choice" list to return.
c1 – the first entry in the choice list. *c1* can be any data type or a range value (arrays, however, aren't allowed).
c2 – the next entry in the choice list. It must be the same data type as *c1*. Additional choice entries can follow *c2*, each separated by a comma.

```
Choose(5,"January","February","March","April","May","June")
```

returns "May".

IIF

Returns a value (the data type depends on function arguments) based on the outcome of a conditional test.

IIF (e, v1, v2)

e – a Boolean expression using comparison operators or other Boolean logic. Returns True or False.

v1 – a value of any data type (excluding an array) indicating what the function returns if *e* is true.

v2 – a value of the same data type as *v1* indicating what the function returns if *e* is false.

```
IIF({Sales.Amount} > 5000,"Bonus Sale","Normal Sale")
```

returns the string "Bonus Sale" for sales over $5,000. Otherwise, returns the string "Normal Sale".

Switch

Returns a value (the data type depends on function arguments) based on the outcome of several conditional tests.

Switch (e1, v1, e2..., v2...)

e1 – a Boolean expression using comparison operators or other Boolean logic. Returns True or False.

v1 – a value of any data type (excluding an array) that's returned if *e1* evaluates to True.

e2 – a Boolean expression using comparison operators or other Boolean logic. Returns True or False.

v2 – a value of the same data type as *v1* that's returned if *e2* evaluates to True.

Additional pairs of expressions and values may be supplied. An equal number of expressions and values must be supplied.

```
Switch ({Sales.Amount} < 100, "Needs Improvement",
        {Sales.Amount} < 5000, "OK Sale",
        {Sales.Amount} < 7500, "Bonus Sale",
        True, "Fantastic Sale!")
```

returns a string value relating to the comparisons of the amount field. If the first three tests fail, the formula returns "Fantastic Sale".

Functions: Ranges

This category of functions test range values to determine if they contain a fixed lower or upper bound.

HasLowerBound

Returns a Boolean (true/false) value indicating whether the supplied range has a defined lower bound.

If you supply a range array to HasLowerBound, *every* element of the array must have a lower bound for HasLowerBound to return True.

HasLowerBound (r)

r – a range or range array.

```
If HasLowerBound ({?Order Amounts}) Then
    "Orders start at " & ToText(Minimum({?Order Amounts}))
```

returns "Orders start at 1,000.00" if the Order Amounts parameter field (defined as a range parameter field) has a lower bound of 1,000 specified.

HasUpperBound

Returns a Boolean (true/false) value indicating whether the supplied range has a defined upper bound.

If you supply a range array to HasUpperBound, *every* element of the array must have an upper bound for HasUpperBound to return True.

HasUpperBound (r)

r – a range or range array.

```
If HasUpperBound ({?Order Amounts}) Then
    "Orders end at " & ToText(Maximum({?Order Amounts}))
```

returns "Orders end at 5,000.00" if the Order Amounts parameter field (defined as a range parameter field) has an upper bound of 5,000 specified.

IncludesLowerBound

Returns a Boolean (true/false) value indicating whether the supplied range has a defined lower bound.

If you supply a range array to IncludesLowerBound, *any* element of the array may have a lower bound for IncludesLowerBound to return True.

IncludesLowerBound (r)

r – a range or range array.

```
If IncludesLowerBound ({?Order Amounts}) Then
    "Orders start at " & ToText(Minimum({?Order Amounts}))
```

returns "Orders start at 1,000.00" if the Order Amounts parameter field (defined as a range parameter field) has a lower bound of 1,000 specified.

IncludesUpperBound

Returns a Boolean (true/false) value indicating whether the supplied range has a defined upper bound.

If you supply a range array to IncludesUpperBound, *any* element of the array may have an upper bound for IncludesUpperBound to return True.

IncludesUpperBound (r)

r – a range or range array.

```
If IncludesUpperBound ({?Order Amounts}) Then
    "Orders end at " & ToText(Maximum({?Order Amounts}))
```

returns "Orders end at 5,000.00" if the Order Amounts parameter field (defined as a range parameter field) has an upper bound of 5,000 specified.

PART II

Functions: Strings

This category of functions allows manipulation or testing of string values, database fields, and other string formulas.

AscW

Returns a numeric value indicating the Unicode value of the first character of the supplied string.

AscW (s)

s – a string value.

```
AscW ("X")
```

returns 88.00 (the Unicode code for a capital X).

NOTE *AscW replaces Asc, which is still supported for backward compatibility. Asc behaves identically to AscW.*

ChrW

Returns a string value indicating the Unicode representation of the supplied number.

ChrW (n)

n – a whole number.

```
ChrW(88)
```

returns "X".

NOTE *ChrW replaces Chr, which is still supported for backward compatibility. Chr behaves identically to ChrW.*

Filter

Returns a string array containing only strings that match the search string.

Filter (sa, s)

sa – a string array containing one or more individual strings to search.
s – a string value to search *sa* for.

Filter (sa, s, b)

sa – a string array containing one or more individual strings to search.
s – a string value to search *sa* for.
b – a Boolean (true/false) value indicating whether the search should return partial matches.
If True, partial string matches will be returned. If False, only complete matches will be returned.

Filter (sa, s, b, n)

sa – a string array containing one or more individual strings to search.

s – a string value to search *sa* for.

b – a Boolean (true/false) value indicating whether the search should return string matches or nonmatches. If True, strings that match *s* will be returned. If False, strings that *do not* match *s* will be returned.

n – a numeric value indicating whether the search is case-sensitive. 0 = case-sensitive search, 1 = non-case-sensitive search.

```
StringVar Array Beatles := ["John","Paul","George","Ringo"];
Join (Filter(Beatles,"o"))
```

returns "John George Ringo" (the Join function concatenates the three elements of the Beatles string array that contain the letter *o*).

InStr

Returns a numeric value indicating the first position in the source string where the search string appears.

InStr (s1, s2)

s1 – a string value indicating the source string to search.

s2 – a string value indicating the string to search for in *s1*.

InStr (n, s1, s2)

n – a numeric value indicating the position in *s1* to start searching for *s2*.

s1 – a string value indicating the source string to search.

s2 – a string value indicating the string to search for in *s1*.

InStr (s1, s2, n)

s1 – a string value indicating the source string to search.

s2 – a string value indicating the string to search for in *s1*.

n – a numeric value indicating whether the search is case-sensitive: 0 = case-sensitive, 1 = not case-sensitive.

InStr (n1, s1, s2, n2)

n1 – a numeric value indicating the position in *s1* to start searching for *s2*.

s1 – a string value indicating the source string to search.

s2 – a string value indicating the string to search for in *s1*.

n2 – a numeric value indicating whether the search is case-sensitive: 0 = case-sensitive, 1 = not case-sensitive.

```
Instr("The rain in Spain falls on the plain","spain")
```

returns 0.00 (the search is case-sensitive).

```
Instr("The rain in Spain falls on the plain","spain",1)
```

returns 13.00 (the search is not case-sensitive).

InStrRev

Returns a numeric value indicating the last position in the source string where the search string appears.

In essence, InStrRev starts searching for the substring from right to left.

InStrRev (s1, s2)

s1 – a string value indicating the source string to search.
s2 – a string value indicating the string to search for in *s1*.

InStrRev (s1, s2, n)

s1 – a string value indicating the source string to search.
s2 – a string value indicating the string to search for in *s1*.
n – a numeric value indicating the position from the right of *s1* to start searching for *s2*.

InStrRev (s1, s2, n1, n2)

s1 – a string value indicating the source string to search.
s2 – a string value indicating the string to search for in *s1*.
n1 – a numeric value indicating the position from the right of *s1* to start searching for *s2*.
n2 – a numeric value indicating whether the search is case-sensitive: 0 = case-sensitive,
1 = not case-sensitive.

```
InstrRev("The rain in Spain falls on the plain","a",25)
```

returns 20.00 (the search starts at position 25 and proceeds left—finding a lowercase *a* at position 20).

Join

Returns a string value consisting of all the elements of the source string array concatenated together.

Join is helpful for, among other things, displaying all the values entered into a multivalue string parameter field in a single formula.

Join (a)

a – a string array.

Join (a, s)

a – a string array.
s – a string value to act as a "delimiter"; it will be inserted between each array element in the output string.

```
Join({?States Chosen},", ")
```

returns "CO, WY, MT, UT" if the four states were supplied to the multivalue States Chosen parameter field.

Left

Returns a string value indicating a limited number of characters extracted from the left side of the source string.

Left (s, n)

s – a string value used as the source string.
n – a numeric value indicating how many characters to extract from *s*.

```
Left ("George", 3)
```

returns "Geo".

Length

Returns a numeric value indicating how many characters are contained in the source string.

Len is functionally equivalent to Length.

Length (s)

s – a string value.

```
Length ("George")
```

returns 6.00.

LowerCase

Returns a string value indicating a lowercase representation of the source string.

LCase is functionally equivalent to LowerCase.

LowerCase (s)

s – a string value to be converted to lowercase.

```
LowerCase ("George Peck")
```

returns "george peck".

Mid

Returns a string value indicating a substring extracted from the source string.

Mid (s, n)

s – a string value to extract characters from.
n – a numeric value indicating the position to begin the extraction from *s*.

Mid (s, n1, n2)

s – a string value to extract characters from.
n1 – a numeric value indicating the position to begin the extraction from *s*.
n2 – a numeric value indicating how many characters to extract.

```
Mid("George Peck",8,3)
```

returns "Pec".

NumericText

Returns a Boolean (true/false) value indicating whether or not the source string contains only numeric characters.

NumericText is helpful for testing the contents of a string value before converting it with the ToNumber function, as ToNumber will fail if it encounters any nonnumeric characters.

NumericText (s)

s – a string value to test for numeric content.

```
If NumericText ({FromMainframe.SalesAmount}) Then
    ToNumber({FromMainframe.SalesAmount}) * 1.1
Else
    0
```

checks that the SalesAmount string field contains only numeric values before converting it to a number with the ToNumber function.

ProperCase

Returns a string value converted so that the first character, and any character immediately appearing after a space or nonalphanumeric character, will appear in uppercase. The remaining characters will appear in lowercase.

This function is very helpful when encountering proper names, such as first and last names, that are stored in a database in all uppercase characters.

ProperCase (s)

s – a string value.

```
ProperCase("GEORGE PECK,JR.")
```

returns "George Peck,Jr."

Replace

Returns a string value where a certain set of characters have been replaced by another set of characters.

Replace (s1, s2, s3)

s1 – the source string to search.
s2 – the characters to search *s1* for.
s3 – the characters to replace *s2* with in *s1*.

Replace (s1, s2, s3, n)

s1 – the source string to search.
s2 – the characters to search *s1* for.
s3 – the characters to replace *s2* with in *s1*.
n – a numeric value indicating the position in *s1* to start searching for *s2*.

Replace (s1, s2, s3, n1, n2)

s1 – the source string to search.
s2 – the characters to search *s1* for.
s3 – the characters to replace *s2* with in *s1*.
n1 – a numeric value indicating the position in *s1* to start searching for *s2*.
n2 – a numeric value indicating the number of replacements to make.

Replace (s1, s2, s3, n1, n2, n3)

s1 – the source string to search.
s2 – the characters to search *s1* for.
s3 – the characters to replace *s2* with in *s1*.
n1 – a numeric value indicating the position in *s1* to start searching for *s2*.
n2 – a numeric value indicating the number of replacements to make.
n3 – a numeric value indicating whether the search is case-sensitive: 0 = case-sensitive, 1 = not case-sensitive.

```
Replace("George Peck","George","Gregory")
```

returns "Gregory Peck".

ReplicateString

Returns a string value consisting of multiple duplications of a source string.

ReplicateString (s, n)

s – the source string to duplicate.
n – a numeric value indicating how many duplications of *s* to make.

```
ReplicateString ("*", 15)
```

returns "***************".

Right

Returns a string value indicating a limited number of characters extracted from the right side of the source string.

Right (s, n)

s – a string value used as the source string.
n – a numeric value indicating how many characters to extract from *s*.

```
Right ("George", 3)
```

returns "rge".

Roman

Returns a string value expressing the supplied numeric argument as a Roman numeral value.

Roman (n)

n – a numeric value to convert to Roman numerals.

Roman (n1, n2)

n1 – a numeric value to convert to Roman numerals.
n2 – a numeric value indicating the type of Roman numeral to return; 0 = Classic; 1, 2, or 3 = various levels of precision; 4 = simplified.

```
Roman (1998)
```

returns "MCMXCVIII".

```
Roman (1998, 2)
```

returns "MXMVIII".

NOTE *The best way to explore the various precision choices is to simply try them.*

Space

Returns a string value consisting of a specified number of spaces.

Space (n)

n – the number of space characters to duplicate.

```
"George" & Space(10) & "Peck"
```

returns "George   Peck".

Split

Returns a string array consisting of elements built from the supplied individual strings.

Split (s)

s – a string containing one or more individual strings separated by spaces.

Split (s1, s2)

s1 – a string containing one or more individual strings separated by the delimiter specified in *s2*.
s2 – a string value indicating the delimiter that separates individual values in *s1*.

Split (s1, s2, n)

s1 – a string containing one or more individual strings separated by the delimiter specified in *s2*.
s2 – a string value indicating the delimiter that separates individual values in *s1*.
n – a numeric value indicating how many elements should be placed in the array.

Split (s1, s2, n1, n2)

s1 – a string containing one or more individual strings separated by the delimiter specified in *s2*.
s2 – a string value indicating the delimiter that separates individual values in *s1*.

n1 – a numeric value indicating how many elements should be placed in the array (–1 for all).
n2 – a numeric value indicating how to treat the search for the delimiter. 0 = search is case-sensitive, 1 = search is not case-sensitive.

```
Split("John Paul George Ringo")[2]
```

returns "Paul".

```
Split("John And Paul And George And Ringo","and",-1,0)[1]
```

returns "John And Paul And George And Ringo", as only one element was added the array—the delimiter search is case-sensitive and "And" is not found.

```
Split("John And Paul And George And Ringo","and",-1,1)[1]
```

returns "John"—the delimiter search is not case-sensitive.

StrCmp
Returns a numeric value indicating how two strings compare alphabetically.
StrCmp returns –1 if the first string is less than the second string, 0 if the strings are equal, and 1 if the first string is greater than the second string.

StrCmp (s1, s2)
s1 – the first string to compare.
s2 – the string to compare to *s1*.

StrCmp (s1, s2, n)
s1 – the first string to compare.
s2 – the string to compare to *s1*.
n – a numeric value indicating how to treat the search for the delimiter. 0 = search is case-sensitive, 1 = search is not case-sensitive.

```
StrCmp ("abc","xyz")
```

returns –1.00.

StrReverse
Returns a string value consisting of the source string in reverse order.

StrReverse (s)
s – a string value to be reversed.

```
StrReverse ("George Peck")
```

returns "kceP egroeG".

ToNumber

Returns a numeric value indicating a numeric conversion of another nonnumeric value.

ToNumber converts other numeric and Boolean values, as well as string values, to numbers. ToNumber is functionally equivalent to CDbl and Val.

ToNumber (v)

v – a numeric, string, or Boolean value to be converted to a number.

```
ToNumber ("5642.15")
```

returns 5,642.15 as a number.

NOTE *You may wish to test the value to convert with NumericText before you supply it to ToNumber, as ToNumber will fail if a string is supplied that doesn't contain all numeric values. If you wish to avoid the test, you may use Val, which will always return a result (perhaps 0), even if the supplied argument isn't numeric.*

ToText

Converts any nonstring data type to a string value.

ToText is an immensely valuable function used to convert any nonstring data type to a string. You'll often use ToText within a string formula to concatenate various types of data items into a single string result.

ToText (b)

b – a Boolean (true/false) value to be converted to a string.

```
ToText({Orders.Shipped})
```

returns the string "True" if the Boolean Shipped field holds a true value or "False" if the field is false.

ToText (n1, n2, s1, s2)

n1 – a numeric value to be converted to a string.
n2 – a numeric value indicating the number of decimal places to use when converting *n1*. This argument is optional.
s1 – a string value indicating the character or characters to use as a thousands separator when converting *n1*. This argument is optional.
s2 – a string value indicating the character or characters to use as a decimal separator when converting *n1*. This argument is optional.

```
ToText(21256.1255, 2, ",", "-")
```

returns the string "21,256-13" (showing two decimal places, a comma thousands separator, and a dash decimal separator).

ToText (n1, n2, s1, s2, s3)

n1 – a numeric value to be converted to a string.
s1 – a string value used to format the number. This argument is optional.

n2 – a numeric value indicating the number of decimal places to use when converting *n1*. This argument is optional.

s2 – a string value indicating the character or characters to use as a thousands separator when converting *n*. This argument is optional.

s3 – a string value indicating the character or characters to use as a decimal separator when converting *n*. This argument is optional.

```
ToText(21256.1255, "#,###,###.00000",2)
```

returns " 21,256.13000" (with leading spaces for extra # characters).

Numeric Formatting Strings

Character	Usage
#	Numeric placeholder. A single numeric character will be placed in each occurrence of #. If there are more # characters than numeric digits, leading or trailing spaces will be added for extra # characters.
0 (zero)	Numeric placeholder. A single numeric character will be placed in each occurrence of 0. If there are more 0 characters than numeric digits, leading or trailing zeros will be added for extra 0 characters.
, (comma)	Thousands separator. Indicates where the thousands separator should be placed in the resulting string. The thousands separator used is taken from a Windows default or the s2 argument.
. (period)	Decimal separator. Indicates where the decimal separator should be placed in the resulting string. The decimal separator used is taken from a Windows default or the s2 argument.

ToText (d, s1, s2, s3)

d – a date, time, or date/time value.

s1 – a string value used to format the date, time, or date/time value. This argument is optional.

s2 – a string value used to as a replacement label for "a.m." for morning hours. This argument is optional.

s3 – a string value used to as a replacement label for "p.m." for afternoon/evening hours. This argument is optional.

```
ToText(CurrentDate, "dddd M d, yyyy")
```

returns "Friday May 9, 2003" if CurrentDate contains May 9, 2003.

```
ToText(CurrentTime, "h:mm tt",
"in the morning", "in the afternoon")
```

returns the string " 4:27 in the afternoon" if CurrentTime is 4:27 P.M.

NOTE *Any nonrecognized characters in the format string will be returned as a literal character. For example, a slash (/) or comma (,) in the format string will simply display within the resulting date string.*

Date/Time Formatting Strings

Character	Usage
M	Month number without a leading zero for single-character month
MM	Month number with a leading zero for single-character month
MMM	Month name as a three-letter abbreviation
MMMM	Month name fully spelled
D	Day of month without a leading zero for single-character day
Dd	Day of month with a leading zero for single-character day
Ddd	Day of week name spelled as a three-letter abbreviation
Dddd	Day of week name fully spelled
Yy	Last two characters of year
Yyyy	Full four-character year
H	Hours without a leading zero for a single-character hour (12-hour nonmilitary format)
Hh	Hours with a leading zero for a single-character hour (12-hour nonmilitary format)
H	Hours without a leading zero for a single-character hour (24-hour military format)
HH	Hours with a leading zero for a single-character hour (24-hour military format)
m	Minutes without a leading zero for a single-character minute
Mm	Minutes with a leading zero for a single-character minute
S	Seconds without a leading zero for a single-character second
Ss	Seconds with a leading zero for a single-character second
T	Single-character uppercase A or P (for a.m. or p.m.)
Tt	Multiple-character uppercase AM or PM (for a.m. or p.m.)

NOTE *CStr is functionally equivalent to ToText. It is provided to maintain compatibility with Basic syntax.*

ToWords

Returns a string value indicating the "spelled out" version of the numeric argument.

ToWords is often used to print checks, but can also be used when required to convert numeric values to text for other situations. For example, ToWords will be helpful if you are required to create a formula, based on numeric data, that returns the string "This contract expires in 30 (thirty) days".

ToWords (n)

n – a numeric value to spell as words.

```
ToWords (1145.31)
```

returns the string "one thousand one hundred forty-five and 31 / 100".

ToWords (n1, n2)

n1 – a numeric value to spell as words.
n2 – a numeric value indicating the number of decimal places to use when converting *n1*.

```
ToWords (100, 0)
```

returns the string "one hundred".

> **NOTE** *An optional third numeric argument specifying the form type can be supplied. Allowable values for the form type argument are numeric and can be 0 (Classic or Check form), 1 (Daily form), or 2 (Casual form). This argument applies only to Asian language versions of Crystal Reports.*

Trim

Returns a string value consisting of the source string with all leading and trailing spaces removed.

Trim (s)

s – a string value.

```
Trim ("    Leading and trailing spaces    ")
```

returns the string "Leading and trailing spaces" with no extra spaces before or after the string.

TrimLeft

Returns a string value consisting of the source string with all leading spaces removed.
LTrim is functionally equivalent to TrimLeft.

TrimLeft (s)

s – a string value.

```
TrimLeft ("    Leading and trailing spaces    ")
```

returns the string "Leading and trailing spaces   " with no extra spaces before the string, but with any trailing spaces remaining.

TrimRight

Returns a string value consisting of the source string with all trailing spaces removed.
RTrim is functionally equivalent to TrimRight.

TrimRight (s)

s – a string value.

```
TrimRight ("    Leading and trailing spaces    ")
```

returns the string "   Leading and trailing spaces" with no extra spaces after the string, but with any leading spaces remaining.

UpperCase

Returns a string value indicating an uppercase representation of the source string.
UCase is functionally equivalent to UpperCase.

UpperCase (s)

s – a string value to be converted to uppercase.

```
UpperCase ("George Peck")
```

returns "GEORGE PECK".

URLDecode

Returns a string with specially defined URL characters converted to readable form.
   URLDecode (s)
   s – a string to apply URL decoding to.

```
URLDecode("http://www.AblazeGroup.%63%6F%6D")
```

returns http://www.AblazeGroup.com, converting the encoded last three characters
to text.

URLDecode (s, n)

s – a string to apply URL decoding to.
n – an integer value indicating what encoding scheme is used in s. Allowable values are 0
for RFC 1738 standards (the default), 1 for application/x-www-form-urlencoded standards,
and 2 for user-defined encoding (alphanumeric characters are returned as supplied, while
other characters are interpreted as coded characters).

```
URLDecode("http://www.AblazeGroup.com/Crystal+Reports.htm", 1)
```

returns http://www.AblazeGroup.com/Crystal Reports.htm (converting the encoded plus
sign to a space).

URLDecode (s, n1, n2)

s – a string to apply URL decoding to.
$n1$ – an integer value indicating what encoding scheme is used in s. Allowable values are 0
for RFC 1738 standards (the default), 1 for application/x-www-form-urlencoded standards,
and 2 for user-defined encoding (alphanumeric characters are returned as supplied, while
other characters are interpreted as coded characters).
$n2$ – an integer value indicating the character set, or codepage, to use when interpreting s.
Allowable values are 0 for UTF-8 (the default), 1 for ISO-8859, and 2 for Shift-JIS.

URLEncode

**Returns a string value containing coded characters that are required for certain web
browser URL encoding.**
This function may come in handy when you need to use hyperlinks within your reports.
In order to allow web browsers to fully interpret hyperlink URLs with special characters

(such as spaces, hyphens, etc.), you may need to encode the initial hyperlink string with URLEncode.

URLEncode (s)
s – a string value to be encoded into a URL-confirming string.

URLEncode (s, n)
s – a string value to be encoded into a URL-confirming string.

n – an integer value indicating what encoding scheme to use when encoding *s*. Allowable values are 0 for RFC 1738 standards (the default), 1 for application/x-www-form-urlencoded standards, and 2 for user-defined encoding (alphanumeric characters are returned as supplied, while other characters are interpreted as coded characters).

URLEncode (s1, n, s2)
s1 – a string value to be encoded into a URL-confirming string.

n – an integer value indicating what encoding scheme to use when encoding *s*. Allowable values are 0 for RFC 1738 standards (the default), 1 for application/x-www-form-urlencoded standards, and 2 for user-defined encoding (alphanumeric characters are returned as supplied, while other characters are interpreted as coded characters).

s2 – a string value indicating characters to never encode when converting *s* (the default is an empty string).

URLEncode (s1, n, s2, s3)
s1 – a string value to be encoded into a URL-confirming string.

n – an integer value indicating what encoding scheme to use when encoding *s*. Allowable values are 0 for RFC 1738 standards (the default), 1 for application/x-www-form-urlencoded standards, and 2 for user-defined encoding (alphanumeric characters are returned as supplied, while other characters are interpreted as coded characters).

s2 – a string value indicating characters to never encode when converting *s* (the default is an empty string).

s3 – a string value indicating characters to always encode when converting *s* (the default is an empty string).

URLEncode (s, n1, n2)
s – a string value to be encoded into a URL-confirming string.

n1 – an integer value indicating what encoding scheme to use when encoding *s*. Allowable values are 0 for RFC 1738 standards (the default), 1 for application/x-www-form-urlencoded standards, and 2 for user-defined encoding (alphanumeric characters are returned as supplied, while other characters are interpreted as coded characters).

n2 – an integer value indicating the character set, or codepage, to use when encoding *s*. Allowable values are 0 for UTF-8 (the default), 1 for ISO-8859, and 2 for Shift-JIS.

URLEncode (s1, n1, n2, s2)
s1 – a string value to be encoded into a URL-confirming string.

n1 – an integer value indicating what encoding scheme to use when encoding *s*. Allowable values are 0 for RFC 1738 standards (the default), 1 for application/x-www-form-urlencoded standards, and 2 for user-defined encoding (alphanumeric characters are returned as supplied, while other characters are interpreted as coded characters).

PART II

n2 – an integer value indicating the character set, or codepage, to use when encoding *s*. Allowable values are 0 for UTF-8 (the default), 1 for ISO-8859, and 2 for Shift-JIS.

s2 – a string value indicating characters to never encode when converting *s* (the default is an empty string).

URLEncode (s1, n1, n2, s2, s3)

s1 – a string value to be encoded into a URL-confirming string.

n1 – an integer value indicating what encoding scheme to use when encoding *s*. Allowable values are 0 for RFC 1738 standards (the default), 1 for application/x-www-form-urlencoded standards, and 2 for user-defined encoding (alphanumeric characters are returned as supplied, while other characters are interpreted as coded characters).

n2 – an integer value indicating the character set, or codepage, to use when encoding *s*. Allowable values are 0 for UTF-8 (the default), 1 for ISO-8859, and 2 for Shift-JIS.

s2 – a string value indicating characters to never encode when converting *s* (the default is an empty string).

s3 – a string value indicating characters to always encode when converting *s* (the default is an empty string).

```
URLEncode ("http://www.AblazeGroup.com/Crystal Reports.htm")
```

returns http://www.AblazeGroup.com/Crystal%20Reports.htm, converting the space to a %20 encoded string.

```
URLEncode ("http://www.AblazeGroup.com",0,"","com")
```

returns http://www.AblazeGr%6Fup.%63%6F%6D, encoding any occurrence of the characters *c, o,* or *m*.

Val

Returns a numeric value indicating the numeric portion of the supplied string.

Val is helpful for converting string database fields that contain numeric data to actual numeric values. In particular, Val will not return an error if it encounters a nonnumeric character in the string—it will simply stop the conversion at that point.

Val (s)

s – a string value to be converted to a number.

```
Val ("12500.1a31")
```

returns 12,500.10 as a numeric value.

Functions: Summary

This category of functions largely duplicates summary functions available via the Insert | Summary option from the Crystal Reports pull-down menus. By using these summary functions, you may include the same summary calculations available from the Insert | Summary option in formulas. In fact, if you add a report summary to a report with Insert |

Summary and then double-click it in the Fields tree of the Formula Editor, the following summary functions will be inserted in your report automatically.

Average

Returns a numeric value indicating the average of the supplied database field or formula.

Average (f)

f – the database or formula field to summarize for the entire report. This must be a numeric field.

Average (f1, f2)

f1 – the database or formula field to summarize for a report group. This must be a numeric field.
f2 – the database or formula field indicating the group you wish to summarize for. An existing group on the report must be based on this field.

Average (f1, f2, s)

f1 – the database or formula field to summarize for a report group. This must be a numeric field.
f2 – the database or formula field indicating the group you wish to summarize for. An existing group on the report must be based on this field.
s – a string value indicating how often to "change" the summary for Boolean, date, or date-time grouping. See **Boolean Conditions**, **Date Conditions**, and **Time Conditions** later in this appendix for available choices.

```
Average({Sales.Amount})
```

returns the average of sales amounts for the entire report.

```
Average({Sales.Amount}, {Sales.Date}, "monthly")
```

returns the average of sales amounts for the sales date group, summarized for each month.

Correlation

Returns a numeric value indicating the correlation between the supplied database fields or formulas.

Correlation (f1, f2)

f1 – the first database or formula field to summarize for the entire report. This must be a numeric field.
f2 – the second database or formula field to summarize for the entire report. This must be a numeric field.

Correlation (f1, f2, f3)

f1 – the first database or formula field to summarize for the entire report. This must be a numeric field.
f2 – the second database or formula field to summarize for the entire report. This must be a numeric field.
f3 – the database or formula field indicating the group you wish to summarize for. An existing group on the report must be based on this field.

Correlation (f1, f2, f3, s)

f1 – the first database or formula field to summarize for the entire report. This must be a numeric field.

f2 – the second database or formula field to summarize for the entire report. This must be a numeric field.

f3 – the database or formula field indicating the group you wish to summarize for. An existing group on the report must be based on this field.

s – a string value indicating how often to "change" the summary for Boolean, date, or date-time grouping. See **Boolean Conditions**, **Date Conditions**, and **Time Conditions** later in this appendix for available choices.

```
Correlation({Sales.Amount}, {Sales.Goal})
```

returns the correlation between sales amount and sales goal for the entire report.

```
Correlation({Sales.Amount}, {Sales.Goal}, {Sales.Date}, "monthly")
```

returns the correlation between sales amount and sales goal for the sales date group, summarized for each month.

Count

Returns a numeric value indicating the number of occurrences (count) of the supplied database field or formula.

Count (f)

f – the database or formula field to summarize for the entire report.

Count (f1, f2)

f1 – the database or formula field to summarize for a report group.

f2 – the database or formula field indicating the group you wish to summarize for. An existing group on the report must be based on this field.

Count (f1, f2, s)

f1 – the database or formula field to summarize for a report group.

f2 – the database or formula field indicating the group you wish to summarize for. An existing group on the report must be based on this field.

s – a string value indicating how often to "change" the summary for Boolean, date, or date-time grouping. See **Boolean Conditions**, **Date Conditions**, and **Time Conditions** later in this appendix for available choices.

```
Count({Sales.Amount})
```

returns the count of sales amounts for the entire report (in essence, this is the number of records on the report).

```
Count({Sales.Amount}, {Sales.Date}, "monthly")
```

returns the count of sales amounts for the sales date group, summarized for each month (in essence, this is the number of records in the group).

NOTE *The Count function will count every record where the supplied field contains a nonnull value. If any occurrences of the supplied field contain null values, those records won't increment the count.*

Covariance

Returns a numeric value indicating the covariance between the supplied database fields or formulas.

Covariance (f1, f2)
f1 – the first database or formula field to summarize for the entire report. This must be a numeric field.
f2 – the second database or formula field to summarize for the entire report. This must be a numeric field.

Covariance (f1, f2, f3)
f1 – the first database or formula field to summarize for the entire report. This must be a numeric field.
f2 – the second database or formula field to summarize for the entire report. This must be a numeric field.
f3 – the database or formula field indicating the group you wish to summarize for. An existing group on the report must be based on this field.

Covariance (f1, f2, f3, s)
f1 – the first database or formula field to summarize for the entire report. This must be a numeric field.
f2 – the second database or formula field to summarize for the entire report. This must be a numeric field.
f3 – the database or formula field indicating the group you wish to summarize for. An existing group on the report must be based on this field.
s – a string value indicating how often to "change" the summary for Boolean, date, or date-time grouping. See **Boolean Conditions**, **Date Conditions**, and **Time Conditions** later in this appendix for available choices.

```
Covariance({Sales.Amount}, {Sales.Goal})
```

returns the covariance between sales amount and sales goal for the entire report.

```
Covariance({Sales.Amount}, {Sales.Goal}, {Sales.Date}, "monthly")
```

returns the covariance between sales amount and sales goal for the sales date group, summarized for each month.

DistinctCount

Returns a numeric value indicating the unique number of occurrences (distinct count) of the supplied database field or formula.

DistinctCount (f)

f – the database or formula field to summarize for the entire report.

DistinctCount (f1, f2)

f1 – the database or formula field to summarize for a report group.
f2 – the database or formula field indicating the group you wish to summarize for. An existing group on the report must be based on this field.

DistinctCount (f1, f2, s)

f1 – the database or formula field to summarize for a report group.
f2 – the database or formula field indicating the group you wish to summarize for. An existing group on the report must be based on this field.
s – a string value indicating how often to "change" the summary for Boolean, date, or date-time grouping. See **Boolean Conditions**, **Date Conditions**, and **Time Conditions** later in this appendix for available choices.

```
Distinctcount({Sales.Acct#})
```

returns the number of unique accounts for the entire report.

```
Distinctcount({Sales.Acct#}, {Sales.Date}, "monthly")
```

returns the number of unique accounts for the sales date group, summarized for each month.

Maximum

Returns a numeric value indicating the maximum of the supplied database field or formula.
   Maximum returns the largest number, the latest date, or the string value last in the alphabet.

Maximum (f)

f – the database or formula field to summarize for the entire report.

Maximum (f1, f2)

f1 – the database or formula field to summarize for a report group.
f2 – the database or formula field indicating the group you wish to summarize for. An existing group on the report must be based on this field.

Maximum (f1, f2, s)

f1 – the database or formula field to summarize for a report group.
f2 – the database or formula field indicating the group you wish to summarize for. An existing group on the report must be based on this field.
s – a string value indicating how often to "change" the summary for Boolean, date, or date-time grouping. See **Boolean Conditions**, **Date Conditions**, and **Time Conditions** later in this appendix for available choices.

```
Maximum({Sales.Amount})
```

returns the highest sales amount for the entire report.

```
Maximum({Sales.Amount}, {Sales.Date}, "monthly")
```

returns the highest sales amount for the sales date group, summarized for each month.

Median

Returns a numeric value indicating the median of the supplied database field or formula.

Median (f)

f – the database or formula field to summarize for the entire report. This must be a numeric field.

Median (f1, f2)

f1 – the database or formula field to summarize for a report group. This must be a numeric field.
f2 – the database or formula field indicating the group you wish to summarize for. An existing group on the report must be based on this field.

Median (f1, f2, s)

f1 – the database or formula field to summarize for a report group. This must be a numeric field.
f2 – the database or formula field indicating the group you wish to summarize for. An existing group on the report must be based on this field.
s – a string value indicating how often to "change" the summary for Boolean, date, or date-time grouping. See **Boolean Conditions**, **Date Conditions**, and **Time Conditions** later in this appendix for available choices.

```
Median({Sales.Amount})
```

returns the median of sales amounts for the entire report.

```
Median({Sales.Amount}, {Sales.Date}, "monthly")
```

returns the median of sales amounts for the sales date group, summarized for each month.

Minimum

Returns a numeric value indicating the minimum of the supplied database field or formula.

Minimum returns the smallest number, the earliest date, or the string value first in the alphabet.

Minimum (f)

f – the database or formula field to summarize for the entire report.

Minimum (f1, f2)

f1 – the database or formula field to summarize for a report group.
f2 – the database or formula field indicating the group you wish to summarize for. An existing group on the report must be based on this field.

Minimum (f1, f2, s)

f1 – the database or formula field to summarize for a report group.
f2 – the database or formula field indicating the group you wish to summarize for. An existing group on the report must be based on this field.

s – a string value indicating how often to "change" the summary for Boolean, date, or date-time grouping. See **Boolean Conditions**, **Date Conditions**, and **Time Conditions** later in this appendix for available choices.

```
Minimum({Sales.Amount})
```

returns the lowest sales amount for the entire report.

```
Minimum({Sales.Amount}, {Sales.Date}, "monthly")
```

returns the lowest sales amount for the sales date group, summarized for each month.

Mode

Returns a numeric value indicating the mode (the most frequently occurring value) of the supplied database field or formula.

Mode (f)
f – the database or formula field to summarize for the entire report.

Mode (f1, f2)
f1 – the database or formula field to summarize for a report group.
f2 – the database or formula field indicating the group you wish to summarize for. An existing group on the report must be based on this field.

Mode (f1, f2, s)
f1 – the database or formula field to summarize for a report group.
f2 – the database or formula field indicating the group you wish to summarize for. An existing group on the report must be based on this field.
s – a string value indicating how often to "change" the summary for Boolean, date, or date-time grouping. See **Boolean Conditions**, **Date Conditions**, and **Time Conditions** later in this appendix for available choices.

```
Mode({Sales.Acct#})
```

returns the most frequently appearing account number for the entire report.

```
Mode({Sales.Acct#}, {Sales.Date}, "monthly")
```

returns the most frequently appearing account number for the sales date group, summarized for each month.

NthLargest

Returns a numeric value indicating the *n*th largest occurrence of the supplied database field or formula.

NthLargest returns the "nth" largest number, the "*n*th" latest date, or the "*n*th" string value last in the ASCII sort order.

NthLargest (n, f)

n – a numeric value (between 1 and 100). 5 returns the fifth largest, 2 the second largest, and so forth.

f – the database or formula field to summarize for the entire report.

NthLargest (n, f1, f2)

n – a numeric value (between 1 and 100). 5 returns the fifth largest, 2 the second largest, and so forth.

f1 – the database or formula field to summarize for a report group.

f2 – the database or formula field indicating the group you wish to summarize for. An existing group on the report must be based on this field.

NthLargest (n, f1, f2, s)

n – a numeric value (between 1 and 100). 5 returns the fifth largest, 2 the second largest, and so forth.

f1 – the database or formula field to summarize for a report group.

f2 – the database or formula field indicating the group you wish to summarize for. An existing group on the report must be based on this field.

s – a string value indicating how often to "change" the summary for Boolean, date, or date-time grouping. See **Boolean Conditions**, **Date Conditions**, and **Time Conditions** later in this appendix for available choices.

```
NthLargest(5, {Sales.Amount})
```

returns the fifth largest sales amount for the entire report.

```
NthLargest(5, {Sales.Amount}, {Sales.Date}, "monthly")
```

returns the fifth largest sales amount for the sales date group, summarized for each month.

NthMostFrequent

Returns a numeric value indicating the *n*th most frequent occurrence of the supplied database field or formula.

NthMostFrequent (n, f)

n – a numeric value (between 1 and 100). 5 returns the fifth most frequent, 2 the second most frequent, and so forth.

f – the database or formula field to summarize for the entire report.

NthMostFrequent (n, f1, f2)

n – a numeric value (between 1 and 100). 5 returns the fifth most frequent, 2 the second most frequent, and so forth.

f1 – the database or formula field to summarize for a report group.

f2 – the database or formula field indicating the group you wish to summarize for. An existing group on the report must be based on this field.

NthMostFrequent (n, f1, f2, s)

n – a numeric value (between 1 and 100). 5 returns the fifth most frequent, 2 the second most frequent, and so forth.

f1 – the database or formula field to summarize for a report group.

f2 – the database or formula field indicating the group you wish to summarize for. An existing group on the report must be based on this field.

s – a string value indicating how often to "change" the summary for Boolean, date, or date-time grouping. See **Boolean Conditions**, **Date Conditions**, and **Time Conditions** later in this appendix for available choices.

```
NthMostFrequent(5, {Sales.Acct#})
```

returns the fifth most frequently occurring account number for the entire report.

```
NthMostFrequent(5, {Sales.Acct#}, {Sales.Date}, "monthly")
```

returns the fifth most frequently occurring account number for the sales date group, summarized for each month.

NthSmallest

Returns a numeric value indicating the *n*th smallest occurrence of the supplied database field or formula.

NthSmallest returns the "nth" smallest number, the "nth" earliest date, or the "nth" string value first in the ASCII sort order.

NthSmallest (n, f)

n – a numeric value (between 1 and 100). 5 returns the fifth smallest, 2 the second smallest, and so forth.

f – the database or formula field to summarize for the entire report.

NthSmallest (n, f1, f2)

n – a numeric value (between 1 and 100). 5 returns the fifth smallest, 2 the second smallest, and so forth.

f1 – the database or formula field to summarize for a report group.

f2 – the database or formula field indicating the group you wish to summarize for. An existing group on the report must be based on this field.

NthSmallest (n, f1, f2, s)

n – a numeric value (between 1 and 100). 5 returns the fifth smallest, 2 the second smallest, and so forth.

f1 – the database or formula field to summarize for a report group.

f2 – the database or formula field indicating the group you wish to summarize for. An existing group on the report must be based on this field.

s – a string value indicating how often to "change" the summary for Boolean, date, or date-time grouping. See **Boolean Conditions**, **Date Conditions**, and **Time Conditions** later in this appendix for available choices.

```
NthSmallest (5, {Sales.Amount})
```

returns the fifth smallest sales amount for the entire report.

```
NthSmallest (5, {Sales.Amount}, {Sales.Date}, "monthly")
```

returns the fifth smallest sales amount for the sales date group, summarized for each month.

PercentOfAverage

Returns a numeric value indicating what percentage an average calculation in one group is of another average calculation in a later group or the entire report.

This function duplicates a Percentage Summary Field created with the Insert | Summary menu option.

PercentOfAverage (f1, f2, s)

This will show the percentage of the group value compared to the value for the entire report.

f1 – the database or formula field to summarize for the entire report. This must be a numeric field.

f2 – the database or formula field indicating the group you wish to summarize for. An existing group on the report must be based on this field.

s – a string value indicating how often to "change" the summary for Boolean, date, or date-time grouping. See **Boolean Conditions**, **Date Conditions**, and **Time Conditions** later in this appendix for available choices. This argument is required only if *f2* is a date, date-time, time, or Boolean field.

PercentOfAverage (f1, f2, s1, f3, s2)

This will show the percentage of the group value compared to the value for a later group.

f1 – the database or formula field to summarize for the entire report. This must be a numeric field.

f2 – the database or formula field indicating the group you wish to summarize for. An existing group on the report must be based on this field.

s1 – a string value indicating how often to "change" the summary for Boolean, date, or date-time grouping. See **Boolean Conditions**, **Date Conditions**, and **Time Conditions** later in this appendix for available choices. This argument (and the comma that precedes it) is required only if *f2* is a date, date-time, time, or Boolean field.

f3 – the database or formula field indicating the later group field to use for the summary. An existing group on the report must be based on this field.

s2 – a string value indicating how often to "change" the summary for Boolean, date, or date-time grouping. See **Boolean Conditions**, **Date Conditions**, and **Time Conditions** later in this appendix for available choices. This argument (and the comma that precedes it) is required only if *f3* is a date, date-time, time, or Boolean field.

```
PercentOfAverage ({Sales.Amount}, {Sales.CustName})
```

returns the percentage that the average sales amount for each customer group makes up of the average sales amount for the entire report.

```
PercentOfAverage ({Sales.Amount}, {Sales.Date},
"monthly", {Sales.CustName})
```

returns the percentage that the average sales amount for each month makes up of the average sales amount for the higher-level customer name group.

PercentOfCount

Returns a numeric value indicating what percentage a count calculation in one group is of another count calculation in a later group or the entire report.

This function duplicates a Percentage Summary Field created with the Insert | Summary menu option.

PercentOfCount (f1, f2, s)

This will show the percentage of the group value compared to the value for the entire report.

f1 – the database or formula field to summarize for the entire report.

f2 – the database or formula field indicating the group you wish to summarize for. An existing group on the report must be based on this field.

s – a string value indicating how often to "change" the summary for Boolean, date, or date-time grouping. See **Boolean Conditions**, **Date Conditions**, and **Time Conditions** later in this appendix for available choices. This argument is required only if *f2* is a date, date-time, time, or Boolean field.

PercentOfCount (f1, f2, s1, f3, s2)

This will show the percentage of the group value compared to the value for a later group.

f1 – the database or formula field to summarize for the entire report.

f2 – the database or formula field indicating the group you wish to summarize for. An existing group on the report must be based on this field.

s1 – a string value indicating how often to "change" the summary for Boolean, date, or date-time grouping. See **Boolean Conditions**, **Date Conditions**, and **Time Conditions** later in this appendix for available choices. This argument (and the comma that precedes it) is required only if *f2* is a date, date-time, time, or Boolean field.

f3 – the database or formula field indicating the later group field to use for the summary. An existing group on the report must be based on this field.

s2 – a string value indicating how often to "change" the summary for Boolean, date, or date-time grouping. See **Boolean Conditions**, **Date Conditions**, and **Time Conditions** later in this appendix for available choices. This argument (and the comma that precedes it) is required only if *f3* is a date, date-time, time, or Boolean field.

```
PercentOfCount ({Sales.Amount}, {Sales.CustName})
```

returns the percentage that the number of records for each customer group makes up of the total number of records for the entire report.

```
PercentOfCount ({Sales.Amount}, {Sales.Date},
"monthly", {Sales.CustName})
```

returns the percentage that the number of records for each month makes up of the number of records for the higher-level customer name group.

NOTE *PercentOfCount calculations will exclude records that contain an null value in the field being counted.*

PercentOfDistinctCount

Returns a numeric value indicating what percentage a distinct count calculation in one group is of another distinct count calculation in a later group or the entire report.

This function duplicates a Percentage Summary Field created with the Insert | Summary menu option.

PercentOfDistinctCount (f1, f2, s)

This will show the percentage of the group value compared to the value for the entire report.

f1 – the database or formula field to summarize for the entire report.

f2 – the database or formula field indicating the group you wish to summarize for. An existing group on the report must be based on this field.

s – a string value indicating how often to "change" the summary for Boolean, date, or date-time grouping. See **Boolean Conditions**, **Date Conditions**, and **Time Conditions** later in this appendix for available choices. This argument is required only if *f2* is a date, date-time, time, or Boolean field.

PercentOfDistinctCount (f1, f2, s1, f3, s2)

This will show the percentage of the group value compared to the value for a later group.

f1 – the database or formula field to summarize for the entire report.

f2 – the database or formula field indicating the group you wish to summarize for. An existing group on the report must be based on this field.

s1 – a string value indicating how often to "change" the summary for Boolean, date, or date-time grouping. See **Boolean Conditions**, **Date Conditions**, and **Time Conditions** later in this appendix for available choices. This argument (and the comma that precedes it) is required only if *f2* is a date, date-time, time, or Boolean field.

f3 – the database or formula field indicating the later group field to use for the summary. An existing group on the report must be based on this field.

s2 – a string value indicating how often to "change" the summary for Boolean, date, or date-time grouping. See **Boolean Conditions**, **Date Conditions**, and **Time Conditions** later in this appendix for available choices. This argument (and the comma that precedes it) is required only if *f3* is a date, date-time, time, or Boolean field.

```
PercentOfDistinctCount ({Sales.Acct#}, {Sales.CustName})
```

returns the percentage that the unique number of account numbers for each customer group makes up of the unique number of account numbers for the entire report.

```
PercentOfDistinctCount ({Sales.Acct#}, {Sales.Date},
"monthly", {Sales.CustName})
```

returns the percentage that the unique number of account numbers for each month makes up of the unique number of account numbers for the higher-level customer name group.

PercentOfMaximum

Returns a numeric value indicating what percentage a maximum calculation in one group is of another maximum calculation in a later group or the entire report.

This function duplicates a Percentage Summary Field created with the Insert | Summary menu option.

PercentOfMaximum (f1, f2, s)

This will show the percentage of the group value compared to the value for the entire report.

f1 – the database or formula field to summarize for the entire report.

f2 – the database or formula field indicating the group you wish to summarize for. An existing group on the report must be based on this field.

s – a string value indicating how often to "change" the summary for Boolean, date, or date-time grouping. See **Boolean Conditions**, **Date Conditions**, and **Time Conditions** later in this appendix for available choices. This argument is required only if *f2* is a date, date-time, time, or Boolean field.

PercentOfMaximum (f1, f2, s1, f3, s2)

This will show the percentage of the group value compared to the value for a later group.

f1 – the database or formula field to summarize for the entire report.

f2 – the database or formula field indicating the group you wish to summarize for. An existing group on the report must be based on this field.

s1 – a string value indicating how often to "change" the summary for Boolean, date, or date-time grouping. See **Boolean Conditions**, **Date Conditions**, and **Time Conditions** later in this appendix for available choices. This argument (and the comma that precedes it) is required only if *f2* is a date, date-time, time, or Boolean field.

f3 – the database or formula field indicating the later group field to use for the summary. An existing group on the report must be based on this field.

s2 – a string value indicating how often to "change" the summary for Boolean, date, or date-time grouping. See **Boolean Conditions**, **Date Conditions**, and **Time Conditions** later in this appendix for available choices. This argument (and the comma that precedes it) is required only if *f3* is a date, date-time, time, or Boolean field.

```
PercentOfMaximum ({Sales.Amount}, {Sales.CustName})
```

returns the percentage that the highest sales amount for each customer group makes up of the highest sales amount for the entire report.

```
PercentOfMaximum ({Sales.Amount}, {Sales.Date},
"monthly", {Sales.CustName})
```

returns the percentage that the highest sales amount for each month makes up of the highest sales amount for the higher-level customer name group.

PercentOfMinimum

Returns a numeric value indicating what percentage an minimum calculation in one group is of another minimum calculation in a later group or the entire report.

This function duplicates a Percentage Summary Field created with the Insert | Summary menu option.

PercentOfMinimum (f1, f2, s)

This will show the percentage of the group value compared to the value for the entire report.

f1 – the database or formula field to summarize for the entire report.

f2 – the database or formula field indicating the group you wish to summarize for. An existing group on the report must be based on this field.

s – a string value indicating how often to "change" the summary for Boolean, date, or date-time grouping. See **Boolean Conditions**, **Date Conditions**, and **Time Conditions** later in this appendix for available choices. This argument is required only if *f2* is a date, date-time, time, or Boolean field.

PercentOfMinimum (f1, f2, s1, f3, s2)

This will show the percentage of the group value compared to the value for a later group.

f1 – the database or formula field to summarize for the entire report.

f2 – the database or formula field indicating the group you wish to summarize for. An existing group on the report must be based on this field.

s1 – a string value indicating how often to "change" the summary for Boolean, date, or date-time grouping. See **Boolean Conditions**, **Date Conditions**, and **Time Conditions** later in this appendix for available choices. This argument (and the comma that precedes it) is required only if *f2* is a date, date-time, time, or Boolean field.

f3 – the database or formula field indicating the later group field to use for the summary. An existing group on the report must be based on this field.

s2 – a string value indicating how often to "change" the summary for Boolean, date, or date-time grouping. See **Boolean Conditions**, **Date Conditions**, and **Time Conditions** later in this appendix for available choices. This argument (and the comma that precedes it) is required only if *f3* is a date, date-time, time, or Boolean field.

```
PercentOfMinimum ({Sales.Amount}, {Sales.CustName})
```

returns the percentage that the lowest sales amount for each customer group makes up of the lowest sales amount for the entire report.

```
PercentOfMinimum ({Sales.Amount}, {Sales.Date},
"monthly", {Sales.CustName})
```

returns the percentage that the lowest sales amount for each month makes up of the lowest sales amount for the higher-level customer name group.

PercentOfSum

Returns a numeric value indicating what percentage a sum calculation in one group is of another sum calculation in a later group or the entire report.

This function duplicates a Percentage Summary Field created with the Insert | Summary menu option.

PercentOfSum (f1, f2, s)

This will show the percentage of the group value compared to the value for the entire report.

f1 – the database or formula field to summarize for the entire report. This must be a numeric field.

f2 – the database or formula field indicating the group you wish to summarize for. An existing group on the report must be based on this field.

s – a string value indicating how often to "change" the summary for Boolean, date, or date-time grouping. See **Boolean Conditions**, **Date Conditions**, and **Time Conditions** later in this appendix for available choices. This argument is required only if *f2* is a date, date-time, time, or Boolean field.

PercentOfSum (f1, f2, s1, f3, s2)

This will show the percentage of the group value compared to the value for a later group.

f1 – the database or formula field to summarize for the entire report. This must be a numeric field.

f2 – the database or formula field indicating the group you wish to summarize for. An existing group on the report must be based on this field.

s1 – a string value indicating how often to "change" the summary for Boolean, date, or date-time grouping. See **Boolean Conditions**, **Date Conditions**, and **Time Conditions** later in this appendix for available choices. This argument (and the comma that precedes it) is required only if *f2* is a date, date-time, time, or Boolean field.

f3 – the database or formula field indicating the later group field to use for the summary. An existing group on the report must be based on this field.

s2 – a string value indicating how often to "change" the summary for Boolean, date, or date-time grouping. See **Boolean Conditions**, **Date Conditions**, and **Time Conditions** later in this appendix for available choices. This argument (and the comma that precedes it) is required only if *f3* is a date, date-time, time, or Boolean field.

```
PercentOfSum ({Sales.Amount}, {Sales.CustName})
```

returns the percentage that the total sales amount for each customer group makes up of the total sales amount for the entire report.

```
PercentOfSum ({Sales.Amount}, {Sales.Date},
"monthly", {Sales.CustName})
```

returns the percentage that the total sales amount for each month makes up of the total sales amount for the higher-level customer name group.

PopulationStdDev

Returns a numeric value indicating the population standard deviation of the supplied database field or formula.

PopulationStdDev (f)

f – the database or formula field to summarize for the entire report. This must be a numeric field.

PopulationStdDev (f1, f2)

f1 – the database or formula field to summarize for a report group. This must be a numeric field.

f2 – the database or formula field indicating the group you wish to summarize for. An existing group on the report must be based on this field.

PopulationStdDev (f1, f2, s)

f1 – the database or formula field to summarize for a report group. This must be a numeric field.
f2 – the database or formula field indicating the group you wish to summarize for. An existing group on the report must be based on this field.
s – a string value indicating how often to "change" the summary for Boolean, date, or date-time grouping. See **Boolean Conditions**, **Date Conditions**, and **Time Conditions** later in this appendix for available choices.

```
PopulationStdDev({Sales.Amount})
```

returns the population standard deviation of sales amounts for the entire report.

```
PopulationStdDev({Sales.Amount}, {Sales.Date}, "monthly")
```

returns the population standard deviation of sales amounts for the sales date group, summarized for each month.

PopulationVariance

Returns a numeric value indicating the population variance of the supplied database field or formula.

PopulationVariance (f)

f – the database or formula field to summarize for the entire report. This must be a numeric field.

PopulationVariance (f1, f2)

f1 – the database or formula field to summarize for a report group. This must be a numeric field.
f2 – the database or formula field indicating the group you wish to summarize for. An existing group on the report must be based on this field.

PopulationVariance (f1, f2, s)

f1 – the database or formula field to summarize for a report group. This must be a numeric field.
f2 – the database or formula field indicating the group you wish to summarize for. An existing group on the report must be based on this field.
s – a string value indicating how often to "change" the summary for Boolean, date, or date-time grouping. See **Boolean Conditions**, **Date Conditions**, and **Time Conditions** later in this appendix for available choices.

```
PopulationVariance({Sales.Amount})
```

returns the population variance of sales amounts for the entire report.

```
PopulationVariance({Sales.Amount}, {Sales.Date}, "monthly")
```

returns the population variance of sales amounts for the sales date group, summarized for each month.

PthPercentile

Returns a numeric value indicating the *p*th percentile of the supplied database field or formula.

PthPercentile returns the "*pth*" percentile value, such as the value that equates to the tenth percentile of the report or group.

PthPercentile (n, f)

n – a numeric value (between 0 and 100). 5 returns the fifth percentile, 2 the second percentile, and so forth.
f – the database or formula field to summarize for the entire report. This must be a numeric field.

PthPercentile (n, f1, f2)

n – a numeric value (between 0 and 100). 5 returns the fifth percentile, 2 the second percentile, and so forth.
f1 – the database or formula field to summarize for the entire report. This must be a numeric field.
f2 – the database or formula field indicating the group you wish to summarize for. An existing group on the report must be based on this field.

PthPercentile (n, f1, f2, s)

n – a numeric value (between 0 and 100). 5 returns the fifth percentile, 2 the second percentile, and so forth.
f1 – the database or formula field to summarize for the entire report. This must be a numeric field.
f2 – the database or formula field indicating the group you wish to summarize for. An existing group on the report must be based on this field.
s – a string value indicating how often to "change" the summary for Boolean, date, or date-time grouping. See **Boolean Conditions**, **Date Conditions**, and **Time Conditions** later in this appendix for available choices.

```
PthPercentile (5, {Sales.Amount})
```

returns the sales amount equating to the fifth percentile for the entire report.

```
PthPercentile (5, {Sales.Amount}, {Sales.Date}, "monthly")
```

returns the sales amount equating to the fifth percentile for the sales date group, summarized for each month.

StdDev

Returns a numeric value indicating the standard deviation of the supplied database field or formula.

StdDev (f)

f – the database or formula field to summarize for the entire report. This must be a numeric field.

StdDev (f1, f2)

f1 – the database or formula field to summarize for a report group. This must be a numeric field.
f2 – the database or formula field indicating the group you wish to summarize for. An existing group on the report must be based on this field.

StdDev (f1, f2, s)

f1 – the database or formula field to summarize for a report group. This must be a numeric field.
f2 – the database or formula field indicating the group you wish to summarize for. An existing group on the report must be based on this field.
s – a string value indicating how often to "change" the summary for Boolean, date, or date-time grouping. See **Boolean Conditions**, **Date Conditions**, and **Time Conditions** later in this appendix for available choices.

```
StdDev({Sales.Amount})
```

returns the standard deviation of sales amounts for the entire report.

```
StdDev({Sales.Amount}, {Sales.Date}, "monthly")
```

returns the standard deviation of sales amounts for the sales date group, summarized for each month.

Sum

Returns a numeric value indicating the sum of the supplied database field or formula.

Sum (f)

f – the database or formula field to summarize for the entire report. This must be a numeric field.

Sum (f1, f2)

f1 – the database or formula field to summarize for a report group. This must be a numeric field.
f2 – the database or formula field indicating the group you wish to summarize for. An existing group on the report must be based on this field.

Sum (f1, f2, s)

f1 – the database or formula field to summarize for a report group. This must be a numeric field.
f2 – the database or formula field indicating the group you wish to summarize for. An existing group on the report must be based on this field.
s – a string value indicating how often to "change" the summary for Boolean, date, or date-time grouping. See **Boolean Conditions**, **Date Conditions**, and **Time Conditions** later in this appendix for available choices.

```
Sum({Sales.Amount})
```

returns the sum of sales amounts for the entire report.

```
Sum({Sales.Amount}, {Sales.Date}, "monthly")
```

returns the sum of sales amounts for the sales date group, summarized for each month.

Variance
Returns a numeric value indicating the variance of the supplied database field or formula.

Variance (f)
f – the database or formula field to summarize for the entire report. This must be a numeric field.

Variance (f1, f2)
$f1$ – the database or formula field to summarize for a report group. This must be a numeric field.
$f2$ – the database or formula field indicating the group you wish to summarize for. An existing group on the report must be based on this field.

Variance (f1, f2, s)
$f1$ – the database or formula field to summarize for a report group. This must be a numeric field.
$f2$ – the database or formula field indicating the group you wish to summarize for. An existing group on the report must be based on this field.
s – a string value indicating how often to "change" the summary for Boolean, date, or date-time grouping. See **Boolean Conditions**, **Date Conditions**, and **Time Conditions** later in this appendix for available choices.

```
Variance({Sales.Amount})
```

returns the variance of sales amounts for the entire report.

```
Variance({Sales.Amount}, {Sales.Date}, "monthly")
```

returns the variance of sales amounts for the sales date group, summarized for each month.

WeightedAverage
Returns a numeric value indicating the average of the supplied database field or formula, given a weight by another field or formula.

WeightedAverage (f1, f2)
$f1$ – the database or formula field to summarize for the entire report. This must be a numeric field.
$f2$ – the database or formula field to use as the weight.

WeightedAverage (f1, f2, f3)
$f1$ – the database or formula field to summarize for a report group. This must be a numeric field.
$f2$ – the database or formula field to use as the weight.
$f3$ – the database or formula field indicating the group you wish to summarize for. An existing group on the report must be based on this field.

WeightedAverage (f1, f2, f3, s)
$f1$ – the database or formula field to summarize for a report group. This must be a numeric field.

f2 – the database or formula field to use as the weight.

f3 – the database or formula field indicating the group you wish to summarize for. An existing group on the report must be based on this field.

s – a string value indicating how often to "change" the summary for Boolean, date, or date-time grouping. See **Boolean Conditions**, **Date Conditions**, and **Time Conditions** later in this appendix for available choices.

```
WeightedAverage({Sales.Amount},{Sales.Goal})
```

returns the average of sales amounts weighted by goal for the entire report.

```
WeightedAverage({Sales.Amount}, {Sales.Date}, "monthly")
```

returns the average of sales amounts weighted by goal for the sales date group, summarized for each month.

Boolean Conditions

The following string values can be used in a summary function when using a Boolean group field.

"any change"
"change to No"
"change to Yes"
"every No"
"every Yes"
"next is No"
"next is Yes"

Date Conditions

The following string values can be used in a summary function when using a date or date-time group field.

"daily"
"semimonthly"
"semiannually"
"monthly"
"quarterly"
"biweekly"
"weekly"
"annually"

PART II

Time Conditions

The following string values can be used in a summary function when using a time or date-time group field.

| "by AMPM" |
| "by hour" |
| "by minute" |
| "by second" |

Functions: Type Conversion

This category of functions is used to convert from one data type to another. These functions are modeled after functions of the same name found in Visual Basic and Visual Basic for Applications.

CBool

Returns a Boolean (true/false) conversion of the source field.

CBool will return False for a value of 0 (zero). Otherwise, CBool returns True.

CBool (n)

n – a numeric value.

```
CBool(-1)
```

returns True.

CCur

Returns a currency value.

CCur (v)

v – a value of number, currency, or string data type.

```
CCur ("1125.13894")
```

returns $1,125.14 as a currency value.

CDate

Returns a date value.

CDate is functionally equivalent to Date and DateValue. See **DateValue** for details.

CDateTime

Returns a date-time value.

CDateTime is functionally equivalent to DateTime and DateTimeValue. See **DateTimeValue** for details.

CDbl

Returns a numeric value.

CDbl is functionally equivalent to ToNumber. See **ToNumber** for details.

CStr

Converts any nonstring data type to a string value.

CStr is functionally equivalent to ToText, including returning the same result and accepting the same arguments. See **ToText** for complete information.

CTime

Returns a time value.

CTime is functionally equivalent to Time and TimeValue. See **TimeValue** for details.

Functions: Xcelsius

This category of functions formats values in an XML format for passing to an embedded Xcelsius .SWF file via Flash Variables. In particular, these functions are useful when the embedded Xcelsius file expects Flash Variables to be supplied in XML format and not CSV format. The functions may be embedded within each another to create an XML <data><row><column></column>…</row>…</data> hierarchy.

ToXMLColumn

Surrounds the supplied argument with <column> and </column> XML tags.

ToXMLColumn (v)

v – a value of any data type supported by Crystal Reports.

```
ToXMLColumn ({Employee.Last Name})
```

returns <column>Fuller</column> for an {Employee.Last Name} value of "Fuller."

ToXMLData

Surrounds the supplied argument with <data> and </data> XML tags.

ToXMLData (v)

v – a value of any data type supported by Crystal Reports.

```
ToXMLData(ToXMLRow (ToXMLColumn ({Employee.Last Name}) &
ToXMLColumn ({Employee.First Name}) & ToXMLColumn ({Employee.Employee
ID})))
```

returns an XML data stream consisting of <data><row><column>Fuller</column><column>Andrew</column><column>2.0000000000</column></row></data> based on values of three database fields supplied to other embedded XML formatting functions.

ToXMLRow
Surrounds the supplied argument with <row> and </row> XML tags.

ToXMLRow (v)
v – a value of any data type supported by Crystal Reports.

```
ToXMLRow (ToXMLColumn ({Employee.Last Name}) &
ToXMLColumn ({Employee.First Name}))
```

returns <row><column>Fuller</column><column>Andrew</column></row>, based on the Last Name and First Name database field values.

Operators: Arithmetic

This category of operators performs standard arithmetic functions, such as addition, subtraction, and so forth.

Add (+)
Adds two numbers.

n1 + n2
n1 – a numeric value.
n2 – a numeric value.

```
2 + 2
```

returns 4.00.

Divide (/)
Divides two numbers.

n1 / n2
n1 – a numeric value.
n2 – a numeric value.

```
10 / 5
```

returns 2.00.

Exponentiate (^)
Raises a number to a power.

n1 ^ n2
n1 – a numeric value.
n2 – a numeric value to raise *n1* to the power of.

```
5 ^ 2
```

returns 25.00.

Integer Divide (\)

Divides two numbers, returning an integer result.

n1 \ n2

n1 – a numeric value.
n2 – a numeric value.

```
10 \ 3
```

returns 3.00, contrasted with

```
10 / 3
```

which returns 3.33.

Modulus

Performs division on two numeric values and returns the remainder of the division rather than the result of the division.

Use the Mod function for particular situations where the remainder of numeric division is required, rather than the actual result. For example, this operator can be used with the RecordNumber function in a conditional formatting formula to shade every other details section.

n1 Mod n2

n1 – a numeric value
n2 – a numeric value

```
If RecordNumber Mod 2 = 0 Then crSilver Else crNoColor
```

when supplied as a conditional formula for the Details section background color, shades every other details section silver.

NOTE *Crystal Reports also includes the Remainder function, which performs a similar operation.*

Multiply (*)

Multiplies two numbers.

n1 * n2

n1 – a numeric value.
n2 – a numeric value.

```
5 * 4
```

returns 20.00.

Negate (–)

Returns the negative equivalent of a number.

–n

n – a numeric value.

```
-14
```

returns –14.00.

```
-{GLDetails.DRAmount}
```

returns a positive debit amount if the DRAmount field is coded as a negative number in the database.

Percent (%)

Calculates the percentage one number is of another number.

n1 % n2

n1 – a numeric value.
n2 – a numeric value.

```
5 % 20
```

returns 25.00.

```
{Sales.Amount} % Sum({Sales.Amount},{Sales.Rep})
```

returns the percentage each individual sale is of a sales rep's total sales.

Subtract (–)

Subtracts one number from another.

n1 – n2

n1 – a numeric value.
n2 – a numeric value.

```
25 - 10
```

returns 15.00.

Operators: Array

This set of operators pertain to arrays. An *array* is a collection of data items stored in a single "bucket," such as a single variable. If an array contains 15 items, it is said to have 15 *elements*. Arrays can contain any supported Crystal Reports data type, such as number, string, date-time, and so forth.

In

Returns a Boolean (true/false) value indicating whether a single value is in an array.

v In a

v – a value of the same data type as the *a* array.
a – an array.

```
5 In [1,3,5,7,9]
```

returns True.

```
If {Customer.Region} In ["CO","MT","UT","WY"] Then
    "Rocky Mountain Region"
Else
    "Rest of Country"
```

returns one of two strings based on the existence of a database field in the supplied string literal array.

Make Array

Creates an array of values.

This is functionally equivalent to the MakeArray function. See **MakeArray** in the Functions: Arrays section for details.

Redim

"Resets" an existing array variable to an empty state with a specified number of elements.

Redim a (n)

a – an existing array variable.
n – a positive number.

```
WhilePrintingRecords;
StringVar Array Beatles;
Redim Beatles [4];
Beatles[1]
```

declares an existing string array and resets it to a string array with four elements, each containing an empty string. The formula returns an empty string to the report (the first element of the reset array).

Redim Preserve

"Resizes" an existing array variable with a specified number of elements, retaining existing contents of the array variable.

Redim Preserve a (n)
a – an existing array variable.
n – a positive number.

```
WhilePrintingRecords;
StringVar Array Beatles;
Redim Preserve Beatles [8];
Beatles[1]
```

declares an existing string array and expands it to contain eight elements, retaining any existing data in the array. The formula returns "John" to the report (the existing data in the first element of the array).

Subscript ([ ])

Extracts an individual element of an array.

a[n]
a – an array value.
n – a numeric value or range indicating the element or elements to extract.

```
WhilePrintingRecords;
StringVar Array Beatles;
Beatles[3]
```

returns "George", the third element of the Beatles array.

Operators: Boolean

This set of operators pertain to Boolean (true/false) values, functions, and expressions.

And

Returns true if both associated Boolean values are true.

b1 And b2
b1 – a Boolean value or expression.
b2 – a Boolean value or expression.

```
2 + 2 = 4 And 10 / 2 = 5
```

returns True.

```
If {Customer.Region} = "CA" And
   {Customer.Last Year's Sales} > 50000 Then
    "California Bonus Customer"
Else
    "Other Customer"
```

returns "California Bonus Customer" if both Boolean expressions in the If test are true.

Eqv (Logical equivalence)

Returns true if both associated Boolean values are the same.

b1 Eqv b2

b1 – a Boolean value or expression.
b2 – a Boolean value or expression.

```
2 + 2 = 4 Eqv 10 / 2 = 5
```

returns True.

```
2 + 2 = 8 Eqv 10 / 2 = 5
```

returns False.

```
2 + 2 = 8 Eqv 10 / 2 = 1
```

returns True.

Imp (Logical implication)

Returns true if both associated Boolean values are the same, or if the second value is true while the first value is false.

b1 Imp b2

b1 – a Boolean value or expression.
b2 – a Boolean value or expression.

```
2 + 2 = 4 Imp 10 / 2 = 5
```

returns True.

```
2 + 2 = 8 Imp 10 / 2 = 1
```

returns True.

```
2 + 2 = 4 Imp 10 / 2 = 1
```

returns False.

```
2 + 2 = 8 Imp 10 / 2 = 5
```

returns True.

Not

Reverses the Boolean value (true becomes false and false becomes true).

Not requires a Boolean value or expression to follow it. As such, you may need to enclose a Boolean expression in parentheses for Not to evaluate properly.

Not b

b – a Boolean value or expression.

```
Not (2 + 2 = 4)
```

returns False.

```
Not 2 + 2 = 4
```

results in an error, as Not expects the first occurrence of the number 2 to be Boolean.

```
If Not InRepeatedGroupHeader Then "New Group Starts Here"
```

returns the "new group" string if InRepeatedGroupHeader is false.

Or

Returns true if either or both associated Boolean values are true.

b1 Or b2

b1 – a Boolean value or expression.
b2 – a Boolean value or expression.

```
2 + 2 = 4 Or 10 / 2 = 1
```

returns True.

```
If {Customer.Last Year's Sales} > 50000 Or
   {Customer.Last Year's Sales} < 0 Then
    "Customer needs attention"
Else
    "Normal customer"
```

returns "Customer needs attention" if either Boolean expression in the If test is true.

Xor (Logical exclusion)

Returns true if the associated Boolean values return opposite values (one true, the other false).

b1 Xor b2

b1 – a Boolean value or expression.
b2 – a Boolean value or expression.

```
2 + 2 = 4 Xor 10 / 2 = 6
```

returns True.

```
2 + 2 = 5 Xor 10 / 2 = 5
```

returns True.

```
2 + 2 = 4 Xor 10 / 2 = 5
```

returns False.

Operators: Comparisons

This category of operators compares values to each other. You may combine comparison operators together with other Boolean operators, such as And, Or, and Not.

Equal (=)

Returns a Boolean (true/false) value indicating whether the two supplied values are equal to each other.

v1 = v2

v1 – a value of any supported data type.
v2 – a value of the same data type as *v1*.

```
10 = 10
```

returns True.

```
If {Sales.State} = "CO" Then "Colorado"
```

returns "Colorado" if the state field is equal to "CO".

Greater or Equal (>=)

Returns a Boolean (true/false) value indicating whether the first supplied value is greater than or equal to the second value.

This operator compares strings from the perspective of sort order.

v1 >= v2

v1 – a value of any supported data type.
v2 – a value of the same data type as *v1*.

```
"abc" >= "wyz"
```

returns False, based on string sort order.

```
If {Sales.Amount} >= 5000 Then "Great Order"
```

returns "Great Order" if the sale amount is exactly $5,000, or anything greater than $5,000.

Greater Than (>)

Returns a Boolean (true/false) value indicating whether the first supplied value is greater than the second value.

This operator compares strings from the perspective of sort order.

v1 > v2

v1 – a value of any supported data type.
v2 – a value of the same data type as *v1*.

```
#1/1/2000# > #1/1/1999#
```

returns True.

```
If {Sales.Amount} > 10000 Then "Eligible for Bonus"
```

returns "Eligible for Bonus" if the sale amount is greater than $10,000. If the amount is exactly $10,000 or less, an empty string is returned.

Less or Equal (<=)

Returns a Boolean (true/false) value indicating whether the first supplied value is less than or equal to the second value.

This operator compares strings from the perspective of sort order.

v1 <= v2

v1 – a value of any supported data type.
v2 – a value of the same data type as *v1*.

```
100 <= 100
```

returns True.

```
If {Sales.Amount} <= 100 Then "Small Order"
```

returns "Small Order" if the sale amount is exactly $100, or anything less than $100.

Less Than (<)

Returns a Boolean (true/false) value indicating whether the first supplied value is less than the second value.

This operator compares strings from the perspective of sort order.

v1 < v2

v1 – a value of any supported data type.
v2 – a value of the same data type as *v1*.

```
#1/1/2000# < #1/1/1999#
```

returns False.

```
If {Sales.Amount} < 100 Then "Improved Performance Required"
```

returns "Improved Performance Required" if the sale amount is less than $100. If the amount is exactly $100 or greater, an empty string is returned.

Not Equal (<>)

Returns a Boolean (true/false) value indicating whether the two supplied values are not equal to each other.

v1 <> v2

v1 – a value of any supported data type.
v2 – a value of the same data type as *v1*.

```
10 <> 15
```

returns True.

```
If {Sales.State} <> "CO" Then "Out-Of-State Sale"
```

returns "Out-Of-State Sale" if the state field is something other than "CO".

NOTE *Case sensitivity of string comparisons is based on the database case sensitivity setting in File | Report Options (applies to the current report only) and File | Options (applies to all new reports in the future).*

Operators: Control Structures

This category of operators might well exist in a separate section of the Formula Editor called "programming constructs." However, as they don't take "arguments" per se, they've been placed in the Operator tree. These operators are most familiar to computer programmers, as they duplicate typical programming logic and flow within a single Crystal Reports formula.

Do While

Loops through formula logic while a condition is true.

Do While differs from While Do in regard to when the loop condition is evaluated. Do While evaluates the loop condition *after* a loop iteration (so that at least one loop will always occur). While Do evaluates the condition *before* a loop iteration (the logic within the loop may not occur at all if the condition is immediately false).

Do <formula logic> While b

b – a Boolean value or expression.

```
NumberVar Counter := 1;
StringVar Accum;
do
(    Accum := Accum + "-";
     Counter := Counter + 1)
while Counter < 100;
Accum
```

returns a string containing 99 dash characters (the loop iterated while the counter was less than 100—once it reached 100, the loop did not repeat).

NOTE *If you wish to include more than one Crystal Reports statement within the loop, separate statements with a semicolon and surround all statements (between the Do and While) with parentheses.*

Exit For

Exits a For loop before its normal conclusion.

Exit For

```
NumberVar Counter;
StringVar Accum;
for Counter := 1 to 1000 step 2 do
(
    Accum := Accum & ToText(Counter);
    If Len(Accum) > 245 Then Exit For;
);
Accum
```

returns the string in the Accum variable consisting of "1.003.005.007.009.00" and so forth. Within the loop, the Accum variable is tested for a length exceeding 245 characters and the loop is exited if this occurs.

Exit While

Exits a Do or While loop before its normal conclusion.

Exit While

```
NumberVar Counter := 1;
StringVar Accum;
do
(   Accum := Accum + "-";
    Counter := Counter + 1;
    If Length(Accum) = 100 Then Exit While)
while True;
Accum
```

returns a string containing 100 dash characters (the loop iterates until the length of the Accum variable reaches 100 characters and the Exit While statement executes).

For

Loops through formula logic a specified number of times.

For v := n1 To n2 Step n3 Do

v – a numeric variable that the loop will increment as it progresses.

$n1$ – a numeric value indicating the beginning value that will be assigned to v when the loop starts.

$n2$ – a numeric value indicating the ending value in v that will stop the loop.

$n3$ – a numeric value indicating the amount to increment v every time the loop iterates. This value, as well as the Step keyword that precedes it, are optional. If omitted, v is incremented by 1 with each loop iteration.

```
NumberVar Counter;
StringVar Accum;
```

```
for Counter := 1 to 100 step 2 do
(
    Accum := Accum & ToText(Counter);
);
Accum
```

returns contents of the Accum variable, consisting of the string "13579111315" and so forth, through "99". The Counter variable increments from 1 to 100, incrementing by 2 every time the loop iterates.

> **NOTE** *If you wish to include more than one Crystal Reports statement within the loop, separate statements with a semicolon and surround all statements (after the Do keyword) with parentheses.*

If Then Else

Performs a Boolean test, returning one value if the test is true and an alternate value if the test is false.

If b Then v1 Else v2

b – a Boolean expression (typically using comparison operators discussed earlier in this section).
v1 – a value of any supported data type that is returned if *b* evaluates to True.
v1 – a value of the same data type as *v1* that is returned if *b* evaluates to False. This value, and the Else keyword that precedes it, is optional.

```
If {Sales.State} = "CO" Then
    "Sales Tax Required"
Else
    "No Tax"
```

returns the string "Sales Tax Required" if the Boolean expression after If evaluates to true. Otherwise, the formula returns "No Tax".

```
If {Sales.Amount} > 5000 Then "Bonus Order"
```

returns "Bonus Order" if the sales amount exceeds $5,000. Otherwise, an empty string is returned.

Option Loop

Specifies how many iterations a loop should go through before an error is returned.

By default, Crystal Reports stops loop processing and returns an error if a loop iterates 100,000 times. This behavior prevents infinite loops from occurring. If you wish to lower the maximum number of iterations, use Option Loop.

Option Loop n

n – a numeric value indicating the number of loop iterations that will occur before an error is returned.

Option Loop must be the first statement in the formula.

```
NumberVar Counter;
Do
    Counter := Counter + 1
While True
```

will iterate 100,000 time before returning an error.

```
Option Loop 100;
NumberVar Counter;
Do
    Counter := Counter + 1
While True
```

will iterate 100 times before returning an error.

Select Case

Returns one of several available values based on a series of conditions.

Select Case duplicates the capabilities of sophisticated If-Then-Else logic. However, Select Case is often easier to understand and maintain than complex If-Then-Else formulas.

Select e Case v1: <formula logic> Case v2 <formula logic>...: Default: <formula logic>

e – a value or expression of any data type to test.
$v1$ – a value or "list" of values (separated by commas) matching in data type to e to test against e.
$v2$ – an additional value or "list" of values (separated by commas) matching in data type to e to test against e.

Additional pairs of Case/<formula logic> combinations may be added. The Default keyword and colon are optional. Formula logic after each Case statement must return the same data type as all other formula logic.

```
Select {Sales.State}
    Case "OR","ID","MT","WA":
        "Northwest"
    Case "CA","AZ","TX","NM":
        "Southwest"
    Case "ME","MA","NH","NY":
        "Northeast"
    Case "FL","NC","GA","SC":
        "Southeast"
    Default:
        "Rest of Country"
```

examines the state field and begins testing it against each Case statement. Once it finds a match, it returns the value following the case statement. If no matches are found, the value following the default statement is returned. Were the Default keyword, colon, and "Rest of Country" string literal to be left out, the formula would return an empty string if no matches were found.

```
Select {Sales.LastYearRevenue}
    Case Is < 100:
        "Improved Performance Needed"
    Case 100 To 1000:
        "Average Year"
    Case Is > 1000:
        "Excellent Year"
```

examines the Last Year Revenue field and begins testing against the ranges specified in each Case statement, returning the appropriate string following the Case statement that matches. No Default keyword is provided, as any number will fall into one of the three Case statements. Were a number to somehow not fall into one of the existing Case statements, a zero would be returned.

While Do

Loops through formula logic while a condition is true.

While Do differs from Do While in regard to when the loop condition is evaluated. Do While evaluates the loop condition *after* a loop iteration (so that at least one loop will always occur). While Do evaluates the condition *before* a loop iteration (the logic within the loop may not occur at all if the condition is immediately false).

While b <formula logic> Do

b – a Boolean value or expression.

```
NumberVar Counter := 1;
StringVar Accum;
While Counter < 100 Do
(   Accum := Accum + "-";
    Counter := Counter + 1
);
Accum
```

returns a string containing 99 dash characters (the loop iterated while the counter was less than 100—once it reached 100, the loop did not repeat).

NOTE *If you wish to include more than one Crystal Reports statement within the loop, separate statements with a semicolon and surround all statements (between the Do and While) with parentheses.*

Operators: Conversion

A single operator exists to convert to one data type from another.

Currency ($)

Converts a numeric value to a currency value.

The CCur function can also be used to convert from another data type to currency.

$

```
$100
```

returns $100.00.

```
${Sales.Amount} * 1.1
```

returns 10 percent above the sales amount as a currency value.

NOTE Crystal Reports prohibits both values in a multiplication formula from being currency—one or the other can be, but not both. If necessary, you'll need to convert one currency value to a numeric value with ToNumber or CDbl.

Operators: Other

This category of operators contains, in essence, operators that don't fit in any other category and perform miscellaneous functions.

Assignment (:=)

Assigns a value to a variable.

In Crystal syntax, don't confuse the assignment operator (:=) with the equals comparison operator (=). In Basic syntax, equals (=) acts as both assignment and equals comparison.

var := v

var – a previously declared variable name.
v – a value or expression of the same data type as *var*.

```
SalesRepBonus := SalesRepBonus + 1
```

adds 1 to the value already in the SalesRepBonus variable and places the result back into the SalesRepBonus variable.

```
NumberVar SalesRepBonus := 0
```

declares a number variable named SalesRepBonus and assigns it a value of zero in a single statement.

Comment (//)

Treats any text following the two slashes as a comment.

Basic Syntax uses the apostrophe (') or the word Rem to indicate a comment. Crystal Reports allows you to add comment slashes or apostrophes to multiple formula lines at once by highlighting them and clicking the Comment/Uncomment button in the Formula Workshop toolbar.

//

```
//The following formula calculates
```

```
//commission based on sale amount
Select {Orders.Order Amount}
    Case Is < 100:
        .01
    Case 100 to 1000:
        .05
    Case Is > 1000:
        .1
```

The first two lines of the formula are ignored by the Formula Editor when evaluating the formula logic.

NOTE *If you are troubleshooting a formula, you may prefer to simply "comment out" certain formula lines that you wish to later use again. For example, you may be working on five different methods of calculating a result. By adding or removing two slashes in front of the various formula lines, you may try various methods of calculations without having to delete and retype each line.*

Date-time literal (#)
Returns a date-time value from the supplied string.

#s#

s – a string that can be interpreted as a date, time, or date-time combination.

```
#1/1/2000 10:15 am#
```

returns a date-time value of 1/1/2000 10:15:00AM.

```
#Sep 10, 02#
```

returns a date-time value of 9/10/2002 12:00:00AM.

NOTE *Crystal Reports is fairly creative in what it will interpret as date or time material between the # characters. If the string can't be understood, an error will occur.*

Parentheses
Used to force evaluation of formula expressions in a certain order.

Parentheses allow you to force calculations to occur in other than the default *order of precedence* (exponentiation, then multiplication/division left to right, then addition/subtraction left to right). In Basic syntax, parentheses are also used to delimit array subscripts.

(<expression>)

```
10 + 10 * 2
```

returns 30.00. The order of precedence causes the multiplication to be done first, then the addition.

```
(10 + 10) * 2
```

returns 40.00. The parentheses force the addition to be performed first, then the multiplication.

Operators: Pattern

This set of operators allow partial string matches to be evaluated.

Like

Returns a Boolean (true/false) value based on a partial string match.

Like uses DOS-style "wildcards" (the asterisk and question mark) to determine if the source string contains the characters specified in the wildcard-based mask. This is helpful for checking for partial text matches. This operator is similar to the LooksLike function.

s1 Like s2

s1 – the source string to be searched.
s2 – the mask string to search against. The mask can include a question mark wildcard to indicate a single-character substitution and/or an asterisk to indicate a multiple-character substitution.

```
"George Peck" Like "G?orge*"
```

returns True.

StartsWith

Returns a Boolean (true/false) value if leading characters match the source string.

s1 StartsWith s2

s1 – the source string to be searched.
s2 – the characters to search for as the first characters of *s1*.

```
"George Peck" StartsWith "Ge"
```

returns True.

NOTE *Case sensitivity of string comparisons is based on the database case sensitivity setting in File | Report Options (applies to the current report only) and File | Options (applies to all new reports in the future).*

Operators: Ranges

These operators either create various ranges of values or test existing ranges. A *range* of values consists of beginning and ending values, and every value in between (some ranges can have no beginning and/or ending value—in other words, the range can be "everything above x" or "everything below y").

Both End Points Excluded Range

Creates a range of values between the two endpoints, not including the endpoints.

v1 _To_ v2

v1 – a value of any data type to act as the lower endpoint.
v2 – a value of the same data type as *v1* to act as the upper endpoint.

```
1 In (1 _to_ 100)
```

returns False, as the lower endpoint (1) is not included in the range.

```
99 In (1 _to_ 100)
```

returns True.

In Range

Returns a Boolean (true/false) value indicating whether the single value is in the range.

v In r

v – a single value of any supported data type.
r – a range value or variable of the same data type as *v*.

```
5 In (1 To 100)
```

returns True.

```
If {Parts.PartNo} In (1000 to 5000) Then
    "Taxable"
Else
    "Non-taxable"
```

returns the string "Taxable" if the part number is in the range of 1000 to 5000 inclusive.

Left End Point Excluded Range

Creates a range of values between the two endpoints, not including the first endpoint.

v1 _To v2

v1 – a value of any data type to act as the lower endpoint.
v2 – a value of the same data type as *v1* to act as the upper endpoint.

```
1 In (1 _to 100)
```

returns False, as the lower endpoint (1) is not included in the range.

```
100 In (1 _to 100)
```

returns True, as the upper endpoint (100) is included in the range.

Make Range

Creates a range of values between, and including, the two endpoints.

v1 To v2

v1 – a value of any data type to act as the lower endpoint.
v2 – a value of the same data type as *v1* to act as the upper endpoint.

```
1 In (1 to 100)
```

returns True.

```
100 In (1 to 100)
```

returns True.

Right End Point Excluded Range

Creates a range of values between the two endpoints, not including the second endpoint.

v1 To_ v2
v1 – a value of any data type to act as the lower endpoint.
v2 – a value of the same data type as *v1* to act as the upper endpoint.

```
1 In (1 to_ 100)
```

returns True, as the lower endpoint (1) is included in the range.

```
100 In (1 to_ 100)
```

returns False, as the upper endpoint (100) is not included in the range.

UpFrom

Creates a range of values including a lower endpoint upward, with no upper endpoint.
    Is >= v is functionally equivalent to UpFrom.

upFrom v
v – a value of any data type to act as the lower endpoint.

```
99999999 In UpFrom 100
```

returns True.

```
HasUpperBound (UpFrom 100)
```

returns False (the HasUpperBound function evaluates whether the supplied range has an upper endpoint).

Up From But Not Including

Creates a range of values from a lower endpoint upward (the lower endpoint not being included), with no upper endpoint.
    Is > v is functionally equivalent to UpFrom_.

upFrom_ v
v – a value of any data type to act as the lower endpoint.

```
100 In UpFrom_ 100
```

returns False (the lower endpoint is not included in the range).

```
HasUpperBound (UpFrom_ 100)
```

returns False (the HasUpperBound function evaluates whether the supplied range has an upper endpoint).

UpTo

Creates a range of values from an upper endpoint downward (including the upper endpoint) with no lower endpoint.

Is <= v is functionally equivalent to UpTo.

upTo v

v – a value of any data type to act as the lower endpoint.

```
-9999999 In UpTo 100
```

returns True.

```
HasLowerBound (UpTo 100)
```

returns False (the HasLowerBound function evaluates whether the supplied range has a lower endpoint).

Up To But Not Including

Creates a range of values from an upper endpoint downward (not including the upper endpoint) with no lower endpoint.

Is < v is functionally equivalent to UpTo_.

upTo_ v

v – a value of any data type to act as the lower endpoint.

```
100 In UpTo_ 100
```

returns False (the upper endpoint is not included in the range).

```
HasLowerBound (UpTo_ 100)
```

returns False (the HasLowerBound function evaluates whether the supplied range has a lower endpoint).

Operators: Scope

This set of operators is used when declaring variables (see "Operators: Variable Declaration" later in this appendix). These operators determine how long a variable retains its value during report processing.

Global

Forces a variable to retain its value in this formula, and all other formulas in the current report (but not subreports).

In Crystal Syntax, this is the default scope for variable declarations that do not include a scope keyword.

Global t v

t – a variable declaration statement.

v – a valid variable name.

```
Global NumberVar BonusCount
```

declares a numeric variable called BonusCount that will retain its value throughout the entire report, but not in any subreports.

```
NumberVar BonusCount
```

is functionally equivalent to the previous declaration, as Global is the default variable scope.

Local
Forces a variable to retain its value in this formula only.
In Basic Syntax, this is the default scope for variable declarations that do not include a scope keyword.

Local t v
t – a variable declaration statement.
v – a valid variable name.

```
Local NumberVar BonusCount
```

declares a numeric variable called BonusCount that will retain its value only during the calculation of this formula. If BonusCount is declared in any other formulas, it will contain zero.

Shared
Forces a variable to retain its value in this formula, in all other formulas in the current report, and in all subreports.

Shared t v
t – a variable declaration statement.
v – a valid variable name.

```
Shared NumberVar BonusCount
```

declares a numeric variable called BonusCount that will retain its value throughout the entire report and in all subreports.

Operators: Strings

This set of operators applies to string manipulation, such as string "concatenation" (the process of combining two or more strings into a single string).

Concatenate (& or +)
Concatenates (combines) strings into a single string.
The + operator requires that surrounding values be strings, while the & operator performs an implicit conversion to string of all surrounding values.

s1 + s2
s1 – a string value.
s2 – a string value.

```
"Page Number: " + PageNumber
```

returns an error, as the PageNumber function returns a numeric value.

```
"Page Number: " + ToText(PageNumber,0)
```

returns "Page Number: 1" if the first page of the report is printing.

v1 & v2
v1 – a value of any data type.
v2 – a value of any data type.

```
"Page Number: " & PageNumber
```

returns "Page Number: 1.00" if the first page of the report is printing, performing an implicit conversion of PageNumber to a string data type.

```
"Page Number: " & ToText(PageNumber,0)
```

returns "Page Number: 1" if the first page of the report is printing.

NOTE *When using the & operator to concatenate strings, you may still need to use ToText or CStr to control how values are formatted when they are concatenated.*

In String
Returns a Boolean value (true/false) based on if the first string is contained in the second string.

s1 In s2
s1 – a string value to search for in *s2*.
s2 – the source string to search.

```
"eor" in "George"
```

returns True.

```
If "(303)" In {Customer.Phone} Then "Denver Area Code"
```

returns the string "Denver Area Code" if the characters "(303)" are contained anywhere in the customer phone database field. Otherwise, the formula returns an empty string.

Insert Empty String ("")
Inserts a pair of quotation marks in the formula.

In Crystal Reports versions prior to 9 (as well as in 9), you may simply type quotation mark pairs in directly.

"" ""

```
StringVar BonusCustomer := ""
```

declares a string variable called BonusCustomer and sets it to contain an empty string.

Subscript []
Extracts a substring from a larger string.

s[n]
s – a string value.
n – a numeric value or range indicating the character or characters to extract.

```
"George Peck"[2 to 4]
```

returns "eor".

Operators: Variable Declarations

This category of operators is used to declare variables within formulas. Whenever a variable is used in any formula, it must first be declared using one of the following operators.

BooleanVar
Declares a Boolean (true/false) variable to contain an array or single value.

BooleanVar Array varname

BooleanVar varname
varname – a variable name that is not the same as any other Crystal Reports formula keyword, does not contain a space, and does not start with a number or certain special characters.

```
BooleanVar Array Workdays :=
    [False, True, True, True, True, True, False];
Workdays[DayOfWeek(CurrentDate)]
```

returns True if the CurrentDate is Monday through Friday. The formula declares a Boolean array variable containing seven elements and then extracts the element associated with the day of the week.

```
BooleanVar BonusReached;
If {Sales.Amount} > 5000 Then BonusReached := True
```

declares a Boolean variable and assigns it a value of True if a sales amount is exceeded.

CurrencyVar
Declares a currency variable to contain an array, array of ranges, range, or single value.

CurrencyVar Array varname

CurrencyVar Range Array varname

CurrencyVar Range varname

CurrencyVar varname

varname – a variable name that is not the same as any other Crystal Reports formula keyword, does not contain a space, and does not start with a number or certain special characters.

```
CurrencyVar Range GoodSales := upFrom 5000;
If {Sales.Amount} In GoodSales Then "Good Job"
```

declares a currency range variable and assigns it all values including and above $5,000. If a sale amount is included in the variable, "Good Job" is returned by the formula.

```
CurrencyVar HighAmount;
If {Sales.Amount} > HighAmount Then
    HighAmount := {Sales.Amount}
```

declares a currency variable. If the sales amount is higher than what's retained in the variable from previous records, the variable is assigned the value of the higher sales amount.

DateTimeVar

Declares a date-time variable to contain an array, array of ranges, range, or single value.

DateTimeVar Array varname

DateTimeVar Range Array varname

DateTimeVar Range varname

DateTimeVar varname

varname – a variable name that is not the same as any other Crystal Reports formula keyword, does not contain a space, and does not start with a number or certain special characters.

```
DateTimeVar Range WorkDays :=
    #6/2/2003 8:00am# To #6/6/2003 5:00pm#;
If Not ({Salary.WorkDate} In WorkDays) Then
    {Salary.DailyPay} + {Salary.OvertimePay}
Else
    {Salary.DailyPay}
```

declares a date-time range variable and assigns it a value of Monday at 8 A.M. through Friday at 5 P.M. The variable is then checked against a work date to determine if overtime should be added to an employee's pay.

```
DateTimeVar OutOfTolerance;
If {Meas.Sample Value} > {Standards.Sample} Then
    OutOfTolerance := {Meas.Sample Date Time}
```

declares a date-time variable and tests to see if a sample reading was out of tolerance. If so, the date-time that the exception occurred is assigned to the variable.

DateVar

Declares a date variable to contain an array, array of ranges, range, or single value.

DateVar Array varname

DateVar Range Array varname

DateVar Range varname

DateVar varname

varname – a variable name that is not the same as any other Crystal Reports formula keyword, does not contain a space, and does not start with a number or certain special characters.

```
DateVar Range Array CompanyHolidays :=
    [DateValue("1/1/2003") to DateValue("1/2/2003"),
     DateValue("2/17/2003"),DateValue("5/26/2003"),
     DateValue("7/4/2003"),DateValue("9/1/2003"),
     DateValue("11/27/2003") to DateValue("11/28/2003"),
     DateValue("12/25/2003") to DateValue("12/31/2003")];
If {Salary.WorkDate} In CompanyHolidays Then
    "Bonus Pay Required"
```

declares a date range array and sets it to the individual dates and date ranges that make up company holidays. The variable is then checked to see if a work day qualifies for bonus pay.

NumberVar

Declares a number variable to contain an array, array of ranges, range, or single value.

NumberVar Array varname

NumberVar Range Array varname

NumberVar Range varname

NumberVar varname

varname – a variable name that is not the same as any other Crystal Reports formula keyword, does not contain a space, and does not start with a number or certain special characters.

```
NumberVar SalesRepTotal;
If {Sales.Amount} > {SalesRep.BonusLevel} Then
    SalesRepTotal :=
        SalesRepTotal + {Sales.Amount}
```

declares a number variable and tests to see if a sales amount exceeded a bonus level. If so, the variable is incremented by the amount of the sale.

```
NumberVar SalesRepTotal := 0
```

declares a number variable and resets it to zero in the same formula statement.

StringVar

Declares a string variable to contain an array, array of ranges, range, or single value.

StringVar Array varname

StringVar Range Array varname

StringVar Range varname

StringVar varname

varname – a variable name that is not the same as any other Crystal Reports formula keyword, does not contain a space, and does not start with a number or certain special characters.

```
StringVar ShippersUsed;
If Not ({Orders.Ship Via} In ShippersUsed) Then
    ShippersUsed := ShippersUsed & {Orders.Ship Via} & ", "
```

declares a string variable. A test is performed to see if the shipper database field is already contained in the variable. If not, the shipper database field is added to what's already in the variable, concatenated with a comma and space.

```
StringVar Shippers;
Left(Shippers, Length(Shippers)-2)
```

declares a string variable and returns all but the right two characters of the variable to the report.

TimeVar

Declares a time variable to contain an array, array of ranges, range, or single value.

TimeVar Array varname

TimeVar Range Array varname

TimeVar Range varname

TimeVar varname

varname – a variable name that is not the same as any other Crystal Reports formula keyword, does not contain a space, and does not start with a number or certain special characters.

```
TimeVar Range WorkHours;
If DayOfWeek({Sales.Date}) In 2 to 6 Then
    WorkHours := TimeValue("9:00 am") To TimeValue("7:00 pm")
Else
    WorkHours := TimeValue("10:00 am") To TimeValue("5:00 pm");
"Store Hours: " & Minimum(WorkHours) &
                " to " & Maximum(WorkHours)
```

declares a time range variable. The day of the week is checked and the variable is given an hour range for weekdays or weekends. The formula returns a string extracting the lower bound and upper bound of the range.

NOTE   *Some of the previous examples illustrate the capability of declaring a variable and assigning it a value in the same formula statement.*

Index

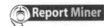